SCIENCE AND MAN'S BEHAVIOR

By the Same Author

THE SOCIAL BASIS OF CONSCIOUSNESS
THE STRUCTURE OF INSANITY
THE BIOLOGY OF HUMAN CONFLICT

Science and Man's Behavior

The Contribution of Phylobiology

by

TRIGANT BURROW, M.D., Ph.D.

Edited by
WILLIAM E. GALT, Ph.D.

:-:

Including the complete text of:

The Neurosis of Man

PHILOSOPHICAL LIBRARY
NEW YORK

Copyright, 1953 by the Philosophical Library, Inc.
15 East 40th Street, New York 16, N. Y.
All rights reserved.

Printed in the United States of America

CONTENTS

PAGE

SCIENCE AND MAN'S BEHAVIOR

FOREWORD 1

CHAPTER
- I. NEED OF A SCIENTIFIC APPROACH . . . 5
- II. AN INVITATION TO SCIENTISTS . . . 13
- III. "NORMALITY" AND THE MEANING OF THE SOCIAL NEUROSIS 23
- IV. THE RIGHT-WRONG DICHOTOMY IN HUMAN BEHAVIOR 34
- V. BIOLOGICAL AND CULTURAL CONSIDERATIONS 45
- VI. THE INDIVIDUAL AND THE GROUP—THEIR PHYLOORGANISMIC CONTINUITY . . 59
- VII. PHYLOBIOLOGY AND THE "LONE WOLF" CRITICISM 75
- VIII. PHYSIOLOGICAL IMPLICATIONS . . . 91

THE NEUROSIS OF MAN

AUTHOR'S FOREWORD 119
PREFACE 127

PART I
INTERRELATIONAL MAN
or
THE SYMPTOMATOLOGY OF HUMAN BEHAVIOR
A PHYLOANALYSIS

- I. MEDICINE TO THE RESCUE!
  INTRODUCTION 135

Phylobiological criteria—Reflex operation of an unrecognized social neurosis—Dualistic factor in human relations—Contrast between man's approach to problems of his external adaptation and of his internal, subjective adaptation—Instances of

v

man's behavioral confusion or his *dis*behavior—Tyranny of arbitrary opinions in respect to human behavior—Inhibitions of "normal" social groups identical with those of the "neurotic"—Each individual the victim of a generic disorder—Fallacy of traditional approach to behavior-disorders—Development of group-analysis as an objective investigation of immediate social reactions—Difficulties—Throughout the phylum a principle of unity runs parallel to a system of deviate reactions—Need of a dynamic anthropology—Man as a social organism must come to reverse his social habituations—Neurosis a medical entity.

II. THE DISSOCIATION OF THE SPECIES OR THE SOCIAL NEUROSIS 156

Universal presence of conflict in human relations—Descriptions in literature of divisive element in man's consciousness—Examples from everyday life—Affect defined —Prejudice—Images of "God" fashioned from systematized prejudices—The social image—Unwarranted burden due to preponderant influence of affect—Man's behavior intrinsically healthy—Inconsistency of customary social reactions—Examples—Defect in man's behavior related to development of symbolic capacity—Sense of "right" in interrelational reactions as mediated by symbolic segment—Inculcation in early years of *amour propre* or "face"—Self-reverting, autopathic behavior constitutes functional impasse in human relations—Principle of species solidarity embodies a common constant—Indications of species solidarity demonstrated on battle-front— Today a battle-front encircles the earth—Emergence of a phylic pattern of reaction.

III. THE MOOD OF MAN OR THE EMOTIONAL FACTOR IN MAN'S DISORDERED PERSONALITY 180

Universal antagonism between individuals and nations an insoluble problem for Freud—Phylobiology investigates this problem experimentally—Early group research into current adaptation classified as "normality"—Mental state of so-called "normality" calls for a community analysis—Criterion of "normality" not basic— Man's monstrous social mood, or the 'I'-persona—Syndrome of Hitler—Autopathic affects invariably motivate leader-follower relationship—'I'-persona ingrained in individual and nation—The bipolar complements of man's moral dichotomy— Illustrative passage from Dostoevsky—As long as the State is autopathic, wars are inevitable—Moralistic attitude toward criminals and neurotics—Need of objective measures of diagnosis and control—In the field of behavior medicine still preoccupied with external symptoms—Analogy seen in history of bacteriology—Artificial reversion of organism's spontaneous motivation—Man must discover a common denominator for a common disorder.

IV. ATTENTION AS A BIONOMIC PROCESS AND ITS SOCIAL ABERRATIONS . . . 201

Attention defined—Whole, undifferentiated attention is essential to survival— Man's facility of symbolic abstraction a special part-function—Intrusion of affect upon symbolic attention—Ditention defined—Effects of ditention—Phylobiological inquiry concerned with neurodynamics of affecto-symbolic manifestations—Biased habits of feeling and thinking preclude objective evaluation of attention—The physiology we *feel*—Interrelational homeostasis disrupted by ditention—"Right-wrong" dichotomy begotten of early child-parent relationship—Various aspects of the social transference—Psychiatric group-therapies contrasted with phyloanalysis— Ditention results in a phylic imbalance expressed in economic inequalities, in war and in insanity.

V. THE GENESIS OF MAN'S DISSOCIATION . . 233

Paleontology of behavior—The nomen, or man's neural conformity to external phenomena—The numen, or the superstitious factor in man's response to external phenomena—Man's compensatory neurosis—Factor of numen in arts of mental healing—Bio-social experiment with a view to uncovering primary elements in human motivation—System of traditional affects and prejudices repudiated—Consistent frustration of affect over many years—Effort to determine basic structures and functions underlying affect—An altered kinesthetic sensation without accompanying ditentive images, rendered perceptible—Group experimentation discloses physiological basis of human conflict—Freud confused symptom of disordered sexuality with its underlying cause—Internal appreciation of 'I'-persona's encroachment upon various functional spheres in man—Examples of segmentation—Man's need to apply the larger function of his brain to the problem of his disfunction as a species.

VI. THE ANATOMY OF PREJUDICE OR THE INDUCTION OF AFFECT IN THE HUMAN ANIMAL 259

Application of experimental medicine to man's disordered behavior an urgent need—Interpolation of 'I'-persona has destroyed functional integrity of phyloörganism—Normal community, no less than psychoneurotic patient, is a prey to ambivalent mental images—Neurosis a problem in anatomy and physiology—Homeostasis—Conditioned response of experimental animal to differential stimuli is analogous to the partitive response of man, or to affect—Subjugation of man to a social system of affective stimuli entails a serious functional dislocation throughout the species—Phylobiological explanation of the mother-fixation—Position of phylobiology erroneously confused with that of the semanticists—Conflict in man's behavior a conflict in neural patterns.

VII. THE SOCIAL IMPLICATIONS OF THE 'I'-PERSONA: A SUMMARY 285

Problem of behavior-disorders a problem in neurodynamics—Man's rigid adherence to partitive conditioning an obstacle to his primary organismic adjustment—Science always preceded by pseudo-science—Need of a phylic principle of behavior as basis of study of behavior-disorders—Affecto-symbolic system of reaction now runs parallel to and controverts man's primary, coördinated principle of behavior—Bionomic shift in phyloörganism's motivation symbolically portrayed in myth and legend—Theocratic affect-pretensions of 'I'-persona—Difference between a collective and an organismic frame of reference—Individual not a summative part of but an integral element within the species as a whole—The method of phyloanalysis.

PART II

ORGANISMIC MAN
or
THE BIOLOGY OF HUMAN BEHAVIOR
A PHYLOSYNTHESIS

VIII. PHYLIC PRINCIPLES IN HUMAN BEHAVIOR . 315

Substitution of numen for nomen has entailed neural modifications in the organism of man—Problem of disordered behavior is phylic as well as physiological—Two discriminable tensional patterns underlie two types of attention—Ditention is secondary, partitive, symbolic; cotention primary, total, organismic—Research became intraorganismic—Intrusion of part-brain, with its affecto-symbolic distortion of total function, is the basis of disordered behavior in man as a species—Deviate motivation identical in "normal" and neurotic—Protoplasm is basic biological norm in structural biology—Cotention is basic biological norm in interrelational function of man as a phyloörganism—Protogenic function and allogenic function—Phylobiologist studies neurology of behavior-disorders as perceptible within him—Principle of species solidarity applied to the interrelational function of man's brain—Ditention an obstacle—Partitive feeling expressed in religion—Organic unity of phylic man the major behavioral actuality—Essential value to man of the symbol within the framework of the total organism—Origin of the social neurosis.

IX. CONTRASTING PATTERNS OF TENSION OR THE PHYSIOLOGICAL SEAT OF THE NEUROSIS 340

Criterion of healthy organism-environment relation—Phyloörganism's balance of function parallels that of individual organism—Homeostasis of phyloörganism deflected—Results of reflexly derouted motivation—Physiological pattern of cotention demarcated from that of ditention—Cotention synonymous with homeostasis—Restoration of organism's cotentive pattern a prerequisite to interrelational health—Defensive reaction of 'I'-persona all but insuperable barrier in early research—Factors in learning to swim analogous to cotention—Examples of discrepancy between mind and mood of man—Study of somatic processes in contrast to mental dichotomy of "right" and "wrong."

X. THE BIOLOGICAL NORM OF HUMAN BEHAVIOR OR THE TECHNIQUE OF COTENTION 365

Need of a broad phylic technique in approach to behavior-disorders—Inadequacy of shock therapies and lobectomy—Early studies of The Lifwynn Laboratory consisted in daily frustration of affect—Later observations revealed affect as an essentially physiological behavior-reaction—Technique for discrimination of the two physiological reaction-patterns—Major difficulties—Analogy between recalcitrance of untrained muscles in acquiring a bodily skill and the bionomic awkwardness of man—Both in ontosoma and in phylosoma cotention is coördination, ditention is conflict—Only the spirit of disinterested research discloses to student of phylobiology the positive aspect of his inquiry—Discrimination of two tensional patterns substantiated by instrumental measurements.

XI. INSTRUMENTAL EVIDENCE OF MAN'S PRIMARY BIOLOGICAL NORM AND OF DEVIATIONS FROM IT 392

Cotentive response an adjustment affecting entire physiology of organism—Physiological concomitants of cotentive pattern experimentally investigated—Instrumental aspect closely correlated with earlier phyloanalytic investigations—Summary of instrumental findings—Discussion of respiratory, oculomotor and electroencephalographic results—Instrumental records possess value only as they corroborate tensional modifications registered through the technique of phyloanalysis.

XII. THE ORGANISM OF MAN 402

Inseparable continuity between organism of man as ontosoma or individual, and as phylosoma or species—Review of different bodily mechanisms mediating phylosoma's total motivation—Third nervous system or "third brain" discriminated on basis of specialization of function—Disordered behavior in both normal and neurotic traced to disfunction of third nervous system—Phylobiology replaces concept of "individual" with concept of ontosoma as an interfunctioning unit in a common species or phylosoma—Rhythmic balance of functions relates whole phyloörganism to environment—Two major constituents of phylosoma consist in the adult and infant generations—Adult contingent performs physiological coördination that relates organism to environment and conveys results secondarily to infant contingent —Adult generation indoctrinates infant generation in pattern of tensions associated with symbol—Symbol a unique bionomic asset—Shift from total physiological plane to one of affecto-symbolic interrelation—Phylic fallacy of "right-wrong" behavior— Third nervous system neural substrate of 'I'-persona—Universal functional maladaptation predisposes phyloörganism to manifold diseases—Continuity basically uniting ontosoma has been disrupted.

XIII. OUR COMMON CONSCIOUSNESS IN A COMMON ENVIRONMENT. A SUMMARY 427

The troubled spirit and the inquiring mind—Sociomoral precepts cannot replace phyloörganism's homeostasis—Serious impediment to unity of the phylic organism—Segmentation of its various functions—Collapse of social institutions inevitable outcome—Primary communication interrupted—Stammering and lying as universal hesitations of speech—Symbolic reaction a miniature behavior-response— Important rôle of the eye in symbolic attention and in total attention—Attention derouted into a restricted part-function—Technique of cotention reviewed—Examples of artificially segregated part-reactions—Man's essential need is a return to the basic pattern of tension in ontosoma and phylosoma.

XIV. PHYLOBIOLOGICAL REFLECTIONS . . . 457

Group-analysis, background of its inception—Obdurate opposition of 'I'-persona to relinquishing its spurious identity—Objective integrity of investigation the sole criterion of phylobiological student—Necessity of physiological approach to problem of human behavior—Menace of atomic bomb traceable to divided tensions in man's organism—Autopathic "rights" versus inherent rights of man—Tyranny of 'I'-persona —Need of a laboratory of human behavior—No occasion for despondency, which is always concern for oneself—Social coördination must ultimately be based upon man's consistently clear mood or feeling—Cotention as a basis for education, government, world union.

APPENDIX 487

Presentation of instrumental recordings showing changes in respiration, metabolism, eye-movements and brain-wave pattern in cotention.

GLOSSARY 525

NAME INDEX 537

SUBJECT INDEX 541

ILLUSTRATIONS

		Page
Trigant Burrow		*Frontispiece*
Fig. 1.	Typical Respiratory and Pulse Curves during Successive Periods of Ditention and Cotention	489
Fig. 2.	Graphic Reproduction of Eye-Movements during Twenty-Second Periods of Ditention and Cotention	496
Fig. 3.	Photograms Showing Eye-Movements and Fixation with Five Exposures per Second:	
	A. Eye-Movements . . . . *after*	500
	B. Fixation . . . . . "	500
Fig. 4.	Photograms Showing Eye-Movements and Fixation with Ten Exposures per Second:	
	A. Eye-Movements . . . . *after*	500
	B. Fixation . . . . . "	500
Fig. 5.	Photograms of Eye-Movements for Periods of Two and Three Seconds:	
	A. Two Seconds . . . . . *after*	500
	B. Three Seconds . . . . "	500
Fig. 6.	Photograms of Eye-Movements when Subject was looking at Black Background without Focusing on any Special Point:	
	A. Ditention . . . . . *after*	500
	B. Cotention . . . . . "	500
Fig. 7.	Drawings of Photograms of Five Successive One-Second Periods in Ditention and in Cotention	502
Fig. 8.	Photograms of Eye-Movements when Subject was looking at a Picture:	
	A. Ditention . . . . . *after*	500
	B. Cotention . . . . . "	500
Fig. 9.	Drawings of Photograms of Successive One-Second periods in Ditention and in Cotention	503
Fig. 10.	Typical Tracings of Brain Waves from Right Motor and Left Motor Areas during Successive Periods of Ditention and Cotention	504

ILLUSTRATIONS

Fig. 11. Typical Tracings of Brain Waves from Right and Left Motor and Right and Left Occipital Areas during Successive Periods of Ditention and Cotention . . 505
Fig. 12. Distribution of Alpha-Percentages in the EEG during Ditention and Cotention (Right Motor Region) . 507
Fig. 13. Distribution of Alpha-Percentages in the EEG during Ditention and Cotention (Left Motor Region) . 508
Fig. 14. Alpha-Percentages in Successive Periods of Ditention and Cotention 508
Fig. 15. Distribution of Alpha Amplitudes in the EEG during Successive Periods of Ditention and Cotention (Right Motor Region) 509
Fig. 16. Distribution of Alpha Amplitudes in the EEG during Successive Periods of Ditention and Cotention (Left Motor Region) 509
Fig. 17. Typical Tracings of Brain Waves from Right and Left Motor Areas and of Eye-Movements during Periods of Ditention, Muscle-Tension, and Cotention . 510
Fig. 18. Spectra of Brain-Wave Activity from Motor Area during Successive Periods of Ditention and Cotention:
    A. Ditention 512
    B. Cotention 512
Fig. 19. Spectra of Brain-Wave Activity from Occipital Area during Successive Periods of Ditention and Cotention:
    A. Ditention 513
    B. Cotention 513
Fig. 20. Spectra of Brain-Wave Activity from Motor Area during Successive Periods of Reading in Ditention and Reading in Cotention:
    A. Reading in Ditention 515
    B. Reading in Cotention 515
Fig. 21. Spectra of Brain-Wave Activity from Occipital Area during Successive Periods of Reading in Ditention and Reading in Cotention:
    A. Reading in Ditention 516
    B. Reading in Cotention 516
Fig. 22. Differential Effect of Reading in Ditention and Reading in Cotention on Brain-Wave Activity from Occipital Area 517

ILLUSTRATIONS

Fig. 23. Spectra of Brain-Wave Activity from Motor Area during Successive Periods of Ditention and Intense Attention:
    A. Ditention 518
    B. Intense Attention 518

Fig. 24. Spectra of Brain-Wave Activity from Occipital Area during Successive Periods of Ditention and Intense Attention:
    A. Ditention 519
    B. Intense Attention 519

Fig. 25. Differential Effect of Intense Attention and Cotention on Brain-Wave Activity from Motor Area . . 520

Fig. 26. Summary Graph Showing Three Types of Physiological Changes occurring most consistently in Cotention 521

FOREWORD

In presenting a scientific frame of reference it is often helpful to trace briefly the development of the discipline—to follow the roots back to the soil where they were originally nurtured. Phylobiology, of which group- or phylo-analysis is a research and therapeutic tool, was initiated and pioneered through the years by Dr. Trigant Burrow whose training was in the fields of medicine, biology and experimental psychology. After receiving degrees in medicine and psychology, he became interested in the psychoanalytic techniques which were developing abroad. During 1909-10 he studied with Carl G. Jung in Zurich and then returned to Baltimore where he played an important rôle in introducing psychoanalysis in this country. It was while working in Baltimore at The Johns Hopkins Hospital and in private practice that he developed the distinctive characteristics of his studies—studies which were later sponsored by The Lifwynn Foundation.

Psychoanalysis had its inception in a social and intellectual climate that stresses individualism in human behavior and mechanistic interpretations in the biological sciences. Dr. Burrow early became dissatisfied with both these emphases. He felt that if human behavior was to be rightly understood and basic principles formulated in this field it was necessary to adopt an organismic frame of reference and to study the emergent properties of the group, as well as the intricate modes of interfunctioning among individuals. Disorders in behavior were for him essentially social or interrelational, and demanded observation and study in their dynamic group setting.

The most striking feature in Dr. Burrow's life was his unremitting interest in understanding and resolving man's behavioral conflict. Years of study and research led him to the view that man is in urgent need of adopting an objective, inclusive attitude in respect to behavior-disorders, individual and social. The development of scientific principles in this field so vital to man's life and effectiveness became the primary aim of his group-analytic studies.

But Dr. Burrow realized that the establishment of such principles must ultimately become a community task—a task for the community of mankind. And he felt that scientists generally, because of their background and training in objective discipline, were eminently fitted to play a leading rôle in bringing about the needed reorientation. When, therefore, in 1948 an unavoidable delay occurred in the printing of his last book, *The Neurosis of Man,* Dr. Burrow took this opportunity to forge lines of communication with outstanding men in various fields of science by introducing certain chapters of his book to them in advance of its publication.

Dr. Burrow greatly valued the opportunity that followed for informal communication with his confreres and felt that the exchange of views contributed much toward the fuller formulation of his position. It was in July of 1949, while at his summer research station in the Adirondacks, that he conceived the idea of assembling in book form the most important aspects of this correspondence, feeling that it would be of assistance generally in clarifying key features of his thesis. He hoped that this book, which he called *Science and Man's Behavior,* would provide a basis for developing new understandings in respect to a scientific approach by man to the urgent problem of his own behavior.

I was fortunate enough to be called upon to assist in the plan from its inception, and I made some preliminary study to determine the topics about which questions were most frequently asked. During the following fall Dr. Burrow had to interrupt his work on the project several times in order to complete writings for which there was a more immediate demand. But he was constantly developing and discussing with me plans for the manuscript, and dictating material for it. Before the onset of his fatal illness in January 1950 Dr. Burrow had outlined *Science and Man's Behavior* and drafted the key chapters, but unfortunately he himself was unable to bring the project to completion. The remaining chapters have been completed by me through drawing material primarily from Dr. Burrow's letters to scientists, and from his unpublished writings. My contribution has been for the most part one of synthesis, of fitting Dr. Burrow's material into the framework of the outline he had planned.

In preparing the material for publication I have been assisted at every stage by an editorial committee consisting of Dr. Hans Syz, Dr. Charles B. Thompson, Miss Aimée Guggenheimer and Mrs. Alfreda P. Sill. I am also greatly indebted to Mrs. Beatrix V. LaGarde for her sensitive and discriminative reading of the manuscript, and for her helpful suggestions.

The Foundation wishes to express sincere appreciation to the scientists whose thoughtful comments and criticisms form the core of the discussion. They gave generously of their time and thought in their correspondence with Dr. Burrow, and without exception consented to the publication of their comments. In this connection it should be mentioned that these comments, as well as Dr. Burrow's response to them, were offered spontaneously and informally and should not be considered as expressing an exhaustive, critical analysis.

We are gratified that Dr. Burrow's correspondence with eminent scientists on the vital subject of human behavior is being brought out in one volume with *The Neurosis of Man*, to which it so closely relates. According to Dr. Burrow's own feeling, this latter book contains the essence of his phylobiological researches. In reprinting it, the text of the earlier edition has been adhered to throughout with only a few minor alterations made by the author himself. The reader who is unfamiliar with Dr. Burrow's studies will probably wish to acquaint himself with *The Neurosis of Man* before turning to the discussion contained in the early pages of the present volume.

These introductory remarks would be incomplete without some word of the meaning of Dr. Burrow for his associates and students. He was an inspiring teacher, an indefatigable co-worker, a steadfast friend. He possessed a rare sensitivity for the needs of others, sparing no effort to assist them toward a full development of their latent ability. He expressed a joyous humor, a natural graciousness and a gentleness of feeling which endeared him to all who were privileged to know him. The completion of his unfinished manuscript has been for me a stimulating and a challenging task. Working daily with Dr. Burrow's writings has served to keep me in close touch with the solidarity of feeling and thinking that characterized his life and work, and I have deeply valued this opportunity. I can only hope that I have succeeded in bringing to the undertaking some small measure of the keen enthusiasm for the intrinsic health of man which imbued his personality and his writings.

WILLIAM E. GALT

The Lifwynn Foundation
Westport, Connecticut
January, 1953.

Scientists whose comments and questions are quoted in the present volume.

Dr. Gordon W. Allport	Psychology	Harvard University
Dr. Arthur F. Bentley	Philosophy	
Dr. George Boas	Philosophy	The John Hopkins University
Dr. P. W. Bridgman	Physics	Harvard University
Dr. A. J. Carlson	Physiology	The University of Chicago, Emeritus
Dr. Honorio Delgado	Psychiatry	University of Lima, Peru
*Dr. John Dewey	Philosophy	Columbia University, Emeritus
Dr. Alfred E. Emerson	Zoology	The University of Chicago
Dr. Ralph W. Gerard	Physiology	The University of Chicago
Dr. Kurt Goldstein	Neurology	Morrisania City Hospital
Dr. Alan Gregg	Medical Sciences	The Rockefeller Foundation
Dr. C. Judson Herrick	Comparative Neurology	The University of Chicago, Emeritus
Dr. Melville J. Herskovits	Anthropology	Northwestern University
Dr. Leland E. Hinsie	Psychiatry	Columbia University
*Dr. David Katz	Psychology	Institutet för Psikologie och Pedagogik, Stockholm, Sweden
Dr. Clyde Kluckhohn	Anthropology	Harvard University
Dr. W. M. Krogman	Anthropology	University of Pennsylvania
Dr. Carney Landis	Psychology	Columbia University
*Dr. Ralph S. Lillie	Biology	The University of Chicago, Emeritus
*Dr. Eduard C. Lindeman	Social Sciences	The New York School of Social Work
Dr. Gardner Murphy	Psychology	The College of the City of New York
Dr. Ornulv Odegard	Psychiatry	University of Oslo, Norway
Dr. William F. Ogburn	Sociology	The University of Chicago
Dr. Nicolas Rashevsky	Mathematical Biology	The University of Chicago
Dr. Pitirim A. Sorokin	Sociology	Harvard University
Dr. George M. Stratton	Psychology	University of California, Emeritus
Dr. Robert H. Thouless	Psychology	Cambridge University, England
Dr. Robert M. Yerkes	Comparative Psychology	Yale University, Emeritus
	also	
Mr. Herbert S. Bailey	Science Editor	Princeton University Press

*Deceased

CHAPTER I

NEED OF A SCIENTIFIC APPROACH

Whether in art, literature, music or science, a fresh departure can expect only uphill going until an increasing facility in testing and perhaps adopting the new orientation creates community-wide sympathy and interest in it. Alan Gregg stresses the point that the writer or teacher needs to bring a note of persuasion, of appeal, to the thesis sponsored by him. In an address to psychologists, he quotes from a letter Wordsworth wrote to Lady Beaumont: "Never forget that every great and original writer in proportion as he is great and original must himself create the taste by which he is relished." Gregg then goes on to say: "As psychologists you are in the enviable position of having a similar freedom to create the taste by which your work is to be relished. You can deliberately create the demand for what you have learned how to do, after you have learned how to do it." [1]

Frankly, the chief mission of the present book is to nourish interest and sympathy in the science of human behavior which I have called *phylobiology*. It is to imbue in students a sense of how acceptable to what is most constructive and fulfilling in man's feeling and thinking, is a thesis that sets free, that gives fullest rein to the inherent capacity of the human organism. But I realize my task is not a simple one. To create a demand for a science whose confessed objective is to turn the student — or nation for that matter — against his own habitual identity, his own inveterate "rightness," is a large order. Nevertheless, it does not seem excluded that the clear and direct statement of the principle upon which the discipline of a *biologically* sound rightness is based should win the understanding and confidence of a sincerely inquiring mind.

In a sense it seems extraordinary that man, having achieved so much in his world of objectivity — in the sphere of the physical sciences — should be so dull and unquickened toward the domain of processes that are the substance of his very life. In other domains he has come to require of himself the application of precise measures to his data; he has been uncompromising toward scientific canons and the establishment of objective criteria of evaluation. Not so, though, toward his own behavior. In this sphere, subjective prejudices, arbitrary preceptive images that may be bent to anybody's whim, everywhere take precedence over exact measurements and scientific standards. It is easier. As we shall see, these arbitrary images are the social reflexes with which we respond to the constant verbal stimuli of "right" and "wrong." On this basis one is sure of securing his own advantage, no matter at what cost to other people.

Of course all science is positive and constructive. It aims at increasing knowledge about; it adds to, it discovers. This is true also for the science of medicine. But there is the additional circumstance that in medicine the objective is largely the elimination of untoward conditions. It is to take away whatever discoverable factors interfere with the organism's naturally healthy processes. In treating pneumonia, for example, the physician does not attempt to add to the lung power of the patient or to increase the efficiency of his breathing processes. He lends his every effort toward identifying and eliminating the hostile agent that has brought about the respiratory embarrassment, knowing full well that processes internal to the organism will restore balanced function once this inimical factor is removed.

This process of discovering and eliminating, characteristic of the science of medicine, has also been the outstanding feature of the discipline of phylobiology or phylopathology. Recognizing that man's habitual behavior is not fully constructive but is in many ways destructive; recognizing disease or pathology as an element conspicuously present in human relations, we of The Lifwynn Foundation set out to discover, if possible, what was the origin and what the nature of this disease or pathology that now interferes with healthy processes in human relations. Our observations indicated that the usual and accustomed in the field of man's behavior does not represent a criterion of health. We sought, therefore, to remove the impediments and distortions we found lodged in the accepted and accustomed, or the so-called normal. Ours was pre-eminently a process in deletion, in excision, in ablation. We wanted to return to native soil, to unearth the *tabula rasa* of the human organism in its primary incitement to action or in its basic motivation.

In the field of human behavior, everybody — any Tom, Dick or Harry — knows the "known" and talks and talks about it, in high circles and low. In the corner pub as in the United Nations

Assembly each knows what his neighbor *should* be doing, and each expresses his opinion with conviction and authority. Yet all the while war, the outstanding symptom of diseased human behavior, has become world-wide. In every field of science, it is the *unknown* that is important; but with reference to human beings and their behavior man tends to cling to the old outlooks he has always cherished. We are now so accustomed to our habitual attitudes that we like them and call them "right" or "good."

It was man's preoccupation with the known, the traditional and habitual in the field of behavior that commanded the interest of my associates and myself, and prompted our efforts of research. Man is "right." He wants to be "right." He will fight; if necessary he will die in defense of his rightness. John Huss, Joan of Arc, Hitler and Cotton Mather are only a few of the many historic examples of this "rightness" though they have no feature in common save a passionately held conviction of the truth of a private preconception. But how correct, how sound biologically is this "rightness" with which man — every man — is now filled to the point of obsession? Our group researches disclosed that for each man the rightness of himself — the rightness of his views, his aspirations, his convictions, his interest and pleasure — is dynamically the strongest urge, the most powerful incitement within his emotional life; that this universal incitement dominates all the other behavior drives within the human breast. We sought to analyze, we sought, wherever possible, to run to cover this popular prepossession that is the fiercest claim, the readiest assertion within civilized man. We found that the "right" which you and I demand and exercise at all times and under all circumstances rests upon an emotional complex that is utterly without warrant. This complex is the basis of the greatest distortion in human life, namely, the domination of the mind of man by emotional preconceptions. Phylobiology, then, challenges everything in this behavioral field of the cherished "known." It challenges known precepts, known habituations that have been our all in all, because our group investigations disclosed that the behavior we call right and good is not biologically sound and healthy.

In the spring of 1947 I had completed a Report of a thirty-year research into the problem of human behavior and its disorders. But it soon became apparent that delays incident to the publication of the volume (it was being printed in England) would postpone its appearance for some time. It therefore occurred to me that this delay would afford me an excellent opportunity to send certain key chapters of my book to a selected number of scientists. It was, I felt, among the scientists *par excellence* that a thesis dealing with the pitfalls of man's habitual ideas would most likely win interest and sympathy, because it is the scientist whose chief function is the adoption of a discipline that at all times places observation and analysis above any preconceived view regarding this or that object, condition, force or relation.

While our researches into the causes of prejudice and human conflict had proved of interest scientifically to my associates and myself, the real value of this study of human relations is, of course, its application to the community at large. Here was an experiment indicative of hitherto unsuspected factors in man, but it was now limited to a small group of investigators. So that whatever theoretical interest it might possess for scientists, it could not possess applicability until the conclusions reached in regard to the genus man were put at the disposal of man as a genus. In short, what had been a restricted, experimental group had to be supplanted by the wider group of man in his daily, practical exercise of the principles uncovered. This, as we know, has been the story of medicine as of all related sciences having to do directly with the health and security of the human organism.

In a matter dealing with man's interrelational behavior we felt strongly the importance of this transition from the closed experimental setting of the laboratory to the actual recognition and adoption of these principles not only by the scientist, but by mankind generally. This was the consideration that prompted my desire to make known to scholars of recognized authority in various scientific fields something of the nature of the processes with which my associates and I had been long engaged. It seemed imperative to enlist their interest and their coöperation in an inquiry having to do fundamentally with their own behavior and that of their associates, as it had to do with the behavior of myself and of my associates, of their families and mine, with the behavior of their community and mine, with the behavior of the individuals and nations composing mankind. Thus in rallying scientists to the recognition and support of principles that underlie and regulate the behavior of man as a species, we sought to invoke interest among leaders of thought in the community.

With this purpose in mind I wrote a letter to outstanding colleagues in various fields of science. In it I stated what our objectives had been, and what I felt to be the kinship between our research efforts and theirs since we had applied to the problem of human behavior the same rigidly controlled scientific principles that govern procedures in their respective fields of inquiry. I also requested the privilege of submitting to my colleagues selected chapters from my book which, without taking too much of their time, might give them an indication of the researches it described.

The letters I received in reply brought me the keenest satisfaction. My correspondents expressed great interest in the direction of the work of my associates and myself, and, wherever possible, indicated a desire to see my material. I think I may say that the response to my letter was the most stimulating experience I have known throughout the many years of my scientific work. Naturally no time was lost in forwarding the selected chapters to these investigators.

I was still more gratified by the earnest interest these colleagues showed after they had read my excerpted material. Not that there were lacking questions and criticisms aplenty. After all, if one is pursuing investigations in a new field, who is in a position to "agree"? If such an agreement were readily forthcoming, the "pioneer" nature of the work in question would be justly suspect. In a truly new field of inquiry there is necessarily lacking the basis for agreement. Agreement can come only when one's colleagues have had the opportunity to verify the results through their own independent application of the same principles and techniques to the same field of investigation.

Of course, in one's conventional interrelational behavior, one likes to be agreed with. People like to agree and to find agreement in others. This makes for pleasant relationships. But such agreement too often rests upon preconceived ideas for which there is no scientific basis, and it affords but an undependable acquiescence. It is social, superficial; not objective or scientific. What seems needed in the field of human behavior is a research method, not a "right" mind. As Sir Richard Livingstone points out in a delightful and penetrating article,[2] we have had this right mind from the time of Plato's *Republic*, with its excellence of thought, to that of Hitler's army, with its excellence of organized discipline. Why can we not seek now a frame of reference in the sphere of human behavior from which men will dissent as violently as they dissented from the views of Galileo, Newton, Darwin and Pasteur? Why, in seeking for excellence, must we adhere to the habitual "right" mind with which we have through the ages futilely sought it? It was the tremendous contribution of pioneers in the field of science that they ruthlessly put aside their own "right" mind and other people's. Setting out with a clean slate, they insisted upon adhering to a process of consistent scientific research.

It is essential that the scientist verify the hypothesis. On no other basis would he want agreement, nor would he himself concede it. The scientist looks for demonstrable evidence regarding the material or data submitted. What is demanded is that, proceeding independently, we be able to examine the evidence together. This was the spirit in which my thesis was tentatively examined by my scientific colleagues as is shown by the type of response I received from them. From this background their reaction was invariably generous. It was the reaction of scientific men, of men who because of their own training, their own experience, were immediately sympathetic to an approach which, however new, however different from their own accepted premises, bore the stamp of scientific systematization and consistency.

These scientists did not say: "You are right because you are saying what I believe." Nor did they say: "You are wrong because you are not saying what I hold to be true." They did not say: "I don't like what you have to say, I don't 'agree' with your point of view. I like what *I* have to say. I like *my* point of view and those who agree with me." Rather their attitude was: "What you have said is interesting, but what is the evidence, what are the grounds, what is the basis for your conclusions? What method have you presented that can be applied by those who repeat your procedure and your controls?" Their reaction was not personal, not affective. They did not take the position: "Since your thesis repudiates criteria I have always known and accepted and that have always been known and accepted by my community, I will have no part of it." On the contrary, as scientists accustomed to controlled experimentation and to dealing with uncompromising, objective data, their reaction was radically different from this. Without preconception or bias they asked for the evidence and for the opportunity to examine it for themselves. In effect, they said: "To question outright the accepted standards of normal behavior is indeed an exacting task, but if your findings are justified, we are with you." This response was heartening. To this unfailingly broad and balanced attitude of students inured to the discipline of observable data and their consistent correlation, I owe my extreme satisfaction with the letters I was privileged to receive from my many colleagues.

Such a scientific attitude is the only one that can be productive in resolving a behavior-dilemma which involves nothing other than man's basic reorientation. But in the field of his interrelational behavior man has nowhere adhered to and been guided by established principles of science. We have for centuries been talking about behavior—about our *ideas* of behavior—the students of law, of government, of religion, education, politics and philosophy. All of us, in lacking an established standard of judgment, have been talking only of what we *think* about behavior. As individuals and communities none of us has hitherto demanded objectively observable data.

For centuries advocates of various schools of thought have sought ways to develop harmonious living among men. They have failed. Today they are seeking as desperately and are still failing because they have continued to discuss ideas rather than acquire a technique for dealing with the basic factors underlying man's conflict and disorder. They have failed because man has not yet raised the problem of his social adaptation to the level of a science of human behavior. He has lacked a consistent principle—a universally accepted criterion of human reactions. And so the years have passed, and war, industrial conflict, religious dissension, political and economic disturbance—these and a thousand other indications of man's disorder and unrest—have persisted without mitigation.

As I said in a recent letter to Professor C. Judson Herrick: "I earnestly hope that my thesis may serve to awaken a broader, more fundamental biological view of human behavior. In saying this, I do not mean broader concepts of behavior. That would indeed be presumptuous of me in view of the able biological formulations we already owe to our many distinguished biologists, including of course your own eminent contributions. But I should be glad if I might assist in furthering the internal recognition of the phylic implications of behavior-disorders—if I might assist in making evident the nature of the subjective feelings and motivations that are the incitement to our behaving, as a species, in the way we do behave. For many years my associates and I have tried consistently to counter our own community habituations by attacking *within ourselves* the affects and prejudices that commonly clutter the 'thinking' of so-called normal man. . . . I have attempted to approach man and his behavior in its immediate subjective experience. With me, as with each of my associates and students, our problem is 'I, myself,' the way 'I, myself' feel. The material of our research in behavior-disorders has at all times been 'my' unwarranted emotions and unreasoning affectivity, 'my' feelings and beliefs, 'my' projections and prejudices as 'I' — as any 'I' — experience them. . . . This research has contributed to alter in no small measure our accustomed frame of reference with respect to the problem of human behavior."

NOTES

[1] Gregg, Alan, "The Profession of Psychology as Seen by a Doctor of Medicine," *The American Psychologist*, 1948, Vol. 3. pp. 397-401.

[2] "Education and the Training of Character," *The Atlantic Monthly*, 1946, Vol. 178, pp. 81-86.

CHAPTER II

AN INVITATION TO SCIENTISTS

In the previous chapter I spoke of the generous response of my colleagues to the letter I addressed to them in the spring of 1948 while publication of my book, *The Neurosis of Man*, was pending. Perhaps the best way to orient the reader in respect to the pages that follow will be to let him read the letter I addressed to investigators in various fields. Their questions and criticisms after reading the advance material referred to in my letter will form the nucleus of the chapters that follow. In the light of comments by these confreres in many fields of science I shall attempt to develop certain themes central to our phylobiological thesis. But let us examine the letter.

Dear Professor........:

I am sending this letter to you and to a few other investigators of eminence in their different fields of science, to announce informally the publication of a Report of the researches in human behavior in which I have been engaged for the past thirty years. In this latest book of mine, *The Neurosis of Man — An Introduction to a Science of Human Behavior* (now in press), I have tried to describe the technical discipline introduced by my associates and myself in our effort to establish a science of human relations — the science I have called *phylobiology*. Only the tragic conditions in human relations we see about us today and your own great interest in the problems and dislocations existing in the world warrant the liberty I am taking in writing you regarding this report of our researches.

The outstanding characteristic of the scientist, of course, is his voluntary relinquishment of personal ways of thinking and feeling in favor of a controlled cultural discipline. Science demands that we replace arbitrarily conditioned determinants of motive and action with criteria of behavior that rest upon a common denominator. This, as we know, has been the substance of all intellectual training — of your training as a physiologist, biologist and educator, and of mine as a student of medicine, biology and experimental psychology.

In these studies, habitually conditioned thinking yielded more and more to scientific discipline. So with the physicists, the mathematicians, the astronomers, the chemists, the engineers, the agriculturists and other students of science. Through these technical disciplines we became specialists in our several fields. In our several fields, our private habits of thought (our wishful thinking and feeling) were brought under the discipline of a special cultural pattern.

In approaching the field of human relations, I was of course compelled to adhere still to the criteria of the technical specialist. If, however, there was to be a science of human relations, it would have not only to conform to a special cultural discipline, but at the same time it would have to include the participation of the common man, since human behavior is common to man throughout. If our experimental groups had not included the layman as well as the scientist—if they had not represented a cross-section of society—our researches in human behavior would have been meaningless. For our inquiry had to do with man's habitual thought and feeling *as a species*. In the test tube of phyloanalysis, man as a species had now to be subordinated not only to the discipline of a special field of inquiry, but to the discipline of a special field in which socially conditioned habit and scientific inquiry, however widely opposed to one another, were regarded as processes common to the race of man. Thus man—common man no less than the scientist—had now to become the material of investigation as well as the investigator of this material. As Professor Dewey says in his recent book, *Problems of Men:* "The initial step is to promote general recognition that knowing, including most emphatically scientific knowledge, is not outside social activity, but is itself a form of social behavior, as much so as agriculture or transportation."

And so, while hitherto my associates and I, like other scientists, had been compelled to submit habitual ways of thinking and feeling to this or that special cultural discipline, we had now to yield our personal habituations to the cultural demands of a common social discipline. In fidelity to the criteria of a science of human relations we were forced to surrender the accustomed interests and motivations entertained by us severally, and embrace the demands of a discipline that was not only special but that was also common to us and to mankind generally. In short, we found ourselves dealing on the one hand with man's common limitations in thought and feeling and, on the other, with the demands of a cultural premise that must be equally shared in common by us. As A. J. Carlson has said: "We hear much today about 'One World,' but not enough about 'One Human Species.' At least we do not always act, at home or abroad, as if we believed this proved biologic fact."

Taking the position of the clinical anthropologist, as it might be called, it became necessary for us to adopt a completely altered frame of reference in respect to the problem of human behavior and its disorders. Our socially credited reactions could no longer be accepted as embodying a norm of health, but new criteria for discriminating between healthy and morbid reactions had to be introduced. For years my analytic quarry has been the state of mind fallaciously yet universally known as "normality"—the social reaction-average of an artificially conditioned species. For our medical investigations showed that abnormal processes motivate also the so-called "normal" behavior of man. They indicated the extent to which a "social neurosis" now dominates human motives and institutions.

So, you see, my book is not primarily concerned with the behavior of the individual. Neither is it concerned with any segregated social group or nation. The unit with which it deals is the species man, and its interpretation of the laws governing man's behavior is addressed to laymen no less than to scientists. In our finding, laymen and scientists are equally victims of social conflicts due to a *disorder in feeling* that has been engendered in man the world over, and both must shoulder an equal responsibility for its understanding and adjustment. Our analysis of groups led us to regard social conflict and war as a medical problem. It led us to view these manifestations as a symptomatic expression of an underlying imbalance within the organism of man. We were led to see that until man has taken upon himself the task of developing a *science of his own feeling*, his conflicts and his wars are inescapable. As a result of this altered orientation we have been interested not in psychiatric symptomatology, but in the neurodynamics of man's behavior as a social organism. For in demonstrating the existence of a biological norm of human behavior, we have indicated the biophysical basis of mental and nervous disorders.

I realize that you are very busy, and under ordinary conditions I should hesitate to intrude upon you. But in this sick and unhappy world today conditions are so far from ordinary that I feel I must appeal to the few scholars long established in the ways of science to lend the support of their interest to a research that attempts to place the study of man's behavior on a stable, scientific basis. It seems to me unquestionable that the scientific specialist, trained as he is in subordinating personal considerations to his special field of inquiry, is preëminently prepared to give impetus to the self-discipline of a science of human relations. In other words, it is the scientific specialist who is outstandingly qualified through his special discipline to bring to common man the discipline requisite to a common science of human behavior. After all, this authority that derives from the scientist's voluntary subordination to the discipline of controlled observation is the sole authority that man looks to in the specialist. It is this discipline that can alone give cultural impetus to the specialist and to the common man alike. In this global discipline, it seems to me, such terms as "communism" and "democracy," which now so largely express only the wishful self-interest of the politician and the commercialist, might give way to a system of world government embodying principles that possess a common phylobiological denominator of thought and feeling.

As I say, my associates and I feel very much the need to have in our work the understanding and interest of other men of science. Our own small group has made but a beginning, and a very small beginning. If disorientation and neurosis are the common lot of man as a species, only the community-wide participation of scientists and laymen in a common phyloanalysis of our human motivations can reach and remedy this universal illness of mankind. It is in this thought that I have presumed to write to you and to others of my esteemed colleagues to ask if I may have the privilege of sending you the manuscript of a few chapters of my book. If I may do this and may have your comments upon my general thesis, it will mean very much to my associates and to me. The material I have selected is the Table of Contents, the Foreword, the Preface, Chapter I of Part I (the remaining chapters of the first part consist of an analysis of prejudice as a social reaction), Chapter VIII or the first chapter of Part II (the remaining chapters of Part II deal with physiological patterns of tension and their instrumental recording), and the final chapter (XIV, a summary). In addition I am including a paper, "The Social Neurosis,"[1] that briefly outlines my book as a whole. The number of pages I should thus be making bold to ask you to read is approximately 160. I hope my request does not impose too great a burden upon you.

Sincerely yours,

Today, the situation with man is critical. The realization of the vital need for the scientific study and remedy of his aberration in feeling and thinking has become almost a commonplace among intelligent men and women. Alertness to the crisis is apparent not only in all departments of science but also in the fields of education and learning everywhere. One cannot pick up a newspaper or magazine without finding an earnest and thoughtful statement regarding the plight of civilization today, and without recognizing in these statements the evidences of man's gradual awakening to a broader, more inclusive social consciousness.

In the letters that reached me in response to my material this comprehensive note is the most frequently sounded. For example, in a letter from Professor Leland E. Hinsie there is this statement:

> ... I think that the "social" revolution through which we have been passing the last several decades may be the forerunner of your hopes. The science of thought, of thinking, seems to be disintegrating, but it is being displaced by undirected, and, hence, ungovernable phylic feelings.
>
> Maybe your observations may not come too late to bring some order out of near chaos. I have enough faith in human nature to feel that man can right his feeling-imbalance to a certain degree "spontaneously," though a far better job is possible, when man himself helps to reëstablish the feeling-balance.

Scientists laboring in many fields of research recognized the need of applying the scientific approach to the pressing problems of human behavior. They were in general sympathy with many of the emphases and objectives set forth in the advance chapters I had sent them. The following comments will indicate the definite trend among them toward a broader, phylic viewpoint in respect to the field of human behavior.

DR. ALAN GREGG: . . . As a general response to your general thesis, I would say that it is something of a relief to encounter your interest in an aspect of biology which encompasses the social aspects of man, and what that invites as well as entails for him as an individual. One of my major reservations regarding Freudian formulations relates to their excessive emphasis upon the encroachments, threats and frustrations imposed by others upon the individual, and the apparent neglect of the fact that man in his healthiest phases could naturally be an exuberantly and effectively social creature.

DR. RALPH S. LILLIE: . . . You have shown skilfully and convincingly how deep-seated a disparity there now is between the biological requirements of man as an animal species and the characteristics and propensities of its individual members. During evolution there seems to have been an overdevelopment of the self-regarding as distinguished from the group-regarding characters of the species; hence a condition has arisen which you describe as a conflict between the claims of the "I-persona" and the real interests of the human phylum; this conflict may well prove a source of disaster unless our scientific knowledge of human behavior advances sufficiently, on both the theoretical and applied sides, to make possible effective preventive measures.

DR. CARNEY LANDIS: . . . That it is impossible to set up a meaningful and consistent distinction between health and disease, between normal and neurosis in terms other than those which you have used, is to me apparent. The necessity for a scientific understanding of affect is most urgent in all of the life sciences. Your methodology has given as much, or more, objective evidence to this field as exists today. Freudian psychoanalysis gave us an understanding of the pathology of affective life and some knowledge of individual behavior but it did not provide any insight into social pathology or social hygiene. Phylobiology does provide a formulation of direct use for social hygiene.

DR. KURT GOLDSTEIN: . . . I agree with you that only a better knowledge of the nature of man can bring about improvements in handling the conflicts, and that a great hindrance to getting that knowledge are the great prejudices by which our thinking, particularly also that of the scientists, is dominated.

I agree with you that the study of behavior by the "layman" is at least as important as by scientists. I would think even more. Scientists have not seldom more prejudices in respect to the relation of man to man than laymen. The usual scientific approach makes the scientist often inclined to consider the phenomena in (artificial) isolation and to overlook therefore the reasons for the difficulties in coming to a natural relationship . . .

You are very right that a better understanding of our own feelings and conflicts is necessary, a better knowledge of the neurodynamics of the "social organism."

DR. ARTHUR F. BENTLEY: . . . I am thoroughly in sympathy with you in your opposition to the other views you observe. I am thoroughly in sympathy with you in your attitude toward the I-disease. Your analogy of "medicine" appeals to me and a medicine-like phylic overcoming is indicated. Probably I would think that this last must be a long slow social-cultural-durational development.

As I say, such sympathetic comments have been most reassuring to my associates and myself. They make us feel that the time is now ripe for a direct, frontal attack upon the behavior of man. They make us feel that this attack can be a coördinated one by scientists in many different fields. We believe that scientists sense the urgent need for such concerted action and that they are prepared to apply the discipline of their scientific training to an objective approach to distorted human behavior as it occurs throughout the tissues of mankind. When scientists have given their wholehearted support to such a study, the layman will not lag far behind. We shall be well on our way to coping effectively with the serious interrelational problems that beset us at every level of social complexity — interindividual, interfamilial, intergroupal, interracial, international.

Most scientists feel that new concepts, new methods, fresh orientations are necessary if we are to break with habituation, and study objectively man's relation to man. Many of those who read the material I sent them felt that the intensive study of my associates and myself in our small laboratory of human behavior had developed techniques and orientations which would be effective in the larger program of study which must follow. Among outstanding scientists, the area of agreement and sympathy was large, although the approach we employed differed considerably from theirs.

Dr. Alfred E. Emerson: . . . Turning my thoughts to your investigations, I find we agree on the "phyloorganism" concept, on the handling of behavior as an adaptation essentially tied in with the physiology of the organism (especially neurophysiology), and the interrelationship between environment and organism, both individual and social. Our methods are somewhat different. You, of necessity, are handling the data on subjective attitudes and actions that are difficult for a biologist to study through scientific method in animals and plants. You thus have a greater opportunity for penetrating important aspects of life, and with this opportunity goes a danger in allowing your own subjective attitudes to dominate scientific objectivity. So far as I can see, you are not only avoiding the dangers, but are investigating the basic problem.

And C. Judson Herrick says: At first glance it might seem that your emphasis on the interindividual relations, the group, the species, and my insistence upon the individual person as the most significant unit of behavior are incompatible. But this is not true. We come out at about the same place.

My correspondence showed, however, that there were real difficulties of communication between my colleagues and myself. This is most natural since I have for years been deeply engrossed in a study which has forced me to change my orientation completely and to abandon all "normal" traditional ways of regarding human behavior. Ours was in a sense a laboratory examination of our habitual ideas in respect to factors having to do with behavior — with one's own behavior. It is precisely in this field of human behavior — in the field of subjective human reactions — that I would urge scientists to observe the same unswerving fidelity to scientific canons which marks their customary approach to their own fields of research.

If we would sense something of the adamant and inhibiting quality of preconceived ideas, we might listen for a moment to a statement of Alan Gregg's along these lines: "No doubt that to be a discovering listener requires exquisite sensitiveness and a lovely freedom of imagination. But it is so evident that what you know or think obscures and limits what you can observe, that I plead with you to regard the amazing receptivity of the clinician at his best. I plead with you because I believe that the greatest handicap to the study of human beings is unconscious preconceived notions. Many a hypothesis is accompanied by preconceived notions, and these may dull our general perceptiveness and blind us to the context and the circumstances of the event observed."[2]

Thus in my attempt to clarify my position in regard to the field of man's interrelationships, I must ask my colleagues to take their responsible part through considering their own affective preconceptions regarding human behavior. Several of my correspondents expressed interest in our studies but spoke at the same time of the difficulty in aligning my thesis with their thinking.

> C. JUDSON HERRICK says: . . . For many years I have read your publications with appreciation, but somehow have found it difficult to fit your formulations into the frame of my own patterns of thought.
>
> In a letter from ARTHUR BENTLEY there is this comment: . . . As a worker at this stage of world-development, I cannot fit your manner of statement and mine together profitably.
>
> LELAND HINSIE puts it this way: Evidently I cannot *feel* your thesis as you do, though I think many have been on the periphery of it. As I read and tried to grasp the meaning of *The Neurosis of Man* I felt a kinship, sensed it, but I couldn't make it fall into any one of my thinking compartments.

An altered frame of reference in any field of science requires the forging of new understandings. By the very nature of the circumstance, one cannot rely upon accustomed thought-patterns in evaluating the new orientation. In other words, my thesis cannot be expected to fall into accustomed thought-patterns. It certainly did not fall into mine or into those of my associates, except under the duress of rigid and long-continued discipline. Our accustomed ways of thinking and feeling were at variance with the experimental discipline we adopted, and with the findings which grew out of this discipline. As with scientists laboring in other fields, our attempt was to hold in abeyance our preconceptions in regard to human behavior, and allow the authority of observable data to determine our formulations. This is the position I am emboldened to urge upon my colleagues because of its alignment with their training as scientists.

NOTES

1 Subsequently published in *Philosophy of Science*, 1949, Vol. 16, pp. 25-40.
2 See note 1, Chapter I.

CHAPTER III

"NORMALITY" AND THE MEANING OF THE SOCIAL NEUROSIS

Many of the letters I received indicated that I had not succeeded in conveying a clear impression of phylobiological concepts in regard to "normality" and "the social neurosis." In order to assist in the clarification of these important issues, I shall quote from some of the letters I received, and formulate our phylobiological concepts in this area in reference to them. In the latter task I shall draw freely from the letters I wrote my colleagues in response to their queries.

PROFESSOR GEORGE BOAS writes: . . . I am not sure that I understand what you mean by "normality," I am not sure whether you use it in a normative or a descriptive sense. Descriptively, as I have no need to tell you, the normal is simply the most usual and I have an inclination to use the term that way. But sometimes you seem to slip over into the other meaning and indeed it is hard for me to understand how therapy can operate without some such meaning to guide it. But if you are trying to get people to behave as most of them do, then clearly you would be re-orienting them towards the social neurosis. And it is perfectly clear that you don't want that!

PROFESSOR A. J. CARLSON phrases his question this way: You evidently are putting a new meaning in the term *neurosis*. It is probably not "neurosis" for man or beast to react initially to the new or the unknown with apprehension or fear. That is probably one factor in survival. Again, if all individuals and social groups are afflicted with the same kind and degree of *neurosis* all the time, where is our standard of comparison? Can behavior based purely on ignorance or faulty understanding be called *neurosis*?

DR. ALAN GREGG says: It seemed to me that the prevalent power of "normality" could be best attacked and disposed of by pointing out what purposes of the I-persona a wide acceptance of normality is made to serve. Is it not probably true that man wants normality in others so that his fellows' conduct will be more predictable for the operations of his I-persona plans? And occasionally, as Ronald Hargreaves pointed out, as a reassurance and protection? And occasionally to give him (when he conforms to its dictates) a sense of "belonging" and so the very sense of cotention he misses much of the time?

Dr. Robert H. Thouless writes me as follows: I do not feel quite clear as to the ground on which you adopt the standard by which you judge men to be neurotic. There is no difficulty for the Freudian since he does not attempt to get outside the current social norms and merely tries to bring deviant individuals back to those norms. I think one needs a stronger argument than I have yet found in your chapters (it may be in the part I have not read) to justify the contention that these norms are at fault and that a better standard of the healthy personality can be formulated. For myself, if I understand it aright, your standard is one that I accept and have long accepted however imperfectly I may have attained it. But what would be your reply to the man who rejects it and believes in patriotism and his own country right or wrong, and down with the Jews, Wops and Negroes? It is not enough to say "You don't accept phylobiological awareness because you suffer from a neurosis which alienates you from all except a narrow group of your fellow-men." That may be true but it is not a sufficient rational support for the statement that phylobiological awareness is a better attitude than patriotism.

There are, of course, many meanings attaching to the word "normal." In a descriptive usage, as Professor Boas points out, "normal" means simply the average or most usual. In the field of psychiatry and other disciplines which deal with man's behavior, however, the term is used in an evaluative significance. "Normal" is applied to that type of behavior that is considered healthy, while "abnormal" is reserved for behavior that is regarded as disordered or pathological. This habit of thinking is deeply entrenched in the psychiatric and, indeed, in the lay mind. It is naturally easy to see how the common, the average and usual should come to be accepted as the healthy and fitting. I have no quarrel with this general extension of meaning in the field of somatic medicine.

Although there may be considerable individual variation in normal body temperature, a temperature of 98° would satisfactorily indicate the absence of fever and a condition of health from this point of view. But where a function is disordered throughout the species, as our researches indicate is the case with man's social behavior, then obviously a grave error is committed in aligning the usual or average behavior with healthy behavior. This is the reason that I have laid so much stress on the matter and have substituted "social reaction-average" for "normality" as it applies to behavioral factors.

In response to Professor Carlson's comment in regard to my use of *neurosis,* it is true that our work definitely advances an altered viewpoint, puts forth new and broader implications in respect to this term. Its customary use, of course, is to designate obviously maladjusted behavior and to differentiate it in type from the usual behavior characterizing social groups. As a result of my early psychoanalytic practice I came to doubt the validity of the differentiation usually made between normal and neurotic behavior. I sensed that the conflict and division which so sorely beset my patients was of one cloth with the conflict and dissension characterizing social groups or communities. I suspected that the irrational prejudices and emotional projections so plaguing my patients were duplicated, in socially accepted form, in the behavior of so-called normality. Resolving to subject my ideas to experimental test, I assembled a group of associates, students and patients, and embarked upon intensive daily sessions in group-analysis.[1]

This step marked the initiation of an inclusive laboratory study of human interrelations. As in other laboratory procedures, the chief objective of our group was independent research. There was not at any time the attempt to acquire greater knowledge *per se,* to achieve clearer ideas in regard to what human behavior ought or ought not to be — what is called "right" and what is called "wrong"— but rather to see if human behavior has been artificially deflected from what it primarily, biologically *is*. The technique employed was internal rather than projective. Unlike the more recently developed group therapies, it was not a study of the reactions of the *other* person. It was a study *of* the group *by* the group in the immediate moment of social interchange. This concentration on a long-term study of disruptive interrelational factors within ourselves in social groups has been the major feature of our phylobiological approach, and accounts for our altered orientation in regard to the field of human behavior and its disorders.

The early years of our group researches convincingly demonstrated that "normal" social behavior is not biologically healthy social behavior. They demonstrated that the same element of basic anxiety, of guilt, of conflicting motivations, of emotional projection, of wishful thinking and feeling, of prejudice and self-bias determines the behavior of normal and neurotic alike. They led us to feel that man as a global community or race suffers from a *social neurosis*. It is precisely because of our subjective involvement in this common social neurosis that the condition is not recognized and dealt with.

The adequacy of the concept of the "normal" as a criterion in respect to nervous and mental disorders has come increasingly under fire in recent years. It is generally recognized today that there is a problem here that is in need of clarification. But the quite radical point of view inherent in the phylobiological orientation is not generally appreciated. Very often the question is phrased to me in this manner. "I agree, of course, that neurotic factors loom large in our life today. There are certainly many evidences in the community of emotional immaturity and even schizoid trends. But don't we also find the well-adjusted, mature personality? Do you mean that all normal people are functioning under the handicap of a neurosis?" To which my unequivocal response is that I definitely do. All of us, normal and neurotic alike, live and have our being in a sea of bias and fantasy. And we are for the most part oblivious to the condition. None of us realizes to what extent the behavior of each of us is governed by a pseudo-identity or *'I'-persona*. We do not realize to what extent unconscious systems of prejudice and wishful thinking have become fashioned into a pictorial self that is biologically alien to the organism. These biologically unrealistic systems were early imbued in us as children, and are perpetuated from generation to generation. We tend to accept them as valid, as "human nature." We do not want to dig in and study them objectively. But we must. A general recognition of the nature of the behavioral illness from which we suffer socially is a prerequisite to a concerted attack upon the problem by scientist and layman alike.

Perhaps an analogy from the field of medicine may be helpful. As we know, the early students of diseases endemic to the tropics brought back with them accounts of communities in which the natives, without exception, regarded the incidence of intermittent chills and fever as a condition natural to their kind as a tribe or group. These clinical manifestations were common to all individuals in these communities. They did not know anything else and, in their lack of acquaintance with modern medical discoveries, the concomitance of intermittent chills and fever and the presence of a pathogenic organism in the blood did not occur to them. They accepted the various symptoms of their infection as a matter of course. After all, the persistence of the symptoms of malaria among them day in and day out was their habitual experience, both as individuals and as a social community. As this experience constituted their sole frame of reference, they had no other recourse than to accept it, however esoteric and false, as evidence of a universal and valid "norm."

Today there is the universal presence in man of disordered interrelational processes, of a deflected mode of attention in relating him to his social environment. The malaria-infected peoples to whom we have just referred did not know the basic biological cause of their disorder until some other individuals of their species came along who had had the opportunity to make an objective study of the underlying factors in their symptomatology, and who were therefore in a position to introduce among them a wholly altered viewpoint. This altered viewpoint came about through consistent bacteriological researches into the physiological cause of malarial fever. Prior to the introduction of this objective approach to their condition, there was malaise and illness in these malaria-ridden communities but no standard of comparison for viewing this disordered condition. It has been similar with the image-ridden and destructive social reactions of modern man.

The typical behavior of man — the typical behavior of ourselves — is neurotic. It is motivated in reference to the behaviorally isolated self rather than to the species. The common motivation inhering in the solidarity of man as a biological organism has been disrupted and distorted. In the field of man's relation to man we therefore have a situation in which the accustomed reaction is unbalanced and maladjusted. There is futile conflict and dissension at each step up the ladder of complexity in social interaction. There is prejudice and hostile competition within the close family group, between one family and another, between groups of differing social, educational and economic status. There is bigotry and conflict between peoples of differing religious convictions, political beliefs, racial extraction and national boundaries. At the most massive level of human interaction is the deadly and implacable conflict between vast aggregates of peoples with divergent ideological concepts and forms of government — between totalitarianism and liberalism, communism and democracy.

Granted the fact that normal behavior does not represent healthy behavioral adaptation, the question of a standard of evaluation is, as Professor Carlson and Dr. Boas indicate, immediately raised. It is impossible for any science or for any therapeutic process to operate without a normative standard. Indeed, it is the disclosure of a norm of behavior consonant with man's biological development, with which our work has been primarily concerned. This question of a comparative standard of values was precisely my quarry in setting out upon group- or phylo-analysis. In the midst of world conflict and disorder, in the midst of insanity and crime, dissension and war, where, I asked myself, is there a criterion of behavior — where the needed standards of comparison? I wanted to find a valid "standard of comparison" between a healthy and an unhealthy basis of human adaptation. Having recognized a certain parallel between the symptomatic behavior of my neurotic patients and that of individuals and communities commonly accounted "normal," I began to search among these two categories for basic factors — for a possible common denominator. This, as I have said, entailed my innovation of the group-method of analysis — an analysis of groups composed of both normal and neurotic subjects, in which each individual served as analyst and analysand, and in which my associates and I were always included as intrinsic elements within this common social medium.

Our studies showed that a system of wishful affects and prejudices clusters about the self-image of each individual, obstructing a common coördination of function within the group as a whole. As Dr. Gregg intimates in his comment, the resultant breach in the phyloörganism's basic unity of function is organically intolerable to man, and the now separated individual, in trying desperately to reunite himself to himself, reaches out interindividually in order to bridge this unwelcome gap. But because the nature of the breach has to do with the interposition of a partitive, affecto-symbolic behavior-motivation, he unconsciously reaches out only wishfully, affectively, in his symbolic effort toward harmonious intercommunication and contact.

This factor of wishful affect proved to be the common denominator underlying our individual and social symptomatology. Further research indicated that this subjective factor in the behavior of each individual was correlated with a disturbance in the function of attention. As we know, man becomes related to his environment through the process of attention. Physiological components play a prominent rôle in any act of attention. Our studies succeeded in differentiating two types of attention in man which were accompanied by discriminable patterns of physiological tension. One type of attention, with its concomitant pattern of tension, results in false social perceptions, in interrelational prejudice and behavioral conflict. I have called this constellation *ditention* to indicate its divisive and conflicting aspects. The other type of attention, and its associated tensional pattern, results in direct, unprejudiced and coöperative behavior. This mode I have called *cotention* to indicate the unified nature of the response and its conduciveness to healthy (whole) social behavior. Instrumental studies of respiratory, brain-wave and oculomotor patterns show that the patterning of these functions is reliably different in cotention and in ditention. These physiological patterns will be discussed more fully in Chapter VIII. I merely wish to indicate here that this demarcation of ditention and cotention gave us a standard of behavioral adaption which we feel distinguishes in a consistent and valid way between health and disease.

I am particularly indebted to PROFESSOR NICOLAS RASHEVSKY for his full and interesting comments on the concept of normality. He says:

> While I entirely agree with you that what is usually accepted as normality in social behavior is quite a relative concept, changing frequently with changing conditions, I feel that you do not complete the logical step in the right direction. You try to introduce a new concept of normality which would have an absolute meaning. It seems to me that this procedure is hardly justified.
>
> You state that such a more or less absolute and objective concept of normality can be established in biology and medicine. I am inclined to challenge this statement. . . .
>
> The same [relativity and inconsistency] would hold about many other so-called norms in biology and medicine. To use a slight modification of your own example, suppose that all

human beings would be carriers of typhoid, but that no one would be susceptible to it. Although the pathologists would find the microörganisms in every individual, they certainly would not have any reason to consider these individuals as abnormal under these circumstances. It is only in a community where a large number of individuals is susceptible to that disease that a pathologist would classify as abnormal those people who are themselves healthy but act as carriers.

Again, if all individuals were color blind or if only a fraction of a per cent would have what we now call normal vision, color blindness would be regarded as normal.

Take another example which illustrates the relativity even of the biomedical norm. It is considered that the basal metabolic rate is normal within a range of $\pm\ 10$. The arbitrariness and relativity of this normalization is, of course, quite apparent. It is based on the observation that individuals with a BMR within a range of $\pm\ 10$ do not show any clinical manifestations of disorders. However if the thyroid functions of such a "normal" individual with a BMR of, say, $+\ 9$ would be affected so that his BMR would drop to, say, $-\ 9$, it is more than likely that the individual's general well feeling may be affected, although he still may not show any clear cut clinical symptoms of thyroid deficiency.

I believe that the concept of normality, no matter how defined, always remains relative. In biology and in particular in pathology, we may define a normal condition or a normal function as one that provides the maximum intensity of well feeling in an individual. One might, however, object against such a definition because, for example, a drug addict certainly experiences some pleasure during those intervals when he uses a particular drug, but in the long run he will suffer periods of distress. Hence, we may improve the definition by defining a normal function or condition as such which maximizes the time integral of the intensity of well feeling taken over the whole life span of the individual. A still further improvement may perhaps be made by maximizing the integral or total intensity of well feeling over the whole society or species. But regardless of which definition we accept, it still remains relative to something.

I believe that the same considerations hold about the normalcy of human behavior. Without having read the manuscript as a whole I am not too clear from Chapter VIII how you wish to define the objective normalcy of which you speak. I can, however, readily see that we could define a normal behavior as one that leads, for instance, to maximum happiness of the society as a whole or, still better, to a maximum integral of happiness in the society over a definite period of time. In my "Mathematical Theory of Human Relations" I have to some extent endeavored to study and classify some types of behavior from this point of view, although I expect to publish in the near future a much more detailed study along these lines.[2]

But again, the normality introduced in any such way is no more objective and no more absolute than the normality arbitrarily accepted by our present society. I believe that it would add considerably to the consistency of your argument if you frankly accept the relativity of the concept of normality. I do not see that it would in any way affect your basic arguments.

The mathematician speaks of normal forms and normalized functions but he is fully aware that these norms are nothing but useful conventions. I am inclined to think that as in physics the realization of the relativity of space and time has led to further progress and outlooks, so will the realization of relativity of some biological and sociological concepts, hitherto assumed to have an absolute meaning, serve the further progress of those disciplines.

I can readily understand Dr. Rashevsky's concern lest the examples I cite in my book in regard to objective and constant norms in the fields of biology and medicine should militate against an acceptance of my thesis rather than foster an understanding of it. I can see that I have been none too clear in the matter of which he speaks. It is evident from Dr. Rashevsky's discussion that a certain relativity is a function of norms, and my thesis really has no disagreement with such an interpretation. In general, our trend is in line with a relativistic as over against an absolutistic, static approach. At the same time, however, we must aim, I believe, at establishing certain principles that are more basic than the ever-changing values of the normal reaction-average. So that I heartily accord with Dr. Rashevsky in his suggestion of a norm of human behavior which insures a maximum of well-being for the species man. The need for this more basic norm of behavioral health is precisely the reason why I am so insistent in my efforts to point out the inadequacy of the present concepts of normality as they apply to behavior and its disorders.

According to our researches, the behavior we regard as "normal" is in no sense biologically sound and coördinated. It insures the essential well-being of neither the individual nor the community. Our highly vaunted behavioral norm is analogous to the situation which would apply in medicine if, through some hardly imaginable quirk, a basal metabolic rate of 140 ± 10 would be considered "normal" although such a rate produced many signs and symptoms of clinical pathology resulting from an extreme physiological imbalance. Our habitual social modes of behavior are today considered "normal" and hence indicative of a fundamental behavioral balance in spite of the signs and symptoms of individual and social pathology present on all sides—unreasoning prejudice and bigotry, neurosis and crime, religious, industrial and international conflict, etc.

What I object to is our custom of applying the concept of normality to the *habitual* in the field of behavior without regard to the inherent fitness of the behavior involved in promoting the health and progression of individual and species. My chief interest is in the urgent need, as it appears to me, of measures for discriminating between disease (disordered adaptation, individual and social) and a relatively constant integral of health.

Just as there is no standard of comparison in a malarial community where all individuals suffer from the disease, there is no valid standard today in the field of human behavior. The "normal-abnormal" dichotomy which we habitually employ is biologically meaningless. "Normality" merely refers to that type of behavior participated in and popularly endorsed by man's prevailing social reaction-average, irrespective of the evidences of behavioral imbalance this artificial standard engenders. Such a norm is invalid since it does not describe a condition that provides "the maximum intensity of well feeling" for either individual or species.

In response to my position in regard to normality, I am sometimes asked if I would have people abnormal. I do not see that. Or super-normal. Nor that either. Not any more than in wishing to protect a physically "normal" society from the germ of tuberculosis, I would contemplate a society of abnormal or super-normal organisms. Correspondents sometimes think, too, that I am pessimistic—that I emphasize the drab and negative aspect of things. But I really can see no less progressive and optimistic a note in a thesis indicting society at large in its behavioral structure than in the bacteriological thesis that holds the whole race of man to be more or less affected by incipient tubercular processes. It does not seem to me any reflection upon the essential health—upon the essentially constructive forces resident in our human tissues—to say and to insist that they are universally liable to, if not actually infected with, a tubercular process. Neither do I feel myself to be unmindful of the beneficent forces operative in the social life of man when I say that his social life has come to be burdened and impaired throughout with processes that are definitely destructive to the rounded and healthy functioning of the individual and the race. So please let me acclaim forthwith my hearty sense of life's basic affirmation and my feeling that, fundamentally, man—original, natural man—is quite sound and wholly delightful!

My emphasis upon the *pathology* of society and my insistently calling attention to this aspect of things is probably what makes difficulty for my readers. Yet I know very well that were I, as a physician, treating, let us say, a case of typhoid fever and giving my undivided attention day and night to the study and treatment only of the various features of the *diseased* condition (assuming, of course, the establishment of a general hygienic program), my readers would not think me heedless of or doubting the primary healthiness of the human organism. On the contrary, they would be inclined to think my confidence in the processes of repair and of health all the greater because I showed my willingness to trust completely to the working of these constructive processes, and devoted my attention entirely to removing such diseased states as interfered with them. And so with man's behavioral health—his clearer sense of meanings and their values within and about him. This, it seems to me, will take satisfactory care of itself, pursue its own integral course, if we can remove those conditions, specific or general, that now tend to interfere with the coördinated functioning of individual and society.

NOTES

[1] A report of an early phase of this undertaking is included in *Our Common Neurosis: Notes on a Group Experiment* by Charles B. Thompson, M.D. and Alfreda P. Sill, New York, Exposition Press, 1953, pp. xxxii + 210. The Foreword to this book was written by Dr. Burrow. [Ed.]

[2] Rashevsky, Nicolas, *Mathematical Biology of Social Behavior*, Chicago, The University of Chicago Press, 1951, pp. xii + 256.

CHAPTER IV

THE RIGHT-WRONG DICHOTOMY IN HUMAN BEHAVIOR

As I have briefly indicated in Chapter I, our phylobiological view in regard to the whole sphere of moral convictions is a radically altered one. It happens that the advance chapters of my book which I sent to my confreres touched only very lightly on this problem and consequently there were few questions from them in regard to it. But through the years, there have been many queries from correspondents as to my position in respect to those dichotomous alternatives for evaluating interrelational conduct known as "good" and "bad," "right" and "wrong." I have therefore thought it wise to include a chapter on this topic, the more so as it constitutes a vital element in our altered behavioral orientation. Since I feel that my formulations with respect to "normal" moral values have become clearer and more specific in recent writings,[1] I greatly welcome this opportunity to restate them here.

Dr. David Katz feels some uncertainty about my challenge of the basis of our accustomed behavioral standards. He questions in what way the education of the child can be brought about without resorting to authoritarian values of "right" and "wrong." He says:

> If I understand correctly your aim to free man from his neurotic behavior, it is to bring him into harmony with nature and with his fellow men, that is, to bring him through the suppression of all egoistic motives, roughly speaking, into the highest coöperation in the interest of the largest community. There are probably few men who would not agree with such an aim. And it could hardly be questioned that we are here concerned with an effort that belongs in the domain of pedagogy. In this connection here is my first question: How can it be accomplished without differentiating between "correct" and "false," between "right" and "wrong," that is, without turning to values and thus to a certain extent making use of the viewpoint of authority? But you seem to oppose that. And that is not clear to me. Do you consider the behavior of a colony of bees as an ideal of human society? But

that does not seem possible, as man can no longer exist under the purely artless conditions typical of nature.

Let me say first that although I attack root and branch the popularly accepted criterion of conduct described as "right" and "wrong," there is no emotional or vindictive element in my position. I am not a cynic or a misanthrope. In an issue that is no less human than scientific, I realize that it is obligatory upon me that I do not sweep away those criteria which have ever been the keystone in the government of human relations, without a deep sense of scientific as well as human responsibility.

I do not for a moment question the importance of values. There is no doubt in my mind as to the existence of a type of motivation and behavior that is biologically right or fitting. In a very true sense all life normally functions in conformity to a principle of action that is fitting or correct. We see its operation in the behavior of animals. It is the unwritten law of growth on every hand. Everywhere there is evidence of the healthy, constructive *right* process, and this may be contrasted with the process that is disintegrative, disordered or *wrong*. The right or fitting function is discernible in all of life's processes, whether in the sphere of microscopic organisms and their interactions, or of human biology and the interrelational behavior of man.[2] The healthy infant represents the acme of what is biologically fitting. It sleeps seasonably; its food intake and elimination are properly regulated. The infant's muscular coördination, its space sense, and the gradually increasing excursions of its interests and activities—all this is right, all this is fitting, all this is biologically sound and healthy. Such a biological right admits of no dichotomy, no alternatives. It is neither moral nor immoral. It is the total organism of man in balanced function. It is the constant and harmonious principle of homeostasis in man's relation to man.

The premise for my downright disavowal of our current standards as to what is right in the behavioral field rests solely upon our research findings. We have already seen in Chapter III that the customary distinction between normal and neurotic behavior could not be supported on the basis of our studies. Our group investigations also demonstrated to us the wishful, unrealistic nature of the prevailing precept governing the behavior of human communities—the precept subjectively experienced by everyone as a sense of right and wrong. They made clear that a conflict has entered into our sense of right, and that our customary moral evaluations bear little relation to an intrinsic biological criterion. Our studies brought home to us the fact that the commonly accepted sense of right governing our human relations is fundamentally so defective as to impair its validity throughout the entire field of man's behavior. They further made evident that this artificial sense of right and wrong is coeval in man with a false sense of identity — with a socially conditioned image of the self. This false principle of the self is the social entity I have called the 'I'-persona. Phyloanalysis disclosed that human society is composed of arbitrary 'I'-personae with their artificial agreements and disagreements based upon a private, esoteric sense of right, and that we ourselves embody just such 'I'-personae.

One of the chief objectives in our group or community studies of man's behavior was the consistent challenge of this state of mind or mood man expresses in his wishful sense of right. The analysis of this inconsistent and emotional criterion was the very crux of our approach to the problem of human relations. Setting aside all question as to whether this one or that one is "right," we turned to the phenomenon of "rightness" — to the systematized self-image, and the private, wishful advantage inseparable from it — as exemplifying a state of mind that affects both sides equally.

In our group-analysis one thing became unquestionably clear: we were all *right* — incorrigibly right. I have greatly valued the privilege of this opportunity that group-analysis gave me for sensing how very "right" we all are — we and our various systems of ideas. Instead of accommodating ourselves to "right" systems of ideas, it has been the unremitting task of our experimental group to challenge our own obsessive tendency toward "rightness." Through investigating this inveterate "rightness" within the subjective processes of each of us, it has been the hope of group-analysis to throw much-needed light upon the tragic moral dualism characterizing the behavior of man — "normal" as well as neurotic.

But I must indicate what our group researches show in respect to the development and cultural transmission of the biologically false evaluations embodied in man's moral concepts. We are first brought to a sense of what is right — to an appreciation of the difference between "right" and "wrong" — in early infancy. As I have said, there exists in the child an inherent, instinctual, biologically healthy feeling for what is right in the sense of man's unity and coördination as a common species. It is as innate to a child as is his sense of physical equilibrium or his visual response to a moving object. Very early in our lives, however, there is inculcated in us a false sense of right that is esoteric, peculiar to "me." By and large, a child's sense of bodily equilibrium remains undisturbed and continues to bind him effectively to his physical environment; his visual responses continue to coördinate him with the objects surrounding him. But the sense of right imparted by the adult generation definitely distorts the child's innate capacity for organismic coördination with his fellows. It is not continuous with the common rights of his kind. It is organically irreconcilable with his inherent, biological mode of feeling and thinking. For the sense of right that is drilled into the child is based upon a divisive mood of private advantage, of socially sanctioned personal gain in respect to one's interrelations with the community. Owing to the development of this type of personal, moralistic rightness and the divisive mood which accompanies it, man has departed from the fitting behavior that is the law of his nature — *the biological norm of behavior* as I call it. It is this organismic norm, this inherent law of function which I believe we have somehow to reinstate.

The parent, then — every parent — invokes a sense of right and wrong that is not biologically sound, that is quite different from the organically fitting and unfitting processes characterizing natural phenomena elsewhere. The sense of right inculcated by the parent is arbitrarily induced through moralistic precepts and cannot be supported by the child's objectively verifiable experience. It is seldom conformable with the coördinating principle of organism-environment rapport inherent in the behavior of the healthy organism. Too generally, in obedience to his or her own childhood training, the parent inculcates in the offspring a course of behavior that has no dependable basis but is merely in line with his private wish or advantage. That is, in the parent's deviation of attention and interest from the biologically fitting pattern of behavior, he automatically induces in the child a pattern of behavior that is also automatically deviate and unfitting. A wish motive has superseded the organism's primary motivation. If the child conforms to what the mother from her wishful basis says is "right" — a "right" for which there is no biological verification — he wins love and reward. If the child does not conform, he is confronted with the parent's ill will, irritation, rejection, perhaps punishment. This love or disaffection, this assurance or rejection, this conformity or non-conformity constitutes the dual mood or motivation induced by the parent's approval or disapproval. The child is thus inducted into a constellation of purely wishful reactions. Wishing to be loved and approved, he comes to pursue a policy of differential advantage rather than one of consistent and intelligent motivation.

With the word "right" as it is applied by the parent in regard to the child's behavior, the child does not receive a signal or symbol of any objectively stable circumstance or situation or law. What conveys itself is the emotional response of the parent, the social *affect* attached to this symbol. The child senses the authoritarian mood of the parent and, like the parent, becomes the possessor of an absolute, authoritarian mood. He, in turn, will henceforth legislate as to the meaning of "right." Were the child employing logic, his reasoning would run something like this: "Says my Mother, 'I am right.' Well, if this 'I' is always right, since I also am an 'I,' I am right too." But he does not employ abstract reasoning, of course. He doesn't need to. The divided, authoritarian mood or affect is inescapably conveyed along with the presenting of the symbol "right," and the child responds affectively to this mood and to the symbol with which it is connected. He is involuntarily imbued with the parental mood that accompanies, or is associated with, the parental symbol. The parent presents a system of involuntarily conditioned stimuli, namely, an affective mood of authoritarian absolutism and autocracy, and the child, in turn, responds with an affective mood of authoritarian autocracy and absolutism.

In effect, the attitude of the parent is one that says to the child: "There is something in this world called 'good' and 'bad,' 'right' and 'wrong' that is not susceptible of objective verification. Your behavior may be 'good' or 'bad' at any time, and the only way you can tell is by my response—by the adventitious symbol 'good' or 'bad,' and the emotional tone associated with it. This 'good' and 'bad' is nothing that you can discover firsthand through your organism's response to the things about you." The implied position of the parent is: "I, as all right-thinking parents, embody a sense of right and wrong that is unimpeachable and that is not to be questioned. Look to your parents and to the community of right-thinking people, and learn to sense the mood or feeling-tone inseparable from this sense of right, this indefinable standard of behavior. You must acquire a similar mood. You must acquire this sense of a right that must be observed at all times but can at no time be questioned, investigated or demonstrated. You must assimilate this mood of rightness that is mine and the community's, and in this way you will enter into a system of customs and beliefs which will henceforth regulate your interrelational conduct and furnish a norm of social behavior."

As I have already indicated, this parental or social norm differs markedly from the child's biological norm. With the biological norm, consistency is the rule. With the social norm, the rule is inconsistency. There is no objectively dependable constant. The child must look into and watch the faces of his elders; he must sense their tone of voice in order to determine what is the "right" as contrasted with the "wrong" response. This is to be "good" or "right" in sheer unconscious obedience to the parental fallacy that in this "goodness" lies the child's constructive adaptation to the environment and to other persons.

And so the morally imbued child sets out prepared to defend with his life, if necessary, a right-wrong principle of behavior that is utterly indefensible. As a matter of fact, the logical outcome is that in defense of this spurious principle he frequently pays the price of his life. For such a sense of divisive "rightness" must lead finally to armed conflict. The ultimate way of exercising this artificial, this objectively indeterminate and indeterminable "right" is the destruction of the individual or community or nation whose "right" presumes to oppose one's own. This adamant adherence to a private and esoteric sense of right explains the utter futility of peace negotiations. It explains the circumstance why men, otherwise intelligent, spend months and even years in efforts to reconcile differences in ideology when these ideological differences rest upon a reflex mood of absolutism and autocracy which of its nature defies all access. Men of good will are constantly saying "We don't want war," and "No intelligent man wants war." But war is an involuntary response of man to an artificial sense of "right," and involuntarily he goes to war. It is an automatic compulsion with him and, on his present basis of thinking and feeling, he can do nothing about it. Under the proper inciting stimulus man must react with the corresponding reflex response. He must be "right" and go to war.

The mood of separate personal rightness constitutes a serious flaw in the behavior of social man. Throughout the entire domain of man's motivation, a private feeling-sense attaches to the word "right" where no intrinsic affinity exists between them. Generation after generation a partitive, emotional tone or coloring is passed down from parent to infant, and this specious standard replaces the biologically right relationship subsisting primarily between the organism and its environment. Yet this counterfeit standard is the paramount determinant of our interrelational thinking and feeling. In consequence, a false start, a false premise of evaluation is inculcated in the child—in all children. Owing to the spurious feeling-tone imparted to the child with the symbol "right," man is under the thralldom of a superstition that is no less active today than in the earliest period of his history.

Mother says "No," or Mother says "Yes," still dominates, still is the accepted authority for us grown-up children the world over. Is it "good"? Is it "bad"? We are obsessed by this empty dualism. The parent—the generation of parents—diverts the attention of the infant organism from direct appreciation of the actual environment, as of actual man, and bids us watch what may be the pleasure of the parental monitors who serve vicariously as our guide to nature and to life. If man will recognize the conditioning, he will recognize the condition. He will recognize that he is, as a species, the victim of a wishful, superstitious mood to which he has been unconsciously subjugated through a *faux pas* in his social development that has placed a premium upon a wishful, autocratic right in contrast to the stable organic right inherent in the biology of man. But to deliver ourselves—for man to deliver himself—from bondage to this ditentive mood demands internal investigation on the part of man, on the part of man's *self*. Man throughout is an invalid. He is a patient.

Professor W. M. Krogman questions whether my thesis may not necessitate the cancelling out of social values. He says:

> ... At all events, I cannot perceive how you can—or propose to—eliminate social values. I cannot as yet grasp a human being with any organic behavior (apart from sheer function) that is not culturally modified (or at least modifiable).

With this position I most heartily agree. But the destructive element in the cultural modification is what I have been driving at over the years. Needless to say, I do not wish to eliminate social values. But social values, if they are to be truly effective, must be an intrinsic aspect of man's basic motivation and behavior. My point is that the social values of civilized man today are largely divorced from biologically sound criteria. They are arbitrary and inconsistent, varying from one culture to another and from time to time within the same culture. Man's sense of right is not continuous and common. It does not lead to healthy social functioning. On the contrary, it is based, as we have seen, upon wishful social precepts in which personal convenience or advantage supersedes principles of common community coördination and health.

As we consider our conflicting individual and international relations, it becomes only too clear that "rightness" is a personal fetish, not a consensual criterion. On the basis of this vacillating and uncertain standard, everyone feels privileged to claim that he is "right" in his opinion concerning the conduct of other people or himself. Every "I" or "me" is arbitrarily right in relation to every other "I" or "me." "I" am right, and those who fail to agree with "me" are not right. Hence in my wishful mood of esoteric rightness, I arbitrarily project "rightness" or "wrongness," favor or blame upon other people; and other people, of course, exercise this same interrelational prerogative in regard to me. This circumstance prevails not only for any and every individual, but for any and every community and nation.

The interpretations of any two individuals or nations, then, no matter how intelligent or cultured, may be as dissimilar as black and white. The Western Allies have their sense of right on the one side, and the Russians and their satellites a diametrically opposed sense of right on the other. The law-abiding citizen holds to a certain set of standards in respect to behavior, and the gangster, the racketeer, the criminal holds to other standards that are no less rigidly established. Lacking a demonstrable constant, all these principles of conduct rest upon a standard that is determined by an arbitrary variable or outer appearance. To be good is merely to observe what in general the community prescribes. This community prescription does not take account of the subjective prejudices or the infinite variety of conditioning among different individuals which from time to time permit of varying interpretations of this general concept of goodness. We all know the prescriptions; we all know the proscriptions. We know them up and down, back and forth. But how inadequate a criterion of behavior are the moral rules may be judged by the endless conflicts and delinquencies existing throughout the community—the dissension in families and between classes, races and creeds. It may be judged by the number of asylums and prisons erected throughout the land to take care of the ever-growing number of psychopaths and criminals.

This unilateral mood of "right," of *my* right versus *your* right—with its inevitable social conflicts—has attained the rank of an obsessive preoccupation among us all. The truth is, people do not think with their minds but with their prejudices. The daily papers carry innumerable headlines illustrative of this trend. Indeed, it would seem that man is the victim of a vast mood-contagion. Today Russia and the United States are the chief protagonists pitted against one another in the international arena. *We* contend that ours is the right sort of right, and that the Russians are wrong; while the Russians respond with equal vehemence: "*Our* right is the proper sort of right, and *yours* is wrong." So it goes. Day after day we witness and are the insatiate participants in this frantic bandying between us of the flighty shuttlecock that is *my* right. On our present ideological basis there is no stopping it. The dichotomy of right and wrong is man's Sisyphus complex. Like that ill-fated outcast, individuals and nations incessantly struggle under the enforced compulsion of this sinister alternative.

For all our unconscious conformity to social custom or morality,[3] for all our vaunted "principles" of right and wrong, the behavior of mankind is in a sorry plight. Contrary to popular prepossessions, the social injunction *pro* or *con* is incapable of giving effective guidance to human behavior. Far from providing us a consensual gauge, it leaves everyone at liberty to regard his own emotional judgment as final. Yet this mutable precept of right and wrong now serves as the backbone of man's relation to man. Our court procedures are determined by it. The laws of Church and State are wholly subservient to this unconscious dichotomy. Our educational systems and the rearing of children begin and end with the arbitrary fallacy of this vacillating precept.

When one questions the prevailing sense of "right," there is an automatic and universal outcry throughout the ranks of mankind. It is said: "If rightness, which is the formula for human behavior is outlawed, then our accustomed human relations, which rest upon this formula, are outlawed." Clearly there is no denying this deduction. But the condition cannot go on. The world is coming a cropper. Man must take a constructive and scientific attitude toward himself and his own behavior. Where conditions are such that something must be done, something will be done. At the moment the cry is, "What are we going to do about it?" This is the call to man's creative energy to which he has always responded with intelligent efficiency.

In this cry there is undoubtedly the implication that there is nothing we can do about it, that "human nature" cannot be changed. But "human nature" is not a fixed condition; it is merely another term for man's accustomed behavior. As Professor R. W. Gerard recently said in a letter to me: "I am profoundly convinced, as you are, that 'human nature' can be changed in certain important aspects, that this is an educational problem, and that mankind will someday have an attitude and organization that effectively prevents wars—if it does not blow itself up first."

There are indications today that man has reached a stage in his evolution when he *can* change his behavior as a race or species through conscious recognition of his own disordered processes. This entails, however, an internal reckoning with the indeterminate, wishful sense of right now dominating his behavior. Because of this mood-contagion seething within him, the drive toward the vindication of his personal "right" is now out of all control, and man is on the rampage. He is throughout neurotic, filled with conflict. As the condition is social, as it is pandemic, the remedy must also be social and pandemic. Apparently, therefore, it would be of profit to both East and West if they would submit to controlled analysis the contradictory mental state now universally expressed by us as "right." It would be of mutual benefit to us if, adopting the broad world-purview of the scientist, we would examine our behavior from this inclusive social premise. In the light of our group-experimentation, such a step would imbue us with an appreciation of the basic structure of man's present behavior-dilemma and, coincidently, awaken us to a sense of our common consciousness. Through such an analysis we shall find that man's common consciousness is governed by laws that are as stable and consistent in determining his behavior as the stable and consistent laws that control the world of outer phenomena. We shall find that a biologically dependable right or fitting reaction still informs man's basic behavioral patterns.

NOTES

[1] Burrow, Trigant, "Emotion and the Social Crisis: A Problem in Phylobiology," in *Feelings and Emotions. The Mooseheart Symposium*, edited by Martin L. Reymert, New York, McGraw-Hill Book Company, 1950, pp. 465-486.
Burrow, Trigant, "Prescription for Peace: The Biological Basis of Man's Ideo-

logical Conflicts," in *Explorations in Altruistic Love and Behavior*, edited by Pitirim A. Sorokin, Boston, The Beacon Press, 1950, pp. 93-117.

Burrow, Trigant, and Syz, Hans, "Two Modes of Social Adaptation and Their Concomitants in Ocular Movements," *The Journal of Abnormal and Social Psychology*, 1949, Vol. 44, pp. 191-211.

[2] As Professor C. Judson Herrick says: "The world is not mad. It is only the people in it who are mad. The world is orderly, and even human madness is lawfully ordered. It has causes and consequences which can be discovered and ameliorated." (From an unpublished manuscript, quoted in a letter to the author.)

[3] From Latin, *Mores*, customs.

CHAPTER V

BIOLOGICAL AND CULTURAL CONSIDERATIONS

Letters from several of my colleagues relate to the comparative importance of biological and cultural considerations in determining man's behavior. Some questioned my emphasis throughout on generic, biological factors and, in turn, stressed the view that disordered behavior is due to the influence of inappropriate conditioning or education. Others wished me to clarify my position in regard to the nature-nurture dichotomy. They asked whether phylobiology regarded neurosis and conflict as innate characteristics of man or as conditions brought about by his social institutions and culture. But I must let my critics speak for themselves.

PROFESSOR MELVILLE HERSKOVITS wrote me: ... You speak again and again of "human nature," or "natural processes," and how such propensities manifest themselves in thought and behavior. Yet everything that cross-cultural study has taught us has caused us more and more to adopt the view that thought and behavior—and I do not mean overt behavior and its sanctions only—take on the multitudinous forms of the many human cultures that have been analyzed. ... Man is what his culture makes of him, and the variety of cultures is such that to reach least common denominators of a formal character is hazardous indeed.

Looked at from the cross-cultural relativistic point of view of modern anthropology, ... it seems to me that you have defined "man" very narrowly, and in essentially ethnocentric terms. That is, your species is not *h. sapiens*, but *h. euro-americanus*. Much of what you say, like so many non-anthropological treatises that discuss the "nature" of man, is applicable to our culture, but scarcely to many others. I think in this connection, for example, in quite another field, of various economic "laws," or of the hypothesis of economic determinism.

The same observation is pertinent to your discussion of "the underlying structure of 'normality.'" I define the normal, certainly as far as psychopathology is concerned, in cultural terms. That is, I am unwilling to concede that what may seem abnormal to us—spirit possession, to cite a dramatic instance from my own field research—is anything but normal to people who accept it as such.

PROFESSOR JOHN DEWEY phrases his misgivings in this way: Without more knowledge I can hardly express my main difficulty or doubt with adequacy. But when you speak of "disorientation and neurosis" as the common lot of man "as a species," I am brought to a pause. That disorientation and neurosis are startling traits of our present world-culture I am not bold enough to question. But I do not know how literally to take the expression common lot of man *as a species*. It seems to be definitely a *cultural* phenomenon, not a strictly biotic one, save as "biotic" is widened to take account of the immense transformation of the physiological wrought by the cultural conditions under which men live. In consequence I think profound *institutional* changes are the precondition of any widely and enduringly successful attempt to deal with the neurotic state of present day man.

That man is now in a bad state is I believe demonstrated by and in every aspect of his life. My own "prejudice"—if an attitude that is the outcome of years of reflection is a prejudice as it doubtless is a pre-conception in approaching new material—is that we have entered a new stage of personal and institutional culture so rapidly that we have neither the benefit of the old stabilities that are disintegrating nor yet of the new, since dispositions formed in the pre-scientific pre-technological and pre-democratic age still rule our *understanding* of what in fact is a very different sort of world. Practically we have to be one sort of thing; intellectually we haven't begun to catch up—consequently we are divided emotionally.

I say this because I think it only fair you should know how definitely I see the problem as a cultural one.

The specific point about which I am most in doubt is the underlying type of concern that your work postulates between what are ordinarily called "individuals" and socio-cultural conditions. I approach this matter with what is doubtless to some extent a prejudice. While I appreciate, I hope, all that psychiatry can do for disturbed and more or less disordered individual persons, it seems to me that it is what I have called socio-cultural conditions that have to be the central and final point of attack in dealing with the spread of disordered personality. In other words, part of my difficulty is that I have not definitely made out just what your underlying postulate may be.

Professor Herskovits feels that I have not employed cross-cultural thinking in my orientation in regard to the problem of man's behavior. This may be true. At least I can readily understand his misgivings. As I said in my letter to him: "There are many scientific disciplines that I wish I might have been able to avail myself of. One of them is anthropology, another sociology. Needless to say, I am without technical training in either field, as indeed in many others. But in pursuing my investigations of the reactions of contemporary groups of people, normal and neurotic, my aim has been only to discriminate between wishfully conditioned habits of feeling and thinking (motivation) and feeling and thinking that is the expression of direct biological incitements. In contrast to the intellectual approach to human problems, this whole process of group-analysis with us has been a somewhat unusual one. There has never been any mental discussion—never any 'thinking things out.' There was the observation of an inter-relational habit of feeling and thinking that was throughout artificial, and the constant challenge of this functional artifact in our behavior as a community."

Certainly as Dr. Herskovits points out, the external expressions of behavior are relative; they differ markedly in different cultures. But there are also constancies underlying the external expressions of human behavior—constancies that reflect biological, organic, bionomic principles. As a result of my experimentation in a group-setting I was brought to recognize that while diverse cultural conditions are important in shaping external differences in maladaptive behavior, the fundamental impairment underlying these varying cultural patterns is common to man as a species. This basic impairment, discussed more fully in Chapter VIII, consists of a functional defect within the central nervous system. It is a defect through which man has lost touch with his natural sense of species solidarity—his sense of total identity as a unitary phylo-organism—and, instead, now everywhere masquerades as a heterogeneous collection of artificially separate individuals motivated throughout by a purely partitive and personal identity-sense. In consequence, our judgments in regard to social and individual values are not dependable. They will not be until there is the repudiation of this false principle of behavior in man. It seems to me that we psychoanalysts, we anthropologists, we sociologists or social scientists, are missing out utterly as long as we fail to take account of the impediment to harmonious interrelational behavior that resides *within ourselves* as a community or species. We are counting without our host when we fail to reckon with the very formidable, autocratic entity in man that I have described as the 'I'-persona.

According to our thesis, the functional impairment of which I speak developed at an early stage in man's prehistory and is reflected in all the diverse cultural patterns developed by him. It had its origin with the development of language. As I put it in a recent paper:

". . . With the beginning of the word, a new adaptation set in for man—an adaptation that has not been appreciated in all its biological significance. From the background of our group experimentation it was seen that this adaptation did not consist only of a peripheral, socio-symbolic innovation, but that it has caused a radical modification in the organismic relation of man to man as well as of man to his physical environment.

". . . With the enormous complexity and reorganization of function that arose coincidently with the invention of language, there took place a special systematization within the brain and organism of man. With the upsurge of the emotive behavior of man and its amalgamation with the highly complex code of symbol-usage, there developed a partitive behavior-organization. In this systematization of man's subjective feelings and interests there was formed a restricted behavioral personality or identity—the partitive identity I have called the 'I'-persona." [1]

I want principally to indicate here that the spurious personality factor represented by the 'I'-persona made its appearance at an early period in man's development and is transmitted from generation to generation irrespective of the specific cultural trappings pertaining in any given society, whether primitive or modern. From a phylobiological viewpoint, any obstruction to complete organism-environment rapport represents disorder. Thus spirit possession in a primitive community, and the hoarding of wealth in our own society are in this sense equally abnormal or unhealthy. Though these phenomena may occur in cultures where they are the customary reaction, they both result from and are the symptomatic expression of a common neurodynamic dysfunction. Both phenomena are the external indicators of a distortion in man's primary feeling and motivation—of a deflection in attention which blocks man from the fullest rapport with his environmental reality. Although the symptoms take different forms and systematizations in different cultures, that is, are culturally determined, the underlying disturbance is internal and common to man as a species.

This point relates to questions sometimes put to me as to the adequacy of the sample studied by us in our group investigations of the social interrelations of man. Naturally, my answer is that our group-study has in no sense been a statistical one. It will be readily understood that in a study of the type we have undertaken it would be a physical impossibility to include the number of individuals necessary for a satisfactory statistical sample covering such items as age, race, sex, national extraction, educational achievement, socio-economic status, cultural background, occupational level, rural or urban habitat, etc. Our purpose has been an intensive, long-term examination of deeply-rooted aspects of behavior rather than an extensive study of external characteristics. It is the underlying biological disturbance or the common denominator of human conflict that our investigations have sought out.

The original research group was initiated in 1918 and consisted of myself, my lay assistant, Mr. Clarence Shields, and a few of my psychoanalytic students and patients. With the progression of the researches, the group grew in number as the members of my family, as well as additional students and patients, professional and lay, joined in the endeavor. Other groups developed as a result of interest in our studies. The composition of the original research group changed from time to time but the maximal number never exceeded twenty-five members. It has continued its work throughout the years, and some of its members compose the nucleus of The Lifwynn Foundation today.

As I said in Chapter III, one of the chief objectives with which we set out was to determine whether the fundamental behavioral processes actuating so-called "normal" interrelational responses were of a piece with the behavioral processes underlying the maladjusted social response of the frankly neurotic individual. With this purpose in mind, the research group comprised not only students with varying degrees of neurotic maladjustment but also socially well-adjusted individuals. It also happened that, as a matter of chance, the group did include persons who differed widely in outer social characteristics. There were individuals of wealth and also those whose sole support was derived from wages for daily manual labor. The students also differed in their educational attainments and in social background. Some had no college training and came from average homes in rural communities; some were college graduates; some were professional men and women possessing exceptional specialized training. The ages of the participants ranged from early adolescence to the middle sixties. In this very limited sense, then, our research group may be spoken of as cross-sectional in composition.

In view of the nature and technique of our researches, we do not feel that accidental social characteristics are important factors. They are most certainly important where one's interest is confined to the social *symptoms* of individual or group, that is, to socially conditioned affect-projections. A conversation between an English nobleman and a New York stevedore, for instance, would indicate myriad differences in social prejudices, conventions and ideologies that would furnish a sociologist with absorbingly interesting material. But, as I have already indicated, our interest has centered primarily upon basic causative factors—upon the common dysfunction underlying the multitudinous and infinitely varied nuances of affect-projection and behavioral symptomatology. After all, the function of the biological organism of man is, like that of other species, universally common and consistent. At this deeper biological level, differences arising from social status and conditioning lose their significance. This certainly proved to be true in respect to these differences as they existed among the members composing our experimental group.

The principle of phylobiology, then, is wholly independent of superficial social discrimination. Surely, a brain surgeon does not have a different operation for the same functional brain-disorder according as it occurs in the aristocrat or the proletarian. Our researches have led us to an analogous orientation. We see ditention as a functional brain-disorder affecting man throughout. It is a disorder of function that interrupts man's sense of his unity and solidarity as a species and, instead, sets each individual, or each ideologically amalgamated group or nation, over against every other individual or nation as a separate and discrete entity. This ditentive mechanism involves the private assumption by each of us that he possesses a valid "right" or prerogative, and that other people are "right" only in the measure in which they agree with him. In short each of us is interrelationally, *in actu* or *in posse*, a self-appointed Czar. Each of us is the private arbiter of the moral "right" he now entertains vicariously in place of the biologically fitting behavior—the basic unity of function—that marks man's primary continuity and solidarity as a species. The 'I'-persona of, say, a professor at a university who is competitive in his behavior toward a colleague is, fundamentally, of precisely the same structure socially as that of an ignorant white southern farmer who is contemptuous of the negro because he is black. The 'I'-personae are the same interrelationally because essentially they embody the same disordered or partitive behavior-patterns.

If I may put it in another way, in phylobiology it is the behavior of the species man that is the material studied just as in human physiology it is the function of the heart, or the liver, or the kidney of man that is studied. There are, of course, as Dr. Lillie points out (Chapter V), individual differences at all levels of organic and even inorganic phenomena. But these variations do not entail differences in underlying principles of structure and function. They do not invalidate our determination of these principles from the study of a *single* human heart, kidney or liver. From such a study we would be able to describe with certainty the basic structure and principles of operation for these organs in individuals of all national or racial groups, as well as in all individuals in any primitive group of people. Similarly with behavioral material at the level at which we have been working. While we do not deny individual and cultural differences and their importance in shaping the external aspects of behavior, we feel that these differences do not affect the underlying principle of operation it has been our attempt to investigate. In passing, I should like to remark that the phylobiological viewpoint does not for a moment detract from the significance and importance of individual man. In the view of my associates and myself it gives added meaning and constructive value to individualized features and special abilities. But this matter will be developed more fully in a subsequent chapter.

I hope that what I have said will set forth my position in a sufficiently clear light to make understandable to Professor Dewey in what ways our views in respect to man's present muddle can be reconciled. I realize that cultural factors are most important in perpetuating man's phylic behavioral maladjustment. As I said in my letter to Dr. Dewey, "Your emphasis upon the cultural factor in man's present-day dilemma does not divide us for a moment. And, incidentally, as I understand prejudice, your emphasis upon the influence of culture possesses no such emotional bias, since your conclusions rest upon the objective analysis and study of the social elements involved. . . .

"The thing that interests me is the question of the origin in man of the tendency to yield more easily to the dictates of prejudice than of reason. This seems to me an artificial condition, artificially created. Some deviate, some abnormal circumstance or conditioning must have intervened, that man should prefer to act counter to what is in his interest as a healthy organism rather than yield to incitements that are sane and clear."

Our observations lead to the conclusion that this abnormal circumstance or conditioning is connected with the function of the symbolic system. My thesis in respect to the involvement of language in the neurosis of man is often misunderstood. I should emphasize that it is not man's use of the symbol with which I have any quarrel; it is with the symbol's use—and very autocratic use—of man, when it assumes priority over his organism's basic affirmation and wholeness. I do not think that language (which I suppose is, in a sense, coeval with consciousness—with intellectual consciousness) is of itself an impediment to consciousness, and an encouragement to man's substituting for conscious action a pattern of behavior that is narrow or biased. I think I make this point quite clear in a paper to which I have already referred.[2] The possibility, though, that coincident with the emergence of language there has occurred a false exaggeration, a false self-centering of the individual's personal identity as over against the larger identity we share in common as a race or species, and that this false identity has blurred man's social vision—this possibility does interest and intrigue me.

I spoke very much along these lines in a recent letter to Dr. S. I. Hayakawa occasioned by a reference to me in which I felt he had misread my meaning. ". . . As I have many times stated, I do not think that man can come to grips with his conflict and division by achieving piecemeal a more extensional orientation in regard to the myriad words with which we are surrounded, or by a greater knowledge or awareness of the process of abstracting, however valuable and important such disciplines may be. To our research unit these factors, like much else in the symptomatology of man's behavior, appear to stem from the presence in man of an interpersonally systematized affect-identity (the 'I'-persona, in my terminology) which has overtly replaced the actual self as a freely functioning unit in a species continuum.

"Not to put the primary emphasis on this phylophysiological dysfunction appears to me to put the cart before the horse. What shall it avail us to recall our affective connotations, our 'intensional' meanings in regard to this word or that, this concept or another, the ideology of one man in contrast to some one else's, if the whole intent, if the entire motivation of the falsely systematized, societally isolated persona is to produce partiality and prejudice in favor of the 'rights' and 'goodness' of his *self* and *his* affiliates in contrast to the 'rights' and 'goodness' of other selves?

"It does seem to me that the 'I'-persona developed in man coincidently with the emergence of the function of communication through speech. . . . It may be that my manner of emphasizing the joint origin of language and man's ditentive behavior has been misleading. I fear, too, that I have not always been explicit enough in my writing. If this is true, I concede that it is up to me as a recalcitrant 'I'-persona to eat humble pie—a dietary régime to which I am not a stranger. In reading passages from *The Biology of Human Conflict*[3] (I have especially in mind portions of the Introduction), I can easily see that I may have given an undue emphasis to the function of language in man's bionomic dilemma. Taken out of the context of my thesis in its entirety, a number of passages could be misleading, and the reader might readily conclude that the theme of phylobiology and that of General Semantics are largely in agreement."

PROFESSOR ROBERT M. YERKES makes the following comments in reference to causative factors responsible for man's social neurosis.

> My inference from your manuscript is that the neurosis of man, although prevalent throughout the species, is individually acquired. In that event the causation must appear in our socio-educational system. You remark that religions and

philosophies have failed us, but you do not indicate that *the neurosis* may be traceable to erroneous religions or philosophies. Does that seem to you probable? . . .

I am not at all clear as to whether you believe that ditention appears in man at birth or is instead acquired, perhaps because of our erroneous assumptions or philosophies of life and resulting social-educational practices. I should be inclined to suspect, as I intimated above, that given proper educative treatment from birth, there would be no neurosis in man. I should especially like your comment on this assumption and also further statement about the nature of the social-educational climate which would assure us freedom from ditention, and the enjoyment of cotention.

In responding to Professor Yerkes' question, I said that I was not inclined to think that the neurosis is "traceable to erroneous religions or philosophies." I would rather be inclined to say the erroneous religions and philosophies are traceable to the neurosis—to the unconscious but universal instilling into the human offspring of a wishful, non-objective sense of right or fitting behavior rather than a biological and objective sense of discrimination between what is fitting and not fitting. As I emphasized in Chapter IV, the attitude of the mature or parental generation to the immature or infant generation begins to operate in very early infancy and to inculcate a ditentive mode in the species man. By "ditentive mode" I mean a mode that disposes the child to adopt a wishful criterion of behavior whose aim is merely the personal advantage implicit in conforming to the parental mood or will. Ditention now automatically places differential advantage above consideration of total biological motivation and health.

Dr. Yerkes' last question interested me no little. But the answer entails a more comprehensive development than is possible here, and I have reserved it for the final chapter of this book. I can merely say in brief that it is only as we of the older generation adopt the principle of cotention as the primary mediator between the organism and the environment that there will be the social-educational climate Dr. Yerkes envisages.

PROFESSOR GEORGE M. STRATTON, under whom I had the privilege of working for my doctoral degree in experimental psychology at The Johns Hopkins University, also indicates that my views need further clarification. He says:

BIOLOGICAL AND CULTURAL CONSIDERATIONS

You must have known that looking at the matter as objectively, as scientifically as I can, some of your main conclusions would to me appear unjustified. And first, of your belief that mankind was once wholly "cotentive," and only later became "ditentive" by an accident of evolution in connection with the development of the fore-brain. But, against this view scientific research into man's past, seems predominantly to indicate that mankind has always, along with "cotention," suffered from "ditention," from self-interest between individuals, and between groups; these groups earlier very small and later increasing in size, each suspicious of groups other than itself, and often in armed conflict.

I am most interested in Dr. Stratton's comments and welcome this opportunity to say that I do not hold the view that primitive man was wholly cotentive. I regret that this impression has been conveyed to my readers. I believe it is due in part to the fact that my colleagues had perforce examined only a fragmentary portion of my manuscript. It is true that certain primitive peoples seem to have a degree of integration and coördination with their fellows which far surpasses that of our highly individualized and sophisticated Western societies. Many anthropologists and ethnologists have called attention to this fact and to the havoc and destruction which comes about in these primitive cultures when civilized concepts of individualism and competition are introduced. I feel that primitive peoples can give us very interesting and valuable data in regard to various types of human adjustment, and to the underlying biological principle of group cohesion and species solidarity. But, if my thesis is correct, primitive man is not exempt from the dislocation in attention and neural function from which we suffer. My position is that man as a biological organism possesses all the potentialities for cotentive living, but that coincident with his acquisition of the symbolic function (a function that has, of course, been of incalculable benefit to man in the course of his evolution), he has acquired a false sense of the self and a faulty behavioral norm for regulating his interactions with others of his kind.

Several of my colleagues called attention to fighting and other evidences of hostility in animal species, and questioned whether the disorder in behavioral adaptation emphasized by me is peculiar to man. PROFESSOR GARDNER MURPHY says:

... I cannot see that the self-preoccupation shows any

evolutionary breaks or discontinuities. Inter-individual hostility is evident at the protozoan level (Jennings), at the level of many invertebrate phyla (e.g.—ants), at the level of fishes, birds, rats, monkeys (and apes). The implication that inter-individual hostility is an evolutionary *new* disorder means nothing to me. Nor is *self-awareness* something that appears *with* language, nor does it appear at any *one* point. *Nor* does it basically *change* the fact of inter-individual *hostility;* it simply focusses it.

PROFESSOR STRATTON writes: ... And among animals, phylic unity by no means invariably produces solidarity, "cotention" in behavior. Nor are language and the forebrain necessary for "ditention." Bees rob from bees of another group; and defend themselves from such raiders by stinging.

PROFESSOR ØRNULV ØDEGARD asks: ... If war is a product of the human fore-brain, what about the wars in the animal kingdom? And neuroses in animals?

And PROFESSOR HONORIO DELGADO remarks that: ... repeated allusions to belligerency and war as pathological phenomena or as manifestations exclusive to man, give the impression that you overlook what is the reality of life in the large part of animal—and even in vegetable—species.

I am grateful to my critics for raising this point. I am not sure that I can answer their questions satisfactorily. But it does seem to me that there is an evolutionary break, a definite difference between the hostility, aggressiveness and conflict which we see expressed in the interrelational behavior of man, and the fighting and aggression that are exhibited by all other animals. One striking difference is that the fighting of animals is closely related to bionomic needs. By and large and under natural conditions, an animal fights to procure food, to mate, or to defend itself from attack. Its fighting is a behavior-pattern that is indissolubly integrated with survival. It is closely related to the animal's total environmental reality. As evolutionary development through the ages demonstrates, it operates in a way that tends to preserve rather than to dissipate the species. What Professor Lillie refers to as the "group-regarding instincts" are in the ascendancy.

My researches clearly indicate to me that this situation has been reversed in man; that with the enhancement of individualism (emphasis upon the self-image or 'I'-persona) the balance in favor of group survival has been placed in serious jeopardy. Today the very existence of the species is threatened because the antagonisms characterizing man have been largely divorced from his biological needs and actualities. These antagonisms are now overwhelmingly determined by projected affects and images that are peculiar to man and that are without biological warrant. On his present basis of adaptation, man's behavior is characterized by an underlying mood of hostility, of suspicion, of competitive and destructive trends toward so-called "others," toward those outside the pale of "me" and "mine." I am reminded of a quotation from Bernard Shaw, "Man is the only animal of which I am thoroughly and cravenly afraid. I have never thought much of the courage of a lion tamer. Inside the cage he is at least safe from other men. There is less harm in a well-fed lion. It has no ideals, no sect, no party, no nation, no class; in short, no reason for destroying anything it does not want to eat."

As I wrote Professor Murphy: "There is not the slightest question in my mind as to the existence of interindividual antagonisms at lower evolutionary levels. But the interindividual conflict in man to which I have attempted to draw attention is, in our finding, not in the category with these spontaneous biological antagonisms. I have attempted to show the quite dissociative state of mind out of which the behavior-conflicts in man habitually arise. My point is that in man the parental generation has put the younger up to 'rights' or prerogatives for which there is no biological foundation and which are answerable throughout human society for the ideological dissensions existing within and among us. I have tried to bring out evidence of the induction in man of an image of the self which is quite fantastic and which, in investing the child with an artificial sense of its personal preëminence, automatically sets the stage for competition and conflict."

Under man's present system of social relations, the private, esoteric "right" of the individual has replaced the organism's biologically fitting response to the environment. As we saw in Chapter IV, this wishful fetish has become the controlling motivation in human behavior. Consequently we do not find man's behavior consistent with the organic laws prevailing in the world outside him. On the contrary, we find each individual a law unto himself. In the abrogation of a common principle man's system of relations is completely lawless. In his social or interrelational values, he is everywhere the victim of wishful thinking and prejudice. Whether it is the "right" of the individual, the group or the nation, it is always *my* right. It is always a principle of "right" that is private, arbitrary, ulterior.

This is the factor to which my associates and I have given long and arduous study and which seems to us chiefly responsible for man's overpowering urge to conflict and destruction—an urge that far exceeds biological bounds. If I may quote from a recent paper: "Man's obsessive self-rightness is at this very moment driving the world headlong into another senseless war despite all our pious ratiocinations regarding the reckless destructiveness and prodigality of war. For war reflects an uncontrollable mood paroxysm that is utterly inaccessible to reason. One could as profitably argue with the convulsive seizure of an epileptic." [4]

NOTES

[1] "Prescription for Peace: The Biological Basis of Man's Ideological Conflicts," in *Explorations in Altruistic Love and Behavior*, edited by Pitirim A. Sorokin, Boston, The Beacon Press, 1950, pp. 96 and 98.

[2] "Prescription for Peace."

[3] Burrow, Trigant, *The Biology of Human Conflict — An Anatomy of Behavior, Individual and Social*, New York, The Macmillan Company, 1937, pp. xl + 435.

[4] "Emotion and the Social Crisis: A Problem in Phylobiology," in *Feelings and Emotions. The Mooseheart Symposium*, edited by Martin L. Reymert, New York, McGraw-Hill Book Company, 1950, p. 483.

CHAPTER VI

THE INDIVIDUAL AND THE GROUP
THEIR PHYLOÖRGANISMIC CONTINUITY

A number of my correspondents questioned my emphasis upon the group, species or phylum,[1] feeling that I neglected the individual. Having always been deeply interested in the development of true individuality, I should like to present some of the correspondence in regard to this point, in the hope that it will make my position clearer.

PROFESSOR RALPH S. LILLIE puts it this way: There is much in what you say with which I agree profoundly, but there are certain points of difference (rather fundamental as it seems to me) which I shall try to indicate briefly in this letter. I am inclined to regard the human species as not so much a unity as a collection of individuals, innately variable and each peculiar to himself. Every organic individual is much more closely and effectively integrated than its race. It is true that all human beings have certain characteristics in common; but a fundamental biological requirement is that each separate individual should have effective self-regarding modes of reaction and conscious behavior if the species as a whole is to survive. This is true for living organisms in general; nature seems to have proceeded on the assumption that if enough individuals can survive until the reproductive period is past the species can be trusted to take care of itself. But in addition to the self-regarding characters certain group-defensive characters are also biologically necessary; and most animals, especially social animals like man, have developed these. The trouble is that in the case of man his enhancement of individuality has created dangers against which the group-regarding instincts seem an insufficient protection.

These dangers (as you point out) arise largely from the fact that the subjective picture which the 'I'-persona forms of his environment is necessarily a partial one, and hence is in defective correspondence with the external reality; it is this lack of realism in the person's subjectivity that makes his behavior so largely maladaptive. In a strictly objective sense every other person is as real as myself; but there is little in the immediate consciousness of the individual to make him aware of this. He tends to regard himself as the only *psycho*-physical system; all others are merely physical! Hence other persons (especially if they belong to different social groups) take on the aspect of merely external, largely obstructive, objects; their inner or "psychical" side is ignored; his behavior toward such persons is in this sense defective in realism. One may take the fighting instinct as an illustration: undoubtedly this instinct has played an important part in human evolution, but not until quite recently has it become a serious threat to the continuance of the race; and just now how to hold it in bounds is the problem. In earlier history the competition between the reproductive and the lethal factors held a safe biological balance on the side of the reproductive; but modern technology seems to have reversed the situation.

You call the maladjustment between the persona-regarding and the species-regarding characters a *neurosis,* and you believe this can be greatly alleviated by an applied science of human behavior. Medical science is, or will be, in a position to cure this as well as other human disorders (cf. your chapter "Medicine to the Rescue"). I should be far from denying that science can be of inestimable service here; but I believe that all scientific men should be on their guard against overestimating the possibilities of science, considered alone. Science has its limitations, inherent in its special nature as a system of abstractions, whose aim is to single out and formulate the stable and regular side of nature. But nature has also a quite different side; I refer to the individualizing feature of its activity. Each individual (even inorganic individuals) is isolated from the others; each "actual entity" has both its generic and its individual properties. In man the individual or non-repeated characters have assumed such importance that they have become the chief determinants of his personal activity. It seems to me unrealistic to refer all individual characters to generic or scientifically definable (hence manipulable) characters. A scientifically defined norm which includes all the possibilities of human individuality is neither possible nor desirable; the important human qualities are precisely those which deviate from the average. The "supremacy of the part-brain" in the individual is the source of whatever originality or creativeness he may have. It is true that this supremacy may also result in maladjustment. Also that certain kinds of maladjustment may be corrected by science. No doubt the autocratic and imperialistic I-persona ought to regulate his behavior in the light of what the welfare of the species requires: but it must be remembered that his autonomy is the source of his creative activity, and that this is also indispensable for the race.

A question is whether the chief emphasis (e.g. in education) should be placed on the general or scientifically definable characters of man which are controllable, or on the individual factors with their uniqueness, unpredictability, and potential originality. Is it true that scientific knowledge is the *only* remedy for the human neurosis (cf. p. 477 of your book)? "We are all common men"; true enough; but the world of separate selves is not illusory; it is a very hard fact; and this very separateness, when it becomes a factor acting under the control of personal ethics and higher ideals (as well as sound knowledge), has been the source of whatever progress the race may have made during its history. At the same time the general or organismic outlook is also a necessary one; this may strengthen and ennoble individuality, as you remark on page 483. My only misgiving is that a purely scientific outlook, with its abstraction from values and its emphasis on conditions common to all human beings, may distract attention from the all-importance of the individual. Every far-reaching advance is made mainly or exclusively through the initiative of superior individuals; what the world most needs at present is the right kind of personal leadership and example. Such leadership should be ethical as well as intellectual; also I believe it should have a background of religious as well as merely practical and human motivation. I mean, of course, religion in the enlightened sense— which would have the support of science.

Before presenting my response to Professor Lillie, I would like to remind the reader that the phyloörganismic orientation I am attempting to establish in the field of man's relation to man is not primarily a theoretical formulation. On the contrary, it has grown out of intensive group-investigations carried on over the past quarter-century by my associates and myself. As a result of submitting the social group itself to a controlled, inclusive analysis; as a result of investigating the so-called normal prejudices, beliefs, wishes, emotions and motivations characterizing our daily social interchange, and relating these phenomena to underlying physiological patterns of tension, certain discoveries have been made and principles formulated which throw new light on the sphere of human interrelations, and offer the possibility of a much-needed reorientation and integration in this field.

I may say that this reorientation, although developing solely from the group researches in human behavior undertaken by my associates and myself, parallels the drastic reorganization in thought, concept and interpretation that has occurred in the past decades throughout many fields of science. As we know, nineteenth century scientists, in line with a traditionally atomistic purview, exalted the fragment, part or element to a position of major importance. They looked upon the whole as the additive sum of its parts and felt that the smallest artificially isolable part was the basic material of science; that only through the study of such isolated parts could larger constellations or wholes be understood. Today this atomistic tendency has receded into the background, and investigators recognize with increasing surety that the whole is something more than the sum of its parts; that they must study the intricate modes of interfunctioning among the parts and the emergent properties of the whole if phenomena are to be rightly understood and basic principles formulated.

This newer trend now flourishes even in the field of physics where atomistic methods of research had been applied with signal success, and from which field this method had been adopted by other sciences. Thus we find that quantum physics and Einstein's relativity have replaced earlier, mechanistic concepts. In neurophysiology, interest has shifted from the discrete reflex to the "total action pattern"; in neurology it has shifted from interest in minute localization and a point for point correspondence between cortex and periphery, to cortical levels of functioning and to organized patterns of cortical response. In medicine, emphasis on cellular pathology gives way to considerations of the organism-as-a-whole and to balanced coördination of function. In psychology, where formulations were formerly based on the reality of elementary sensations, on isolated conditioned reflexes and on specific stimulus-response connections, emphasis is now placed upon the configuration or pattern of excitation and response, and upon the intimate interrelatedness and interdependence of behavioral processes. Such similarity in trend in respect to fundamental conceptions in varied branches of science is one consideration leading to Bertalanffy's postulation of a new scientific discipline which he calls *General System Theory,* and which formulates and deduces those principles valid for "systems" in general.[2]

Scientists, however, have not yet accepted the full implications of an organismic position as it applies to man's interrelational behavior. While our views have become increasingly less mechanistic, we fall definitely short of the type of orientation that we now consistently require in many other fields of science. Although modern biologists have gathered much objective, incontrovertible data on the importance of social interdependence, mutualism, and basic coöperation throughout living forms, although ethnologists and anthropologists have stressed the bonds of social integration and internal coördination in the life of primitive tribes, and the scientific world in general has turned more and more to the study of functioning wholes, the accustomed approach to man's behavior in relation to his fellows is still essentially atomistic. It is true that we speak much today of "the organism as a whole" and of the interrelatedness of behavioral processes. But even where there is the recognition of a unifying principle underlying man's behavior, it is still largely on a verbal or theoretical plane. It has not yet been incorporated into the vital motivational processes that shape and determine our behavior. In our feeling-life we are all isolationists. We are discrete and often conflicting entities, prejudiced in favor of the self and what we conceive to be its unilateral advantage.

But let me quote from my response to Professor Lillie: "I am most grateful to you for your thoughtful letter with its kind and helpful comments. Your remarks about the relationship between the persona-regarding and the species-regarding trends in man are most interesting. I believe that, fundamentally, I agree with most of what you say. Certainly I do not disparage the great evolutionary advance in creativeness made possible by the development of the forebrain, especially as exemplified in the genius of the leaders in various fields of human enlightenment. My position is that the individual will function more originally, more creatively when the blight of the false sense of the self or 'I'-persona has been removed and he is more clearly oriented in respect to phylic principles of behavior."

I do not for a moment wish to detract from the importance of individual differences among men which Professor Lillie has rightly emphasized, or to impugn the original, creative powers that mark the man of genius in any field of endeavor. I have no desire, of course, to hamper initiative; to reduce man to a general level of mediocrity. There are, I realize, individual differences at every stage of organic and even inorganic development. I am told each snowflake if examined miscroscopically will show some slight difference from all other snowflakes. I know also that each paramecium, each flowering plant differs slightly from its neighbor. Nature has no mechanical pattern, no mass production. And this is one of the significant sources of the exquisite beauty, balance and artistic creativity exhibited in nature's handiwork. Such differences offer pleasurable variety; they do not entail inimical conflict.

This same type of variation, of course, applies also to the species man. But in man's interrelational behavior there occurs a type of difference that my researches lead me to feel is biologically ill-founded. This difference is based on a private systematization of affects and prejudices which each individual or 'I'-persona builds up about his image of himself, and which potentially pits each such systematized individual against all others of his kind. Of course, 'I'-personae do get together socially. They pool their affects and prejudices in the formation of families, working groups, communities, political parties, nations, etc. But no matter how large the social extension, the amalgamation is not a true integration. It is a superficial association of many 'I'-personæ with their privately systematized core of affects and prejudices.

In our group-analysis, the essentially discrete and discordant nature of the individual's affect-systematizations came readily to the fore. The motivating factors in "normal" and neurotic behavior were again and again demonstrated to be inextricably linked with the subjective image of "all-might" which each 'I'-persona holds in respect to himself. This inflexible core of "rightness" and all-might determines the behavior of the individual. It results in the assumption of a type of difference and hostility for which there are no biologically valid grounds.

As we know, the biological identities among human beings far exceed their differences. There is in man, as in other animal species, a structural and functional identity of tissues and organs throughout the body, and this leads to a consistency in the structure and function of individual organisms. The dependability of all our observational processes rests essentially upon the identity of sense receptors and perceptual processes. When exposed to the same visual, auditory, or olfactory stimuli, men by and large (barring, of course, physical abnormalities) see, hear, and smell the same thing. A *consensus* among observers, as the etymology of the word implies, is ultimately dependent upon a commonness of sense impressions.

It is the position of phylobiology that in the internal sphere of motivations relating the organism as a whole to the external environment, and interrelating it to others of its kind—in the internal domain of reactions that compose the feeling-life of man—there is inherently the same continuity, the same consistent uniformity of response that characterizes the sensory behavior of the organism's peripheral field of reactions. This principle of continuity determines the biologically fitting behavior of man and is equal and one throughout the species. Residing within the tissues of mankind, it is a criterion or right of which our moral dogmas and religious creeds are but symbolic and insubstantial representations.

But with man this commonness of feeling-impressions native to his organism as a species has been interrupted. With the extraordinary emergence of the selective function of language, a wholly new system of reactions began to take place in man—a system of reactions which in its wide and rapid growth socially has disrupted the continuity of motivations and interests that primarily govern the behavior of man as a solidaric species. Here was created an artificial delusion of separateness and a corresponding denial of species solidarity. Where unity and consistency had prevailed, there now occurred a splitting, a division and a conflict at the heart of the individual's identity. "I," or the self, being now the governing center in the scheme of things, "you" are acceptable to me only in so far as you contribute to the authenticity and suzerainty of this esoterically arrogated autocracy. If you like or favor me, our two selves are in tentative, temporary accord. But there is no guarantee of the lastingness of this bond between us. It subsists only by virtue of a purely arbitrary and tenuous affinity. And if you do not like or favor me, our separateness is certified to in ill-will, disparity and conflict. Because of the development of such an arbitrarily systematized identity, the organism's feeling, its motivation is now *my* feeling, *my* motivation; the right or balanced reaction has been replaced by what is good for *me*. Man's primary empathy for his kind has been replaced by reactions of personal sympathy or antipathy. As we saw in Chapter IV, there was introduced the extraneous element of morality among individuals in place of a principle of interrelational coördination that rests upon the common function of the species as a whole.

The purpose of my investigations is to find a method for freeing the individual organism for greater creative achievements, especially as these achievements have to do with his feeling-life—with his artistic and cultural attainments, with the whole sphere that is symbolically represented in high ideals and ethics. The individual is now very much hampered in his creative expression by the weight of the social neurosis, with its emphasis upon external appearance and the image of the self. His feeling is greatly curtailed in its expression and turned back upon this image of himself—his 'I'-persona. It is this 'I'-persona with its rigid isolation, its inaccessible systematization of affects and prejudices of which I feel man's organism needs to divest itself.

The highest level of artistic and creative accomplishments is not opposed to but consistent with the individual's continuity with his species. In this connection it is interesting that the words *genius* and *genus* are derived etymologically from a common root. Our experimental studies indicate that when man adopts a technique which dissipates his conditioned concerns with the projective affects of the 'I'-persona, the fullness and continuity of his feeling-life will be restored. These studies give full support to the position that inherently the feeling-processes of individuals are continuous and consistent with one another, and that the individual's originality, his creativeness, his rapport with the environment is in direct proportion to his internal appreciation of this continuity. This principle of feeling-continuity seems to me to be the tangible substance underlying what Professor Lillie speaks of as sound religion and ethics. My endeavors have been directed toward developing a technique through which man can overcome the partitive obstructions that now block his clear, whole feeling.

PROFESSOR R. W. GERARD states his reservation as follows:

. . . I am particularly bothered by, what seems to me, your main thesis: that individual man is completely subordinated to racial man in his psycho-social organization. While I think it extremely healthy to emphasize that each human individual is a unit in a greater human community or epi-organism, especially since the emphasis on man as an individual has been so extreme through much of this century, I cannot but feel that your own position errs in the opposite direction. To me, any failure to recognize that man is *both* a complete organism in himself (biologically and psychologically) as well as a unit in a larger organism, necessarily falls short of the whole story.

Evidently I had not made myself clear to Professor Gerard since he suggests that my thesis holds to the view "that individual man is completely subordinated to racial man." As I wrote him, "There is no question of subordination. My researches have led me to the view that the principle of motivation primarily informing the behavior of individual man is phylic in its scope; that the 'normal' objectives of the 'I'-persona constitute a social dissociation from a healthy pattern of human behavior that is generic. But I fully recognize the continuity of the ontogenetic and phylogenetic aspects of the behavior of man as a functioning unit in relation to the environment."

The student of phylobiology knows that, true to its name, this science deals with mankind as a unit. He senses always in the erratic behavior, in the deviate pattern of the individual, the expression of a phylic condition. Where a reaction is consonant and whole, it is *man's* whole reaction; where a reaction is partitive or affective, it is also *man's* reaction, the one a reaction of balance and health, the other of pathology and division.

What we have most to keep in mind, it seems to me—to keep in our *feeling* would better say what I mean—is the all-encompassing nature of our conflict and neurosis. We need to make this phylic feeling so real, to bring it so close home to us that there can be no room for any division, any discrimination in our condition as a species. The discrete, private ache—the ache that seems so engrossing to any phylically isolated you or me—is just another misappropriation on the part of the 'I'-persona. The ache is really man's, not the ache of any separate you or me; just as the 'I'-persona is an appropriation on the part of social (affecto-symbolic) man, and does not indict any individual or group of individuals as we, in our divisive "wrongness," like to "think." Organismically, or in the phylobiological reckoning, you and I are man too, just as any nonplussed Dmitri behind *his* iron curtain of affect is also man, and shares with us in this ache that is man's. This basis of feeling and thinking, however, depends upon our foregoing an habitual brain-function based upon differentiation and projection, and recovering a pattern of reaction that is integrated and unitary. As I shall attempt to show in Chapter VIII, it depends upon the discipline of converting "impacted" affect into the sensation of neuromuscular stress that underlies it—a biophysical discipline to which the prevailing 'I'-persona does not readily yield in its habitual supremacy over the processes of individuals and social groups.

Ultimately, of course, group-analysis must extend to the species man. In that day it will be an intolerable thought to mankind that any one individual should suffer the mauling and the permanent mutilation that all men suffer today and accept meekly and without protest as the common lot.

In his letter to me Mr. Herbert S. Bailey says:

> I found your approach interesting and original, and no one could disagree with your objectives, but I found a general tone and underlying scheme that made me uncomfortable and doubtful. This is the approach to man as a phylum, implicit in the the very name of phylobiology. The same is true of your title the neurosis of man, which seems to say that man as a phylum is troubled by a single neurosis. In any work of this kind I am always on the lookout for the organic fallacy; after all, "man" is an aggregate of *individuals* acting and interacting on each other. The action and interaction produces the group or social attributes of "man," but in the deepest analysis they must go back to the individual. And the troubles of "man" are the troubles of individuals, which are many and complicated, organic and neurotic. Perhaps it is possible, looking at the whole as you have tried to do, to find large symptoms that cannot be found in individuals. But individuals are individually important, and I am skeptical and fearful of any approach that pushes them into a background mass.

I can appreciate Mr. Bailey's misgivings. But it is only as we recognize the phylopathological scope of this behavior-disorder that we shall be in a position to attack it with the degree of patience, intelligence and ingenuity this radical innovation demands. In a sense medicine had its beginning in the recognition of a phylic norm of health and in the definition of disease as a deviation from this phylic norm. Only with the bacteriologists' recognition of the community-wide nature of infection was there the beginning of medical science upon a broad and inclusive scale. It is a digression from a phylic norm of health that has given definition to such a widespread infection as tuberculosis and to so prevalent a disease as cancer. It is similar with the widespread functional disorder that characterizes the behavior of social man.

Until just the other day, relatively speaking, when one's child became ill from an infectious disease, one called in the doctor to cure *his* child of the *symptoms* corresponding to the disease in question. The parent's only thought was of *"my* child." Today he recognizes that the cause and course of infectious disease is community-wide. Consequently the modern emphasis is upon isolating the bacterial agent responsible for the disease, and instituting public health methods for preventing its spread. And this, of course, demands a scientific program that is world-wide. In a word, man has been brought to adopt a generic attitude toward infectious disease, and he must now be brought somehow to adopt a generic attitude toward the field of his behavior and its manifold disorders. He must realize that effective treatment and prevention of individual disturbances in adaptation can come about only through the recognition of the fundamental factors responsible for the widespread aberrations in behavior which I have spoken of as the "social neurosis."

It is not possible to study and treat such disorders in isolation. As things stand today, we tend to rise up in wrath and condemn this or that individual or this or that nation because their customary (conditioned) behavior does not agree with the behavior customary among ourselves as individuals or as a nation. In this judgment our diagnosis is based upon bias and not science. It is personal and parochial, not generic and inclusive. Such a narrow view precludes the acceptance of a phylic principle and the recognition of the deviation in behavior in respect to this principle embodied in the neurosis of man.

I hope it will be clear from what I have said that I do not, as Mr. Bailey fears, set the species man over against the individual. On the contrary, our group researches led us to feel that the most potent factor in maintaining the compactness of the individual's identity is his sense of compactness or solidarity as a species. I try to show that there has developed in man a spurious or artificial persona which is not in harmony with the organism's basic interests and needs. It is only because of the spurious and image nature of this personality-construct that there could be any question of differentiation or conflict between individual and species. I try to treat the organic solidarity of the species and that of the individual as two aspects of the same biological process—the phylogenetic and the ontogenetic. To me the individual without its species is as unthinkable as the species without its individuals.

I shall select passages from several letters from PROFESSOR C. JUDSON HERRICK with whom I have had a most interesting and illuminating correspondence in regard to the interrelation of individual and group. He says:

> In my phylogenetic analysis I find that behavior begins as an individual affair. It is the person who behaves, and the pattern of behavior is determined primarily by the organization of the person not by the environment. The social environment plays a progressively larger part as we ascend the phyletic series, becoming dominant in man; but even here behavior is still personal and every attempt to correct disorder must ultimately come down to correcting persons. So, as I see it, though we are emphasizing different things, these things are but different aspects of the same problem.
>
> By way of general criticism, I think you have weakened your argument by over-emphasis on the phyletic, the universal, components of normal and abnormal behavior. More attention to individual differences in both innate and acquired components of behavior and the part they play in social adjustments would give better balance. But you are, of course, playing the part of an advocate of one method of approach, and I am the advocate of another. I see no ground for conflict here.
>
> Social relations of various kinds play an increasingly important role in the determination of behavior patterns as we pass from the lowest to the highest animals, and in mankind they play a dominant role. But when you say that "human society is but another name for the species man," you are mixing categories in a way that is biologically inadmissible.[3] The "social norms," however defined, are not "species" norms

as biologically defined. The human species is not a social unit. The integrity of the species defined biologically and the "solidarity of the species" viewed sociologically are quite different things. The two evolutionary trends may reinforce each other or they may be antagonistic, and both of these movements have occurred.

The primordial unit of behavior is the individual person. In animal evolution the social units come later, and at the transition from brute to man there is the revolutionary change which you so graphically describe. But throughout this change and up to the highest level of cultural advancement yet attained the individuals with their individual differences are the crucial units in all social movements, and, as you clearly show, the social neurosis resolves into personal neuroses, and remedial measures must be applied by these persons to persons to be effective. We are not dealing here with man as a species nor with an impersonal "culture," as Leslie White and the other social positivists contend, but with the disordered mentality of the separate people who compose the society affected.

Professor Herrick makes the point that "the 'social norms,' however defined, are not 'species' norms as biologically defined." In my reply I said: "That is just the rub as I see it. It is my position that social norms which ignore certain intrinsic continuities with biological norms are the bunk. Look at our ditentive society today. Look at our chaotic international situation. Look at our hopelessly muddled United Nations that sets itself up to adjust our disordered human relations. . . . But man pretends—he acts upon the assumption that he is a social unit, that there is something 'unitary' in his social get-togethers, his religions, his politics, his families, his brotherhoods and whatnot.

"Yes, the two categories are, as you say, 'independent variables.' But there are biological correspondences also.[4] There are correspondences in tissue and function which are not recognized and hence not reckoned with in our efforts to attain saner social relations. My experiments in social groups compel me to insist that these biological functions common to man as to other biological entities must be scientifically reckoned with. A defect in man's attention, a defect in the instrument of our ecosomatic [organism-environment] balance is a defect in brain-function, and we shall not attain any benevolent rallies among communities of men until this essential impediment in the function that mediates interindividual rapport is reckoned with as a physiological process calling for physiological adjustment. . . .

"What I am saying makes for me such perfectly good sense that I can only think its failure to make sense to you is due, as you have yourself said, to our widely differing premises with their widely differing experimental techniques. I would say that I do not deal at all wth cultural man [that is, with behavioral differences due to various cultural factors]. It is outside my field. We are, it seems to me, one phylic organism, and in our social community we've gotten our wires hopelessly crossed. For the life of me I cannot see that adjusting persons as single units, and not adjusting the unit man, with its widely confused interpersonal relationships, can be effective. I would as lief try to repair an organ of the body in an organism that was diseased throughout as attempt to heal an isolated individual or a thousand or a million isolated individuals in a community when it is their interrelations that are their disease—when they are related not cotentively or as organisms with a common basis of tensions in respect to the environment, but ditentively, that is, with an attentional function that assumes a basic division between each such individual and every other. This is the 'individual' I call the autocratic 'I'-persona—the individuals or the groups or nations of individuals that now completely rule the world. . . .

"I just cannot see the 'I'-persona as other than a phylic or species-wide process. If one single individual became self-conscious overnight and went about inducing this self-reversal in motivation among his fellows, taking each of them in his benighted confidence as to his new acquisition, my position would be of course different. But the . . . advent of 'me' and self-consciousness and 'my right' seems to me to have come along as generically as the invasion of the tissues by a species of bacteria."

Professor P. W. Bridgman emphasizes the distorting effect which society has upon the individual. He writes:

> . . . For some time I have been coming to certain views which, in some respects, are similar to views expressed in your manuscript, but in other respects are diametrically opposed. It seems to me that the fundamental difficulty is that society forces every individual to ignore a dichotomy in the structure

of the world which to every individual must be the most fundamental feature of experience. The world of my experience is not one, but two. What shall I mean by saying that your pain is the same as my pain? But society forces its members to think in terms of a universal unity and so forces every individual to adopt as fundamental what amounts to a palpably false description. How can neuroses and frustrations be avoided in the framework of a strait jacket like this? Every human being from the beginning of time has been blinded by society and forced to shirk his fundamental problem, namely, to find within himself the springs of his own conduct.

It seems to me that the authoritarian rôle assumed by society, and so rightly stressed in Professor Bridgman's comment, is fundamentally traceable to the falsely organized sense of the "self" that has developed in man in the course of his conscious evolution. Certainly, as we have seen in Chapter IV, a society of 'I'-personae has the effect of "blinding" the developing organism and diverting it from an appreciation of its fundamental behavioral problem. There is a corroboration and systematization of 'I'-persona trends that tend to make them as inaccessible as the grotesque but personally infallible systematizations of the psychotic. It is for this reason that I have made such an insistent plea for a reëxamination of our "normal" behavior. Our laboratory work has been a concentrated analysis and challenge of this factor of social consolidation as it affects man's relation to man. Our studies have had the effect of bringing about an orientation in regard to the problem that is internal rather than projective. In this orientation one cannot think of society as doing something pernicious (or for that matter salutary) *to* the individual. For the phylogenetic and the ontogenetic spheres are not separable functionally any more than structurally. Functionally, as well as structurally, the individual *is* society. So that I cannot but think that we are again a prey to reflex social images when we believe we are standing apart from, are looking at, passing judgment upon and offering external advice or palliation to this abstraction we call society.

NOTES

[1] Some of my colleagues commented upon the unusual sense in which I use the term "phylum." In a letter to Professor W. C. Allee, I said that I realize "I am not strictly consistent with accepted zoölogical categories when I speak of man as a

'phylum.' By this term I do not mean to separate man from the rest of the vertebrates. I am merely trying to discuss man, with his social needs and interests, as a biological organism. I want to recognize a biological principle that does not countenance the superficial preoccupations of this man and that, of one nation and another on the basis of their purely private self-interests—preoccupations that now dominate the interrelational processes of mankind throughout.

"In the matter of terminology I am really up against it. But a biology of behavior that recognizes man as an organismic unit apart from our petty ideological differentiations — national, political, religious — is the concept I have attempted to establish." The term "species" would be zoölogically more correct but, unfortunately, this term has no adjectival form. In order to fill this breach, I adopted "phylic," from *phylum*, which in its original Greek had the meaning of "tribe." In line with my usage I have adopted the combination "phylobiology" to describe our researches into the behavior of man as a biological organism.

[2] Bertalanffy, Ludwig von, "An Outline of General System Theory," *The British Journal for the Philosophy of Science*, Vol. 1, pp. 1-32.

[3] The remarks in this and the following paragraph refer to the manuscript of "Prescription for Peace," which Dr. Burrow had sent Dr. Herrick. [Ed.]

[4] And I am heartened that in an addendum to his letter Professor Herrick says: "Let me add also that in this chapter I have recognized that the human species is in a legitimate sense a social unit as well as a taxonomic unit." Dr. Herrick refers to a chapter in his unpublished book, *The Evolution of Behavior*.

CHAPTER VII

PHYLOBIOLOGY AND THE "LONE WOLF" CRITICISM

Throughout the years of our researches there has been the criticism that I am an isolationist, that I do not encourage students or confreres to participate with us in our studies, that I do not relate my results to similar research and findings by other investigators. Perhaps this impression was unavoidable. In any event it has caused me no little concern.

Actually I incline to be gregarious by nature, enjoying close and varied social and professional contacts. Furthermore, it is the nature of my thesis that its full meaning can come only through its application to the community of mankind. As I said in a letter to a colleague more than twenty years ago: "The fact is that I am not without a sense of social responsibility in regard to my thesis. If there have been findings that have scientific significance and social value, they belong to my colleagues and to the community. And then, too, however it may seem to the contrary, I do not cherish being as much alone in my work as circumstances have compelled me to be. So that if in my effort to reach others I sometimes overreach the mark I hope you will understand."

And in a recent letter to a writer who had become interested in our researches, I said: "I do want to disparage the idea too common among friends or students interested in the thesis of phylobiology, that I alone embody the creative spirit responsible for the work of our organization. This is not said out of a spirit of humility or out of the wish to be generous, though I hope I am not a stranger to those motives. I say it because it is the simple truth. As you may have surmised, the thesis of phylobiology could not arise—it is organically excluded that it should have arisen from the mind of one individual. The 'I'-persona marks a universal dissociation within the species man, because in its interrelational blindness this false self or identity has virtually cut itself off from connection with the biological organism (individual and phylic) which presumably it represents. That anyone should come forth from this distorted biological medium and turn a clear, objective eye upon this subjective disturbance would be comparable to an insane patient on the ward of a mental institution suddenly turning about and presenting a clear analysis of the disordered feeling and thinking characterizing himself and his fellow patients. Mentally, theoretically, I did see very early that normality does not present a dependable criterion of healthy human behavior. But behavior is motivated by feeling; feeling is the basis of behavior, and my own feeling, of course, was compactly interwoven with the feeling pattern characteristic of the 'normal' mode of adaptation. . . . In our phylobiological premise the organism of man was the physician, and normality (socially unintegrated man) the patient. As you see, this was not and could not be a one-man job. Here was a social disorder involving man at large, and only organismic man could possibly tackle objectively this problem of his own social disorder."

In speaking of the small group composed of my associates, students and myself I have often emphasized that it would be absurd to expect that a small gathering of people, whatever their earnestness, whatever their insight, whatever their reorientation in respect to their own inner feeling and thinking, could do more than verify their group findings in the limited test tube of their own group experience. The real crux will be the application of our phyloanalytic researches within the larger group that is mankind.

But let me turn now to the comments of my friendly critics and my replies to them. PROFESSOR GORDON ALLPORT has put the matter directly and forcefully:

> In your letter to me you expressed a desire to enlist wider attention among social and psychological scientists for the central problem that you have long endeavored to bring into focus. It is regarding this issue that I shall try to speak most frankly, even though I may sound to you unjustly critical.
>
> Progress in psychology (this is my guess after 35 years of study in the field), has come in two ways: (1) through a lone wolf who is brilliantly separatist (one thinks of Freud, to a lesser degree of Gestalt psychologists); or else, (2) through the more eclectic scholar who fits his contribution into the mainstream of current thought, building upon the foundations of his predecessors and contemporaries (one thinks of most of the academics and eclectics: James, Boring, Tolman, etc., etc.).
>
> It is characteristic of Type (1) that the author is polemic against the errors of his forerunners, thinks everyone else

misses the "right" formulation, invents his own concepts, and turns prophet. A circle of "followers," a "school of thought" results. I don't deny that these brilliant insights are a greater contribution in the long run, precisely because they provoke controversy by their one-sidedness and isolation of concepts.

But most of us are lesser mortals and contribute by the Type (2) formula. We read what others have written, and try to integrate our thought with contemporary work of a comparable order.

Would it be fair of me to judge you a Type (1) worker, rather than Type (2)? For example, much that you say has relation to current work in group therapy, group dynamics, general semantics, industrial relations, sociometry, semantic therapy, etc. I find no references in your work to these movements, excepting a short and separatist reference to Lewin, whose group dynamic work surely offers a technique for achieving the remedies you desire. Are you perhaps prone to emphasize the *differences* between your conceptualization and that of your co-workers in this generation of human misery?

To sum up: It seems to me you fail to meet other social scientists half way. Your terminology and concepts beckon them to come 100 per cent of the distance to you. The "nomen" of social science today cannot be established by a solitary worker (even with a circle of followers), but only by the joint efforts of all social scientists. It is not quite fair for one worker to expect *all* other workers to come *all* the distance to join forces with *him*. An unkind reader might even say that an air of "autopathic numen" marks such an attempt.

Now I have said frankly the worst that I can possibly say. Let me hasten to re-state my admiration for the courage you have shown, the persistence, the tireless emphasis upon the social basis for man's miseries, also for the workmanship that marks your productions.

Professor Allport's thoughtful letter was the occasion of a review on my part of the course and method I have followed through the years. An important point had been raised and I wanted to meet it as best I could. In my reply I wrote as follows of some of the many factors that have contributed to an impression of aloofness on my part.

Far from feeling that your criticism was severe, I thought

your letter extremely generous and understanding. On the rare occasion that anyone writes me so liberal a letter as yours, I am naturally no little heartened. But at the same time I am spurred to dispel, if I can, whatever needless differences appear to underlie our viewpoints. I hope that in this intention I am not merely trying to defend the 'I'-persona (*my* 'I'-persona), though, knowing this reflex trend as intimately as I do, I would not put it past me! But, however reflex one's subordination to this social impostor, I do want to secure the utmost scientific accord between us in an endeavor having to do with man's behavior, since of its nature it involves us both in a common social problem. To this end, in responding to your letter, I should like to assist to the utmost your helpful criticism and coöperation.

With regard to your interesting comparison of the method of the "lone wolf" with that of the more eclectic scholar, I do not think that either designation really defines the position of my associates and myself. I would say that we are all students of quite ordinary qualifications. To me it is precisely this equalization of aptitudes that is our chief asset. It happened, however, as not infrequently is the case among students in a particular field, that a few of us, having entirely different backgrounds and experience, found ourselves by accident consigned to a common objective in the field of behavior, and to common conditions for approaching it. So that I would say, rather, that in our basic unity of purpose lay our strength—a unity coeval with the common nature of our problem, namely, the common mood or motivating pattern of behavior underlying the social processes of man.

Ordinarily, when students of research hit upon some trend of inquiry, they set their separate *minds* to work, whereas in our study of the basis of human behavior and its motivation, our chief objective was to *set our separate minds aside,* to set aside our *separate aptitudes and attainments* and, as far as possible, to discount the commonly accepted processes of the projective mind of man in its habitual attitude toward behavior. As I recently wrote another colleague, "our group work has consisted solely in the effort to define a mood we definitely recognized in the reactions of the individual and of social groups as being arbitrary and unstable, and to challenge this arbitrary mood as a falsely imbued sense of the 'self.' We set out (associates, students and I) to study our *selves*—the *social self* of man and his motivation as a phylum."

Had there been anything of intellectual interest or novelty to offer to other colleagues working in the field of human behavior—had there been anything that seemed to me of mutual interest to compare with or set beside their mental investigations—I think I could not have refrained from the fullest communication with them in order to assist in clarifying our objectives and possibly welding any related points of view. But we did not have anything of the kind. Primarily, our work held little of mental or academic interest. Besides, what we had to offer was neither stimulating nor inviting in the ordinary sense of the word. There was only the monotonous and exceedingly irritating process of challenging—and then only with awkward and fumbling attempts—the constant and uncontrollable social habit of affect-projection discernible among us as individuals. Here was a reflex social process involving us all as equal and common affect-elements in a homogeneous social matrix. In this common disorder and its common menstruum lay our research interest.

It was the origin and structure of this unconscious social matrix with which we were working, as we were working with the problem of developing a technique with which to withstand and offset its coincident pathology. Over the years we persisted in the effort to discover, if possible, the common denominator responsible for this self-defeating social mood. For the most part our efforts met with failure, or only meager results—a situation hardly calculated to invite the participation of our colleagues!

We would have been glad, only too glad to include other investigators in our all but hopeless efforts to attain a consensual, objective observation of our socially conditioned *selves*. Realizing that other investigators were not less the victims of this common phylic maladaptation, that they too were not less "normal," not less conditioned reflexly in their social prejudices and projections than we were, we would have been the more glad to share our research-endeavors with them. But as for years our work brought us only frustration and defeat, we felt that our sole recourse was to pursue our laboratory studies of man's affect-self until we might reach, or at least be able to indicate, a remedial measure sufficiently positive to invite welcome and acceptance among our colleagues. It is only in the last few years that that expectation has seeemed to offer the prospect of realization. Surely this sort of "lone wolf" inquiry has not been without its scientific precedent.

From the viewpoint of our colleagues generally I can well understand that our position should have appeared aloof and inhospitable. But as the work of our group had not reached the stage of adequate scientific solution, as it was not yet susceptible of formulation in scientific terms, we were compelled to await the fuller development of our research and, except for a few occasional published articles about the general aspect of our investigations, remain silent. Taking into account the domain of our own partitive reactions—I am prepared to admit that no procedure could have *seemed* more inhospitable, more aloof in the accepted sense. But because of our altered frame of reference and because of the incompleteness of our experimentation during the major part of our investigations it was simply not possible to dispense scientific hospitality. Not through any striking intellectual brillance or insight of mine or my associates but through quite fortuitous circumstances we found ourselves committed to a strange and unwonted research assignment. Lacking previous preparation or training, and faced with a situation in which intellectual capacity *per se* could not be of the slightest assistance to us, we were compelled to cope with a problem that was all but insurmountable. This was due to the fact that our experimental setup demanded that we be at one and the same time both the investigators and the material investigated. This was, I assure you, no small order. For a long time it was a case of the blind leading the blind. Such an unprecedented "method" could hardly be expected to invite confidence and accord in the absence of results that show for themselves. But if we were not hospitable to our professional friends, at least we were not inhospitable in the breadth and in the timeliness of our scientific thesis which (however lame our procedure) attempted to challenge the unconscious and universal mechanism of projection—a *reflex social mechanism* which we were obliged to recognize in the immediate actuality of our own behavior inadequacy if we were to resolve this obstacle to balanced community behavior through methods of scientific analysis and resynthesis.

If there has anywhere been a group of research students who have derogated or have attempted to derogate their own accustomed motivation throughout—if they have discovered a technique through which they succeeded in disparaging their habitual feeling even to the point of discrediting their very identity in so far as it is systematized of man's spurious affects—there is no doubt that the fullest acknowledgment of such colleagues should have been given. But I do not know of any group of students that has followed this type of research. On the contrary, in the group procedures with which we are acquainted, the participants have set their *minds* to work. In the midst of their—of man's—irrational mood projections they have not felt compelled to thrash out among them an affective group situation that was socially impossible. . . .

Had the work of my associates and myself grown out of some exceptional hunch or intellectual insight on the part of any one of us, the situation would be different. But whatever has grown out of the coalition of persons and groups that form The Lifwynn Laboratory has been in large measure accidental. We followed a certain consistent procedure and awaited the results. The results followed, but in their own sweet time and, after careful study and examination, they were found to be of an entirely different structure and to lie in an entirely different field from what we had expected. . . .

We are still feeling our way, but there is no question that our research procedure has necessitated the adoption of a fundamentally different basis of reference in respect to human behavior. As I remarked in a recent paper, "to lock oneself in a house for years with associates and students, with normal and neurotic personalities, all of whom have voluntarily pledged themselves to a schedule of unremitting challenge of their own habitual reactions, personal and social, is an experimental discipline that definitely gives pause to one's customary prepossessions—to one's reflex affects and projections."

Dr. Allport was not the only correspondent who felt I had

slighted advances toward interrelational harmony made in other fields of endeavor. For example, Dr. Robert H. Thouless thinks I have not adequately recognized the contribution of religion to an understanding and betterment of human behavior. He says:

> I feel that something might be gained in the present stage of your research by studying its relation to the ideas of these other explorers of the same general principles. I gather that you have no use for the idea of God and regard this idea as one dividing the individual from the rest of mankind. But it is arguable that as religion has superseded the idea of personal or tribal gods by the idea of a God who is the father of all men, it has succeeded in bringing some men nearer to phylobiological awareness than any other system has done. Obviously it has not always or even generally succeeded; the majority of men have formed religious sects and allowed their religious sectarianism to divide them further from their fellow men. This may, however, be due not to the defect of the ideas but to the resistance of the average man's neurosis (or sin).

Professor Pitirim A. Sorokin also feels that I have overlooked religious concepts and other historical antecedents in formulating my thesis. In part, he writes:

> Your complete disregard of all social, psychological, and philosophical disciplines and their discoveries appears to me also unwarranted; ...
>
> Your ... attitude towards religions, ethics and so on is also unjustifiable: side by side with their errors and misdeeds they discovered many a valid truth and performed, sometimes in the most efficient and finest manner, many a function of cotention for millions.

I would like to assure Dr. Thouless that my thesis does not brush aside religious insights as unimportant. I realize that they embody an intuitive though symbolic attempt on the part of man to reach a more coördinated type of experience and behavior, and I have mentioned this parallel from time to time in my writings. I have more than once emphasized that the *mental concept* of harmony, of the interrelatedness of the parts that compose the whole, is as old as philosophy and religion. The fact that the idea is not new makes it all the more pertinent to our thesis. Mankind has thought and talked harmony from the earliest days of his use of sign, symbol or word. He has written beautiful poetry, painted beautiful pictures and composed beautiful music; he has established beautiful dogmas of duty and faith as the basis of his various religions; he has established equally beautiful dogmas of law and order as the basis of his various governments, and he has built beautiful structures to house his religious and political institutions. But he has not yet turned to the observation of those physiological and biological processes internal to him in order to find the cause of the incessant discord in his interrelational life. Throughout the centuries and in all directions man's thought has abounded richly in manifold *theorie*s of harmony, particularly in respect to human behavior; but man's relation to man, his interrelational behavior, is still inharmonious, still consistently divisive. In the moment it is more universally destructive than at any time in his history. Obviously, the richer man has grown in theories of harmony the more outstanding has become his proneness to conflict, crime, insanity and war. Here is something for man to consider soberly and to the best of his scientific ability.

From the point of view of phylobiology, the mental concept of harmony as expressed in the theories of religion and philosophy represents a substitution of symbol and metaphor for the biological continuity of feeling that is inherent in man, both as phyloorganism and as ontoörganism. The systematization of affects associated with the symbol interposes itself between the organism and its environment, causing a break in the spontaneous flow of man's feeling.

The individual, so-called, must become one with mankind and *feel* the common disorder of man as a species. The pain we are experiencing is really due to our individual separateness and conflict arising from the loss of our human solidarity. In truth, we are one vast self—one vast global self. The free and capacious functioning of this self is the phylic reality of which the moral proctors men call their "Gods" are but a vicarious image. It is not God with whom we need all day to walk and talk, but Man. Man is within us; God is an image which self-interest has set in front of us for our own satisfaction. No God is worth the price we pay to travel after him. Religion and devotion are not necessarily related. Religion, as its etymology attests, is bondage.[1] Devotion never binds; it is at all times completely spontaneous and free.

In reference to Professor Sorokin's remark, I may say that those who know me and my work have never regarded me as holding to a superior attitude toward religion and ethics. I am not myself religious as people ordinarily understand religion. But it could only be a very narrowly religious person who would condemn my view regarding man's place in the universe because of my inability to follow the wishful trends currently known as religion. As I said in a recent paper, "It devolves upon us to remove the problem of human behavior from the entire field of tradition and speculation—from religion, as now understood, from morality and other supernatural instrumentalities—and make plain to ourselves and to the community that the understanding and control of disordered behavior-processes is a discipline that lies within the category of the biophysical sciences. . . . And it seems to me that the men and women who have laid aside wishful fantasies and beliefs and have set themselves to study the universe of observable phenomena without fear or favor are the real servitors in the world of thought and feeling, and that it is the self-righteous 'believers' who, if any, should come in for challenge. . . . As the term 'atheist' is used today, it is synonymous with 'infidel' (literally, one who is unfaithful), whereas it would be more consistent to apply such a term to those who adhere to wishful emotions and beliefs rather than to stable scientific principles." [2]

Several other scientists called attention to what seemed to them my failure to integrate my approach with other approaches to the problem of human behavior. PROFESSOR WILLIAM F. OGBURN writes:

. . . There is a good deal of research done on the building of a social organization which will prevent wars, and I am inclined to think they may meet with success, certainly the effort is not to be tossed out. We have had considerable stretches of history without serious wars. These stretches might be prolonged. I believe the cultural anthropologists conclude that war is a cultural phenomenon. But how ever this particular point may be, there has been a good deal of work done on war and on social disorganization by very competent scholars. But you make no citation to this work. . . . [In the portion of the manuscript sent me] you have 24 citations in footnotes of books and articles but 17 of these are from yourself and your associates and only 7 from others.

PROFESSOR ØRNULV ØDEGARD says: . . . You have built up

your own system, without any systematic attempt to show its relations to other systems in psychology and psychiatry. It strikes me that there are interesting parallels—for instance the Russian investigations on cortical and sub-cortical motility (Gurewitch, I believe)—and the two types of Jaensch, B. and T., are certainly closely related to your own. He even speaks about one as integrated and the other one as disintegrated. An investigation in phylic psychology should in the main be based upon studies of animals, small children and primitive people—as far as I can see you have to some extent neglected the findings of these branches of psychology. . . . This isolation of your own system from the rest is accentuated by the introduction of a special terminology—was it necessary to introduce as many new terms? It is at times rather bewildering, particularly for one whose command of the English language is limited. I have always regretted that Adolf Meyer introduced his own terminology, and I feel that his ideas would have been more readily accepted if he had expressed them in the ordinary psychiatric language, which is in fact easily done. If you read E. Bleuler's book on the autistic thinking in psychiatry, you will find ideas closely related to your own, but without any new and bewildering terminology.

In my response to Professor Ogburn I said that there are many disciplines that I would have liked to avail myself of in the writing of my book. I realize that all those fields which have a bearing upon the individual, social, and cultural development of man are of significance in a study of behavior. A background in anthropology and sociology would have been most helpful to me. But, as I have indicated, I am without technical training in either field, as indeed in many others, and have been obliged to pursue my investigations in the reactions of contemporary groups of people, normal and neurotic, under the handicap of many limitations. The concentration of my associates and myself upon internal physiological tensions as the basis of interrelational disorders must plead for some mitigation in my failure to cite anthropological and sociological approaches.

I was especially interested in Dr. Ødegard's remarks about the parallels to my studies which he sees in the work of other investigators. I am not familiar with the Russian researches he mentions on cortical and sub-cortical motility and so cannot express an opinion. It seems to me, though, that the similarity which Dr. Ødegard posits between the B. and T. types of Jaensch and the behavioral modes of ditention and cotention is merely on a superficial and descriptive level. In my usage, the term ditention is applied to a socially divisive attitude and type of motivation characteristic of man throughout. It is characteristic of normal (socially accepted) as well as of abnormal individuals. That is, it applies to all personality-types, to extroverted as well as introverted; to seemingly well-integrated as to obviously schizoid types. In our studies we found that, irrespective of symptomatology, the individual invariably embodies the socially systematized 'I'-persona, with its self-conscious, competitive preoccupations and affect-projections. Equally, it is our thesis that the shift to cotention may occur in all the different types. So that it would be a mistake to give the impression that a certain personality type (for instance, the integrated type of Jaensch) has a specific affinity for the cotentive mode. In phylobiology we are dealing with very basic differentiations in modes of behavior that cannot be determined by accustomed psychiatric and psychological means of discrimination.

Many of my colleagues shared Dr. Ødegard's dissatisfaction with the number of new terms I have introduced. But in order to communicate the new concepts and point of view I am attempting to advance, I felt the need of an altered terminology. I do not wish to minimize my own inadequacies in my attempt to set forth my position. I realize they are many. In presenting our radically altered thesis in respect to man's behavior, it seemed to me there were two courses I might follow. I could either use established terms and attempt to impart different meanings to them, or I could coin new terms to convey these meanings. Knowing how tenaciously accustomed meanings and connotations adhere to words, it seemed to me less confusing in the long run to adopt the latter course. With my colleagues I believe the difficulty was due in part to the fragmentary nature of the material I sent them. In the development of the book as a whole, I tried to indicate rather carefully the meaning of each new term as it is introduced. In addition, there is a full glossary that defines the unaccustomed terms employed.

Professor E. C. Lindeman expresses a criticism similar to that of Professor Allport. In writing me of the advance material from my book he says:

... Two claims seem to pervade this text and unless I am wholly mistaken these are in contradiction. One is the claim of Science and the other appears to be claim of complete originality. Now, if your inquiry is a part of a scientific enterprise, then it must be also a part of some continuity in which other persons and other facts are involved. It seems to me that you fall into a type of Solipsism by placing your inquiry outside the realm of continuity.

My chief reason for mentioning this logical problem is this: I want very much to have your ideas dispersed and utilized because I believe you are pursuing a trail which will ultimately become the gateway to a genuine understanding of human nature and its involvements, but I wish there were fewer barriers such as now keep strategic persons from making use of your material. I recognize the importance of the barrier, the "definite behavioral difficulty," which you mention on page 151, but it seems to me that you erect other barriers which are not really essential to your thesis, and one of these is the failure to associate what you are doing with the work of other persons. I have made use of your material, for example, because I was a student of C. H. Cooley's and it was he who first pointed out the serious fallacy of placing individuals and groups in antithesis. Further, Dewey prepared me for your insights by his doctrines of false antitheses, but it was also Dewey who taught me the value of never losing sight of the law of continuity. What I am striving to say, and very awkwardly I fear, is that I do wish that somewhere in this new text you could find place for indicating the relation between what you and your associates are doing and what is being done by others. It would please me, of course, if some of these others might be philosophers, since all of your work rests upon certain philosophical assumptions which are important, and once the philosophers become acquainted with you they will build new channels of acceptance. You may dismiss this suggestion entirely and on grounds similar to those denoted on page 151 of your text but if so, you will I believe, find yourself involved in a continuing battle for which there can be no victory, or rather a battle in which the victory will go to others and not to you, the others being those who first recognize the strategy of placing your ideas within the stream of continuity. Of course, there may be considerations involved, considerations of a more subtle psychological nature, which I do not comprehend and in that case you will, I hope, forgive me.

In replying to Professor Lindeman's very thoughtful and tempered criticism, I said: "I am quite sympathetic with the emphasis you place on the matter of continuity and I hope I have not been too incorrigible an offender in respect to the work of other colleagues. From the beginning of my investigations I have tried to make clear that my thesis regarding the social neurosis is an outgrowth of my early interest in Freud's rich contribution to the understanding of unconscious mentation within the individual. In more recent years I found in Pavlov's study of conditioning an undoubted analogy with my investigations of the social conditioning I have emphasized in phylobiology. . . . As for Coghill, I do not know of anyone who has laid more stress on his neuroembryological investigations than I have."

In earlier writings my associates and I have mentioned considerable supporting data from other fields of science. In *The Biology of Human Conflict,* for example, I made numerous references to the work of investigators in many fields of endeavor. In the portion of *The Neurosis of Man* that presents our instrumental studies, I have also frequently referred to the work of other investigators—notably to that of Berger and his development of electroencephalography. In other sections of the book there is a discussion of experimental neuroses in animals and of prefrontal leucotomy as they bear upon the physiological aspects of my thesis. In this latter book, however, I felt it necessary to focus particularly on the internal and generic aspects of our phylobiological researches—on the drastic reorientation in behavioral concepts resulting from our consistent group effort to negate the projection of interrelational affects, and to focus upon internal physiological tensions as the basis of behavioral disorders. As far as these essential aspects of our thesis are concerned, we have attempted to blaze an uncut trail. So far as I know there are as yet no established standards with which to compare our phylobiological findings.

I am really up against an unusual difficulty in communicating our phylobiological researches. Such difficulty of communication is present, of course, wherever there is the attempt to introduce a radically altered frame of reference in respect to any field of endeavor. But where that field has to do with behavior—with one's own behavior—the difficulties, both internal and external, are increased a thousandfold. Any "normal" person interested in our researches inevitably says, "Let me see your patients, let me see your methods." But he himself is a patient because he is normal and therefore neurotic, and if he would really see, that is, feel the condition of the patient, he will feel it in himself, the only patient with whose feeling he is in direct and immediate contact. To learn about phylobiology, really to take part in it, one has to become the patient, and that goes against the accustomed grain.

We are all reflexly in favor of our partitive feeling and our partitive physiology. Our training since childhood has been overwhelmingly in this direction. Our accustomed judgments, our very perceptions are biased in favor of an affecto-symbolic, partitive view in respect to behavior. Generations of mankind have lived predominantly on this basis. So in a very real sense we are all reflexly against the development and community acceptance of phylobiological principles. It has therefore been necessary for me consistently to recognize and study such a tendency within myself, and to observe this trend as it expressed itself in the co-workers and students closely associated with me. It is no less my responsibility to call to the attention of professional colleagues and scientists generally the tendency to negate reflexly and without considered study a phylic or organismic view in respect to man and his behavior. I have often emphasized this point in my correspondence and at scientific meetings where I have delivered reports on the progress of our studies. I mention it in the following excerpt from an early letter (1926) to a psychiatric colleague:

> "Your experience with the laboratories of objective investigation has not left you any doubt that it is the laboratory that is authoritative and not the individual. In your letter you tend, as I have done and as was the experience of others of my associates no less, to take the ground of one who would inspect the laboratory from his own viewpoint rather than of one who submits himself and his viewpoint to the laboratory. It has seemed to me, along with others of my co-workers, that this misapprehension occurring time and again within ourselves is due to a certain subjective self-favoritism that is unconsciously bound up precisely in the attitude which one habitually calls his 'viewpoint.' In all discussion it is the *sine qua non* of the individual that he has a viewpoint. But it is

the *sine qua non* of the behavioral laboratory that he has not, that what one calls his 'viewpoint' is the reflection in him of deeply imbued social images which have never been subjected to the test of an unbiased laboratory observation. It is one's own viewpoint—yours or mine—that is precisely the material of a laboratory that examines into subjective processes.

"Under ordinary circumstances I should not take this time to speak of this quite routine tendency. It is one with which we shall be dealing over and over again in our group sessions. But I should not be willing—and I know you would not—that those who are approaching the work largely under your stimulus should be misled at the outset as to the nature of such work through any misapprehension on your part of which I might be the occasion. Together we shall somehow have to make certain to ourselves that the laboratory in which we shall attempt to deal with the subjective processes of the organism, has to do with aims that are as uncompromising and as unnegotiable in terms of theory as those we confront in the laboratories of biology elsewhere."

As I have remarked on more than one occasion, my thesis is not popular. But I believe it can be. I am convinced that just as there is nothing on the instinctual level that is more "popular," more welcome organismically than the feeling of mutuality and common kinship, so a thesis that attempts to expound the biological basis of this instinctual trend should become equally acceptable within the community.

NOTES

1 Religion, from Latin, *religare*, to bind.
2 "Emotion and the Social Crisis," pp. 485-86.

CHAPTER VIII

PHYSIOLOGICAL IMPLICATIONS

In this final chapter I shall discuss the physiological aspects of our thesis and attempt to answer the questions of my colleagues as they relate to this sphere of our researches. I shall lay special emphasis upon the contrasting patterns I have called *ditention* and *cotention* and indicate the profound differences in behavioral and physiological orientation occurring in these two patterns—the one discrete, partitive; the other confluent, total. The technique which my associates and I have found helpful in developing an internal appreciation of the two patterns and of demarcating them functionally will be mentioned briefly for whatever value it may have to others working in this general area of research. As in Chapter IV, I shall take the liberty of including material from sources other than the correspondence regarding the advance chapters of *The Neurosis of Man*.

Writing of these matters to Mr. Herbert Read I said: "With regard to the discussion of cotention . . . where it comes to bridging the interval between theory and experiment, it will relieve your puzzlement, I think, if you attempt the connection in the opposite direction, because it was in the opposite direction that the linkage between them was first made. I had not the remotest idea of cotention until cotention quite unexpectedly took hold of me—until the tensions concomitant to the social affects I had been observing became internally appreciable. My *ideas* regarding cotention and ditention came as an aftermath to the actual physiological appreciation of these opposed patterns. . . . With us the experimental data were thrust upon us unawares, and whatever conscious formulation took place followed these findings. There was not anteriorly, as I say, the theory. I was never in my life more taken aback than when I suddenly perceived an internal sensation hitherto unfamiliar to me (the stress in the anterior zone of the head) and learned through repeated experiment and observation that 'affect-images' and striving were completely irreconcilable with the awareness of this cerebral stress or tension. . . .

"People do not at all credit the physiology of their social tensions, the tensions coincident with group interchange. We know very well the physiological tensions that accompany individual states of health, as of ill health. We know, for example, the physiological stress or tension of an individual's revulsion as expressed in the reaction of nausea. But the contrast in physiological tension that accompanies man's healthy and his unhealthy social interrelations we do not realize. We do not sense the internal difference between one's falsely separate sense of identity and our sense as a common race or species of our common identity. I do not think we shall heal the pain of our differences except as we learn to define within ourselves the presence of these contrasting patterns and have learned to discriminate the positive from the negative type of tension. Unless I am greatly mistaken, we social 'normals' do not faintly suspect, in the habitual give-and-take of our conventional interchange, how far we are from an objectively reliable biological norm."

The social factor is, indeed, a major difficulty. We humans do not really think socially any more. We think convivially perhaps, but not socially in the sense of our being basically members of a common and continuous organism from which the organism of the individual is biologically inseparable. We are all so accustomed to employ our earnestness at every moment in the pursuit of our own personal interests that to turn with earnestness to an impersonal interest in the organism of man as a species entails a wholly unfamiliar pattern of behavior. Yet the pattern is there, and its presence is one of strong affirmation and dependableness. The task is to set aside the distractions, the ditentive impediments that crowd it out.

The cotentive pattern is not a thing to be enticed, coaxed, driven, forged out of iron or compelled by the "will." It does not respond to any of the fervors that characterize man's present level of contact with his kind, whether religious, intellectual, mystical, oratorical; whether loud-mouthed or soft-tongued. Cotention is not *for me*—the outstanding personality, a big, strong, wonderful person. Nor is cotention for me as a sweet and lowly person—an outstanding, patient person. The cotentive pattern is neither for me nor against me, neither for you nor against you. Nor is it something I can give to you or you to me. It is not a thing of "face," of opportunity, of bargaining, of intellect, of "good" and "bad" behavior. It is not a thing of virtue, nor is it a thing of steel. No, it is not a thing of money, might or humility; one cannot go after it hammer and tongs nor can one get it through the virtue of self-effacement.

The cotentive pattern is a pattern of physiological function, as commonplace yet as delicate as the growth of a blade of grass; as simple yet as complex and as powerful as the ray of light that beckons the budding flower to unfold and produce. The cotentive pattern is quite simply the healthy functioning of organismic man — the healthy functioning of the individual as an entity that is inseparable from the species.

In recapturing the organism's cotentive pattern, all mental images are excluded, and the experimenter yields himself to whatever physiological sensations may arise spontaneously within the cephalic segment. As a result of focusing upon the physiological stress in this area, one involuntarily resumes the total body tension for which the partitive tensional pattern has been artificially substituted. With growing familiarity with the organism's total pattern of tensions one automatically accepts more and more the authority of the basic pattern of behavior which relates him effectively and realistically to his objective and social environment. Since man is now abjectly committed to habits of inter-relational prejudice and wishful thinking, his problem is the blocking of the partitive tensional patterns underlying these behavioral trends, and the reactivation of the physiological pattern that relates him cotentively to his surroundings. The induction of cotention is the undoing of the wishful, unilateral affect-interest that now impedes the constructive action consistent with a biosocially integrated personality-structure.

Cotention is not to be achieved through words. We shall not *think* our way into this pattern of organismic function. It is difficult for the sophisticated adult to refuse to "think," because to set aside thinking (with all the affect that now attaches to it) is to seem to set aside one's very *raison d'être*. It is to turn away from the means of "survival" as we know it, that is, of getting ahead in a so-called normal world of competitive 'I'-personae. This, it would seem, is the rub. I am, however, unacquainted with any recourse other than sticking to the effort — or rather to the effortlessness — to maintain a blank mind, to render null and void all that now represents one's social interest or motivation.

According to our findings we do not live *in* our behavior but talk *about* it, the while we firmly believe that this *is* behavior. Cotention is never knowledge *about;* it is experience *with.* It is like any skilled physical activity—tennis, dancing, horsemanship or skating. Everyone is familiar with the characteristic adaptation in habitual tensions that he must make in acquiring an unaccustomed technical skill. In the case of the tennis player, for example, everyone knows that only with consistent drill and practice can he eliminate a faulty stroke and replace it with the technically correct stroke. In the acquirement of such a skill the player is setting aside a familiar, habitual way of performing for one that in the long run is more effective. He is relinquishing an erratic, ill-adapted behavior-reaction that feels satisfactory, and substituting one which, although momentarily seeming less "natural" and desirable, may be more readily systematized within the total pattern of the organism's behavior. This systematization consists in integrating erratic part-reactions within the economy of response of the organism as a whole. This is the process we recognize in the ease and grace with which an accomplishment may be performed.

So with the cotentive pattern of the cerebrum in its interrelational function; knowledge *about* won't do the trick. It can be acquired only through the doing. One has somehow, through repeated trial and error, to grope his way into it. He has to learn from technical experience to set aside his constant preoccupation with self-advantageous images and gradually sense this quiet, secure, basic mode of organismic man. For, as I once wrote Leo Stein, "The total reaction-process — the systemic or integral function as contrasted with the partitive or symbolic function — is as completely intact and operates as efficiently and as persistently today as in the days of our earliest prevertebral meanderings."

There are certain objective conditions and simple procedures which I have found of assistance in the discipline of coming to physiological grips with the tensional patterns underlying behavior.[1] It is necessary, at least at first, to secure conditions that permit one to be unhurried and in a quiet atmosphere. If, then, with eyes closed, one will look straight ahead at the forecurtain of blackness, he will find that he gradually develops an increasing awareness of the muscles about the eyes that maintain them in a position of equilibrium. With the growing kinesthetic awareness of the tensions about the eyes, these tensions automatically tend to relax and one finds that he begins to shut out the restless images that make of us such mental gadabouts. This is not surprising since the processes of thinking and projection are so closely interwoven with the visual function. As one first undertakes this experiment he will probably become drowsy and will fall asleep. Our experience has been that one must return again and again to the exercise. It is merely an entering wedge in differentiating two patterns of physiological functioning. My own procedure has been to set aside daily experimental periods in which I have adhered consistently to relaxing the eyes and to getting the kinesthetic "feel" of the tensions in and about the eyes and in the cephalic area generally. But this is by no means the whole story. With us the study and consistent frustration of social affect afforded the indispensable background of this technique.

I early observed that my work with internal tensional patterns as they relate to man's behavior brought about a marked slowing in respiration, and that this slowed respiratory rate occurred coincidently with the checking of partial, affecto-symbolic patterns of tension (ditention) and the reactivation of the total pattern of action of the organism as a whole (cotention). This preliminary observation led to a series of intensive instrumental studies of physiological functions in my associates and myself in the hope of securing other measures which might be used as objective indices for differentiating these two modalities of behavior. In addition to a slowing and deepening of respiration in cotention, we found that there were certain consistent differences in frequency and extent of eye-movements as well as in brain-wave patterns in the ditentive as over against the cotentive pattern of the organism's response. The instrumental studies to date are summarized in an appendix to *The Neurosis of Man*. They give concrete, objective evidence of differences in the physiological functioning of the organism in the two modes of attentional adaptation.

The technique of working with physiological tensions is not, as some students seem to think, a mere handy recourse for furthering one's personal comfort or convenience. In fact, in first working with the tensional patterns of the organism that underlie behavior, one finds the task uninteresting and difficult. All the customary incentives are for not continuing with the somatic discipline. To exclude from one's mind, in the very moment that they clamor for projection, ideas that are affect-laden is not a simple procedure. Dominated by affect and prejudice, the pattern of our interrelational behavior has become so deeply ingrained within us that it appears now to be a pattern intrinsic to the organism. It has become attached to one's very personality, and the effort to dislodge this ditentive pattern of behavior and restore the organism's primary cotentive mode meets with definite opposition and stress. Thinking, especially emotional thinking, is so much a habit with us now as a race or people that it is easier to be pushed on by this habit than to let go of it. It is so much more diverting to pursue heedlessly the projected affect-image than to determine how the organism feels. But it is precisely this restless mental preoccupation with emotionally toned images which man needs to eliminate.

Whatever the difficulties, we really must become internally acquainted with the cotentive pattern — not my cotention or yours, but man's; not now and again, but as the permanent reinstatement of an intraorganismic configuration. The physiological pattern of cotention, when it becomes a *fait accompli*, entails a fundamental alteration in one's basis of motivation, in one's very center of identity. It will mean the induction of a fundamentally altered mode of behavior throughout the human race. In the absence of this radical readjustment, man's behavior must remain partitive and unreal. With ourselves as an experimental group, our ditentive inertia and its developmental inhibitions were an inevitable part of our research experiment. It was necessary to nurture our condition if we were to study our condition. And so, we had to remain together, to stick close day in and day out — at meals, in the instrumental laboratory, in the office and in my study — in order to fulfill our appointed job of interindividual affect-baiting. With a view to dissolving the affective bonds of family tradition, we had to reproduce an affect-situation redolent of the family, redolent of the pseudo-relationship between parent and child. In other words, we had to invite and foster an experimental dilemma. It was necessary to fashion a setting that encouraged the very dichotomy that was our disease and that we, as students, were supposedly examining dispassionately. We were each an element of a group which was compelled to countenance within its social milieu the same behavioral pathology which it was our business to eliminate.

Of course, there never would have been a science of bacteriology, had not the bacteriologists induced and studied under controlled conditions the very disease they wished to understand and eradicate. Except for the fact that the disease we studied was already present within our processes, our procedure was like theirs. Without doubt, ours was a difficult and hazardous undertaking. Many were the impasses and the false turnings in our experimental attempt to arrive at the basic factors responsible for the manifold symptoms of behavioral imbalance. But with the gradual unearthing of the physiological pattern of cotention, the whole situation became greatly simplified.

A scientist, of course, must have his basis of observation. He brings phenomena into his field and studies them from the basis of his background and training. What we did in The Lifwynn Laboratory was to move ourselves into a new and different field. Instead of using the cortical segment to observe the behavior of man, we moved back into the organism-as-a-whole to observe the behavior of the cortical segment. Abandoning all attempts to offset mental habits with different mental habits, we tried to deal with contrasting neural patterns of behavior. We tried to differentiate between a pattern that governs the behavior of man's organism as a phylic unit, and a pattern that is secondary or partitive and that governs the reactions of individuals in their symbolic relations to one another. We placed our primary emphasis upon the whole organism, both in its ontogenetic and its phylogenetic aspects, and upon *feeling,* or the primary expression of the total organism. We found that man's feeling — the feeling of every you and every me — is seriously disturbed and unbalanced. Through our group approach we attempted to get an internal and generic appreciation of this common disorder in our feeling-life, and to see how it determines our behavior — our thinking, our perception, and convictions. As a result of this procedure there was a lessening of emphasis upon the adroit manipulation of symbols, upon mental convictions, and the infallibility of one's "knowledge." Interest shifted in the direction of research, of acquiring firsthand knowledge through experience.

DR. DAVID KATZ raised several questions in regard to physiological findings as they relate to the cotentive behavioral pattern. He phrases his queries as follows:

> If I understand you correctly, "cotention" is the ideal attitude toward which you are striving. It is what can be accomplished after freeing one of all neurotic traits. Now . . . you say the breathing rate during cotention is on the average

4.63, 3.73 for Subject A. If I understand you correctly, cotention is the final attitude toward which you strive. But can any human being survive with a breathing rate of about 4?

Another question: You present certain behavior patterns with relation to the eyes, that one could consider as relaxation exercises that would restore health. Do these exercises alone suffice, independently of long and tiring group-therapeutic efforts?

Naturally, these are important considerations and I am grateful to Dr. Katz for voicing them. In responding to him, I called attention to a sentence on page 397 of my book which reads as follows: "Needless to say, increased experience in cotention may add further indication of physiological changes, or may materially modify the indications already obtained." In my letter I went on to say, "In those of us in whom cotention has become a quite customary procedure there is already an indication of modification in recent experiments. There is not now the very marked retardation in the breathing-rhythm, with the shift to the cotentive pattern. Apparently the extremely slow breathing-curves we obtained in the early period of our investigations of cotention are to be explained in part as a function of that initial stage in the experimentation. It was necessary to overcome our habitual conditioning to the ditentive pattern, and this presented an obstacle which had to be surmounted with the induction of cotention. That is, in opposing itself to the ditentive pattern, cotention came up against definite physiological resistance. It would seem that this conflict-situation is responsible for the very slow respiratory rhythm. Certainly, as cotention became more habitual—as it became more a matter of routine among us—the characteristic respiratory rate increased. It still differs, however, from the rate prevailing in ditention. I am just now in the process of getting together some experimental data on this matter and hope to publish it in the near future.

"As to your query in regard to the behavior of the eyes, it has been our experience that in bringing about the pattern of cotention, the tensional pattern in and about the eyes plays a significant rôle. It plays a significant rôle because this pattern of tension would seem to be the physiological substrate of the ditentive (affect-projective) mode. The appreciation of this biologically alien pattern could not be brought into relief except from the basis of the organism's total behavior-pattern. But for the organism's total pattern (cotention) there would not be the needed background from which to observe or sense the extraneous (conditioned) pattern of ditention. I believe I describe this in the chapter on technique.[2] But whether this readjustment can be obtained without some background of discipline in group-analysis is not a question which I am at the moment prepared to answer categorically. Certainly the long and intensive schedule followed by our original research group will not need to be repeated by other groups in order to achieve the cotentive pattern of behavioral adaptation. I go into this in my Symposium paper,[3] and I hope that that rather careful discussion may be of assistance to you on this point. The paper attempts to show very specifically how in a group there is brought about the transition from a naïve dichotomy of right and wrong to a common appreciation of the neural pathology (cerebral stress or tension) underlying this behavioral dilemma."

The conceptions I have advanced in regard to the neurobiological substrate of man's disordered behavior seem to have caused considerable difficulty for my colleagues. PROFESSOR C. JUDSON HERRICK has been particularly generous of his time and thought in discussing with me the physiological, neural aspects of my formulations. He writes:

> Your neurological excursions . . . confuse and puzzle me. They seem to me out of step with current neuroanatomy and neurophysiology. I know of no neurological evidence that justifies some of the distinctions that you make which seem inconsistent with principles of cerebral activity as I understand them. This is a pity because your basic concepts are, I think, fundamentally correct. And my confusion may be due to lack of knowledge on my part or failure to grasp the full significance of your statements.
>
> The key to my difficulty lies perhaps in footnote 13[4] . . . The "mixture of categories" clarifies nothing for me. "The transition from the symbolic behavior level of sociology and psychiatry to the non-symbolic level of phylobiology and medicine" is meaningless to me. In your phylobiology you are simply substituting a different series of symbols for those

of conventional sociology, biology and medicine. This is a legitimate thing to do, but your symbols stand for concepts that are fuzzy in my mind.

"In phylobiology the factors involved are neurodynamic, biophysical." Very good. We can look for these factors in individual persons, in social structures and cultural patterns, and in their interrelationships. This, I take it, is your program. But the categories involved should not be mixed.

In responding to Professor Herrick's thoughtful comments, I said: "For my own sake I earnestly hope I can clear up any difference between us on neuroanatomic grounds. I am no neuroanatomist, as I am sure you know. It would be preposterous of me to presume any ground in this field that is not in accord with that of accepted authorities. As my Symposium paper ["Prescription for Peace"] I think shows, I am strongly of the view that a significant shift in man's emotional behavior has taken place within his organism, with a concomitant modification in neuromuscular function. It is always *function* that I am talking about. It is always the displacement of the total by the partitive pattern of behavior, individual and phylic. My theme is the misplaced identity throughout man, as a species, caused by the inadvertent channeling of feeling or affect into the circumscribed symbolic area. When I speak of the 'third brain,' I am speaking of this affecto-symbolic reaction-pattern that has become functionally separated from the organism's pattern of behavior as a whole — the whole pattern, phylic and individual. I have no structural alteration in mind. Far be it from me, with my inexperience in neurophysiology, to presume to suggest concrete neuroanatomic variations.

"You say that my statement that 'the transition from the symbolic behavior level of sociology and psychiatry to the non-symbolic level of phylobiology and medicine' is meaningless to you. This I regret. For me there is nothing in my entire thesis that is more meaningful than this — than the difference between discussion, concept and recommendations of external social adjustments in behavior (the interrelational sphere), and direct experimental research based upon the immediate observation of the organism's interrelational mode as it makes contact with the environment. So that I would like to indicate briefly its significance for me. It seems to me that in our traditional psychiatric, psychological and sociological concepts in regard to disorders in human behavior, we are dealing with the *symptomatology* of behavior, not with the disordered process itself. It seems to me that we are working at the same level that characterized the medical approach to infectious disorders before the advent of bacteriology. As we know, there were many diverse concepts in regard to the cause of these diseases before their bacterial origin was demonstrated. As I see it, the contribution of the bacteriologists was that they advanced concepts in regard to causation that could be objectively verified. They removed infectious disorders from the sphere of traditional (superstitious) belief and disbelief to a sphere involving concrete and observable phenomena. This substitution of concepts with its altered frame of reference was, of course, of enormous value to man.

"It is an analogous reorientation which I feel it is most imperative to adopt in the field of behavior-disorders, individual and social. My studies . . . have shown that most of the problems with which we attempt to deal in behavior are the symptoms of the disorder; not the causative factors. It seems to me that concepts which remove man's behavior from the field of the mental and moral, from the sphere of the projective, the symptomatic and the ideological, and posit a dysfunction in physiology in man as a species as the causative factor in his behavior imbalances, may offer a significant reorientation in regard to our pressing human problems. The physiological aspects of our researches which have developed coincidently with our altered orientation give objective data in regard to the physiological coördination and dysfunction of the organism as a whole in its relation to its environment. Given an acquaintance with the phylobiological technique in tensional readjustment, these data are susceptible of check in other laboratories.

"So that I cannot but feel that the trend of our concepts toward the objective and the verifiable should be a rewarding one. But I hasten to add that I realize my work is still incomplete. It has yet to be adequately formulated. It greatly needs the participation of other research workers interested in the common problem of man's behavior. I earnestly trust that this will come about, and I believe that my efforts in this direction have not been unavailing."

Professor Carney Landis stresses the general lack of knowledge in respect to brain-function. He says:

On the negative side I find myself in a mental muddle with respect to your acceptance and reliance on the functional supremacy of the fore-brain. The review of all the hypotheses regarding brain function which I made in connection with the Columbia-Greystone project together with our findings in the project have left me at a loss for a satisfactory working hypothesis. To my mind no theory so far advanced can encompass the evidence.

The major difficulty comes from the absence of a satisfactory scheme which will provide a place for affective phenomena in functional neurology. The generalizations which you advance are interesting speculations for which I know of little factual evidence in support nor do they seem to offer avenues for verification.

Dr. Clyde Kluckhohn contributes the following comment:

In the article at the end[5] you say, on page 35, that disorders are not sociological, not moral, but neural. On the other hand, on page 39, you say that neurosis is social. I would feel very strongly that both things are true, but that there is an apparent contradiction in your statement as it appears here. And such phrases as "functional brain twist" bother me because, while the implication may be correct, I have not seen any evidence.

In responding to Professor Landis' comment, I said: "My thesis really does not hold to the hypothesis of the functional supremacy of the forebrain. But as a medium of affect, this arbitrary, socio-symbolic segment does seem to have forced its dissociative charades into the foreground, and in this sense to have usurped the functional supremacy of the brain as a whole. As I see it, because of affect-involvements that are universal, this segment now mediates a spurious social process throughout and plays a dominant rôle ... in the determination of human behavior. ...

"What seems to me true is that 'thinking with our mouths,' as children sometimes put it, has to a degree far beyond our suspecting, involved *feeling* with our mouths' — by which I mean feeling partitively, personally, or from the point of view of the 'I'-persona, with its unilateral restriction of interest and motivation.

" ... I am not a sufficiently competent neurologist to presume to define the relation of affect-drives to specific brain-areas. I doubt if anyone can. My thesis is as yet far too general for the finer neural localizations and discriminations."

I believe it will be generally agreed, however, that the brain of man possesses a function that is quite different from the brain of any other animal. It is the only organ in the history of evolution that possesses the peculiar faculty of making contact or establishing communication with other similar organs throughout its species. In man, the brain of one organism communicates with that of another through the use of agreed signs or symbols, and this mechanism that has become systematized into speech or language establishes a unique nexus or continuum among all individuals. This social mechanism of symbol facility or speech has brought about an enormous expansion of function within the brain of man. The possession of such a systematized function is the basis of human consciousness. It forms the entity that each of us experiences as the self, thus distinguishing man from all other animal species.

Of course, the fact that man should have had recourse to the use of symbol and metaphor in relating his processes to the external universe is an incident in his development to which our very civilization owes its rise. Science itself could not have existed but for the employment of the symbol or metaphor in part-replacement of the organism's whole relationship to the actual objects and conditions in the external world. But where man's feeling, where his own motivation, where his very identity is transformed into symbol and metaphor, the story becomes a very different one. For feeling and motivation are not to be so transmuted. They are not with impunity to be displaced to the area of the forebrain and to be mediated through sign and symbol. Though overtly such a transformation has taken place, the circumstance entails a vital contradiction in man's feeling and motivation. It entails an organic contradiction. In the process, feeling has backfired. It has recoiled upon itself and become locked and impacted. The problem presented, then, is not a mental but a physiological one. Man is confronted with a problem internal to his own organism. It is a problem in the physiology of man's own feeling or motivation.

Dr. Kluckhohn calls attention to an apparent contradiction when I speak of the neurosis as "neural" in one place, and "social" in another. It seems to me that what often appear to be inconsistencies in conception are but differences in the aspects emphasized. In my usage, the term "social" applies to the common interrelational symptoms of man's disordered behavior, while "neural" applies to the physiological seat of the lesion involved. For example, the widespread pathology expressed in the social image — my preoccupation with what I think of myself and with what you think of me — is a subjective, symptomatic condition. This symptomatic aspect is, I believe, quite inaccessible to me or to you on man's present social-image basis. (Naturally, I'm speaking of any "me" or any "you.") On the other hand, the neural substrate of the reactions reflected socially in these countless "mc's" as in these countless "you's," and in their social interrelationships, constitutes for me the objective, physiological process involved in man's common behavior-disorders, both normal and neurotic.

Several other colleagues wrote me about the neurological implications of my thesis and I shall quote portions of their letters. Dr. Alan Gregg said:

> Probably because I had only parts of the presentation I was able to form only an inadequate impression of the evidence you offer for your ideas of the dislocation of the forebrain. It would seem to me (perhaps because I have not seen the presentation as a whole) that the relationship of man's consciousness of self, his tendency to projection, and his rather extraordinary penchant for symbols and conditioning by symbols, deserves a more explicit and closely reasoned exposition or proof than I was able to follow in what you sent me. Together with a fuller discussion of what you mean by neurosis, these points would seem to me to be central and essential to your general thesis. In connection with the function known as conditioned reflexes I suspect that there may be considerable significance in the fact that it is in fact by means of variations in the conditioning stimuli that dogs can be made to experience a state of being closely comparable to neuroses. Is it our ability and tendency to accept and live by symbols that makes it possible to have neuroses? And, rather tangential to that question is the curious observation of Charles Stockard that man is the only animal that gives deliberately false signals to his own kind — the I-persona at work?

I was no little interested in Dr. Gregg's comment regarding the establishment of experimental "neuroses" in animals through variations in the conditioning stimuli. In one chapter of *The Neurosis of Man* I attempt to develop the analogy between the disintegration in the behavior of the experimental animal when consistently presented with conflicting or ambiguous stimuli, and the neurosis which has developed spontaneously in man as a result of conditioning to a conflicting *system* of wishful, arbitrary thinking and feeling. In an earlier book,[6] I describe a hypothetical situation (analogous to the actual situation in man) in which dogs are represented as reflexly conditioning one another, and indicate the biologically spurious character of the interrelational conflicts that would be engendered in such a procedure.

Dr. Gregg's remarks on the relation between man's symbolic capacity and the neurosis also interested me, and especially his citation of Stockard's pertinent observation that man is the only animal that gives deliberately false signals to his kind. I heartily agree with Dr. Gregg's comment on this observation. It is my position that this anomaly in biological development *is* to be traced to the 'I'-persona; that the egocentric, partitive self with its systematization of affects and prejudices is the motive power, the neurodynamic factor in man's behavioral impasse today. Accordingly, I feel that it is this spurious self or 'I'-persona—the subjective identity of each of us — which must be brought to objective observation and awareness if we are to achieve a scientific approach to the problem of human behavior, individual and social. It is toward this major aim that our researches have long been oriented. In the effort to understand the factor of behavioral conflict, our work has made at least an entering wedge through its internal differentiation of the contrasting tensional patterns that are the physiological concomitant of ditention and the 'I'-persona on the one hand, and of cotention and man's phyloörganismic adaptation on the other. Furthermore, this technique has resulted in the demarcation of cotention, or the organism's total pattern of behavior, as a practical instrument for reorienting and controlling the organism's behavior in relation to other organisms and to the environment. In order to be effective, of course, cotention must be community-wide. It must become as widespread socially in man as his prevalent ditentive adaption is today.

Dr. Arthur Bentley writes: On a general proposition

that there is no technically "human" behavior, and of course no "lower" behavior (in time-line) that is found except through and in physiological process, just as this latter is through and in physical process, I am 100 per cent in agreement.

But when it comes to setting the fore-brain, or the language process, over against physiological process, I can't go along. There are many stages of "new" process lower down along the evolutionary lines — chemical reactions, primitive perception-traces, variously developed stages of perception, cue-shrinking and cue-naming, and so on up. I cannot forget that while the brain (or fore-brain) thrives in distortion, also it transforms the world through mathematics. One might take issue with you on this last point. I do not. I know what you are after, and am in thorough agreement with the campaign.

The main difficulty for me is cutting off part of the brain as though it could act by itself, and thus presumptively could set over against certain interior parts of the organism's body. I see nothing like this. I see the behaviors involving all there is organically around. When you use the word "reaction" as applied to happenings inside the skin, and class them with reactions found as between the skin-included parts of the world and the extra-skin parts, I find no interpretation by you. Unfortunately this is the one region of inquiry in which I am most concerned. "Reaction" is the word, i.e., on which my eye clamps down hard every time it shows up.

This main difficulty shows itself in your use of words implying production or causation starting from physiological processes, organs, or regions, as interpretive of behavior as outcome. I cannot see this at all. . . . My view sees the behavioral development growing through, in, of and with neural complexity; neither as causal to the other — both, so to speak, as "the same thing."

In respect to Dr. Bentley's comments, I feel that there is less difference in our positions than they would seem to indicate. And I am encouraged in this feeling by subsequent correspondence with him. For instance, my thesis really does not set the forebrain or the language process apart and over against other physiological processes. But as a mediator of affect, the socio-symbolic segment does seem to have interfered with the functional supremacy of the organism as a whole. It is not that I have any quarrel with language *per se*. It is the imposed, the tutored, the conditioned twists of feeling away from their common center that apparently have come about with the acquisition of the function of language and projection—with the acquistion of the partitive and biologically unwarranted proposition "me and you" — at which I demur. This, as I see it, is a derivative of the fatuous anomaly I call the social 'I'-persona.

My views are very much in sympathy with what I understand of Dr. Bentley's "situational" or "transactional" approach. As I said in letters to him: "I believe that in so far as I am capable of thinking in your way — on your lines — I am quite in accord with all that you say. . . . Unless I am even more abysmally mistaken than I think, all philosophy, like all science, proceeds from an established principle — a standard or criterion that cannot be argued or gainsaid, but that is common, permanent, unitary and immutable. Well, why may not man himself embody such a unitary principle, and why exclude the thesis that all our conflicts and self-interests have derived from the violation of this central principle in man? All I ask is that we try out some such principle, and adopt a procedure in our human relations that is consistent with it.

"Differentiation is the emphasis everywhere. It has always been. Always and everywhere man is occupied with differences that either overtly conflict or are covertly reconciled. Man would achieve peace through war. He would 'join issues,' as the phrase fondly runs. But the issues are not joined. Peace and war are not reconciled. Differences are of their nature mutually unassimilable. *Dissimilia dissimilibus non curantur.*

"Why may we not try to discover somewhere a basis of unity and accord? Why may we not turn from our age-old preoccupation with dissimilarity, and embrace a premise of similarity? I really don't believe I am trying to do anything more spectacular, more exceptional, more original than just that. All that I have tried in my faltering way to suggest is that *as a genus* we somehow attempt to forego a brain-function that habitually rests upon a basis of differentiation and projection and, instead, recover a pattern of reaction that is integrated and unitary. Why, then, can we not interrupt, at least momentarily, our tendency to emphasize differences, and see what our resemblances may be — what common identity may underlie our habitual contrasts and disagreements? It seems to me that, come what will, it is worth trying.

"To begin with, there is evidence that our differences are really imposed upon us, not inherent. I don't like being imposed upon. I don't like being made to think or do anything that isn't natural to me — that hasn't the full and spontaneous sympathy of my organism. And harboring still some faint remnant of man's early communal sense, I don't like to see anyone else imposed upon against the dictates of his native organism. So, I want to get back — I want the community of man to get back to the primary, undifferentiated sense of the organism and its basic motivation."

The partitive mood of the 'I'-persona is synonymous with differentiation. It is preoccupied with projective interests, with pointing. It points to itself as estimable, and it points to others as inestimable. The aim of The Lifwynn Laboratory has been to undermine this unilateral systematization of the 'I'-persona and to allow man's total reaction-pattern — his organismic behavior — to reassert itself. The organismic pattern of behavior is inclusive, common — necessarily so. The partitive pattern on the other hand is preëminently special, restricted to "me." The line of demarcation is clearly drawn. We have a vital challenge here in these two opposed patterns—the partitive and the organismic—with all the world caught up in the part-reaction and not suspecting the anomaly our substitutive behavior entails socially.

Throughout the years a number of my colleagues have asked me what I mean by the terms "partitive" and "organismic" in their application to man's behavior. In writing some time ago to Dr. Adolf Meyer, with whom I was closely associated at The Johns Hopkins Hospital, I took up these questions and tried to clarify my meaning.

> About "partitive" and your question regarding this term, I only know that I find myself feeling things *mentally*, as my feeling appeals to "me"; that I am affectionate mentally, and equally disposed to be mentally disaffected; that mentally I am drawn to this person or that, and like as not am tomorrow critical toward him and withdrawn. All this upon analysis shows itself of one piece with the shifting affects of the mentally disturbed patient—these oscillations from like to dislike, between comfort and discouragement, these transient prerogatives of the "me" and the "mine." And I am no bio-

logical sport; this "me" and "mine" represents quite the normal vacillations of mood occurring everywhere mentally. So that this "I," I insist, isn't restricted to me. The frailty is one I share equally with the community because of our common part in a common community infirmity.

And yet, basically, biologically, there is a more solid foundation upon which the race of men has builded. True, "the genesis has already been done," as you say, but in our normal mood criteria may we not have forgotten the genesis that took place ages ago — whether in life's womb today or yesterday? May not the accustomedness of our mental feeling and thinking have come to lack, inadvertently, the communicative, the unifying quality that inheres in all genesis? Does not the effort of all peoples "to get together"—not to mention our own effort toward a clearer understanding of one another—indicate just this? So that one wonders whether our thinking (and our feeling with it) has not become too detached from our organisms, like a clock that gives time on its face and lacks a balance wheel. And perhaps this has happened to us as a race of word-using people. And is not this precisely your teaching, as I first came to know it and to set my course by it years ago?

These are the thoughts that lead me to speak of a mental disease as a functional imbalance in man's social development as a phyletic organism. There appear to have occurred definite shuntings — side-trackings and reversals in this organism's primary motivation. Of course one might ask and very pertinently, I think, "what of it? If this is all, why all the pother—why pick upon these reversals as responsible for the presence of serious behavior-abnormalities?" But this isn't all. These shuntings have led to definite impactions within the organism. They have led to our placing a definite obstacle in the path of the organism's basic feeling or motivation — an obstacle in the path of the organism of man at large and therefore perceptible as an obstacle within *my* organism. I cannot disconnect me and the phylum. That is why I harp so constantly, though perhaps injudiciously at times, upon the phylum as well as upon the individual. And when the individual or organism gets into communication with another individual or organism of its species, it does so through a delimited behavior-process, or mentally, not with all of itself as was man's wont (and mine) originally, natively, pre-mentally. That is all there is to "partitive."

And what with me would be "a sample of the whole?" I'm sure we are at least both agreed that, within the realm of whole processes, samples or symbols are of their nature contradictory of the very wholeness they would affirm. Description or symbol is secondary to the whole it stands for. In this sense the whole or total function, as I just said, always precedes the image. It precedes the image or part-consideration of the self just as with the individual who has turned about before mentally planning turning about, or as your effectiveness with me or with a student took a prior position in relation to your word or verbal meaning. To cite an analogous example: a mirror will afford me an image of myself but once I set about behaving spontaneously my self-image is necessarily effaced in the total spontaneity of my behavior. I may be enjoying music and I may want to describe my inner enjoyment by taking notes on the *phenomenon* of my enjoyment, but with the entrance of the "phenomenon" the music and its enjoyment necessarily recede. This is trite but it is probably on this account the more illustrative. Organically the part just won't stand for the whole. This whole of which you ask—this absolute affirmation or reaction—may not be defined in symbols or in the language of part-function except as one resorts to negation or to the absence of affirmation. This total function is present and effective only when the itemized, detailed or part function is not present and dominating the scene. . . . .The whole toward which my interest directs itself is rather an indivisible *summum organum* —a primary, integral function into whose totality no part-function, no symbol of the self or self-occupation can intrude without embarrassment and contradiction to the organism's total behavior.

And so in my interpretation the individual in his part-function is split off in feeling or motivation from this *summum organum;* and similarly a nation, whether the American nation or that of Hitler, is split off in feeling or motivation from this *summum organum* that is biologically its central core. For this whole, this affirmation, this racial commonness and continuity of function is the very substance of man's motivation. It is the *prima materia* of his behavior.

It was here before .... language, and if language were suddenly effaced from man's catalogue of part-reactions, this primary reaction-principle would still remain.

In bringing to a close this interchange of views with my scientific confreres, I wish again to express to them my deep appreciation, and to voice the earnest hope that this material will prove of assistance in answering the thoughtful questions they raised. Above all, I trust it will help to forge and consolidate bonds of communication and understanding that will promote an intensive, scientific study of the pressing problem of man's behavior.

Such a synthesis of purpose is greatly needed. Our research group is small and limited, and there remains much work to be done in resolving the impediments to man's healthy interrelational functioning. As I said to colleagues at the Second International Symposium on Feelings and Emotions: "My associates and I recognize, of course, that in our group approach to the problem of behavior we have made but a beginning, and a very meagre beginning. We recognize too that even this meagre beginning of an understanding of social man must abort in mere futility unless there is the coöperation and participation of scientists the world over in defining and accepting the larger biological pattern of behavior native to man as a social organism. I assure you that we have no illusions as to our limitations as a special experimental unit or group. For a long time we have fully realized that no single group, no restricted section of the social community, can perform a task which, of its nature, belongs to man as a species. The scientist who studies infectious disease or cancer does not restrict his investigations to a single group or community. Neither can the scientist who studies the forces and relations that determine human behavior adopt a parochial attitude toward his problem. Science, like art, is a universal language. It is necessary that scientists everywhere recognize and impart to the wider community of man the global nature of his behavioral conflict."

NOTES

[1] Cf. pp. 365-90.
[2] See Note 1, Chapter VIII.
[3] "Emotion and the Social Crisis."
[4] The footnote is from "Prescription for Peace" which appeared subsequently to

The Neurosis of Man. It reads: "To link the concept of social feeling and that of physical trauma or impaction involves us, of course, in a mixture of categories. But this solecism is, I hope, a permissible expedient in making the transition from the symbolic behavior level of sociology and psychiatry to the nonsymbolic level of phylobiology and medicine. In phylobiology the factors involved are neurodynamic, biophysical. They have to do with the conflict and irreconcilability between the total physiological pattern of cotention and the partitive pattern of ditention. It is the disparity in neuromuscular tensions that constitutes the element of trauma or impaction."

[5] "The Social Neurosis," the manuscript of which had been included with the advance chapters Dr. Burrow sent to his colleagues. This paper was subsequently published in *Philosophy of Science,* 1949, Vol. 16, pp. 25-40. [Ed.]

[6] See Note 3, Chapter V.

THE NEUROSIS OF MAN

THE NEUROSIS OF MAN

An Introduction to a Science of Human Behavior

by

TRIGANT BURROW, M.D., Ph.D.
SCIENTIFIC DIRECTOR, THE LIFWYNN FOUNDATION
WESTPORT, CONNECTICUT

Today we are faced with the preëminent fact that if civilization is to survive, we must cultivate the science of human relationships—the ability of peoples of all kinds to live together and work together in the same world, at peace.

FRANKLIN DELANO ROOSEVELT.

**PROPERTY OF WASHINGTON
SCHOOL OF PSYCHIATRY
LIBRARY**

AUTHOR'S FOREWORD

The history of phylobiology is the history of the thirty years' association of Clarence Shields and myself in an uninterrupted research in human behavior. This book is the history of that association. It is the embodiment of it. With us there was also associated a small group of co-workers, professional and lay. The history of this group is the history of The Lifwynn Foundation.

The thesis with which Mr. Shields and I began our investigations may be stated quite simply: What man is overtly, is not what man is basically. The externals of man are not man. And this thesis, of course, we applied equally to ourselves. We too, however "normal," however comfortably "adapted," were, as social individuals, not what we appeared outwardly to be. Today human relations are throughout superficial, not fundamental. They are psychosocial, not biological. Wherever it is a question of his own feelings and the relationships begotten of them, man ceases to be objective or scientific. He is subjective, wayward, undependable. This discrepancy in human behavior is the problem our group attempted to bring to practical test in the relationship of its members to one another and of each of us to the group as a whole.

From the outset of this interrelational self-study my accustomed interest in individual behavior, social and professional, began gradually to fall away. Human behavior took on a different meaning. From now on man became for me the center of interest, and from now on I began studying and writing only of man—of the muddled sum of parts that had become dissociated from the organism of man as a primary biological whole. I was no longer interested in the separate personality of this or that patient, or in the tangled processes which, in his separateness, he brought me to unravel. As if the tangled threads of his life—of any individual's life—were not just part of a vast knotted skein extending throughout the interrelationships of man the world over. For in my altered outlook it had become clear that the problem of human adaptation was infinitely larger than this. It was a problem of science and research, and the job of behavioral medicine was that of tackling a disorder existing within the biosocial processes of man throughout.

In a moment of evident vexation, Freud once remarked to a mutual colleague of ours, "Does Burrow think he is going to cure the world?" to which my unequivocal reply was, "I most certainly do"; adding, "What is more, I know of no physician worth his salt who is not interested in curing the world, in employing medical measures applicable to the world at large." This business of employing esoteric methods for a privileged few is completely at variance with the essential principles of science. A method that has not value for everyone is not a scientific method. The medical sciences are based upon principles that possess a universal value. Indeed, I'd like to know where we'd all be today, had not the students of bacteriology promoted an all-out program for "curing the world"!

Freud, of course, had his own esoteric system, and was not to be disturbed. But in the coördinated effort in social analysis with which our groups set out, whatever savored of esoteric systematization was excluded. As a group or community we were agreed not to countenance the customary premises, personal or interpersonal. Starting out with the clean slate of an unbiased research into the social behavior of man, we were bent upon finding a remedy applicable to man everywhere. Basically, Freud was not interested in a research in human relations. He started with human relations as they were—his own and other people's—and built on this established social order. Our whole purpose, on the contrary, was to discredit all there was of man's behavior prepossessions—all the inherited mental and social constructions habitually cherished by us—and to build anew. But to my thesis of the wider social implications of the neuroses Freud turned a deaf ear. Freud, who had himself done so much for the world at large through his dynamic conception of human personality and its disorders, was too firmly set in the mordant of his personal systematizations to countenance the broader social involvements of a research in human behavior.

Yet in any other course medical interest and incitement inevitably become contracted into a purely formalized "practice," in which physicians devote themselves to the business rather than to the profession of medicine. All medical research, on the contrary, is necessarily a form of community medicine. But there is also the need of community law, economics, housing, education and play, of civic and domestic research. In a clear view of man, anything other than research in whatsoever field is a distortion of interest, of natural devotion to one's subject. Devotion to work is the whole meaning of systematic activity and interest. How often do we see physicians who are too interested in their practice to give time to their patients! One cannot make an enterprise of medicine or of any other interest. Through enterprise, work becomes mere formalization and routine. It lacks the spirit of devotion and research.

Considering the failure of religion and philosophy, and of the various political, social and economic schemes presumed to answer the need of man, it would of course be silly for any person or any group, especially a group of quite ordinary people like ourselves, to imagine they could devise a program of welfare for the human race. But it is precisely the failure of efforts based upon mental and social programs for the betterment of human relations that gives point to our effort—an effort that has nothing whatever to do with mental or social measures of reform, but that rests squarely upon a basis of disinterested research into the impaired structures and functions that are the underlying cause of man's unhealthy social relations. Essentially our aim has been the application of principles of internal medicine to the problem of human behavior.

Clearly, ours is the record of an experiment that was no one-man job. It was a biosocial experiment in which the experimental conditions laid down by us were rigid and uncompromising—far more so than we knew upon first setting out. For our criterion of investigation demanded the consistent discrediting of all our habitual "manifest" social expressions. It demanded that in the interest of a common interrelational reorientation the motives of human relations as they exist today be granted no quarter. We had lowered the barriers surrounding the personal sympathies and confidences we had thought to be bonds, and found that inter-human relationships which we had believed were close and dependable were everywhere shifting and insubstantial. In the process of phyloanalysis, however, these relationships became far closer, far more dependable and secure.

In view of the earnest work of those who have participated in this endeavor, and in view of the many years they have participated in it, this Report should be a worth-while and representative one. It should be as distinguished in form as it is distinctive in substance. But to be daily embroiled in the devastating task of recognizing one's own part in an ugly, crippling community defection, and at the same time put into beautiful, balanced form one's scientific formulation of this disfiguring behavior-process—one's own and everybody else's—is truly no light undertaking. It is all very well for the "artist" to skip lightly over the most inartistic, the most crudely naïve and unconscious expressions of his organism's relation to the environment, and yet compose exquisite nocturnes, paint lovely landscapes, or write line after line of melodious words in graceful cadence. But the task—the internal task of phylobiology in which composition and composer are its inseparable materials, its indispensable media, calls for the artist of far broader perspectives as well as a far deeper sensitivity to life's basic values. Am I equal to this task? Hardly. But however awkward or fumbling the effort, there is no choice. After the experience of so many years in analyzing and correlating the behavior-reactions of social groups, I must go on. I must set down our findings. I must complete the record of our group undertaking— a record that represents the drastic compression of slowly gathered laboratory material as it developed within our experimental groups.

As I said, this Report embodies the analysis of Mr. Shields and myself. But this analysis of ours is a social analysis. It is the analysis of the reader as well. It is the analysis of man. In this group or social analysis I shall say the same thing many times under different aspects, because the group process is necessarily a process in repetition, in education—in the reëducation of fixed social habituations. But this social education, this pedagogic drill is disturbing to social groups. It will be disturbing to the larger group comprising the wider community. It will be disturbing, not because of the awkwardness of repetition but because it tends to force upon us all an unwelcome pattern—a pattern that is strange to man's habituations. Herein lies the irritation. The reëducation of social man through the adoption of an altered pattern of behavior is irritating to man. But all social education through repetition involves an altering of accustomed patterns. In phyloanaysis it is the unaccustomedness, the strangeness of the process, not its repetition, that is irritating.

Whatever the significance of phyloanalysis, however, this process of man's social reëducation is interesting only to future man. It is not interesting to habitual man. Habitual man prefers his habituations. He resents a challenge to his social habits of adaptation. There is no circumventing this personal incommodity. Education through phyloanalysis necessarily entails an insistent drill in the breaking up of accustomed social adhesions. Even within our own groups, notwithstanding relentless repetitions, there has been little catching on, little sensing of inept patterns of adaptation. No separate individual, no separate group can catch on to what belongs essentially only to man, to man as a unitary organism. Over the years there have been here and there many attempted interpretations of the work of The Lifwynn Foundation but they have almost without exception been wholly subjective and gratuitous. They have not caught on. So that I heartily welcome this opportunity to give a full exposition of our principles and aims and set our cause aright.

May I say that for me this book is in no sense an enterprise. If anything, it is a deliverance. It is a supreme effort to put into the hands of man what belongs in the hands of man, and not in the hands of a few absurd mental healers. Quite simply, phylobiology is the application of the scientific method to the field of human relations. This phylobiological Report, therefore, presents an account of the inquiry into disorders of human behavior which through the leaven of our experimental group-association ripened into the medical research represented by The Lifwynn Laboratory.

* * *

Acknowledgments[1]

The material of this thesis was in large measure dictated and discussed in daily group seminars composed of associates and students. Needless to say, in these sessions I have been afforded many helpful criticisms and suggestions. The fact is that my associates have been so integral a part of the work on which this thesis is based that customary acknowledgments are not possible in the ordinary sense of the word. Where day after day, early and late, students have been united in a common endeavor for nearly thirty years, any such formal expression would be but a feeble gesture. Then too, as will become apparent throughout the pages of this

---

[1] For the assistance given me in carrying out the instrumental experiments and in the preparation of the graphs and tables special acknowledgments will be found in footnote 1 of the Appendix.

book, the steadfast collaboration of my co-workers and myself has been in no sense the social or interpersonal affiliation that commonly amalgamates the interests and aims of working units. The bond among us was far closer, far more basic than the conventional ties that usually cement the interests and activities of social groups. As elements in a common research in human relations, it was our endeavor to set aside the accepted covenants and amenities of customary social interchange and, instead, make it our uncompromising quest to attain a fresh basis of human understanding and accord. In this quest it devolved upon each of the participants in our community experiment to discover within himself and for himself in what that basis consists. If there was to be affiliation, this affiliation must rest upon the altered basis which it was the business of each of us to discover and utilize on behalf of his own untutored organism. This was the premise of groupor phylo-analysis as Mr. Shields and I saw it in respect to our own interrelationship. This was the premise on which was based the phyloanalysis of the interrelationships existing within the laboratory groups generally.

Naturally in an investigation of man, it was an inevitable part of our phylobiological experiment that we abrogate the usual distinction between "professional" and "lay" individuals. For Dr. Hans Syz, for Dr. Charles B. Thompson,[2] for Dr. William E. Galt (as also for those professional or lay students, who for longer or shorter periods became associated with our group effort), the task has been, as it has been for Mr. Shields and myself, a wholly independent one. Only upon such an organismically democratic premise was it possible to conceive of a science of human relations. This task was that of discovering, each within himself, the nature of the organism's relation to the environment and to other organisms. On no other basis could we dignify our work in human behavior as a laboratory process.

This same independent concentration of purpose has characterized no less the lay students composing our laboratory base. Among them I wish especially to mention Miss Flora A. Guggenheimer, whose care and management of the living conditions of our group quarters has throughout the years been as devoted as it

---

[2] The demands of a full-time position at Bellevue Hospital have naturally limited Dr. Thompson's participation in the daily activities of The Lifwynn Laboratory. His interest, however, and his unfailing services to the Foundation as a member of our unit have been of incalculable assistance.

has been gracious; Miss Aimée Guggenheimer, whose service as secretary and supervisor of the Foundation office during all these years has been equally steadfast and capable; and Mrs. H. A. Sill, who for many years has given unstintedly of her time and talents in her effort to promote the purpose and interest of our laboratory endeavor.

In so far as the voluntary efforts of any individual or group may withstand the accustomed involuntary habituations of the larger social community of which they are an inseparable part, the achievement of associates and students has been a truly notable one—so notable, as I say, as quite to beggar the ordinary expressions of personal indebtedness. Indeed I think it has been the privilege of few men to be surrounded by co-workers so consistently devoted to the work in hand as has been my good fortune. But for the untiring services of my co-workers throughout our daily association, the preparation of the present Report, which is essentially an extension of the method and aims of our laboratory technique to the wider community, would have been an impossible undertaking.

Among these co-workers none was more loyal, more devoted to the work and aims of The Lifwynn Foundation than Miss Nelly Hölljes, R.N. It is with deep regret that I must record her untimely death. I cannot adequately express our great sense of loss in her absence. This loss has been felt not only in the cessation of her intensive study with Mr. Shields—a study and an association that formed an intrinsic part of the larger research undertaking—but also in the surcease of a genial companionship that through the years was shared by us all.

May I say that for me there is still another group, and a very significant one—the group composed of my family and friends, of children and grandchildren. It need hardly be pointed out that to this intimate group that constituted my home, nothing could have conformed less to their idea of exciting entertainment than an experimental research into the behavioral ineptitudes of the Hominidae! As our interest had always been just the joy of life as we knew it, an unsolicited analysis of personal and social reactions was the more unwelcome. And so there was, understandably, no little discrepancy between the customs and conventions of the group contingent comprising my home and the innovations in social or group coördination I was attempting to initiate.

In almost every undertaking, however, there is the personality whose unheralded presence contributes to blend and reconcile conflicting differences, to harmonize old ways with the new. It is usual that this rôle, "unhonored and unsung," falls to the lot of a woman, and it has not been otherwise within the personnel composing the complex of elements that formed our research group. But for this silent, unseen intermediary, but for the graciousness and gallantry of my wife, the situation would have presented to me a vista too bleak to contemplate. It is with particular pride and devotion that I salute her courage, her understanding and her steadfast loyalty throughout these formidable years.

* * *

A scientist is no little favored whose work receives the recognition of a man of letters who is himself interested in promoting scientific research. In respect to two earlier books of mine Mr. C. K. Ogden stood in this relation to me. And now in the publication of this Report I am similarly fortunate in having the benefit of Mr. Herbert Read's scholarly interest. I want earnestly to express my indebtedness to these two outstanding students of life and letters who are not only gifted writers but sympathetic editors as well.

TRIGANT BURROW.[3]

THE LIFWYNN FOUNDATION,
  WESTPORT, CONNECTICUT.
    1947.

---

[3] Because the author's name is invariably mispronounced by those who are acquainted with it only in the written form, the reader may care to know that the first name is French and that the last name is accented on the second syllable.

PREFACE

With this Report there is concluded a significant phase of an investigation into behavior-processes that began nearly thirty years ago, or about the time that the first world-war came to assume its global proportions. I recall that in the larger reckoning of phylobiology that first world-paroxysm seemed to me but a trivial bout, a preliminary skirmish. It was, as I expressed it at the time, "but the detonator preceding the crash that is to come—a crash that has been gathering momentum within the unconscious of the race through centuries past and that will descend upon the world with inevitable fatality in the absence of a more societal and inclusive reckoning among us." [1] I was not thinking then in terms of actual combat only, nor am I today. But then, as today, I was interested in war as the symptom of an underlying condition that resides within the organism of man. That earlier world-war seemed to me the expression of a universal syndrome that betokened a hidden defect within the latent processes of man. However incompletely, I had in mind the existence of an unrecognized impediment in the function of man as a species or phylum—an impediment or impasse that was organismic or, as I would now say, phyloörganismic. Already at that time the thought that occupied me had to do with a behavioral process that was phylic in scope but of which there was as yet no adequate sense, no phylic awareness in man.

In the present world-war, as in the first (I say "present" because the rumblings of war have by no means subsided), everyone is trying to do his part toward the founding of a saner, safer world. Now, as then, it is the effort of everyone to assist as far as he can in bettering man's condition. And it has not been otherwise with the research efforts of my co-workers and myself. From world-war to world-war those efforts of ours have continued unabated. But war is for us not a sudden episode in the midst of peace. It is a state of mind in man that is constant and unremit-

---

[1] *The Social Basis of Consciousness.*

ting, and throughout this book we shall so regard it. On this premise we have sought to study the underlying motives of man's habitual feeling and thinking, the customary incitements to man's behavior or to his doing what he does at all times. The pages that follow attempt to give some idea of what a saner world means to us in accordance with the researches in the field of human adaptation we have been privileged to pursue with unbroken purpose these many years.

Above all, our studies have disclosed man's very great need of a *science of feeling*. Basically, man has the capacity for the development of such a science. In his natural—in his biologically normal—behavior, phylic man is activated precisely as the scientist is activated. Primarily he looks at the objects and conditions about him from an unbiased viewpoint. But this primary capacity has been inadvertently side-tracked. Where human affections and disaffections or the interrelational behavior of man is concerned, he no longer sees objects and conditions with the consistency and precision of the objective scientist. Owing to this handicap in his behavior, the objects and conditions that relate to man's own life are now colored and distorted by nostalgic memories of the past or wishful fantasies of the future. The result is that his habitual outlook has befuddled his senses in relation both to the external world and to his own behavior. Man's projections in respect to the future are now dictated by his beliefs in respect to the past. Because of these beliefs, his interest and activation have been shunted into false expectations at the cost of the immediate present. This deviation is contrary to recognized principles of science, as it is contrary to the native reaction of man in his unbiased orientation as a total organism. Until man has taken upon himself the task of developing a science of his own feeling, his conflicts and his wars are inescapable. They are inescapable as long as man continues to place confidence in rationalized ideologies that can only compass a rationalized peace. As in the first, so in the second world-war—not to mention the third débâcle he is already busily promoting—man confidingly hopes that these conflicts he is waging will result in a permanent adjustment. But such is man's state of mind today that he is bound to wage periodic world-wars without end, just as in a not too remote past man had to submit blindly to the inevitable ravages of periodic infectious diseases.

By this I mean precisely that man's present difficulty and confusion, that the difficulty and confusion of us all, lies not in our external institutions, but in our internal motivations and in the distorted sensations and reactions arising from them. To understand this situation it is necessary to consider the existence of an organismic factor that is as yet unrecognized by man. Such a demand is not without precedent. It is one with which science has always been confronted. Whether in biology, physics, chemistry or any other field, science has always demanded the observation of some factor that man has not yet recognized. And so today when the world of man's behavior is enveloped in conflict throughout, he must before all else turn scientist and consider the possibility that his conflict is due to some factor he has as yet failed to take account of. He must look for some biological entity not yet existent for him, an entity not yet brought into being within the field of his own behavior. Like the bacteriologist, he must search for a biological factor that resides within the organism of man himself and that requires to be brought to his conscious recognition. He will not find this anthroponomic factor in this individual or that, nor in this nation or some other nation, but only in man as a species or phylum. Briefly, man must give his *whole* attention to the *whole* condition expressed in his confused and disordered behavior-processes. In the field of his behavior he must set aside his accustomed thoughts and opinions based upon fantasies of past or future and, like the scientist, center his whole attention upon the immediate present.

Today the urgency of this need is indicated by a crisis in human affairs that is both global and unprecedented. Confusion and conflict now rage throughout the total processes of man as a race. The disorder exists in such virulent intensity and in such vast proportions as utterly to surpass all that man has hitherto experienced. Only an adjustment commensurate with both the global and the unprecedented aspects of man's problem will be commensurate with man's need. Although everyone is trying in his way to do his part—although philosophers, psychologists, economists and statesmen are earnestly and zealously proposing new ways and means for reorganizing man's disordered world, their efforts do not meet the unprecedented global condition with which we are faced. Their "new" ways are patterned on the old and inevitably they bear the stamp of the very traditions that are answerable for man's present chaotic impasse.

Whether as soldiers or civilians, whether in the prosecution of war or in efforts to build a permanent program of peace, we are as individuals and nations in fairly close agreement as to the need that something decisive and adequate be done. But unfortunately men are faced today with issues with which no former experience qualifies them to deal. If, then, in proposing new ways with which to adjust ourselves to the future we are merely adhering to old ways of escaping from the errors and misconceptions of the past, it is clear that our thinking and feeling are not abreast of the immediate moment, that we have not yet lock-stepped with the present.

In the case of our fighting men at the front, the old aim describes itself in seemingly direct and immediate terms. They expressed it when they said that they wanted to get this war over and go back home. They yearned for scenes of the past. These men longed to return to their own shores, to their own country. They felt the need to renew old acquaintances, old customs, old creeds. They craved the things of memory and association. But, both for those on the war front and on the home front there is no longer the home to return to. There is no longer even one's own country in the old sense. These cherished havens have become but artificial confines. The bounds of home and country have been obliterated by the impact of a larger world community. The old beliefs, the old customs do not any longer await these men who hope to return to them. They are no longer there. Civilians and soldiers are merely beguiling themselves with false promises of the past, and in their retrogression would build another future only to be beguiled once more. They face a world of new opportunities but they have not yet faced the present. Thus their fantasies of the past can only culminate in fantastic plans for the future. Home and country too are but the lingerings of fantasy, and plans based upon retrogression and fantasy can only lead to further conflict and confusion.

Hitherto people have everywhere lacked the perspective for recognizing that their home, their country, the social system in which they live is not home in the sense of a basic security, of a place of abiding values. They begin at last to see that these sanctuaries are not all that they had reckoned them to be, and in their confusion they do not know where to turn. Yet they do turn. They must turn. They must turn notwithstanding that they do not know where to turn. But this, as its name implies, is revolution. It is revolution on a world-wide scale. After all, it is not alone the "enemy" that is preparing to wage a third world-war.

The impetus to war springs from a world-wide illusion, a universal fantasy. It springs from a disease within the mind of man.

When men come to realize that the drive toward war is world-wide, that the disease is universal, they will begin to recognize for the first time what is their real, their inherent need. This need is the stabilization of their own processes, of their individual and social processes. It is the need of a deep and abiding acquaintance with their own feeling, their own motivation, with the feeling and motivation of man as a race or species. It is the need to see that disorder resides within the tissues of phylic man, and that only an immediate phylic approach to the *present*—to man's immediate global insecurity—can disclose the cause of his conflict and confusion.

Man may delude himself only with respect to past and future. His integrity, his security, the dependability of his relationship to the environment are inevitably bound up with his relationship to the present and to himself. When man will be brought to a sense of the plight in which he finds himself today; when, refusing to indulge in either memories or hopes, he is brought up short with the stark immediacy of the moment, man will at last take hold of his environment and he will take hold of his own processes in relation to that environment. This round-up, this turn-about, this coming to grips with the present has been the sole purport of my researches in human behavior during the past thirty years.

But what do we mean by the present? Of what is its substance? The scientist can tell you as he broods searchingly over the material of his problem. He will tell you that it consists of the direct correspondence between his unbiased senses and the objective data before him. The scientist asks himself the simple question, what is the structure before me *now?* Abrogating past and future, abrogating the longings of yesterday and the hopes of tomorrow, setting aside all personal preoccupations, the student of science seeks to know the what and the why of this or that material or condition. But this unbiased functioning of the scientist's total senses in their relation to the environment is but a specialization, a refinement of the attitude latent in mankind at large. When man, global man, becomes equally interested in a science of man and his relationship to the world about him, he will not ask himself what was or what is to be, but he will put himself the simple question, what have I here and now? What is the true nature of this or that process or circumstance as my impartial senses are applied to the direct study of it?

And so in regard to human behavior and its relation to the immediate present, man will ask himself, what is the nature of the human organism, of *my* organism here and now? What is the structure of the feelings and reactions that motivate my behavior, the behavior of man? Do they serve or defeat, do they build or destroy, are they healthy or diseased? While fundamentally man is a scientist, while basically the common sense of phylic man, of man at large, is objective and scientific in its approach to the immediate condition or circumstance to be investigated, the common sense of man has not yet addressed this direct method of observation to the immediacy of his own global behavior. Instead, he invariably looks back or forward, that is, away from his problem. His direction is a misdirection, a dissociation in man's time relations, in his relation to the environment and to his kind in the actuality of the moment. In respect to man's behavior it is the present, the global present, that is man's immediate material of observation. In the observation of himself the immediate global attention of phylic man is the indispensable instrument. Only in this common immediacy lies the safeguard to the life and happiness of man.

While everywhere men and communities have contributed their part, and while the part they have contributed has been a valiant one, this is not enough, nor has it been adequate. Man stands in need of a *phyloanalysis*—an analysis of his own organism, an analysis of the phyloörganism of man. This effort to meet the present, to see what is to be done in regard to man's own behavior, his own feeling, and to do it now—has been the central endeavor of my co-workers and myself of The Lifwynn Laboratory. This has been the contribution we have tried to make toward the aspect of man's reconstruction that has to do with his understanding and synthesis of feelings and motivations resident within himself—feelings and motivations which relate man to the external world about him, and through which he is interrelated to his fellows as individuals, communities and nations, members all of a common race.

PART I

INTERRELATIONAL MAN

or

THE SYMPTOMATOLOGY OF HUMAN BEHAVIOR

A Phyloanalysis

The words of his mouth were smoother than butter, but war was in his heart...

PSALM LV, verse 21.

History does not prove the inevitability of war, but it does prove that customs and institutions which organize native powers into certain patterns in politics and economics will also generate the war-pattern.

JOHN DEWEY.

CHAPTER I

MEDICINE TO THE RESCUE!

Introduction

In writing this essay in regard to the springs of human behavior I cannot pretend to express the conventional personal view—either my own or that of anyone else. The material with which these pages deal has not been gathered from the usual sources of individual opinion or belief. In the realm of human behavior, unfortunately everyone, by dint of his pre-established beliefs, already knows all there is to know about his own behavior and everybody else's. The present thesis, however, has been the outcome of a study of the motives of behavior in which the criteria of evaluation, as tentatively adopted by a small group of investigators, rested upon a wholly altered basis.[1]

Thought is synonymous with communication or speech. Such phrases as "they say," "people tell me," "rumor has it"; or "listen to me," "get this," "have you heard?", are repeated on every hand and attest our interest in communication through thought. But these current modes of address betoken only a superficial, symbolic form of interchange. They bespeak a contact that is implemented merely by means of words. These vocal signs or gestures afford the individuals of the species only a pseudo-articulation. In this book we shall attempt to reach, or rather recover, a level of understanding and communication that is more fundamental. We shall try to attain a deeper level of contact and articulation. We shall be interested not so much in man's acquired forms of verbal thought and interchange as in an internal communication among people based upon the continuity that primarily knits them into a common and unitary race or species. In our researches we were not concerned with what the intellectualized and sophisticated individual thinks about the genus man but with what the genus man thinks about the intellectualized and sophisticated individual. It was the avowed purpose of our investigations to discover and, if possible, restore those biological principles of behavior that are intrinsic to us and that insure man's basic relation to the external universe and to his kind. Abrogating personal opinions and beliefs, we regarded only internal feelings and reactions directly observable within and by the observers themselves as data pertinent to our inquiry. I mention this circumstance at the outset not only in the interest of reportorial accuracy but also because the recognition of it will be of help to the reader as the course of this thesis unfolds.

In his list of the world's one hundred worst books Oscar Wilde assigned a prominent place to "all books which attempt to prove anything." I find myself heartily in sympathy with this facetious dictum of Wilde's. Only, as a student of behavior I wish he might have said, all books or all preoccupations of whatsoever sort that attempt to prove anything *to other people*. It is this very prevalent urge to prove things to other people, as it is people's urge to have others prove things to them, that too often accounts for their attitude of abject complacence toward the lecturer or writer on human behavior who places himself opposite a defenseless audience and, assuming the rôle of parent, undertakes to say what he feels especially appointed to tell them about their own adaptation. This tendency to bring people to one's own way of thinking by telling them how they should think and feel and do is characteristic of our interrelational ideologies generally. Telling other people what one presumes to believe they ought to know is the very keelson of our religious, political, educational and psychiatric systems.

This situation is one which should possess a very special interest for students of behavior. But as yet, unfortunately, it possesses for them precisely no interest whatsoever. The reason is that this arbitrary disposition of an individual to exercise projective control over others, coupled with a reciprocal subservience on the part of his listeners, is but one of many behavior-reactions that owe their explanation to the reflex operation of a quite generally unrecognized *social neurosis*.[2]

By virtue of this authoritarian give-and-take that now characterizes man's interrelational level of behavior, there is today early imbued in him—in us all—a dichotomous attitude of servile dependence upon other people on the one hand, and of vindictive repudiation of them on the other. The social fabric of human relations is now shot through with this dualistic factor of personal attraction and repulsion. This bipolar reaction is universal. Our mental world is divided between those toward whom we feel kindly disposed, and those toward whom we feel unkindly disposed. People with whom we agree, or who agree with us, are those for whom we feel affection, while people with whom we do not agree, or who do not agree with us, are those with whom we do not share our affections. So that some people please us and others displease us. This one finds certain persons interesting, while another finds these same persons an utter bore. Again, the person toward whom one is friendly today, one is unfriendly toward tomorrow; and the person who was on his black list yesterday is today restored to favor once more. It would appear, then, that our interpersonal feelings are quite undependable. The choices to which our affections and disaffections incline us would seem everywhere helter-skelter and unpredictable. Dependent as they are upon the arbitrary and variable interpretation of each individual, there would appear to be no stable or dependable criterion within the domain of human relations.

Because of this early defect in human behavior, people are at all times psychologically disposed to enact either the rôle of the parent or that of the child. They approve and are approved of; they disapprove and are disapproved of. In the field of behavior one alternately persuades or is persuaded; he enjoins or he obeys; he counsels or invites counsel. We shall find that society is composed exclusively of these two complemental phases of reaction. Because of this dichotomy extending throughout the domain of behavior, people the world over alternately feel either that they must be ever teaching others to feel and think as they themselves were once taught to feel and think; or else that they must be constantly receptive to the teaching of others as to what to feel and think. And, needless to say, their preceptors were, in turn, once equally susceptible to the same teaching on the part of their antecedents. Thus people's habitual feeling and thinking is passed down to them from generation to generation, and their behavior is at all times arbitrarily divided between these two reaction-alternatives.

On the basis of observations pointing to the existence of a social neurosis, I should like to consider this habit of behavior-adaptation according to which people commonly assume a position opposite others, and from this position attempt to prove things to them or try to influence their behavior on grounds of what they naïvely believe to be their superior knowledge, qualification or authority. This dependent reciprocity entails a far-reaching confusion within man's behavior-processes generally. To understand this social maelstrom in which the world is today universally embroiled, and to appreciate how completely man fails to recognize this confusion affecting his own subjective processes, let us consider the special feature that characterizes man's approach to his own motivation or behavior in contrast to his approach to the motivation or behavior he observes in other forms of animal life.

Owing to his adoption of controlled scientific methods in his relation to the outer environment, man has learned increasingly to maintain a clear-cut precision, a streamlined objectivity in respect to data that lie to his hand in the field of his external adaptation. What man has accomplished in respect to the outer world through his practiced accuracy of adjustment between head and hand, between his seeing and his manipulation of the external phenomena that come within the compass of his senses, is quite extraordinary. This facility with which man coördinates his seeing and his manual dexterity he has attained through his increasing appreciation of the delicate internal adjustment of his subjective senses in relation to the object or incident presented before him—an adjustment whose fruits we recognize in the fields of chemistry, mathematics, physics, biology, electrical and mechanical engineering, in experimental psychology and in the various branches of medicine. To take bacteriology alone, the achievements which through the refinement of the scientific method in this field so sensitively relate the eye and hand of man to the outer environment have in the last brief eighty or ninety years enhanced his capacity of accomplishment to a degree that surpasses the measure of his performance during all the ages preceding this short span. So too in our dealings with the reactions of animals and their motivation, our procedure is unfailingly objective and experimental. We observe and test the behavior of a given animal in relation to its environment and to other animals of its kind.

But with regard to processes that are internal to man himself the story is a very different one. With regard to processes that motivate and control the behavior of man's own organism as a species or phylum—processes that primarily influence his interrelational behavior—man has failed to apply these same objective measures of observation. Thus in the course of man's evolution, the field of his development that undoubtedly has shown by far the greatest lag is the field of man's relation to man. Indeed, where it is a question of man's knowledge of himself and his underlying motivation as a community or species—where it is a question of man's relation to man—it would appear not only that he doesn't know anything, but, to use the proverbial Frenchman's laconic phrase, that he doesn't even suspect anything. The fact is that in the sphere of man's own reactions—in regard to those habits and motivations that prompt our own behavior—the more people "know," the less they tend to suspect!

It has been aptly said that in any scientific inquiry, if one is to find the right answer he must first ask the right question. This means adopting a direct approach to the material under consideration. We have only to recall man's consistent achievements in the sphere of biology, agriculture or geology, and note his recourse to scientific controls in the domains of physics, engineering, cytology, chemistry, etc., to recognize how direct has been the application of man's processes to these various fields. And of course this same direct relation of man to his outer circumstance or environment exists no less in the attitude of medicine toward man himself when it is a question of somatic disorders objectively observable within the organism. Again, we need only consider the wide field of infective diseases and the efficient experimental measures we owe to the bacteriologists for the marked decrease in the incidence of these disease-processes in both men and animals. And where there has occurred disease or disorganization within the various external domains of man's community life, he has been no less direct and effective in his effort to provide the proper remedy. Consider, for example, such work as that of the Red Cross or the Quakers and the immediate and effective response of these organizations to sudden calamity as it occurs anywhere throughout the world, whether in peace or in war; or the work of The Rockefeller Foundation in promoting medical research, regardless of nation or locality. In short, where distressing conditions occur in the life of man as a result of disturbance or disease caused by external disaster, man has learned increasingly to apply immediate objective controls to their alleviation or adjustment.

But where disorder occurs in the relationship of men interindividually, we have a very different picture. Where there occurs inept behavior or *dis*behavior in man's relation to man, the needed adjustment has not been forthcoming.[3] In every behavioral phase of man's relation to man there has been the failure to apply the suitable objective remedy in accordance with the objective need. This, of course, is not a new situation. It has existed for thousands of years. The only modification through the centuries has been the slow, consistent extension of man's external expression of disbehavior to their present world-wide proportions. There was the time, for instance, when war was an isolated phenomenon. Today it is inescapably global. There have been periods in the past when man seemed to experience something he dared call peace. Now clearly there is no peace. Not only do peace conferences fail of their objective, but everywhere civil strife breaks out afresh like the rash of a contagious disease. Of course the acknowledgment of this condition is on the lips of everyone. On the lips of everyone throughout the world—soldier or civilian, young or old, rich or poor, educated or uneducated—there are the words, "There is no peace"; and some few even dare to say there can be no peace.

But still man does nothing. Essentially he is capable of studying his own behavioral confusion, but obviously he has not yet recognized this confusion as a problem within himself. And now after these many thousands of years he has become inured to the condition as a fish to water. His behavioral confusion has actually become his standard of living. This inadvertence in man's feeling and thinking is now his norm, the universally accepted norm by which he measures all things. So that, in failing to observe and correct this ineptness of behavior internal to himself, man is not merely blind to his own confusion but actually enslaved to it. Throughout the species or phylum, man is enslaved to his own habitually subjective, wishful reactions.

Is it any wonder, then, that even members of the highest judiciary courts betray this rigid authoritarianism, that instead of presenting a coördinated effort to reach an objective agreement, each contends for what he has been taught by others to think and feel and do? Is it any wonder that in face of a vital international behavior-problem involving the fate of civilization, the delegates from the various nations of the earth should sit around a "peace" table and fight one another! It is evident that in response to such subjective, interrelational situations people are not primarily interested in regarding their own behavior—their own thinking and feeling in relation to an objective situation or circumstance—but that they are ever under the alternating behavior-compulsion either to teach others or be taught by them how they *ought* to behave—in what manner it behooves them to think and feel and do.

Through the force of this subjective habit—through the domination of mere wishful preferences—oppositeness now everywhere prevails over man's mental and social processes, and disbehavior, in supplanting his basic behavior-reactions, has become the order of the day. The evidence of this widespread disharmony in human relations is seen in the prevalence of crime, war, industrial dissension, domestic infelicities, political, economic and religious discord. Today some of us begin to realize that man's effort toward interindividual coöperation rests upon motives which only promote opposition and antagonism among us. It would appear, then, that through some ineptitude in his development man's behavior bears the the stamp of a form of maladaptation or disbehavior in respect to himself and others that has superseded the primary reaction of his organism in relation to the immediate environment.

Let me emphasize again that this condition of disbehavior, albeit an expression of man's habitual wish, is not a condition that man basically desires. The wonders of discovery and invention that man has achieved in his relation to the physical world about him are also an index of his potential capacity for healthy balanced behavior in his interrelational life. But with all his knowledge, man is still in the dark in this vital interrelational sphere of his own behavior. With all his science, and his poetry too, man's insight, his understanding, his vision, and his feeling as one people or race still lie dormant. His apparent sureness of opinion, seemingly so real today, turns to confusion tomorrow; and the next day in turn brings its own subjective illusions that only further obscure man's underlying perplexity and division. With all his commercialized internationalism, ably supported by his increasing acquaintance with the physical elements—by his discovery of steam, electricity and the radio—man is still beyond the reach of man.

It has been the business of our phylobiological laboratory to examine this widespread anomaly in man's subjective behavior and, if possible, to discover what precisely is the chief factor answerable for it. To do this it was necessary to proceed as the scientist proceeds in any other field of observation. It was necessary to discover a method whereby the habitual bias that now colors and dominates man's subjective judgments and reactions would be automatically eliminated. In the effort to attain this aim we found ourselves faced with a very interesting observation in respect to the broad field of reactions that has to do with the relation of man to himself and his own motivation. This observation consisted in the *internal* recognition of the wide and irreconcilable difference there is between man's approach to objectively demonstrable phenomena and his approach to those subjective phenomena that involve his own behavior.

We know that throughout the entire field of science the feature that has especially characterized man's objective observation and study has been his willingness to yield himself to the direct evidence of his senses as they report the immediate data before him. Needless to say, every scientist accepts this circumstance as a matter of course. But I should like to point out the specific debt that man owes to this circumstance. I should like to point out that thanks to it, that thanks alone to his consistent observation of objective data lying in front of him, man has learned to replace subjective prejudice with objective judgment. Indeed the progress of science has been coterminous with man's capacity to withhold judgments that precede observation,[4] that is, that are antecedent to the fact, and instead, to compel his judgments to wait upon observation. In this way it has come to be the general characteristic of man that he approaches the data of science in an attitude of frank ignorance and submission. But the fact to be noted—the observation with which we were confronted in our group researches—is that man concedes this attitude of ignorance and submission *only in face of objectively observable material*.

In the sphere of human behavior, in the sphere of those subjective processes that mark our disbehavior as a race or species, we shall find that this criterion of science is entirely absent. We shall find that the objective attitude of science as it prevails in other fields of investigation is completely lacking in the field of man's relation to man. Where man's own behavior is involved—where it is a question of man's relation to himself and to those about him—we come straightway upon the tendency in man to look to those who will *tell* him what he should think and feel and do. In our laboratory analysis we found that in his early-imbued wish to lean upon others for knowledge in respect to behavior—in his habitual dependence upon sentimental indoctrination rather than upon scientific observation in this sphere—man has assumed an attitude toward his own motivation that is not objective but that is habitually subjective and esoteric. Further, we found that because of this unreasoning attitude, man's behavior—his feeling or motivation—is completely rigid and inaccessible to objective approach. Instead of adhering to an attitude of submission in respect to data presented for observation, instead of maintaining an attitude of subordination to the controlled report of one's own senses in respect to the observable material, the "observer" already knows all about it. Since, however, he lacks the substantiation of objectively controlled data, his knowledge is not real. His knowledge consists merely of an automatic submission to and dependence upon words or statements that express the arbitrary, preceptive opinions and beliefs of other people.

But though words may be misleading, no one of course would deny that as instruments they are indispensable. Obviously they are not to be scorned as a medium of communication. Indeed their service through the ages cannot be adequately estimated. But where words perform a function that substitutes for the continuity and consistency of man's behavior as an organism, they not only cease to be aids to communication, but these symbols of exchange become an actual hindrance to mutual understanding and accord. They become incitements to subjective and esoteric fantasy. Pope's oft-quoted line, "The proper study of mankind is man," is very pleasing talk, very graceful poetry. And even the words of the homely hymn, "Rocked in the Cradle of the Deep," are not without their own quaint charm, their own rhythmic appeal. But what *is* man, and what are these deep, primordial processes that cradle him? Poetry, like the other arts, undoubtedly has its place. It is a subtly expressive and beautiful form of communication. But in this dynamic age—in this new age of science, of physiology and the laboratory—the interrelationships of men call for a new implementation. In face of our world-wide dissensions, in face of our complete distortion of the essential media of understanding and communication as a race or people, the crying need of dynamic man in respect to his behavior is his immediate recourse to objective investigation and action.

The habit of listening to rumor and hearsay discloses a tendency in the human organism that has not been adequately reckoned with. All knowledge was once rumor and hearsay. Rumor is not only contemporary but traditional. From his earliest years one yields oneself to what others say, and thenceforward a certain arbitrarily appointed course becomes "right," while another is "wrong." People pattern their thinking according to these popular hand-me-downs. Again it is the tyranny of hearsay and beliefs[5] of which our words are only the external vehicle. Again it is the inept habit of people to think and feel as others have taught them to think and feel. But, basically, experiment is more native to man than tradition. Man is by nature the forager, the hunter and the digger. We see this in the child. The child's very security depends upon his being an inquirer. Leaning on tradition is quite a secondary, foreign trait in man. It came about as an accidental by-product in the course of his social evolution.

Medicine had its beginning in the science of anatomy. It began when man dropped those practices of subjective therapy which in early days constituted all there was of "medicine," and of which the starry-eyed methods of the psychopractors with their esoteric talk—with the words and symbols expressive of their habitual opinions and beliefs—are the descendants today. Medicine began when the brain of man examined into actual somatic processes; when it looked into the anatomy and physiology of the organism and finally turned to the microscope. But these scientific principles have not been applied to the interrelational field of man's behavior. Where it is a question of man's behavior, the charm of the word, the wish, the belief, still prevails. Instead of the needed objective correctives in human adaptation, the element of the psychic, the symbolic, the metaphysical, still holds sway throughout our far-flung systems of "mental healing."

From the very outset our experiments in group-analysis left no doubt that this element of the subjective and esoteric holds a position that is completely dominant in the attitude of man toward his own behavior. They made evident that even trained students who commonly see eye to eye in the various laboratories of scientific observation are no less subject to an esoteric and inaccessible dogmatism where it is a question of their own conditioned prepossessions and habituations. We found it to be the unfailing characteristic of social groups that, owing to people's habits of dependence upon what others think and feel, automatic inhibitions and frustrations now wholly dominate the sphere of man's thought and action wherever it is a matter of opinions and assumptions having to do with man's own behavior. What is more, these inhibitions and frustrations were seen to be of an identical structure with the impediments and repressions observable analytically in the neurotic patient, and to constitute no less a condition of pathology in social groups or communities.[6]

The outstanding example of this universal dependence of

people upon the preceptive habituations of others in replacement for their own capacity to see and observe clearly is their infatuation with the particular *social image* they call the "personality."[7] According to one's habituations it would seem that the "personality" is an indispensable factor in achieving the ends of existence. Wherever there is any teaching to be done or learning to be attained within the domain of our subjective human relations, the personality is at a premium. In all attempts to inculcate interest in the sphere of politics, religion, philosophy and psychiatry, students require the dominance of the "personality" and his "ideas" upon which they may focus and upon which they may depend; while in the various spheres of the biological and other sciences the importance of the teacher is wholly submerged beneath the significance of a student's direct relation to the material under observation. As Huxley said: "Authorities, disciples, and schools are the curse of science; and do more to interfere with the work of the scientific spirit than all its enemies."[8]

These personality appeals are in line with the method of the metaphysical healer with his wide and enthusiastic following, as they are in line with the method of the pseudo-scientist everywhere. It is especially, of course, in the so-called mental or psychological field that the advocates of the come-hither approach find ready adherence among their devotees. There have not been lacking evidences of this interrelational phenomenon as they were observable in social groups.

In a laudatory address upon the work of Dr. James B. Conant and Dr. Karl T. Compton, Bernard Baruch has ably described the qualities requisite to the method of the objective scientist.

> A trained, and, mind you, I say trained, scientific researcher [he declared] thinks only of the object he has before him, not of any ideology, not of himself, not of his publicity, not of what anybody thinks of him or his associates, not of another job—but only of one thing—what do the facts justify? How helpful it would be if we could have more trained minds to see errors, to pass judgment and guide action before it is too late.[9]

We might all profitably take to heart this unequivocal test of the scientific method as voiced by Mr. Baruch. For even in fields of observation that relate to purely external phenomena and that in no way bear upon the criteria of man's own behavior, it is often only too apparent that the motives of the observer are far from chemically pure. As for the student who sets out to tackle the inconsistencies of man's subjective behavior in general and of his own in particular, it becomes straightway evident that he represents precisely the opposite of Mr. Baruch's trained student of research. For many are the subjective digressions into which he slips because of ideologies which are completely subjective and automatic, and over which, therefore, he has no objective control.

But before going further let us again remind ourselves that we are confronted with the behavior of man as a species or phylum, and that we may not righteously single out any individual or group as being recalcitrant and hence answerable for this or that expression of inadequacy in the source of his thinking and feeling, or in the motives to his doing as he does. In other words, we cannot look at and disdain this disorder of adaptation as it evidences itself here and there in other people. There is hardly place for an attitude of superiority or aloofness toward an infirmity which of its nature is common to man.

And so let us be quite clear in regard to a proposition of central importance in the present thesis: If the neurosis of man is inseparable from the specific conditions of his adaptation socially, if his reactions are now coeval with the subjective inferences with which we have all been traditionally imbued, then in the absence of an adequate remedy the present writer and the reader are likewise no exception. If behavior-disorder is an infirmity common to man as a species; if, in short, the neurosis is social, then you and I have got it, and the material of our inquiry lies wholly within ourselves. Were the disease in question an epidemic of measles, or an endemic of malaria, or even a pandemic of tuberculosis, some of us might have escaped with a clean bill of health. But where it is a question of a disharmony of function that is incurred by the very nature of man's social adaptation, we are all necessarily victims of this generic disorder. Our need is not the shattering of traditions on the other side of the world; it is not benevolence to a group of people dwelling on some island thousands of miles away. What is needed is that we break the mold of our own would-be normality. It is ourselves and our own social habituations that we need to jolt into seeing things as they are. In the field of human behavior clarity begins at home.

As in other fields of science, then, so in the field of behavior, if we are to obtain the right answer it is necessary that we first ask the right question. It is necessary that we keep consistently within the field of our material—within the field of man's reactions as a hominid. Our inquiry into disordered reactions has nothing to do with the behavior of the annelid or of the paramecium. Nor, indeed, has it to do with the *genus homo* in any remote, abstract or symbolic sense. It has to do with the concrete and immediate actuality of man himself as a phylic organism. But to repeat, as things now stand, nothing is further from the interest of students of behavior than a direct, systematic inquiry into their own mode of adaptation. Instead, all manner of symbolic substitutions and interpretations enter in to replace the immediate consideration of the organism's reactions.

A good many years ago, having been led to the view that the world of man is a pretty sick world; having seen in my work with individuals and with groups that socially, economically, politically we are as a people seriously maladjusted, it became evident to me that the commonly entertained notion that I, as a psychiatrist, represent an organized entity in relation to the patient who, on the other hand, represents a disorganized entity, was no longer tenable. This fallacious attitude that places the physician occupied with behavior-disorders in a biologically artificial relation to his patient—an attitude, need I say, in which the physican heartily concurs—is one which it is hoped the present essay may serve to dispel. It will, I think, be possible to show that where a patient places the physician or psychiatrist upon a pinnacle and, having placed him in so unique and exalted a position, credits him with special powers of "psychic" healing, it is because by virtue of their mutual frailty the physician represents to his patient a purely arbitrary, esoteric symbol. Of course the psychotherapist may *say* to his patient, "I am just like you," but watch his emotional reaction if anybody else says so! Observe how quick is his resentment in face of a direct challenge to his own neurotic lack of social inclusiveness.

According to our phyloanalytic findings, it is this very general tendency to replace the actuality of an individual with one's own social image of him that is the source of our distorted human relationships. It is hoped that these pages will make clear that our many distortions in human behavior are traceable to this habitual employment of the symbol to serve purely emotional outlets wholly irrelevant to the actual situation.[10] The observation of this misuse of the symbol socially was the specific occasion of my withdrawal from the practice of psychiatry, as ordinarily understood, and of my effort to establish in the community no less than in the patient an objective attitude toward unclear, misdirected feelings and reactions. For these feelings and reactions are now governed by factors that are subjective and unconscious, and hence distort the symbols of communication and incite misunderstanding and division in individual and community.

When it comes to this or that person with his particular type of misadaptation, there is no question that psychological methods of healing may under certain circumstances solace or allay many symptoms occurring in the sporadic instance of neurosis or psychosis. But these methods fail to reach the core of the disturbance or to offer alleviation for the disordered condition of man's organism as a phylum. The superficial assuagement of these ills is at present achieved only through shifting such displaced trends from less comforting to more comforting lodgments. It is not unusual that such lodgment is found in the personality of the physician. But, as we have seen, what is called "personality" in the accepted social sense is too often again but a snare and a delusion. It does not stem from the organismic pattern of man's behavior individually and as a phylum.

Working, however, with groups which, as biological units, necessarily included myself—just as the present thesis is based upon observations which include myself—the attempt was to adopt an objective method toward our own subjective social or group behavior. Our aim was to abrogate motives based upon prevailing standards of "right" and "wrong"—the esoteric standards of behavior derived from what we have been told by others to do, feel or think. For this business of "rightness," of teaching other people what to feel and think is merely stimulating their behavior through the symbol and necessarily inciting a behavior-response that is also only symbolic. In confronting this spurious criterion now everywhere activating human behavior and arbitrarily differentiating individual from individual and group from group, it was our effort to discover and credit whatever healthy behavioral elements remained as a residue after we had eliminated these specious standards. In other words, our objective procedure led us to seek a basis of discrimination between disorganized or deviate behavior and organized or healthy behavior—a basis that would wholly disavow the commonly alleged difference between one individual and another, between one group or nation and another, upon grounds of the specially claimed prerogative of each. Repudiating habitual moralisms, the method of phyloanalysis made evident a *condition of organization or unity of function that extends throughout the species or phylum as a whole, while parallel with this unitary principle of behavior there was likewise traceable throughout the species a system of reactions that is definitely deviate and disorganized.*

The technique, therefore, in which I invited the participation of experimental behavior-groups was one in which we attempted to disclaim habitual social evaluations and, instead, study behavior as it may be observed in its immediate social reactions. The procedure was not without its difficulties. These difficulties, however, were due precisely to the mental and social habituations we had come together to investigate. Years ago when first we undertook the research of which this book is the report, the utter inaccessibility of individual or group to any challenge of their subjective opinions and beliefs constituted the chief stumbling-block to our inquiry. The cause of this subjective obstacle was not far to seek, yet it was all but impossible to find. For the inquiry and the obstacle to it were inseparable. Unlike researches in other fields, our quarry and our inquiry lay wholly within ourselves. But if there were difficulties, there was at least the merit of novelty in an approach in which we ourselves were the patient as well as the physician and in which the disorder we sought to remedy was as widespread as human society itself.

Hence in seeking material requisite to our investigation of human behavior and its disorders, it was not necessary to go beyond the confines of our own research group. As a social group we ourselves constituted the experimental material for studying the behavior-reactions of man at large. While our own group-behavior was not more disordered than the behavior of any other social group, it was imperative that in attempting to deal phylobiologically with subjective anomalies of behavior the subjects embodying these phenomena apply their examination to themselves—to their own subjective reactions. For the circumstance is inescapable that only a subject's own experiential self presents immediate behavior-material. It is this immediate material that has occupied the biosocial investigations of my associates and myself as constituting the only material that satisfies the conditions of an exact scientific inquiry into man's behavior.

But, as I have said, our *selves*—the constellation of feelings and reactions that make up our own subjective processes—do not readily prove in the beginning the fertile field of inquiry that maturer investigation shows them to be. In approaching the internal habituations of oneself, one enters upon sacred ground. The subjective entity that each of us knows and cherishes as the "self" is hemmed in by a wall of reservations. This wall is social as well as individual. With most people their reservations are adamant. They are decisive in the determination of their behavior. These rigidities constitute their "personality." And yet one finds here and there an attitude of greater breadth and inclusiveness, a willingness to tread more softly in face of an untried experiment. I think I cannot better illustrate this attitude than in quoting from a letter written to one of my students by a man who was both an able scholar and a person of more than usual flexibility in feeling and perspective.

> I'm sure it must have annoyed you that I have delayed so long in commenting upon Dr. Burrow's book [*The Biology of Human Conflict*] and the pamphlets you were kind enough to send me. My delay has not been due to indifference, but, as you may have guessed, to an internal conflict that has stayed my hand. You may have guessed too, and I want to assure you very clearly on this point, that my primary emotion is one of affection for you and that I want to be sure that nothing I may think or say will obscure this fact.
>
> Therefore I feel that I must write to you as honestly as I can and as directly. It won't do for me to remain silent because silence is too easily misconstrued.
>
> Very simply, then, I find it quite impossible to accept these writings as I know you would like. It is not only that I find them hard to read because of the unfamiliar vocabulary and locutions. In spite of my basic sympathy with what I conceive to be the author's objectives, in spite of my respect and affection for you who are coöperating with him, I experience a positive feeling of opposition every time I read his work.
>
> Naturally, I am puzzled by the vigor of my reactions. I never forget what Dr. Burrow has done for you and I am deeply grateful for this. As I said before, I think I agree with his general attitudes and objectives. The mere fact that he uses language that taxes my intellectual powers ought not to make me so intolerant.
>
> But there I am—for better or for worse. And I feel much better for having expressed myself to you. It was necessary if we are to preserve the mutual affection that we have enjoyed for so many years.

The feeling of resentment toward phylobiology of which this

writer speaks is only too familiar to me. But the kindliness and the generosity that underlie this expression of his response to my thesis are rare indeed. Admittedly the thesis whose principles I have attempted to incorporate in my writings presents for the reader a definite behavioral difficulty. But ordinarily one masters a difficulty by approaching closer to it, not by backing off from it. Nevertheless, it is the automatic tendency of the student confronted with the principles of phylobiology to shy away from them, and in support of his irresolute policy to indict my formulations as being obscure and unacceptable. Certainly in the present inquiry progress will be fraught with serious impediment if the reader does not reckon clearly with this inevitable reaction on his part. After all, communication is a form of art. It is the expression of art in the written word. Much needs to be said about the art of communication through writing and about the science of phylobiology in relation to art. It is simple enough to write if one has nothing to say—if one follows the accustomed patterns of thought. It is where one has something to say—where one has abandoned the beaten path and must forge his own way amid new and uncharted areas of thought that writing or the selection of the adequate symbol becomes difficult. One needs be especially mindful of his own limitations where one is writing of a neurosis he shares in common with the community—in common with man.

Whatever my personal inadequacies as an author, the student must recognize that in these pages he is entering upon *an analysis of himself and his community*. He must come to see that preceptive opinions and beliefs, resting as they do upon purely emotional premises, will not only fail to assist him but will actually hinder the adjustment of his basic feeling-processes. To the degree in which man has lost touch with the principle of motivation that is basic to him; to the degree in which he has become insensible of the principle that determines his organism's behavior in accordance with the primary laws of action and reaction governing the world of matter and energy, he has yielded to the domination of emotionally toned precepts that have been covertly inculcated in him through the medium of other people's words. In his thraldom to the "personality" of other people, he has adopted a course that departs from the behavior inherent in the natural polarity of his organism's balance between stimulus and response. Instead, he now vacillates between the arbitrarily prescribed alternatives of a symbolically substituted "right-and-wrong" dichotomy. But man's present dichotomy of "right and wrong" is not what we think it is. It is not primary and central, nor does it represent an elemental balance that ensures the health of man.[11]

In the absence of a central and consistent principle of logic there can be no science with respect to man's external world of objects and their relations. In the absence of a central and consistent principle of motivation within the organism there can be no science with respect to the internal world of man's behavior and *its* relations. In the relation of man to the external environment there is required, of course, a basic and consistent pattern of attention and interest; and concomitantly, in the relation of man to the internal environment that comprises his own subjective reactions, there is required a no less basic and consistent pattern of attention and interest. For these biologically complemental patterns are native to us as elements in a common race or species. But as yet they have been given no place in the curriculum of medicine.

In the field of human behavior—in the field that pertains to the various functions and relationships of the organism of man as a whole—the medical sciences have not yet observed the basic and essential material requiring observation. The organism of man and its motivating principle has lacked concrete definition and study. For reasons which students have as yet neglected to take account of, the study of man has remained essentially reminiscent, historical. Anthropology has been restricted to bygone ages or to scattered tribes of primitive people. Instead of studying the actions and reactions of the human organism in its relation to the environment as this organism exists today and now, anthropology occupies itself with biological data that pertain to man's paleontological past. The interest of the anthropologist has centered so largely in the study of ancient fossils, whether anatomical or sociological—it has centered so largely in the unearthing of the vestiges of prehistoric man—that he has quite overlooked the social implications of man's present-day adaptation to the environment. He is more interested in securing structural measurements than in understanding the anthroponomic functions and relations of man's organism here and now. Where the student does attempt to examine the behavior of the hominid in its functional interrelationships, he does not apply himself to a science of dynamic anthropology, to a science of man that is concrete and immediate. Instead, he is caught up in concepts of behavior and its disorders that are as parochial in method as they are ephemeral in aim. We are only too familiar with these tedious concepts and with the trivial, interpersonal premise upon which they rest. There is needed a frank repudiation of this narrow, ideological interpretation of man's behavior. There is required an approach that is consistent with the scientific envisagement of an *applied anthropology*. Man's study of man must deal with the vital phenomenon of the organism's action and reaction precisely as it deals with this phenomenon in all other living forms. In short, there is demanded an anthropology that is not purely traditional or historic, but an anthropology that offers the student direct functional impact with the daily reactions of himself and his fellows—an anthropology that is medical as well as social and in which material and observation have to do with behavioral processes of immediate and dynamic instancy. It will have to do with subjective sensations and reactions as they arise out of the generic solidarity of man as a species.

It should be understood that in consistency with our phylobiological technique our investigations demand in a very special sense the initiative of each investigator. Each investigator finds the material of his phylobiological observations in his own reaction-patterns. But the reaction-pattern of the individual is not confined to his own behavior and, therefore, he cannot find it in himself alone. It is part of a larger social pattern. The individual and his conflict are part of a pattern that is phylic. Man's behavioral *faux pas* cannot be limited to any specific element, to any special personality, community or nation. It is a *faux pas* of the phylum man as a whole. As part of the whole, the individual is inevitably part of a disorder affecting the whole and he necessarily shares equally with others the responsibility of its investigation. In this way our research becomes the spontaneous investigation, by individual and group, of an internal conflict embodied in our common phylic reactions.

War—the outstanding symptom of man's disordered behavior—has today reached the acme of its expression. It has involved all peoples on the earth. It has become a phylic phenomenon. And with this climax has come the atomic bomb. It is in keeping with the disordered development of internal man that atomic energy should first have been used as a destructive agent, when in reality its discovery is but another token of man's capacity for efficient, constructive thinking in his relation to the external world. Obviously man's disordered behavior is in the moment more powerful than his clear thinking, feeling and doing—than his own basic adaptation in respect to the external surroundings. This circumstance is a commentary upon man as a species. But in the disturbed state of man's feeling-life it could not be otherwise. The fact remains that atomic energy was first employed as a means of destruction, and by nations that presumably represent an enlightened form of government. This circumstance, however, is relatively negligible beside the appalling fact that science itself should have approved of its use as a means of destroying human life. It is indeed significant that in its largest opportunity even the creative inventiveness of science should have succumbed to the domination of the generic disorder in adaptation that marks the behavior of man as a species.

This brings us back to our crucial problem. How can man as a social organism be led to reverse his own social habituations? What is to stay the hand that is poised to smite man if the hand that menaces him is the hand of man himself? In other words, how can man be brought to adopt a course that is contrary to what is now his own deeply imbued and automatically cherished preference—his traditionally ingrained wish? This is the question which I believe is the right question to ask ourselves if we are to achieve a science of human behavior; and it is this question that the present essay seeks to answer. Disregarding man's multifarious ideologies—his various philosophies and religions, his governmental policies, his clashing economic and political systems; disregarding the vacillating opinions, customs and habituations that occur in this individual and that, in this country and that, in this race or nationality and that, our interest will be not in these external, superficial differences but rather in the common denominator of organismic motivations and reactions that are the universal heritage of us all.

* * *

In Part I we shall discuss the aspects of man's behavior that reflect the superficial disparities observable in the external differences now existing among us and constituting the outer symptoms of man's antagonism to man. Part II will be devoted to a consideration of the underlying cause of man's conflict and neurosis as disclosed through the study of the basic biological factors that determine man's health and coördination of function as a unitary phylum.

NOTES

[1] Burrow, Trigant, "The Group Method of Analysis," *The Psychonalytic Review*, 1927, Vol. XIV, pp. 268-80.

———, "The Basis of Group Analysis," *The British Journal of Medical Psychology*, 1928, Vol. VIII, pp. 198-206.

———, "So-called 'Normal' Social Relationships Expressed in the Individual and the Group, and their Bearing on the Problem of Neurotic Disharmonies," *The American Journal of Psychiatry*, 1930, Vol. X, pp. 101-16.

Syz Hans, "Remarks on Group Analysis," *The American Journal of Psychiatry*, 1928, Vol. VIII, pp. 141-8.

[2] Burrow, Trigant, *The Social Basis of Consciousness—A Study in Organic Psychology*, The International Library of Psychology, Philosophy and Scientific Method, New York, Harcourt, Brace & Co., Inc.; London, Kegan Paul, Trench, Trubner & Co., Ltd., 1927, pp. xviii + 256.

———, "Our Mass Neurosis," *The Psychological Bulletin*, 1926, Vol. 23, pp. 305-12.

———, "Neurosis and War: A Problem in Human Behavior," *The Journal of Psychology*, 1941, Vol. 12, pp. 235-49.

[3] The word *dis*behavior should not be confused with the commonly used word *mis*behavior. In order to indicate the specific type of behavior-defect I have in mind, I found it necessary to coin the term *dis*behavior to signify behavior that deviates from a biological norm, without reference to the moral connotation inherent in the word misbehavior.

[4] Prejudice = *pre*-judgment.

[5] In its basic etymology the word *belief* means a preferred manner of thinking, or an emotional choice of opinion. Cf. Anglo-Saxon, *geleafa*, also *léof*. Such "beliefs" should be carefully discriminated from inference regarding objective data, based upon inconclusive evidence.

[6] See note 1, page 135.

[7] Burrow, Trigant, "Social Images versus Reality," *The Journal of Abnormal Psychology and Social Psychology*, 1924, Vol. XIX, pp. 230-5.

[8] Huxley, Thomas H., letter to Professor Weldon, February 9, 1893, *Life and Letters of Thomas Henry Huxley*, New York, D. Appleton & Co., 1902, Vol. II p. 336.

[9] This statement from an unpublished address by Mr. Baruch was made on the occasion of the meeting of the American Chemical Society on September 15, 1944, *The New York Times*, September 16, 1944.

[10] Burrow, Trigant, *The Structure of Insanity—A Study in Phylopathology*. Psyche Miniatures, London, Kegan Paul, Trench, Trubner & Co., Ltd., 1932, pp. 80.

———, *The Biology of Human Conflict—An Anatomy of Behavior, Individual and Social*, New York and London, The Macmillan Company, 1937, pp. 186-91, 229-31.

[11] Burrow, Trigant, *The Social Basis of Consciousness*, p. 81.

———. *The Biology of Human Conflict*, p. 47.

CHAPTER II

THE DISSOCIATION OF THE SPECIES
OR
THE SOCIAL NEUROSIS

The present moment is a portentous one in the history of human behavior. Only yesterday the armies of half the world were locked in a death struggle with the armies of the other half. And even now, as the representatives of the various governments are gathered together in an attempt to organize an international state, the shadow of a weapon that threatens to end all life upon this earth lies athwart their deliberations. The moment with which we are faced is the more portentous because of the persistent hope man vainly entertains that a world of wholeness and peace will somehow issue out of these two warring and divided half-worlds. Even the student of behavior fondly believes that out of this divided world an undivided peace will come. Along with the rest of mankind even the seasoned student fails to see that the overwhelming impetus to man's feeling and thinking now stems from a social artifact of division. He does not see that owing to a discrepancy in man's mental and social processes the ideological world that man has projected is necessarily a world of conflict. In this hour of universal dichotomy and discord it would appear that we who study the problems of human adaptation are confronted with nothing less than a false, unilateral basis of motivation and behavior within the organism of man throughout.

As in all wars so in the war of yesterday and of today division exists not only between opposed nations but also within the opposed nations themselves. Every country and every group of countries is honeycombed with economic and political ideologies that breed suspicion and disorganization throughout the life of these countries. The self-interested greed of one nation or coalition of nations is pitted against the greed and self-interest of other nations in peace no less than in war; and among nations that are momentarily allied, it is only a matter of time before a rift that is no less arbitrary and dictatorial divides them once more. So with human relations upon every hand. It is a commonplace to see covenant turn to discord, affection and marriage ending in disaffection and divorce; international treaties dissipated in war. Labor and capital are sworn enemies, Negro and white stand in sullen opposition to one another; Jew and gentile, East and West, communism and democracy, the so-called lower and the so-called upper strata of human society are all at daggers drawn. Even man's various religions—Mohammedanism, Judaism, Christianity, Shintoism, Buddhism and the rest—are irreconcilable one with the other. Each is a separate world unto itself. Surely if the Gods themselves are unable to get along together, it is no wonder that the peoples over whom they preside are not on speaking terms. There is conflict in the individual, in the family, in the community. Everywhere we see sectionalism and competitiveness. Everywhere the part stands against the part, and all the parts contend against the whole. No matter what the superficial pattern, there appears to be a deep-seated dislocation within the domain of human interrelations. This partitiveness, this dichotomy is not personal or local; it is universal. Apparently the very identity of individual and nation rests upon a hidden premise of division.

The newspapers offer daily clinical histories of man's social and economic conflicts. Their columns are a veritable syllabus of behavior-disorders. Such records of antagonism and division are the fascination of our current news items. They constitute the sales value of popular journalism. Reports of dissension are found upon every hand. Automatically taking sides with one faction or another, we like nothing so much as "a good fight." I am sure that the ill-fortune of even one's dearest friend stirs a hidden sense of satisfaction.[1] After all, it is not oneself who suffers the affliction, and seemingly this momentary assurance reflexly offsets all sense of sympathy for another's pain. None of us accustomed to look within himself is unfamiliar with this subtle trick of man's divided consciousness. This universal division and conflict within the mental processes of man, this 'I'-versus-'you' dichotomy, appears to reflect a socially unconscious factor that is typical of the interrelational behavior of human society throughout.

Literature, whether of history, novel, poetry, philosophy or religion, teems with descriptions of this divisive element in human behavior. Take, for instance, the familiar soliloquy of Hans Sachs in Wagner's *Die Meistersinger*.

> Craze! Craze! Ev'rywhere craze!
> In vain my looks I cast
> O'er present things and past,
> The reason ever seeking
> Why men so fiercely fight;
> Each one his malice wreaking
> In aimless frenzied spite! . . .
> Ah, who shall tell its name?
> The craze is still the same. . .[2]
>
> ACT III, SCENE 1.

The well-known passage in Shakespeare's *Coriolanus* is also very much to the point:

> O World, thy slippery turns! Friends now fast sworn,
> Whose double bosoms seem to wear one heart,
> Whose house, whose bed, whose meal and exercise
> Are still together, who twin, as 'twere, in love
> Unseparable, shall within this hour,
> On a dissension of a doit, break out
> To bitterest enmity; so, fellest foes,
> Whose passions and whose plots have broke their sleep
> To take the one the other, by some chance,
> Some trick not worth an egg, shall grow dear friends.
>
> ACT IV, SCENE 4.

Sherwood Anderson's reflections on this secretly antagonistic trend in human behavior come still closer home. Years ago, during the leisure hours of long summer days spent together in the Adirondacks, Anderson and I used often to discuss the many quaint and pathetic instances of behavior that seemed to me even then to hint of some hidden quirk in the social processes of us all.[3] I remember our speaking especially of this lurking tendency among people to opposition and conflict. Anderson has reverted to this theme in his published *Memoirs*.

> I have always, from the beginning [he writes] been a rather foxy man, with a foxiness which at times approached slickness. If ever by chance you get into a horse trade with me, be a little careful.
> This slickness. It is the curse of the world. It is in too many of our diplomats, our statesmen, governors, politicians. Business is lousy with it. It invades the world of art, is in families, in groups of so-called friends, it is everywhere.
> How can I use this man or woman? What can I make this one do for me?

We do it under the cloak of friendship. You do it and I do it. It is a disease. When I was a boy I heard it on all sides.

Go to it, boy. Be on the alert. Watch your chance, then push forward. Oh, onward and upward, over the shoulders of others, trample them down.[4]

There is ample evidence of this tendency to antagonism and conflict even in the most commonplace instances of human relationships. Too commonly we find it in the human bond so piously revered everywhere as motherhood. It is not seldom that one hears a thoughtful young mother confess that she is greatly irritated with her child. She acknowledges that her little one is not difficult or unruly and that she feels herself fortunate in having a child who is so gentle and coöperative and to whom she is so devoted. Yet there are times when she finds herself inexplicably irritated and impatient at the claims that the child's insistent dependence makes upon her. This feeling of impatience with persons of whom one is fond is so general as to be quite taken for granted.

At the slightest occasion one readily becomes critical and inimical toward others. They "get on one's nerves." One is irritated with the salesman in a store, and in turn the salesman feels no less put upon by the demands of the customer. We see this attitude between employer and employee. So with the waiters and guests in a café, with the personnel of a bus or train and their passengers. One feels at any time that he may justly complain of the conduct of others, of their viewpoint or their manner of feeling and thinking and doing. Whether it be members of one's own family, or servants, or even persons who are utter strangers to us, we do not hesitate to feel that they are something they should not be or that they do something they should not do. How often one is heard to say that this or that person "makes me tired," that he "just can't stand So-and-so!" And of course the "family squabble" is a stereotype.

Because of the supreme importance of one's beguiling image of oneself, a single and even slight offense is often sufficient to cancel out a lifelong friendship. And the irritated or offended person is always quite sure it is the behavior of the other person that is responsible for their estrangement. For in the world of man's interrelations the cause of a misunderstanding appears always to lie outside oneself. Always it is someone else who is to blame. This fatuous attitude we owe to the fact that our social or interindividual relations invariably stem from the illusory self-righteousness of each separate self. Says the aggrieved one, "He did such and such to *me. Think* of it!" In this general imbalance in social feeling one's love for a woman is not more sweet than the grudge into which it is instantly transformed at the slightest hint of her alienation. So with the putative disloyalty of a friend.

In phylobiology these interpersonal reactions are called *affects*. The affect is an unwarranted feeling bred of the individual's wishful self-interest or his self-bias. The folk mind plainly senses this deviation in feeling-tone when it describes certain aspects of this self-conscious, introverted trend as an "affectation." But psychiatry has not recognized this affective self-bias; far less has it recognized that affect is an habitual attendant of man's social reactions generally. Everywhere there is lacking any systematized knowledge of this affect-impediment as it bears upon man's interrelational adjustment to his environment and to others of his kind. There is lacking any recognition of this phenomenon as a social condition.

Affect is really but another name for prejudice. This is important. It matters not whether the affect be positive or negative, favorable or unfavorable, whether an expression of love or hate, it is still prejudice. It is still biased thinking. If I uphold the cause of the Negro in the South because of an affective opinion in favor of him and against the whites, my presumable devotion to the Negro is prejudice. If I espouse the cause of the yellow race on the ground that they are "good" as contrasted with their foreign oppressors who are "bad," my reaction is undependable because again it rests upon prejudice. If in response to affect, I am a member of some particular political party, Church, sect or other ideological persuasion, once more it is prejudice. If in deference to a right wrong dichotomy, if in my disposition to think and feel as I have been blindly taught to think and feel, I am for or against isolationism, labor unions, reciprocal trade agreements, equal rights for women, race discrimination, the poll tax, anti-inflationism or what not, I am prompted by prejudice. If in my subjugation to the way I have been told it is proper for me to feel and think and do, I am for or against Germany, England, Russia or Japan, it is necessarily affect or prejudice. If, out of conformity to what I have been told by other people, I am more devoted to one parent than the other; or if I like one neighbor better than another, once more it is due to my subordination to affect or to the influence of prejudice. My attitude is a response to an opinion that is biased. It is incited by covert self-interest.

We are admonished to stand by our convictions. But oftener than not our convictions are the last thing we should stand by. It is one's convictions that clutter the symbol with affect-impediment or prejudice. As James Harvey Robinson said, we have knowledge aplenty and endless resources to make a far better world than that in which we live, but we are fond of our prejudices.[5] Whatever the circumstance or condition, if one is motivated by affect and prejudice he fails to apprehend what is before him. His reaction is subjective, self-interested and, in the absence of objective grounds of judgment, processes that naturally link organism and environment are no longer operative. Clear, direct judgment has ceased to function.

An overwhelming number of people build up entire systems of prejudice, and pattern their lives in accordance with these systems. Indeed, to a far greater extent than we realize, people fashion their "God" out of the material of their own systematized prejudices. In their interrelational dissociation they design their deity out of an arbitrary image of the parent, and they like nothing better than to pin this fanciful label upon other people. I recall a patient—an unusually sensitive, intelligent woman—for whom the image she had fashioned of me had up to now proved an entirely adequate parent-surrogate. There was, however, just one reservation. But, "knowing me," she could not doubt that I would satisfy her affect-longing on this point, too. Only, as yet, she was not quite fully assured. Finally she decided to settle the matter. "Dr. Burrow," she said, "there's one question I must ask you. Do you believe in God?"

I replied wholeheartedly that I did not believe in anything else! Her face lighted with seraphic satisfaction, for she wanted nothing to interfere with her liking for me. But on my adding that I could not guarantee that I believed in *her* God or in the personal God of anyone else, her face fell perceptibly. But I went on. I said that the concept of "God" is too generally fabricated out of the wishful yearnings of man's self-interested affects. I explained that the God of wishful hearsay and tradition is at variance with the principle of action and reaction, of cause and effect existing throughout the world of objective experience. I said that religion does not consist in believing in the comforting image of an all-powerful parent; that what is needed in this disordered world is living in and by the principle of unity that abides alone in the prevailing order and consistency of the surrounding universe. I reminded her that the processes in man that enter into his relation to the unknown are identical with the processes that relate him to the world of known phenomena. I said that in his relation to every known object or condition man had first to yield over his superstitious notions in regard to it, that all phenomena were once falsely apprehended, that they once belonged to the realm of sheer fantasy.

I said that man today has likewise to yield over his superstitious notions with respect to the unknown; that if he is to apprehend objective reality as experienced throughout his interrelational life, he must surrender his entire realm of wishful fantasy or affect, including the principle of causation he fancifully portrays as his "God." I said that this principle when shorn of its affect-trappings is one in which I had complete confidence; that in this sense it was a principle in which I devoutly believed, and that fundamentally it is a principle in which I was sure all men likewise feel a natural confidence except as they are lured from it by flattering beliefs in "Gods" they have been taught to project out of their falsely inculcated affects and prejudices. These are the Gods begotten of a "right-wrong" dichotomy, the Gods man has set up as authoritarian parents who will tell him what he *ought* to think and feel and do—Gods to whom he may turn in abject dependence for guidance and help, and on whom he may lay the blame for his difficulties and inadequacies, for his ignorance, crime and disease. I said that people who want to know whether you believe in God always have in mind whether you believe in *their* God—whether you believe in the cherished family idols handed down to them through family legend and repute. I held to my point that what people really want to know is whether one was taught to think and feel and do as they themselves were taught to think and feel and do. I said that this is affect, that it is prejudice, that it is biased thinking and feeling. I repeated that on man's present interaffective level of communication and contact this is the sole condition on which people like or dislike one another, that our social system is throughout fashioned in accordance with this fallacious interrelational pattern of behavior.

From now on we began to recover our former rapport. For now we were once more upon the ground of a common neurosis, a neurosis common to man. We began to see in common the fanciful nature of the family "Gods" to whom all of us have been drilled to conform in deference to the arbitrary images we have projected in our pious folk-obeisance. Here we came upon the recognition of an attitude automatically imbued in everyone. Once more we found ourselves confronted with the fallacy of the *social image*[6] or transference[7] and with the servile response it inculcates in us all. We saw that the presence of this artificial attitude in our community relationships marks a social transference in which a purely fanciful image of deity is made the over-all sponsor of man's relation to the phenomenal universe.

This matter of man's traditional beliefs is serious. It is an aspect of his habitually prejudiced or affective state of mind—a state of mind that is inseparable from man's conflict or neurosis. The preponderant influence of this socially prevalent state of affect and its automatic replacement of man's basic relationship to himself, to his environment and to the wider universe is a defect in human adaptation that is in urgent need of thoughtful reckoning and analysis.

War and other crimes are expressions of prejudice. Our habits of living, our habits of feeling and thinking and doing are largely governed by prejudice. So are our traditional virtues, our apocryphal precepts, our cherished "principles of conduct." Of course, for the affectively conditioned reader such things are painful to hear. One does not like their implications. None of us like to have our prejudices impaled in this way. It wounds our pride. But our wounds and our pride are prejudice, too. Our obsessions, our fetishes, our loves and hates, our sentimental pity, our justice, our nobilities and charities, our righteous approbations and indignations, our patriotisms and our party loyalties—all these, as currently actuated, are prejudices, and all place a useless, stupid and unwarranted burden upon our lives that quite spoils whatever sanity and happiness we might otherwise enjoy.

Perhaps what is said here may seem rank cynicism. Certainly such a reaction would not be an unnatural one. I well remember the occasion of my speaking in somewhat similar vein at a psychological meeting, and the very unsympathetic response that pervaded the gathering.[8] I particularly remember how irate some of my foreign colleagues became, and vividly recall the dreadful faces they made. They appeared to feel that this was just too much, and voiced the objection that my position was "pessimistic." But no scientific observation is ever pessimistic. As I said at the time, the recognition in man of the element of affect as a deterrent to his balanced behavior is no more pessimistic than the bacteriologist's recognition of the widespread and infectious nature of tuberculosis or other communicable diseases. These early investigators did not say that it was the nature of man to be tubercular, that tuberculosis must be regarded as intrinsic to his organism. They recognized, of course, that the health of man as of other living organisms is primary, that it is basic to man as a phylum. Realizing this, they merely pointed out that the germ of tuberculosis is an impediment to the natural health of the organism. Similarly, my position is that man's behavior is intrinsically healthy, that basically the function of man's organism rests upon a principle of balance and coördination that is consistent throughout the phylum, but that the unsuspected presence of affect or prejudice has become a serious impediment to man's behavioral balance and integrity.

Like affect and prejudice, feeling-inconsistency and behavior-imbalance are synonymous. Owing to the universal presence of bias or affect and the behavior-imbalance it entails, people are invariably inconsistent in their customary social responses. We cannot stand a person at one time and yet fairly dote on him at another. And it is pitch and toss when to expect the revulsion and when the doting! So with the behavior of people the world over. One can never predict when some such reflex will be touched off—whether a reaction will be friendly or unfriendly. What is equally common, as likely as not the fault or habit that one cannot endure in others, he himself reserves the privilege of indulging at will. In fact, it is the universal rule that defects of behavior which one cannot tolerate in others are precisely those which are most often present in himself, though seldom if ever disclosed.

It is also characteristic of an individual that, while he feels entirely at liberty to criticize the conduct, the opinions or the habits of others, he himself is painfully sensitive to and even bitterly resentful of criticism directed toward him. Indeed, it is precisely the criticism one directs at others that he most strongly resents having others direct at him. One does not see or for a moment suspect the utter inequity of his judgment even in the circumstance in which he violently condemns a certain course of conduct in another while condoning the same conduct in himself.

Apparently his habitual bias of feeling precludes all dependable estimates. And if these instances do not offer sufficient evidence of emotional instability within the wider social community, it is only because the wider social community is likewise impervious to the least suggestion that inculpates *its* emotional behavior. These interrelational mix-ups, these ever-present "incompatibilities of temper" due to the subtle intrusion of affect, would of course be silly and even amusing were it not for the tragic condition deep within man's organism betokened by these behavior-contradictions.

The other day a neighbor was speaking with no little amusement of the vast sums of money the New York spiritualists are sweeping into their coffers these post-war days. He mentioned a mutual friend as being a devotee of such a cult. "Of course," he said, "I could not take any stock in that sort of thing myself. To me, it seems just sheer nonsense." But, in the same breath, he added that upon hearing of the illness of this friend of ours he had entered immediately into earnest prayer in her behalf because, he said, he had always believed in the efficacy of divine intervention! Apparently it just depends on the line of the particular "God" one happens to believe in.

I might also mention the instance of a lady whom I knew years ago. She and her father lived alone, and their relationship over many years had been a very close and devoted one, the more so as they were the only remaining members of a once large and unusually gifted family. But now the father wished to marry again. His first marriage had by no means been a bed of roses owing to the semi-invalidism of his wife during the greater part of her life. The daughter had no valid reason for objecting to her father's remarrying beyond the fact that he was now growing old. His fiancée was acceptable in every way, and besides being truly devoted to him, she had been a lifelong friend of the daughter. Yet the woman strenuously opposed her father's marriage. Avowedly she did so on the ground that he had in her a companion who also was devoted to him and that no home life could be happier than theirs. Not only was she opposed to his wishes, but she was deeply resentful and "hurt." As a result of her attitude the engagement was broken off, and shortly afterwards the father died. Yet hardly had six months passed when the daughter, already well beyond middle years, up and marries an old man with a houseful of devoted daughters! It is the old story. Yet this lady, otherwise highly intelligent, to this day sees no inconsistency whatever in her behavior.

A physician of my acquaintance offers another example of the subjective inability of people to see conditions in balanced perspective. Again the situation is typical. Here was a man outstanding in his profession who had devoted a long life to capable and untiring service in the interest of his patients. But many years ago his son married at an early age and accepted a commercial position instead of continuing his medical studies as his father had wished. From this moment the son became anathema and was forbidden to enter his father's house. Because of this spite-reaction on the part of the father, neither the son nor his wife or child was ever received at their parents' home. The mother entertained no such resentment toward her son, but to the embittered father her feeling in the matter was of no consequence. She was devoted to her son and daughter-in-law and to their child, and would have been only too happy to be able to invite them to her home. But the mother's pain and disappointment was neither here nor there; the father was adamant. And though thirty years have now passed, the self-righteous old man is still enjoying the bitter relish of his resentment. The large and luxurious home of this aging couple still stands empty and cheerless.

This physician was justly prominent in his medical work. He was a valued director on many important medical boards and a man whose judgment was sought on vital questions of civic action, as well as those relating to his profession. His competence was unquestioned and his kindliness equally so. Yet he could see no inconsistency in his behavior toward his son or the latter's family, or toward his own wife, in contrast to his recognized services to the community generally. Any such acknowledgment on his part was completely excluded. Again an old story. But it is an old story that people do nothing about, that is accepted in every community as "just one of those things." One could go on endlessly with instances of such needless emotional strangulations. But the point to keep in mind (and to keep it in mind calls for a violent wrench to one's own personal prejudice) is that the instances cited are not alone typical of the individuals from whose lives I have drawn them. They do not reflect, as our habitual prejudice would have us believe, only upon the particular persons I happen to have mentioned. Anyone, if he will, can readily recall instances in his own life of the rigid tyranny of some such blinding grudge, and how it has choked his sense of wider human values.

Admittedly nothing, of course, could be more petty, more trivial than the examples I have cited. These instances of affect are indeed a commonplace. They are characteristic occurrences in the lives of us all. On its present level of adaptation the race of man is activated throughout by such emotional trivia. But it is not realized that this condition of unrecognized affect has us all in its grip, that the condition is social. Indeed its triviality, and the very fact that it is commonplace and seemingly negligible, is precisely its significance. Not recognizing our affect, not sensing the insidious influence of this distortion in man's feeling-life, each of us cherishes this socially prevalent impediment beyond all things else. So that, if affect bespeaks a picayune condition, it is a picayune condition that characterizes the behavior of everyone.

Take, for example, this instance included in the editorial column of the *New York World-Telegram*.[9]

Language in Government

Scene: a Senate subcommittee hearing. Subject: renewal of Reciprocal Trade Act.

Sen. Alexander Wiley of Wisconsin asks Secretary of Commerce Wallace whether reduced tariffs might eventually cause American shoe workers to lose their jobs.

Secretary Wallace: "You're just talking for a third world war."

Sen. Wiley: "That's a hell of an answer. You're getting cockeyed, that's what's the matter with you."

We submit this scene as a sample of how some men talk in pursuing the duties of federal government.

Rather silly, rather childish, rather undignified, is it not? But I should like to submit that this unseemly bit of Billingsgate is an example of how *all men talk* in response to a sufficiently provocative affect-stimulus. And when I say "all men," I mean you and me, Reader, and our own families and our own friends. Our affects are really coextensive with our human relations. In the phylobiological view such a verbal exchange is not indicative of the behavior of Secretary or Senator; it is indicative of the behavior of man. It represents the anthropological level of our human behavior today. Being common to man, it also expresses the behavioral level of us all. It is the level of the affect-reactions that characterize man's social system throughout.

In the domestic instances I have cited—one the reaction of a daughter, the other that of a father—it is the love-affect that is the dominant motif. The woman's "love" for her father had, of course, nothing whatever to do with any thought of or interest in him. Similarly with the relationship of the physician to his son. In both cases the outstanding reaction was one of personal affect. Consistent with her personal bias or wishful self-interest the daughter wanted the father for herself. In the case of both the daughter and the physician, the apparent love-object was but the manifest interest. Each was interested solely in his own self-love, in his introverted, affective love for himself and his self-assumed "rights."

This clinical picture is one that is of frequent occurrence throughout social communities. It is a form of inveterate self-interest that should be known as *affect-paranoia*. In this condition the symptom-complex consists of an insatiate emotional greed. The patient himself does not suffer from the greed. Not he. He has never a qualm. It is everybody around him that suffers. His only suffering is the pain of not having his greed satisfied, of not receiving the flattery his self-image craves. Such self-love, when viewed objectively, will shed much-needed light upon our too-ready irritation and resentment toward others, as well as upon our so-called "affection" for them.

These illustrations of affect are unquestionably commonplace, but the affect that incites these everyday behavior-reactions is the selfsame affect that incites men to conflict and war the world over. It is the same affect that divides Negro and white, Jew and gentile, labor and management, British and Hindu; that separates the imperialistic, democratic and communistic States, that sets one half the world against the other half, that alienates man's various "Gods" from one another, along with the various religions or minor sects subsisting under each. Yes, these incidents separating daughter and father, father and son, are commonplace and insignificant, but not more commonplace, not more insignificant than the incidents of affect that separate nations and peoples and that divide and segment the entire world.

It is not alone, then, in the individual that we find such inconsistencies. These reactions are national and international. We speak of the "barbaric Japanese," but the barbaric element in the Japanese soul does not date from December 7, 1941, when they committed their "sneak attack" on Pearl Harbor. Nor must it be forgotten that at that time our own nation was on terms of friendliness and equality with the Japanese. Indeed, the Japanese owe to our aid the successful conduct of their "barbaric" war against the people of China through our steady shipment to them of scrap metal. In fact at the very moment the Japanese guns were being trained on Pearl Harbor, the representatives of this Government were engaged in amicable discourse in the White House parlors with representatives of the Japanese nation. Our friendliness with so barbaric a nation as Japan, and the assistance we rendered her in her assault upon China would seem to offer evidence that there is not absent this barbaric element within our own nation. Viewed phylobiologically, it offers evidence of the unrecognized presence of affect within our own national soul as within the soul of all individuals and all nations upon this benighted earth. It is this common vindictive element, this common element of affective viciousness and cruelty upon which all of us, scientist and layman alike, would do well to direct our unbiased observation. For these unscrupulous affects and prejudices that we so readily "see" in other people, in reality reflect upon the health and sanity of us all.

And so if the examples I have cited appear trifling, they are for this very reason the more insidious, the more elusive factor in our human pathology. It is therefore urgent for us to recognize that of all the impediments to man's clear thinking and feeling, his affective reactions are the most subtle and persistent. We must come to see that this condition of affectivity embodies a disordered state of mind whose morbidity infects us all, that *it is a defect in the behavior of man as a species*.[10] For the natural course of the organism's attention and interest is seriously altered and impeded by these mental obstructions, these private affects and prejudices that now interpose themselves between the organism and the outer world.

Of course, all literature is glutted with mental, moral and social nostrums for adjusting our dislocations in behavior. The Law is a veritable Bible of behavioral precepts. Religions have for centuries taught and preached mental measures for the repair of these disorders afflicting our human kind. Philosophy is an inexhaustible source of such behavioral counsels.[11] But, however elaborate, however ingenious, none of these mental discourses *about* conduct, personal or social, in any way touch the physiological actuality of human behavior. None of them hit the biological nail on the head. For they in no way make contact with the structures and functions answerable for the symptomatology to be seen in man's distorted relation to man. They fail to take account of these somatic factors. In short, these mental interpretations do not reckon with the soma, with the organism that is the seat of these outer manifestations or these mental symptoms in man.

It would appear that the secret defection and hostility we find to be second nature in man, exists in no other species but man and that, oddly, it is related to the particular type of developmental variation that most clearly "elevates" man above all other animal forms, namely, the type of consciousness that emerged in man with his attainment of the capacity of symbol formation and language. This aspect of man's evolution is one that we shall examine more fully in subsequent chapters. At the moment I should like to consider the mental and social involvements observable in this inimical tendency we now sense only in its outer or symptomatic expressions. An acquaintance with the social or symptomatic aspect of this development will, I believe, be helpful to us, both as individuals and communities, in our effort to understand the deeper causations that underlie the many disabilities to be found in human behavior.

In our social relationships we seem ever at pains to preserve what is known as our *amour propre,* our mental and social "right" or prestige.[12] Phyloanalysis shows that this sense of one's "right" or prestige is the most cherished of all human prejudices. The measures we adopt for its protection and security now operate automatically among us. These measures are both defensive and offensive. The defensive mechanism is seen in one's effort to achieve credits, to be thought approvingly of, to be "somebody." The offensive aspect of the mechanism is shown in the tendency to disparage others, to indulge in personal criticism and irritation toward them. Thus one shows a reflex readiness to uphold at all costs this affective image he calls his "character." "Pity that man who has a character to support," said Thoreau, "it is worse than a very large family."[13] Yet one insists upon preserving at all times this social image of his "right," his "character" or prestige, and by the same token he belittles the rights and deprecates the prestige of others. We demand our rights with special virulence when the rights of others conflict with our own magnified self-image, when the opinions or the prejudices of others are not sympathetic to our own and so do not contribute to sustain our *amour propre* or private prerogative.

Affect or prejudice is a heavier blight upon the processes of man than he at all suspects. We do not think with our minds but with our prejudices. You do this, I do it, everyone does it. Two people may look at the same thing and see something quite different because of the difference in the prejudices with which they "think." Because of prejudice, our mental concepts are falsely colored, our minds biased, our feelings divided, our thought refracted, our facts factional.[14] Sometimes it is the differing prejudices of governments that come into conflict. When sovereign governments clash there is war. This is because prejudice does not permit the free operation of one's whole thought. The circumstance or object engaged does not embody one's true interest. It does not express one's organic self, but only the picture or image that is one's social self, his *amour propre*, "face" or prestige. Prejudice is always imposed from without. Like money, prejudice is not something we possess; it is something that possesses us. To get square with his prejudices, man must learn to suspect himself. We shall have more to say about affect and prejudice and about their underlying physiology in Chapter VI, and throughout Part II.

It is in the light of our privately assumed prestige that we *like* some people and *do not like* others. This, in a social analysis, is the test that qualifies or disqualifies other people in our regard. "I 'like' or 'admire' such a one" means that such a one is *like* me,[15] that I may readily identify him with me, this identification resting upon the mere outer appearance or social image I assume to be my private prerogative or prestige.[16] But if he is not like me, if he is not in agreement or affiliation with me and with my cherished self-opinionation, I do not "like" him. Consider Shakespeare's "It likes me not," meaning *I* do not like it, that it is not like me, that it does not match or accord with me.[17] This exaltation of one's prestige, of one's esoteric right or *amour propre* has become bound up with and inseparable from our use of symbols, or our social interchange through speech. It marks a psychosocial process that tends to center or to focus chiefly in the interrelational reactions mediated by the head and face—the particular segment of the organism that subserves the function of symbol formation or language. In the organic *naïveté* of the Oriental mind, the word "face" and the expression "saving of face" are, as we know, synonymous with one's sense of his reputation, with his prestige, his mentally precious "right," indeed with his very identity. Even in our own country one often hears the expression, "to save one's face," meaning, of course, one's standing or social prestige. This usage further evidences the degree to which one's proprietorial[18] standing or prestige has come to be associated with the face and with "saving one's face." This is the great desideratum, this the security that not only the Chinese and the Japanese, but that we ourselves and the rest of the world covet above all things.

We need hardly be reminded of the extent to which the face is decorated, treated, manipulated by the beautician, not to mention the art of face-lifting practiced by the plastic surgeon, or the cosmetic effects provided by the gruesome artistry of the morticians. These ornamental recourses are a commentary on the socially aberrant position the face occupies in the community in contrast to the natural interest and motivation of the organism as a whole. The face is man's "front," his social façade. It is the individual's card of introduction, the persona's self-advertisement, its interpersonal placard. "Face" is the symbol of one's entire personality. One's honor, one's right, one's integrity as a person—all center in the face.

The entire structure of man's morality or the all-important emphasis he places upon social custom is again preëminently related to the head and face with its socially developed function of speech. In view of the outstanding position which this segment occupies in man's interrelational behavior, our universally spurious apotheosis of the face or physiognomy is not without phylobiological warrant. For it is through the specialized senses of the face that the younger generation learn as children those precepts that are to fashion and mold their subsequent behavior as social beings; just as it is through the face that, as parents, we of the older generation impart to our children these current interrelational precepts—the words we use, the quality and tone of the voice, the expression of the eyes and brow, etc. It is the face, with its specific function socially, to which the mother or the older generation cunningly shifts the child's primary government of its organism and induces those self-conscious, those affective maneuverings with which the child must henceforth mediate its relation to the outer world. This injection of "right" or "face," this construction of a social façade, this interpolation of interrelational prejudice or affect marks the organism's initial induction into politics, into diplomacy and self-seekng. For in telling the child how it should think and feel and do symbolically, partitively, the mother unknowingly deroutes from their natural channels the processes of interest and attention native to the child's organism as a whole.

In truth, this matter of "face" disrupts all man's natural bionomic interest and motivation. For spontaneous action there is substituted mere pretence. It is this pretence that colors and determines our habitual feeling and thinking and doing. It displaces our natural relation as organisms to the environment. The child is early initiated into this family pretence, this social charade. For the parent only pretends that such and such is "right," and that such and such is "wrong." He has no proof, no objective ground for his position. This false tenet is induced through mere insinuation. Yet this pretence on the part of the parent is the key to the child's future behavior, to the child's own pretence, to its own reflex charade in place of the organism's natural response to its environment. Pretence is synonymous with "face" and neurosis.

It is not surprising, then, that the factor of "face," with its attendant self-conscious affects, possesses untold meaning in its influence upon disorders of human behavior. This self-enfoldment, this retroversion of the individual upon his own image has seriously dislocated processes that are basic in mediating man's relation to man. It has muddied the springs of native feeling and thinking and has distorted the primary coördination of man's organism as a species. The self-reverting, self-conscious type of behavior expressed as "face" constitutes a functional impasse in human interrelations. This dissociative factor, which I shall describe as *autopathic* or *retropathic*,[19] exerts a profoundly deleterious influence upon the behavior of man, and in the present thesis we shall devote much study to it.

It is within the pattern of the "face" that we have communication through speech, that we have "*my* opinion," and the autopathic mode of human relations generally. Here are the motives to self-interest, to the covert advantage of me versus you, of this party or nation against some other party or nation. Here are the distorted aims of sex, as there are here those distorted processes in human economy that replace the natural interests of peace and security among men. Here within this artificial realm of affect we learn to inform others and be informed by them how to think and feel and do in accordance with the arbitrary teaching of social custom and tradition. Here are born the spurious laws that demand artificial differentiation among organisms of the same species and foment social conflict and neurosis among them.

After all, it is the face that is the social instrument *par excel-*

lence with which we negotiate our world, with which we must constantly orient ourselves in our relation to the vast social medium of impacts and reactions in which we are habitually immersed. And so, because of the position the face occupies at the upper or fore part of the organism, and because of the obligation this special part constantly feels itself under to maintain a symbolically acceptable appearance, right or prestige—to secure a favorable mental and social relation to others—this social contact-plate, as it were, justly merits a place of the utmost socio-biological importance in the study of man's interrelational life.[20]

Politeness, politics, affability, diplomacy,[21] with their striving for personal distinction and self-exaltation, are the very special function of the facies or face, just as the opposite reactions of irritation and resentment also subsist under the sponsorship of this hallowed icon of the self. In fact, affability is too often but a cover for one's irritation. But the reader should be reminded that, in the strict sense, neither affability nor irritation is basically a *mental* reaction. Both responses are expressions of prejudice; they are expressions of "face." Like the affective reactions of prejudice, these reactions of the face, or social façade, are not primarily sponsored by man's mental or symbolic capacity and its social plexus of interchange. As we shall see in the following chapter, "face," "rightness" or the importance of the *persona* is due to an emotional complex of reactions that has nothing to do with "mental" in the sense of pure or total reason.[22]

Owing to the interpolation in man of affect, of face, of autopathic thinking, man's spontaneous attention and interest have been seriously deflected and impaired. The organism's primary orthopathic relation to the objective environment and to the organisms of others has been ruthlessly intercepted and its basic processes turned awry. In the sphere of feeling, of behavior, attention has become self-attention. When we consider the importance that is artificially given to this human façade or face; when we consider the extent to which children are trained to shift their spontaneous, involuntary behavior into the social appearances or symbols of behavior that are reflexly relegated to the face or autopathic segment, is it any wonder that there should be universal discrepancy in human interrelations? Is it any wonder that there should exist the socially widespread disorders in man's behavior-adjustment we see about us today upon every hand? Surely, when we consider the terrific trauma to the mind of childhood of this early affront to the young and growing organism, we need go no further afield in seeking to account for the distorted reactions observable in the more dramatic expressions of social disharmony clinically diagnosed as nervous disorders and insanity.

These are serious impediments to man's healthy growth and functioning. But notwithstanding their widespread existence today these impediments, if clearly, if objectively apprehended are of relative insignificance biologically when compared with the deeper motivations of man as a balanced, unitary organism. Like the organisms of other animals, the human organism is primarily motivated by instinctual interests common to the species throughout—the interests of work and play, of mating and the rearing of young, of securing shelter and warmth, of procuring food for the survival of the individual and the species. These are the common, undifferentiated interests that are primary to the life of man in his individual and in his phylic behavior. In man, as we know, there later developed reactions in which the organism's primary instinctual motivation combined with its symbolic capacity to promote those socio-intellectual pursuits that are the distinctive feature of man's unique evolution—the social inventions of language, literature, craftsmanship, of science and art. But these expressions only sublimate the motivations that arise from the primarily integrated processes of man and that preserve his continuity of function as a phylic organism.

We may gain some idea of the primary solidarity of the human species, of the basic cohesion among the elements composing it, if we consider the strength of the bond that often unites individuals in the pursuance of a common purpose or need, or in protection against a common danger. Time and again we have read of the distress of our men at the front when they were placed on the inactive list, when they were suddenly withdrawn from participation in activities with which they had long been identified—activities often involving great hardship and danger to life.

While war inevitably entails extreme confusion and disorganization, while it causes the disruption of many personal and conventional ties, its mere massing of men in a common endeavor brings them a sense of far deeper, far more elemental bonds. It causes them to feel their common blood, their common need, their identity as one vast human organism. Together men have known unremitting hardship and grim, unrelenting struggle. Together they have faced danger and death. But in this they have found, they have rediscovered this forgotten, yet unforgettable primary bond, this matrix of a common identity. As for our own boys, many of them returned home wounded, some badly wounded. Of course they were given every care and attention and all that medicine affords or surgery can supply. But as these young soldiers rested in the security and comfort of their convalescence, as they were attended by thoughtful nurses and once more experienced the luxury of clean, cool sheets and days on end of rest and easement, their thoughts were not merely of their personal good fortune; they did not reflect "how lucky *I* am!" Not at all. Many of them were constantly haunted by thoughts of the buddies they had left in the fox-holes and in the forward trenches—buddies with whom they had suffered and fought as one organism. Their only thought as they lay there was to return and fight again beside the men with whom they had shared life as common pals in a common cause.

This instinct of our oneness as a people, as a race, represents a common constant that preserves man's unity of function as a species, and I hope to show that this common constant, this principle of species unity and solidarity, is biologically the most powerful, the most deeply motivating principle in human behavior. It is in times of war as of any desperate mass urgency, when men are again thrown back upon their elemental unity, that all the petty personal ties, all the vain striving for one's own self-interest — one's personal wealth, success or distinction—become empty of meaning. It is therefore not difficult to understand how a sense of gloom, of desolation should become most poignant for them precisely at the moment when in their own comfort and well-being one would expect their personal happiness to be at its peak. For these boys have known what it is to be one with their kind in a desperate fight for their common life, and in this they have known comradeship in its deepest meaning. Having found it, they have realized something they are unable to put into words. As one war correspondent wrote:

> War is ugliness. War is death. War is destruction. War is heartbreak and sorrow. The men who fight wars, when they fight them, hate war. They hate its blood and carnage, its grime and filth, its demands on their bodies. They hate its separations, its regimentation. But when wars are over, day after day that's easier to forget.
>
> You don't forget the other side of war. You don't forget that in war

you found the only . . . brotherhood you ever knew. You don't forget that in war you found complete selflessness. You don't forget learning in war that a man could love the other fellow more than himself, if only for a minute, an hour, a day. You don't forget that in war you saw men who loved life give their lives for you.

I didn't know that kind of living before I went to war. I haven't known it since. I miss it. The absence of it, the brutal contradiction of it in peace makes it the harder to forget. . . . It's insane that war should bring out our best qualities and peace our worst.[23]

And so, even in the safety and security of home, the thoughts, the interests of these men take them back to the more heartening, if only fleeting, solidarity of a life under arms. They do not go back in mere sentimental contemplation. There is the spontaneous, wholehearted reversion to an experience that nothing can ever quite replace. They have become alerted to a call that is primordial, that lies deep within them. So that today, in face of a needed readjustment to a partitive, divisive world, these men are confused, and in their confusion are seeking desperately to attain a form of social articulation in keeping with their biological articulation as elemental human beings. But their quest is hopeless. They will not find it in politics, collective bargaining, in labor-relation negotiations or in diplomatic conferences. They will not find it in the peace talks of the United Nations, but only in the unity of their own phylic organisms.

Such a reversion to elemental ties, to a comradeship that is basic to the organism, occurs naturally, spontaneously with us all, once we are removed from the artificialities of an autopathic adaptation and brought back to the impact of life in its organismic actuality. With an understanding of this native mood, one begins to understand the mood of our returning soldiers. We shall, I believe, understand it increasingly. For the attitude of these men who have known battle and death side by side is the forerunner of the altered attitude that must take its place in the world of interrelational adjustments that undoubtedly lies ahead of man.

This mood is not new. It is one that has appeared among men on battle fronts throughout all time. But this time the battle front has encircled the earth. It has included both men and women, and everywhere the home front has dovetailed with the battle front. Today, then, there is truly a new situation, a new pattern of action involving all the peoples on the earth—a phylic pattern. With the emergence of this pattern the consciousness of man has for the first time in history begun to assume phylic proportions. We see it in the widely prevalent unrest and dissatisfaction with conditions as they exist in human society throughout. For despite all its blundering and ineptness, despite its reversion to division in its very effort to remedy division, the mind of man is finally forced to seek a remedy commensurate with a global situation. Man's global disorder demands a global remedy. In this social crisis there are signs that the mind of man is at last groping toward a wisdom that is racial—a wisdom without which there can be no true evaluation of the motives to man's behavior as a species. Without this racial wisdom man will continue to wage war in spite of laws, philosophies, ethics, religions, politics and the best of man's intentions.

NOTES

[1] "Nous avons tous assez de force pour supporter les maux d'autruy," Maxime XIX, La Rouchefoucauld, François, *Les Maximes de La Rochefoucauld*, Paris, E. Flammarion, p. 40

"I am convinced we have a degree of delight, and that no small one, in the real misfortunes and pains of others." Burke, Edmund, *On the Sublime and Beautiful*, New York, John B. Alden, 1885, p. 39.

[2]
    Wahn! Wahn!
    Ueberall Wahn!
    Wohin ich forschend blick'
    in Stadt- und Welt-Chronik,
    den Grund mir aufzufinden,
    warum gar bis aufs Blut
    die Leut' sich quälen und schinden
    in unnütz toller Wuth!—
    Hat keiner Lohn
    noch Dank davon: . . .
    Wer giebt den Namen an?
    's bleibt halt der alte Wahn,
    ohn' den nichts mag geschehen,
    's mag gehen oder stehen.
                  Act III, Scene i.

[3] Burrow, Trigant, "Psychoanalytic Improvisations and the Personal Equation," *The Psychonalytic Review*, 1926, Vol. XIII, pp. 173-86.

[4] *Sherwood Anderson's Memoirs*, New York, Harcourt, Brace & Co., 1942, p. 5.

[5] Robinson, James Harvey, *The Mind in the Making*, New York and London, Harper & Brothers, 1921, pp. 235.

[6] See note 7, page 155.

[7] Burrow, Trigant, 'The Problem of the Transference," *The British Journal of Medical Psychology*, 1927, Vol. VII, pp. 193-202.

[8] Burrow, Trigant, "Crime and the Social Reaction of Right and Wrong—A Study in Clinical Sociology," read at the Ninth International Congress of Psychology, Yale University, 1929; published in the *Journal of Criminal Law and Criminology*, 1933, Vol. XXIV, pp. 685-99.

[9] Issue of May 10, 1945.

[10] Burrow, Trigant, "Insanity a Social Problem," *The American Journal of Sociology*, 1926, Vol. XXXII, pp. 80-7.

[11] There is perhaps no abler, no keener expression of the conventional mental and moral viewpoint with respect to behavior than the recent essay by Emery Reves, but this competent treatise also follows the same age-old, divisive, moralistic

pattern of ancient rite and precept. (*The Anatomy of Peace*, New York and London, Harper & Brothers, 1945, pp. 275.)

[12] Prestige < L. *praestigium*, a delusion.

[13] Sanborn, F. B., *The Life of Henry David Thoreau*, Boston and New York, Houghton Mifflin Company, 1917, p. 247.

[14] The words *fact* and *faction* have a common origin in the Latin *facere*.

[15] Admire < L. *ad + mirari*, to go before the mirror, and also, to wonder at.

[16] As we know, the verb *to favor* means both to resemble or be like, and to gratify or to indulge. In this combination of the two meanings we may detect the element of affect inseparable from the idea of *liking*. Likeness and likeableness are seen to be really synonymous. (*The Biology of Human Conflict*, p. 315.)

The verb *to fancy*, meaning both to like and to entertain dreams, is also interesting in this connection.

[17] The reader will recall the phrase, "That's more like," meaning more *my* way hence more fitting.

[18] The words, *proprietary, proper, property*, etc., = one's own. (*The Biology of Human Conflict*, p. 58.)

[19] It may be recalled that the Greek word πάθος possesses two meanings. Like the English word "affection," it signifies both *feeling* and *disease*. In my combination of *pathos* with *auto*, the word *pathos* is used in the sense of *feeling*. Phylobiologically, it corresponds to sentimental or self-conscious feeling, for it expresses feeling that has been battered and mauled by affect and prejudice. *Autopathic* is to be contrasted with *orthopathic*—a term which I shall use to describe direct, whole feeling ('ορθος=straight). Similarly, I suggest the term *retropathic* to indicate feeling that has recoiled upon the subject and has been converted into bias or *self*-conscious affect. It is feeling that is retroactive.

[20] "Of all expressions, blushing seems to be the most strictly human; yet it is common to all or nearly all the races of man, whether or not any change of color is visible in their skin. The relaxation of the small arteries of the surface, on which blushing depends, seems to have primarily resulted from earnest attention directed to the appearance of our own persons, especially of our faces, aided by habit, inheritance, and the ready flow of nerve-force along accustomed channels; and afterwards to have been extended by the power of association to self-attention directed to moral conduct. . . . We may conclude that blushing originated at a very late period in the long line of our descent." Darwin, Charles, *The Expression of the Emotions in Man and Animals*, New York and London, D. Appleton & Co., 1916, p. 363.

[21] Diplomacy = Gr. διπλόος, double.

[22] *Persona* is etymologically synonymous with face (L. *persona* = mask or false face). In the view of phylopathology our much revered postulates of person, personableness, personality, etc., are expressions of the self-exaltation we experience as "face."

[23] Lucas, J. G., "Nostalgia for War," *New York World-Telegram*, January 14, 1946. Reprinted in *The Reader's Digest*, April 1946, p. 74.

CHAPTER III

THE MOOD OF MAN

OR

THE EMOTIONAL FACTOR IN MAN'S DISORDERED PERSONALITY

In Freud's essay, "Reflections on War and Death," there occurs a passage that points up significantly the problem of man's interrelational discord and conflict. Says Freud, "Why it is that even in times of peace every nation and all the individuals within a nation should disdain, hate, and abhor one another is indeed a mystery. I do not know why it is."[1] In making this statement Freud was not speaking of any insular tribe or sect. He was not speaking of people dwelling in the remote fastnesses of some fantastic Ultima Thule. Freud had in mind people everywhere, the general run of individuals and groups that make up normal society. He had in mind human behavior the world over, the behavior of you and of me. In short, his thoughts were concerned with the popular social reactions of human beings whose feelings and interests, identical with yours and mine, are those of normality.

Though purely academic, this question of Freud's is interesting. It is a question that I too had asked myself very early in my psychoanalytic work. It happened, however, that circumstances led me to approach it not as a mere philosophical inquiry but as a very pressing problem in human behavior that called for precise experimental research. It was to find an answer to this question—what is the matter with normality?—that in conjunction with Mr. Clarence Shields and later with the assistance of other associates I undertook to investigate the basic composition of human communities or groups. As voluntary guinea-pigs, it was our aim to discover, if possible, why there exists this social undercurrent of conflict throughout the processes of normal groups—why there exist disdain and hatred among nations and individuals throughout the world.

In order to assist our inquiry we felt the need first to determine the structure and function that enter into the composition of these social units. We asked ourselves: What is the essential make-up and motivation of these behavior-aggregates comprising normal communities? What is the biology of the social self and in what way may this social entity be brought to the test of scientific diagnosis and control?

Our group-research, then, set out with the purpose of analyzing the current adaptation popularly classified throughout human society as "normality"—the social reaction-average which, though dubbing itself healthy, is compelled from generation to generation to maintain permanent prisons and asylums for the individual and to provide periodic wars for the community. This state of affairs appeared to us a condition of disorder, not of health, and our research was undertaken with the object of promoting a plan of group or community health through the discovery of measures of examination and adjustment that ultimately might be applicable to the reactions of man at large. For years I had suspected that the criterion of social and individual adaptation represented by "normality" was not all it was cracked up to be. This accepted consensus of behavior is shot through with inconsistencies and conflicts too numerous and too persistent for it to constitute the valid norm claimed for it. It lacks the basis for establishing within the domain of human behavior a stabilized criterion of objective diagnosis and treatment.

Let us look into this attitude of "normality" upon which individuals and communities commonly pride themselves. Let us consider the accepted covenants upon which this social syndicate rests. For the prevailing premise of normality embodies habits of behavior that are sacrosanct. Indeed nothing so commands the fealty of human communities as the socially established average of conduct known by universal assent as normality. Nothing exerts a more irresistible influence over the processes of men than this criterion of behavior represented in the currently accepted social reaction-average. This criterion of conduct dominates man's thinking and feeling and doing no less today than in the earliest period of human history. Its traditions are preserved in literature, art, religion and philosophy. Its tenets are securely embalmed within the processes of the law. It is the warp and woof of politics, the *raison d'être* of psychiatry, the foundation of our educational systems. Adherence to the vacillating standards of an arbitrary normality has for generations been regarded as the guarantee of mental and social health. Among all individuals, professional as well as lay, among all groups and all communities, it is normality that guides and determines the behavior of family, home and country. Normality enjoys the solemn endorsement of Church and State. It is the measure by which we judge all behavior and indict as subversive or pathological whatever behavior deviates from this popularly cherished "norm."

Very early in our analysis of the group we found that this social confederacy, this mental state we know as "normality," possesses three special and distinctive marks—marks that cannot be too strongly emphasized. First, the standards of normality are completely mutable and arbitrary; they are alterable at any time in accordance with varying personal volition. Though socially ubiquitous, this mental habitude rests upon no determinate premise; its dicta are wholly esoteric. Second, the motivation underlying this esoteric norm activates equally the behavior of the isolated psychoneurotic and that of the socially adapted individual. It activates the teacher as well as the pupil, the governing alike with the governed, the parent no less than the child, the presumably strong and upstanding personality along with those presumed to be weak and ineffectual. Third, normality, as now constituted, consists in a secret and unconscious prerogative that jealously preserves this habitual reaction-level against all inquiry. The shrine of normality at which all of us devoutly worship must on no account be examined into. The old-time religion is good enough for normality, and any investigation into its sacred rites and ordinances is taboo. The least infringement upon it calls forth a reflex defense-reaction in individual and community. To question the prerogatives of this social consensus of behavior is the unpardonable sin, the irreconcilable affront. As the sworn custodian of a hidden, ulterior aim, normality promptly frowns upon any suggestion that presumes to question its accepted tenets. By the universal manifestos of unwritten law this criterion of human adjustment we call "normality" is the great Sir Oracle. According to the adherents of normality its subjective implication of rightness and security leaves nothing to be desired. Enjoying supreme authority over man, this social pattern of human conduct possesses the credibility of a superstition and hence is by common consent immune to the scientific tests of objective actuality.

As to the variability and inconsistency of the standards of

normality, examples are legion. We are supposedly a democratic country but we are largely ruled by professional lobbyists. Overtly we support a war for world-unification, but our ulterior intention leans strongly to the side of nationalism. In our international relationships secret cartels take precedence over our boasted policy of good neighborliness. Everywhere codes of morality have been juggled beyond recognition. Only a few years ago children stood in awe of their parents; now it is the parents who stand in awe of their children. Divorce was formerly anathema, but today no stigma whatever attaches to it. One advocates principles of liberty in his public life, but not infrequently subscribes to tenets of imperialism in his home. Such will-o'-the-wisp "principles" of human behavior and a thousand other catch-as-catch-can precepts are shared in varying forms by all peoples and bespeak once more the perennial imbalance and dichotomy, the vacillating factionalism and partitiveness that mark the habitual mode of adaptation we cherish as "normality." The fact is, normality is but a pious euphemism for the social reaction-average of the two billion people who subscribe to it.

It has now been many years since it first occurred to me that it is just here in man's rigid adherence to the mental state of normality that we shall discover the needed challenge to our human relations—a challenge that can only be met in the vital reality of an actual community- or group-analysis. I have spoken many times of man's automatic defense-reactions in support of the accustomed habits and mores characteristic of the normal level of adaptation. As these reactions were at all times and under all conditions shown to be dominant in our social groups, they seemed to offer the most promising clue to whatever processes might lie beneath them. It seemed to us profitable, therefore, to try to discover what lay beneath this protective social covering of spurious authority and its reflex self-defense. And so, in spite of the relentless opposition among us, in spite of the rigid resistances existing within ourselves, we continued to probe mercilessly day after day into the underlying processes of our so-called "normal" group-behavior.

After the travail of much painstaking research it became apparent that beneath this artificial criterion of behavior and its autocratic inconsistencies there was to be traced the presence of a monstrous *social mood* of systematized prejudice and absolutism. This powerful and disrupting mental bias—this social mood begotten of partitive feeling, or affect—we found to be due to the presence of the insidious element or social image I called the *'I'-persona* or *'I'-complex,* an element which was seen to be unilateral and divisive to its core. This socially autocratic mood or mode proved itself a match for all our efforts to reach and understand it.[2] Inaccessible to every avenue of approach, it defied inquiry. It yielded to neither threat nor persuasion. Nothing entered into or touched this deep-seated mood of the social 'I'-persona with its implicit 'I'-versus-'you' dichotomy. Its autocracy and self-sufficiency were adamant and all-supreme. It was as if this specious form of social conditioning embodied in the mental state of "normality" were the expression of a vast and compactly interknit social transference.[3] It was obvious that this spurious mood of normality embodied a systematization of opinions for which there was no warrant apart from the affect that underlay them.

One thing became clear: whether manifesting itself singly or collectively, in the individual or in the group, this impervious mood of competitive affectivity or prejudice was of one cloth throughout the entire social structure. What appeared to be a unified reaction in a particular personality turned out to be only his successful connivance in this socially consensual affect-bias. Where there appeared to be unity and accord in the interpersonal relationship of any two individuals, again it rested upon the mutual satisfaction of mere reciprocal affects. Similarly, an appearance of unity and accord in any segment of a group or in the group as a whole was traceable to sheer mood-affinities and their successful social exploitation.

It is not difficult, therefore, to account for disdain and hatred among individuals and nations. There is really no mystery involved when, lurking beneath the customary social amenities of individual and group, there is invariably found this unilateral element constellated of the 'I'-persona with its affect-consensus of secret self-interest and autocracy. In its subservience to the mood-entrancement of the 'I'-persona and its "right-wrong" dichotomy, normality of necessity negates all its vaunted principles of organized decency in human relations. To cite but one of many typical instances of the symptomatology of the 'I'-persona in its social ramifications, we might ponder for a moment the syndrome embodied in Hitler and Hitlerism—a disturbance in interrelational behavior that was global in its scope. For this unilateralism and autocracy resident within normality explains why it was possible for the German people to make the dupe they did of Hitler and why Hitler could turn about and from the false eminence he had now attained could make the dupe he did of the German people. Such, it would seem, is the lot of all so-called great men—that is, men made "great" by the autopathic thinking of their community—as it is no less the lot of the masses who constitute their autopathically "great" followers.[4] For "great" were the youngest tyros in the Nazi military ranks, as great and as paranoid in their autopathic pretensions as the Führer himself.

Hitler wrote a book in which he said that the way to conquer people is to lie to them. He said the bigger the lie the more acceptable it would prove, the more it would fool people. And we all remember the pious assurances that followed in its wake. He would never enter the Saar, he said. He would never attack Poland. He would not overrun the Low Countries. He would not attempt to annex Austria. He lied. But his prophecy was correct; he said we would believe his lies, and we believed them all, one after another. Notwithstanding that he said we would be fools to believe him, we did just that. What is more, with each lie we became more furious with Hitler because we believed lies he plainly said we would believe and that we would be fools to believe. It would seem, therefore, that the Führer outsmarted us—that this sick and tortured psychopath pulled the wool over the eyes of us all.

But did he? Or was it our own lies we were all the while believing—lies born of our own wishful affects and prejudices? Certainly at the outset Hitler freely laid his cards on the table when he said he would pursue a consistent policy of inconsistency and lying. And as it turned out, this statement of Hitler's was the unvarnished truth. Consistent, however, with our own inconsistent habituations, we did not like it. It offended our customary habits of "right" and "wrong." It conflicted with the traditional way we have been taught to feel and think and do. True, in his lying Hitler made it clear that he knew nothing of whole human relations, that he had no appreciation of the organism of man as a unitary entity. But on the other hand neither had we. For we did not reckon with the element that is basic in subverting the primary motivation of man, namely, the *affect-dichotomy* that underlies our so-called "normal" social reactions. We did not reckon with the secret absolutism that prompts our own dichotomous affects and prejudices. And so as Hitler proceeded to pile up lie upon lie and promise upon promise—promises which, in compliance with his published schedule, he did not keep—we still clung to his lies; we still insisted on believing them one after another against the testimony of our own senses. Was it after all, then, Hitler's lies to which we were so receptive; or was it not our own? Was it really Hitler who deceived us, or was it not our own autopathic thinking—the unconscious wishes of our own social 'I'-persona—that led us by the nose?[5]

The behavioral dissociation that an autopathic community calls a leader is seen upon every hand, but is nowhere better illustrated than in the dissociation of Hitler and the German people. To the group or community that is partitive, autopathic, dissociated, nothing is so fascinating as the authoritarian mood of a partitively dissociated father-surrogate. It takes the mountebank to draw the crowd. But, in reality, the "leaders" of such crowds are not chosen by the community, nor are such communities chosen by their leaders. Master and master race are of one piece. Held together like the elements in a chemical compound, their common identity is their common bond. History is the record of such affective wedlocks. But while history is replete with instances of these autopathic "unions," these unions only reflect the artificial polarity of man's hidden affect-dichotomy. These inflammable affect-tensions underlie the superficial structure of human relations everywhere. It is such "chemical affinities" that too often lead to violent social explosions. Consider the negative transferences that separate former military allies.

Here social man is confronted with a problem. But let us not be too lofty in tackling it. Let us not fall a prey to the common illusion that a disorder in social behavior is a disorder *outside* of man. While these interrelational combinations and their destructive forces urgently require man's recognition and adjustment, let us see that the unilateral fallacy of man's 'I'-complex is subjective and universal, that this symptom, coterminous as it is with a dichotomous basis of feeling and thinking, extends throughout the race of man. The sinister little Nazi soul abides within us all, for its essence is the partitive 'I'-persona. There are the Hitlers and the Czars over Russia no less than there were the Hitlers and the Czars over Germany and Japan. There are the Hitlers and the Czars over England too, as there are no less the Hitlers and Czars over our own country as over all other partitively segmented States. And each Hitler, each Czar, whatever the country, claims the sole right to determine, by whatever means, the way to peace throughout the world. This is an old, old condition. For these Hitlers and these Czars are but the epitome of a phylic neurosis that is ingrained in the 'I'-persona of each of us. Man is really in a jam.

Everyone knows the history of nationalism and its disorders. Everyone knows the history of Russia, and everyone knows that it is a history of Russian pathology. But, lacking a phyloanalysis of one's own 'I'-persona, no one knows that the history of Russia is the history of all nations. No one knows that it is the clinical history, the social pathology of all countries and all individuals. If the Russian Soviet Union is in need of a basic, internal adjustment, the United States of America is also in need of a basic, internal adjustment. Two autopathic half-worlds cannot make a whole one. Phyloanalysis is no discriminator of either persons or nations. It recognizes but one patient, and that is disorganized, autopathic man. It recognizes but one union, and that is the union of organized, orthopathic man.[6] On no other than phylobiological principles can there be the union of man, and a united world. Adopting the viewpoint of a *dynamic anthropology*, it is imperative for us to see that the 'I'-persona is a universal social symptom that is dominant and operative *now* and that it is dominant and operative *in ourselves;* that the laws of human behavior activating ourselves are as much the problem of man as are the laws of physics, chemistry or bacteriology. It is imperative for us to see that in the symptoms of Hitlerism, for all their cultural depravity, there is exemplified a divisive and undependable attitude of mind that prevails in varying degree among us all, and that this symptomatic state of mind is in urgent need of stable scientific investigation. The view that Germany is a psychiatric patient and should be treated as such by the rest of the world is utterly superficial, restrictive and without phylobiological warrant. Until man has learned to fashion a method of studying the mind of man as a whole—as individuals, nations and peoples—there will continue to be this division, this tragic dissociation within the mind, within the partitive mood of man.

The 'I'-persona is the skeleton in man's family closet. Its sovereign prerogative is the social blind spot that man must reckon with or be destroyed by. For, despite all its popularity, the 'I'-persona is biologically fictitious. It is the ulterior and subversive entity that all of us are keen to detect in everyone else, but covertly preserve unseen within ourselves. Because of the intrusion upon the organism of the 'I'-persona, whole feeling and thinking and hence whole interrelations are precluded. There is only the personal, retropathic affect and its rationalizations. In the realistic view, the disorder of behavior implicit in the unilateralism of Hitler, as of any other political 'I'-persona, is but the counterpart of a unilateralism and dichotomy now endemic to man as a social organism.

We should try to grasp the full import of man's affect-dichotomy. Lacking a clear sense of this self-defeating dualism, man can only leap from the frying pan into the fire. Moral, like immoral people, are in a bad way. Children who disobey their parents think they escape their parents through infractions of their law. Surfeited with "good" behavior, they think the alternative is "bad" behavior. Under the Nemesis of their dualism, they must be—they are under compulsion to be—"good" and docile or "bad" and defiant. They cannot see that either course is equally their subservience to the parental image, that the authoritarian image we hate possesses the same power over us as the authoritarian image we love. So with man's subordination to his images of "God." The atheist fondly thinks that in flouting religion he has freed himself from the fetters of divine authority. But he has struck off one set of chains only to be shackled by another. Whether acquiescing or rebelling, his acknowledgment of Deity is equally automatic. In his fealty to a dichotomous image, he is still bound. If he but knew it, hating God involves as devout a belief as loving Him. In his recalcitrance the militant agnostic still bows to an autopathic image of paternalism.

On man's present divisive plane of behavior his reactions are throughout but bipolar complements in a fatal moral dichotomy. These Janus-faced reactions possess no biological solidarity. They do not represent the primary organism of man. They are not consonant with the organism's total, phylic motivation. Our virtues and our vices are but the writhings of an organism that has forfeited its unity as a functioning whole. Feeling, thinking and doing in accordance with a pattern to which one is conditioned by other people is autopathic, reversed, repercussive feeling, thinking and doing. Autopathic feeling, whether "right" or "wrong," is retropathic feeling; autopathic thinking, whether "right" or "wrong," is retroceptive thinking; autopathic doing, whether "right" or "wrong," is retrofective doing. With all his carryings-on, man's morality is but an interpersonal fetish. In view of man's quarrel with himself we need not wonder at the interpersonal wranglings of affectively biased nations.

Apparently there begins to stir within the depths of our consciousness a faint awareness of the presence in the heart of man of this inimical, this violent and antagonistic trend—a trend at which, oddly, Freud expressed surprise. To return to literature, we find numerous instances which seem to presage the widespread emergence of this divided condition in man. I think that in all my reading I have come upon no passage more strikingly indicative of a sense of this autopathic state of mind than that embodied in the prophetic dream of Raskolnikov in Dostoevsky's *Crime and Punishment*. In Dostoevsky's obvious self-identification with his hero, it would almost seem that in the preconscious vision of this epileptic seer there is prefigured the universal conflict in which the world has become convulsed today.

He dreamt that the whole world was condemned to a terrible new strange plague that had come to Europe from the depths of Asia. All were to be destroyed except a very few chosen. Some new sorts of microbes were attacking the bodies of men, but these microbes were endowed with intelligence and will. Men attacked by them at once became mad and furious. But never had men considered themselves so intellectual and so completely in possession of the truth as these sufferers, never had they considered their decisions, their scientific conclusions, their moral convictions so infallible. Whole villages, whole towns and peoples went mad from the infection. All were excited and did not understand one another. Each thought that he alone had the truth and was wretched looking at the others, beat himself on the breast, wept, and wrung his hands. They did not know how to judge and could not agree what to consider evil and what good; they did not know whom to blame, whom to justify. Men killed each other in a sort of senseless spite. They gathered together in armies against one another, but even on the march the armies would begin attacking one another, the ranks would be broken and the soldiers would fall on each other, stabbing and cutting, biting and devouring each other. The alarm bell was ringing all day long in the towns; men rushed together, but why they were summoned and who was summoning them no one knew. The most ordinary trades were abandoned, because every one proposed his own ideas, his own improvements, and they could not agree. The land too was abandoned. Men met in groups, agreed on something, swore to keep together, but at once began on something quite different from what they had proposed. They accused one another, fought and killed each other. There were conflagrations and famine. All men and all things were involved in destruction. The plague spread and moved further and further. Only a few men could be saved in the whole world.[7]

This prescient dream of Raskolnikov suggests vividly the great divide in the life of man today, of which there is certainly not lacking patent evidence in individual and in community, within the family, the group and the nation. Because of this division traceable to the mood of man, and because of our obstinate refusal to recognize the symptoms of this autopathic mood as they apply to ourselves and to our daily activities, we have failed to sense the universality of these symptoms within man as a species or phylum. We have blinked the recognition of the universal cause that underlies these universal symptoms and inconsistencies, and that resides within the tissues of man himself. The failure to recognize the generic, organismic, indivisible nature of man's behavior and of the problem of its adjustment accounts for the circumstance that man—man as an organism, individual and societal—has not raised the problem of his social adjustment to the level of a science of human behavior. It is because of his lack of systematized knowledge in respect to human behavior that man's healthy phylic function yet remains to be established, that a confused situation exists among us individually and socially, and that universally disordered functions are now decisive in determining man's behavior.

We have need to recognize the social character of the 'I'-persona. We have need to see that this lesion in our human behavior is of one piece throughout the structure of human communities. But this unilateralism and dichotomy in man is today completely elusive. Along with our allies we have conquered Germany and Japan, but we have not conquered the 'I'-persona in either Germany or Japan, for we have not conquered this spurious factor in ourselves. If, in these countries, we have temporarily broken the backbone of the social systems bred of the 'I'-persona, our achievement will prove but short-lived. For if the power of this social artifact has been momentarily checked, it does not mean that the seeds of this same imperialism, of this same political system of affects and prejudices are not still thriving in these conquered countries and in an equally rich soil within our own. In the regimes of dictatorship in Argentina, Spain, Russia and other nations, whether overtly democratic, communistic or monarchical; in the lawlessness and uprisings we are now witnessing in Orient and Occident, we have already seen the breaking out of this same autopathic rash. Nor are there wanting blatant evidences of this social exanthema in ourselves.

In a universal ideology of self-contradiction and division, governments too embody but a disturbed mental condition in which there can be nothing but war, whether declared or undeclared. For it must be recognized that the State is a state of mind and that this state of mind betokens an autopathic, dichotomous, self-contradictory mood. A democracy is not democratic, communism is not communal, and the monarchies lack a monarch. A ruler today is but a puppet of the State—of an autopathic state of mind. He is a puppet in royal trappings, a doll dressed up in the apparel that best befits the delectation of the State's momentarily dominant political group. Whatever the name, whatever the ideological platform—monarchy, democracy, socialism, Fascism, communism, Labor Party, Right or Left—the State is always a state of mind, and this state of mind is always unilateral, inconsistent and divisive.

In the midst of a universally autopathic state of mind one is apt to be misled by the spectacular episodes of warring aggression and to overlook the equally pathological, if less obvious, expressions of dissociation and conflict existing in so-called times of peace. One may usually discount the words of the casual commentator in respect to human behavior, but statements by so illustrious a scientist as William James may profitably be cited as an appreciation at least of the symptomatic aspects of man's neurosis.

"Peace" in military mouths today [wrote James] is a synonym for "war expected." The word has become a pure provocative, and no government wishing peace sincerely should allow it ever to be printed in a newspaper. Every up-to-date Dictionary should say that "peace" and "war" mean the same thing, now *in posse,* now *in actu.* It may even reasonably be said that the intensely sharp competitive *preparation* for war by the nations *is the real war,* permanent, unceasing; and that the battles are only a sort of public verification of the mastery gained during the "peace"-interval.[8]

Certainly James's position is amply corroborated in the situation the world now has on its hands, or rather half the world, when it finds itself committed to the permanent policing of the other half—to keeping it in submission, *or else!*

No psychiatrist in his right mind, having in his care a patient with a homicidal trend, would consider this behavior-disorder cured because the nurses and attendants had, to date, successfully intercepted the patient's efforts to kill his enemies or persecutors, whether fancied or actual. So with the behavior-disorders that afflict peoples or nations. No nation with homicidal trends due to causes, either fancied or real, can be considered cured as long as its tendencies to violence are merely kept in check through the safeguards of an international system of policing. Of course it is the fervent hope of police and psychiatrist that the recalcitrant element may be restored to an orderly process of behavior, and accordingly both exert their utmost ingenuity to this end. We cannot be unmindful of, indeed we cannot be sufficiently grateful for the services of both psychiatry and the law in their care and control of the disturbed or the delinquent individual everywhere to be found under our present system of society. But the fact remains that under our present social system it is chiefly the function of psychiatry as of the law merely to police people who fail to conform to the prevailing system of pseudo-normality.

Throughout the world there are many thousands of mental and penal institutions housing unnumbered millions of inmates all of whom are under constant guard. This deplorable situation, this matter of the larger pseudo-normal community assuming disciplinary charge of its refractory members means that both in the fields of mental disorder and of social infringement our pseudo-normal majority does not really know what the morbid condition is with which it is supposedly dealing. In short, both psychiatry and the law have failed to employ objective measures of scientific diagnosis, and therefore lack a scientific criterion for the treatment and control of the condition. All they can do in their autopathic unenlightenment is to punish it and to keep forever punishing it. This complete misconception of the subversive individual or community is probably the most tragic chapter in all human history. As things stand, we tend to regard the unruly delinquent or psychopath as a vicious and dangerous cut-throat. Again we fail to sense the viciousness and the danger within our own unilateral or pseudo-normal selves. We fail to see that we who are "normal" are also cut-throats, that we do not hesitate to knife these delinquent minorities wherever the opportunity is favorable, but in our "normal" smugness we do it, of course, in a nice way.

At no time in man's history has there been greater need for science to come to his aid in the study of his own behavior. For man's situation—his state of mind—is desperate. In the arguments concerning human conflict and war that are set forth again and again in book, periodical and newspaper editorial, we find the same level of motivation, the same affectivity that characterizes the very type of behavior which presumably is under intelligent and encompassing criticism. In man's complete lack of understanding of his own behavior, intellectual rationalization everywhere attempts to cope with intellectual rationalization. Man has not recognized that his ever-present social affectivity is symptomatic of a dislocation within his own basic processes and that this dislocation calls for objective measures of physical diagnosis and control. We need no stronger evidence of the global character of man's division and dichotomy than is to be found in the global conflict of the all-enveloping world-war we are still struggling to bring to an end. We need no stronger evidence unless it is to be found in the deep-seated dread with which men are silently watching the hurrying processes of a political peace based, as it inevitably is, upon an equally dichotomous pattern of motivation.

As no scientific remedy has yet been applied to this disorder within the organism of man, there is no assurance that a like pandemic will not also divide those of us who now stand allied as United Nations. There is no certainty that the momentarily combined 'I'-personae of these nations, notwithstanding their "Four Freedoms" and their system of world police, will not break out with the same eruption and consequent virulent division among themselves. The social pathology of this disturbance is such that it may as readily erupt within a class, race or section of any one or all of these nations. For the 'I'-persona never learns. It is completely uneducable. It does not hear what is said unless what is said is to its advantage—unless what is said contributes to the inviolability of its own arbitrary systematization. Obviously, a disorder within the tissues of man requires the approach of a scientific principle and method capable of reaching the seat of this disorder.

Based on the trend of the investigations I have indicated, it would seem that we must face without flinching the unflattering fact that in the sphere of behavior-disorders medicine is woefully befogged. We would do well to see that in the sphere of man's interrelational behavior we still carry the blighting burden of a bias descended from traditions which in other domains of scientific inquiry have been summarily abandoned. While in spheres of investigation lying outside man's own behavior the student of medicine has done outstanding scientific work, in the sphere of human behavior he still adheres to the ancient folkways of mere symbol and psychopractice. Like the medicine of yesteryear he still clings to ancient precept and superstition. Only a few years ago—some ninety or so—physicians invoked mere ideological concepts to account for infective and other somatic processes. And today we see the residua of this same esoteric ideology in current efforts to account for the neuroses and kindred disorders of behavior. Where in earlier times we believed in evil spirits, black magic, witchcraft, healing amulets and the imposition of spells and conjures, psychiatrists still invoke today such conceptual artifacts as "the unconscious," "the psychic censor," "the super-ego," "the transference," "interpersonal domination." And recently, in reading an article on psychotherapy in a leading medical journal, I even came upon the term "spiritual imprisonment."

It is not surprising, though, that behavioral medicine is still far in arrears when we consider how short a time ago medicine ceased to be occupied with mere outer signs and symptoms even in relation to constitutional and infectious diseases.[9] As we know, such symptoms of tuberculosis as cough and fever were for years regarded as the disease itself. It was only following the work of Pasteur and Koch that these disease-accompaniments were recognized as being but symptoms of an underlying disorder.[10] Behavioral medicine is still limited to psychiatry or to the study of symptoms. But it must be remembered that the attitude of all medicine was originally psychiatric, that all diseases, including the infections, were for centuries referred to mental and moral causations.[11] In other fields of medical investigation, as we know, all this has altered; but not so in the field that deals with problems of human behavior. Still believing that the cause of these disorders resides in realms of mental imagery projected outside his own organism, man continues to deal with these disorders in terms of their outer signs or symptoms. He still adheres to purely ideological "causations." He still attempts to apply psychic treatment to those individual signs and symptoms which are but indicators of a conflict reflexly induced within the organism of man as a species.

When man discovered the bacterial origin of infectious disorders he necessarily based his procedure, albeit unwittingly, upon the inherent consistency of the phyloörganism as a whole. He proceeded on the biological principle of generic solidarity that unites the organisms of a species as a unitary behavior-structure.[12] Only on this unitary premise of the organism's solidarity as a species was it possible for medicine to establish the common denominator answerable for a disorganization within this common unitary structure. It is equally important today that in his outlook upon behavior-disorders man put aside his psychosocial thought-patterns, and that on the basis of the organism's *generic solidarity* he set about discovering the common physiological denominator responsible for his autopathic conditioning and for resulting disorders in the behavior of his organism as a whole. Viewing the world at large, there is no blinking the fact that we have come to a turning point in our social and economic outlook as it bears upon human relations; but we have need to come to a turning point in our medical outlook as it bears upon these same human relations.

Notwithstanding that we are now, as a species, daily swayed by the mutable and arbitrary criteria of a pseudo-normality, it is nevertheless the inescapable obligation of medicine to acquire an objective insight into this widespread distortion in human adaptation. If we are to reckon effectually with a disorder of function affecting the organism of man and appreciable within ourselves, it is demanded that we dispel our spuriously partisan standards based upon the moralistic dichotomy of "right" versus "wrong," and apply to disorders of man's behavior—of our own behavior—the same objective criteria we have applied in other fields of medicine. No one can be both organismic and unilateral. No one can serve Man and Mammon. In this tragic hour of man's history when the conflict within himself has attained the violence of the world-wide war we lived through only yesterday, it is more than ever required that man recognize the impediments to his consistent conduct in terms of concrete somatic processes and that he adopt a course of action consonant with a science of human behavior.

We speak of the individual neurotic, but the individual neurotic is but the myth of an habitually unilateral point of view. Everywhere throughout "normal" society we find the counterpart of the disorders we designate clinically as hysteria, psychasthenia, dementia praecox, manic-depressive reactions, obsessive and phobic states, etc. In the larger generic view these reactions are seen to exist throughout the community. The psychiatrist who sits in his study or in the hospital clinic or at the bedside of a mentally ill patient is but one of many thousands of psychiatrists who at that moment are sitting with corresponding thousands of patients similarly afflicted. These patients represent specific social reactions to a generic social condition. It is the social condition that is the disorder. But to the individual psychiatrist the disorder of such a patient appears to be an individual disorder. From the partitive basis of psychiatry—from the basis of the psychiatrist's social and professional habituations—the patient is unique and all-important. But the physician's partitive basis, like the patient's, is an erroneous inference based upon an erroneous social premise. It is only as we summon the broader recourses of an organismic purview that we shall recognize the narrow, unilateral premise upon which man's current social systems—political, religious, psychiatric, economic, international—now operate.

The trouble is, all the world is a psychiatrist. All the world thinks it can heal partitive aberrations with partitive remedies. True, the individual psychiatrist is now beginning to *say* that mental disorders are social. But while he says it, he continues to maintain his personalistic interests, his partitive mood, in respect to the partitive disorder of the single individual before him. Lacking the broader outlook of phylopathology, the psychiatrist does not comprehend the phylic basis of the neurosis. His mood, the unilateral mood, does not compass a sense of the larger social nature of disorders of behavior and of the psychiatrist's own share in this wider behavioral structure. My own background, of course, is that of the psychiatrist. So that whatever indictment I bring against psychiatry, I have for many years directed against myself. My interest, however, is not in myself or psychiatry or the normal community. It is in man's clear conception of himself and his behavior. I am interested in bringing to evidence the habitual acquiescence of individual and group in man's neurosis as this acquiescence was repeatedly evidenced in myself and my associates. I am interested in the analysis of this social neurosis with a view to recovering the more orderly processes resident within the organism of man.

From what I have said we may begin to recognize that the habitual reaction of the 'I'-persona as evidenced in affect, in "face," in autopathic thinking and feeling, is an essentially social reaction. With the development of "face" and the necessity to preserve one's own self-interest as a consecrated image or icon, there came about an element of differentiation and competition in human motivation. Instinctual motivations that naturally issued in pursuits possessing a common interest for individuals and communities as a unit or whole underwent a profound alteration. They were suddenly turned back. Their course was reversed. Instead of phylic unity as an organism, there developed an interindividual rivalry in the quest for "face." Because of the interposition of personal motives begotten of one's private right or prestige, because of man's preoccupation with the merely "right" symbol or appearance created by him mentally, affectively, there occurred throughout the phylum a strange repercussion or back-firing in individual and social feeling. The feeling that had flowed naturally from organism to environment was now checked by retroactive concern for one's personal interest—a personal interest which, in enthroning itself and its prestige as the supreme consideration in human behavior, necessarily obstructed the primary interest and motivation of the phyloörganism.

In this artificial reversal or introversion of the organism's spontaneous motivation and interest there was born the social image or the mental element of interpersonal oppositeness and contrast, of competition and antagonism. This social dichotomy and antagonism superseded spontaneous and instinctual thought and feeling as they function on behalf of the well-being and survival of man's organism as a species. This repercussive trend that developed socially, this reversion of the organism's natural feeling or interest toward considerations of one's mentally cherished "face," his social façade or appearance, his own prestige or right or social importance, introduced the factor into human behavior to which we refer in phylobiology as partitive motivation or affect. This all-pervading social affect, this factor of personal prestige or "face" is coterminous with man's interpersonal relationships as mediated through the production of speech. Man's entire interrelational life is constructed of the affect. War itself is but a mass paroxysm of affectivity.

Perhaps it may now become clearer not only why man has recourse to philosophy in his search for solutions of his behavior-confusion, but also why these philosophies are endlessly, intricately devoid of solutions and beget only still more philosophies. Philosophies are spawned of man's supreme effort to *think* his way through the maze of his affects without taking into account that his thinking is of the same texture as the affect. And so, too, we may begin to see that our pseudo-religions, like our pseudo-philosophies emerge out of the very conditions they would correct. Our pseudo-religions with their fabulous construction of wishful empires of security are the product of man's desire for "face." The mood-constellation that is coterminous with social affect or "face" has invented these intellectual designs for living—these mythical images of deity—purely for our autopathic comfort and self-flattery. The system of affects that man has built around these theocratic constables, with their authoritarian "right" or "goodness," is utterly arbitrary and alien to man as an organismic entity. Authoritarian Gods, being divorced from the natural laws governing man's orthopathic processes, are purely fanciful constructs begotten of fanciful social images. As Montaigne has said, "Man is certainly stark mad; he cannot make a worm, and yet he will be making Gods by the dozens."[13] If we are to escape the arbitrary dictates of others as to what we should think and feel and do, we shall abrogate the mental rhetoric and metaphor that has set up these tutorial personages as guardians over our behavior and we shall try instead to understand the motivating principle that activates the processes of man as a phyloörganism.

What appears to be needed in this disordered and unhappy world is a return to the organismic principle that will permit of man's conscious and intrinsic self-government. There is need, not of theoretical mechanisms or of projective preoccupations with the behavior of others, but a frank concern with the behavior of ourselves through the subjective appreciation of a disorder existing among us socially. When some years ago a few of us organized into a group of behavior-students and became the voluntary patients, individually and collectively, of the unit consisting of that same group as a societal whole, it was with a view to confronting the problem of behavior as it exists internal to man himself. Our concern was not with the deviation of the obviously disordered individual opposite us but, for all our seeming (symbolic) security as individuals and as a group, with a wholly unsuspected disharmony within ourselves—within the social system of "normality." Regarding ourselves as integral elements within a racially organismic whole, it was our endeavor to initiate an objective inquiry into this socially continuous lamina of conflict and disbehavior.[14]

However well intentioned the political psychopractors, professional and lay, their machinations have throughout the pages of history shown a complete incompetence to deal with the objective problems of either the State, the family or the individual. The reason is that within a world-organization that is itself subjectively, affectively arbitrated throughout, these would-be students of behavior are necessarily barred from an objective investigation that has to do with their own subjective motivations. Truly, in regard to his own behavior man has signally failed to ask himself the right question, and as a consequence he is today no nearer the right answer.

NOTES

[1] "Warum die Völkerindividuen einander eigentlich geringschätzen, hassen, verabscheuen, und zwar auch in Friedenszeiten, und jede Nation die andere, das ist freilich rätselhaft. Ich weiss es nicht zu sagen." Freud, Sigmund, "Zeitgemässes über Krieg und Tod," *Imago,* 1915, Vol. IV. p. 12.

[2] The words "mood" and "mode" are traceable in their meaning to a common kinship with the word "pattern."

[3] See note 7, page 155.

[4] Burrow, Trigant, "The Heroic Rôle—An Historical Retrospect," *Psyche* (London), 1926, Vol. VI, pp. 42-54.

[5] Burrow, Trigant, "Fallacies of the Senses," "*Scientia,*" 1935, Vol. LVII, pp. 354-65, 431-41.

[6] See note 19, page 179.

[7] Dostoevsky, Feodor, *Crime and Punishment,* translated from the Russian by Constance Garnett, New York, The Macmillan Company, 1917, pp. 489-90.

[8] James, William, "The Moral Equivalent of War," *International Conciliation,* Bulletin No. 27, 6-7 (February), 1910.

[9] Burrow, Trigant, *The Biology of Human Conflict,* Chapter V.

[10] The work of Carl R. A. Wunderlich (1815-77) on the relation of animal temperature to disease forms the very foundation of our present clinical thermometry. (*Das Verhalten der Eigenwärme in Krankheiten,* Leipzig, 1868.) Before Wunderlich's time volumes had been written on fever as a disease. But "by utilizing the advanced thermodynamic knowledge of his time, Wunderlich made his book a permanent scientific classic. He found fever a disease and left it a symptom." (Garrison, Fielding H., *An Introduction to the History of Medicine,* Philadelphia and London, W. D. Saunders Company, 1922, pp. 452-3.)

[11] Garrison, Fielding H., *An Introduction to the History of Medicine,* pp. 20-1.

[12] Galt, William E., 'The Principle of Cooperation in Behavior," *Quarterly Review of Biology,* 1940, Vol. 15, pp. 401-10.

[13] "L'homme est bien insensé! il ne sçauroit forger un ciron, et forge des dieux à douzaine!" *Essais de Montaigne,* Paris, Bibliothèque-Charpentier, Vol. 2, p. 417.

[14] How different the actual experimental work in group-behavior from any theory or intuition regarding the neurosis of man! It is a far cry, indeed, from the objective experience of neurosis or dissociation in one's community or group as one participates in a phyloanalysis of it, to the position, for example, expressed by me thirty-two years ago in my paper, "The Origin of the Incest-Awe" (*The Psychoanalytic Review,* 1918, Vol. V, p. 253). At that time I wrote:

"Man's 'morality'—the code of behavior that represents psychologically the zealously courted standard of conduct he designates as 'normality'—is, in my view, nothing else than an expression of the neurosis of the race. It is a complex of symptoms representing the hysterical compensation of society that are precisely analogous to the compensative reactions manifested in the hysteria of the individual. As morality is essentially the pain of the neurotic due to an intuitive sense of his inadequacy to the demands of his own individual code of behavior, so morality expresses equally the pain of the social organism because of its inaptitude to the requirements of its generic social code. The 'hysteria' of the one is the 'normality' of the other, but in both the inherent psychological mechanism is identical—the mechanism in the one as in the other representing vicarious compensations due to the frustration of principles of organic truth. So much for the morality representative of 'normality'."

This is all very well as far as it goes, but it does not go beyond mere theory. Man's disordered behavior, though, is no theory; it is a very deep-seated disturbance in processes that are internal to man's organism. Compared with formulations that rest upon my maturer investigations in more recent years of the neurotic *mood* of man, this early statement seems to me now almost naïve.

CHAPTER IV

ATTENTION AS A BIONOMIC PROCESS AND ITS SOCIAL ABERRATIONS

In the search for the right question in the field of behavior-disorders, I think we shall find that inquiry into the process of attention will go far in assisting our quest for the right answer. Attention is all but synonymous with the relation of an organism to its environment. Attention is thus an essentially bionomic or ecological process. Without attention there would be no contact with the outer world. There would not be man's apprehension of the objects and conditions that surround him. There would not be his ecosomatic or organism-environment relationship.[1] And so, in looking for a clue to the processes that determine man's behavior, we cannot do better than devote ourselves to a consideration of the ecosomatic function of attention as it links together organism and environment.

We have all been accustomed to use attention before troubling to define it. Attention is everywhere taken for granted. The vast majority of people come into the world and go out of it without ever considering what attention is or even knowing that they possess this handy commodity. If interest or attention is examined at all, it is examined only after adult life has been attained, and then only by a few academic specialists. In the meantime this phylic process has directed *us* quite as much as we have directed *it*, because attention has already established in us certain habits of looking at things, certain habits of feeling and thinking. And these habits now determine our behavior reflexly. When we do come to examine it, the process of attention, which by now has already been long under way, proves highly complex. It is complex both in its personal and in its community expressions. For the individual or the community that in due course is led to examine the function of attention is the same individual and the same community that has been using attention wholly unconsciously or unknowingly up to the moment of examining it. Because of the subjective involvement of us all in the present inquiry we would be greatly assisted if we would regard the process of attention from a basis that, as far as possible, is objective and impersonal.

In saying that attention is the process that primarily relates the organism to the outer world, our definition of attention covers the most instinctual and elementary, as well as the most intellectually specialized or symbolically complex reactions of the organism. If we consider the simpler mode of attention as manifested in the animal, we find it to consist of a process that relates the whole organism physiologically to the whole environment.[2] There is not the intrusion of the partitive or symbolic itemization through which the symbolic or part brain of man separates outer objects into mentally differentiated entities. In this cerebral process the special senses of vision, hearing, taste, smell and touch constitute the media of contact with the external world. Undifferentiated or whole attention, as it exists in the animal, and primarily of course in man, is essential to viability and survival. Through the organism's instinctual attention it secures food, finds shelter, adapts itself to changes in temperature, senses danger, seeks its mate; and in all its external relations the health and integrity of the organism is dependent upon the process of attention.

Among the animals primarily dependent upon this function in relating them to the external world, the animal man of course must also be included. With man, however, attention has been elevated to a far more delicate and refined mechanism. Through the employment by man of the symbol and its unique facility of sensory analysis, a special part-function has been added to this instinctual asset whereby the organism may now separate out and detach the object or condition from the environment as a whole. That is, through the use of the symbolic or part brain man is capable of dealing with *imaged* parts or items. If I may quote from an earlier essay, *The Structure of Insanity*:

> The function of symbolic attention performed by the organism in relation to its object is selective or partitive. It is selective or partitive because, contrary to the integral mode of attention, it is restricted to the part represented by the cerebrum and its exteroceptors, and because the contact made with the outlying world of objects is made correspondingly with a selective or partitive feature of the object as a whole. That is, the whole object is cerebrally symbolized through this imitative part-function of the organism.[3]

Later, in *The Biology of Human Conflict,* I said that

> In attempting to deal at all specifically with the process of attention, it would be well if we might discourage in ourselves certain prepossessions which we now entertain as a result of the type of attention we habitually apply to the process of attention itself. Attention has come to mean for us only the function we habitually experience when focusing "mentally" upon this or that object, or image of an object. The sharply directive pencil or focus of interest with which we apply ourselves mentally to a specific object or phenomenon constitutes an example of what is for us now practically the sum of the process understood as "attention." This mental penciling upon an item, whether actual object or retained image, is, however, from the point of view of man's evolution, a very recent and specialized acquisition. In an earlier period in the history of the race the organism's bionomic relation to its outer environment was something very different. Whatever was external to the organism engaged its interest as a total function. In its relation to the outer world the process of attention originally represented far more a coördination of the organism *with* the object than the directing of its interest *at* the object.[4]

It is through the interpolation of this special symbolic function in man, whereby he mentally pencils upon an item, that there was begotten the elaborate system of relationships observable in the external world and constituting the basis of science.

But if through his acquirement of the symbolic faculty man is endowed with a tremendous asset, if through his facility of symbolic abstraction he has lifted himself to heights infinitely beyond the level of other animals, he has by the same token incurred very heavy liabilities—liabilities so heavy that it may be truly said that man has descended as far below the animals as he has risen above them. These liabilities are traceable to the incident of the affect and to man's concomitant mode of private distinction we have seen in the accidental interpolation of the 'I'-persona. For in passing from the cerebral mechanism of attention that relates the whole organism to the whole environment, there occurred a serious modification in man's primary thinking and feeling. Owing to the impingement of affect, instead of his whole brain employing the symbol as the part-function that it is, the part-function of the brain tended more and more to become systematized and to encroach upon the function of man's organism as a whole. In permitting the symbolic segment to supersede the motivation of his organism as a whole, man got the cart before the horse.[5] His bionomic processes were henceforth at cross-purposes. The organism's ecosomatic function became reversed. In consequence, man's feeling, man's motivation became seriously involved and confused. Part-interest or self-advantage—advantage accruing to the 'I'-persona—came to alter and obscure man's total outlook or attention. Attention became partitive, digressive. It became self-attention. Affect and "face" intruded themselves between the brain of man and his environment, shunting his objective thinking into mere autopathic thinking. As we shall later see, the deviations of behavior we witness in individual and social conflict are traceable to this inadvertent form of attention. This mode of attention that tends to divert interest in the object to interest in oneself—in one's self-image and its secret gain—I have called *ditention*.[6]

In our phylobiological consideration of the function of attention we have asked ourselves what attention *does* rather than what it *is*. Ordinarily one regards attention as a purely symbolic, ideational function and deals with it in strictly intellectual, scholastic terms. But the process of attention needs also to be considered in its influence upon the motivation of the organism as a whole, particularly as this influence facilitates or impairs man's social interrelations. In man, as we know, attention is now closely tied up with language or with the verbal symbols acquired through social contacts. These mental tokens are imparted to us by others from earliest childhood. For symbolic attention is an interrelational function. It is a process that is conditioned socially, or from *without in*. Phyloanalysis has made evident that this type of attention is characterized by the unconscious dominance of an autopathic trend—of a personalistic image that tends to differentiate individuals composing social groups, upon a quite arbitrary basis. In its interrelational capacity attention is too often linked with affects that are merely interpersonal and that obstruct the course of felicitous social interchange. In contrast to this socially infelicitous form of attention our observations in group-analysis led to the recognition of a species of attention that maintains the neurodynamic relation of organism to environment prior to and independently of the individual's acquisition of mental or symbolic attention. This type of attention rests upon primary, unconditioned feeling or motivation and is consonant with societal solidarity and coördination. It is a process that flows from *within out* and that relates the organism as a whole to the environment as a whole.[7]

This is of course the primary, spontaneous type of attention in which the organism relates itself directly to the objects of the environment. By virtue of the neuromuscular orientation involved in this form of attention the soma makes contact with the objects about it, and these objects become a functional part of man's ecosomatic or organism-environment relationship. We found, however, that this direct attentive process is too frequently impaired through the insinuation of a biologically obstructive factor. We found that an affective element enters into the function of attention and distorts the organism's primary rapport with the environment. "Intellect," as Herbert Spencer said, "being framed simply by and for converse with phenomena, involves us in nonsense when we try to use it for anything beyond phenomena."[8] An object or situation, for instance, toward which one is unfavorably prejudiced or conditioned possesses for him a perceptual value that is very different from that of an object toward which he is favorably disposed, notwithstanding that inherently there may be lacking any valid differentiation between them. Similarly, the personality of an individual may seem praiseworthy or reprehensible in one's view. That is, one's customary "liking" or "disliking" an individual is the response of a wholly prejudiced, affective or socially conditioned attitude of mind. As I said, because this type of attention is deflected by affect, and causes an impediment in social rapport, I have designated it partitive attention or ditention.

Ditention is of more general occurrence and has become socially crystallized to a far greater degree than is commonly recognized. While this type of behavior is markedly characteristic of the neurosis, it is by no means limited to "neurotic" individuals. There is ample evidence that the unsuspected presence of social affects causes this same blurring of the object in the habitual reactions of "normal" persons. The affect-object loses perspective because the attention has been deflected into purely interpersonal involvements. Consider the first five or ten minutes of waking as the various interests of the day begin to lay claim upon one's attention. Take, for instance, the period of returning consciousness in the daily life of the average man. He recalls, let us say, the letter that came from the University the day before, saying that his son's record is far below standard. This incident brings up an unpleasant train of thought. How much more trouble is his son going to cause him? He has been unamenable from his earliest childhood. These reflections occasion the father a distinct sense of irritation and disapproval toward his son. Or perhaps he recalls that his wife told him yesterday that she needed a new fur coat. Why must she have new furs at a time like the present? Why can she not be satisfied with those she has? There are so many more important needs just now. And anyhow the coat she has looks quite presentable. Here again his reaction is one of irritation. He feels no little put upon by his family, and finally gets up with a marked sense of self-commiseration. In his mood of general gloom and dissappointment, the attention of our family-man is markedly dominated by subjective affects. The outlines of the objects in question—in one case the purchase of a new coat and in the other the adjustment of a deficient academic record—have been clouded because of the subjective feeling-tone that has entered into his relationship to his wife and his son.

Apparently the community's prevalent preoccupation with such interpersonal affects is related to the fascination people commonly find in the diversions of social gossip, whether expressed in the invidious small talk of a Sairey Gamp or in the lurid reports of the daily newspapers. The mutual self-infatuation that underlies social man's interpersonal exchange of affects is of course psychiatry's stock in trade. Today even the radio has its clinical bureau with which to while away the twilight hour. Through this handy device one may listen to an endless ventilation of ditentive affects and to equally ditentive efforts at their adjustment. The widely featured appeal of these socio-psychiatric clinics succeeds in capturing the attention of millions solely because of the salacious relish that people the world over are prone to find in the beguiling savor of interpersonal rumor and report. Here again there is the proneness of people who have been taught how to think and feel and do, to teach others how they should think and feel and do, their disciples being the only too-willing victims of their didactic solicitude.

Everywhere there are ditentive differences requiring to be settled—differences between individuals, differences between nations, differences between economic or political groups, differences between one half the world and the other half. And always these differences originate in the 'I'-persona with its dichotomous impasse. As we saw in earlier chapters, this situation is not innocuous nor are its social consequences isolated. The ditentive type of reaction is universal. This all-too-human mode of reaction has its social ramifications throughout the entire system of man's social interchange, whether in clinic, forum, or Senate Chamber; whether in formal academic debate or in the touch-and-go relationships of casual domestic intimacy. Indeed phyloanalytic investigations make clear that this ditentively colored mode or pattern of adaptation is of one piece with subjective reactions which in their more intense form are expressed in the social antagonisms of religious dissension, political conflict, crime and war.

But whether their mood is one of satisfaction or disappointment, the process of attention in the individuals concerned is predominantly occupied with subjective affects. The outline of the problems confronting them is not clear. It has been obscured by subjective feeling-elements that have entered into their relationship to their social congeners. In this way a definite affective impediment stands between them and the objective circumstance to be met. Personal prejudice has superseded orderly thinking. Were the issues not clouded by the presence of affect, the normal process of attention would lead to direct and decisive handling of them. A clear objective course would automatically define itself. But direct action is now precluded. Subjective irritation has replaced efficient purpose. One is like the irate man who, though finally conceded all that he asked for, was by now too overborne by his aggravations to be appeased, and declared that he "would rather be mad!" This is ditention. It is attention that has become affectively conditioned. It is retroceptive or self attention. With this type of attention the direction of the drive or motivation is from periphery to center or from without in, owing to the fact that external circumstances have indirectly stimulated subjective reactions that are wholly irrelevant to the immediate situation.

Most of us know the countless distractions throughout the days that are incident to some passing worry or dissatisfaction, to grievances, true or alleged, to unassuageable anger or apprehension, to a lingering disappointment or regret, and scores of similar mood-vacillations. And if we examine the opposite column of man's dichotomous ledger of emotions, we find again the same hindrances to his interrelational function, and once more the same complemental balance between the characteristics of neurotic and normal. One's image-raptures, one's sentimental dependence, his nostalgic reversions to memories of the past, his sick empathies due to self-identification with the mother-image are equally obstructive and occur no less in the affects and prejudices of the community mind than in the affect-withdrawal of the isolated neurotic patient. The obtrusion of such affect-interludes and the interruption entailed by them are a heavy liability upon a program of work calling for vigor and enthusiasm. No psychiatrist need be reminded of the cumbrous moods of despondency or the correspondingly light and irresponsible waves of elation his patients bring to him—their fears, their dispiritedness, their cynicism and irritability, their unpredictable excitements, the obsessive quality of their love-interests, and all the suspicion, jealousy, hatred and possessiveness with which their sick minds are too commonly beset. Students of behavior are only too frequent a witness to the sentimental broodings, the self-absorbing concerns of such patients, and know too well how these affective reactions contribute to a disorganization of purpose in these personalities.

But these customary instances are trite and inconsequential. They hardly constitute material deserving of scientific evaluation. Obviously in themselves they do not. The interest of our investigations, however, does not center in these trivial community preoccupations, or even in their more violent expressions. Neither does it center primarily in the affects they betray. Our inquiry centers in a neurodynamic mode of behavior that exists throughout the phylum and that underlies these socially impulsive, affecto-symbolic manifestations. It is only the phylic pattern underlying such universally prevalent interactions that raises this social maladaptation to a plane of scientific importance. These more fundamental processes must be considered in detail in subsequent chapters.

After all, our autopathic dreams of the night are but the hangover of our autopathic activities of the day. Man's wishful interests are operative throughout the twenty-four hour cycle. But to say "wishful" is not biological. It is yielding to merely subjective, autopathic habits of interpreting a condition that is itself subjective and autopathic. It is not to see that our waking hours, too, are obsessed by motives that are equally "wishful." It is to describe symptoms in terms of the selfsame symptoms and fail to recognize that in man's social anomalies of function the disorder and the so-called remedy are of one piece. There is the need, therefore, for a more biological—for a more phylobiological approach to the problem of human behavior, if we are to reach an objective understanding of the nature and meaning of human conflict.

When one considers the great importance of the function of attention in mediating between the brain of man and his environment, one would think that investigators of our interrelational behavior and its disorders would long ago have turned to the field of man's attention, that students would have been interested in this preëminently significant function in the domain of man's behavior. But the social interest of these investigators, along with that of the rest of mankind, was already too much engrossed in the partitive preoccupations dictated by the ditentive 'I'-persona to be attracted to the larger problem of man's environmental adaptation as a phylum. In other words, their own affective involvement in their problem precluded their objective envisagement of it. They were too much a party to the situation to permit disinterested attention to direct itself upon their self-attention or ditention.

As man did not become earlier interested in investigating the physiological aspects of attention—as in the course of his mental evolution he was not earlier prompted to study the neural implications of this function in relating his organism to the environment—the priority of his subjective prepossessions regarding attention has now quite impaired his subjective comprehension of this biological function as it operates *within himself*. And so when at last we come to confront the phylobiological implications of attention as it functions within us affectively, there is urgent need that we stress the bias of our own subjective habits of attention and their tendency to befog our own inquiry into it. There is urgent need that we take account of the factor of the 'I'-persona, of our inveterate *amour propre,* of man's universally sophisticated façade or "face," and of the whole constellation of secondary affecto-symbolic formations that now serve as a social mask, derouting the organism's interest from its environment and shunting it back toward the self or subject. Because of ingrained habits of autopathic thinking that are coeval with socially disturbing factors, man's whole trend, as we have seen, is now deflected toward ulterior affect-images of self-interest and security.

Impaired attention is unbalanced behavior, for attention is ourselves in action. It is the physiology of our organisms reacting toward and in response to the physical objects of the outer world. This is the interrelationship between organism and environment which the biologists have called relational physiology or ecology.[9]

But the physiological science of ecology as it applies to man has been seriously neglected by man. This science of the organism's physiological relation to the environment has been neglected because of the subjective precedence that affect-deviations or habits of ditention have assumed over man's behavior. Where it is question of the behavior of man, his thought and feeling is not governed by objectively clear-cut and unbiased mental or symbolic functioning, but is befuddled and distorted by affect-images or ditention. This mental quirk in man's interrelational life is a grave interruption to his healthy interrelational adaptation, and it is perhaps the most important task of man today to overcome the partitive habits that give preference to this ditentive trend. When we have prepared ourselves to shoulder this anthroponomic task, we shall be able to correct an impediment that now markedly impairs the bionomic processes of man and encourages the inharmonious functioning to be seen in our painfully muddled human relations.

One morning years ago at a session of the philosophical seminar at Johns Hopkins, Professor James Mark Baldwin was speaking of the field of mental disorders, and I recall his mentioning the names of Charcot, Janet, Forel and other prominent European psychiatrists. But he said that none of them had as yet "ignited the spark" requisite to bring about an understanding of the basic cause of mental disease. This interested me, and I remember that I then and there recorded the pledge to devote my life's work to the effort to contribute what I could toward igniting this spark necessary to throw light on the nature of abnormal mental conditions. I had just enrolled for my doctor's degree in experimental psychology and I straightway decided that my doctoral thesis would deal with a problem in the field of attention.[10]

So that, when years later it happened that through a combination of fortuitous circumstances I came upon the idea of the social nature of behavior-disturbances and established the method of group-analysis, it was natural that I should have been led to return again to my early field of interest and to investigate anew the function of attention. As the function of attention mediates between the brain and the environment, it seemed to me that this was the field to which one must look for an understanding of man's interrelational behavior and its disorders. For, to examine the function of attention is necessarily to examine an ecological or interrelational process that links the organism to its environment.

It was therefore the interest of our researches in behavior-disorders to adopt a procedure that would recover the organism's basic motivation in relation to the environment. It was our group aim to discover measures for circumventing the habitual element of affect that now attaches to symbolic processes of attention and blocks constructive action. To this end we sought to reinstate a mode of attention and motivation whose direction, being primary, is from center to periphery or from within out. We sought to recover a sense of the basic physiology of man and his primary interest or motivation quite apart from the mental and social images with which man now negotiates his world of outer, symbolic relationships. In short, we undertook to reinstate attention and action arising from the aspect of man's behavior that is motivated by whole feeling.

A paper of mine, written some fifteen years ago, set out with a statement that seems rather pertinent to the trend of the present pages:

In the wide range of experience that relates to the study of human behavior, there is the physiology that one looks at and there is the physiology that one feels. The physiology that one looks at is classically exemplified in the jerk of a frog's leg in response to electrical stimulation, but it is exemplified no less in the response to nervous excitation one witnesses socially in a Wall Street brain panic. The physiology that one sees, whether manifested in the reaction of a single isolated nerve or in the spasmodic response expressed in some collective social excitation, is a condition that lends itself to objective definition. For these objectively seen physiological expressions belong to a category of phenomena that are subject to scientific correlation under a common and consistent phylic principle of reaction. To the objective observer of frogs and men there is no brain state private to man or frog —no biologically detached or esoteric reflex, individual or social. This is the meaning of the objective biological sciences—of the physiology that one may *see*. For in this field, as we know, it is the basis of scientific observation that the phenomena observed pertain all and equally to the phylic whole that unites the individuals of the species upon a principle of behavior that is common and consistent.

With regard, however to the physiology we *feel*—the physiology of love, dependence, sentimentality, admiration, etc., and their opposites anger, fear, hate, jealousy etc.—the attitude of man is not phylic, not objective, not scientific. We do not relate the functional reaction subjectively experienced by the individual to a common generic whole, but, on the contrary, within the physiological feeling of man such reactions are subject to the private interpretation of each individual who reacts. So that as yet the entire field of the physiology you and I feel is, at best, a very vague experience. Our customary approach to it has been and still is only through such symbolic media as art, literature and religion.

Because of the lack of a common and consistent phylic background of inquiry, this absence of a science of man's feeling-life constitutes an impasse to the intelligent functioning of man's life throughout and tends constantly to impair the natural interchange occurring interindividually among us. This is amply demonstrated in the physiology we can see, in such impaired community reactions as exist in the more marked divergences of insanity and crime, not to mention the impaired interactions that characterize man's relationships conjugally, industrially, economically and politically. These objective social reactions to be *seen* are readily classified with reference to a phylic norm. But the crux of the situation lies within the strict domain of the subjective inter-physiological reactions we *feel*. Here there are similarly impaired reactions but here there is as yet no generally accepted acknowledgment of these impaired interactions as they occur subjectively both within the individual and the community. Here at the base of man's biology and of all that which is finally sociological, there is as yet no common and consistent phylic method of observation and study." [11]

Undoubtedly the outstanding factor in the external symptomatology of neurosis is the cleavage between the individual and his environment. Where this anthroponomic relationship is impaired, it is due to a disturbance in the process of attention or in the process that mediates between the individual and his surroundings. With the separation of the individual from his environment the organism's motivation and interest are distorted and confused because the direction of its basic attention is deflected.

If organismic processes underlie and activate the ideas of man, or man's symbolic attention, and if his disorders of attention, or man's ditention, are but the outer reflection of internal physiological deviations, no amount of mental or theoretical rationalizations can adjust these basic physiological disturbances of the soma's behavior in its relation to the environment. *Whether in individual or nation, it is not one's thinking that determines his pattern of reaction, but one's pattern of reaction that determines his thinking*. If in man's symbolic usages he has unknowingly employed affects or deviate feelings instead of feelings that are consistent with his organism's primary relation to the environment and to others, symbolic interpretations are of no avail. These symbolic interpretations with which students of "mental disorders" attempt to account for this basic substitution in man's interrelational life can only further confuse and postpone the solution of man's problem in relation to himself and to the outer world. It is imperative that man recover his inner sense of his disorder—that he somehow get back into the *feel* of the deviate internal stress we find to be the inseparable somatic accompaniment of his superficial affects. Surely, if anywhere, it is here that Goethe's provocative line, "Wenn ihrs nicht fühlt, ihr werdet's nicht erjagen," applies most aptly.

Basically, every organ maintains an internal balance of function within the larger function of the organism as a whole. This physiological balance within the organism is governed by the conditions of the internal environment to which the physiologist, Claude Bernard, first drew attention. It is the principle which Cannon called homeostasis.[12] But phylobiology offers evidence that every organism as a whole, and every species or phyloörganism as a whole, equally maintains its internal balance of function in relation to the external environment.[13] This bionomic balance, however, does not now prevail in the sphere of man's consciousness or attention. Through a *faux pas* in man's conscious development, through an inadvertence in the process of substituting the symbol for the actual object, man's attention was deflected into part-attention or ditention. The result was conflict and discrepancy in the interrelational processes of man. Had man's biological norm of interaction with the environment been maintained within the sphere of his consciousness or attention, the physiological balance or homeostasis within man's anthroponomic processes would have remained intact. But, as I have indicated, the internal balance of man's organism has been interrupted in its conscious rapport with the environment and there has occurred the imbalance in the interrelational function of man we see today in the social neurosis.

The ditentive element constantly present in human interchange was first brought to awareness through our systematic study of social groups or units. As participants in the analysis of social groups, it became necessary for us to discount the influence of the extraneous factor of affect by consistently observing the intrusion of ditention in interindividual reactions. Through this consistent challenge of affectively colored elements, we were led to the increasing recognition of the ditentive process and of the obstacle it forms to the individual's direct and unbiased approach to the environmental object. We saw that it is ditention or the organism's dichotomous motivation that is answerable for the early split in the consciousness of childhood and for the child's subsequent approach to its environment as a separate, autopathic or affecto-symbolic entity.

While our researches are by no means restricted to a particular aspect of human behavior, parents may well consider the factors implicit in this finding of phyloanalysis. The contrast between friendly and unfriendly, between responsive and unresponsive reactions toward people is begotten of the early child-parent relationship of favor or disfavor, praise or blame, as it is passed down from generation to generation and is inculcated in each individual by the mother or by parents generally. This is the community obsession *par excellence* that expresses itself in the moral dichotomy of "right" and "wrong"—a dichotomy which according to man's fond belief represents his free choice of alternatives, but which really embodies in every instance but a response to his early conditioning by external agents. In the mind of the parental generation what is called "right" bears no relation to a determined constant. It possesses no biological foundation. Injunctions based upon this sense of "right" have no regard to the organism's consistent behavior, to its functioning in accordance with the nature of its being. Resting upon a purely moralistic tradition, this sense of "right" is ditentive. It is not the result of observation or inquiry but is arbitrarily transmitted to us in response to a purely autocratic social code. We all learn to behave either at the parental knee or across it.

We are solemnly taught to revere the alternatives "right" and "wrong" as representing "principles," but the sole authority for these principles is traditional habit. They rest upon no firmer support than the fanciful standards of fairy tale and folklore. They are throughout but the product of man's ditentive thinking. Our habitual alternatives of right and wrong represent no tangible, stabilized criterion, but are a criterion bred of man's affective conditioning. Phyloanalysis shows that these moral alternatives are but autopathic symbols and that they are in no sense basic to man's organism. Yet this false dichotomy now forms the hub of our human relations. Its influence radiates throughout the entire body social. This affect-dichotomy is induced in us so early and has become so intimate a part of man's social development that its existence is now wholly unrecognized by him. Indeed, so great is the subjective influence of this dichotomous social reaction that it has become an unconscious part of our social processes and the major determinant of them.

The tendency of parents to block the native spontaneity of children is traceable to this moralistic dichotomy, this factor of ditention. Of course our intention is to give the child our utmost care and interest. But we ourselves, as parents, have already been caught up in the meshes of a moralistic, right-wrong dichotomy that deflects our own attention and blinds us to the real needs of our children. Being unaware of the child's inherent needs, each parent pursues the traditional course that "appears best" to him and, in accord with behavioral traditions, this is no other than the course that "appeared best" to *his* parents. It means that the parent (father or mother), following the line of apostolic succession, inevitably tells the child what *he,* the parent, has been taught to think and feel and do.

Were we free to observe even such a simple and lowly process as the internal motivation of the so-called "wild"animal in its eminently successful approach to its young, we might at least begin to reconsider our own internal motives. But who ever heard of a human being taking lessons from a bird! And so we fail to inculcate in the child a sense of its relation as an organism to its environment but, instead, incite him to depend upon a certain vague authoritarian shibboleth called "right" and presumably personified by the parent.

Naturally, in setting out from so fanciful, so non-objective a premise, it is impossible to be truly united with the child in thought or feeling, no matter how earnestly we may desire to be so. Instead, we inculcate in him an image of ourselves and of the external, vacillating law we call "right," and upon this purely imaginal basis we teach the child to be in love with us and our arbitrary command. We teach him to "love" or to be identified with a mere *image* of dependable law, just as we "love" in him this image with which we seek to identify him in turn. This is not to be thoughtful of the child. This being "in love" with him and having him "in love" with us is not union in any true biological sense. And I use the word "love" in the quite accustomed, if unsuspected, sense in which people use it when they speak of being "crazy about" or "fond" of someone.[14] In all this there is the presence of a transference that is social. We have not recognized this social transference. We have not recognized that it inculcates in the child ditentive habits of dependence upon the parent,[15] and that this dependence inevitably throws the child upon a mere affective image or symbol of authority. Teaching the child what to do and think, or stimulating its behavior by means of the symbol, is necessarily to secure a response that is also only symbolic. This is the social image.[16] This is the impediment to man's health of function and the bane of his "civilization."

This mutual self-admiration pact that rests upon a mere exchange of affect-images automatically displaces the unity and continuity of feeling that primarily identifies the organisms of parent and child. To adopt such a course is to set up an 'I'-persona in place of the child's organism. It is to pit this 'I'-persona of the child against that of the parent. It is to launch him upon a career of imitation and competitiveness, of false dependence and of corresponding resentment. It is to inculcate ditention, dichotomy and conflict. It is to insinuate between parent and child the presence of a socio-symbolic transference that is as insidious as it is sentimental.

Biologically all animals are so constituted that the instinctual parent-factor passes on to the succeeding generation those evolutionary qualities that are favorable to the continuation and development of the species. Undoubtedly there have been "errors" in this selective process. But when we consider that man himself is the product of this integrative evolution, it may be said that the process has in the main been a constructive one. What is important in the over-all picture is that in man as a species there developed the potential capacity for conscious selection. As a phylically conscious organism, the parent would naturally wish to give to the child the benefit of his own experience. He would wish the child to be as consciously selective in organismic adaptation as he himself would be, or even to improve upon his own adaptation. But this does not happen. Unknown to parent or child, something has occurred in man's development to obstruct the organism's conscious adaptation. Though we regard ourselves as thoughtful of the child, as conscious of his need, we are as a matter of fact only divisively conscious—not wholly conscious, as we are accustomed to believe. Instead of consciousness there is self-consciousness;

instead of attention there is ditention. Because of their autopathic complicity in the biased feeling and thinking of children, parents should be included in all group attempts to widen a child's outlooks and surroundings. After all, parents were once human too.

Regardless of its superficial aspects, the underlying transference-pattern is always the same; it always imbues in the child habits of dependence upon a mere *image* of authority—a dichotomous right-wrong image of authority that now prevails throughout the species or phylum. Though there are as many aspects of this social image as there are varying cultures, the dichotomous right-wrong mechanism is identical throughout the species. Again it is to employ the symbol with an autopathic coloring that reflexly diverts its intention into self-interested aims or into unilateral channels. It is to displace the symbol's direct intent with obliquity and ditention. Such is the despotism of the good-bad alternative in human behavior.

Man needs to recognize the tremendous handicap our pseudo-integrity—what we call our "right" or "goodness"—places upon the life of everyone. We all know people who have so much "character" that there is no living in the house with them. This lugubrious sense of "right" applies equally to nations, and in nations it is no less spurious. When we come down to it, we find that our virtues are only the qualities we like to inflict upon other people. Nations are like individuals, they have a high sense of other nations' honor. We shall find that all conflicts, all wars are ultimately traceable to the subtle operation of this little international commodity. And how often we see two people whose cherished "character" is such that, although they have no sympathy or affection for one another, they feel bound to cling together throughout a lifetime because it is "right." The excuse they offer themselves is that they do this for the sake of the children, when in truth nothing could be more disastrous for the developing child than the extremes of partitive tension that mark a divided home.

Of course, with the advent of Freud the tendency has been toward the opposite pole of this affect-dichotomy. In his arbitrary interrelational projections, anyone these days finding himself "unhappily" married cavalierly proceeds to dispose of his consort. This has come to be a conspicuous factor in the treatment of the psychoneuroses in the absence of a more basic reckoning with an imbalance that is internal to the organism. For whether the course adopted is one of enforced "fidelity" or reckless divorce, it is the interrelational fetish of one's "rightness" that decides the issue. As a matter of fact, phylobiology shows that each individual holds this identical *inter*relational position even in respect to himself when, identifying himself with his autopathic preceptors, he permits himself to be held to a code of behavior known socially as "right" and "wrong," and accordingly adopts at one time the "good" course, at another the "bad," depending upon the conditioning compulsion of the stakes offered. He "likes" or he "dislikes," he is elated or depressed, cheerful or despondent, hopeful or discouraged, wanting this and wanting that, being satisfied only to be dissatisfied again, and obsessively seeking solace in the acquisition of more gains, more property, more self-flattery for his partitive mood, when his real need is the healing of a lesion internal to the organism of man as a phylum. In their interrelational dilemma, the participants in an autopathic union are in a bad way. Whether the contracting parties stand by, or take to the road, an interrelational policy necessarily overlooks the organismic need of both parent and child. In either case the effect of a unilateral course is equally detrimental to the offspring of unions that are unilaterally motivated.

We have much to ponder here—many points on which as parents and educators we may profitably question ourselves. It is because people have been taught by others what to think and feel that, like our family-man, they turn to others with complaint and vilification when their inept thinking and feeling gets them into trouble, when they become involved in affects, falter in attention and communication and go to pieces mentally, or when their inability to meet reality causes conflict and gets them socially, politically or economically into hot water. It is commonly recognized that the insane are most violent against their own relatives. And the closer the relationship the greater the violence. As is well known, in the handling even of the milder nervous disorders, patients are better off when removed from their families—from those directly answerable for their ditentive confusion. I once asked the eminent psychiatrist, Adolf Meyer, what in his experience he felt to be the single measure most essential in treating nervous and mental patients. "To place their families under lock and key," he replied dryly.

In man's addiction to a moralistic dichotomy that possesses all the tenacity of a social transference, it is not alone the parent who is blind to the child's needs, nor is it alone the child who subsequently becomes blind in respect to the needs of the parent. Neither is it in families alone that we find a deflection of attention leading to inept habits of feeling and thinking. This same autopathic deflection, these same ditentive habits are equally present in those professional students who are obligated to bring to the problem of human behavior the mature product of their unbiased thought and feeling. For a situation that is world-wide in its scope necessarily includes the professional student as well. Where it is question of a problem that involves man, where it involves the social image or a transference that is social, the professional student too is powerless to observe this social condition from an objective basis. He too is part and parcel of this same constellation we have described as the transference or the social image.[17] And so, unconsciously throwing his objective obligations to the winds, the psychiatrist or any other conventional student of behavior likewise automatically protects this transcendental image he shares with the rest of the community. The truth is, neither layman nor psychiatrist recognizes this universal, this socially systematized transference that has inculcated in us all an habitual dependence upon the social parent as a mere *image* of authority.

To meet the problem of human behavior, therefore, in all its social implications, our procedure in phyloanalysis has included the professional student and the neurotic alike in our attempt to deal with the ditentive reactions of social groups. But, as I have said, these ditentive reactions are perceptible only within the subjective processes of the investigators themselves, and are susceptible of observation only in the immediate moment.[18] Needless to say, our handling of group material is essentially a matter of releasing distorted feelings, or feelings that give notice of an interference in the phyloörganism's harmonious functioning. We do not permit personal affects to hide beneath words, nor do we attempt to expose personal affects merely to give vent to interrelational disharmonies. Affects are brought to book for the purpose of challenging a pattern of behavior that is partitive or ditentive and that artificially replaces the organism's basic homeostasis or its primary process of attention and adaptation to the external world. "Normal" opinions and beliefs, or ideas and convictions based upon what other people have taught us to think and feel and do, play no part whatsoever in our group technique. Personal and social tradition, symbolic or mental preoccupations are excluded. Within the sphere of our interrelational life, or within the sphere of man's symptomatology, the material of observation consists solely of the partitive affect—of an affect that marks an arbitrary and unwarranted discrimination between one individual and another upon a wholly extrinsic and superficial plane and that is irreconcilable with a common biological principle of behavior coördination. Our group process has not been concerned with differentiations between socially approved and socially disapproved behavior, between "right" and "wrong," between neurotic and normal, man and woman, native and alien, between white and Negro, or between people who are "important" and people who are not "important." Nor has it been concerned with any other of the blighting dichotomies with which man is socially beset upon every side. The common denominator recognized by our research unit was not the individual or a collection of individuals, but organismic man—the phylum of man as a whole. Our excavations into human behavior were applied to man's behavioral tensions, to the primary, virgin soil of his organism's physiology.

I can think of no more striking example of man's benighting dichotomies than is offered by students of behavior themselves. I have particularly in mind the position of the psychiatrists who in recent years have adopted a procedure they call group-therapy. The position of such students is important in relation to the problem of ditention and its wide social ramifications. It must not be thought, however, that the influence of deflected attention, or ditention, as it may be observed in these group-therapists, is a condition to which I or my associates are strangers. From the very start of our researches we found ourselves fairly overwhelmed with ditentive habitudes. We found that our ability to direct clear objective attention upon habitual personal and social reactions was constantly impeded by our customary ditentive processes. But with the discovery of ditention as a condition internal to the organism, the observation of these reactions became increasingly simple, and as more and more these ditentive trends were brought to evidence, they were shown to be the very substance of man's neurosis. Since these affect-deflections of attention and interest showed themselves to be the root of man's interrelational disorders, naturally they became the systematic material of our group or phyloörganismic investigations.

Unfortunately in their writings the group-therapists often tend to line up their principles of procedure with what they conceive to be the principles of phylobiology. I do not wish to disparage the work of these students. However non-objective, however devoid of data derived from an acquaintance with the organism's behavioral physiology, their studies will undoubtedly possess academic value from the viewpoint of an interpersonal psychiatry. From this angle they will at least have the merit of indicating what phyloanalysis is *not*. It seems fitting, though, to explain that inasmuch as these psychotherapists have lacked the opportunity to undertake a phyloanalysis of their own ditentive affects and motivations, their accounts can hardly present the method of phyloanalysis as practised by the group of investigators who are the sponsors of it.

A sharp line of distinction should therefore be drawn between the group-analysis of my associates and myself and the procedures of more recent adoption among psychiatrists. These group procedures have all the external semblance of our own, but only the external semblance. As regards internal material and method, the gulf between us is an impassable one. For in our approach to disorders of behavior our interest and attention has centered solely in the phenomenon of ditention as a disordered phylic process; while, on the other hand, our colleagues in group-therapy, as in individual therapy, have centered their interest and attention upon every manifestation of behavior-disorder *except* ditention—the one disturbance which, in our finding, is responsible for all the rest!

As "normal" personalities, therefore, these therapists, as was originally the tendency with ourselves, are constantly under the subjective domination of this inadvertent form of attention. They do not bring this deflection of attention under their objective observation as a physiological impediment to the organism's balanced function. Yet this clear line of demarcation between our work and that of our colleagues is one they have persistently failed to recognize. They will in one breath speak of their procedure and that of our laboratory as though their method were susceptible of alignment with the technique of phyloanalysis. As this very general misconception of our position is needlessly misleading, I am prompted to draw attention to certain erroneous inferences which, in their ditentive interpretations, psychiatrists too commonly make regarding our basic thesis.

In the work of my associates and myself we have attempted to abrogate customary mental or psychiatric interpretations of disorders of behavior, including our own habitual psychiatric methods, and instead have sought to blaze a new trail in the field of human reactions. But too frequently the work of our laboratory has been identified with group measures which are purely mental and with which our researches have nothing in common. It is not seldom included in descriptions of group procedures in which the groups discuss "mental" problems, ideologies and reactions under the guidance and supervision of a psychiatrist whose own ditentive ideology directs these mental meetings. But not even in the very early, immature beginnings of our group investigations, dating as far back as the year 1918, have we encouraged any such mental interchange. Nevertheless our colleagues continue to assume that our work includes such discussions, and that we do not differ from the group-therapists who try to bring their patients to react in a more "mature" and more "normal" manner. With my associates and myself, however, the essential point is precisely that the presumably "mature and normal manner" is the whole trouble; and as for "guidance," any such interference with other people's thinking or feeling or doing is, in the very premise of phyloanalysis, automatically excluded.

One feature of their method cited by group psychiatrists is that patients gain deeper insight because of the presence of others with difficulties like their own. But it has been my experience over many years that nothing more effectually aggravates the blindness of a patient to his own condition than getting into a huddle with other people who are insisting upon the recognition of their right to attention for the same condition.[19] It is the family situation all over again, with its separate 'I'-personæ and their separate "rights." The "group" therapists further claim that the presence of other patients stimulates problems and thoughts in a way that serves to promote successful treatment. There is no question that the presence of other persons has the effect of stimulating "problems" and "thoughts" but, however profitable in these get-together situations —and nowadays the world is surfeited with get-together situations —the problems and the thoughts that are stimulated do not offer the slightest advantage or even meaning in a laboratory of phylobiology.[20]

In order to understand the significance of ditention and our group-method of approach to it, it should be recognized very clearly that the term "group" has never meant for us a conventionally assembled collection of individuals. For us the concept "group" is not an external connotation, but a biological principle. I have at no time thought of groups as a landscape gardener thinks of an arrangement of trees, or an educator, of a class of students.

Biologically, such grouping is purely extrinsic and artificial. No inherent principle binds the individuals composing these arbitrary units. Such groups represent but a fortuitous collection of heterogeneous elements. In my use of the term group, I have had in mind from the outset a biological group and a biological principle of behavior. As I said in one of my early papers:

> We were at once connoting an assemblage of elements that is grouped into one integral whole by reason of an inner organic bond common to the several elements of which it is composed. It is this type of group that unites the elements of the species. In such organic groups the connecting link among them is an essential and instinctive one. It is not one that is separable by any arbitrary or external process of arrangement.

And again:

> Man is not an individual. He is a societal organism. An analysis, whether individual or collective, that is based upon differentiations assumed to rest upon legitimate scientific ground rests in fact upon very transient social artifices and lacks the support of a true biological basis. Man's analysis as an element means his isolation as an element. And his isolation is an essential affront to an organic group principle of consciousness.[21]

It is because of this organismic principle of behavior underlying our researches that in the course of time I discarded the term "group-analysis" in favor of the term "phyloanalysis."

As "normal," psychiatric units must inevitably set out from the partitive basis of the unilateral 'I'-persona with its affects and prejudices, its *amour propre,* its "face" and its inaccessible social system of autopathic thinking, feeling and doing, these conventional therapeutic groups, like normal communities everywhere, can only discuss as collective 'I'-personæ what is "right" thinking and feeling and what is "wrong" thinking and feeling. Lacking recognition of a homeostatic basis of motivation as a phylum, or a basis of motivation that rests upon man's internal balance of reactions, a social collection of 'I'-personæ, like the individual 'I'-persona, can only adopt the dichotomous premise embodied in man's traditional *mores,* and act and counsel action solely from the point of view of current tradition as descended to us from the 'I'-personæ that are our racial antecedents.

Such mental or symbolic ratiocinations do not reach the core of the matter. They represent mere affect-thinking. Man needs to give more consideration to his internal balance and less to the external symptoms of ditention and "face." We will reason rightly only when our feelings rest upon physiological motivations that are rightly centered. With man's ditentive behavior taking precedence everywhere over his clear thinking and feeling, resort to analysis, individual or collective, is futile. "My" affect, and the organism's distorted physiology are phenomena that belong to two separate and distinct categories. Physiological modifications are subject to objective observation, but "my" affect is something that "*I*" will never observe. Backed by the long years of our research battle with the obdurate 'I'-personae that made up our research unit, I feel qualified to say that the individual and the group therapists, if they but knew it, are no different from the healers of old. While presumably analyzing disordered behavior, they are in fact but employing disordered behavior in analyzing the behavior that is disordered!

As the analytic interchange inhering in individual and group procedures is based upon mental precept and cogitation, this analytic interchange rests upon ditentive premises that are not germane to the bionomic situation. This is why such interchange too easily leads students of behavior to the ditentive habit of seeking cover in alien tongues, as in the resort to such surrogates or mental subterfuges as the "id," the "ego," the "super-ego," the "psyche," and similar *quid-pro-quo* recourses. Alien tongues, of course, are all very well in their place. Science could ill afford to dispense with these handy tools. But describing one's behavioral infirmities in Latin or Greek is not a fortunate practice. The difficulty with us all, whether "normal" or neurotic, is not Greek; it is not something rare or exotic. It is one's own partitive persona, and to come to grips with a condition so familiar to us, we will do well to use familiar language in addressing ourselves to it. One's "I" is a far more intimate resident of one's own bosom than this thing remotely referred to as "the ego." But it is only as a broad phyloanalysis succeeds in placing this ditentive persona in proper internal perspective that one brings himself to speak in simple objective terms of this subjective abstraction now emotionally cherished by us all.

From the point of view of a research into the processes responsible for disorders of behavior, there is in principle nothing whatever new about such group-therapies as the psychiatrists have recently adopted. There have, of course, always been the philosophical devotees of the group-method—Socrates, Plato, Aristotle, Spinoza and Kant, among others. In the minds of the religious schools St. Francis Xavier has been for centuries an outstanding group-therapist. Paul, the Apostle, too, had his day; likewise Savonarola, Luther, Calvin, Brigham Young and a host of others. For that matter, with the ringing of the bells for service each Sabbath Day all the world is called to sessions in group-therapy.

The ditentive factor in man's behavior which we consistently brought to light within our own groups, and which obviously exists unobserved in the procedure of the group-therapists, is the sort of thing that exists universally, if entirely casually, throughout the social community of man everywhere. In a sense all social interchange, all communication among individuals that has to do with behavior is a form of group-therapy, that is, therapy based upon the "normal" dichotomies of agreement or disagreement, of favor or disfavor, of praise or blame, of the "rightness" of one individual as over against another. This is why our popular healers have ever made quarry of group therapeusis. It gathers additional safeguards about the partitive, ditentive self. Disseminating a welcome parental suggestion throughout all man's social processes, the ditentive mode or tone offers an enticing guarantee of individual and community welfare. The countless religious fanatics who decoy the unwary "normal" with promises of the abundant life here and a cheerier one hereafter habitually imbue their audience with a sense of lasting security through recourse to just such ditentive appeals. Whether in individuals or in groups, ditention is the backbone of normality.[22] It is the old story of telling other people what they should think and feel and do. This they cannot better accomplish than by trading upon popular gullibility precisely in respect to this matter of the revised life through oratorical precept and admonition. It is characteristic alike of ditentive group procedures, whether ancient or modern, religious or secular, sincere or fraudulent, that they all embody mental, symbolic, external attempts to induce mental, symbolic, external cures. But whatever may be their academic merit, I wish once more to reaffirm that they are no more related to phylobiology than the methods of Charcot or Freud are related to the science of serology.

There can be no societal science in the absence of societal material. One could as well propose a science of chemistry in the absence of the elements that are the material of chemistry. It is the indispensable characteristic of a science that only its material and the unbiased observation of it constitutes decisive authority within the domain of that science. Within the domain of phylobiology it is the physiological function of the organism as a whole, and the observable disorders occurring within that organism, that constitutes the material of decisive authority. The special distinction of phyloanalysis consists in the fact that verbal interchange *per se* has no part in it, that these symbolic expressions are epiphenomena that are implicitly discredited from the viewpoint of the organism's basic motivation. The sole aim of the phyloanalytic technique is to demarcate between habit-reactions that are ditentive or falsely motivated, and habit-reactions that are biologically integrated and organismic. Our inquiries into behavior have to do with internal physiological processes affecting the organism of man as a species. The major proposition that has been the outcome of our researches is that so-called normal personalities and the so-called neurotic are equally ditentive and are equally victims of a conflict and obstruction in their interrelational life, and that this obstruction and conflict is traceable to internal patterns of behavior that are only internally appreciable by physician, patient, and community alike.

What we saw in Chapters I and II as world-wide conflict due to affect and prejudice, what we discussed in Chapter III as mood, we have now traced to ditention or to a deflection in the physiological function of attention. As prejudice is synonymous with ditention, the recognition of this deflection in the physiological function of attention brings us a step nearer to an objective, scientific comprehension of the social phenomena of affect and prejudice, of our good-bad, or right-wrong dichotomies or the dilemma of neurosis. In recognizing this factor of ditention, man is on the way to discarding his interrelational moralities, his affect-images of behavior, along with the prejudices that are their unconscious concomitants. He is on the way to taking conscious reckoning of disturbances within the organism that may be as clearly observed objectively as are conditions that exist external to the organism.

Our researches have shown that partitive attention or ditention, in replacing an organism's total pattern of behavior, results in a disturbance in various functional reactions. The cerebral reactions, in particular, present disfunction because of their constant involvement in the wide sphere of man's interrelational processes—his social contacts and communication. Behavior that is based on ditention or cerebral part-thinking—on compulsive images of "right" and "wrong"—is based on a partitive dichotomy. It is to sin and repent, to grow mentally ill and mentally well, to be inimical and become reconciled, to make laws and to violate them. It is to vacillate between economic inflation and economic depression. It is to implement life through vested interests, political blocs, spheres of influence, secret cartels, international intrigues, partisan alliances, and adopt divisive, autopathic ideologies generally. It is to fight for one's own "rights" and deny these same "rights" to others. It is to advertise far and wide and make a great show of sympathy for the "neediest" once a year with heart-wringing poems and prize-winning pictures, and to devote the rest of the year to the promotion of an economic system that makes the condition of the unclothed, unfed, unhoused and uneducated—of the neediest generally—inevitable. There is no denying that there is occasion aplenty for heartbreak in this partitive and unhappy world. One individual alone left naked and hungry would be ground enough for a whole community's grief. But my point is that we who do the grieving are those who make the whole occasion for the grief. This same fallacy of attention, this same persistent error of mental refraction, we see expressed over and over again on the part of everyone, but in it all no one suspects the obsessive dichotomy, the habitual ditention beneath which mankind is pinioned.

Over and over again we see this dichotomy in the individual called "normal" and in the individual called "neurotic." It is extraordinary to what extent ditentive people will persist in bringing illness upon themselves and then have a wonderful time getting the doctor in to set them aright once more. It is like a patient who is under compulsion to cut his finger repeatedly, and repeatedly to apply a healing lotion to it. In his compulsive obsession a man will drink to excess, bite his nails or incur ulcers of the stomach, and then turn about and apply various remedies to these various ills. Barring this universally compulsive dichotomy in feeling and thinking, how much more intelligent it would be not to cut one's finger or bite one's nails or cherish habits that can only bring on gastric ulcers. In their uncontrollable dichotomy these victims get precisely nowhere. They are in no better pass than today's emissaries of peace. These emissaries can talk peace, but they cannot make it. They remind one of the religious-minded who cry that the remedy for war is to return to God, quite forgetting that it was precisely from "God" that we set out when we went to war. Surely this is not the God to return to. The trouble is that in men's purely symbolic concept of "God," in their sense of a mere shifting and dichotomous *symbol* of the consistent principle of unity governing the world of phenomena, they have no basic, organismic sense of the reality of this principle. In the affecto-symbolic or ditentive dissociation of "normal" and "neurotic" alike, they are unable to recognize what, in truth, this principle is, or where it may be found. This dichotomous inconsistency is only too graphically illustrated in the spectacle of armies going forth for the purpose of maiming or killing one another and at the same time taking along with them a host of doctors and nurses and stores of penicillin to insure recovery following the assault! How much simpler it would be to remain home in the first place. But no; man cannot. He is under the compulsive drive of a too-powerful inner dichotomy.

As long as men prefer ditention and the personal affect to an inclusive process of attention—as long as they prefer a partitive system of feeling and thinking to man's organismic unity of behavior as a phylum—the poor and needy will be always with us, and incidentally their dichotomous complement, the rich. And speaking of the rich, the absurd lengths to which this opposite pole of man's economic dichotomy carries them are simply not to be measured. If the following is not an expression of ditention, I don't know ditention when I see it.

Mrs. Quadruple X, who was at the Pierre, sailed yesterday on the *Queen Mary*. At Cherbourg, France, she will board her yacht, the *Arethusa*, and with a party of friends will sail for the Florida coast planning to arrive there about Christmas. Later they will visit Honolulu and South America. In the Spring they will go to her villa at Marrakesh, Morocco. She will return to pass the summer at Newport, R.I.

This gem culled some time ago from the social notes of a current periodical was not intended as a joke. It was published as a serious item of news. But this glamorous epic only *seems* a more extravagant program of self-entertainment than may be found on every hand. There are no end of people whose chief problem in life is trying to make week-ends meet. Once more, though, let us not be too superior and look disdainfully at these expressions of unbalanced behavior. It is the social neurosis—a neurosis that is really not alien to you, Reader, or to me. All that is required in us both, as in everyone, is sufficient social stimulus to induce an expression of just such spectacular antics. Give us a yacht, some bags of money, and a few villas, and we are all Quadruple X's. It is the 'I'-persona. It is ditention. It is "face," or the repercussive image of the self. It is autopathic feeling and thinking and doing as an autopathic society has taught us to feel and think and do.

Whoever handles money for money's sake handles affect. Until we have recognized this fact—until we have recognized man's mass affect, there can be no resolution of his economic problems. Originally money may well have been part of the total environmental situation. It may well have stood to man as but the earnest of his susbsistence and security, and have been as little associated with affect as the seed the birds gather for food. The seeds they gather are not gathered partitively. They are not associated with a sense of "right," for they do not belong to any one bird. With us today money is always for "me." Today, wherever there is money there is ditention and affect. Having been taken over by the 'I'-persona, the use of money is now entirely separated from its early interrelational function. But man's adjustment has not to do with money or with any of the symbols of behavior. It has to do with the systematization of affects that constitutes his partitive identity or 'I'-persona. The problem of man's distorted attention is a serious one. It is the most serious problem that has yet faced man, and in it is included the whole gamut of man's behavioral problems, not excepting the problem of world coördination and peace.

Our books, our periodicals and our newspapers are just so many autopathic, ditentive 'I'-personae, each out-thundering the authoritarian pronunciamentos of the other. For each has its religious, its social, its economic, its political affects and prejudices. And woe to the individual or community that does not subscribe to these religious or political beliefs, these social creeds, these racial dogmas as propounded by this or that particular organ. As with individual, group or nation, the process of attention exemplified in these literary sheets has become dislocated. Their direction of feeling and thinking has become deflected. They have adopted an esoteric dichotomy of "right" and "wrong" in substitution for the organism's inherent law of action and reaction. So that in relation to the social world and to the behavior of man as a species, our "normal" literature represents a mere ditentive impersonation of a principle of law and order—the organismic principle of homeostasis governing the biological world of phenomena. The authoritarian 'I'-persona, with its arbitrary dogma of "right" and "wrong," is thus but a retroactive, repercussive, predatory innovation that offers a mere travesty of the organism's inherent balance of attention and coördination.

From the point of view of an organismic stability and balance of health we are, as individuals and as groups, a dreary lot. We lack the even keel of balanced attention in respect to one another and to our surroundings, and in our human relationships flounder and falter at every turn. Because our attention is engrossed solely in the asset or advantage to be gained by *me*—"me," the autopathic, unilateral 'I'-persona—it is inevitable that "I," as the twin of "me," am unable to reckon with this deflective attention within my own organism. Man must come to see the over-all clinical picture and the under-all lesion that phylobiology, as a science of behavior, takes cognizance of. This is no time for picayune, affective thinking and feeling according as some picayune and affective community dictates. If our symptomatology is universal, the underlying condition is universal also. There is no one individual, no one group, nor is there any aggregate of individuals or groups to be held answerable for their behavior. The disorder is common. Educators, religious leaders, philosophers, statesmen, writers and, above all, psychiatrists who as professional specialists presume to heal the disordered personality of all comers, are equally victims of this common disorder. When the condition will be seen as a disturbance affecting the pattern of attention in man throughout, we shall have come to recognize the true implications of the bionomic function of attention in relating man to his environment.

As has been said, the whole trouble goes back to the habit of giving precedence to thinking as a determinant of the phylo-organism's basic pattern of behavior, when in fact it is the phylo-organism's basic pattern of behavior that is the determinant of man's thinking—of all his processes of whatsoever sort. The personality that is congenitally late cannot by taking thought give the slightest impetus to a program of greater promptness. He cannot add one cubit to his stature as a balanced organism. Because affect is linked with and fetters his attention, he will be late over and over again, and over and over again he will be "so sorry." In the larger reckoning of the mass expression of this fatal dichotomy man goes to war again and again, and again and again he too is so sorry. That is, he is so sorry until the next occasion of his being late, or of his going to war.

Our thesis demands the recognition within man of the presence of a balance of function or a principle of homeostasis that is as essential to the healthy interrelational functioning of individual and community as is the healthy balance of function or the homeostasis of the organs of the individual in their relation to one another. According to our investigations, it is ditention or the interruption of this balanced function in relation to the environment, and of men to one another throughout the species, that is the cause of the phenomena we have subsumed under the term phylopathology—phenomena which psychiatry mistakenly restricts to a special group it calls the mentally disturbed or psychoneurotic. It is, therefore, the task of phyloanalysis to make evident this impediment in the function of man's attention, to restore the natural course of the organism's motivation from within out and to bring about such adjustments as will reëstablish man's primary coordination of function or the organismic homeostasis of man as a species or phylum.

NOTES

[1] The phrase *organism-environment* relationship seems a bit awkward, so that I propose the adoption of the handier term *ecosomatic* relationship (ὄίκος = environment, σῶμα = organism) in discussing the broader aspects of man's bionomic adaptation. In this connection the reader may recall Haeckel's use of the term "relational physiology." (See Haeckel, Ernst, *Generelle Morphologie der Organismen*, Berlin, Georg Reimer, 1866, Vol. 1, p. 238.)

[2] Max Wertheimer and other proponents of the Gestalt theory have emphasized the need of understanding configurational laws in the perception and behavior of living organisms as well as in the field of external phenomena. The individual event is an integral part of the larger whole, and a partial, discrete view of it gives a distorted picture of reality. (See Wertheimer, Max, *Über Gestalttheorie*, Erlangen, Im Weltkreis-Verlag, 1925, p. 60.)

Researches in phylopathology make evident that in man's interrelationally conditioned life the sovereignty of the whole has been discarded and that this has resulted in a distorted interpretation of the component parts. As this partitive misconception is habitually active throughout man's affect-life, we are faced with a world-wide interrelational disorder.

[3] Burrow, Trigant, *The Structure of Insanity*, pp. 27-8.

[4] Burrow, Trigant, *The Biology of Human Conflict*, pp. 115-16.

[5] See note 5, page 199.

[6] Burrow, Trigant, "Neurosis and War: A Problem in Human Behavior," *The Journal of Psychology*, 1941, Vol. 12, pp. 235-49.

———, "The Neurodynamics of Behavior. A Phylobiological Foreword," *Philosophy of Science*, 1943, Vol. 10, pp. 271-88.

[7] Burrow, Trigant, *The Structure of Insanity*.

———, *The Biology of Human Conflict*.

[8] Spencer, Herbert, *First Principles*, New York and London, D. Appleton & Co., 1910, p. 108.

[9] "All the various relations of animals and plants, to one another and to the

outer world, with which the Œkology of organisms has to do, and especially such interesting phenomena as those of parasitism, of family life, of the care of young, and of socialism,—all admit of simple and natural explanation only by the Doctrine of Adaptation and Heredity." Haeckel, Ernst, *The Evolution of Man,* New York, D. Appleton & Co., 1897, Vol. I, p. 114. See also Burrow, Trigant, *The Biology of Human Conflict,* note 3, p. 273.

[10] Burrow, Trigant, "The Determination of the Position of a Momentary Impression in the Temporal Course of a Moving Visual Impression," (Doctoral Thesis), *The Johns Hopkins Studies in Philosophy and Psychology,* No. 3, *Psychological Monographs,* 1909, Vol. XI, pp. 1-63.

[11] Burrow, Trigant, "Physiological Behavior Reactions in the Individual and the Community—A Study in Phyloanalysis," *Psyche* (London), 1930, Vol. XI, pp. 67-81. (See pp. 67-8.) With a few minor revisions this paper was recently republished in *Etc.*, 1946, Vol. III, pp. 265-278, under the title, "Phylobiology: Physiological Behavior Reactions in the Individual and the Community." (See pp. 266-7.)

[12] Bernard, Claude, *An Introduction to the Study of Experimental Medicine,* translated by Henry Copley Greene, New York, The Macmillan Company, 1927, pp. 63-5, 98-9, 118-22.

Cannon, Walter B., *The Wisdom of the Body,* New York, W. W. Norton & Co., 1932, pp. xv + 312.

[13] For a discussion of homeostasis in its phyloörganismic implications, see Burrow, Trigant, "Neurosis and War: A Problem in Human Behavior," *The Journal of Psychology,* 1941, Vol. 12, pp. 237-8, 247-8.

———, "The Neurodynamics of Behavior. A Phylobiological Foreword," *Philosophy of Science,* 1943, Vol. 10, p. 273,

Burrow Trigant, and Galt, William E., "Electroencephalographic Recordings of Varying Aspects of Attention in Relation to Behavior," *The Journal of General Psychology,* 1945, Vol. 32, p. 273.

Galt, William E., "The Male-Female Dichotomy in Human Behavior—A Phylobiological Evaluation," *Psychiatry,* 1943, Vol. 6, pp. 12-13.

[14] *Fond* has also the meaning of "crazy about"—ME *fonned,* past participle of *fonnen,* to be foolish.

[15] Note the etymological relationship between the words *parent* and *apparent* or *appear* in the sense of seeming. *Apparent* is from L. *apparēre, adparēre,* < *ad,* to + *parēre,* appear, to be apparent, and *parent* is from the secondary form of *parēre,* to produce, to beget.

[16] See note 7, page 155.

[17] See note 7, page 178.

[18] See pages 148-49, 198.

[19] See note 3, page 178.

[20] Syz, Hans, "Phylopathology," *Encyclopedia of Psychology,* edited by Philip L. Harriman, New York, Philosophical Library, 1946, pp. 519-22.

[21] Burrow, Trigant, "The Group Method of Analysis," *The Psychoanalytic Review,* 1927, Vol. XIV, pp. 269, 280.

[22] See pages 180-84, 195-96.

CHAPTER V

THE GENESIS OF MAN'S DISSOCIATION

It will be well to consider briefly what may be called the paleontology of behavior and of human consciousness. After all, it is only in the early generic implications of the 'I'-persona with its systematization of affects that we may attain an adequate phylobiological sense of its social significance. No biologist studying a structure or process immediately before him would fail to take account of the evolution of this structure or process, of its original morphology and function. It is no less essential that the phylobiologist take account of the functional morphology that lies at the back of man's interrelational life and that is coeval with the evolution of his consciousness.

All processes are governed by laws that are intrinsic to them. Animal organisms react to their environment in accordance with these inherent laws. This basic response preserves an organism's interactive consistency. With the acquisition by man of the symbolic faculty, or of knowledge—with his acquirement of a secondary, mental plane of reactions—man was still subject to this same law of the organism.[1] For with the intelligent use of the symbolic or semiotic capacity there was the increasing submission of man's senses to the consistent interactions of the objects and conditions in the world about him—to its dependable order and sequences. This is man's subordination to objectively observable data.[2] Man's consistent relation to the outer world came about through the agreement of his own sequence of sense-reactions with the sequence of reactions existing outside him. This is the external constant. Only man's neural conformity to the observable consistency of external phenomena has made possible the intelligent consistency of his own behavior in respect to the outer world. Only the unvarying correspondence between external stimulus and internal response has established the law or *nomen,* as I have called it, that determines the validity of man's mental reactions.

This consistency gives authenticity to the symbol. This is what the indices of science are. It is the meaning of scientific law and of *nomen*clature. The nomenclature of a science consists of a systematized body of symbols or indices that mean what they say. It consists of symbols and meanings that have back of them a dependable body of experimentally controlled data. The data obtained through such a system of symbols express man's neural reaction to the objects and processes for which these symbols stand. Heat and cold, gases and solids, solubility and insolubility, electrons and protons are states of matter to which the senses of man maintain a consistent relation because of the consistency with which man's senses respond to these environmental manifestations. This organismic consistency embodies a principle of reaction that insures the organism's unity of behavior. In this organismic generalization there is contained the sovereign principle upon which all scientific knowledge rests.

But in man's early use of the symbol his mental reactions were not always in accord with the manifestations occurring in the external world. Man did not always adhere to the consistent relation between his senses and the outer object. In the distortions of his early mental perspectives he "believed" the sun to be "God." The shadows that lay upon the hills or on the sea he took to be "spirits," friendly or menacing. Man did not reckon with the physical law or nomen that accounted for the violent repercussions accompanying an electrical storm. To him, the thunder was the anger of God. Principles of astronomy and meteorology were as yet unknown to him. The scientific laws of chemistry and physics were a closed book. Nowhere had the nomen established its anchor of validity within the newly acquired sphere of man's symbolic behavior in its response to the external universe.

This was of course inevitable. For the development of consciousness through the medium of the symbol was beset with many obstacles to man's clear thinking and feeling. As we know, the evolution of man's organism traces back to a very low form of life. It is not different with the evolution of his mind. Man's symbolic mind undoubtedly originated in psychosis. The birth of man's self-conscious thought was coeval with affect, superstition and prejudice, that is, with pre-judgment and the wish. This explains man's ready regression to mental disorder or psychosis. While the names of objects and conditions in the immediate environment came easily and with more or less precision—the words for shelter, food, water, and for implements—the names of such mysterious phenomena as rain, the running brook, the vast ocean, the immensity of the snow-capped mountain and of the moonlit heavens presented difficulty. This difficulty lay not so much in the naming of objects as in the inescapable tendency, in face of the incomprehensible, to personify, to deify or add to the symbol, to the name, a quality or attribute not inherent in it. The major pitfall lay in the circumstance that man could not employ the symbol in his relation to the objects of his environment without employing it also in his relation to others of his kind. And if, through the projective faculty of naming or of his use of the symbol, man could call the sun "God" and thus isolate it from its true relations, so in his symbolic attitude toward those of his own kind he had of necessity to isolate them and set them opposite him. That is, the tendency to add to the symbol a quality or attribute not inherent in it applies also to man's symbolic or mental attitude toward others of his own species. The recognition of this inescapable pitfall in man's mental outlook is important, for the same organismic consistency that gives warrant to man's scientific knowledge of outer objects and conditions is demanded of the relation of men to one another.

And so, as more and more man took over the sign or spoken word in substitution for the reaction of his organism as a whole, as more and more he adopted a secondary, mental plane in place of his primary, organismic plane of behavior, the extraneous and deviate factor of affect began to enter in, and man inadvertently lost touch with the hard and fast impact of outer actuality. As the symbolic function came to dominate man's processes, there was no longer the sure touch of objective solidarity, but only the symbolic authority of this or that autopathic or partitive reaction, of man's recently acquired ditentive or affecto-symbolic code. The "face" or the fore-end of the organism began to take on more and more the function of a socially vicarious mask or persona.[3] With the replacement of man's primary, orthopathic behavior by a purely affecto-symbolic, autopathic mechanism, man's organism was seriously thrown out of balance in its relation to the environment.[4] With the interposition of autopathic behavior or ditention there occurred a fundamental dislocation within man's interrelational function or within the ecology of his organism as a species. As regards man's behavior-motivation there was not now the consistent correlation between the response of his sense organs and the object or stimulus external to them.

Phylobiological investigations indicate that this interruption to the consistent reactions of man has influenced his entire symbolic behavior as a species. It has set up a barrier to man's consistent reactions to the outer world. While this barrier did not result directly from the acquisition of the symbolic function, it was incidental to it. As I have said, this disturbed reaction is social and is to be traced to a peculiarly insidious image that unconsciously colors man's mental processes through the inadvertent intrusion of affect. But there is evidence that this social image with which man's interrelational life has become invested is tied up with early anthropomorphic strains, that it is linked with intimations of the supernatural. For the sake of convenience I have given to this superstitious factor in man's behavior the specific name of *numen*, a word that means "divine will" and that implies the presence of some mystical, non-objective immanence governing man's behavior.[5] We shall trace in the paleontology of the numen the mental pathology we have recognized in the ditentive phenomenon of the social 'I'-persona and its unilateral affectivity.

Because of its radically distorted feeling-tone, this insidious numen that characterizes the symbolic persona has given a false color to the sense of self expressed socially as "I," "me" or "mine." In its superstitious dissociation this cherished numen, individual and social, disavows the organism's primary basis of motivation— its basic principle of behavior in relation to the environment— and, instead, assumes a secondary, mental self-impersonation that is esoteric and without biological warrant.[6] By virtue of the artificial mental prerogative of this secondarily improvised social numen, the 'I'-persona came to regard itself as something hallowed, as something set apart and sacrosanct. From its affective, partitive pinnacle this numinal immanence that now pervades man's processes has become socially untouchable. Yet the existence socially of this fond illusion has been all the while wholly unsuspected by us. Indeed so unsuspected is it that this inflated self-image now everywhere exercises complete supremacy over the interrelational processes of man.

The casual employment of the numen may be seen in the habitual intonation accompanying such early nursery admonitions as "Mother said *'no,'*" the implication being that "mother" is some manner of rare, transcendent spirit, a being not of this earth. Usually the ultimatum is bolstered by a look of relentless finality as devastating as it is prolonged. In this connection the reader will recall how, according to legend, Columbus consciously invoked the numen for his own practical purposes when, in anticipation of a lunar eclipse, he affected to possess supernatural powers and by threatening to extinguish the light of the moon effectually coerced the Indians to his will. Columbus was canny. Knowing the superstitions of primitive communities, he was adroitly trafficking with their ditentive susceptibilites.

Having fashioned an esoteric image of himself, it was not difficult for man arbitrarily to fashion the esoteric wonder-image he called God. Through this ventriloquy of the affecto-symbolic function there was begotten the phylic illusion of anthropomorphism. This early anthropomorphic or, more correctly, automorphic mechanism established an affective kinship between man's image of himself and his image of God. If the God of day and night, of the thunder and lightning was wonderful, so thought man, was he himself wonderful in having created God in his own likeness. In his esoteric distortion of interrelational values, man effected an autopathic ("unconscious") transference toward the all-powerful image he called God, and in his numinal transference, man and God became really one. The next step was simple. Automatically man now proceeded to establish arbitrarily the mutual interests of these complemental images upon a reciprocal basis. Deprived of a sense of his organism's dependable reciprocity in relation to the environment, man had no other recourse than to seek compensation in this purely artificial image-dichotomy. Having lost contact with the principle of harmonious interaction between his organism and the environment, he was compelled to atone the loss of his organism's primary balance through the vicarious security he conjured in the mere symbol of a benign and all-embracing Father-protector. It is by virtue of this numinal dichotomy and the contradictory basis of feeling and thinking implicit in it that in one and the same breath one may with entire complacency "praise the Lord and pass the ammunition."

Through this handy process man was no longer subservient to the fixed nomen governing all dependable experience. The power that makes for harmony and order in the universe of matter and energy had now become something quite alien to him. The basic organism of man was no longer an expression of this universal motivation, but a thing apart and subject to the private will of each and every man. Now that a whimsical numen or false image of authority had replaced the authority that resides in the consistent correspondence between man's senses and the external world, his interrelational continuity was interrupted and his organism was no longer bound by a consistent law of behavior. The omniscient and omnipotent principle or nomen that resides within man and that governs his relationship to the environment lacked the organismic support of conscious correlation. Henceforward man could believe as his fancy dictated, not as his senses ordained.[7] Such is the autopathic dictatorship of the numen over the social processes of man.

Here was impediment, with its inevitable repercussion and introversion. Here was first incurred man's compensatory neurosis—the obsessive compulsion of labor and toil, the relentless dichotomy of "right" and "wrong." Here was exacted of man the awful toll of self-division, of the ulterior aim, of partitive retrofection. This divisive element has played havoc with the folk mind. Throughout the chronological descent of our various cultures theologians and metaphysicians have called it by different names—the Devil, the Bad Angel, the Evil Genius or the Unconscious. Through this impediment in the basic feeling of man, man unwittingly tricked himself into a mere charade of behavior. Henceforth there was only pretense of feeling, or an affective replacement of the organism's motivation and interest. Man had succumbed to the lure of the social image, with its *self* reflections, its *amour propre*, its false personal identity. In the introversion of his sick empathy—in his *auto*-empathy—man saw only the falsely begotten *image* of himself—an image in which his whole world was transmuted into mere affect or into autopathic thinking.

This psychic transformation, this sleight-of-head magic, man wrought within himself through his false use of the symbol. But this device of man's symbolic ingenuity recoiled upon man himself and henceforward he could only seek to explain with more symbols his own disordered state of mentation. In the semiotic systematizations of pseudo-religion, philosophy and metaphysics, man could only employ further elaborations of the symbol in attempting to explain himself to himself.[8]

This was man's fall. This was his entrance into sin and transgression—into *original* sin and the numen.[9] For man had sullied the original springs, the organismic principle of his very own identity. But it is not true, as the pseudo-religionists would have us believe, that man's trespass is irretrievable, that the earth is cursed in his name. If, repudiating the false Gods born of autopathic images, man returns to the primary source of his defection; if, regardless of his own habitual wishes, man applies to man a scientific principle of behavior, the secret of his own secretive infoldment and introversion will appear to him in as clear and objective perspective as the once mysterious sources of infective disorders appeared to the bacteriologists only a few decades ago.

With the interruption of man's organic fidelity to external stimuli, with the accession of the partitive, autopathic persona and the intrusion of private affects upon the organism's symbolic function, man sustained a biological trauma of incalculable severity. Through this phylic trauma his primary behavior in relation to the environment—his orthopathic feeling and thinking—was artificially shifted to a level of response that was purely autopathic and fictitious. Substituting for the world of objective reality a superstitious, numinal interpretation of the phenomenal world, man unconsciously abrogated the law or nomen that governs his primary interrelational behavior. Under the sponsorship of a whimsical social image, or numen, there was no longer the consistent correlation of man's senses with external phenomena. There was no longer the external constant. From now on man's world came to be tinged with fanciful attributes of his own making, with affective intimations and discolorings wholly alien to the objective circumstance, so that henceforth man's behavior was exempt from the inexorable control of organismic law. He was now enveloped in a *social neurosis* with its manifold behavior aberrations.[10] In the interpretation of phylopathology this anthropomorphic mechanism, this early fantasy-system, represents the biological origin of the clinical deviations in the individual long known symbolically to psychiatry as persecution mania, ideas of reference, delusions of grandeur and related psychopathic manifestations.

The numen is the factor that has for centuries operated unconsciously throughout the arts of mental healing. The numen with its artificial projection of the father-image is indeed the very mainspring of methods of therapy based upon interpersonal projections. Freud, of course, was the first to give this factor of the parental image explicit recognition, and under the name of "the transference" he presumably raised it to the level of a conscious therapeutic technique. "No transference," said Freud, "no psychoanalysis." But Freud failed to reckon with the phylic implications of the numen because he failed to reckon with the social images or the numen in the community around him. Freud failed to reckon with this unconscious behavioral numen as a deviate phylic process, because he was unable to reckon with the numen that colored and fashioned his own ditentive or autopathic persona. And psychiatry, in its transference to Freud, has religiously failed to recognize it along with him. The result is that this factor of the numen as it operates in the physician-patient relationship remains still an unrecognized impediment in psychiatric procedure.

As I remarked some years ago, the transference or the social image is not a sporadic phenomenon.[11] It is by no means limited to particular personalities. It is the early and persistent prepossession of every individual living under the sway of our present social system, and the autopathic mechanism of the transference so essential to the technique of psychoanalysis has not been raised to the level of a conscious program of healing after all. Like the rest of individuals and communities, psychiatrists, too, still labor under the yoke of this prevalent affect-impediment as it exists within themselves and within the larger social community. As yet the psychopathologist does not see that the inconsistencies of the individual patient stem from a phylic inconsistency that characterizes equally the social mind of man. Within the limited scope of the numinal outlook it could not be otherwise. The psychopathologist constantly witnesses inconsistency and vacillation in the attention and adaptation of his patients, but he can get no further. Being blocked in his own ditentive perspectives, his observations achieve nothing more than a catalogue of personal symptoms.

Had Freud had the opportunity to recognize through phyloanalysis the social implications of his own autopathic images, of his own transference, and had he seen this socially esoteric superstition or numen as symptomatic of a social neurosis, he would have found no difficulty in recognizing interindividual conflict as the phylic disorder that it is.[12] Man's neurosis is man's stumbling-block. If we cannot understand the conflict that exists interindividually and among nations, neither can we understand the conflict that exists in the neurotic personality. But unless we understand the conflict that is recognizable within our own neurodynamic processes, we cannot understand the conflict of either the nation or the neurotic. Just as the psychoneurotic construes his socio-symbolic affects as real in the absence of a phyloanalysis, in the same way the so-called normal community construes its sociosymbolic affects as real in the absence of a phyloanalysis. It was Freud's limitation in respect to human behavior and its disorders that he remained aloof from a neurosis that affects man as a species. This limitation is one in which Freud does not lack company today both among psychopathologists and within the pseudonormal community generally.

But we have to take off our hats to the psychoanalysts when it comes to the treatment of the *symptoms* of behavior-imbalance. They do go after the crucial symptoms, namely, the symptoms expressed in emotional conflict. If psychoanalysis cannot cure the actual disease, at least it succeeds in keeping the fever down, and this is certainly more than can be said of other psychic ointments. But while the psychoanalyst keeps the libidinous temperature under control, he does so only by restoring the patient to the dubious level of the social behavior-average represented by the community's pseudo-normality. The process, however, does meet the great desideratum; it does fit the patient into the great symptomatic cure-all of "normality." It does satisfy the popular estimate of health based upon the autopathic 'I'-persona with its currently prevailing social system.

We shall not tackle the problem of human dissociation with its ditentive aberrations ("wish-fulfilments") as long as we confine our inquiries to states of isolated mentation and withdrawal, to the fantasies occurring in the dreams of sleep, to the dissociations of schizophrenia, hysteria, and of psychoneurotic processes generally. It is necessary that we include expressions of deviation in their social manifestation. It is necessary that we discover in the historical records of language, in the processes of politics and economics, as well as in the conventional interests of our daily human interchange, the ever-present earmarks of neurosis and disorganization. We little recognize the dictatorial influence of the fatherimage in our current social relationships. We little suspect the presence of this numinal or authoritarian impersonation within our own psychiatric ranks. We have yet to see the extent to which the pseudo-authority of this ditentive or so-called wishful image obstructs all possibility of an objective inquiry into the behavior of man as a species. Under its blind impositions we fail equally to realize that the underlying processes of democracy, depending as they do upon the "votes" of the people, are again a wishful form of government or patriarchal jurisdiction—that in the etymology of the word *vote* and the word *wish,* for example, there is betrayed a common phylobiological origin.[13] In our dissociated *naïveté* we proceed upon the day's activities with competitive "avidity," and in the absence of phylobiological sources we do not sense that the motivation that is marked by *avidity*[14] is again the motivation that is marked by ditention and the wish. Owing to the habitual decoys of our traditional social numina we have not begun to be aware of the degree to which our own processes are shot through with the sick lures of unreality.

It was the recognition of this same ditentive or numinal limitation in my own outlook upon the problem of the neuroses that led me to question my whole psychoanalytic or individualistic approach to my clinical work. The upshot of the inquiry upon which I entered was the development of the group-method of analysis.[15] It was with a view to uncovering, if possible, the primary elements in the motivation of human behavior that I organized the bio-social experiment which I first called group-analysis. Under the conditions of this social set-up my associates and I sought to question not only the personal and social activation of those of our group-units recognized as neurotic, but to question also the prevailing activation of those of us commonly regarded as normal.

Our preliminary purpose was to lay bare as far as possible the primary elements entering into the behavior of ourselves, as individuals and as groups, quite in defiance of habitual *mores* or the traditional affects and prejudices with which we found ourselves shackled, but which we now recognized as the common heritage of us all. In this social process our effort was directed toward divorcing ourselves from the medium of habituations that now constitutes the basis of man's personal orientation and security—from our socialized opinions, judgments, moralisms, dependencies and beliefs. Repudiating the dictates of apostolic descent in favor of objective demonstration, disavowing the transference in favor of coöperation, we challenged among us the entire system of ditention now thwarting man's interrelational life. Need I say that this consistent questioning of our inter-affective relationships entailed a condition of personal and social frustration whose scope and intensity one can only dimly imagine.

As a social individual, constituting in my separate 'I'-persona a supreme entity, *my* opinion and *my* wish is, of course, supreme. But John and Mary are also social beings and equally supreme in their affectively encapsulated 'I'-personae. They and everyone else are as "right" in their private absolutism and autocracy as I am in mine. The result is that there can be among us only social conflict and disparity with its various recourses to external amenity and disguise. Lacking the motivation or behavior that is physiologically continuous, having substituted the premise that the organism's motivation rests upon a basis that is private and dichotomous, our reactions can only be private and dichotomous also. We may only *deal with* one another; we may not be *united as* one another. If there is conviviality and accord, it is not because of a phylic union between the organisms involved, but because momentarily the self-interest of each of us happens to correspond in its outward form. Beneath this outer covering of social suavity there is inner conflict, and this hidden conflict entails a constant attitude of diplomacy. It entails a studied concealment of the ulterior aim lying beneath a relationship that rests upon two secretly opposed directions of self-interest.[16] This is man's affecto-symbolic pain—a pain which, however bitter, he now holds sweeter than life and is, therefore, disinclined to recognize or acknowledge.

It may be said that in its subjective implications our experimental frustration of the affect may be compared with the objective induction of pain which the physiologist, Henry Head, experimentally imposed upon himself.[17] While our group purpose was not primarily, or indeed secondarily, the induction of distress or pain, it was definitely our purpose to intercept whatever deflections of feeling—no matter how pleasant or habitual—evidenced themselves in personal and social affect, in customarily autopathic feeling and thinking, or in ditention. This process necessarily entailed marked mental and emotional discomfort. Such a reaction, however, was but an experimental by-product of our group procedure. I stress the quite devastating character of this frustration we consciously brought upon ourselves, because of its direct bearing upon the phylobiological phenomenon I am about to describe.

First, though, it should be understood that in our work in group- or phylo-analysis there was no definitely preconceived goal or plan of adjustment on the part of the individuals participating in it. Our procedure held consistently to an experimental basis. There was, of course, the ultimate objective of securing a foundation of healthy social relations. For there was only too evident the persistent presence of disabling affects and prejudices and the automatic tendency throughout all the groups to protect and defend to the death these besetting emotions. In their habitual autocracy the participants were without exception completely rigid in their defense of the 'I'-persona. In their tenseness and sensitivity to criticism these champions of the "normal" or partitive mode knew no bounds. Their self-defensive alertness possessed the quality of an inevitable reflex. Mentally, intellectually, their need was obvious enough to them, but the mode of self-interest and automatic defense of habitual affect and dition was obdurate.[18]

It was, therefore, our explicit task to remove these impediments which now constituted barriers to a clear inquiry into the underlying motives of human behavior. It was our task to set aside ideational feeling or affecto-symbolic habituations born of what we had been told by others we ought to think and feel and do. If the bacteriologists could succeed in altering habitual numinal *thinking* in regard to the causation of infectious diseases, why, I asked myself, might not the student of phylobiology compel habitual numinal *feeling*—our accustomed "normal" affects and prejudices—to give way to the authority of intelligent interest and motivation? Unlike prevailing methods of procedure in psychotherapy, including my own traditional trend, phylobiology did not set out knowing in advance what was the desired goal for either the individual or the group. We sought merely to clear away whatever ditentive elements obstructed man's path to the recognition of what that goal might prove to be. There was no "normal," no gratuitously assumed social reaction-average to pin our faith to or direct our effort toward. Our ultimate finding, like that of the early bacteriologists, was admittedly an unknown quantity. Like theirs, ours was a field of original research. And so, adhering strictly to our experimental basis, we sought to maintain an open mind as to what we might find to be the natural interrelational function of man—his basic feeling and motivation—when the artificialities that now submerge this function should be eliminated.

Emphasis, therefore, should be placed upon the essentially somatic or physiological nature of the experiment to be described and upon the entire absence of the usual ideological or philosophical inducements commonly presumed to bring about an alteration in individual behavior. Whatever alteration in motivation or behavior took place was a result not of a change in thought, but of an alteration coincident with processes within the organism of which there existed no preformed conception for the guidance of resulting orientations. With regard to the approach to the problem of human behavior employed by my associates and myself, I have already drawn special attention to the physiological aspect of our methodology as contrasted with the methodology of investigators whose formulations and methods have rested upon traditionally preconceived ideas.[19]

In a world which undoubtedly must come to be recognized as neurotically deviate and distorted, the mental and social processes of even the ablest scientists and scholars are no less marked with inconsistency than those of the humblest and least favored of individuals or groups. Our purpose therefore had to do, first, with the effort to remove the heavy pall of affective or autopathic habituations under which we are all now socially blanketed. Second, it was our purpose to discover, if possible, what basic structures and functions might be found beneath these befuddling affects and strivings concomitant to man's purely superficial, ditentive efforts of interchange and communication. It was only after several years of this relentless personal and social discipline among us that there was accidentally noted the phenomenon which I shall now attempt to describe.

If I may speak of my own personal reaction, this phenomenon occurred during the rare moments when the sense of frustration or defeat of my habitual interests and activations had reached its acutest phase. As far as concerned the tone of my customary social interests and exchange, the dearth of my "normal" interests and incentives seemed to have reduced me to a state approaching inter-relational nihilism. It seemed to me that in these moments the sense of frustration had reached the saturation point. At these times of intense social frustration and feeling-disparagement, all affective response to affective stimuli, as ordinarily experienced, appeared to have become non-existent. It was in this setting that there occurred a most unexpected phenomenon. It consisted in a reaction which at the time I could only describe as a sensation of pressure or tension in the head.

This sensation was not at all clearly outlined at first as to location or quality. It lasted for only a few seconds, and was not sharply defined or vivid; nor had it a quality of either pleasure or pain. There was merely my conscious recording of a barely perceptible sensation of pressure, stress or tension seemingly within the anterior cerebral zone. I could in no way account for this reaction, but it is quite unthinkable that such a subjective sense or sensation as I have described could ever have come to awareness had there not been the interruption of the social interests and distractions that ordinarily occupy man's projective trends. It was only by virtue of the enforced suspension of congenial activation and the complete negation of the conditions and surroundings which commonly promote human interest and interchange that this very slight neurodynamic impression acquired sufficient prominence to awaken recognition of it.

Anything less interesting, anything possessing less the quality of excitement than this vague intimation of tension in the anterior region of the head could hardly be conceived of. Only the utterly drab and uneventful background against which this sensation was outlined can at all account for its having elicited my attention. In the unmitigated frustration of mood coincident with the rigid routine of hourly imposed affect-negation, and in the complete withdrawal of the customary supports of convivial social activity, with their quickening tone and impact, there was a total void of affective interest and incitement.

If wholly new and alien, here at least was something tangible, something directly palpable, so to speak. A sensation, a perceptual impression had presented itself which was unconnected with my habitual sphere of sensations and perceptions, as also with my habitual sphere of mental and social interests—sensations, interests and incitements which for purposes of experimentation I had encouraged to be ruthlessly frustrated among us on every hand.

Apparently, in this altered bionomic orientation there was a correspondingly altered kinesthetic or, should I say, coenesthetic response. Needless to say, this unexpected intimation of a new field of observation, however faint and however uncorrelated with my habitual experience, constituted an impression of no little significance for me. For having recognized in myself the constant presence of affect as the underlying motive in so-called normal human relations, and having seen this affective motivation in others who along with me recognized its presence within themselves, naturally I was no little intrigued to find that with the assertion of this sense of internal tension, affect-images correspondingly fell away. My thought was that perhaps here in this scarcely appreciable sensation arising from what was an utterly new and unfamiliar field of perception—perhaps here at last there might be something affirmative to hold to, something savoring of restoration to a more basic, a more solid plane of interrelational interest and activation in contrast to our accustomed habits of affective communication and interchange.

So that my newly, if faintly, awakened interest begain to center upon recovering and sustaining this internal sensation. As I had, of course, no hint whatever of its origin or incidence, I found this sense of stress wholly beyond the reach of customary efforts of recall. After the lapse of many weeks, however, in which there was this same unremitting routine of unanswered affects, of general social frustration, there was the spontaneous recurrence, if only momentary, of this same phenomenon. With the passing of the months, the intervals between its recurrences became shorter and shorter until finally the feeling of stress or tension occurred with relative frequency and would last over slightly longer periods of time—possibly for half a minute.

As time passed—and under conditions of complete environmental frustration time passes at a snail's pace—there was a still further lengthening of these periods of stress or tension. Finally it happened that in a period considerably longer than usual the feeling of stress appeared to be more definitely located in the anterior part of the head or in the region within and back of the eyes. But since we possessed as yet no considered technique for regaining this unaccustomed sensation of tension, my recourse and that of my associates adhered still to the seemingly thankless task of our common group frustration. Gradually, however, the incidence of cerebral stress took on increasingly definite form. The observation of particular interest connected with this internal stress was its indication of a physiological reaction that was unaccompanied by any mental image or critique.

With this reaction we began to efface increasingly the running commentary of mental images, with their ditentive affects and numina, that apparently constitute the daily routine of both normal and neurotic. And with a sense, however vague, of the coincidence between the feeling of stress and the elimination of ditentive images, our effort now directed itself more and more to the appreciation of this physiological sense of tension or stress. Later the induction of this cerebral stress came to be our sole recourse in the effort to eliminate affective imagery or ditentive motivation.

The objective recognition of this physiological anomaly resulted solely from our direct experimental observation of the interrelational operation of man's brain as it functions in the activities and interests of "normal" groups. This experiment in social behavior caused a marked frustration of so-called normal interpersonal projections along with their affects, and pointed up a concomitant awareness of strain or discomfort within the region of the brain itself. *Thus, behavior which under the excitation of projective affect appeared normal or healthy, appeared abnormal and even distressing when referred back to the brain and its related tensions.*

The professionally rigid, conventional mind is stabbed to the quick and raises an unholy hue and cry at the very mention of sensations of stress or tension "in the brain." The neurological students have got it firmly planted in their heads that brain tissue is not susceptible to the mechanical production of local sensation, and their conclusions, of course, rest on well-established neurological findings. This is all quite true. But these same students would not question the propriety of speaking of a "painful memory" or a "painful association," of a "distressing thought or item of attention," all of which they would quite naturally refer, at least in part, to the brain, and all of which would in general terms be sensation. Likewise with grief, pride, joy, satisfaction, anger, covetousness, etc. One regards these general sensations and their accompanying neuromuscular and vasomotor modifications as concomitants of brain stimulation and response. Well, it is in an analogous sense that I refer to the brain when I speak of stress in this organ due to its lifelong conditioning to habits of response that are totally at variance with the organism's natural biological behavior. Such stress is concomitant to the complex of cerebral tensions that are associated with the 'I'-persona. If components of this stress with its habitual alterations in attention and association are not cerebral, neither is memory cerebral!

Here, then, there was a practical effort within social groups to recover the consistent reaction of the brain of man in its relation to the external object or circumstance. In ditention man has reverted to the generic *faux pas* of the numen. He is now partitive, affective, prejudiced, or a prey to arbitrary, unilateral judgments. But in consciously referring our affect back to the brain we found ourselves on solid ground. Here man was engaged consciously, experimentally, with the immediate concern of discriminating sharply between the numen and the nomen—between ditentive, affectively colored images, on the one hand, and the organism's direct neural response to external stimuli on the other.

Having to do with the neurodynamics of behavior, this phase of the experiment was of interest chiefly to the professional members of the group—to the physicians and experimental psychologists. I say of interest, but it will be understood that a scientific interest in a direction of behavior that runs counter to one's habitual behavior is not precisely what one would call enlivening. Nor is it easy sailing. The attempt to oppose an unaccustomed physiological pattern to a pattern that has crystallized itself into a fixed interrelational reaction-habit is not readily fraught with success. In this subjective task the experimenter necessarily prefers to be habitual rather than experimental. But the incitement to further experimentation in the field of interpersonal reactions rested upon the thesis that, if the withdrawal of habitual affect-projections induced in their place a sensation of stress or discomfort in the region of the brain, then the invoking of the cerebral sensation of discomfort and stress might conversely eliminate habitual affect-projections. We therefore resorted to efforts to reinstate the sense of local tension and stress in the head and, following years of experimental trial and error, it finally became possible to eradicate habitual affects and their attendant pathology by centering attention upon the local tensions concomitant to them and permitting their redistribution throughout the system of tensions that governs the behavior of the organism as a biologically unitary whole.

Reasoning from biological analogy, it had seemed to me very early in my psychoanalytic work that the basis of mental disorder is to be finally traced to a demonstrable physiological substrate.[20] The unexpected discovery of a sensation of tension within the cerebral zone (if one can speak of "discovery" where it is merely a question of observing something to which one's attention has not hitherto been drawn) tended to confirm my thesis that the basis of interpersonal impediment and conflict, like impediment and conflict observable elsewhere in medicine, is physiological; that the obvious dissension and antagonism manifested individually and among nations is ultimately traceable to a physiological conflict within the organism of man as a species or phylum and that, basically, man's real conflict is phylophysiological. From this altered frame of reference we began to see more clearly the phylic significance of the numen and its contrast with the phylic significance of the nomen.

Many are the pitfalls that may be traced to the widespread presence of the numen. For example, because of their partitive subservience to this hidden mental quirk, it has been the great mistake of scientists as of pseudo-scientists that, having hit upon some universal symptom, they have regarded it as the universal cause of the disorder underlying this symptom. This error of reasoning characterized very generally the early days of medicine. For instance, when confronted with the universality of fever as a symptom, physicians concluded that the fever was the disease.[21]

It is, however, the mark of distinction between the scientist and the pseudo-scientist that the scientist eagerly welcomes competent challenge of established findings. He cheerfully welcomes the consistent challenge of data he himself has laboriously gathered. In his adherence to scientific canons he even encourages whatever evidence tends to show that his own results have been fallacious. He does not hesitate to consider evidence that he himself has committed the error of confusing the universal symptom with the universal cause.

It was the regrettable fallacy of Freud that he confused the universal symptom of disordered sexuality invariably present in the psychoneuroses with the underlying cause of these conditions. But, of course, to have recognized the broad underlying cause, Freud must have ceased to be the clinical therapist, or to be the sworn deputy of any professional group or clique. In fealty to an uncompromising principle of scientific research, he would have had to indict all mankind and its pseudo-normality, beginning with himself and his own pseudo-normality, in order to discover the cause of man's disorders of behavior, including man's sexual disorders. That, needless to say, Freud could not possibly do. That, no one man—not even the humblest—could do unaided. And certainly no "great man," whose premise of thinking stands as an unchallengeable system, as the great untouchable talisman throughout the world of healing, could bring himself to so radical a reversal of his established premises. Only the circumstance—only the accidental circumstance of the consistent challenge interindividually *by* one's community or group *of* one's community or group could possibly have led to the discovery of the universal cause of man's universal neurosis.

Disorder in the sexual sphere, of which psychiatrists have made so much in recent years, is but one element in a wide-embracing constellation of disordered functions. We can only understand the sexual element in this constellation in the measure in which we understand this constellation as a phylic whole. We can understand it only in the sense in which we achieve an internal appreciation of the 'I'-persona, of ditention, of the numen, of pseudo-normality and its autopathic feeling and thinking. In a word, we can understand the function of sex and its disorders only through our internal, subjective appreciation of man's dissociation as a species.

The inroads of the 'I'-persona upon the various spheres of man's function—gastronomic, respiratory, cerebral, sexual, etc.—are dire. Itself a segment, a bias, a part-function, the semiotic 'I'-persona inevitably divides the function of the organism over which it has assumed partitive supremacy into correspondingly semiotic part-elements or segments of function. These segments now constitute, as it were, partitive, separative principalities subsisting under the partitive, separative sovereignty of the 'I'-persona. For example, the segmentation of the function of sex is answerable for the travesties of the healthy function of procreation we now see in the various auto- or homo-sexual *divertissements* that constitute the pseudo- or semio-sexual life of so-called normal man.[22] We are, indeed, far from suspecting the part played by the 'I'-persona and "face" in man's distortion of his basic sex sensations—on the one side, in the "normal" or gregarious perversions of man's instinctive feeling; and, on the other, in his isolate or schizophrenic misadaptations such as are to be seen in reversions to the mouth, lips and tongue as sources of partitive sexual gratification.

Man's pseudo-sexuality is the inevitable outcome of his pseudo-normality. Under its semiotic or pseudo jurisdiction the function of sex has become partitive, separative; it is but an image, a symbol, a part-function of sex. As it exists today, what is called sex is merely a metaphor of sex. In the obsessive intensity of this compensatory part-function there has developed the most far-reaching dichotomy in the bionomic life of man. As a result, the reproductive instinct of man is now alternately either compulsive sexuality or "badness," or it is compulsive repression or "goodness."[23] In short, sex is self-reflective, self-conscious, and in its self-consciousness it can only vacillate between morality and immorality. For the function of sex is now the restricted and distorted function of the self-image or 'I'-persona. Under the domination of the 'I'-persona a man who loves a woman, loves a symbol. She "looks good" to him. Everybody, the man and the woman, is now but a symbol each to each. In their sexual relations, they are, as Rupert Brooke put it,

> but taking
> Their own poor dreams within their arms, and lying
> Each in his lonely night, each with a ghost.[24]

Such are our *affaires du cœur,* such our pride of "sexual conquest," such the invariable element in our autopathic affiliations, marital and extra-marital. So that in its self-reflective image-drives, the sexual life of man is a very light, a very superficial and episodic quest. In truth, in the partitive conceit[25] of the pseudo-normal personality, the "heart" proves on careful diagnosis a very chesty organ indeed.

In the mutual narcissism of the "in-love" state, the participants do not see that in attraction begotten of mutual affect-images, whether expressed between individuals of the same or opposite sex, their "love" is but a unilateral ownership of one another. Resting, as it does, upon covenants that bear the impress of a mere surface likeness or a superficial appearance of unity and accord, such affinities are auto- or homo-sexual (homo = like).[26] To be consistent, autopathic lovers should not address each other as "my own" but as "my owned." For, Freud and normality to the contrary notwithstanding, deviation from man's natural organismic impetus to sex-fulfilment is synonymous with his substitutive, affecto-symbolic or image sexuality. Auto- or homo-sexuality, neuroticism or pseudo-normality are deviations from man's total organismic basis of motivation, including of course the organism's primary impulse of sex. Owing to the monopoly of man's behavior by an autopathic 'I'-persona, his sexual life is throughout retropathic, retroceptive, retrofective. In short, in man's lack of an organismic basis of feeling and thinking, sex has become an interrelational fetish and all its manifestations are but homogenic perversions of the primary instinct of mating and reproduction.

The enormous amount of money, the enormous amount of time spent, the enormous crowds that assemble daily, almost hourly, to attend motion pictures displaying the partitive love-relations of this or that individual, and the millions of dollars paid annually to our popular "stars" and their managers are indeed a commentary upon the social image and upon the partitive segmentation now rampant throughout social communities. We read of some absurd boy with a yen for crooning, or some slip of a girl with an equally naïve propensity, who clears a million dollars a year out of the pockets of the vast section of the community willing to pay for just the sort of pranks they have to offer; while a dozen scientists, laboring to improve the condition of man, to increase his comforts, to facilitate transportation, to combat disease, etc., would, combined, do well to make a million dollars in a lifetime. Naturally the boy—and the girl, too—is going to "cash in" on this sort of community madness. They aren't to blame. They are quite as sincere as any other limelighted celebrity. But the community, the partitively sick and benighted community, is sorely in need of a phyloanalysis.

A functional segment that is no less distorted through the partitive encroachments upon the organism is the function of the gastronomic system. We see this distortion in man's all but universal excesses of eating, his unbalanced diet and in his habit of eating inappropriate or merely palate-tickling foods. We need only look at the monstrously misshapen physique of the great majority of people in their middle years. But within the guild of normality it is the unwritten code that we must not call attention to these disfigured abdominal conditions. A humped back is a deformity, but a humped anterior is quite *comme il faut*.

Partitive dislocations of function within the cerebral segment, due to the 'I'-persona, are too patent and too common to call for specific comment beyond the general thesis of this book. Nor need we cite man's cerebral stress and pain, and the desperate measures to which he resorts for its relief in his excessive use of alcohol and drugs. Alcohol, drugs, and man's auto-sexual excitations are anodynes with which man vainly seeks to atone (be *at-one*) for the loss of his organism's primary unity as a phylum. Opiates, alcohol and tobacco will continue to be popular palliatives as long as they remain the handy substitutes they are for the organism's primary pattern of behavior.

As for the modifications in the function of the respiratory segment due to the partitive encroachments upon it of the 'I'-persona, we have in disorders of speech only too frequent instances of emotional reactions associated with this segment. We see impediment and reversal of function due to the involvement of partitive affect in the production of words, or language. Indeed the emotional disturbances that center in the respiratory segment are proverbial. These disturbances are further illustration of the many functional impairments we have recognized as affecto-symbolic interferences. A "remedy" for the discomfort of this segment, as of others, is one that again must not be openly spoken of as such, yet nothing is commoner among pseudo-normals than resort to the excessive sucking on a weed fashioned into a tube and ignited at one end, in the effort to secure relief in this area of tension. But, like alcohol, the smoking habit is a social remedy for a disorder that may no more be admitted socially than the protuberant abdomen. Is there anywhere a keener bit of irony than the spectacle of a group of educators or of psychiatrists, or a federation of mothers or of religious leaders, seated in an auditorium dense with the fumes of their tobacco, solemnly descanting on the baleful effect upon infants of the habitual use of pacifiers! Surely it is time we settled down to a serious study of the needs of the unadjusted parent.

Obviously we cannot indict either religionists or psychiatrists, parents or educators. We are, as a race, ditentive. We all have our pacifiers in one form or another. We all have our blind remedies for easing a disorder the symptoms of whose presence in us we do not even dimly suspect, much less its basic cause. There is dislocation within the interrelational processes of us all. We are all "normals." We are all dissociated elements within a dissociated species, and we have all got somehow to discover this disease in ourselves before we can discover a remedy for this disease. In the wider reckoning, man's neurosis is, after all, an acute case of mistaken identity in which the scope of the mistake is phylic or anthropological, and in which the remedy must consist in a phylic or anthropological approach to it.

The segmentation by the social 'I'-persona of the primary phylic coöperation and continuity among the elements of the species is evidenced not only in the impediments within the immediate interrelational life of man, but also in the distortions of communication and rapport occurring within the wider world community and frequently cited in this book. This general segmentation and distortion within the various functions of man's organism calls for serious phylobiological reckoning. With the recognition of the impediments within man's interrelational life, one may expect that scientists and physicians will heed the cry of man's organism for a re-unification of its disordered processes, however offensive, however unwelcome may be the indispensable acknowledgment on the part of each scientist and each physician of a segmentation caused by his own 'I'-persona and appreciable only within his own organism. If this process initiated by the laboratory of phylobiology is an offensive thorn in the flesh of partitive man, professional and lay, the process of adjustment which the laboratories of bacteriology ushered in with their recourse to the use of serum was once no less a thorn in the flesh of physicians of restricted perspectives in the domain of infectious diseases.

Today there is, on the one hand, partitive feeling or affect with its ideation correspondingly controlled by the numen and, on the other, there is balanced, organismic feeling with its ideation subsisting under the corresponding control of the nomen. Man has the intelligence and the artistry and the science to meet his problem and re-order his life, but under the sovereignty of the numen there can be only ditention, affect, "face." There can be only thinking and feeling and doing partitively as we have been instructed by our partitive forbears to think and feel and do. Under the restrictions of this behavioral impasse man flounders in vain for a solution of his behavior-problems. His partitive thinking, his personality, man's identity itself is bound up with this inhibiting numinal premise. Man is enclosed within an affective, wishful world, and on his present affective premise man desires only to remain undisturbed within this self-encapsulating system, while he rants hysterically in his subjugation to the unrecognized powers of a blindly motivating dichotomy. Because of this artificially induced cosmogony within the phyloörganism of man, my associates and I have through the years attempted to challenge this ideological basis of human relationships as it is sponsored and motivated within the social community and as it lent itself to observation among ourselves as an integral contingent of this wider group.

Through the sciences of physics, chemistry, mathematics, geology, physiology, ecology and the rest, the brain and senses of man became related by means of its symbolic function to the consistent order of the external universe. But phylobiology requires a further step. It requires not only that man's brain and senses but also that the harmonious function of man's own processes—the consistent behavior of man's own organism—be related to and coördinated with the consistent harmony prevailing in the outer world of phenomena.

This may seem a large order. Indeed, from the narrow viewpoint of the conditioned part-brain of man it is a large order—so large, in fact, as to appear quite beyond the possibility of fulfilment. But from the viewpoint of the organism's basic orientation, this position becomes infinitely simpler than the position maintained by psychopathologists today in respect to man's disorders of behavior. As Willard Gibbs has said, "The whole is simpler than the sum of its parts." In the finding of phylobiology, it is only because man has been divisively or partitively conditioned from infancy that his habit of outlook is now biased by the limitations of a part or personalistic view of his own organismic reactions. It is for this reason that he does not see the problem of behavior as the phylic whole that it is. It is for this reason that each separately conditioned unit, whether individual, community or nation, now strives obsessively to promote its separately conditioned claim or advantage above that of others in defiance of a common principle of species solidarity.

To the phylobiologist nothing appears more urgent than the application of the larger function of the brain and senses of man to the problem of his behavior-disfunction as a species. Nothing appears of greater interest and significance than the discovery of measures that will make possible the demarcation between man's partitive mode or motivation and the mode or motivation expressive of man's total pattern of reaction in relation to the environment.[27] To this end it has been our effort to give physiological definition or delimitation to man's partitively (affectively) conditioned brain-segment as it mediates man's symptomatic or symbolic sphere of behavior. In demarcating the affecto-symbolic substrate underlying the behavior of man, we have attempted to define the motivations that pertain to this conditioned reaction-segment and thus separate the organism's partitive behavior-reactions from the motivation of man's organism as an orthogenic whole.

It would seem that in the interest of the larger sphere of the senses future students of behavior will repudiate the supremacy of the part-brain and with it the narrow domestic preoccupations of a purely interpersonal psychiatry. The time is undoubtedly approaching when instead of clinging to such partitive interpretations as rest upon a false dichotomy of motivation—instead of adhering to psychiatry's affecto-symbolic system of *numen*clature—we shall cultivate the larger function of the brain as a whole, and with it such symbols as will be commensurate with a wider employment of the senses. When this moment arrives we shall no longer limit ourselves to interpersonal preoccupations based on the organism's secondary, ditentive conditioning. In our newer outlook we shall envisage such neurodynamic concepts as the primary behavior of the organism in its phylic motivation, and adopt a concept and a nomenclature befitting the organismic solidarity of man as a species. This envisagement should afford an insight into the universal conditioning of man in his present social adaptation. It should permit us to sense the dislocation that has occurred in the function of the brain of man as a whole, because of the false priority of a partitively constellated brain-segment. From such a background it will become possible for man to disavow the currency of mere partitive affects and reëstablish the organism's total function in relation to the environment.[28] In this consummation there will be reëstablished the phyloörganism's bionomic homeostasis. Man's anthroponomic motivation will flow from within out. In this readjustment it will become possible for man to correct his numinal deviations of behavior through promoting laboratories of investigation whose material will be none other than the phyloörganismic processes of man himself. In these laboratories there will be opened to man the possibility of encompassing in the sphere of man's own behavior a systematized body of facts within the frame of a universal premise.

NOTES

[1] Burrow, Trigant, "The Law of the Organism—A Neuro-Social Approach to the Problems of Human Behavior," *The American Journal of Sociology*, 1937, Vol. XLII, pp. 814-24.

[2] See page 142.

[3] See note 22, page 179.

[4] The term *orthopathic* (ὀρθὸς = straight, πάθος = feeling) refers to the organism's primary pattern of reaction and is synonymous with man's basic motivation. It is contrasted with the term *autopathic* which, as we noted previously (note 19, page 179), refers to reactions that are affecto-symbolic and are deflectively motivated. In the preceding chapter on attention the distortion of symbolic reactions was described as ditention.

[5] The primary meaning of numen is nod, acquiescence. As it happens, the term *numen* possesses special terminological aptness in the present context because both in form and pronunciation it presents a sharp contrast linguistically to the word *nomen* from which it differs by only a single vowel.

[6] Superstitious = Latin *super*, above + *stare*, to stand. Cf. Greek, επίστασις, standing above.

[7] See note 5, page 155.

[8] See page 224.

[9] Burrow, Trigant, "The Origin of the Incest-Awe," *The Psychoanalytic Review*, 1918, Vol. V, pp. 243-54.

[10] See note 2, page 155.

[11] See note 7, page 178.

[12] Syz, Hans, "The Concept of the Organism-as-a-Whole and its Application to Clinical Situations," *Human Biology*, 1936, Vol. VIII, pp. 489-507; cf. Lillie, Ralph S., "The Problem of Synthesis in Biology," *Philosophy of Science*, 1942, Vol. 9, pp. 59-71.

[13] An interesting discussion of the phylobiological implications of language may be found in William E. Galt's "Our Mother Tongue—Etymological Implications of the Social Neurosis," *The Psychoanalytic Review*, 1943, Vol. 30, pp. 241-62.

[14] From Latin, *avēre*, to wish.

[15] See note 1, page 155.
[16] See note 21, page 179.
[17] Head, Henry, *Studies in Neurology*, London, Oxford University Press, 1920, Vol. I, pp. 225-329.
[18] See page 183.
[19] See pages 220-25.
[20] Burrow, Trigant, "The Psychological Analysis of So-called Neurasthenic and Allied States," *The Journal of Abnormal and Social Psychology*, 1913, Vol. VIII, pp. 243-58.
———, "The Meaning of the Psychic Factor," *The Journal of Abnormal and Social Psychology*, 1913, Vol. VIII, pp. 322-30.
[21] See note 10, page 199.
[22] Burrow, Trigant, *The Social Basis of Consciousness*, pp. 201-04.
———, *The Biology of Human Conflict*, pp. 347-51.
[23] Burrow, Trigant, *The Social Basis of Consciousness*, p. 158.
———, *The Biology of Human Conflict*, pp. 349-50.
[24] Brooke, Rupert, "Love," *The Collected Poems of Rupert Brooke*, New York, John Lane Company, 1916, p. 138.
[25] *Conceit* means both an idea and overweening self-esteem.
[26] Burrow, Trigant, "The Genesis and Meaning of 'Homosexuality' and its Relation to the Problem of Introverted Mental States," *The Psychoanalytic Review*, 1917, Vol. 4, pp. 272-84.
———, "The Origin of the Incest-Awe," *The Psychoanalytic Review*, 1918, Vol. V, pp. 243-54.
[27] Syz, Hans, "Burrow's Differentiation of Tensional Patterns in Relation to Behavior Disorders," *The Journal of Psychology*, 1940, Vol. 9, pp. 153-63.
[28] See note 6, page 231.

CHAPTER VI

THE ANATOMY OF PREJUDICE
OR
THE INDUCTION OF AFFECT IN THE HUMAN ANIMAL

Having in the preceding chapter considered the broader "paleontological" viewpoint with respect to human behavior, we may now turn to a consideration of the minute element to which the specific mechanism of the affect must ultimately be traced. We saw that the partitive interpolation in man of the numen or the 'I'-persona has obstructed the phyloörganism's balanced relationship to the environment. With the numen and its compensatory rationalizations there occurred an interference with the consistency and solidarity of man's organism as a species. Its relation to the environment was no longer spontaneous, endogenous, essential. Because of this distortion in relational and interrelational values it would seem that serious scientific reckoning with man's disordered processes of behavior is now the indispensable step in man's social and cultural development.

The application of experimental medicine to the behavior of human communities is probably the most urgent need within the entire sweep of man's scientific and cultural perspectives. As yet medicine has not recognized that the community is composed of common organismic reactions and that these reactions are susceptible of a common organismic approach. Only in relatively recent times have we appreciated the necessity of this point of view even in respect to the single individual. But an organismic approach to the single individual, whether man or animal, remains inept and anomalous in the absence of its extension to processes that affect the community or species as a whole. In the light of the desperate conflict of arms that has recently raged throughout the world and that offers a daily increasing threat of fresh eruption, such a phylobiological approach to the study of man's behavior would appear especially urgent. And the war's immediate aftermath of dissension—political, economic and industrial—further accents this urgency. As I write these lines, the radio announces a strike of 450,000 American coal miners—an industrial conflict that promises to be more far-reaching in its disruptive consequences than any this country has ever known.

It was with a view to establishing dependable methods of medical experimentation regarding the community's reactions as a whole that my associates and I have devoted many years to the development of a program of research based upon man's biological behavior as a species. The present chapter deals with certain aspects of these researches and with their bearing upon the ecology of the hominid as a unitary social organism.

Individuals and communities must eventually come to see that man's inconsistencies of behavior are of quite common occurrence. One readily sees this inconsistency in the simultaneous adoption by one and the same agent of two mutually opposed courses of action. Not only scientists and educators, but statesmen and journalists are today calling attention to an especially conspicuous instance of this behavioral paradox. They point to the discrepancy in man's behavior when, side by side with his discovery of medical agencies for safeguarding human life, he invents the most deadly devices with the direct object of destroying life. Such widespread contradictions would seem to indicate a serious disturbance in the function of the human organism in its relation to the environment. They would seem to indicate an impediment in man's biological articulation as a species. But mere concepts and commentaries, whether of scientist or layman, cannot cope with a breach in the functional integrity of man as a phyloörganism. We must look deeper than this. There is required something far more radical than mere words or concepts if medicine is to deal with the actual pathology involved in man's contradictions of behavior. We have here a problem in medicine and biology, a problem in physiology and anatomy.

Those of us who have devoted ourselves to the analysis of patients with mental or nervous illness know the extent to which these individuals are a prey to the nostalgic lures of a purely fantastic security, to the subtle enticements of the mother-image. We know that in their regression toward this fanciful basis of behavior these personalities are invariably confronted with a two-way policy of action. Because of the reversal of their interest toward mere symbolic images of motivation in place of the organism's primary kinesthetic pattern of action, the capacity of these patients is not applied naturally or with balanced ease to the environmental object or situation. Beneath the outer manifestations of these personalities the wish is father to the thought, and ambivalent mental images obstruct a free passage to the task or incident before them. Fair is foul, and foul is fair. They earnestly want to do "right," but they are as earnestly prone to do "wrong." This behavioral dichotomy is inherent in the very concept "mental conflict" first introduced by Freud—a concept with which the formulations of psychiatry are in essential agreement today.

Those of us, however, who have for years devoted ourselves to the analysis of social groups have not felt content any longer with this purely mental interpretation, but have sought to study the problem of human behavior in the immediate reactions of man as an organismic group or species. In this analysis our observations rested on the principle that there exists within the organism of man as of other animals a primary basis of motivation that is unitary and cohesive, and that is therefore equal and common among the individuals composing the community or group. From the background of this organismic analysis we have seen that beneath the outer covering of social amenities there exists in the behavior of man as a community a dichotomy that is identical with the dichotomy we have observed in the individual patient. We have seen that ambivalent images intervene no less to defeat the unitary purpose of social groups or communities. The community also is lured by nostalgic fantasies, by the enticing invitations of the mother-image. The aims of the community are likewise beguiled and diverted by wishful interests. It, too, is dominated by the urge to do "right" but, like the neurotic patient, the community is equally motivated by secretly recalcitrant wishes, and so is no less dominated by the alternative urge to do "wrong."

With the increasing interest of physicians in social medicine and in measures for dealing with community problems, it becomes increasingly important to recognize the primary organismic principle of behavior underlying social or community reactions.[1] Only in this way may we appreciate the part played by the community in the deviations of behavior responsible for mental and nervous disorders. In this wider purview of phylopathology it may its natural approach to the environment, that within the group or be seen that with the community, too, there is an obstruction to community, as within the individual, a barrier of ambivalent mental images constitutes an impediment to the organism's basic behavioral goals. As yet psychiatrists have not explained either the image or the barrier that is formed by it, nor have they explained the bearing of this obstruction upon man's primary organism-environment relationship.[2] What is more, psychiatry has given no biological account of the factor of *affect* or of so-called wishful thinking as it bears upon the organism's immediate reaction as a whole to the interrelated environment. This is not to be wondered at, however, since a biological account of affect or of ditentive thinking and feeling would have required an acquaintance with the physiological matrix that underlies this interrelational impediment.

This barrier of ambivalent images, whether individual or social, needs to be more carefully reckoned with. What is called the wish or the affect needs to be reduced to explicit neural terms rather than left suspended in the thin air of mere mental abstraction. Do we really know the nature of these affect-images, or the nature of the barrier formed by them? After all, what composes the fabrication of wishful thinking which the neurotic habitually substitutes for factual thinking? Superficially, of course, we are familiar with the dichotomous moral element inherent in the conflict of the nervous patient. His dilemma, in face of a division between "right" and "wrong," is a commonplace. But what actually is the substance of this dilemma? What is the objective structure of his "conflict" as contrasted with psychiatry's subjective concept of it? We know how close kin is the neurotic's sense of obstruction and insecurity to the insecurity of what he calls his "conscience." But obviously the moral element in these personalities, of which their conscience is an index, calls for clearer medical definition. What is this moral dichotomy that determines the individual's choice of conduct—the ever-haunting alternatives of "right and wrong" we know as "conscience"? Here, again, psychological terminology must be brought to the bar of biological analysis. For if these manifestations of disordered behavior occurring in the personalities of our patients, and no less in the community, are traceable to a problem in anatomy and physiology, it is essential that we relate these mental manifestations to the definite physiological alterations actually responsible for them.

It may be of assistance if, before going further, we try to orient ourselves in regard to general biological premises and perspectives as they bear upon our inquiry. In dealing with behavior or with the functional relation of the organism to its environment, it is well to consider the scope and implications of this broad bionomic relationship. It is well to take account of the vastly systematized complex of reactions, chemical and physiological, that compose the unit we know as the organism, and to recognize that the relationship of this organismic unit to the outer world is normally one that preserves a state of constant balance and reciprocity between them. As has been said, the maintenance of the organism's balanced function is known as homeostasis.[3] On the basis of the writer's observations it is essential that a comprehensive study of human as well as of animal behavior set out from this primary principle of homeostasis as a fundamental premise.

The principle of homeostasis is universally operative throughout living forms. It is present in the single cell, in each organ, in the composite of organs constituting the individual and in the unit of individual organisms that constitutes the phyloörganism or species. The maintenance of an organism's homeostasis is synonymous with the preservation of its balanced tone or tension. The basic balance or syntonicity of organisms is a principle inherent in all life. In the absence of this balanced consistency in the soma's reactions there would be no health, no integrity of function. Indeed, disease may well be defined as an interference with this primary syntonic state of the organism through the incidence of deviation in tensional balance or consistency. In contrast to the syntonic pattern this interruption represents a ditonic condition.

The syntonic state of equilibration whereby the soma of animal or hominid preserves its integrity of function in respect to the environment constitutes the consistent balance of reactions we know as "instinctive behavior." With the lower animals their adjustment to the environment is wholly instinctive, automatic. They do not possess, of course, the psychic adjuncts to behavior that relate them to their surroundings through a process of intellectual reflection or judgment. With the bionomic modification in man incident to his acquisition of the symbolic faculty or language, there occurred a marked differentiation between the adaptation of animals and the human species in respect to the outer world. If through this bionomic modification man was lifted to a level of adaptation that opened to him a horizon which was enormously expanded and enriched, at the same time there was introduced an element of conflict that curtailed and impoverished man's primary syntonic function or the instinctual life of man as a phylo-organism. In other words, because of the inadvertent miscegenation of affect with language or consciousness, there occurred a ditonic disturbance in the organism's balance. Where there had been syntonicity and health, or a homeostatic balance of tensions, this functional consistency was now disturbed by the introduction of affective factors, or of retropathic elements that tended to replace the organism's spontaneous reactions with reactions that had undergone disturbance through man's secondary processes of self-consciousness and sophistication.

The universality of man's increasingly disordered behavior is, in a superficial, mental sense, generally accepted. Man's contradictory behavior, his division and competitiveness, his emotional instability and general inconsistency of behavior are more or less commonly admitted. But had man a reliable scientific perspective upon these traits of his in relation to his kind, they would of themselves indicate to him a serious disturbance in organismic values. They would mean to him not a problem of words, ideas and mental programs, but a problem of medicine. They would mean not merely a problem of the single individual, nor even a problem of man socially, but an organismic problem, a biological and physiological problem of man as a species or phylum. In short, it is not alone the superficial picture of behavior but also its basic physiological matrix that is universal.

With a view to the clearer exposition of the nature of man's emotional instability—with a view to uncovering the extraneous factor of affect—let us consider briefly the work done on animals by the experimental psychologists. In experimenting with the external reactions of animals, much has been accomplished toward gaining a knowledge of the behavior of these lower organisms in their relation to the environment. By placing an animal in a box or cage and presenting it with certain stimuli, we have learned a great deal in regard to its drives, its capacities and the influences that determine its "choice" in this or that given set-up. By introducing into the experimental chamber certain artificial conditions selected with a view to obtaining special responses, all manner of somatic reflexes have been induced that have added to our knowledge of the animal's behavior and its motivation.

These selective modifications in animal behavior represent, of course, the type of experimentally induced reactions we know as conditioned reflexes. A conditioned reflex is produced through the substitution of a symbolic for a normal physiological stimulus.

There is here a relatively simple situation. The animal is, of course, naturally stimulated to salivate at the sight of food. If now, through expert handling, the sound of a bell is substituted for food, the animal may eventually be made to accept this substitutive stimulus in place of the food-stimulus and to salivate at the sound of the bell. Among the experiments employed with animals—with dogs, let us say—there is also that in which differential stimuli or symbols are applied within a given behavioral situation. That is to say, there is the stimulus which, in calling forth a definite response, leads to a specific action, and there is the stimulus which, in calling forth the contrary response, as definitely interdicts this same action. Of course, nowadays almost everyone capable of reading knows the nature of conditioned reflexes. He knows than an animal normally, physiologically stimulated to salivate at the sight of food may be conditioned to accept a substitutive, symbolic stimulus in place of the food-stimulus and to salivate at the sound of a bell.

The classical example of the induction of differentially conditioned reflexes is seen in the experiment in which a dog is conditioned to salivate (the hunger-reflex) in response to a metronome having a rate, say, of 120 beats per minute, while at the same time he is conditioned not to respond to a metronome having a rate of 60 beats per minute. These differing reactions are induced because, simultaneous with the oscillation rate of 120 beats, the dog was given food, while with the 60-beat rate food was withheld from him. The two stimuli may now be slowly approximated to one another by gradually reducing the higher rate and increasing the lower until the two rates approach a point at which the animal is unable to distinguish between them. With prolonged repetition of the two opposed stimuli, the resulting confusion leads to frustration and to the breaking down of the dog's discriminative capacity. If pushed still further, the result may be a complete disintegration in the animal's behavior. This has been called, though rather loosely it seems to me, the production of an "experimental neurosis." [4]

But there is a type of animal conditioning that entails a reaction of more immediate interest to the present thesis. This type of conditioning is brought about by means of an experiment in which, as before, there is produced a physiological reaction to a purely arbitrary symbol in place of the physiological stimulus that normally calls forth this reaction. But now the response elicited is one that entails the animal's selective behavior or its "conscious" choice—conscious in the sense that the animal does not now follow a pattern already established experimentally. In this altered type of set-up the experimenter places at one end of the cage a cup containing food and one that is empty. In front of the cup containing the food he places, say, a white card four inches square in the center of which is a black surface two inches square. In front of the empty cup he places a similar white card of the same dimensions but having a central black area one inch square. The animal is now allowed to enter the cage at the end opposite the cards and to make its choice between the two visual stimuli. With repeated experience the animal learns to associate the larger black square with food-reward, and the smaller black area with food-denial. That is, the symbol represented by the larger black square elicits the animal's positive response, and the symbol represented by the smaller black square calls forth its negative response.

After this series of responses has been well established and the animal discriminates readily between the larger square that symbolizes food and the smaller square that symbolizes denial, the experiment may be complicated in such a way that the animal is no longer competent to discriminate consistently between the rewarded and the non-rewarded symbol or stimulus. It now hesitates in its choice and shows marked evidence of confusion. If the experiment is continued, the animal's confusion mounts to the point of complete frustration. On pushing the experiment still further, its behavior becomes disorganized and "neurosis" results.[5]

In this experiment we have an instance of an animal's response to a selective or symbolic stimulus that involves the issue of a right choice or a wrong one. It involves the issue between success and failure, gain and loss, the advantageous and the disadvantageous course. Thus the conditioned response elicited in the animal may be compared to the partitive reaction we have already recognized in man as affect. Because of the similarity of the animal's artificially induced reaction to partitive or affective behavior in man, perhaps we may describe the reaction of the animal, in the experiment just cited, as an experimental affect.

The animal man has also been subjected to various conditioning stimuli. Man, too, has been gradually brought to respond to artificial stimuli or to the symbol of an object or circumstance in substitution for the object or circumstance itself. There is a difference, however. With man, his conditioning is far more general and varied. Without having recognized it, man has become conditioned socially through his gradual subjugation *as a species* to a social *system* of symbolic stimuli. Though experimentally unpremeditated, these symbolic stimuli are present today in the vicarious mechanism of the spoken word, or language. These verbal stimuli have artificially produced in us endless conditioned reflexes. They have caused substitutive modifications in the physiological behavior of the hominid similar to the substitutive modifications produced in animals under conditions of laboratory experimentation. The houses in which we live—our homes, schools, offices, factories, our various halls of legislation and, I might add, our current peace conferences—constitute the experimental cages, so to speak, into which affect-inducing stimuli have been accidentally introduced. But, as I say, there is a difference. For not only has man been gradually trained over generations to respond reflexly to certain selective words or symbols, but the conditioned reflexes thus induced by these systems of stimuli have become *socially consolidated into affectively conditioned systems of reaction*. In man's conditioning, then, there is induced the physiological mechanism of affect to which the affect artificially induced in rudimentary form in the animal is analogous. But in man this mechanism of affect now motivates his interrelational life throughout, and it does so to the exclusion of his organism's primary reaction as a whole.

The complex of impressions received from the personality of one individual—his ideas, his appearance, his moods, gestures, intonation of voice, his interests, his enthusiasms and his doldrums—may constitute the symbolic system of stimuli by which one is conditioned. Or it may be that certain systematized habit-formations prevailing within an entire family or community constitute the substitutive stimulus. In this way a social system of reactions—for example, a system of religious beliefs as it characterizes an individual, family or community—provides the complex of exciting stimuli; or the conditioning stimulus may be constellated of this or that political or economic system of ideas. At one time the subject presents the characteristic reaction of the convert; at another, that of the dissenter. In former days to be a Southerner was to be a Democrat; to be a Northerner was to be a Republican. The physical boundary between North and South defined by the Mason-Dixon line marked no less sharply the demarcation between these two political ideologies. Such a socially systematized form of conditioning acts positively or negatively upon the subject, whether individual or community, according as the affective response is pleasurable (gain) or displeasurable (denial) —according as he lives on one or the other side of the line! In this conditioning of one individual by another, or of two individuals mutually, lies the substance of the reaction known in psychoanalytic parlance as "the transference." This general systematization of affects within and about the individual is the crystallization of behavior-motivations we have recognized as the 'I'-persona with its compulsive dichotomy of "right" or "wrong," of gain or loss, of advantage or disadvantage for oneself, that is, for one's ditentive or autopathic *image* of oneself.

We must now point to a further parallel between the differential conditioning of the experimental animal and that of man. For, as in the animal, the conditioning of the hominid has also been marked by the presentation of two or more stimuli that are mutually opposed to one another. The father of a family, or the head of a business organization may have one system of ethics under one set of circumstances, and a wholly different system under another; or one person may provide the stimulus at one time, and another at another time. The result is disorientation and confusion within the family or business unit. Such inconsistencies within human communities do not exist in isolation. On the contrary they are universal, and their effect, whether familial, religious, political, economic or industrial, is to cause a corresponding conflict of responses throughout the world of man's individual and social reactions.

With man, therefore, as with the experimental animal, there are the stimuli which in inducing a part-interest or response promote certain definite actions and, contrariwise, there are the interest-inducing stimuli which contravene these same actions. In man, however, conflict has been introduced not only between two systems of response, but in the process of man's social evolution—with the inadvertent intrusion of a dichotomous 'I'-persona—a condition of conflict has been induced between many such systems. This condition of conflict within physiological reaction-systems has brought about a confusion in the natural interests and activations of man. Man has been reflexly caught up in part-reactions—in ditention and the numen—at the expense of his whole attention with its consistent relation to the nomen. So that there has now resulted an unpremeditated condition of dispartment or conflict throughout the species.[6] This discrepancy in physiological reactions represents a basic phylogenetic anomaly in man's development, and underlies the symptomatic or outer expression of the world-wide confusion and conflict I have called *the neurosis of man*. In Part II we shall enter more fully into the discussion of this basic physiological disturbance in man's processes.

But let me turn aside for a moment and call attention to the prevailing tendency among experimental psychologists and among lay audiences to infer that what happens in the conditioned animal may be taken as a criterion of what happens in the behavior of man. Our phylobiological interest bears solely upon the basic physiological aspect of animal conditioning. In so far as we are dealing with physiological mechanisms, the conflict or neurosis premeditatedly induced in the experimental animal quite obviously bears a certain analogy to the social confusion or neurosis of the hominid. But needless to say, the neurosis as experimentally induced by single stimuli in the single animal cannot be compared in scope, intensity or duration with the complex system of conditioning that tends to the production of neurosis as it has occurred in man. So that man's knowledge regarding a conflict experimentally induced in animals by no means warrants him in inferring that this conflict is in all respects identical with conflict or neurosis as it exists in himself. In so far as he has attempted to do so, he has only confused the issue with forced analogies, grossly exaggerating the situation on the one side and seriously minimizing it on the other. For when the student of behavior regards conflict in the experimental animal as a "neurosis," he is unwittingly invoking anthropomorphic assumptions, while in accounting for conflict in the hominid he fails to reckon with the phylogenetic substrate of man's behavior as a species. He has thus disregarded entirely the socio-biological implications of man's neurotic disorders and has in the same measure precluded a clear reckoning with those phylogenetic implications requisite to man's study of his own behavior.

As we have seen, in conditioning the laboratory animal the experimenter presents an inert visual or auditory stimulus (a card or a tuning fork) simultaneously with a physiologically exciting stimulus such as food. In this way the innocuous visual or auditory stimulus becomes, by association (or conditioning), the sign or symbol of the potent physiological stimulus. Of itself the arbitrary sign or symbol is not competent to evoke an emotionally colored reaction or interest. But, as we have also seen, after many repetitions the experimenter may present this substitutive stimulus without the accompanying food and still call forth in the animal a response (muscular, visceral, glandular, etc.) appropriate to the physiologically potent incitement. The animal will move toward the large black square which now stands to him as a symbol of food (satisfaction or reward) and he will avoid the small black square which now symbolizes the absence of food (dissatisfaction or denial). In this situation an interest-inducing *symbol* has been substituted for objective actuality. There has occurred in the animal's behavior a shift from the natural bionomic object to the mere sign or indicator of it.

As already mentioned, the response of man to the actual objects of the environment has also been largely replaced by a response to mere signs or symbols of them. With man the stimuli represented by vocal sounds or words have, through conditioning or association (affect-linkage), gradually assumed the provocative quality of the actual objects or circumstances for which they stand. Like the bell or the card presented to the experimental animal, these words or symbols presented to man now call forth in him the physiological reaction originally appropriate only to the actual objects themselves. With man the repeated presentation of stimuli and their increasingly complex association have come to be systematized within a special functional pattern of the brain—the associational function situated largely in the frontal lobes. This is the area of neural function whose social or interrelational crystallization has gradually formed in each of us the symbolic systematization of affect-awakening responses that underlies the partitive (ditentive) 'I'-persona or 'I'-complex.

It may be added that while the conditioned reflex of salivation induced in an animal at the sound of a bell is a definite physiological response, this reflex is not identical with the total response induced by the physiologically adequate stimulus or by the presentation of actual food.[7] The substitutive stimulus causes less flow of saliva and the flow is of shorter duration. Similarly in man: though the reaction to substitutive stimuli or verbal symbols is definitely physiological, my associates and I have been able to show through instrumental experimentation that the organism's reaction is of a different character when responding to the affect-laden word or symbol (ditention) than when induced spontaneously through the organism's direct contact with the environmental object or situation as a whole (total attention).[8]

Experimentally we may attach a spontaneous or physiological stimulus to any inert sign or symbol arbitrarily chosen by us. In this way we obtain, in man or animal, a pseudo-stimulus. The response to this artificial or pseudo stimulus is an artificial or pseudo response. It is not spontaneous or organic, but is a substitute response, experimentally induced. This is the production experimentally of the partitive or affect response. Here a syntonic stimulus is replaced by a ditonic stimulus, and correspondingly the resulting response is ditonic rather than syntonic. Here in elementary form we have pseudo-feeling or the affect. Similarly, man has built about him a socially conditioned menstruum of give-and-take affects that are purely substitutive. These are the affects now systematized into man's pseudo-identity or 'I'-persona.

In its response, then, to a selective, symbolic stimulus the reaction of the animal represents the physiological rudiment of the part- or affect-response we have seen in man. For in the animal, no less than in man, the selective reaction always entails a response that is discrete, apart from, and that is substituted for the natural response that characterizes the species in accordance with the law intrinsic to it as a phyloörganism. The difference between the partitive response of the animal and the partitive response of man is that man's symbolic or partitive reaction has become socially or interrelationally systematized throughout the organism of the species. This systematization, as I have said, is represented subjectively in the pseudo-identity each of us reflexly impersonates as the "I" or 'I'-persona—a constellation of affects and prejudices that replaces man's species solidarity or his primary identity as an organism.

The animal, of course, possesses no 'I'-persona. To the dog, the sense of "I" or "me" is an unknown quantity. But in the conditioned dog there is a situation that, in the main, sufficiently resembles the situation in conditioned (ditentive) man to invite comparison. There is much to consider, though, before we can claim this similarity. For the moment, however, let us take a situation in the behavior of man that is analogous to that of the conditioned dog. A man builds a house. The house is good; it shelters and protects him. Along comes a friend who, as it happens, is a competent architect, and says, "I don't like the house." Says the owner, "This is my house. If you don't like it, go your way." There is defense and offense on the part of both, and in a moment both are angry. The house is still a good house that shelters and protects, but suddenly a difference has arisen subjectively between the two men that has nothing to do with the original actuality of the object, house. A "right' opinion (an affect or prejudice) has interposed. The building is no longer a mere house. To the angry owner it is *my* house—my possession. To the angry friend or architect it is also now not a house. For him, too, it is a possession; it is *his* reputation or authority as an architect. It is now the house equally of two identical 'I'-personae whose unilateral interests or "rights" stand to one another in the relation of a mutually obdurate dichotomy. In the eyes of the owner, *the* house has been replaced by *my* house. In the eyes of the architect, *the* house has been replaced by *my* opinion. With both, a conditioning stimulus has been substituted for an object of reality, much as in the case of the dog a bell has been substituted for a delectable bit of meat.

We cannot emphasize too strongly that part or selective reactions in the animal bear only a remote resemblance to part or selective reactions in man. For in man, part-reactions are an invariable expression of the 'I'-persona. They involve in every instance the substitution of secondary affect for primary feeling, the part-reaction being an expression of the systematization of affects that now separates the individual, and the affectively clustered community or nation, from the total principle of motivation governing the organism of man as a phylic unit. In short, affective or partitive conditioning in man constitutes a conditioning that is phylic. Man as a species has unconsciously been led to adopt a substitutive, symbolic, partitive plane of reactivity or behavior that now constantly replaces throughout all man's waking state (as well as during certain levels of sleep) the primary reaction of the phyloörganism as a whole.

This vast system of conditioning in man differs from the type of conditioning observable in the experimental animal not only quantitatively but also qualitatively. Man—interrelational man—begins and ends with disturbed, affective behavior. For the interrelational behavior of man begins and ends with affectively conditioned reflexes. The behavior of the experimental animal, on the contrary, begins with biologically whole reactions. A dog must first be conditioned to biologically inadequate stimuli. And if after a dog has been abnormally conditioned he is allowed to go free, he begins automatically to return to his biologically normal behavior. With the withdrawal of the animal from its conditioning stimuli, it automatically reverts to the organism's primary *status quo*. With man, such a return to biologically normal behavior does not take place. As things stand at present it cannot take place. For man is now abnormally or affectively conditioned throughout. In the course of his evolution man as a species has accidentally conditioned himself socially or interrelationally through the gradual interpolation of language or the signs of objects in substitution for the primary reaction of the phylosoma as a unitary whole. Thus, with man, an autogenous system or entity has been created whose operation throughout the species is now automatic, partitive and, to all intents and purposes, self-sufficient. Unlike the animal, therefore, man is enveloped in a compact mesh of conditioning stimuli. The difference is that in the experimental animal the partitive becomes *in the moment* its whole interest; whereas in the human animal the whole interest is *at every moment* partitive. Man's very identity is now partitive. He is now partitively or affectively conditioned throughout the species or phylum. But so universal is the conditioning of man, and so compact is it socially, that he now regards his partitive or conditioned behavior as "normal," and the society made up of such conditioned responses as "normality."

If the hominid is to recover its elemental balance and restore its biologically normal behavior, it may do so only as it undertakes its own regeneration as an organismic group or community. It may do so only as a species or phylum. The individual who theoretically might make the effort to return to a healthy biological norm would be straightway reconditioned environmentally, interrelationally. His affective conditioning is systematized not only socially but also phylically. This affective conditioning of man is handed down from generation to generation. The behavior of man that is held by man to be normal throughout the phylum is not normal; it is abnormal. Though every infant born to the species must be newly reconditioned, this substitutive, this conditioned phylic mechanism has become crystallized throughout the hominid and is now everywhere sufficient unto itself. Man's conditioning is autogenic.

We cannot induce the anomalous condition of affect in an animal, but we can induce in him a momentary part-interest. In this sense we do get in the animal the rudiment of what in man is the affect. But affect or prejudice exists and can exist only in man. Affect is the crowding of man's whole feeling and motivation into a physiological sector that cannot possibly accommodate it. The affect may be a woman, yet it cannot be a woman; it must be *my* woman. It may be property, yet it cannot be property; it must be *my* property. It may be religion, an opinion, or God, or a political party, but it cannot be any of these; it must be *my* religion, *my* opinion, *my* God, *my* political party.

Unlike the artificial conditioning of the animal, the self-conditioning of man is reflexly self-sustaining. This system of inter-relational self-conditioning is responsible for the phylically disparate and incongruous 'I'-persona with its affective autocracy and absolutism—a situation which we have seen in its extension throughout the species. In the discrete conditioning of the animal we have only the physiological rudiment of the affect; in the social conditioning of man we have the physiological systematization of the affect into spuriously separate and independent personae.[9]

It is here in this affect-systematization that the trouble began to brew. For the 'I'-persona, being autopathic or numinal, is essentially an isolationist. It is ditentive, partitive, as contrasted with the primary orthopathic organism which, in adhering to its basic principle or to the nomen, is undifferentiated, unitary, total. Again it is the 'I'-persona, or man's pseudo-identity that is at stake. The cogitations that prevail at our various peace conferences do not take account of the 'I'-persona with its ulterior, unilateral, numinal bias. So that the proceedings of these autopathic panels are embarrassed, obstructed by each representative's prior commitments to his affective "opinion," "right" or "rights." Naturally, the delegates cannot apply the criterion of the nomen to their several affairs of State in the absence of the opportunity to apply this orthopathic test to their own partitive or numinal state of mind—to their own rightness. And so with the United Nations Organization. As these lines are written, the proceedings of that gathering are cluttered and obstructed with the ditentive, affective elements that are the inescapable prerogative of each nation's collective 'I'-persona. The mind of man will not be free of its affective rightness until it has rid itself of its autopathic polemics and verbigerations. Man is chronically "right."

There is then, as mentioned earlier in the chapter, the total response to an actual object, or what we may call the organism's *orthonomic* response on the one hand, and the affective or part response to a mere partitive symbol, or the organism's *metanomic* response, as it may be called, on the other. Notwithstanding that this altered pattern of orientation with respect to the environment is limited in neural area, it entails a profound alteration in the organism's behavior. For where the organism confronts an affect-laden sign in place of its natural bionomic object, there occurs a shift in the soma's internal tonicity. That is to say, where there occurs a response to the partitive symbol of an object, there is induced a functional dislocation whereby the organism's total reaction is displaced in favor of its symbolic or part response. Correspondingly, where the physiological stimulus is whole and undifferentiated, the organism's response is whole and undifferentiated. From the standpoint of phylobiology the type of behavior to which I have applied the term orthonomic—an infant's response to light, a craftsman's response to his tools—coincides with the organism's total reaction to the environment. The corresponding internal tone may be conveniently referred to as the *orthotonic* pattern of response. The metanomic type of behavior, on the other hand, coincides with the organism's partitive reaction to the environment. In this instance the corresponding internal tone may be distinguished as the *paratonic* pattern.

With regard to the metanomic type of reaction it is important to hold tight to the fact that man, like the dog, never responds to the stimulus as such. *With man, as with the animal, it is the affective impression associated with the sign or signal, to which the soma reacts.* For the individual dog this sign is associated with its need of an actual environmental security, namely, food; but for the species man the sign is now invariably associated with the spurious promise of security held out by an elaborate *system* of affecto-symbolic substitutes or *social images*.[10] From the parochial angle of our conventional mental symptomatology, the system of deflected responses that is represented most outstandingly in man is the reaction-constellation that psychiatrists regard as peculiar to the "neurotic" individual and have subsumed under the term "mother-complex" or "mother-fixation."

In the phylobiological reckoning, the notion that the "mother-complex" connotes a reaction to a single and special individual must be relinquished. The mother has her mother-complex, too. She has her mother-complex no less than the child, for both are reacting to a form of conditioning that is social. The mother-complex is thus a social complex, and the individual mother but the symbol of it. This is the social reaction that is responsible for man's prejudices, for his ditentive or repercussive behavior. What man really fears and is ever abjectly dependent upon is the prevalent social image begotten of social opinion or approval. It is again the obstinate hang-over of his social reverence for what he has been told by others to think and feel and do. So that in applying the principles of phylobiology, it is indispensable that one see neurosis—his own and other people's—as a social reaction to a social condition of spurious affect, to one's pseudo-identity or "face." We shall never compass the scientific view of a whole disorder as long as we cling automatically to a mere selective part of it.

Phyloanalysis, therefore, regards the mother-image and its influence upon the child as a phylic conditioning and classifies this generic mother-complex as an affecto-symbolic reaction specific to the hominid. What each mother is in her community-conditioning, all mothers are in their community-conditioning—and fathers too, of course. For phylobiology the question is not how or in what manner individuals are verbally conditioned. The interest of phylobiology lies in the social influence of the process of verbal conditioning as transmitted from organism to organism, and in the *physiological* effect of this phylic conditioning upon human reactions from generation to generation. On this basis the neurosis is not a sporadic disease but a disorder of behavior that is pandemic.

Speaking of behavior, it should be said that through some ineptness in habits of human reckoning the position of phylobiology is not infrequently confused with that of other schools, most often perhaps with the school of General Semantics. But I really must demur at the persistent tendency among students of behavior to align the researches of my associates and myself with the principles of schools to which our investigations in the field of behavior are in no way related. The method of phylobiology does not make contact with the school of the semanticists at any point—nor, as far as I know, with any other school. After all, where we are dealing with behavior, it is primarily the method, and only the method, that is decisive in any school. It is not what it *thinks*, but what it *does* that defines a school of behavior.

I have yet to see a psychiatrist, a semanticist, a representative of any school or system of behavior subsisting within the frame of "normality" whose principle rests upon the thesis that the identity, the central constant, the very substance of the organism's motivation is decentered and its behavior dissociated in all its interrelational processes, and who has devised a technique consistent with that thesis. I have yet to see or hear of a laboratory of behavior in which students and director recognize a distortion in man's pattern of feeling and motivation throughout, and in which the corrective method consists in repudiating the entire sum of the students' and the director's socially motivated habits of behavior. In the premises of phylobiology, it is our explicit position that the attempt to cope with neurosis by disparaging the symbols of language or any other external item or manifestation is putting the cart before the horse. From the outset we have insisted upon the essentially veridical character of man's verbal forms of interchange within the social setting in which they are employed. It is not the distorted meaning or symbol that is responsible for the incited affect; it is the incited affect that is responsible for the distorted meaning or symbol. Primarily it is the dislocation in the organism's motivation as a whole that is responsible for conflict and ineptness in the organism's interrelational reactions generally.

Far from concerning ourselves with the symbol or with this or that affect with which this or that symbol of language has become burdened, our attack has centered solely upon man's affective (autopathic) identity. It has centered upon the affective replacement by the 'I'-persona of the phyloörganism's reaction as a whole. Our procedure has nothing to do with situational "revaluations," with altered "identifications" or with improved "cortical control." It has to do with the inadvertent substitution in man of a basis of identity that is false because a process of social conditioning has replaced the organism's primary principle of identity throughout the processes of man as a phylum. Rather than seek, therefore, to explain the evidences of man's distorted behavior-motivations upon a purely interpersonal, ideational basis, it has been our effort to trace these disorders of affect to their phylophysiological substrate. We have regarded the verbal frames on which the community's behavior-distortions are hung as relatively quite innocuous epiphenomena, and have consistently emphasized the biophysiological basis of behavior-disturbances. In our finding, it is not the letter but the spirit of the word that betrays the underlying pathology of its meaning—a spirit coextensive with the decentering or dissociation in man of the organism's central constant of motivation. What, indeed, avails the letter of the symbol against the spirit of the affect? Does any of us in his heart of hearts doubt the answer? But "the heart" is not consulted. The truth is, we are not interested in the organism's basic mood or motivation, but are completely caught up in the social reflexes of the part-brain and its affecto-symbolic habits of behavior.

To the phylobiologist, the part-brain is responsible for the 'I'-persona. And to the phylobiologist, all affect entails the part-brain or 'I'-persona. That is, it entails man's pseudo-identity or his dissociation of personality as a species. So that when I say that the semanticists do not base their thesis upon the same premise as that of the phylobiologists, I mean simply that they do not base their thesis upon the affective displacement of man's motivation or behavior throughout all his interrelational reactions. Not to do this means, for me, not to confront man's actual pathology—man's actual disorder of behavior. And not to confront man's basic disorder of behavior in dealing with the problem of behavior means, for me, merely to deal in words. If, among those words, there is the phrase, "the organism as a whole" and kindred expressions, it is still mere words, mere theory; it is still the use of the letter in place of recognizing *as an organism* the primacy of man's organismic feeling, and abrogating whatever reactions are not consonant with this primary principle of behavior. Psychiatrists are special offenders in this regard. They speak frequently of "the organism as a whole" and use similar conceptual phrases. But in these expressions they are but beating the air. No such artifactual entity as the 'I'-persona and the barrier which this pseudo-identity erects against man's total organismic feeling receives any recognition in this psychiatric symbol-usage. Like my associates and myself, psychiatrists cannot attain the needed bionomic adjustment in respect to problems of behavior except as they have adopted the discipline of phyloanalysis in relation to their own behavior-processes.

We have already noted the two-way policy of action characteristic of the nervous or mental patient due to his partitive identity or to the 'I'-persona. We have seen that he tends to do "right," but that he also tends to do "wrong." In the conditioning of the neurotic, however, the cherished prize, as I have said, is not food, but the mere affecto-symbolic security based upon mother-love or sympathy. Linked with his pseudo-security—with his affective memories of the mother—there are words and phrases possessing for the patient as strong associations or affects, as the associations or affects that link the bell and the meat for the dog. In his dichotomous images of self-satisfaction the neurotic wavers between the affectively approved and the affectively disapproved response, between the comfort of parental protection and the hazards of parental rejection. Thus in his alternative conditioning the neurotic, no less than the experimentally dissociated animal, is faced with a critical choice between the issues of gain and denial, between "right" and "wrong"; and from the point of view of his ambivalent images he feels no permanent security as to the direction in which his advantage lies.

Phyloanalysis, or the bio-social analysis of individuals and groups, has made evident also the existence of an inhibiting division in the motivation of social man. It has made evident that the socially "normal" individual is equally at a loss to distinguish between an advantageous and a disadvantageous behavior-response, between the "right" and the "wrong" choice, between prejudice for and prejudice against. Our investigations show that with the normal personality as with the experimental animal, his advantage or satisfaction (as affecto-symbolically incited) must be weighed in the balance against his disadvantage or dissatisfaction. So with the conditioned mind of the social community and *its* dichotomous images. On the basis of its ditentive adaptation the community too is divided between conflicting images as to its ulterior, unilateral choice—as to a course of behavior that is "right" and a course that is "wrong," the one entailing images of social assurance, the other, of social disfavor. But where it is a question of the organism's homeostasis, the situation is very different. The organism's homeostatic balance is, of course, not a "choice" between two opposites. The alternation is instinctual, organismic. The response is determined by the organism as a whole, and upon this response depends the organism's viability and survival. Here we are dealing with balance and polarity, not with conflict or dichotomy.

Comparing the reflexes induced in man interindividually or socially through the employment of the word or symbol, with the reflexes experimentally induced in an animal through the presentation of a card or a bell, our research organization has sought to define in terms of the organism's group-motivation the common element embodied in these reflexly induced reactions in both man and animal. In accordance with our phylobiological formulations this common denominator consists in a process that induces in both man and experimental animal a mere abstract, selective enactment of the organism's primary response as a whole. This altered response consists of an excerpt, as it were, of the soma's total potential behavior-reaction.[11] The induction of socially conditioned reflexes in the species man, therefore, constitutes a form of partialization or decentering of the organism's primary pattern of behavior as a whole. Like the response of the animal to a bell or card, the verbally induced reflex in man constitutes a response that is extracted from, or lifted out of, the organism's central motivating context. In this semblance or sample, so to speak, of its basic behavior, the soma's response, whether in animal or man, takes on the form of a physiological metaphor.

Needless to say, the use of symbol and metaphor is an invaluable economic asset in man's anthroponomic adjustment, but in his partitive zeal man has carried partitive allegory to the point of actual obstruction of the organism's behavior as a species. Admittedly, man's partitive pattern of reaction has provided him with a language and a literature of behavior that has enormously enriched his experience socially. But, owing to the partitive linkage of the affect with the symbol, it has at the same time seriously impaired man's capacity to react as a unitary organism in relation to the environment. This substitution of metaphor for factual response throughout the human organism—this replacement of ortho- or phylo-pathic reactions with reactions that are purely autopathic—has fundamentally altered the social or interrelational behavior of man as a species.

That this alteration in man's behavior is profound need hardly be emphasized. Whether in dog or man, this internal alteration—this semiosomatic process due to an organism's reflex conditioning—finds its motivation in the autonomic or parasympathetic nervous system. An internal shift, therefore, from the total basis of motivation to a level of motivation that is partitive and symbolic throughout the species is deep-seated. The conditioning induced in the animal through a single pair of contrast-stimuli is one thing, but the interindividual conditioning of the hominid by means of affectively toned words or verbal stimuli is quite another. The latter involves a partitive or symbolic modification that extends throughout human society, and this internal bionomic alteration is necessarily reflected in man's social institutions—political, economic, industrial, religious, and educational. It need hardly be pointed out, therefore, that these social institutions are as partitive and as ulterior in their origin as the internal alterations of which these institutions are the external reflection.

With the recognition on the part of my co-workers and myself that man is, throughout, socially conditioned, we were enabled to develop our socially controlled technique in human experimentation.[12] In the course of our analysis we soon came to recognize the parallel that exists between the reaction of the experimental animal in its laboratory compartment and the reactions occurring in the natural confines in which the activities of man have become spontaneously conditioned—the home, the school, the office, the industrial plant, our halls of Congress, and momentarily the United Nations Security Council. In accordance with the conditions of this experimental set-up, our procedure entailed the consistent frustration of both alternatives of the conditioned reaction.[13] Through session after session of laboratory analysis it involved the frustration of the socially ambivalent affects and prejudices (differentially conditioned reflexes) that occur habitually in groups or communities and that reflect the partitive, decentered motivation of man as a species. So that the "good" response and the "bad" were equally objects of challenge. It was not only the subjectively "wrong" affect or the socially incriminating response that constituted the object of our experimental interest, but the subjectively "right" or socially approved behavior-reaction received equal consideration in our objective inquiry.

The partitive confusion in the response of social man to the differential affect-stimuli "right" and "wrong" is, then, the origin and meaning of the ambivalent sensation he experiences subjectively as his "conscience"—a sensation which determines man's moral (affective) "choice" of action and which in its wider community-extension constitutes the highly muddled system of "ethical" values whereby man now attempts to adjust his social, political and economic life. As the social, economic and political life of man with its conflicts and disparities is but the reflection of a division in his internal patterns of innervation, scientific consistency requires that we reckon directly with these basic neural elements. It must become man's interest to derogate the many conflicting and irreconcilable social motivations in his behavior—his so-called moral life—by reducing them to their simplest physiological components. Seen in biological perspective, prejudice is a somatic, neural reaction, not a conventional, moral reaction. But a somatic reaction can be interpreted only in relation to the somatic stimulus that incites it. It is meaningless to attempt to understand and discuss the reactions produced in the hominid in response to the differential stimuli "right" and "wrong," unless we know the nature of these stimuli in their elementary physiological motivation. Only a broader knowledge of man's physiology in relation to this conditioned dichotomy of motivation will serve to restore the problem of man's behavior to its proper place within the domain of medicine and biology.

Repeated experiments with the behavior of social groups offer increasing evidence that the conditioned reflexes which accidental stimuli have produced in communities of men are basically of one piece in their physiological mechanism with the reflexes we have produced with experimental intent in the single animal. The conflict in man's behavior, like the conflict in the differentially conditioned animal, is a conflict between neural patterns of conduction. But as yet students of human behavior have noted only the outer, mental symptoms of this physiological conflict in man, and as a consequence they have attempted to deal with it only in its outer or mental symptomatology. Today when we have seen the entire world uncontrollably enveloped in a mass-reflex of antagonism and combat, the social nature of neurosis or conflict is really too patent to require emphasis. What requires emphasis is the fact that in human societies no less than in the single experimental animal the essential conflict is somatic or physiological. This somatic aspect of human behavior will be discussed in Part II.

NOTES

[1] It is not unadvisedly that I say "underlying." For in such broad community activities, let us say, as the Public Health movement, the purpose of these endeavors in behalf of community welfare is to discover the diseased process underlying the superficial manifestations. The public hygienist is concerned with the protection of the community against the disordered physiological processes answerable for the outer symptoms of disease. With regard, however, to the activities of our societies for Mental Hygiene, the outer manifestations of disease and the alleged "cause" rest upon the same plane. The symptom and the supposed causation are of one cloth. Contrary to the procedure of the physiological hygienist, the pathogenic incident determining "mental" maladaptations is not sought in the distorted physiological processes lying beneath them. Our programs of behavior-hygiene approach the symptoms of behavior through methods that are as symptomatic or "mental" as the symptoms they approach. So that in speaking of the need to recognize community pathology in the field of behavior, I have not in mind the com-

munity's superficial symptoms as shown in mere mental reactions. I have in mind the underlying somatic disturbances within the social organism that are ultimately answerable for the community's superficial or mental disorders of adaptation.

[2] See note 7, page 231.

[3] See pages 212-13.

[4] Anderson, O. D., and Liddell, H. S. "Observations on Experimental Neurosis in Sheep," *Archives of Neurology and Psychiatry*, 1935, Vol. 34, pp. 330-54.

Gantt, W. Horsley, "An Experimental Approach to Psychiatry," *The American Journal of Psychiatry*, 1936, Vol. 92 pp. 1007-21.

———, *Experimental Basis for Neurotic Behaviour* New York, Paul B. Hoeber, 1944, pp. xv + 211.

Maier, Norman R. F., and Glaser, Nathan M., "Studies of Abnormal Behavior in the Rat" *Comparative Psychology Monographs*, 1940, Vol. 16, Serial No. 80, pp. 30.

Pavlov, I. P., *Conditioned Reflexes—An Investigation of the Physiological Activity of the Cerebral Cortex*, London, Oxford University Press, 1928, pp. xv + 430.

[5] Such an experiment has been carried out on monkeys with resulting "neurosis" in the animal.

Galt, William E., "The Capacity of the Rhesus and Cebus Monkey and the Gibbon to acquire Differential Response to Complex Visual Stimuli," *Genetic Psychology Monographs*; 1939, Vol. XXI, pp. 387-457.

Other experiments have been performed in which neurosis was induced by pushing the animal to the limit of its discriminative ability in the learning of intricate mazes and in the mastering of complex visual discriminations.

Fields, P. E., "Contributions to Visual Figure Discrimination in the White Rat, II," *Journal of Comparative Psychology*, 1931, Vol. XI, pp. 349-66.

Karn, H. W., "A Case of Experimentally Induced Neurosis in the Cat," *Journal of Experimental Psychology*, 1938, Vol. XXII, pp. 589-93.

———, "Experimental Neurosis in Infrahuman Animals," *Psychological Record*, 1941, Vol. IV, pp. 35-9.

[6] Burrow, Trigant, *The Biology of Human Conflict—An Anatomy of Behavior, Individual and Social*, New York and London, The Macmillan Company, 1937, pp. xl + 435.

[7] Gantt, W. Horsley, "Relation of Unconditioned and Conditioned Reflex: Effect of Prolongation of the Work Period from the Usual One Hour to a Period of Ten to Twenty Hours," *The Journal of General Psychology*, 1940, Vol. XXIII, pp. 377-85.

Razran, G. H. S., "Conditioned Responses: An Experimental Study and a Theoretical Analysis," *Archives of Psychology*, New York, 1935, No. 191, pp. 124.

[8] Our instrumental results are reported and discussed in Chapter XI and in the Appendix. See also:

Burrow, Trigant, "Kymograph Studies of Physiological (Respiratory) Concomitants in Two Types of Attentional Adaptation," *Nature* (London), 1938, Vol. 142, p. 156.

———, "The Economic Factor in Disorders of Behavior," *The American Journal of Orthopsychiatry, 1939*, Vol. IX, pp. 102-8.

———, "Kymograph Records of Neuromuscular (Respiratory) Patterns in Relation to Behavior Disorders," *Psychosomatic Medicine*, 1941, Vol. III, pp. 174-86.

———, "Neurosis and War: A Problem in Human Behavior," *The Journal of Psychology*, 1941, Vol. 12, pp. 235-49.

———, "Preliminary Report of Electroencephalographic Recordings in Relation to Behavior Modifications," *The Journal of Psychology*, 1943, Vol. 15, pp. 109-14.

Burrow, Trigant, and Galt, William E., "Electroencephalographic Recordings of Varying Aspects of Attention in Relation to Behavior," *The Journal of General Psychology, 1945*, Vol. 32, pp. 269-88.

[9] For a discussion of the phylobiological inferences to be drawn from animal conditioning, see *The Biology of Human Conflict*, Chapter XII.

[10] See note 7, page 155.

[11] G. E. Coghill says: "The conditioned reflex, like the unconditioned, is acquired by analysis of a total pattern which under normal conditions is from the

beginning perfectly integrated." ("Individuation versus Integration in the Development of Behavior," *The Journal of General Psychology*, 1930, Vol. 3, pp. 431-35.) He also says: "Local reactions or reflexes are of secondary origin, and arise within the total pattern." ("Integration and Motivation of Behaviour as Problems of Growth," *Journal of Genetic Psychology*, 1936, Vol. 48, pp. 3-19.) And again: "Normal behavior requires that the total pattern maintains sovereignty over all partial patterns." ("The Biologic Basis of Conflict in Behaviour," *The Psychoanalytic Review*, 1933, Vol. 20, pp. 1-4.)

[12] Burrow, Trigant, *The Biology of Human Conflict*, Chapters X and XI.

———, "So-called 'Normal' Social Relationships expressed in the Individual and the Group, and their Bearing on the Problems of Neurotic Disharmonies," *The American Journal of Psychiatry*, 1930, Vol. X., pp. 101-16.

Galt, William E., *Phyloanalysis—A Study in the Group of Phyletic Method of Behaviour-Analysis*, Psyche Miniatures, London, Kegan Paul, Trench, Trubner & Co., ltd., 1933, pp. 151.

Syz, Hans, "On a Social Approach to Neurotic Conditions," *The Journal of Nervous and Mental Disease, 1927*, Vol. LXVI, pp. 601-15.

"Remarks on Group Analysis," *The American Journal of Psychiatry*, 1928, Vol. VIII, pp. 141-8.

———, "Socio-Individual Principles in Psychopathology," *The British Journal of Medical Psychology*, 1930, Vol. X, pp. 329-43.

[13] See pages 243-48.

CHAPTER VII

THE SOCIAL IMPLICATIONS OF THE 'I'-PERSONA: A SUMMARY

As individuals and as communities we have suddenly awakened to find ourselves enveloped in a welter of unprecedented changes —social, political, economic and scientific. If our minds are to keep pace with the restless current on which we are being carried along, if our senses are to become alert to the teeming dislocations that mark the present, it will be necessary to raise our sights to the farther reaches of a rapidly oncoming future. In this hurrying hour the outstanding domains of man's thought are found wanting. Accepted tenets in many fields of his activity are giving way to rapidly broadening concepts. In this moment of new assessments it is safe to predict that a system of psychotherapy based upon mere autopathic thinking must also gird itself for very radical alterations. It is safe to predict that present-day preoccupations with interpersonal affects, domestic transferences, psychosexual irregularities, marital conflicts, psychotic episodes, and the vast array of neurotic symptoms that comprise our psychiatric systems will in the scientific reckoning of the future appear to us quite obsolete and inept. They will, I feel sure, appear to us as humdrum and archaic as old wives' tales, when contrasted with the basic and encompassing constructs of an organismic phylobiology.

On the basis of phylobiological investigations, human behavior and its disorders will be seen as a problem in neurodynamics. The science of human reactions will attempt to deal with the relationship of organism to environment in terms of matter and energy. Such a program will entail a searching study of the function of the brain and its appendages as they mediate man's organismic adaptation to the outer world. Like all other sciences, phylobiology will perforce extend the function of man's brain and enlarge the sphere of his senses. But, unlike the sciences that deal with the data of the external universe, phylobiology will deal with data internal to the universe of man's behavior. It will deal with the internal universe of reactions that underlie man's feeling and thinking and doing.

In the midst of the obsessive drives and inhibitions that reflect man's level of thought today—drives and inhibitions to which man has become socially conditioned—an adjustment of his social behavior that is primary and organismic can hardly present a welcome or inviting prospect. The very nature of man's social conditioning makes impossible a viewpoint that transcends his conditioning. It would be idle, therefore, to expect the psychopathologist to embrace the prospect of so radical a change with enthusiasm, or even equanimity. His traditional thought-patterns, his customary employment of the senses in his personal, social, economic, and political relations have too firm a hold upon him readily to permit so vital a reversal of their habitual course. Indeed the reaction of the psychopathologist can only cause him to cling the more tenaciously to his accustomed thought-patterns.

So that I would not be understood as wishing to intrude for a moment upon the habits of feeling and thinking of prevailing psychiatric schools. I realize that man's socially conditioned habits of behavior are not susceptible of perfunctory modification. I wish merely to predicate, on the basis of experiments that have been conducted by a small group of investigators, what revaluations the future holds for a science of human behavior, and to suggest the likelihood that with further investigations these revaluations may prove comparable to the reconstructions now taking place in other fields of man's endeavor.

How difficult it is for the psychiatric mind to achieve a phylic sense of its own involvement in a neurosis that is phylic, The Lifwynn Laboratory has had ample opportunity to observe in the rock-bound inertias of those of its students, including myself of course, who are themselves psychiatrists. Yet how could it be otherwise? After all, the behavior of psychiatrists is inherently no more basic or unified than that of other people, for obviously psychiatrists are not any more immune than the rest of the community to a disorder intrinsic to man. But as the accredited guardians of the community's health of mind, it is inevitable that in our reluctance to disclose our own social involvement we psychiatrists should discreetly screen from view any evidence of ineptness of adaptation on our part.[1]

When we consider the modifications that have taken place in

the various fields of man's thought, we recognize that all scientific advance has been preceded by an arbitrary sciolism or pseudo-science. Owing to the insidious presence of the monarchical 'I'-persona or numen, traditional superstition, as we saw in Chapter V, has always antedated systematic inquiry. This was the story of the science of chemistry with its antecedent system of alchemy; of astronomy with its predecessor astrology; and of the science of medicine itself whose forerunners may be seen in the mysticism and magic that long prevailed in regard to the structure and function of the human body.[2] But with the introduction of the science of astronomy and the telescope, "the wide and starry skies" became the intimate laboratory of man. With the advent of chemistry the world of matter became equally man's scientific workshop. And in the sciences of physiology and bacteriology, man was once more faced with the practical materials of laboratory analysis.

In these progressive transitions metaphysical theory and symbol-juggling have been replaced by the direct observation of structures and their demonstrable function. Habits of mental rationalization have been discarded as outmoded and of no avail. Not so, however, with the domain of man's interrelational behavior—with the domain of reactions that relate the organism of man to his environment and to others of his kind. While it is true that this domain of human ecology, too commonly symbolized as the mental sphere, is coming to be known more precisely today as the sphere of human behavior, nevertheless superstition and symbol-juggling continue to dominate this wide domain of man's interrelational experience. The accepted approach to the sphere of human relations still goes hand in hand with the parochial outlook of the astrologer, the alchemist and the tribal medicine man.

In the field of man's behavior then—in the field of our so-called mental reactions—there is equally the need that the symbols of sciolism and metaphysical speculation now give way to a science of behavior. There is the need that the realm of man's environmental interrelations—interrelations that knit organism and environment into a dynamic unit—serve man likewise as a laboratory of investigation. This primary homeostasis that unites man and his environment constitutes the matrix of phylobiology. For phylobiology is the science that makes possible man's study of his own motivations as these motivations mediate between brain and environment and are rendered perceptible within man's own organism. Instead of studying the vast multiplicity of symptoms that characterize the part-brain of man, or crediting with mental labels the endless differentiation of personal motives conditioning this and that individual or group under this or that ever-changing circumstance, phylobiology seeks to reach the common phylic basis of this infinite complex of shifting and accidental symptoms.[3] It attempts to bring to clear definition the physiological substrate of this personal and social symptom-complex by means of an analysis of phylic processes, and it attempts to render this phyloanalysis as objective as it is comprehensive.[4]

The work of Willard Gibbs in vector analysis, his penetrating formulations regarding energy and "entropy" as factors in the thermodynamics of chemistry[5]—a research in which he was in certain respects the forerunner of Einstein; the work of Einstein himself in mathematical physics with its concept of quantum dynamics;[6] the discoveries of Marconi in the field of wireless telegraphy, and the more recent developments in radio transmission and in electronics; the investigations of Darwin into the developmental processes of animal and plant that led to the concept of evolution; the commensurate researches of Koch and Pasteur in relating the physiology of infectious processes to an unseen agent which they later identified as pathogenic bacteria—all these departures from customary patterns of thought introduced man to a new sphere of the senses, and with it to a new application of the function of man's brain to the environment. But none of these extraordinary discoveries had anything to do with the interrelational behavior of man. They placed him in control of new domains of matter and energy and greatly enriched his understanding of the palpable universe of experience, but they did not place man in organismic control of himself and his own processes in their whole relation to the environment and to others. They have in no way clarified man's relation to man.

While these sciences extended the function of man's brain and its special senses, they had nothing to do with human behavior. They had nothing to do with internal imbalances of function as evidenced in the widespread symptomatology of social man with his compulsive and erratic wishes, with his vacillating choices between what he arbitrarily calls the "right" course and the "wrong," with his sudden and morbid volitions, his unpredictable moods, gay or dark, with the infinite sphere of his conative impulses and unreasoning desires, nor with his equally sudden compulsions and capricious inhibitions. In other words, the physical and biological sciences have thus far had nothing to do with the ever-pressing problem of man's disposition to internal conflict. They have had nothing to do with a conflict that is internal to man as a species and that manifests itself symptomatically throughout the world in an unequal allotment of economic opportunity and the right of survival, with a conflict that has resulted in adaptive regression and neurosis, in industrial disturbances, in political and international disorders, in crime and war.

It was the reassertion of the whole brain of man that made possible the discovery of the bacterial origin of infectious diseases with all its sweeping phylic implications—implications that consisted in man's recognition of his susceptibility as a species to the pathogenic invasion of his tissues by an alien species of organism. Through this restoration of man's larger faculties, communicable diseases were for the first time in man's history accorded their true phylic import. Disease was no longer the special distinction of the isolated individual. In this new field of medicine there was no longer the palling influence of the private self-image or numen, and there could no longer be the prerogatory isolation of the individual as a separate biological entity. The myth that explained disease as the expression of a divinity who in his infinite wisdom selected this or that individual or community for special immolation or punishment ceased to exercise over man its hitherto potent charm.

But this sudden awakening to a science of bacteriology—and this awakening occurred, be it remembered, but two or three generations ago—took place only in the sphere of those reactions that related man's organism to a condition in the external environment. Like the sciences of chemistry and electrodynamics, the science of bacteriology had nothing whatever to do with the organismic behavior of man himself. As far as concerns the sphere of those reactions that embrace the relations of individuals in their behavior toward one another—as far as concerns those subjective affects and prejudices that now everywhere color and distort the natural coördination of man as a species—no phylic principle of behavior and hence no phylic concept of the organism's behavior-deviations has as yet penetrated the consciousness of man as a community or phylum. Within the sphere of man's own reactions the numen or the 'I'-persona continues to hold unchallenged sway. Because of his abject subordination to this numinal legerdemain, any individual or any nation is at liberty to believe whatever he likes to believe in regard to his own conduct or that of any other individual or nation. Within the field of man's behavior, even today no biological law has been established for determining the validity of the organism's reactions. As yet no scientifically accepted nomen declares the biological veridity of the organism's reaction in its relation to the environment or to others of its kind.

How then is man to recover the consistent function of his senses in the domain of his own behavior? How is man's participation in the dependable sequences that preserve the universal order of his responses to the objects of the outer world to be reëstablished? Only in the measure in which man succeeds in throwing off the influence of the social numen will he be able to employ the larger resources of his senses and restore the function of his brain as a whole in relation to the objects and conditions about him.

As has been said, there is evidence that this numinal impediment to the accurate correspondence of man's senses in respect to outer relations and events is ultimately traceable to a dislocation in the neurodynamic function of the brain of man as a phylum, and that this phylic impediment is therefore susceptible of objective definition and localization. In its symptomatic aspects this neurodynamic deviation first manifested itself in the reactions we were able to observe socially through our group-method of analysis—a method that posits the total organism as the instrument of observation and from this total basis proceeds to analyze reactions that are autopathic or partitive and that therefore deviate from it. We found through this phyloanalytic technique that a persistent affect-distortion pervades the reactions of the social community generally and obstructs its interrelational function throughout.[7] We found that because of this numinal obstruction the private opinions of social man with their personal criteria of interpretation constantly override the natural acquiescence of man's senses in response to data presented to them.

In Chapter V we considered the law or nomen whereby the organism's dependable response is unfailingly linked with the accurate correspondence between its sense impressions and the objects or conditions impinging upon them in the surrounding world. We considered the extent to which this law is vitiated through the encroachments upon it of the numen, or through the interposition of quite arbitrary opinions and judgments in violation of this basic law or nomen. We saw how inferences in regard to the surrounding world, which are wholly lacking in objective warrant, have come to replace the dictates of sound reason, and how the features of the external world are blurred and its true lineaments distorted through the extravagant insinuations of this esoteric numen.

We found it incumbent upon us to consider the extent to which the processes of man's own behavior have been travestied through the false opinions and beliefs that have intercepted man's relation to himself—man's relation to man. We have considered how man's false subjective response has warped his objective world. We have considered what the brain of man has done to the objects and events of man's external cosmogony. But more important still we have considered the result of the inept action of man's brain upon the world within him—upon his own subjective behavior. We have seen how man's subjective world, the world of his own feeling and thinking, is perverted by man's subjective premise of thought and feeling or by the numen. Man's opinion of himself, his opinion of others, his artificial projections, his affiliations and his segregations, his accommodations or regressions, his sympathies or revulsions, his coöperation or disaffection, his ability to get on with others or to fail of contact with them, his moods, his prejudices, his unaccountable enthusiasms and his apathies—all these reactions are ditentive expressions of the 'I'-persona or the numen, and all have distorted man's adjustment as a conscious organism to the environment.

By the term 'I'-persona, then, I mean the artificial system of prefabricated affects and prejudices that underlies man's present level of "normal" feeling and thinking and that leads to inferences that are lacking in biological warrant. I mean the social conditioning that has placed a premium upon man's subjective emotions at the expense of his objective relationships. This affective constellation of feeling and thinking that developed in the course of man's mental and social evolution has seriously clouded the unitary motivation of individual and group. The developmental modification that obscured the subjective outlook of man as a unitary organism was due to a unique mechanism operative within the phylum. I refer to the subjective mechanism of projection. This phylic phenomenon of projection emerged in man coincidently with his acquisition of the language-forming function of the brain and is therefore peculiar to the human species. With the development of language there was developed a consciousness of self. There was developed a subjective process that had heretofore been non-existent and that was all unconsciously brought into being. This process came into being through the emergence of the symbol-complex or 'I'-persona and its oblique, unilateral premise of motivation.

With this subjective entity, man incurred the self-attentive impedimenta we have recognized as the social image, as man's private systematization of affects and prejudices, as his *amour propre,* as the symbolic foundation of his many Gods, and finally, as the symbol that man has invoked in substitution for his own organism and that is now everywhere devoutly cherished by him as "face," prestige or "goodness." The 'I'-persona is one's "right." The 'I'-persona or one's "right" is one's sovereignty—one's spurious sovereignty. And a nation's "right" rests upon this same spurious, autopathic sovereignty. Owing to the preëminence of the 'I'-persona, all right, all sovereignty is based upon an arbitrary, esoteric self-identification that is metanomic rather than orthonomic. Such a "right" marks a reversal of function or motivation that is ditentive, partitive, self-interested. It is a reversal of the basic behavior of man. Because of it, the individual, group or nation has become completely detached from man's primary organismic principle of motivation. "Right" or the 'I'-persona has replaced man's basic homeostasis, his orthonomic balance of reaction in relation to the environment.

In consequence, what was at first only a superficial differentiation in man's interrelations—what was a mere peripheral self-consciousness, or a purely symbolic, extrinsic distinction between "you" and "me"—began to seep into and slowly permeate man's organism in its internal motive and interest. A discrimination or division that was at first only mental or projective began to enter into the deeper reactions of the total organism, until gradually, unconsciously, man's *feeling* became divided too. The feeling of man as an integrated species or phylum became divided. For the originally unitary purpose and incentive of organismic man now became split up into the private and ulterior interests of each individual or group as a separate and independent persona. Whether in the single persona of the individual or in the collective persona of the group, it became split up into the self-conscious image of *my* feeling or interest versus *your* feeling or interest. A wedge of secret competitiveness sundered the primary coördination of man's organism as a biologically functioning whole. Self-attention had entered in—self-attention and "the knowledge of good and evil." There was now no longer the united pursuit of the common welfare of individual and community as a phylically integrated entity. Instead, there developed a partitive, disunited lamina of feeling and thinking which ran parallel to and controverted the unitary and coördinated principle of behavior that was man's primary biological equipment.[8] I should like to explain in some detail the division between these parallel systems extending throughout the phylum.

With man's acquirement of the use of the symbol, with his increasing facility in handling the verbal *signs* of objects in place of objects themselves, man acquired a mechanism of symbolic projection that was mediated chiefly through the eye and ear and the special laryngeal system. This application of the special senses constituted, of course, the development of speech.[9] It would seem not unlikely that originally man made concrete use of the symbol without bionomic mishap. It would seem that the misadaptation involved in the development of the 'I'-persona, and hence of affect, marked the inception of man's neurosis as a phylum. It is even possible that man's use of concrete symbols antedated by a considerable evolutionary interval the partitive development of the 'I'-persona and its ulterior, unilateral affect.

But with the introduction of this restricted part-mechanism, the life of man began to assume a restricted, partitive basis of behavior instead of adhering to its originally organismic pattern of behavior as a species or phylum.[10] This part-mechanism is the mechanism with which individuals are related to one another upon a dichotomous basis of "liking" or "disliking." They are related to one another pleasantly or unpleasantly, approvingly or disapprovingly according as they find or do not find other people in agreement with what they have been taught is the proper way to think and feel and do. And so affect or "goodness" appeared upon the scene. Affect is always *my* affect, goodness is *my* goodness, my right. Where there is affect there is only personal judgment; where there is personal judgment, the final criterion of behavior is a private determinant, an absolute ultimatum, an arbitrary interpretation. Affects are now inseparable from our symbolic mechanism of interrelation. They are the structure of our interpersonal attractions and repulsions. This affective basis of man's interrelationships is the pitfall of man's ditentive or autopathic mode of communication.

This matter of inept communication, of a false basis of contact among people because of the intrusion of retroactive affects accounts for the heavy score man has to settle with himself by reason of his misdirected development of the highly useful instrument of language. As I remarked elsewhere:

> Through a phylic study of the physiology we *feel*, it becomes apparent that our predominant habituation to the use of the symbol as a means of communication has seriously jeopardized the natural instinctive avenues of communication among us. It becomes apparent that the overwhelming absorption of the activities of man in the symbols of cerebral interchange has unnaturally repressed the feelings of interchange that belong to the instinctive, autonomic life, with its internal sensations and reactions. Phylogenetically, the mechanism appears to be somewhat like this: The instinctive feelings—the sense of community-identification and wholeness as individuals of a common phylum—are forces which of their dynamic nature must seek expression. Because man is now all-engrossed in the outlets of social communication afforded him through the avenues of the symbol—the intercerebral channels of contact—he is denied an outlet in the natural interbehavioral reactions of the race, i.e., in the continuity of expression of the organism as a whole that belongs to the instinctive interactions of work and play, of industrial activities and economic conservation, of creative construction, of relaxation and spontaneous sex-fulfillment.
>
> In this situation our incontrovertible instinctive trends crowd upward toward the cerebral paths of egress and seek projection through the medium of the external senses and the symbol. They are dislodged from their natural seat within the organism as a whole, and are compressed within the confines of the cerebral segment. In this recourse a conflict ensues. Feelings that are organic reside only in organic structures—in our muscular, neural, vasomotor and visceral tissues. Feelings are not something aerial and symbolic. Feeling-sensations are not subject to projection into the external forms of communication afforded by physical sound- or light-waves as employed in our symbol or intercerebral interchange. Physiological feelings can reside only in the solid flesh of which they are the subjective coefficient.[11]

It is not the word, then, but the flesh that calls for indictment in the matter of man's disorders of behavior. The semanticists, I believe, have laid undue stress upon the ineptitudes of the word.

They have failed to see that it is the organism as a whole whose reaction is involved, whose function is misplaced. They have failed to see that it is man's total identity as a phylum that has been dislocated as a result of the systematization of affects lying back of the symbol. In the final analysis it is neither the "weakness" nor the "unwillingness" of this or that one's flesh or spirit that has got us into trouble. The difficulty is phylophysiological. For the function of the flesh or organism is now autopathic and divided within man as a species, and the "spirit" or the organism's outer mental and verbal expressions are necessarily autopathic and divided also.[12]

I would not make all this ado about the wide disparity between the methods of General Semantics and Phylobiology, were not Korzybski so determined to proselytize me on the ground that "we are saying the same thing." Perhaps we are. But do our organisms *feel* the same thing? For I hold that the problem with Korzybski, as with myself, is not our *mental* reconcilability with one another. Rather it is our common recognition of our common social neurosis, of a disorder of feeling common to man, and of the irreconcilability of every individual's affective insistence upon the uncommon nature of *his* particular 'I'-persona. The 'I'-persona with its fallacies of motivation will continue to prevail until man— man as a species, and not merely a few behavior specialists—assumes the burden of his own behavior-problem.

The development of speech or the word constituted, of course, a tremendous asset for man socially and economically but, at the same time, owing to a *faux pas* in his evolution, the acquirement of the symbol and of language exacted of man a very onerous toll. For concomitant with the use of this handy instrument of symbol-projection as applied by man to external objects, the mechanism of symbolic projection, as stated earlier, reverted upon its inventor, and in so doing came to apply itself unconsciously to man himself.[13] Because of this projective attitude of individuals of the species toward one another, this partitive mechanism gradually came to muddle very seriously man's primary relationships interindividually. So that while the elements of the species undoubtedly enjoyed a greater facility in communicating with one another in respect to outer objects and conditions, man's increasing symbol-usage gradually led to its imperceptible encroachment upon his own organism and upon its primary pattern of behavior. His symbol-usage encroached upon the phylum until the coördination uniting the species as an organismic whole was largely superseded socially by a purely projective or affecto-symbolic interrelationship of individuals to one another.[14] In this retrofective reaction, motivation was turned back and interest reversed. For affect is resurgent feeling.

This alteration in the adaptation of man as a species entailed profound consequences phyloörganismically. It entailed an alteration in man's bionomic frame of reference that affected the basic physiology of man's relation to man. The behavior of the phylum no longer arose from its original pattern of motivation—a pattern of motivation in which the individual is the outgrowth of a confluent, organismic whole—but the individuals of the species came to be symbolically projected by one another as discrete, disjunctive elements. There was established the artificial existence of the biologically separate 'I'-persona, or the affecto-symbolic "I." In accepting the priority of this socially discrete "I," the individuals of the species assumed a basis that was henceforward numerical rather than continuous. They became an extrinsic association rather than an intrinsic unit. As a community or phylum man's frame of reference from now on was collective rather than organismic.

Let us turn once more to the genealogical implications of this bionomic shift as symbolically portrayed in the early legends of man's conscious descent. At its very outset the story of man is the story of an interrelational impasse. With the beginning of consciousness man was set at odds with himself and with his environment. Man first became conscious when he became a person—when he ate of the fruit of knowing and *knew* he was a person. In knowing he was a person, in becoming a separate subjective "I," man lost contact with the solidarity of his organism as a species; he lost contact with the very soil that had nourished him. His motivation as a total species in relation to the environment was now interrupted by the innovation of the symbol, of language or of knowing. Through man's constant substitution of the symbol, or of separate, ulterior knowing, he himself became but a symbol. He became part of a separate and ulterior system of symbolic knowing. This was the genesis of man's partitive behavior. This the rudiment of man's psychosis. Having been affectively taught by means of the symbol what was "right" and what was "wrong" *feeling*, having been told by others how he should feel and think and do, man became part of a socially affective system of behavior, of a divisive system of feeling and thinking. This was man's persona-consciousness, his self-consciousness. This was man's fall. For man had become discrete, unilateral, ulterior; he had become an automatically projected pseudo-identity, and man himself now stood apart from himself. The phyloörganism of man was split up into the knowing elements or social images constitutive of the 'I'-persona of each individual, as of each group, and the earth was accursed in the symbolic division man had wrought.

In the intolerable dichotomy and conflict of his self-awareness— in his unbearable separateness as a person—man felt naked and alone and he sought to hide himself. He had forfeited his organismic security as a total entity in relation to the environment, and from now on man was repressed, secretive, divided, introverted; he was guilty and full of fear. In short, man was neurotic. Fanciful images had begun to replace factual reality. In his psychoneurosis, in his biologically insupportable isolation, man was driven to project the image of a larger Presence than his own. He was driven to compensate for the loss of his organism's bionomic integrity as a total functioning unit by conjuring the presence of a stronger, wiser Persona who, as an all-powerful parent, would henceforth counsel and protect him. In the need of social man for parental domination and authority there entered upon the scene of his conscious evolution the hallucinatory image man created in his own likeness and called "God." In his phylic plight, in his loss of a sense of species articulation, it is quite understandable that man should have employed this social numen to compensate for the absence of his organism's primary unity of motivation and behavior. It is quite understandable that he should have projected a *symbol* of unity to which he might henceforth appeal for protection in substitution for the order and continuity inherent in the observable universe and no less in man's own organism.

All this, though, is but allegory. It merely reflects man's religious intuition and the unconscious symbolism in which the folk mind has through the ages been wont to account for man's early division or his "original sin." [15] This trespass against the law of "God" was a trespass against a merely fanciful, autopathic image of "God." It was the God of man's own making. Having been wrought of man's wishful, autopathic thinking, this God represents but the numen. But this God is not in unison with the central, integrative principle or constant that governs the orderly processes underlying all phenomena and that governs no less the processes of man. The organism of man in its primary integral functioning is one and continuous with the consistent harmony of the physical world of matter and energy around him. According to phylobiological findings it is only as man's motivation or behavior is consciously coördinated and at one with this harmonious principle operating within and about him that he gives to this principle a consistent, intelligent, living acknowledgment.

I realize that whoever presumes to write objectively of Deity treads upon ticklish ground. And in a sense this is as it should be. For the forces that make for order and constructiveness in the world of outer phenomena man has always acknowledged with instinctive reverence. But in the shallowness of his fanciful superstitions man has failed to sense the unity and continuity of his own organism with the wider harmony governing the manifestations in the physical world of matter and energy. Instead, he has arbitrarily set up false images of personal authority before which he cringes or upon which he fawns according to his whim. Repudiating the integrity of his organism and its continuity and coordination with the phenomenal world, man continues to worship the false Gods or the numina he himself has constructed in his own image and likeness. And so, while the theocratic affect-pretensions of the 'I'-persona undoubtedly merit the thoughtful examination of the scientist, to attempt to bring to book these anomalous factors in man's adaptation is to appear to desecrate the age-old sanctuaries of our most sacred institutions.

Originally, of course, all science was an affront to habitual wishful creeds. But in man's larger, organismic view this has not mattered. However inept his digressions of fantasy, at heart man has been profoundly conscious of those cosmic motivations that underlie and integrate the processes of the phenomenal world. To some of us this universal order and harmony is all we know, all that we care to know as God. And to the phylobiologist these unitary principles abide no less within the internal universe of man's own organism. It is only as the 'I'-persona usurps the rightful place of man's organism in relation to the external universe that man has been led to set up mere images of authority, human and divine, in substitution for the healthy functioning of his organism. Man's images of a theocratic presence, vicariously set up at the behest of the 'I'-persona, are responsible for the dethronement of the basic power and authority resident within man's own organism. Man must see—and in the restlessness existing today throughout his world there is earnest that man *will* see—that the numen, the God of his superstition, is nothing other than the projection of this artificial 'I'-persona now residing within himself. Man will see that this numen has been, and today still is, his undoing; that it is an entity whose malevolent inventions threaten to destroy the very life of man.

In this organismic account of the "fall of man" we shall find the biological basis of ditention, of man's dualism and self-consciousness—of his conditioning and neurosis as a species. For it is not in religions or in philosophies or yet in theories of man's mental evolution, but in ourselves that we must look for a criterion of diagnosis and correction in respect of deviations occurring within ourselves. But recourse to measures of systematic diagnosis and repair occurring within ourselves calls for a very special physiological technique.

Phyloanalysis set out with the attempt to analyze the affecto-symbolic 'I'-persona and its special prerogative as commonly assumed by social man; and it undertook to differentiate this pseudo-entity from the organism's biological basis of integration and behavior. Our analysis of social groups made evident that there was nothing special or prerogatory about this affective "I". Analysis made evident that it is artificial, ditentive, autopathic throughout, and that the arrogating of special distinction, merit or privilege to the symbol we call the "I"—the *self* or *me*—is a socially current fallacy common to us all.

From man's ever-present collective frame of reference born of clashing 'I'-personae, each with its own separate premise of behavior, all our efforts of unity represent mere get-together programs of accord. Resting on a basis of mere "collective" security, as it has come to be called, these efforts of peaceful affiliation, however well-intentioned, are merely additive, accumulative, acquisitive. Stemming from a purely partitive, ditentive, unilateral basis of motivation, they represent an entirely spurious effort of unification that compensates with mere symbol or index the loss of man's primary unity and coördination as a phylum.

Phylobiologically there is only one quality that counts. That quality is oneness. In the absence of this quality of oneness, all other qualities are meaningless, insubstantial. In the absence of the quality of oneness, "I" must at all times be affective, partitive toward others. "I" may not be united organismically with anyone. And this is true of everybody. There is no wholeness, no unity. Everybody is something to everybody else—a little here, a little there. But always the interest is fragmentary. Though it may seem at times very great, very deep, yet in the absence of man's articulation as a phylum, in the absence of the oneness of man, interest or feeling or affection is still only partitive. It is all things to all men. It is not one.

From its illusory background of self-importance and self-sufficiency—from its delusional sense of itself as a complete entity or whole—the 'I'-persona necessarily regards every item about it as also a complete whole, as *its* complete entity or whole. Whether the item or part be a woman, property, reputation, success at cards, business or what not, in relation to this absolute "I" it becomes "the whole." In the artificially enlarged affect-perspective of the personal "I," the part or item is all there is; within the limited range of its partitive vision there is nothing else.[16] But where there is the organism's sense of its primary ontogenetic wholeness as an element within the phylum, the item assumes its proper place in the field of interest. It is then but a part, and this part is readily assigned its proportionate rôle or meaning in relation to the larger organismic whole. But because of the spurious absolutism of the 'I'-persona, one's every interest, one's motivating drive, is distorted beyond all bounds. For the 'I'-persona, as one says in vulgar parlance, has a keen eye for the main chance. Says the 'I'-persona: "This or that is for me, therefore it is all; it is the whole, it is the sum of meaning." That is to say, for me, for the 'I'-persona, the part is always the whole.

Accordingly, there is need to recognize that man's adaptation has come to be almost exclusively partitive, episodic, disjunctive. Dealing indiscriminately, as we now do, with the symbols or indices of objects and with the symbols or indices of one another, man has come to assume a projective basis of behavior that is wholly insular and discrete. Where he does think in terms of mass behavior, his background is collective, numerical, summative. As in one's attitude toward the sum of single elements that constitutes a set of checkers or dominoes, the student of behavior has come to assume that numbers of individual men make up or constitute the mass motivation or behavior embodied in the organism of man as a phylum. Here, I believe, is a fatal and widespread fallacy, and upon its shoulders rests the responsibility for the chaos of behavior that exists throughout our social, political and economic life today.

The individual is, of course, not just a part of the species or phylum in the sense in which a domino is part of a set of dominoes. An individual organism is the outgrowth of an organismic principle of behavior that is motivated within the phylum as a whole and, as an outgrowth of this phylic principle of integration, the individual remains always an integral element within the organism of man as a unit. As such an integral element within the species or phylum, the individual is not a summative part, but is himself ontogenetically a whole, just as the species of which he is the outgrowth is phylogenetically an integrated whole. As individuals we are fundamentally not separate; we are integral wholes within an integral whole. This is the conception we need somehow *to transmute into a physiological pattern of behavior and incorporate biologically within ourselves as a species or phylum*. Security for the partitive, symbolic system of man that is merely collective, acquisitive, means only insecurity for man's primary pattern of behavior based, as it is, upon his organismic coördination as a total phylum.[17]

Where it is a question of behavior, the mere symbolic awareness of disturbance, or "thinking" about it, is one thing, but the objective appreciation of a subjective dislocation, of a dislocation internal to the organism, is quite another. Correspondingly, it is a far cry from a mere symbolic awareness of unity to an internal sense of the phyloörganism's common basis of interest and motivation. One sees, one senses two wholly different aspects of behavior according as he employs one or the other of these two different ways of approaching it. If the reader happens to have thought of this distinction, if he happens to have dwelt upon the difference between these two aspects of man's behavior, what I am saying is not new to him. And if he has habitually thought of it, he has habitually recognized the vast contrast there is between the group that is conventionally arranged according to external distinctions of class, creed or opportunity—political, economic, social and educational groups—and the group that constitutes a species such as man by reason of the inherent identity of the structures and functions that unite the elements composing this phylic total.[18]

As a phylobiologist, it had become only too plain to me that wherever affects and prejudices have superseded the unitary feeling of man as a common species—wherever they have led to confused adaptation, or to man's disbehavior—there is the crying need in the social life of man for developing a technique which will clearly demarcate between the two major spheres of man's bionomic adaptation, between the mode of unification and the mode of partition. It was in order to establish this demarcation and to discount the common social bias which regards individuals and their behavior, whether single or collective, as discrete and separative phenomena, that with a few associates I entered upon the process of group-analysis.

In initiating this process we undertook to challenge among us, as a group or community, whatever behavior-reactions had assumed a discrete or independent position in relation to the organismic unit represented by man as a species. In order to assist the more objective, scientific study of this social situation and secure an inclusive, bionomic setting in which to observe it, I had recourse to the social experiment referred to in Chapter V. Among the individuals assembled some were physicians or psychologists, others laymen; some aristocrats, others proletarians; some rich, others poor; and of them all some were neurotic, others "normal." So that in their collective sum they represented a quite heterogeneous gathering of social elements. It was my idea that in this concentrated bionomic colony with its extensions into the wider social community, we should be able to study the phenomenon of behavior-disorder apart from any private, restricted position such as might favor a private (affecto-symbolic) and therefore restricted interpretation of it.[19]

From the point of view of my medical practice in the field of behavior-disorders I had come to see that my neurotic patients came to me as presumably discrete entities; that they were activated by affects which they conceived to be quite private to themselves; that they were looking for help in the form of acquisitions, comforts, reassurance, love or what not. They came in quest of additive elements which were to contribute to the fund of the individual's assets as a collective sum. Their quest was linked with their habit of feeling and thinking as others had told them to feel and think. Their attitude was wholly subjective, traditional, dependent. And so the remedy they sought was also one that they wished to find within the category of the subjective, traditional and dependent. As the question they asked was personal and subjective, the answer they sought was likewise required to be personal and subjective. The patient had established an arbitrary social image of himself, and this he gratuitously related to the social image of the physician—an image that he had also arbitrarily established. He wanted to be told what to think and what to do. But following many years of group investigations, my conception of a patient's need came to be quite different from this. He was no longer to be made whole through any summative process—through the acquisition or accumulation of discrete conditions or advantages represented in this or that delectable circumstance or self-satisfaction existing outside himself. The unity or totality of function in relation to the environment of which he stood in need was only to be realized by his organism as an integral element within a phylically unitary whole. It was apparent that the physiological actualization of an internal sense of phylic coördination was the patient's, as it is man's, essential need.

We have noted the fact that recent innovations in the mental therapy of groups have nothing whatever in common with phyloanalysis, and that the technique used by my psychiatric colleagues in group-therapy inevitably consists in an intellectual (affecto-symbolic) procedure.[20] It is an attempt to reach and analyze the patient's symbolic mind, but not synthesize his organismic mood. For this reason it must fail of the mark if the mark is the readjustment of man's disordered behavior as a community or phylum.

The method of phyloanalysis, on the other hand, is not transmissible mentally or symbolically. It is not a mental or symbolic procedure. It does not attempt to deal with either the symbolic or the affective aspects of behavior. These are the outer symptoms of the disturbance. The phyloanalyst is interested in employing an organismic, biological basis for adjusting a biological disorder in man. In this attempt he is interested in affording an opportunity to alter the affect-mood or motivation not only of the student or patient but also of himself, through a phyloanalysis common to them both. But it is not a phyloanalysis of ideas or of their adherent affects. It is a phyloanalysis of components lying far deeper than the symbol and its affective adhesions.

Laboratories have been established from time to time in various fields of observation where materials are presented at which man's brain may *look* and report its findings—laboratories in which man's projective capacity is at a premium. But scientists have not yet, as a consensus of observers, established a systematically controlled body of facts within the frame of man's own organismic capacities as a phylum. In their habitual preoccupation with affecto-symbolic elements—with the segment of the brain that mediates the function of attention affectively in relation to the outside item or event—they have lost sight of the function of the brain that mediates an awareness of behavior indigenous to the phylo-organism itself. In having yielded themselves entirely to the field of attention and observation as a function of projection, they have in the same measure neglected the field of interests that are internal and organismic to themselves. It is not to be expected that the devotee of pseudo-normality, of affect and the part-brain can be interested in the problem of human behavior as it affects himself—not any more than a drunken man can be interested in the problem of chronic alcoholism as it affects himself. Partitive indulgence and whole interest are not to be reconciled with one another.

On the basis of the part-brain, however, with its manifold unilateralisms, human behavior discloses strange concinnities. It is extraordinary what alien reaction-types make intimate bed-fellows. Indeed, it is the most divergent contrasts that most often lie down together. For the widest characterological antithesis are not irreconcilable with one another. There is here again the duality of the 'I'-persona, the dichotomy of normality. This reconcilability of mutually exclusive traits explains why a man may be an outstanding surgeon, an expert medical diagnostician or otherwise brilliant professionally, and yet in his interrelational life be an autopathic nincompoop. It explains why one may be an intellectual lion and at the same time an emotional ass, why politicians are invariably religious people, and religious people invariably politicians, why there persists an incorruptible core of goodness in the "bad" and a no less indomitable nucleus of badness in the "good." Unless one is a psychiatrist, he may witness all these disabling contradictions *within himself*. It does seem at times that of all normality the psychiatrist is phylobiology's most difficult problem child.

While I have all my life been profoundly interested in the extraordinary biological development expressed in the consciousness of man, I have been even more interested in the pathological liabilities coincident with this bionomic attainment. After all, though, it is not intellectuality that is important; it is sensibility and consciousness—consciousness of the relations of external phenomena and of one's internal relation to them. The time has come for adult man to recognize that information is not learning. It is the mere mechanics of memory. Yet information is the great desideratum. Apparently, the goal is to make of one's mind the largest possible barrel for containing the largest possible number of mental items. Witness the puerile performances upon our public forums of grown-up men competing with one another as to who has collected and held on to the largest mass of factual material, material that is accessible to anyone with sufficient itch to accumulate more than the other fellow. It is like people who think it is a distinction to gather and collect and display the largest number of money bags—of stocks, bonds, debentures, dividends, not to mention their desire to display big estates, big art collections, a big assortment of jewels, to acquire big stables, be a "big shot," and make a big noise generally. Too much of what we call information is merely this big noise, this large display, this bid for the widest advertisement of the 'I'-persona. Yet in this situation there can be no criticism, no indictment of any person or class of persons. It is man's autopathic, ditentive behavior. It is an infirmity of the mood of man and this infirmity is shared equally by us all. Man has an inordinate appetite for pottage, and in his relish for it he cheerfully sells any and all other commodities, including his organismic birthright.

Students of human behavior have not recognized that ditention or autopathic feeling and thinking has virtually become the very structure of the individual's personality, as of the personality of the community or State. They have not recognized that this is the personality with which we now think and feel. In the absence of phylobiology, they have not seen that this personality with which we think and feel is incompetent to alter the various symptoms of neurosis that are expressions of its very own structure. In other words, they have not seen that there is involved the individual's spurious identity, and that this spurious identity is powerless to destroy itself—its own intrinsic self-identity, composed, as it now is, of a systematization of unwarranted affects and prejudices fully accredited by this personality. Yet it is this artificial personality, this pseudo-identity that must be destroyed, root and branch. Only the dislocation of the phyloörganism's center of gravity and the consequent shifting of its identity to a false pivot of interest and motivation—the substitution of the 'I'-persona and its part-function —has caused man to feel and act from the artificial premise of seemingly separated and disjointed 'I'-personae. We have, therefore, endeavored to seek a basis of observation that lies outside the material to be observed. In repudiating ditention and affectivity, we have found it necessary to invoke an organismic form of attention and observation that rests upon a different principle of identity.

So that some twenty-five years ago, with several co-workers and students, I sought to establish a laboratory in which reactions that are *felt,* in contrast to reactions that are *looked at,* would constitute the material of investigation. I entered upon an experiment in group-living and in group-analysis that had as its purpose the discrimination between habitual affecto-symbolic behavior-reactions and reactions that motivate the organism as a unitary whole. The aim of our experiment was the blocking and frustration of such behavior-expressions as gave evidence of an overlapping and confusion between the primary feeling-sphere and the affecto-symbolic sphere of man's adaptation. In our experimental group the many affecto-symbolic interchanges or dichotomies of motivation among the participants—the loves and the hates, the irritations and the flatteries, the praise and the blame, the dependencies and the aggressions—were the constant material of direct investigation. Affective responses and behavior-inconsistencies, commonly glossed over or mutually accepted socially, came in for direct challenge by the participants. The expressions of each, whether on a verbal or on a more dynamic behavior-plane, were by formal consent at all times open to analytic challenge. Thus each individual was essentially subject as well as experimenter.

As a result of these experiments we became gradually aware *within ourselves* (some of us more, some less) that the priority of man's motivation has come to be artificially vested in the 'I'-persona or, as I then called it, the social substantive "I." We became aware through practical research into our own inner processes that this transposed basis of behavior is now wholly credited by us all—and wholly without warrant; that this behavior-level is permitted to hold a position of sovereignty within each of us as a presumably discrete element. Unlike the subsequent groups of the psychotherapists, we did not work with personal symptoms and their symbols as such. We worked with the systematization of prerogatory affects that now constitutes the "I" or pseudo-personality of each of us and that replaces entirely the biological entity that is man's primary organism. We saw that affect or prejudice is encysted feeling. It is feeling that has become impacted in the socio-symbolic segment whose restricted, partitive channels do not permit it organismic egress. This impacted feeling, as we saw in the preceding chapter, is the concomitant of the ditentive or part pattern of behavior—the constellation of "psychic" reactions belonging to the "unconscious" and responsible, according to the older schools of psychiatry, for a patient's "repression."

With the pseudo-authority of the 'I'-persona maintaining universal precedence among us, it may well be imagined how difficult was the effort to place even a momentary check upon this commonly accepted prerogative now so deeply ingrained within social groups. Nevertheless, barring as far as possible all symbolic or ideational sponsorship of human motivation, with its discrete and wholly acquisitive function, our procedure led increasingly to the abrogation of traditional ideologies respecting human behavior. It tended gradually to induce, instead, a position that was objective and experimental toward our hitherto subjective behavioral trends, as well as toward our continual prepossessions with regard to these trends. The accepted interpersonal, congregational or collective basis of interchange was no longer accredited. Behavior began to be seen as a phylic phenomenon, and our effort was directed toward reaching back of man's prevailing collective, affecto-symbolic basis of motivation to the basis that is integrated or organismic in man's behavior as a species.

In questioning the isolated, symbolic approach of psychopathologists to the presumably sporadic patient, we must repeat that this is not a criticism of psychopathology. The absence of a recognition of the organismic basis of man's behavior is universal throughout medicine as throughout "normality" everywhere. Naturally, therefore, a clear observation of the behavior of man as a phylically integrated whole automatically excludes the singling out —the separating from the phyloörganismic whole—of any particular element or part or system of parts as being especially inadequate or undependable. We are, therefore, not pointing to any discrete or isolated mental method or system as it reflects the conduct or behavior of this or that individual, school or community. As the very frame of reference from which my associates and I set out in our experimental inquiry into the reactions of groups was the behavior of man as a species, our position is precisely the abrogation of an attitude that directs criticism or even attention to any specific part-reaction within the community or group, whether professional or lay. This altered frame of reference is coterminous with the capacity in man, as a phylum, to view his own behavior from the scientifically disinterested basis of the objective observer. But in view of the complete lack of a stable, scientific criterion in the field of man's interrelational life, man has yet to develop and utilize this capacity. It cannot be too strongly emphasized that the greatest lag in man's processes of attention and observation lies in the sphere of his own behavior as a species or phylum. As I said in *The Biology of Human Conflict*:

> In speaking of the "total organism" and of the "behavior of the organism as a whole," it may be recalled that I am using these terms to express not the collective whole, but the organic whole. There is a difference here that calls for very careful discrimination. As I have said, while the collective whole means, of course, the entire sum of the parts composing a structure or substance, the organic whole means the underlying principle of motivation on which depends the organism's primary unity of function.
>
> The scholastics expressed this difference in the distinction of meaning rendered by the Latin *in toto* as contrasted with the meaning defined by the phrase *totum in illis*. The latter may best be paraphrased as "whole-heartedly" or "without reservation," but the former as "comprising every part of" or "including every element in." If this distinction is kept in mind the reader will be spared much needless anguish. Even where an organism undergoes serious mutilation and loss of its parts as an original collective whole, its primary motivation or its function as an organic whole remains completely intact and unimpaired. Hunger, love, fatigue and curiosity may, in the sense of the organic whole, still continue as undiminished as when the body possessed all the parts belonging to it as a collective whole. So that the organism's function as a whole, as I use the term, means simply the function that is uncomplicated, undivided by partitive reactions that are differentiated from the organism's primary basis of behavior. The distinction is the more important as the meaning of "the whole," as here used, involves the organism not only as an individual but as a phylic unit. But in any event the organic whole that is functional or behavioral has to do with the organism's unitary principle of action.[21]

With this very different premise from which to observe, correlate and adjust the organism's deviate reactions, it began to appear that, in its approach to disorders of behavior, medicine had set out with the wrong foot. Of course, where there is question of a localized deviation in any part or organ—say, a visual error of refraction, a tubercular infection or a broken arm—the physician may to all intents and purposes look at such a manifestation as something wholly discrete and discontinuous in relation to man's organism as a phylum. Where, however, a physician is dealing with symptoms indicative of a disturbance in a patient's interrelational processes or with so-called nervous or mental maladjustments, there is no question of deviation in a discrete part-function. The situation is organismic; it is phyloörganismic. It involves a disorder in the field of man's bionomic motivation and in his orientation in respect to the total environment. This discrimination between the discrete behavior of a part or organ on the one hand, and the organism-environment relationship controlling individual and species on the other, is of major importance in our approach to the problem of behavior-disorders.

As our investigation as a social community continued from day to day, there developed progressively the tendency for us to look for a wholly altered accounting of man's motives of behavior. Through such an accounting the motivations to behavior were to be found, not in any discrete agencies—not by looking to reactions, whether benign or malevolent, as they exist in isolation in organisms other than one's own—but in processes common to the organism of man as a species. As an experimental group our repeated challenge and defeat of our accustomed level of interrelationships, and the consequent disparagement of these relationships, had the effect of forcing our attention and interest away from these socially current affectivities and directing it instead toward the internal sensations that pertain to the organism's immediate behavior-reactions. Instead of being occupied with the behavior of ourselves and of others from the point of view of commonly prevailing affects and prejudices, we became aware of factors that are to be found within a wholly different sphere of behavior.

What was of chief interest to us in the process of frustrating the interpersonal reactions which on the basis of man's secondary, collective frame of reference are commonly regarded as normal, was its apparent physiological shock to the entire affecto-symbolic segment. Under ordinary circumstances, this personal trauma is the inevitable stopping-point in all studies of human behavior. The cry, like that so often heard from the neurotic patient, is "I just can't understand"—really meaning, "I can't endure it, I can't stand what you are saying." For an affront to the symbolic behavior-segment constitutes an affront to what one feels to be the very core and meaning of his personality as an individual. But as students faced with a specific scientific task, we adhered to our investigation in accord with our altered frame of inquiry, and consistently included this rebuff to our cherished "personalities" as part of the routine analysis of the behavioral material before us.[22]

The problem of phylobiology is the problem of the 'I'-persona —the problem of man's self. This self of man is the self of everyone. It is the self of every "you" and of every "me." For the neurosis of man is phylic, it is world-wide; and a science of human behavior is truly a science for the millions. I hope the reader begins to realize this. I hope he realizes that a biological science of the self is a science that necessarily applies to us all, that it applies to him—to his self, as it applies to my self and to every other self; that, like every science, the science of man is universal. I hope he understands that just as medicine applies the remedy to the individual organism in which the disease occurs, so in the field of human behavior, if the disease resides within the organism of social man, the remedy must be applied to the social organism. I hope I have made clear that as our inquiry is universal, as it deals with the subjective material of the distorted self or 'I'-persona—with *my* prejudices, *your* prejudices, and *the prejudices of us all*—our approach to this material can only be universal in its scope. But in this inclusive approach it is required that the student of human behavior become an *internal experimentalist;* that he attain an altered frame of reference with respect to the internal feeling or mood of man.

The purpose of the group experiment, then, was that of divorcing from the concept or symbol the entire sum or system of affects which, through their linkage with the symbol, have established in man a falsely systematized personality, a spurious center of identity, and hence an artificial basis of human motivation. Whether these affects happened to be pleasant or unpleasant, was immaterial. Our unalterable purpose was to sunder them from the mental concept or symbol as prior motivating elements, and to allow such dislodged affects to be dissolved and reabsorbed into the total organismic stream of behavior as bona fide feeling or motivation.[23] But our continued experiments with groups and with the affects that "normally" motivate them, gradually made clear that our method thus far was more valiant than decisive. A factor still remained to be accounted for. This factor, however, began now to disclose itself increasingly. The phenomenon was alluded to in Chapter IV as an internally perceptible stress or tension, and it is with this phenomenon that we shall deal in detail in Part II.

So much, then, for the symptomatology of disorders occurring in man's interrelational life as they are reflected in the 'I'-persona and are extended outside the organism in the manifold projections of our affecto-symbolic or autopathic behavior. So much for the superficial or currently "normal" aspects of our human adaptation due to processes that heretofore have remained unrecognized and unsuspected. They have remained unrecognized and unsuspected because our hitherto restricted approach to habitual interpersonal disorders has of its nature precluded the recognition and adjustment of a disturbance affecting communities of men as a species. But we shall now proceed to a consideration of the more fundamental conditions responsible for our manifest interrelational disturbances.

NOTES

[1] See pages 194-96.

[2] Haggard, Howard W., *Mystery, Magic and Medicine*, Garden City, N. Y., Doubleday, Doran & Co., Inc., 1933, pp. 192.

Castiglioni, Arturo, *A History of Medicine*, New York, Alfred A. Knopf, 1941, pp. xxviii + 1013.

———, *Adventures of the Mind*, New York, Alfred A. Knopf, 1946, pp. 428.

[3] A phylobiological discussion of the function of the affecto-symbolic segment or part-brain of man may be found in the author's essays, *The Structure of Insanity*; and "The Human Equation," *Mental Hygiene*, 1941, Vol. XXV, pp. 210-20.

[4] See note 6, page 283.

[5] Gibbs, Willard, *Collected Works of J. Willard Gibbs*, London, Longmans, Green, 1928, two volumes. See also Rukeyser, Muriel, *Willard Gibbs*, New York, Doubleday, Doran & Co., 1942, pp. xl + 465.

[6] Einstein, Albert, and Infeld, Leopold, *The Evolution of Physics*, New York, Simon & Schuster, 1938, pp. 63-7.

[7] See Chapters II and III.

[8] See pages 148-49.

[9] The theory has been advanced that communication by symbols first came about through imitating objects or actions by means of movements of the arms and hands, and that these symbolic expressions were only later transferred to the tongue and lips supplemented by the mechanism of laryngeal sounds. (Paget, Sir Richard, *Human Speech*, New York, Harcourt, Brace & Co., 1930, pp. 360. For a brief version see article by the same author, "The Origin of Language," *Psyche* (London), 1927. Vol. VIII, pp. 35-9.

[10] Burrow, Trigant, "The Law of the Organism—a Neuro-Social Approach to the Problem of Human Behavior," *The American Journal of Sociology*, 1937, Vol. XLII, pp. 814-24.

———, "The Organismic Factor in Disorders of Behavior," *The Journal of Psychology*, 1937, Vol. 4, pp. 333-41.

———, "Bio-physical Factors in Relation to Functional Imbalances," *Human Biology*, 1938, Vol. 10, pp. 93--105.

[11] Burrow, Trigant, "Phylobiology: Physiological Behavior Reactions in the Individual and the Community," *Etc.*, 1946, Vol. III, p. 272. This paper was published in its original form under the title, "Physiological Behaviour Reactions in the Individual and the Community—A Study in Phyloanalysis," *Psyche* (London), 1930, Vol. XI, pp. 74-5.

[12] Burrow, Trigant, *The Biology of Human Conflict*, pp. 254-5.

[13] See pages 203-04.

[14] See note 6, page 283.

[15] See note 9, page 257.

[16] See pages 203-04.

[17] See pages 222-23.

[18] See note 1, page 155.

[19] Galt, William E., *Phylonalysis—A Study in the Group or Phyletic Method of Behaviour-Analysis,* Psyche Miniatures, London, Kegan Paul, Trench, Trubner & Co., Ltd., 1933, pp. 151.

[20] See pages 220-25.

[21] Burrow, Trigant, *The Biology of Human Conflict*, p. 176.

[22] Burrow, Trigant, "Speaking of Resistances," *Psyche* (London), 1927, Vol. VII, pp. 20-7.

[23] Burrow, Trigant, "The Reabsorbed Affect and its Elimination," *The British Journal of Medical Psychology,* 1926, Vol. VI, pp. 209-18.

PART II

ORGANISMIC MAN

or

THE BIOLOGY OF HUMAN BEHAVIOR

A Phylosynthesis

Considering the close connection between the phenomena we distinguish as somatic and psychic, one may predict that the day will come when our knowledge and, it is to be hoped, our control of the biology of organs and their chemistry will enable us to approach the domain of the neuroses from this angle. This day seems still far distant, for at present these disturbances are wholly inaccessible to us from the standpoint of medicine.

SIGMUND FREUD.

The end of society is peace and mutual protection, so that the individual may reach the fullest and highest life attainable by man. The rules of conduct by which this end is to be attained are discoverable—like the other so-called laws of Nature—by observation and experiment, and only in that way.

THOMAS HUXLEY.

CHAPTER VIII

PHYLIC PRINCIPLES IN HUMAN BEHAVIOR

In Part I (Chapter V) we noted the basic fidelity of man's senses in relation to the external world and saw that the neurodynamic principle expressed by this law or nomen has been violated throughout man's social adaptation. We had earlier seen (Chapter IV) the result of the imposition upon man's natural processes of partitive, autopathic trends, of his purely arbitrary interests, opinions and beliefs; and we saw that these trespasses upon the organism's natural response were the result of a distortion in man's basic attentive processes or of the impairment of function we called ditention. In these chapters we considered the consequence of an interception of man's faithful rapport with the environment and dwelt especially upon the rôle played by the cerebral process of attention in mediating the organism's primary relationship to the environment. These early chapters had to do with our group investigations into the operation of the brain of man as it makes contact with or "perceives" the environmental object or circumstance. Still earlier (Chapters II and III) we considered the influence of subjective affects and of man's autopathic mood upon his general outlook and behavior; and in Chapter V we again considered this private mood or affect in its numinal systematization, together with the formation of the false entity or identity we called the 'I'-persona. In Chapter VI we traced the physiological origin of affect or prejudice in conditioning man's social behavior.

In setting out upon the second part of our thesis we shall examine the modifications that have taken place *within* the organism of man and that are concomitant to his substitution of the numen for the nomen. We shall consider the effect of these modifications in the human brain upon man's relation to man or upon his relation to himself and to others. For through the interposition of the numen and ditention man has placed an arbitrary interpretation upon the manifestations of the surrounding world and, as a result of the numen or of ditentive feeling and thinking, man has correspondingly misinterpreted those subjective processes that govern and motivate the behavior of his own organism. As we saw, the numinal error into which man fell was traceable to his private or part interpretation of external phenomena. It was traceable to man's withdrawal from a sense of his organism's continuity and consistency in relation to the processes existing in the external world about him. We saw that this numinal blind spot has turned man away from an organismic sense of himself as a phylically articulate whole or as an organism whose structure and function is delimited only by the species itself.

As man owes his capacity of symbol-formation to a unique segment or part-function of the brain, to understand human behavior is to understand the operation of this unique part-function. This cerebral part-function or segment now relates individuals only vicariously to one another, as it also relates them for the most part only vicariously to the environment. That is, an autopathic, affective process gradually systematized itself into a specific part-function of the organism. This part-function represented by the 'I'-persona with its autopathic feeling, or affect, has thrust itself between the organism and its environment. With the recognition of this socio-symbolic segment or partitive function of the brain, my associates and I found ourselves faced with a problem in neurophysiology. As this cerebral process of symbol-formation relates not only the organism of the individual but also the organism of the species to the environment, our problem—as ultimately every medical problem—became a phylic as well as a physiological one. This finding and its organismic significance in relation to human behavior pointed to a new field of investigation as well as to a new method of investigating it.

With the discovery that our problem was physiological it became evident that we were dealing with a form of social conditioning with which no mental or theoretical approach could anywhere make contact.[1] It became evident that our obstinate conditioning—the kind of behavior man has unwittingly adopted and that is now everywhere prevalent in the social life of the species—was due to alterations in neural function that modify the internal behavior of man as a phyloörganism. Here then was a hint as to the structural background of "normality," and with it the way had been opened to the field of *phyloneurology*. Here was a clue to the biological substrate of the unilateral affectivity and absolutism that everywhere motivates social communities or groups. And so, both as individuals and as a group, we were now upon wholly new ground. We were faced with a problem that had to do directly with a neurodynamic adjustment of the social organism to the environment.[2] Dismissing interpersonal affects and prejudices as epiphenomena that no longer lent themselves to scientific inquiry, we began to touch neuroanatomical bedrock. Disregarding the mental and social factors of partition and factionalism existing throughout human communities, we had now to deal with an alteration in behavior occurring immediately within the organism.

With this complete shift in material and objective there went hand in hand the discovery of two patterns of tension that were internally discriminable from one another. These tensional patterns are effective in relating the organism to the environment through the process of attention. The first or the symbolic part-pattern, which involves the 'I'-persona, I have already spoken of as *ditention*.[3] This is the pattern through which the numen has inadvertently come into operation. The second or total pattern, which governs the primary motivation of organismic man and which relates him to the nomen, I have described as *cotention*.[4] It was upon the differentiation of these two neuromuscular patterns of behavior and their relation to the function of attention that our efforts were henceforth centered. They were centered upon these internal reaction-patterns with a view to the possibility of affording systematic diagnosis and control of behavior-disorders, both individual and social. In the next chapter we shall return to the more detailed consideration of these two contrasting patterns.

May I say that in this altered procedure the organism of man was for the first time attempting to examine into its own organismic processes as they relate him directly to the environment. Repudiating the unilateral, self-reflective basis of behavior that relates individuals vicariously, ulteriorly, to the environment—repudiating the socially collusive system of affects and prejudices, the wishful opinions and beliefs upon which the vacillating covenants of normality rest—our research became essentially *intra*organismic. Reactions internal to the organism of man were now to be investigated through methods and processes which were also internal to man.

As we continued to delve into the underlying structures answerable for man's bionomic deviations in behavior, our inquiries led us further and further into the organism's deeper genetic systems of reaction—systems and reactions whose function, like that of other animals, primarily relates individuals of the species to the environment and to others of its kind. The basal brain and its ganglia govern the reactions of man's organism in its total phylic behavior, while the part-brain with its more recently acquired symbolic function governs man's interindividual behavior and is the seat of the functional artifact in his social system of interrelationships we have identified as the 'I'-persona.[5] The 'I'-persona and its psychosocial development appeared to be incident to a shift of innervation from the basal nervous system of man to the specialized areas of the brain that mediate his symbolic behavior. With this shift and the concomitant development of the 'I'-persona, man's mental and social adaptation—his interrelational behavior—had become partitive or divided in its inception. A divisive, sectional interest or motivation henceforth replaced the total motivation and interest arising from the primary central nervous system of man. Dichotomy and conflict now assumed supremacy over the organism's unity and centralization of function as a species. It was natural, therefore, that this basic shift in bionomic behavior should occupy a foremost place in our phylobiological investigations.

Early in the course of our group investigations it had become apparent that beneath the outer expressions of so-called normal communities there are the same fears, the same repression, insecurity and evasion; the same substitution and guilt; the same unilateral secrecy and self-defense; the same superstitions, anxieties and suspicions; the same elations and depressions, however transient or prolonged; in short, the same neurotic reactions that characterize the isolated patient. It had become apparent that in dealing with groups of people commonly regarded as "normal" we were dealing with the identical undercurrent of mood-affectivity and absolutism—with the identical dichotomy and conflict—with which we are confronted in the ambivalent symptoms of the psycho-neurotic personality.[6] But with the clear delineation of a phylic background of tensional conflict in human organisms, it was now seen that the physiological mechanism underlying the behavior of social man is also essentially identical with the mechanism activating the behavior of the clinical patient.

From this physiological background, Freud's quandary as to

why individuals and nations should disdain, abhor and despise one another becomes quite simple.[7] Indeed it is amazing that cultural man should have gone on these many thousands of years naïvely rejoicing in a form of social adaptation which, though it calls itself "normal," rests upon no organismic principle of biological balance but, on the contrary, is beholden to the shifting whimsies of mere superficial *mores* and moralities.

It would seem especially fitting, then, that students of human behavior somehow brace themselves to understand the underlying structure of "normality"—the social reaction-average within which each of us daily lives and has his being. This would seem the more pertinent undertaking inasmuch as the clinical cases we are accustomed to study as discrete, isolated manifestations are the habitual outgrowth of this same normal reaction-level. The neurotic youth, whether girl or boy, who is brought to the psychiatrist because of serious mental disturbance merely presents the same reactions that are present in his parents, except that in the parent these reactions exist in a form that has been comfortably assimilated within the constellation of reactions expressed by the "normal" community. For the normal community is unconsciously agreed upon certain cherished and untouchable madnesses common to us all, and the individual patient is stigmatized with mental dereliction only because his deviation or neurosis is not in line with the deviation or neurosis of the wider community.[8] But to reckon deviations by the standards of reaction of a numerically larger group that arbitrarily calls itself "normal" is at variance with the canons of science. To classify the mechanism of a special group of reactions as mentally and socially pathological without regard to a norm of behavior that is consistent and universal, is scientific heresy. Such a procedure possesses no precedent throughout the entire range of scientific methods.

As we know, there are backward communities in which certain individuals have hemorrhages and kindred symptoms of tuberculosis. The majority of the community, however, have no such symptoms but are going about apparently well; and these individuals say that the others have "consumption" or "wasting disease." But a scientist comes along and draws a different line between the two groups. He finds that among those who believe themselves healthy, there are also many who are diseased. Accordingly, he classifies them clinically along with those who are manifestly ill. For he is able to demonstrate that the germ of tuberculosis is active in these apparently healthy individuals as well as in those who are obviously sick. This he does by virtue of an objective norm that has been scientifically established.

In the behavioral life of man there exists a parallel situation. The phylobiological scientist finds that deviation from a biologically established norm is present no less in the average social reaction than in persons who obviously are clinically maladapted. Strictly speaking, only newborn infants can be considered healthy from the inclusive viewpoint of phylopathology. For even children are all too soon subjected to a distortion of behavior through the social conditioning of their organisms and the concomitant inculcation in them of divisive or aberrant affect-images.

Only when there have been established in social man behavior-reactions that are universal and constant, may we determine those reactions that deviate from this universal principle of behavior. This position of phylobiology in respect to the field of man's social reactions possesses not only the merit of resting upon definite scientific findings, but it is consonant with the attitude of science in other fields of biology. It would be well, therefore, if in our effort to understand our own behavior and that of "normality" generally we would consider briefly what those scientific principles are that prevail in other fields of biological inquiry.

In the domain of structural biology, medicine has established the substance whose chemical composition constitutes the structural norm of the tissues and organs throughout the body. This element that is basic and constant throughout all organisms is known as protoplasm. Disease or pathology of the organism is recognized and denoted by the incidence of deviation from the physico-chemical constancy and balance of this primary substance or norm. Healthy structures are characterized by healthy function. The healthy condition of the organism's protoplasm is essential to the health of the organism. This is the organism's basic biological norm. All organic disturbance is characterized by alteration in the protoplasm. Instead of healthy tissue or protoplasm there is defective protoplasm or what may be called *alloplasm*.

If a patient has scarlatina, cataract or cancer, it is because of diseased tissue or a disturbance in the physiological norm that medicine has established as protoplasm, and the problem is the restoration of the protoplasmic substance through the elimination of pathological elements. Disturbance or disease of the protoplasm is recognized in the alterations of function observable in the *symptoms* of disease. The appearances or symptoms of disease lead to its recognition by means of examination and physical diagnosis. Medicine, however, may recognize conditions of disordered health or disease within the organism where there is present no observable deviation in the structural norm we know as healthy protoplasm. These are called functional disorders, and consist not in organic disease but in a disturbance in the function of the tissues or organs, or in their relation to one another.[9]

It seems odd that medicine should never have demanded specific recognition of a *functional* principle of health in respect to the organism of man as a species. It seems odd that medicine should not have recognized an interrelational sphere of function, that it should not have required at least a conceptual definition of a phylic principle of health corresponding to the definite structural principle of health posited in the use of the medical term protoplasm. This circumstance undoubtedly ties up with normality's wholly erroneous conception of itself as the embodiment of a dependable norm, when in truth it embodies but a purely mutable social reaction-average. Even with respect to the individual, medicine recognizes health of function only through the exclusion of disordered function. Its criteria of function are negative, not affirmative. When the clinician speaks of findings being negative, he means that there is an absence of disease, not of health.

It is, of course, quite unthinkable that there should not exist for the phylosoma as a whole a definite functional norm, a determinable central constant that is as basic and dependable as the universal structural norm recognized as protoplasm. It is unthinkable that there should not exist a primary principle of functional constancy or interrelational balance within the phyloörganism that discloses deviations in function correlative to those existing in the structural sphere. The presence of such a primary balance of function is inherent in the principle of phyloörganismic homeostasis. Deviations from this consistency of function are to be seen in the various expressions of mental disorder, individual and social—in phobias, hysterical paralyses, unwarranted suspicions, states of elation and depression, disorders within the sexual sphere, etc., as well as in crime, industrial conflict, political dissension and war.

Phylobiology, therefore, requires that we recognize within the phyloörganism a principle of behavioral function that is primary and that corresponds to the primary structural principle of protoplasm. This principle of the organism's primary function, or motivation, may be called *protergy* or *protogenic* function. And so, just as we may describe disturbances in protoplasm as alloplasm, we may describe concomitant deviations in the organism's protogenic function as *allogenic* function or allergy—a term of common medical use in characterizing certain deviate reactions occurring in the individual. *In this broader medical premise of phylobiology we must regard the symptoms embodied in interrelational disorders or neurosis as the expression of a basic* intra*relational disfunction or allergy.*

In the sphere of reactions that pertain to the behavior of individuals of the species man, we are dealing, then, with a disorder of function, but with a disorder of function that affects the interrelation between the organism and the environment as also the interrelation between one individual and another, or between one community and another. We are not dealing with disordered protoplasm; we are not dealing with disorder in relation to a structural norm. We are dealing with a deviation in behavior or with disordered function as it affects the elements of a common phylic organism. This was the problem with which as phylobiologists we were faced. As experimenters in the field of human behavior, we were interested in discovering the physiological basis of man's social symptomatology, of his interrelational disharmonies. To this end we centered our attention upon certain disparities in the organism's internal tensions as these disparities were brought to our conscious awareness in the immediate moment through the technique of phyloanalysis.[10] We thus shifted emphasis from the external or interrelational symptoms here and there to an internal or intrarelational modification in man's behavior. We shifted emphasis to a modification caused by deviation from a biological norm of function that is internal to the phyloörganism and that is, therefore, perceptible only *within* the organism of individual and species.

When I speak of an intrarelational disorder I have in mind a condition of disturbed tension that affects the organism's bionomic relation to the environment and to others of the species. I have in mind a condition of stress or tension that is as yet unrecognized and that affects the organism's ecosomatic function. What is habitually called one's transference—one's love, anger, dependence or disaffection, his competitiveness or superiority in respect to someone else—is a quite superficial interpretation that rests upon the fallacy which maintains that external symptoms constitute the internal disorder. Man's real disturbance is a physiological conflict, a disorder in intrarelational function that dislocates the organism's basic homeostasis—its balanced relationship to the environment and to others.

Where we come to deal with the biological process that regulates the interrelational behavior of man, the functional norm required to be established is the norm that governs man's internal processes of feeling and thinking in relation to the external environment, and the feeling and thinking of individuals and communities in their relation to one another. This norm of behavior which concerns man's attentional or adaptive processes is the pattern of behavior I have called cotention. Cotention is an expression of the phyloörganism's protergy or primary motivation. It is synonymous with the solidarity of the species. Like the criteria of health established by medical science in regard to bodily structures, cotention also is a criterion of health. But there is a difference. Cotention represents healthy, in contrast to unhealthy, behavior-reactions *within the field of man's interrelations.* In the sphere of man's interrelational adaptation, the criteria of cotention are sharply contrasted with manifestations of ditention or with man's partitive, autopathic feeling and thinking. A person with typhoid fever is restored to health when the typhoid germ has been eliminated from his organism and he presents no further symptoms occasioned by this bacterial infection. So with the organism's interrelational health. The healthy, cotentive adaptation of man is automatically present when the intrusion of ditentive elements has been intercepted. Again, to compare our position with that of the physician who deals with structural disease occurring in the individual, if we are to restore man's healthy interrelational processes, it is necessary that we discount the external symptoms of his interrelational disorder and examine into the underlying functions responsible for these outer manifestations.

Because of the physiological consistency inhering in the basic substance called protoplasm, there exists throughout the tissues of a species or phyloörganism a consistent pattern of structure and function. This pattern is coeval with the principle of species articulation. *The individual organism is a consistent unit in itself only by virtue of its consistent adherence to the pattern of structure and function that constitutes the solidarity of the species.*

The solidarity of individual and phylum, then, represents a biologically consistent norm of behavior. The establishment of this norm in respect to the individual was the prerequisite to the development of the medical and biological sciences. For it has been typical of these sciences that they have first determined the healthy character of the structures and functions existing within a given species, and from this universal norm have proceeded to demonstrate the nature of the processes that mark the individual's deviation from this experimentally determined constant. Had medicine not established the biochemical consistency of protoplasm, it could not have discovered measures for tracing pathological deviations in an organism's structure and function. It could not have established measures of objective diagnosis and therapy, but would still be floundering amid mere superficial symptoms that bear no relation to a consistent biological criterion.

As yet medicine has not recognized the need to apply this principle of an established norm to disorders occurring in the field of man's interrelational behavior. It has not recognized the principle of an established norm that holds equally for functions and reactions that interrelate the species organismically to the environment, and for those that interrelate the organisms of the species to one another. Instead, it has permitted a purely subjective social reaction-average arbitrarily *called* "normality" to stand as the criterion of healthy human relations. In the absence of a biological norm within the sphere of man's interrelational functions, there is not the possibility of systematic diagnosis and treatment of man's disorders of behavior. Students attempting to observe disturbances within this sphere are perforce dealing with a mere hodge-podge of symptoms having no relation whatever to a constant and dependable principle of behavior. Until we have established a reliable norm within the field of man's function as a phylum, we cannot recognize in the observable symptoms either the nature of the structures involved or the character of the function impaired. This lack of a consistent norm with which to contrast deviations in interrelational behavior has been the basic concern of the small group comprising my associates and myself. Our recognition that disordered behavior, whether of the individual or the community, represents a pathological deviation throughout the entire sphere of man's interrelational function first led us to develop measures for determining the intrarelational health of man as a phylum, or the science of phylobiology.

The phylobiologist then, like the internist, must also look deeper than mere symptoms. The social symptoms of hate, disdain, antagonism, crime and war; the symptoms evidenced in the sense of guilt, fear, repression and violence; and the complemental symptoms of transference with their clinging dependence, their nostalgias and sentimentalities; in short, the symptoms of partition characterizing the social neurosis are, like the symptoms of the individual patient, but superficial manifestations. They are like the fever or prostration of the typhoid, malarial or tubercular patient, or of a community of patients. Like these diseases, the interrelational disorders of man are not diagnosed and treated by translating them into mere words or symbols. Conversational therapy, whether interpersonal or group, does not touch the problem of man's neurodynamic dislocation in relation to the environment.[11] This phylic dislocation has entered too deep into the physiology of man's daily life. In this hour it is ravaging the very tissues of man. The phylobiologist must demand to know the *neurology* of behavior-disorders, both individual and social. But he must demand to know the neurology of these disorders internally, organismically, or as *reactions perceptible within himself.*

As we know, it is the mark of science that it recognizes the element as a complete and integral expression of the total structure of which it is an elemental part. In short, science always sees in the part or element the potential structure and function of the whole, whether healthy or diseased. And as a scientist, man has not departed from this principle of observation and study in respect to the structure and function of his own organism. But this principle requires to be applied to the *behavior* of man, to the motivation or *function of man as a phylum.* Only on this basis may we recognize deviations in phylic and in individual behavior. Only on this basis may we study deviations of function occurring in the wider social community, and measure them in relation to a biological norm or in relation to man's cotentive solidarity as a species.

Once we have assumed a medical interest in the function of the phylum as a basically unitary organism, we shall adopt the same attitude toward the social symptoms of disorder and conflict that we now maintain toward symptoms occurring in the individual organism. Just as we examine the function of the individual organism, we shall also examine the function of the phylic organism in order to understand the cause of its symptomatic manifestations. Just as a feeling of distress or pain in any part or organ of the body is a gauge of disorder in the function of that part or organ; and just as a feeling of distress or pain in the organism of the whole individual is a gauge of disorder within the function of the individual as a whole, so it is with the feeling or motivation of the organism of man as a species. If there is disturbance and pain in the interrelational feeling or motivation of man as a species, there is a condition of disease within the whole function of man as a phyloörganism.

In making a plea, then, for studying man's behavior from the basis of the organism's species solidarity, I am after all but returning to principles that form the accepted understructure of science. There is no organ of the body except the brain to whose function we bring an interpretation that is not based on the principle of phylic solidarity. We could not possibly treat disease or deviation of function in the liver or the lungs or the kidneys of various individuals of a species dwelling in widely separate regions of the earth, were we not aware that we are dealing with a phylically uniform and consistent structure—if we did not know that primarily livers and lungs and kidneys and the rest of the human organism perform a constant and uniform function by reason of a constant and uniform histological architecture throughout the species. In each organism, or in each complex of organs, we look for and we find a uniform principle of function, organ for organ, tissue for tissue, cell for cell. Only by virtue of this species solidarity, of this unity of structure within the organs and in organisms, is it possible to adopt a consistent procedure toward deviations of function or disease-processes in these organs. Whether the patient is a resident of Flatbush or Kamchatka, medical science applies the same objective procedure in the diagnosis and treatment of diseased organs and tissues.

Objectively, of course, I may know the liver, the heart or other bodily organs by reading about them in some book or dissecting them in an anatomical laboratory. As I dissect the cadaver of some Tom, Dick or Agnes, or read of this or that particular organ or part, I know it is not peculiar to this or that particular person. I know that I am reading about or dissecting the liver or heart or kidney of man; that I do so because said organ in each healthy (biologically normal) individual is, as we say in medicine, "typical." "Typical" of what? Typical of the species.

Where it comes to a subjective knowledge of *my* organs, however; where it is a question of my own liver or heart or kidney as it functions within myself, I have no direct acquaintance with it. I have no direct acquaintance with these organs typical of man as they function within my own organism. Subjectively, I lack all knowledge of them. The organs that function within me—within man—are brought to subjective knowledge or awareness only if there is *dis*comfort, *dis*order, *dis*ease due to some lesion, some division or deviation in the function of these organs.

So with the organ that is the brain of man. With the brain, too, there is the same contrast between my objective and my subjective observation of it. I may study the brain in the text and illustrations contained in a book, or more directly, more adequately, in a laboratory of anatomy. But of my own brain, of the brain of man as it exists in myself, I have no conscious awareness under conditions of biologically normal, healthy, typical functioning. As with the kidney or the liver, so under healthy, typical conditions, the brain of man functions automatically, imperceptibly. Man is unaware of the organ with which he is aware of all things else. In his solidarity as a species, man has no subjective contact with, no direct appreciation of his own brain or its function.

Of course, like the liver or kidney, the brain of man may suffer a structural lesion—a tumor, for example—and because of the disfunction and pain caused by this tumor, the individual may become aware of this disorder within the brain. But with the organ that is the brain of man there is a difference as compared with other organs of the body. Man's brain possesses a projective, interrelational function. By virtue of this function the brain of man is the only organ of the body that makes direct contact with this same organ in other individuals. The liver and the lungs and other organs of man do not intermesh with each other. The brain is the only organ capable of interindividual consort. This projective, interrelational function, then, relates the individual not only to the environment but also to other brains within the species man. It is this projective or interrelational function that I have specifically in mind at the moment. For, unlike the situation in respect to disfunction in the liver or kidney, even where there occurs interrelational partition or disfunction within the brain—even where the projective function of man's brain deviates from the biological norm represented in the solidarity of man's organism as a species—man has no conscious recognition of this disturbance in brain-function. Though the organism's direct articulation with its surroundings is everywhere impaired; though man's interrelational behavior is shot through with affects or with ditentive habits of feeling and thinking that cause universal disturbance in communication interindividually and in respect to the environment; and though this ditentive factor is synonymous with autopathic adaptation, with "face," with man's *amour propre,* in short, with the pseudo-identity we have recognized as the 'I'-persona, man does not sense the cerebral stress or pain that underlies this misadaptation. He does not recognize that these interrelational disorders are traceable to a disturbance in the interrelational or projective function of his own brain.

It is apparent, then, that with the functioning of the brain—with the projective functioning of the brain of man—there exists a phylogenetically unique situation. This situation consists in the fact that the whole organism of man, that man's very being, is now identified with his affecto-symbolic personality, with the affecto-symbolic part-function that constitutes man's dissociation as a species, and that man's identity has become a pseudo-identity. It is highly expedient for us to look carefully into this circumstance. But to do so, we shall have to bring the matter closer home. We shall have to bring it back to ourselves in all its daily, subjective implications.

My brain—and that of my readers—performs its function in relation to the environment by virtue of the special process of mental projection. That is, in the functioning of our brain, the attention or interest is conveyed outward to the object envisioned.[12] But, as I have said, there has occurred functional impairment or disorder in the use of this brain, yours and mine, and because of our preoccupation with the external object or condition which we project and in which we have now come to be wholly absorbed, we do not become aware of a disorder or impairment of function within this organ that is our own brain.

Thus partitive feeling, or affect, has seriously distorted the subjective function of our brain. To illustrate: in my substitution of a ditentive or partitive premise of motivation, I may say that a person who is harshly critical of me offends me, causes me pain, whereas the real occasion of my pain or offense is my organism's lack of cotentive balance or integration. Or, I may say that there is a ghost or evil spirit in my room because of the repeated sound of knocking close to my bed. In this latter instance my false inference must be laid to the numen and its ever-present tendency to invoke arbitrary images or spectres. I do not allow for my unfamiliarity with the physical laws of contraction and expansion that operate under changing conditions of heat and cold. Thus in both circumstances, the one interindividual, the other environmental, there occurs a definite disfunction or deviation in the neural response of brain to environment. The brain is led to false and unwarranted perceptions or inferences through its lack of consistency in relation to the external law or nomen. And, because this ditentive pattern of reaction now involves my whole organism (man's whole organism), instead of seeking a remedy for my deviation or disfunction I tend (man tends) to contribute further to my difficulty by falsely ascribing my brain's inharmonious functioning to the circumstance or person on whom my interest is projected. So that a strange thing, a biologically anomalous thing has happened to the brain of man, to the organ we know subjectively —that man knows subjectively—as "my" brain.

Of course man, as an objective scientist, deals with the structure and function of man's brain with controlled objective standards of evaluation. Correspondingly, man recognizes—man the scientist recognizes—the function or behavior that is biologically normal to the brain of man in its relation to the objective environment. But where it is a question of the observation of the function of man's brain subjectively—where it is a question of man's own feeling and thinking as mediated by his own brain—the element of ditention, of autopathic thinking, or the numen, operates to intercept healthy or whole subjective behavior. The accurate correspondence between sense-reaction and environmental object, which we have called the nomen and which governs healthy observation and behavior, is set aside in favor of esoteric inferences that are due to the systematization of affects we earlier recognized in the arbitrary partitiveness and unilateralism of the 'I'-persona and the numen. A biological norm is set aside in favor of an arbitrarily assumed "normality."

Consistent with the law of species solidarity, no individual function can deviate from phylic function and still preserve the health of the individual. The kidney of each individual of a given species must function in the manner that is biologically typical of kidneys throughout the species. Deviation of individual function from phylic function entails disorder and pain. Similarly, to be healthy, the brain of each individual of any species must function as it is biologically typical of brains throughout that species to function. In man, however, owing to the intrusion of ditention or the numen, the individual brain throughout the species does not function typically or in accordance with this biological norm. *In the species man, the brain has assumed a function that departs from the behavior typical of the phylic brain of man.* Through a functional inadvertence that has occurred in the course of his development, man's brain—the brain of man throughout—has assumed a part-function. Both ontogenetically and phylogenetically —individually and as a species—man has substituted for his whole brain an autopathic, affecto-symbolic part-brain or segment whose function digresses from the function typical of the brain of man as a whole. In consequence, there is disorder and pain. But, as already said, unlike disfunction in the stomach or kidney, disorder in the interrelational function of the brain of man is not experienced as pain in the brain. Just as man projects everything else in his use of the brain, so in his use of the brain he also projects its own pain. Moreover, the pain and disorder due to a deviation in the function of man's brain constitutes a social as well as an individual anomaly. Man's conflict and pain entails a social neurosis —a phyloneurosis which, though universal, is still projected outward and man is still at war with man, still at war with himself, whether in peace or in war.[13]

Perhaps it will be said that no competent physician, that certainly no neuroanatomist or neurologist, would in his sane mind think of regarding the brain of man as calling for a less phylic interpretation than other organs or tissues of the body. Quite true. He would not do so in his *sane* mind, in the mind that proceeds with objective consistency to study objective material. But when the neurologist attempts to study the function of man's brain in its subjective operations, when he attempts to study the function of the brain that is his own brain with all its partitive affects and prejudices, he definitely fails to bring objective consistency to these intrafunctional observations. He fails to bring to bear the function of his whole brain upon the disfunction of his affecto-symbolic or part brain. For if we will accompany this same neurologist to his home or to his club, where his surroundings are part and parcel of a social tissue of subjective affects, we shall find that he enters wholeheartedly into this prevailing milieu of ditentive reactions and that his behavior is no different from the behavior of the most commonplace and illiterate of laymen. We shall find that, like the layman, he becomes partitively irritated or unctuous at the slightest provocation, that, tossing objective consistency out of the window, he becomes a prey to reactions based upon purely arbitrary, personalistic affects and prejudices.

It becomes plain, therefore, that the subjective behavior of our neurological scientist cannot be reconciled with his cherished criteria of objective science, that in his subjective processes he too preserves an artificial, prerogatory numen which, in his sane or whole mind, he would frankly repudiate as being inconsistent with a logical program of behavior. Yet this is the brain that man applies to the rearing of children, to the enactment of laws, to congressional debate, to governmental administration and to international deliberations. It is the brain with which he "makes wars to end wars" and with which he sets up principles of a lasting peace that never lasts, but whose inevitable transience is ever obscured by man's cherished social numina. It is the brain with which he establishes his social and religious institutions, endows universities, with which he marries, pursues his business or professional career, fashions his ethical values, his family standards and his philosophy of life generally. Of such is the stuff of our social images and transferences. This is the subjective blind spot, this the illusion of personal priority and privilege on the part of the 'I'-persona that has everywhere muddled man's interrelations. This muddle in social motivation is the basis of my plea for a consistent objective recognition *within ourselves* of these behavior inconsistencies throughout the field of man's environmental adaptation, both individual and social. It is highly expedient that the scientific mind bring itself to take account of the unscientific mood within itself.

We have seen that throughout the organism as a species man's brain has assumed a function which deviates from the function that represents the biological norm of that species. In no other species except man has there occurred a deviation in function that characterizes the individuals of the species throughout. Only in man does there exist a socio-symbolic form of behavior that has been grafted upon the organism's biologically normal brain-function, causing an inadvertent distortion in his feeling and thinking by reason of a repercussive, autopathic mode of adaptation. Normally, the part-brain is an integral element within the function of the total brain. Affect or mentalized feeling—affecto-symbolic or ditentive behavior—is the result of an abnormal deviation from orthonomic or cotentive behavior, or from the biologically normal relation between the part-brain and the brain as a whole. In its production of affect the forebrain has assumed a position that disregards the primacy of the whole brain or the total organism. In other words, the forebrain has assumed a spurious supremacy, and the phylic brain of man as a total organism no longer functions as a phylically integrated entity.

Instead of there being a consistent uniformity of function throughout man's brain as a whole, the autocratic claim or right advanced by each individual or by each community or by each nation supersedes this basic consistency of function throughout man's organism as a phylum. Owing to a dislocation of function within the brain of man, this organ in each individual of the species, as well as the socially composite group or community brain, has arbitrarily set aside its primary unity and integrity as a phylically common organ.

This is not consistent with the organism's solidarity as a species. It is not conformity to the law of action and reaction. It is not *intra*relational balance and integrity. It is not protergy, cotention and health, but allergy, ditention and pain. It is confused interrelationships rather than the intrarelational function of man as a unitary whole. In man's allergy and pain there is persistent antagonism and conflict. The violence of war is succeeded by political clashings among nations, large and small. And within our own nation that played so effective a part in the recent world war, there is at this moment the spectacle of incessant strikes of nationwide dimensions. What is sought is not the clear thinking and feeling of man for man, but only thinking and feeling for *my* nation, *my* State, *my* country or community, *my* family, *my* self as opposed to other nations, other families and other selves. Such feeling and thinking is not consistent with the organism's syntonic pattern of behavior. It is not common feeling with and for the organism of man as a phylum. It is partitive feeling, or affect—feeling or affect for me, for my advantage, my gain. In all this the object sought is not balance, not equanimity and coördination, but the subjectively assumed "right" of person against person, class against class, party against party, of nation against nation. Each would enforce his own right in favor of his own personal advantage or that of *his* group. But one cannot be false to the phylum and remain true to the individual. Whoever cheats his kind cheats his kin.

This business of pitting Russia and the United States against one another, which is the vogue at the moment, is just another figment of the sick brain of man. In its partitive dichotomy, man's divisive brain is under the inevitable compulsion to make bullies of the largest and most powerful countries and, by egging them on to a competitive race for national preëminence, to stage another grand knock-down and drag-out fight between them and their several allies. But boys will be boys. And so in the records of "normality" the escapade will be registered as just another world-war, while on the clinical chart of phylopathology it is in truth just another hysterical paroxysm due to the divisive function of man's brain. The fact is that what is called "peace" has always been but underground warfare. Today this underground warfare extends throughout the world. With our world-wide labor strikes and our internal political dissensions, war has become *intra*national as well as international.

In the division within man's whole brain there is division within his whole organism, within the whole motivation and behavior of man. It is because of this division in man that he seeks to find compensation in the fanciful unity of imaginal Gods rather than in the actuality of his own unitary organism and its continuity with the environment. Nor are those nations which in their autopathic strivings have set aside their Gods in favor of their own autopathic political State in any different pass. Their State is but another God. In his love of his imaginal Gods man destroys himself, but he still continues to cherish and depend upon his Gods. We may not forget that Nazism is also a religion, that the massacre of St. Bartholomew's was a religious ceremonial, that the crucifixion of Jesus was also the performance of a religious rite. Did they not rend their garments and cry: "He hath spoken blasphemy"?

Though, through war after war, man pleads with his Gods for deliverance from strife and bloodshed (and not infrequently both contestants plead with identical Gods), the strife and the Gods and the pleading continue hand in hand without arousing in man any suspicion that all are of one texture; that the strife, the Gods and the pleading are of one piece with a conflict that is not outside man but within him. This is inevitable as long as man remains unaware that in apotheosizing his many symbolic recourses to unity he wholly misses the internal sense of the strength and solidarity of his own integrity as a phylum.

In all poetry, in all great art, as in all religions, we find allegorical expressions of this sense of man's organic unity, and we find corresponding expressions of his sense of the lack of its fulfilment. The Book of Job with its paeans of praise to the Almighty is a symbolic manifestation, albeit unconscious, of man's feeling of his own phylic integrity. In Matthew Arnold's salutation to "the enduring power, not ourselves, which makes for righteousness," there is but the symbolic exaltation of the power and unity of man as a phylum. The whole epic of the life and death of Christ, and of the Christian ideal is again a symbolic portrayal of man's organic continuity, as also of the partitive betrayal of his phylic continuity by the 'I'-persona. One thinks of the majestic epic of Æschylus, *Prometheus Bound;* and nothing in our own day could more beautifully symbolize the loss of the organism's primary wholeness and integrity than Francis Thompson's *Hound of Heaven.* Throughout all great literature this underlying theme of man's struggle, as of his defeat, is the substance and meaning of the folk dramatization of man's partition and neurosis.

I cannot speak of art without alluding to the robust and far-reaching conceptions of Herbert Read. The theory of art advanced by him automatically presupposes the abolition of the restrictive part-interest of the entity we have called the 'I'-persona. The goal toward which he seems to me to direct his insight (and he does so with a quite extraordinary intuitive aim) is a phylobiology of aesthetics. For the teaching of this author requires a powerful artistic sublimation that is necessarily phylic in its scope. It bespeaks a new order in the field of art, and presages the shaping of things that are to come in the sphere of man's feeling and thinking. In the domain of art today, affect too easily betrays itself in mere affectation.

In the fresher rehabilitations of phylobiology, art expressions will not be dominated by the affect. Read's work tends toward a restoration of the saner, more inclusive objectives of art. In his *Education Through Art,* as in other writings,[14] he has shown that art forms have their basis in the laws and organizations of inorganic as well as of living things, in the processes of biological growth and function as well as in the mathematical and mechanistic properties of matter. Art, Read says, is the representation, science the explanation of the fundamental structures and processes within and around us. But, according to this critic, art has become separated from living; it has become the departmentalized occupation of the few rather than the expression of the community's fundamental functions and capacities. There is thus a wide gulf between artistic creation and the actuality of life. Under the dominion of the social neurosis, there is the exclusion of any truly organic expression of art. Because of the intrusion of the 'I'-persona and its false "Gods," the individual artist does not enact in his own behavior—in his own interrelational life—the continuity and harmony of which his creative expressions are the symbol.[15]

But in forfeiting the 'I'-persona and its foolish Gods, in forfeiting an allegorical numen to which he may vicariously cling, man need not forfeit the service and facility he derives from his expanded use of the symbol. The symbol is not without honor in its own domain. Indeed, the play of mental metaphor, as such, is wholly consonant with man's primary belief in man and in the consistency of his organism's cotentive relation to the order of the phenomenal universe. The recognition of the need of consistency between organismic function and the symbol is Read's outstanding contribution to the field of art. I need not like Shakespeare less because I like phylobiology more. Because one delights in an actual landscape he does not become less fond of painting it. In his fantasy one may construct a drama of life and yet maintain a no less active interest in the vicissitudes of his own daily living. The loveliness of a finely proportioned cathedral with its graceful arches, its sombre interior, is not less beautiful because one has ceased to believe in the fanciful God of which it is the symbol. A Beethoven symphony, sunsets, the play of children, starry skies and the open sea do not mean less but rather more when felt within the frame of the organism's cotentive pattern.

But, for all man's symbolic recourses, for all his appeals to the grace and loveliness of art, man is restless. In his conflict and neurosis he is trying desperately to adjust a disarticulation in his processes that is phylic, universal. Yet always his efforts are restricted to the adjustment of purely superficial, affecto-symbolic epiphenomena. I feel I cannot more fittingly conclude this chapter than by quoting a statement prepared by Mr. Shields a few years ago and originally written as part of his annual report as President of The Lifwynn Foundation. At that time Mr. Shields wrote: "Throughout the human species, diseases are many and widespread, and in every instance there is the consistent effort of medicine to restore disordered tissues and organs to a state of equilibrium and harmony that is biologically normal to the species. When one cuts a finger and severs its tissues, one disinfects the wound and protects it. If necessary, the physician assists the healing process and even guides it. This, however, is as far as the skill, knowledge and wisdom of man can go. The physician cannot do the healing itself. It is the total organism that is the sole power and final authority in the task of reuniting severed tissues. Immediately upon sustaining a wound anywhere within its domain, the total organism sets to work quietly, methodically, surely. Though the orderly function of the organism may be threatened, there is no confusion, no division of motive, no partitiveness, no ditention. Everything moves harmoniously toward the single objective of closing the breach, and in due time the wound is healed and order is restored.

"There is this same authority within the framework of man's behavior as a phylic organism—an organismic power and final authority in the task of reuniting the severed tissues of human relations. This phylic organism with its central constant is not only a powerful authority; it is a past master in an art that is coeval with the origin of life itself—the art of living wholly and in unison, both internally and externally. But, singularly, man does not evoke this power. Nor does he assist it. For he does not know that it exists—he does not know in any objective, diagnostic sense. And not knowing, he feels no urge to know. Yet man has never ceased to ruminate, to indulge in images and fantasies of this central organismic constant. Ever since man lost contact with the organismic force of this central principle he has vaguely sensed its existence within him. As yet, though, he has been unable to do more than invoke a mental, ditentive concept of it—a concept that invariably breaks down when faced with the test of actual human relationships. And so man has spent endless centuries arguing, moralizing and philosophizing, even though the end product is only dispute, confusion and conflict. This state of conflict in the life of man with its 'moral' issues is not fundamental, as he mistakenly supposes. In its beginning this conflict of motive within the species man was a quite simple accident, an inadvertence in his neurodynamic evolution; and all moral, all affectively 'right' and 'wrong' issues are but the symptomatic reflection of this accident, not its cause. It is like the pain accompanying a gastric ulcer. It is not the pain but the ulcer that is the disease. This inadvertence was associated with the development of the forebrain, the part-brain or with the symbolic segment and its concomitant use of gestures, signs, symbols and words that eased communication, expanded the function of the brain and senses of man and widened environmental frontiers.

"The evolutionary trend of the total organism in creating a specialized organ of attention and interest was biologically most felicitous. It assisted in refining the process of total attention, and thus increased the adaptive capacity of man, individual and phylic. Nevertheless, in spite of this favorable outset, things began to go amiss. They need not have gone amiss. Merely because man found this developmental trend apt and handy, he need not have lost touch with the whole brain and the total organism that lies back of it. But he did. And as a result the part-brain more and more assumed supremacy. The process, however, was extremely slow. Obviously, its beginning took place before the advent of historical records, and then for ages and ages went on so gradually that man did not know what had happened, until finally the function of the part-brain all but completely displaced the function of the whole brain and its matrix, the total organism.

"Naturally, this *faux pas* entailed a serious sidetracking of the primary, unified processes that are vital to total, balanced development. At the same time the phenomenon of awareness or consciousness took a new and unexpected turn. It now differed markedly from the balanced, phylic consciousness that had been evolving slowly, but steadily, surely and constructively. This new awareness, while acutely sensitive as a socio-symbolic mechanism, became increasingly erratic and uncontrollable. It simplified intercommunication, but it cut corners. And somewhere in the long line of its development this new awareness disclosed to man the *image* of self. Inevitably he grabbed this image of self, hugged it and never let go of it. Man had become image- or persona-conscious. This was man's undoing. Instead of continuing in the direction of an increasingly sensitive, phylically whole consciousness, he became part-or self-conscious. The part-brain had assumed the dominant rôle and a cleavage began to appear not only within single organisms but, as was inevitable, between one organism and another, between 'me' and 'you,' between man and man, and so throughout the phylum. Wholeness—phylobiological, constructive wholeness—was set aside for an image of wholeness.

"From now on man began his agelong trek down the enticing but precarious slope of a self-beguiling moralism and dichotomy.

His part-brain was now supreme. No matter how desperately he strove to retrieve a fancied golden age, or find the equally fancied spring of whole living, his reward was only impasse and confusion. His wishful 'goodness' turned to 'badness,' his love to hate. His 'getting together' with his kind resulted in isolation and conflict. However fervently he espoused peace, he found himself at war. It was inescapable. Man was at war with himself. He had forfeited the pattern of whole living and with it he lost completely his sense of direction. He lost the only means of healing the breach between himself and his kind.

"Today man is still faced with this relentless dilemma, and his habitual partitive, ditentive recourses are without avail. Over and over throughout the centuries he has tried them all. But in the final accounting there is always confusion, conflict, impasse, disease. This conflict does not grow less. It increases. Until today man is fighting man throughout the world, throughout the species, the while the identical age-old confusion and conflict continues unabated within the political bounds of man's divisive and warring half-worlds—within each nation, each State, each community; within each family, home and individual. Biologically, this dilemma was not necessary, but socially it was inevitable. It was the inevitable result of an accident in man's social development—an accident through which the symbolic part-brain and its 'I'-persona assumed a dominant rôle and thenceforth masqueraded under the guise of the whole brain. It was through this accident that ditentive deviations came to take precedence over the organism's primary pattern of integration or cotention."

NOTES

[1] See Chapter VI.
[2] See note 6, page 283.
[3] See pages 204-10.
[4] Burrow, Trigant, *The Structure of Insanity*.
———, *The Biology of Human Conflict*, pp. 116, 152, 214--16.
[5] See pages 183-88.
[6] See Chapters III and VI.
[7] See page 180.
[8] Thompson, Charles B., "A Psychiatric Study of Recidivists," *The American Journal of Psychiatry*, 1937, Vol. 94, pp. 591-604.
[9] Perhaps with the development of finer measures of inquiry we shall find that in all functional disturbance there is also present some element of structural change, either potential or actual. (Elsberg, Charles A., *The Story of a Hospital, The Neurological Institute of New York, 1909-1938*, New York, Paul B. Hoeber, Inc., 1944,

pp. 31-2.) And it may be found more profitable still to consider the part that a rudimentary disturbance of function plays in inciting structural disease. The extent to which disturbance in the sphere of man's interrelational life constitutes this functional causation will, I believe, become of major interest to future medicine.

[10] See pages 244-49.

[11] See pages 220-25.

[12] See Chapter IV.

[13] While under the blinding domination of his habitual affect-projections man has no objective recognition of the resulting pain within his organism, he has nevertheless always had a ditentive or distorted sense that all is not well with him. But while finding himself resorting obsessively to all manner of anodynes—tobacco, alcohol, drugs, not to mention his insatiate recourse to mollifying transferences—he could only wring his hands and struggle the more desperately to make his ditentive dreams of peace and good will come true. Man's energy is great but it is misdirected.

[14] Read, Herbert, *Art and Society*, New York, The Macmillan Company, 1937, pp. xix + 282.

———, *Education Through Art*, London, Faber & Faber, 1943, pp. xxiii + 320.

———, *The Grass Roots of Art*, Problems of Contemporary Art, No. 2, New York, Wittenborn & Co., 1947, pp. 92.

[15] Syz, Hans, "Education Through Art," A Review, *Psychiatry*, 1947, Vol. 10, pp. 104-9.

CHAPTER IX

CONTRASTING PATTERNS OF TENSION
OR
THE PHYSIOLOGICAL SEAT OF THE NEUROSIS

With the acceptance of a science of human behavior it will become the interest and the business of man to set aside the multifarious expressions of his unpredictable mood or his vacillating affects. It will be our interest to learn in terms of practical neurodynamics what differentiation has taken place in man's organism coincident with a shift of function from the basal nervous system to a functional brain system that is socio-symbolic or partitive. Setting aside familiar theocratic accounts of the origin of man and his relation to the universe; setting aside political, philosophical, moralistic evaluations of man's behavior, it will become our business to familiarize ourselves with the neuromuscular modifications involved in this shift of innervation from man's primary organismic interrelationship with the environment to a social relationship that is purely interpersonal or affecto-symbolic and that has its origin in the social image or symbol-complex embodied in the 'I'-persona. In a word, we shall turn from the outer aspects of conflict, ditention or autopathic motivation—a conflict expressed interrelationally in the social dichotomy of right and wrong, praise or blame, love or hate—and, instead, deal directly with the organism's violation of its primary or cotentive basis of motivation, a violation expressed in a discrepancy between man's internal tensional patterns.

In man the acquisition of the symbolic segment and the gradual conformity of the organism to the laws operating in the external world—the organism's response to the nomen—provide an avenue of conscious correlation between these external laws and the law intrinsic to the organism. The law intrinsic to the organism controls the coördination of function that unites the cells and organs of the body and preserves the balanced function of the organism as a whole. This coördinating principle is the central constant of which we spoke earlier.[1] The central constant regulates the behavior of the organism's internal processes; its organismic fidelity to the external constant or to the consistent principle regulating the phenomena of the outer world constitutes the nomen. The nomen or the consistent correlation between internal constant and external constant reaffirms the principle of man's species solidarity or his bionomic homeostasis. This internal consistency is the criterion of healthy organism-environment reciprocity. It is the biological norm to which man must return if he is rightly to evaluate whatever deviations in interrelational function have inadvertently impaired his organism's healthy balance of behavior.

While the motivation of man is, of course, primarily governed by the autonomic or involuntary nervous system, the genetically recent acquisition by man of the socio-symbolic system marked an evolutionary variation in the human species and introduced a new factor in the adaptation of man's organism to the environment. This new bionomic system has assumed a function that now mediates only vicariously between the organism's involuntary or autonomic system of behavior and the world of external phenomena. As long as the complemental interaction between the socio-symbolic and the autonomic systems remains intact—as long as this functional correlation remains unimpaired by ditentive or autopathic interpolations—man still maintains a consistent relation to the prevailing order and sequence observable within the external world and, correspondingly, the interrelation of individuals to one another is equally unitary and consistent. Moreover, as has been pointed out, this symbolic system has immeasurably expanded the function of the brain and senses of man and has correspondingly enlarged the field of observable phenomena.[2]

In discussing the function of attention and ditention (Chapter IV), I spoke of the phyloörganism's maintenance of its balance of function, of its action and reaction as a whole in its relation to the environment.[3] Here in the reaction of the phyloörganism we have the parallel to the principle of reaction-balance which, in its manifestation within the organism of the individual, was first described by Claude Bernard and later called by Cannon homeostasis.[4] Like the motivation of other animals, human motivation is mediated by the thalami and the autonomic nervous system and is therefore spontaneous and involuntary throughout. In the lower orders of animal the autonomic system controls the behavior of the organism, and this instinctual reaction of the animal is all that is required in initiating its healthy adaptation to the environment.[5] But with the acquisition of the symbolic function and the relating of man to the environment through a process of symbolic attention, the organism's primary attention, or cotention, was thrown out of kilter. The phyloörganism's basic homeostasis or its primary interrelational function was interrupted, and ditention henceforth replaced man's primary cotentive pattern of adaptation to the environment. It is therefore in the social or interrelational sphere of attention that the phyloörganism's homeostasis—man's primary relation to the environment—has undergone deflection. It has undergone deflection through the intrusion of the 'I'-persona with its concomitant ditention and affectivity. It is in this sphere— in the sphere of attention as it mediates the interrelational life of man—that the solidarity of man as a species or the organism's biological norm has been violated.

It is, then, through a biological inadvertence in the basic function of man's ecosomatic behavior that the organism's total homeostasis or its cotentive adaptation underwent a deflection or derouting. As a result of this interruption in the phyloörganism's interrelational function or in its species solidarity, man's behavior is at all times subordinated to a ditentive pattern of adaptation or to the systematization of digressive affects and prejudices we have traced to the 'I'-persona. These ditentive ("wishful") excursions man now fondly takes to be his voluntary choice of conduct, when in fact his "wishful" behavior is his inevitably autopathic response to this reflexly derouted or decentered pattern of motivation. Thus man's wishful moods—his so-called will—are in fact quite involuntary reactions. What man in his ditentive mode calls his choice is but his partitive, his reflex social conditioning. That is, the total involuntary system in man has been sidetracked by unilateral or autopathic interests that are subversive of the organism's internal nomen or its consistent reaction to the laws operative in the external world. This is the phylopathological phenomenon of ditention; this the dislocation in man's primary cotentive relation to the environment—a dislocation in phyloorganismic homeostasis that is responsible for the numen and man's world-wide social neurosis.

On the basis of group studies of the organism's phylic patterns of tension I have elsewhere attempted to describe the principle of homeostasis in relation to man's ecosomatic function as a phyloorganism.[6] Cannon has given a most able description of homeostasis as it governs the organs and their interrelated functions within the individual.[7] But unfortunately this competent investigator becomes lost amid the abstractions of mere symbol and metaphor when he attempts to trace a parallel between the disorganization and imbalance that occur within the physiological processes of the single organism, and the disorganization and imbalance we see projected socially in man's political and industrial institutions.[8] Cannon has dealt most ably with the physiological functioning of the individual organism, but naturally he failed to recognize the serious impediment that has occurred in the *physiological functioning of man as a phyloörganism*. And so, in dealing with the phenomenon of homeostasis with its testimony to "the wisdom of the body," he neglects to take account of the *un*wisdom of the head (his own and the community's) when, through the interposition of the partitive 'I'-persona, the head attempts to make social symbols and images substitute for the homeostasis of the phyloörganism as a whole in its relation to the environment as a whole. Otherwise, in seeking to explain man's social expressions of disharmony and conflict, Cannon would not have drawn the highly artificial analogy he does when he endeavors to extend the functional disharmony of the individual organism to the disorganization in function that is secondarily projected in the industrial and political disturbances of the social community. These purely social expressions of man, belonging as they do to his partitive or symbolic plane of adaptation, are only secondarily related to the somatic functions of man's organism. The attempt to correlate man's purely social, external disturbances of function expressed in impaired industrial production and distribution—strikes, riots, race conflicts and wars—with the manifestations of physiological disorder witnessed in the individual organism lacks biological warrant. The two phenomena do not belong within the same category. Disturbances in the sphere of social interactions coincident with man's symbol interchange, and disturbances within the physiology of the individual organism possess no common ground, no basis of contact. Such a correlation rests upon mere philosophical theory. The external manifestations of social conflict are the symptoms of a phylic disorder in physiological tensions, and it is only in the domain of these phylic tensions that a correlation may be established between individual and community disorganization. Cannon's theoretical analogy again exemplifies the tendency to arbitrary excursions into symbolic abstraction so common to the social community. The frequency of these erroneous habits of thinking and feeling in dealing with the problem of man's interrelational behavior should warn us of the ease with which even the scientist of proved capacity in his special field may, in his partitive dissociation as a separative individual, fall a prey to the extravagances of mere metanomic or ditentive speculation. It is obvious that scientific or intellectual capacity is no guarantee against the inroads of man's socially pandemic neurosis.

With a view to the controlled study of man's behavior as a phyloörganism, the efforts of my associates and myself were directed towards the investigation of those processes which would best assist the conscious correlation of man's habitual reactions with the exigencies of an ever-changing environment. To this end we sought objective means of differentiating between the affecto-symbolic pattern of behavior and the total behavior-pattern both of ontoörganism and phyloörganism. In this attempt we did not adhere to the usual distinction between normal and neurotic individuals, "normals," as we have seen, representing merely those who measure up to the arbitrary rules of conduct embodied in the social reaction-average, and "neurotics" representing those who do not. Instead, as I have said, we sought to establish the biological norm that underlies and governs the reactions of social man as a species. We sought to establish this central constant or biological norm in order that it serve as a basis in respect to which deviations in man's social behavior might be recognized in as sharp outline as we now recognize deviations from the social norm in the individual clinically regarded as pathological. The behavior expressive of this bionomic basis comprises those organismic functions that primarily relate man to the environment independently of his affecto-symbolic or his "right"-versus-"wrong" adjustments.

We mentioned in the last chapter that in searching for these fundamental behavior correlations our interest had centered specifically upon the process of attention as the essential factor mediating man's ecosomatic adaptation. As was said, we applied ourselves to the study of attention in its function both as a total pattern of action and as a partitive pattern of action. The functioning of the organism's total bionomic processes—its primary homeostatic balance in respect to the environment—is the process to which I have referred as cotention, while divisive attention or adaptation (man's affecto-symbolic reactions), whether occurring in the neurotic subjects or in the social community, is the process to which I have referred as ditention.

I should again like to call attention to the circumstance that from the outset of our researches there was the effort to sense the basic internal factors responsible for disorders in man's social life. In this connection perhaps I may quote a passage from an earlier study that is pertinent to the trend of the present pages. In speaking of the distortion of attention and interest in the human species and its influence upon man's behavior, I said in *The Structure of Insanity*:

Before the introduction or invention of language, of socially agreed signs and symbols, or before the adoption by man of the projective, intellectual mechanism of attention as we now know it, the organism's adjustment to its surroundings was effected by means of certain general tensional alterations. These reactions constituted an integral, a systemic or an organic mode of adaptation or attention. Through this process of attention the organism as a whole encountered its environment as a whole. That is, the total object of the environment engaged the total interest or feeling of the organism. In response to this integral species of attention the organism performed its various "instinctive" functions— the function of locomotion, of rest, the function of nutrition, of elimination, of herd or family interplay, of sex activity as of the corresponding interludes of sex quiescence. By virtue of these functions, alternately cumulative and dissipatory, the animal procured its food, gathered for the winter, sought shelter, found repose, grew tense or relaxed, slept or wakened. There was thus maintained that physiological balance of tensions and releases through which the total organism secured "its continuous adjustment of internal relations to external relations." [9]

This organic reciprocity, this synergy between organism and environment is, of course, no less the biological basis of the organism's total function today. This organic rapport between internal tension and external stimulus tends equally today to maintain in man, as in the lower animals, an equal balance of adjustment between inner and outer processes. Of special interest to the present theme, however, is the fact that, in their racial homogeneity, these internal tensions constituted for man, as for the lower orders of animals, a medium of interindividual communication as comprehensive and as efficient for the purposes of the organism as a whole as the sophisticated symbols of interchange that have come to serve the purposes of man in his social intercommunication today. Whatever "mental" agreements have come to be interpolated socially in the course of man's functional evolution, this organic mode of attention that mediated the adjustment of the organism as a whole still maintains unabated its physiological primacy.

These internal postural tensions that relate the total organism to the environment and to other individuals of the species I have elsewhere described as the *co*tentive processes in contrast to the *at*tentive, and the state or condition in general as *co*-tention.[10]

Psychiatrists, and indeed many laymen these days, frequently make reference to "tensions" and the harmful effect upon childhood of these "tensions." They speak of individual tensions, of family tensions, of social tensions, national and international tensions. They speak of the importance of psychiatry's dealing with these tensions, particularly with a view to creating a healthy environment for children. But what *are* these tensions? What is their seat? What is their origin, their history and development? What structures and functions are involved? How may one reach them, and what may one do with them when he has reached them? These are practical, anthroponomic questions which neither psychiatrist nor layman asks himself, and it is not surprising that in thus failing to ask the right question they should fail to find the right answer. This answer is one that would take into account man's dissociated identity due to a miscarriage in the function of his affecto-symbolic segment with its creation of a disparate pattern of tension—a pattern of tension that may be objectively discriminated from the pattern of behavior belonging to the organism's tensional balance as a whole. But we cannot talk of tensions and not satisfy the conditions of science by establishing data which permit a conscious correlation between these alleged tensions and the behavior-disturbances of which they are presumed to be an index.

Viewing attention or adaptation from the basis of the group or the phyloörganism as a whole, my associates and I sought to bring to evidence the organism's partitive tensions, or the divisive motivation that is expressed not only in each separate individual but also in the social reaction-average of the community as a partitive clique or cluster. We attempted to contrast man's attention or motivation in its habitual partitive expression with the attention or adaptation of the phyloörganism in its primary total motivation. Having succeeded in defining the presence of part-reactions which, in both neurotic and normal, are ditentive or autopathic, our efforts centered upon the fullest abrogation of these part-tensions as the dominating motivation of man's behavior. Through the repeated and consistent frustration of ditention or part-motivation in both individual and group, the whole or total pattern of man's behavior came more and more to the fore, until finally the phyloörganism's cotentive pattern gave definite indication of its primacy as a totally integrated behavior-reaction.

The process of cotention as well as the process of ditention, as I use these terms, should be defined very clearly because of their specific bearing upon the experimental investigations of my coworkers and myself. Let me return, then, to the definition of the retroceptive type of attention represented in ditention. In Chapter IV ditention was described as the situational reaction in which ulterior advantage supersedes direct interest in an object or condition for itself. Our interest in ditention lay solely in the reflex linkage of affect and symbol involved in this attentional mode. In our finding, this type of affecto-symbolic attention is invariably accompanied by an irrelevant, partitive interest—an interest that supplants and divides man's cotentive adaptation or the native attention of the phyloörganism. It is for this reason that I have called it *di*tention. The mechanism of ditention is automatic. It is not a condition one has himself induced. But, through a phylic accident in man's development and the encouragement in us all of ulterior motives of behavior based on what others have bid us think and feel and do, ditention is induced with the inculcation of speech in each growing organism. It is this partitive process of ditention that ever preserves in individual and community its secret aim of private advantage in contrast to the total interest of the species as a whole.

Cotention, on the other hand, may be defined as the neurodynamic relation of organism to environment as it exists natively and undifferentiated within the cerebro-sympathetic system. Cotention represents the balance of internal tension and stress that primarily relates the organism kinesthetically to the outer world. It is the phyloörganism's basic tensional constellation or its total matrix of sensation in its relation to the environment. This tensional mode represents the non-differentiated pattern of motivation that mediates primarily between man's organism and the external world.

When we consider it, all functional balance is a form of cotention. Cotention is a form of homeostasis that operates normally in all bodily activities. It is cotention that maintains the organism's balance in walking, that coördinates the movements performed, for example, in dancing, in bicycling, skating or in horseback riding. Where one first acquires facility in any of these activities, a preliminary stage of awkwardness makes him aware of the somatic discipline required to bring about the needed coördination or correlation with the environment coincident with the organism's homeostatic function or cotention.[11] Where an individual's cotentive pattern becomes momentarily suspended through so unwonted an activity as swinging, parachuting or riding the racer dip, he becomes painfully aware of a physiological disturbance in the organism's total balance of tensions.[12] One may also become painfully aware of an interruption in cotention by purposely disturbing this natural function of the organism in any of its parts. If, for example, one holds the unsupported arm outstretched for a sufficient length of time, he begins to experience an unnatural tension which, if prolonged, may become quite unbearable. Such a localized state of stress is a disturbance in the organism's normal homeostatic balance in relation to the environment. It is an interception of the organism's primary tensional equilibrium.

But our interest in man's interrelational adaptation has to do with the interruption of cotention upon a far broader biological plane. The symbolic segment as it operates interrelationally in the function of speech possesses social involvements that interrupt the natural cotention of man's behavior as a phylum. There is entailed disturbance in a part-function of the phyloörganism that affects man's behavior throughout. The function of attention as a total reaction in relation to the environment has given way to the function of attention as a purely affecto-symbolic perception, and the cotentive correlation of the organism with the outer environment has in the same measure yielded to a socially habituated part-pattern of attention, or ditention. Because of the social involvements in this part-reaction, it is only through bio-social measures or through a broad phylic approach that the partitive process of ditention can be resolved and the phyloörganism's primary condition of cotention reëstablished. This shift from affecto-symbolic (ditentive) part-pattern to syntonic (cotentive) total pattern is a prerequisite to the organism's conscious correlation with the environment.

Cotention or the phyloörganism's primary tensional pattern has been superseded by ditention over so long a period of man's evolutionary descent that the effort to recall the internal sense of this deeply submerged pattern now involves a definite affront to the organism's habitual mode of adaptation. No one knows better than I the unwelcomeness of cotention as compared with the ditentive blandishments of man's socially constellated 'I'-persona. With everyone, and with me no less of course, the reaction of the 'I'-persona shows all the reflex persistence of a confirmed tic. There is no reasoning with it. It has become one's very self—the partitive self that is ever foraging for images of security that are purely fanciful. Yet for all its unpalatableness, the pattern of cotention is not beyond the reach of man. It has been definitely established by The Lifwynn Laboratory that this ancient pattern of wholeness is accessible to the organism's deeper levels of sensation and perception. But as the very first step in the conscious recapture of this integrative principle there comes the recognition that not only the individual but also the community is now wholly insensible of and hence inhospitable to this larger basis of feeling, and that with all of oneself, with all that one now knows as "oneself," he is rigidly set against this inclusive, organismic basis of behavior.

In a scientific investigation, however, a student sets no store by his personal wants. And this rigid disregard of his personal wants marks the second step in man's return to his primary cotentive matrix of feeling and thinking. For it is the obligation of research that it break with every cherished tradition and that, single-minded and unsponsored, it set out upon the virgin soil of experimental material. It is our premise that the balance and integrity of one's observation of perceptible data existing outside one, is controlled by the balance and integrity that resides within one's own organism. In approaching the cotentive pattern one is entering no less upon an objective research, but now the field of that research—the material to be observed—lies within one's own organism.

As is well known, under conditions favorable to bodily quiet and rest one quite readily discovers muscular zones of tension or contraction in the various body-parts. These physiological reactions, these chance muscular contractions within the organism, are inconsistent with the complete quiescence of the body as a whole. They are out of harmony with the design of the organism's total cotentive pattern. But immediately on observing these localized contractions, one has a distinct sense or sensation of their disparity in relation to the rest of the organism. With this kinesthetic awareness, the contractions are released and the tensions subside, because these muscular discrepancies are automatically brought into conformity with or reintegrated into the pattern of the organism as a whole.

When, however, this tensional discrepancy occurs within the sphere of man's interrelational behavior, the situation is a very different one. In the interrelational sphere the physiological disparity consists in neuromuscular contractions that are coincident with the use of man's socio-symbolic capacity. For in this sphere we have to do with the physiological substrate of tensions that we experience in the unreasoning affects and prejudices systematized within the 'I'-persona. As noted in Chapter V, these tensions and contractions are localized in a definite feeling of stress in the forepart of the head, chiefly in the region of the eyes and forehead. Unlike the contractions just cited, this physiological stress that underlies man's 'I'-persona—a stress that he experiences interrelationally only as affect—does not readily yield to immediate control. This discrepant pattern too long established, too long operative in us since our early infancy and since the early infancy of the race, is not to be lightly brought into line or reintegrated into the phyloörganism's total pattern. Yet the reintegration of this deviate pattern into the pattern of the total organism is the task that faces the student of phylobiology.

Apparently this anthropological modification in internal behavior is the most urgent adjustment that lies ahead of man today. Apparently it is only in such a direction that man will meet intelligently the tremendous conflict and chaos he himself has created out of ditentive processes resident within himself. And so, in seeking the solution of man's problem of behavior, it is wiser to follow the course of science—of the biologist, the chemist and the physicist—and discover in what direction a social process lies than adhere to the habit of the philosopher, the religionist and the politician, and insist on the direction one would like a social process to take. To attempt to see what lies ahead of man in the natural course of his development, and to contribute one's utmost to the cotentive understanding and furtherance of this inevitable course, is surely the part of the realist in contrast to the dreamer and the wish-ridden.

It is because the course of man's behavior shows today so strong a bent toward newer and broader evaluations that the realistic position of phylobiology with its outreaching toward a conscious bionomic order and harmony becomes especially pertinent in a scientific study of man. Coupled with these intimations of a broader social orientation, there are on every hand the widespread breakdowns of man's partitive systems of behavior—social, industrial, economic and religious. The present accession of conflict and self-destruction throughout the world should offer sufficient evidence of the social welter of affects into which man has been plunged. In face of this widespread disorder of function in our bionomic life we can hardly disguise from ourselves the extent to which distorted thinking and feeling, or ditentive outlooks, have replaced the constructive aims of the organism's balanced motivation, or cotention.

But if anyone supposes that to attain the pattern of cotention is to attain a state of Nirvana, that with the discovery of this pattern he has come into possession of "spiritual meanings" hitherto undreamed of in the philosophies, that he is about to adopt some manner of Yogi practice or experience something akin to the "beatific vision" of the mystics, let him be warned that his trend is definitely away from his biological base, not back to it; that he is riding the runaway steed of ditention to a lather. None of these comforting self-propitiations, none of these flattering self-appeasements, play any part in man's quite simple physiological appreciation of the function of his own organism as a total entity.

On the contrary, in approaching cotention the organism finds itself upon quite prosaic, pragmatic ground. The problem is really a simple one. Perhaps an analogy may be found in the altered pattern one must attain on learning to swim. To one who does not know how to swim, the water is a quite alien medium, and he invariably sets out to make its acquaintance along lines of his habitual reaction to the solid ground—a reaction precisely contrary to the behavior required of the swimmer. Where one is on terra firma and there is question of his security, of his footing, he seeks automatically for a more solid base. His tendency is to grab for something that will help sustain his poise. So it is at first with the venturer into the unfamiliar medium of water. With the very first threat to his accustomed balance, his reaction is a frantic effort to secure a firmer hold. His impulse is to grab. Over and over again he grabs. But his grabbing avails him precisely nothing. It is, in fact, the most inappropriate response he could make. What is needed now is that he let go of his usual physiological pattern of security and, instead, make use of a wholly different pattern—a pattern adjusted to his wholly altered environment. While on land one's instinctive reaction is to hold on, to maintain a firm solid medium beneath him, now the organism's need is to let go of solid, unyielding ground and to abandon all effort to secure a firm footing. For he must exchange a solid for a fluid medium of security, and the organism must entrust itself completely to the support of this new menstruum.

On land, of course, the organism supports itself through the proper adjustment of the external skeletal muscles, or through the appropriate adjustment of the body's tensions in relation to its surroundings. In the water an internal readaptation is required, and the would-be swimmer must learn to abandon his accustomed adjustments. In maintaining its balanced support in the water, the body must seek before all to maintain its air-supply intact. One's security is dependent upon his air-intake, and one needs to place full confidence in the ability of his organism to support itself with this aim in view. Once the swimmer ceases to rely upon his breath-control for his support, immediately distrust and fear take hold of him, and he sinks beneath the surface. For in his fear he begins to grab again. He begins to clutch for the security of a firm environment where there is no firm environment. Thus the swimmer accustomed to a bionomic pattern in which he depends upon solid ground for his security must, on entering the water, adopt a pattern that depends upon the balanced pliancy of his internal respiratory and general motor adjustment to the altered medium. In this way he finally learns to swim.

Needless to say, a person does not ordinarily give himself airs on learning to swim—not any more than on learning to walk. On acquiring the facility to swim, marked as this departure is from his habituations on land, he does not feel he has attained the millennium. Adopting the requisite pattern of balance, he quite simply swims, and there is no more to it. After all, as the evolutionists have taught us, man was an aquatic animal many eons before land became his natural habitat. Similarly with respect to man's internal behavior: the pattern of cotention antedated the pattern of ditention by countless thousands of years, and to reëstablish this original pattern, so long forgotten, presents little occasion for special pride or affectation. To be anything but cotentive is to be deviate, autopathic, dissociative; it is not to be one's bionomic self. Surely to be merely what one is, is not an achievement to be signalized with a fanfare of trumpets. For man to be man can hardly be set down in the record as a noteworthy attainment.

In comparing swimming with cotention, I am resorting, as I

said, to mere analogy. Nevertheless, the two reactions possess certain common features. Under the dominion of ditention or of affect-images one is ever grabbing on behalf of the 'I'-persona. He is ever grabbing for the fleeting image of his preëminent "right." For it is the law of ditention that, at whatever cost, one must somehow preserve a policy of unilateralism. He must get ahead in a partitive, competitive world. He must be first. He alone must be secure; he must have the best there is for himself. Above all, he must create an appearance of success in competition with others. This is what I have called "face"; it is the social affect; it is one's autopathic self-propitiation, his *amour propre*. Even though it destroy his very life, he must keep scheming, lying shoving and fighting in the interest of what he calls his personal prerogative. And so he must grab. He must grab everything and he must grab it *first*. Such is the ditentive pattern of behavior with its short, quick, staccato movements ever alert for this and that interrelational advantage or opportunity. In this mechanism the organism's spontaneous grasp reflex has been transformed into a sophisticated and monopolistic grab reflex. This grab reflex has no connection with man's environmental security, but only instigates a socially competitive response in the interest of a retrofectively conditioned 'I'-persona. Biologically, therefore, we may not fail to see that the grab reflex is but the perversion of a healthy instinctual reaction, that our unilateral grabbing is a ditentive distortion of the organism's biologically normal grasp reflex.

With the pattern of cotention, on the other hand, motivation arises from the internal need and interest of the organism. In cotention one assimilates from the environment; he does not grab; he reacts spontaneously to the organism's need. Though effortless, cotention is productive. There is a great difference between the grabbing impulse and the reflex of grasping in the interest of the organism's assimilative function. In the cotentive pattern one seeks only what is his own organismically, and he seeks it only by reason of the natural interest of the object in relation to his own capacity or endowment.

Ditention rests upon a subjective, unilateral interpretation of behavior; cotention on an interpretation which, being organismic, is consistently objective and inclusive. Cotention is synonymous with functional balance, organismically and intraorganismically. It is identified with ease, quiet, clarity and preparedness, both in feeling and in thought. **Cotention** is a function that is free and capacious. It is steadfast and dependable both in normal function and in emergency. Cotention deplores the partitive step before taking it. It crosses the bridge before coming to it.

With the reëstablishment of cotention and the reintegration of organism with environment, the necessity to struggle, to leap for this and that advantage in competition with others, falls away. From now on the outlook becomes broad, impersonal, affirmative. The spirit of disinterested research, and with it the disinterested spirit of living and letting live, now takes precedence over a fancied prerogative of affectivity and unilateralism—the affectivity and unilateralism of the social 'I'-persona. With the attainment of this altered mode, the student automatically begins to function as man, to think and feel as man, to recover his organism's basic primacy and with it the experience of a full and mature consciousness. He begins to sense the basic principle of his organism's motivation before there was inculcated a sense of "I"—the social image of separateness, of distinction, of private or personal importance. He begins to transmute into terms of consciousness the undifferentiated preconscious mode of behavior that was his in early childhood, as it was man's in the early preconscious childhood of the race.[13] This is cotention. This is integration. This is Man come to himself.

Man's fallacious inferences in the past respecting the physical universe of energy and matter were serious, and long impeded the expansion of his sense-relations in respect to the surrounding world. But these obstacles to the correct functioning of the brain of man affected only his intellectual or projective appreciation of the objects and situations about him. A far more serious and formidable impediment to man's clear adaptation exists in the hindrances and confusion that obstruct his appreciation of the origin and meaning of his own behavior and its underlying motivation. In man's confusion before the world of outer facts and relationships the obstacle besetting his path is to be traced merely to a false habit of reasoning. But the obstacle to man's clear perception within the field of his own behavior is to be traced not only to a false habit of reasoning but also to a false habit of mood, feeling or motivation. This is a vitally significant distinction. It is a distinction that points up with new insistence the very urgent problem of man's needed reconstruction in relation to an increasingly complex environment. It points up this problem as one calling for the enlargement of the senses of man and a broadening of the function of man's brain as it relates his organism to the outer world.

The discrepancy between the outer manifestations of the schizophrenic and his internal mood has long been recognized by psychiatry. It is the rationalizations of this autopathic mood to which Bleuler gave the name "autistic thinking."[14] This type of patient will relate the most tragic personal experience but, in relating it, he will wear a countenance of beaming complacency. The condition of the schizophrenic mind is not unique. This behavioral inconsistency is characteristic equally of the social mind of man. Socially the mind of man may quite sincerely assume an outer aspect that completely belies the undependable vacillations of mood that lie beneath it.[15] This is a situation with which we need carefully to reckon.

Twenty-five years ago we resolved that the world war—"the first world war"—was to be also the last world war. That was the *mind* of man. That was what man thought. But we did not reckon with his *mood*. We did not reckon with the shifting and uncertain caprices of man's feeling. And so today we have just finished fighting what we call the second world war. Yet with our guns still smoking from this second world war, the mind of man is already busy laying plans on the one side to promote, on the other to offset, a third world war. But once more the mood of man—his covert, unpredictable affect—is not taken into account. We do not take into account the devious machinations of the 'I'-persona as it operates socially among us. Accordingly, we persistently fail to reckon with the fact that wars are not fought in response to a mental attitude, but that these recurrent episodes are invariably the outcome of man's recurrent moods.[16]

In his welcoming address to the United Nations Organization (*The New York Times,* October 24, 1946) President Truman quoted the opening lines of the Charter of the United Nations Education, Scientific and Cultural Organization which declares: "Since wars begin in the minds of men, it is in the minds of men that the defenses of peace must be constructed." But it is just here in the minds of men that the defenses of peace have been constructed from time immemorial, and without avail. Mr. Truman and the Charter are furbishing anew the old fallacy that the motivation of man is of mental or intellectual origin. But it is only the fallacious mind of partitive man that voices this thesis. It is only the part-brain of man which in defiance of the repeated evidences of history still lays claim to the belief that man can solve the problems of war through a mental process, when in fact it is the underlying mood, the underlying neurodynamic pattern of ditention that continually motivates the human organism and that, if not remedied, will continue to drive man to unceasing conflict and war.

In an able and delightful article, "Man's Long Story," Lewis G. Westgate reviews the life span of the *genus homo* and assembles an imposing list of its vast assets and achievements.[17] No one could better have described the progress of man's mental growth. Toward the close of his impressive summation the author pertinently adds: "Millions are spent for research in technology, for improving glass, rubber, corn and hogs; very little for the study of man himself. One sickens at the billions now necessarily given for war, all of which would be unneeded in a decently ordered society; and thinks what tremendous advances the wide use of a fraction of that wealth would bring about if devoted to the problem of man." Finally he asks whether man shall not readjust his behavior in the interest of a better world for all people. In answer he says: "There is no question but that he has the necessary intelligence. The mind that can weigh the infinitely distant stars and tell their make-up, that can track down the minute carriers of disease . . . can solve its social problems when and if it decides to do so."

This is all very well, but the mind of man can solve its social problems only when and if man decides to examine objectively his own false mood, his habitual social numina. This disordered mood of man the author does not reckon with. He does not reckon either with man's sick mood or with the obstacles this sick mood of man stubbornly opposes to the clear operation of his intelligence wherever it is a question of his own behavior. That man can accomplish all that he has accomplished in intellectual fields and yet spend billions upon a world war which would be unthinkable in a decently ordered society is due, in the finding of phylopathology, to the present impassable gulf between the mind and the mood of man, between the function that is sponsored by the brain of man acting as a whole and the biased part-function of man's socially conditioned brain, or 'I'-persona. Yet in spite of the manifest inadequacy of the part-brain in dealing with disordered human relations, man continues to employ this behavior-segment with all the ditentive affects or mood-impediments with which it is beset.

From the point of view of man's biased reason or mood, from the point of view of the organism's autopathic behavior, man continues to cling to the fanciful image of divine protection which his private mood, his ditentive "reasoning" has arbitrarily created in behalf of his personal comfort and safekeeping. In his secret apotheosis of an esoteric 'I'-persona, or social numen, man still demands exemption from the phylic principle implicit in an organismic science of behavior. This is the essential mechanism of man's dissociation. The ditentive vagaries that issue from man's partitive 'I'-persona—the superficial reactions that have their collective expression in the social neurosis—are in no way related to man's primary behavior-motivation. The organism's primary motivation is as fundamental to its behavior as protoplasm is to its structure. Whether or not man likes to challenge his own cherished mood, it is the mood of man and its distortions upon which his scientific observations need most urgently to be directed.

Keeping in mind the decentration or the partialization of motivation that has been induced by man's verbally conditioned reflexes—his symbolic affects and prejudices—it has been the aim of The Lifwynn Laboratory to analyze this artificially disorganized pattern of behavior against the background of the organism's primary motivation as a whole. Our object has been to eliminate this barrier of dichotomous images and affects with a view to the ultimate restoration of the organism's basic pattern of cotention. We have sought to give to the symbol or to the verbal stimulus its proper place in negotiating interindividual contact within social communities without permitting its untoward encroachment upon the organism's centrally motivated processes. In short, as participants in the wider human community sharing common interests and ideas, it was our effort to preserve the social convenience of external symbol or metaphor without allowing it to decenter the phyloörganism's primary pattern of behavior.

I cannot repeat too often that, notwithstanding its distortions into metanomic (autopathic) avenues of motivation, I am in no sense deprecating the symbol or underrating the great economic asset to man of this vicarious usage. The symbol that man has invented should stand, however, as a dependable constant to the phyloörganism, serving as a convenient handmaid to the phylum as a whole. Instead, shifting and inconstant affects or partitive motivations have become attached to this primarily consistent sign or gesture. It is these partitive adhesions to the symbol that constitute the unstable element in effecting man's partialization of function or his organismic dissociation as a phylum.

Naturally, the interest of medicine can, in the last analysis, direct itself only to the concrete somatic processes, anatomical and physiological, that are the seat of man's behavior-conflict as a phyloörganism. Regarded from a neurological angle, these processes obviously involve, on the one hand, the symbolic functioning of the cortex of man and on the other, the functioning of those basal brain-areas—the thalamic and hypothalamic structures —that mediate the primary reactions of the phyloörganism. Phylobiologically, the impasse expressed in man's phylic disunity in behavior—a disunity caused by a functional disparity between the symbolic (socio-cortical) and the organismic (phylothalamic) processes—marks a decentration or partialization within a primary function of the human organism. This phylic disturbance of function has shifted the neural basis of man's behavior from its central unitary areas of motivation and has led to interindividual reactions which, by dint of this very maladaptation, man now interprets purely socially or symbolically. As a result, it is the universal attempt of man today to adjust the organism's phylic disorders of behavior only upon a purely interpersonal or symbolic basis. Man is forever seeking ineffectually to correct his behavior-disorientation with mere differentially conditioned (moralistic) alternatives, or with the socially imposed image-precepts he calls "right" and "wrong."

Whatever our interest as laboratory students in basic anatomical conceptions, as phylic elements finding themselves inadvertently led astray through a false course of bionomic development, our major concern was not with formal anatomy, but with such a physiological adjustment within our own processes as might once more set us in the path natural to our growth and integration as a species. This is no less the immediate need of man the world over. It is the realization of this need that I wish I might bring home to the student of this thesis. To this end I cannot do more than invite the reader's participation in a common effort to recover the organism's primary integrative basis through the function of cotention. In the next chapter I shall describe as concretely as the data permit, what I have found through repeated experimentation to be the most effective technique for reclaiming this integrative or cotentive basis of man's immediate relation to the environment.

But first let us return for a moment to the contrasting patterns of motivation which I said earlier constitute the underlying physiology of the symptoms we automatically enact under the sponsorship of a spurious normality with its shifting moods and varying affects. Let us examine the tensions which upon physical diagnosis we find to be concomitant to these external symptoms of neurosis, or to man's phylic dislocations in behavior. For we are now dealing with the very fine discrimination between the interrelational function that mediates man's socio-symbolic capacity of interchange, and the intraorganismic function that mediates the adaptation of man's total organism to the environment. The perception of this delicate differentiation in neuromuscular adjustment is not easy. The displacing of the ditentive in favor of the cotentive pattern of behavior, whether in the individual or in the community, is not an adjustment to be blithely achieved.

If, however, through a device of the total organism the agitated 'I'-persona can be induced to hold still long enough for us to allay the go-getting drives of self-interest and competitiveness that now obtrude upon this intraorganismic sphere, we may materially assist the restoration of man's primary pattern of motivation. For by this process the organism recovers its total pattern of innervation and thus checks the intrusion upon it of a pattern that is partitive and that necessarily issues in sectionalism and dichotomy. In other words, through this technique one may perceive within his own processes the contrast between the pattern of tension and motivation that innervates the symbolic segment of the brain with its partitive affects and prejudices, and the pattern of tension and motivation that belongs to the basal nervous system and that is consonant with the organism's total biological behavior in relation to the environment. We may distinguish between a pattern of tension that has artificially disintegrated the behavior of the phylo-organism in its basic motivation, and a pattern of tension that reintegrates the behavior of man in its organismic solidarity. In a word, we may eliminate unilateral or partitive tensions manifested in the interpersonal affects and prejudices of our pseudo-normal society and coincidently restore those behavior-tensions that are the basis of unitary and constructive behavior throughout the phylum.

It was through our gradual exclusion of interest in these wholly proprietary social affects in respect to ourselves and others that there came about the increasing perception among us of the clearly defined tensional patterns just mentioned. Of these, one pattern (ditention) characterizes the behavior of the organism's symbolic segment as a discrete and separative expression of the 'I'-persona and is clearly discriminable from the pattern of neuromuscular tension (cotention) that integrates individual organisms within the phylum as an organismic whole. Our aim, therefore, was henceforward directed toward the clearer organization of these internally appreciable tensional patterns.

The contrast between these two patterns of tension is a contrast between health and disease—between the health and disease of the community in its external, social manifestations. For the contrast between these internal patterns of tension is the basis of the contrast between two interrelational modes of behavior. In one mode we have the social expressions observable as man's autopathic thinking, his spurious assumptions of "face," the morbid dichotomies of feeling and thinking that rest upon his purely fanciful "rights" and the numen. In the other mode—in the mode that is consistent with the biological law or nomen—we see those expressions that further the confluent interest of man in progressive programs of social activity and growth.

Upon this contrast in internal tensions and reactions, therefore, depends the harmony or disruption of man's social reactions. Where there is disruption and disease, or autopathic motivation, there is the social dominance of the pattern whose complex of tensions corresponds to the 'I'-persona—the divisive entity that represents the behavioral standard of normality and that *forms the social background from which the artificially segregated neurosis of the individual has emerged*. Desperate disease entails desperate pain. And the pain caused by the tensional complex embodied in the 'I'-persona is no exception. Yet this tensional complex, this phylic pattern underlying the social 'I'-persona has thus far thwarted all man's attempts to observe human behavior in the scientific spirit in which he has consistently observed other objective phenomena. For it is the tragedy of the social neurosis that its pain is by common consent disguised. The disease of the 'I'-persona contains its own social opiate. But there must be the intelligent recognition of pain before there can be the intelligent treatment of it.

For the community no less than for the individual, pain is the great reducer, the great leveller. If it asserts its law with sufficient force and persistence, none of us can resist its authority. Its word is supreme. But with man as an organism afflicted with the pain of tensions that are partitive and that denote a condition of pathology within the phyloörganism, quite the reverse is true. Not only does this generic pain fail to bring man to his knees in obedience to its authority, but thus far man has absolutely refused to recognize his pain and, instead, resorts desperately to every diversion, every irrelevance that serves to distract his attention from it. The reason is that his partitive tensions are now his very own identity or 'I'-persona, and thus man's actual condition, his true pathology is disguised from his own organism. Hence our failure to recognize the pain of conflicting patterns of tension.

The objective recognition of the stress or pain involved in this conflict, and the differentiation of the internal tensional patterns is the task of the laboratory of phylobiology. This differentiation with which we found ourselves unavoidably confronted—a differentiation between secondary affect and primary feeling—may, it is true, appear a somewhat large and over-ambitious order. Indeed, it may appear to lie quite beyond the reach of man. Yet it is extraordinary what people can do when they have to. Only a short time ago the attitude of physicians toward infective diseases rested upon a basis as subjective and traditional as the ideological prepossessions that too commonly offer a "scientific" account of behavior-disorders today. Only yesterday, as we have seen, the attitude of medicine toward infective diseases was such as ascribed these processes either to the discretion of a Divine Will whose displeasure it sought to appease through the medium of prayer, or to certain "humors and distempers" vaguely assumed to bear a causal relation to the disease in question. But so widespread was the devastation of communities throughout the world by reason of these disorders in man's reaction as a community that, violent as was the wrench from established theological ideologies, man was forced to discover in the actual tissues of man himself the cause of deviations occurring within those tissues. However bitterly the early students of infective processes were assailed by their conventional colleagues, the time had come when man *had* to find a remedy in man himself.

In a situation demanding a scientific approach, there are people who think anteriorly of the condition, and these are the people who meet the crisis with ingenuity and invention. In view of the close intercommunication between individuals and races brought about by the frequent shifting of armies and the widespread displacement of civilian refugees during the recent war, many, if not all, contagious diseases would have spread throughout the world like wildfire but for the check that had been placed upon these processes by the early students of medicine and bacteriology. This fortunate circumstance resulted solely from the resort of science to measures of invention and discovery.

With our close social intermingling today, individually and racially, there is still the pernicious contagion of affects arising from our social 'I'-personae and a consequent intensification of disharmony and conflict throughout the world.[18] So today when man wages universal wars against man—when autopathic "reasoning" and ditentive superstition, or the numen, prevail upon every hand—we must perforce depart from our accustomed partitive, metanomic ways of thinking and feeling, and face at last the inexorable dilemma of our own unilateral and divisive selves.

As the 'I'-persona is an internal, *endopathic* lesion, only an internal, endopathic recognition of it can possibly control or eradicate it. In order that the organism make contact with an object or condition, its approach to it must lie within the same category as the object or condition itself. I do not approach the sphere of mental concepts except as I approach it mentally, nor do I make contact with elements or conditions within the domain of feeling or sensation except through the avenue of feeling or sensation. One could no more do so than he could see with his ears or hear with his eyes.

Subjective, autopathic, neurotic thinking and feeling has its corresponding pattern of tension internal to the organism. Purposeful, practical, effective thinking and feeling has also its corresponding pattern of reaction internal to the organism. According to the intraorganismic study of man as a phylum undertaken by my associates and myself, the solution of the problem of man's adjustment to man and to the world of actuality lies in his capacity of objective discrimination between these two patterns of tension automatically operative within him. The organism of man is a very delicate instrument. It is a mechanism requiring very fine adjustment. But man has as yet not approached, in any objective sense, this instrument of adaptation that is his own organism.

NOTES

1 See pages 321-24.
2 See pages 138-39, 288-89.
3 Burrow, Trigant, *The Biology of Human Conflict,* pp. 142-72.
4 See note 12, page 232.
5 In connection with the principle of homeostasis as it relates the organism of the individual as a whole to the environment—in reckoning with the function of the special senses (smell, vision, hearing) in their relation to the total organism's internal needs—Curt P. Richter's experiments with rats are of interest. In these experiments he demonstrated that the principle of homeostasis operates not only among the organs and tissues of the body *inter se,* but that it also influences the behavior of the individual organism as a whole in its relation to the outer world. Richter found that when his experimental rats had free access to as many as fifteen dietary elements, they chose those substances which served to provide a well-balanced diet, while avoiding those less appropriate to the organism's needs. (Richter, Curt P., "Biology of Drives," *Psychosomatic Medicine,* 1941, Vol. 3, pp. 105-10. See also his "Total Self-regulatory Functions in Animals and Human Beings," *The Harvey Lecture Series,* 1942-3, Vol. 38, pp. 63-103, and Albrecht, William A., "Discriminations in Food Selection by Animals," *The Scientific Monthly* 1945, Vol. LX, pp. 347-52.)

With the process of human evolution and with the tremendous growth of the intellectual faculties associated with the cerebrum, man's external vegetative senses, chiefly the sense of smell, have become correspondingly less acute. But unquestionably this liability has been more than compensated by man's symbolic facility in the analysis and correlation of objects and phenomena. It is only in the misapplication of the symbol through the interposition of ditention and the affect that man's capacity for symbolic discrimination and judgment has seriously fallen behind the instinctual aptitude of the animal.

6 See note 13, page 232.
7 Cannon, Walter B., *The Wisdom of the Body,* New York, W. W. Norton & Co., 1932, pp. xv + 312.
8 Cannon, Walter B., "The Body Physiologic and the Body Politic," *Science* 1941, Vol. 93, pp. 1-10. See also *The Wisdom of the Body,* pp. 293-8, 302-6.
9 The phrase "internal relations to external relations" is, of course, taken from Herbert Spencer's *First Principles,* New York, D. Appleton & Co., 1897, p. 86. See also J. S. Haldane's discussion of the organism's "internal environment," *The Philosophical Basis of Biology,* 1931, pp. 14, 67; and the latter's quotation from Claude Bernard, p. 66. Cf. also W. B. Cannon's *Bodily Changes in Pain, Hunger, Fear, and Rage,* New York and London, D. Appleton & Co., 1929, pp. xvi + 404.
10 Burrow, Trigant, *The Structure of Insanity,* pp. 22-4.
11 Indeed the individual's bodily expressions of the organism's tensional balance or norm might perhaps be more fittingly called coten*sion* instead of coten*tion,* the latter term being reserved to describe the balanced tensions that pertain specifically to man's projective or interrelational behavior. A corresponding distinction might also be made between diten*sion* and diten*tion.*
12 I well recall my experience when as a boy I rode a roller coaster for the first time and felt the disconcerting, if wilfully induced, pang that accompanied the sudden "drop into space." I remember that the spasmodic intake of breath that occurs simultaneously with the sense of falling, and the surge of fear concomitant to it were readily inhibited through my voluntary recourse to a slow, forced expiration during the moment of sudden descent. I shall never forget the immense relief on finding that this improvised countermeasure served to efface completely the feeling of anxiety. It is evident, as I look back, that the organism's cotention had been rudely interrupted by so unexpected a shock, and that my "orthopathic" resort to a compensatory physiological measure had restored the organism's balance of reaction.
13 Burrow, Trigant, "The Preconscious or the Nest Instinct," paper (unpublished) read at the Seventh Annual Meeting of the American Psychoanalytic Association, Boston, May 25, 1917. The trend of the preconscious thesis is outlined in Chapter IV of *The Biology of Human Conflict.*

[14] Bleuler, E., *Das autistisch-undisziplinerte Denken in der Medizin und seine Ueberwindung*, Berlin, Julius Springer, 1919.
[15] See pages 183-84.
[16] See pages 190-91.
[17] Westgate, Lewis G., "Man's Long Story," *The Scientific Monthly*, 1943, Vol. LVII, pp. 155-65.
[18] Burrow, Trigant, "An Ethnic Aspect of Consciousness," *Sociological Review* (London), 1927, Vol. XIX, pp. 69-76.

CHAPTER X

THE BIOLOGICAL NORM OF HUMAN BEHAVIOR
OR
THE TECHNIQUE OF COTENTION

When we come to the technique of cotention, we have for the first time in the field of human behavior to reckon with a technique that is anthroponomic. We have for the first time to reckon with the neurosis of man as a maladaptation in the function of man's brain in respect to its environment. We have, accordingly, to let go of habits of thinking and feeling that have characterized the attitude of psychiatry and of "normality" generally toward mental disease. This attitude consists essentially in the belief that a person who is a mental patient does not think and feel as the community thinks and feels, and that in this consists his illness. In such an outlook the physician does not see behavior in its broad phylic aspect. He does not recognize that the community itself is merely pseudo-normal. This attitude has been the social vogue for generations.

True, in recent years psychic treatment has been replaced in part by physical measures of relief. Electro-shock therapy and convulsive doses of insulin and metrazol have been used with a view to breaking up a patient's neural paths of association. But here too the approach is not anthroponomic. It does not envisage the neurosis in its broad, phyloneurological aspect. It still deals with a person whose thinking and feeling is not in accord with the popular feeling and thinking of the community. Once more, as is customary in our "normal" psychiatric procedure, the physician does not reckon with the pseudo-normal "associations" of the community and with the need, therefore, of breaking up those associations that characterize the adaptation of the brain of the physician as well as of the patient. The psychiatrist does not recognize that the system of associations (the interrelational mode) characterizing the community is of one piece with the associational system of the individual patient, and that the patient is regarded as clinically deviate only because he fails to accord with the prevailing associational habits of this wider, pseudo-normal community. In other words, the psychiatrist lacks the criterion of a biological norm and therefore does not recognize that the brain of the pseudo-normal community is quite as deviate or "dissociative" in its interrelational function as is the brain of the clinically aberrant patient.

In saying this, I do not forget that I, too, am a psychiatrist and that, as I said earlier, my criticism of psychiatry necessarily involves the traditional procedure of myself as well as of others in this field. And so I cannot point at psychiatry or at any other expression of normality as though these mentally systematized reaction-modes did not apply equally to myself—as though my own involvement in the restricted perspectives of "normality" had not been the whole incitement to my interest in a broader orientation in respect to the field of human behavior. But instead of telling other people in the community how to feel and think and do, we psychiatrists need to come down into the community and enter into its feeling and thinking. As an integral part of the community we need to examine neurosis, our own and the community's, as a condition common to the phylum man—so common that no individual, sect or nation can assume a pontifical attitude toward this infirmity but must envisage it as an anomaly in behavior present within man as a race or species.

In the past few years, as we know, recourse has been had to operative procedure for the relief of certain types of mental disorder, notably the agitated depressions. Through this technique certain neural fibers within the frontal lobes have been severed. This type of surgical intervention is designed to reach paths of association which, to judge from the clinical cases reported, relate to the differential reactions referred to in Chapter VI, or to the system of socially conditioned reflexes localized within the area comprising the organism's affecto-symbolic segment of behavior. This segment contains the neural tracts which, according to phylobiological experimentation, mediate the interrelational behavior of man—the reactions I have referred to as partitive, affective, or autopathic.[1]

From the cases described by the neurosurgeons, it would seem that in some instances the extirpation of portions of the frontal lobes has proved helpful, although scientific conservatism would commend our withholding judgment until there has been a longer time for observing the cases reported and a larger number of cases to report. But however handy in the specific emergency, it is hardly to be hoped that the neurosis of man, or the age-old conditioning of the phylosoma with its resulting decentration of man's primary adaptation as a whole, can be reached and eradicated with a mere scoop! Certainly, from a phylobiological angle this more or less random dredging amid none too definitely localized brain-areas is hardly reconcilable with an organismic approach to the problem of man's associational or autopathic disorientation as a phylum. Besides, removing tissues that are the seat of a functional disorder occurring within the brain is not in keeping with accepted medical practice. Rather is it customary to apply a functional remedy for a functional disturbance. In seeking a cure for indigestion one would hardly think of removing the stomach.

But whether the method followed is that of the functionalist or the structuralist, psychiatrists and the schools of behavior, generally, need to recognize the anthroponomic nature of the disorder requiring investigation. Only in this phylic purview can we avoid the hit-or-miss measures that are now applied to the relief of conditions universally misapprehended as "mental and nervous disorders." Only in this wider outlook can we realize the necessity of reckoning with these disorders as alterations in phylophysiological function, and of dealing directly with the organs and tissues involved in these functional alterations. The neural areas whose function controls the partitive or paratonic pattern of tension we may call the *parencephalon,* while the functional areas of the cerebrum that regulate the organism's orthotonic pattern of tension as a whole we may call the *orthencephalon*.[2] These terms will be of assistance in describing the practical discrimination between the socio-cortical functions presiding over man's symbolic capacity and those phylothalamic processes that regulate his behavior as an organismic whole.

The area I demarcate functionally as the parencephalon corresponds, in part at least, to the area which the anatomists circumscribe with more or less definiteness as the prefrontal zone. Undoubtedly, future scientists in the field of human behavior will more and more focus attention upon this area of neural conduction because of its relation to the over-accentuation in man of symbolic affects or of man's metanomic behavior. In this connection there is evidence that the diminution in a psychotic patient's symptoms following chemical or electrical shock-therapy is coincident with the occurrence of tissue disorganization within the parencephalon or within the frontal associational areas.[3]

But in face of man's desperate maladaptation today, how wide of the clinical mark is his remedial aim! What, after all, has been accomplished by resort to lobectomy, or to the use of insulin, metrazol and electro-shock therapy in this or that patient, other than the mere chance relief of certain outer symptoms? Of course, through the use of these techniques, individual patients may be relieved of some of their external symptoms, but in the relief from their associational habits they too often have to pay a very heavy toll in a serious aftermath of personality-alterations—alterations that are hardly less burdensome, and certainly no less pathological, than the original symptoms. As well be unduly agitated as rendered dull, apathetic and unresponsive, as is the case with so many of these operative patients. Such techniques illustrate once more the irony of an operative procedure which may be eminently "successful" but from which the patient dies or is crippled for life.

We might for a moment review the rudiments of man's associative process and consider anew the primary composition of this psychosocial phenomenon. In Chapter VI, in which we dealt with the elementary physiology of the affect or prejudice, we saw that conflict is introduced in the experimental animal through the artificial induction of a dichotomous situation in which motivation is divided between the issues of gain or loss, advantage or disadvantage, the "right" or "wrong" choice. We also saw that the condition of conflict, as it has been brought about spontaneously within ourselves in the course of man's evolution as a species, rests upon this same elemental dichotomy. We saw, however, that in man the opposed alternatives in his behavior-conflict or neurosis are reactions to a complex constellation of differential affect-stimuli—affect-stimuli which in each separate organism or group of organisms have become systematized into the spurious entity we called the 'I'-persona.

In the course of our study of the conditioned motivation induced in man no less than in the experimental animal, we found that the induction of dichotomous or two-directional affects entailed an affront to the organism's integrity of function as a whole. This affront which, in the beginning of our laboratory work, registered itself in the "normal" interrelational reactions of affect and its inevitable defense, was now observed among us as an essentially physiological behavior-reaction—a physiological reaction which in man, as in the case of the animal, is hemmed in or partitive (metanomic) in contrast to the organism's total (orthonomic) reaction. Ordinarily, of course, affect is drained off in the alternative satisfactions of acquiescence or resentment. But under the impetus of systematic laboratory challenge, affect is robbed of its validity and denied the satisfaction of its customary outlet. The affect becomes blocked and impacted, so to speak, and causes insult or trauma within the organism. It was the immediate physiology of this congested affect with which, as laboratory students, we had now to cope. And so, instead of seeking to explain behavior-disorders as a conflict of dichotomous images, as a mental tug between the alternative affects of right and wrong, advantage and disadvantage, or as a conflict between the fulfilled and the unfulfilled "wish"—the perennial concern of psychiatry as of all behavior-schools, religious and secular—we set aside these purely projective or socio-symbolic epiphenomena and attempted to reach the deeper physiological causations lying beneath these socially manifest antitheses.

As indicated in Chapter V, under conditions of prolonged group challenge and frustration I had more than once had a fleeting sensation of unusual stress or tension within the forward cephalic region. With the gradual maturing of the experiment this sensation of stress, which was experienced partly as tension in the eyes, became a factor of central importance in our behavior investigations. It became important to us in discriminating between tensions originating in the partitive segment or 'I'-persona and relating the organism affecto-symbolically to the environment (ditention), and tensions that relate the organism to the environment through its balanced function as a whole (cotention). As the 'I'-persona employs the same neuro-muscular area (the symbolic segment) in its partitive motivation as does the organism in its behavior as a whole, it was in this area that there occurred an overlapping and conflict between the organism's total and its partitive pattern of tension.

As our laboratory procedure led increasingly to the abrogation of a mentally dichotomous basis of adaptation and of the endless symptoms of conflict and neurosis that flow from it, we sought more and more to discriminate between the two physiological patterns of behavior I have described.[4] We sought to discriminate between the physiological tensions that constitute the phylo-organism's differential ("right-wrong") behavior-pattern on the one hand, and the balance of tensions (homeostasis) that primarily relates man to the environment on the other.[5] Our efforts centered upon demarcating in clear objective terms the phylosoma's total pattern of reaction from its reaction as a partitive behavior-response.

As the brain constitutes the central nervous ganglion, so to speak, of man's organism as an entirety, the brain of man constitutes the neural reaction-system of special interest to us. We repeat that of the two major functions of the brain, the first is that which relates the organism as a whole to the outer environment. The second consists of the specialized function of that part of the brain through which individuals are related to one another and to the environment by means of commonly agreed tokens or symbols of objects in place of the objects themselves. This function which is mediated through the use of symbols or language relates man to the environment projectively rather than organismically. The study and analysis of differences in behavioral adaptation between the soma's organismic relationship to the environment and its symbolic or projective relationship has led to a discrimination within the bionomic adaptation of the brain of man that is distinctive in the work of The Lifwynn Laboratory of behavior experimentation. This discrimination consists of a demarcation in function between the affecto-symbolic part-brain and the brain of man when acting as a whole.

We have emphasized the pattern of reaction that characterizes the numen, or man's fanciful relationship to the external world, as contrasted with the nomen or the relationship to the external world that is consistent with bionomic law.[6] We said that there is need for wider perspectives not only regarding phenomena existing external to man but also regarding reactions having to do with man's own behavior—with man's relation to man. We said that in respect to this latter sphere of behavior there is required the same expansion of the brain and senses of man that has characterized his approach to the biological sciences elsewhere. For in the sphere of man's interrelational behavior no less than in his consistent appreciation of the phenomena of the external world, it is necessary to discriminate carefully between the internal pattern of reaction concomitant to the nomen and the internal pattern concomitant to the numen. The effort to restore the pattern of cotention as over against ditention is no other than the effort to enlarge the function of the brain and senses of man. For ditention constitutes the obstruction to man's unhindered use of his brain as a whole. Ditention is synonymous with the numen and is thus an obstacle to the nomen or the conformity of the brain of man to the consistent order prevailing in the external world of interrelated phenomena.

But the student of behavior will wish to have a definite understanding of our phyloanalytic technique. He will wish to know in concrete terms just how the response to the nomen may be distinguished from the response to the numen. He will be interested to know how to discriminate between the basic reactions that are an expression of the whole brain and that mediate the organism's primary security in relation to the environment, and the affecto-symbolic reactions that are an expression of the partbrain and that seek mere metanomic satisfactions on the basis of sheer fanciful images of security.

In the effort to differentiate these two physiological patterns, the tensions in the region of the eyes were at first our only index. They were, however, an unfailing index because of the key position the eyes occupy in relation both to the organism's partitive or reflexly induced behavior-pattern and to its primary or central pattern of behavior.[7] They were an index because man's socially ambivalent images (the intrusion of differentially conditioned reflexes) are, according to our previous finding, concomitant to an internal physiological alteration. This alteration consists in the circumstance that the tensions in the ocular musculature have become dissociated from the organism's center of control or from its internal system of tensions as a whole.[8] The reason for this dissociation lies in the fact that in the course of man's social (affecto-symbolic) evolution the total pattern of neuromuscular control was largely abandoned and the eyes left to the accidental influence of reflexly induced stimuli, that is, to the influence of partitive, decentered habits of innervation. In other words, we found ourselves making direct contact with the neuromuscular substrate of man's secondarily conditioned (associative) pattern of motivation—the interrelational pattern of motivation which with its affect-linkages now entirely supplants the primary behavior of man. This development gave the first indication of the neurodynamic basis underlying the indirect, haphazard system of ditentive (paratonic) responses that now replaces the phyloorganism's cotentive (orthotonic) pattern of reaction as a whole.

It was this unique finding, based upon repeated experimentation, that brought to evidence the existence in this area of a subjectively appreciable pattern of stress or tension—a pattern of stress or tension due, doubtless, to our conscious arrest of a partitive behavior-reaction grown habitual to the organism.

At first this sense of stress or of internal shear, so to speak, was only of sporadic occurrence and stubbornly eluded all efforts to recapture it at will. But gradually the tension in the cephalic segment grew to be more frequent and more pronounced, until finally, after long-repeated experimentation, it was possible to elicit this localized tension at any moment. As the pattern of tension associated with autopathic thinking, or ditention, is connected with a specific type of eye-behavior, the procedure which seemed at first of greatest assistance in getting in touch with this localized partitive pattern was that of sensing the pattern of tension in the region of the eyes. It consisted in differentiating this localized pattern from the organism's pattern of tension as a whole. In doing so, one automatically intercepts not only the images concomitant to the oculomotor tensions, but also whatever affects are linked with them.[9]

The first step in the method followed by my associates and myself consisted in closing the eyes. While in one's attempt to restore cotention the eyes need not necessarily be closed, it seemed helpful, at least in the beginning, to employ this procedure. With the eyes closed and with only the sense of complete darkness before them, our aim was to maintain a steadfast internal sense of the balance and tension connected with the eyes. In my own case, the effort, as I looked at the curtain of uniform blackness, as it were, before me, was to rest the eyes on the point (not visible of course) that was felt kinesthetically to be directly in line with the normal visual axis. That was all. This "all," however, consisted, in fact, in the sustained awareness of an indeterminate physiological process subjectively appreciable by the organism.

Where it was possible to sustain this cerebro-ocular posture over any considerable period of time (such a period amounted in the beginning to a few seconds only), the elimination of customary affect-images took place automatically. The mental and emotional pain and disappointment resultant from the frustration among us of ditentive social feelings and impulses was suddenly dissipated.[10] If imagery occurred, it was of a different quality or character from that which prevails in the field of man's customary social images.[11] This altered mode represented a reaction that could be quite clearly differentiated from the mode accompanying the affect-stimulation and self-concern of ordinary social interchange. In general, I would say that this mode of feeling and thinking was characterized by a constructive, impersonal type of interest that is inclusive or organismic as contrasted with the type of thought and feeling characterized by personal self-interest or the unilateral dependence of the individual in his relation to others of the community. While our experiment in the field of mental and emotional reactions was at that time only tentative, it seemed to us even then that the alteration in the individual's reaction in response to the discipline of group frustration consisted in a shift from an affecto-symbolic basis of motivation to a basis of motivation that is primary and organismic.

Through the kinesthetic balance of the ocular muscles it became possible, following long-continued practice, to maintain the eyes in a state of equilibration for increasingly longer periods. In thus holding to an internal awareness of the tensional balance of the muscles controlling the eyes, there was, as I have said, the coincident occurrence of a sensation of stress or tension in the region of the eyes and in the anterior part of the head.[12] With the maintenance of this more steadfast and centralized position of the eyes, it was disclosed that the sense of physiological strain or tension was due to the opposition of the affecto-symbolic pattern (ditentive thinking) to the primary pattern of cotention.

For this localized strain or tension in the region of the eyes and forehead stood out in ever sharper contrast to the more balanced and diffuse sense of tension that now began to supersede more and more the organism's part or ditentive pattern of reaction. With our progressive facility in this technique of subjective oculomotor balance, the steadfast position of the eyes became linked increasingly to a steadier tone or pattern of tension within the body-musculature generally, while the occurrence of oculomotor unrest was associated with cephalic tenseness, particularly within and behind the eyes. It became apparent, however, that in the kinesthetic awareness of stress in the ocular and retro-ocular region we were now dealing with a behavior constellation or complex which apparently was integrated within a larger part-system of motivation. To judge from the deeper sensations lying back of the eyes, this behavior system appeared to be connected with a special zone of cerebral activity. Our subjective inference in this regard was supported objectively by further observations. For we found that, concomitant with the maintenance of balanced oculomotor tensions, other physiological systems, presumably not primarily connected with the innervation of the ocular musculature, underwent correlative modifications. So that there seemed indication of the presence within the organism of a powerful neural pattern of behavior more or less narrowly circumscribed within and demarcated from the neurodynamic pattern of motivation governing the organism as a whole.

Of special interest to our experimental group was the circumstance mentioned earlier that symbolically induced reactions—ambivalent mental images and the dichotomous motivations accompanying them—were automatically excluded so long as the balanced position of the eyes was maintained through the organism's internal control of the ocular muscles. In the initial stage of the experiment the attainment of this internal muscular balance of the eyes was, as already indicated, an indispensable prerequisite in differentiating the organism's primary, orthotonic balance of function from the partitive, paratonic pattern of function mediated by the symbolic segment.

It was our finding that, unlike the sense of ease present in any other coördinated group of muscles in a state of rest, complete relaxation of the oculomotor system of muscles does not exist at any time (unless, perhaps, in profound sleep), nor may relaxation of these muscles be induced at will. Even under conditions most favorable to quiet and repose, there still persists a feeling of stress or tension as one directly observes, or becomes aware of, the eyes. With progressive experimentation this phenomenon came to be lnked more and more unmistakably with the symbolic level of motivation or with the dichotomous efforts of adaptation that correspond to man's preoccupation with ambivalent mental images. As our experiments continued, the perception of this tension, now definitely identified internally with affects that are linked with the symbolic mechanism and with autopathic habits of thinking and feeling, became a matter of routine in controlling the organism's external adaptation. In other words, this physiological tension in the forepart of the head became immediately appreciable as belonging to the plane of partitive reactions associated with the 'I'-persona or with the organism's response to differential stimuli—with man's "right-wrong" behavior-dichotomy as contrasted with the homeostatic balance of tensions that relates the organism primarily to the environment.

Henceforward, then, the efforts of my associates and myself in maintaining the organism's balanced behavior were directed toward a consistent discrimination between two neuromuscular systems of tension—between the organism's partitive pattern of tension (man's secondary, associational system of tensions) and its primary pattern of tension (man's deeper, organismic system of tensions). The first or partitive mode of reaction is concomitant to ditention or to the organism's paratonic (socially conditioned) excitations; the second or organismic mode of reaction is concomitant to the total orthotonic (unconditioned) type of adaptation I have already described as cotention.[13] Intensive experimentation with reactions occurring individually and in social groups has shown increasingly that projective attention or ditention, as it now prevails universally throughout the hominid, is characterized by an arbitrary secession of motivation from the organism's central governing pattern of behavior, while cotention is an expression of the phyloörganism's sovereign pattern of behavior as a whole.

As a result of these findings, our interest came to center less and less upon the ocular element in the tensions pertaining to the symbolic or associational processes and, instead, was directed more and more to the tensions pertaining to the symbolic segment generally. This was an important step in our phylobiological researches. It brought into sharp objective relief the entire neural segment underlying man's affecto-symbolic function—the segment in which we (man generally) had from childhood been completely enmeshed and with which we were now wholly identified. For, as the reader will recognize, here was nothing other than the partitive element we have defined as the 'I'-persona. With the organism's attention centered upon this symbolic zone of tensions, there was correspondingly a clearer appreciation of the organism's total background of tensions—its primary pattern of cotention.

Through the gradually increasing awareness of the total or basic pattern of cotention, it was now possible to give clearer definition to the organism's affecto-symbolic segment. With the growing physiological sense of our experimental field we were able to bring into ever sharper relief this functional segment that now completely dominates man's interrelational behavior, with its autopathic thinking, its *amour propre,* its assumption of "face," and its concomitant social dichotomy of gain or loss, advantage versus disadvantage, of "right" or "wrong." Naturally, with the heightened perception of this demarcation between the deviate or ditentive pattern of motivation (the social reaction-average or man's pseudo-norm) and the primary system of cotention (the phylo-organism's basic biological norm), a marked physiological impetus was given our phylobiological observations and, correspondingly, the field of our research took on an increasingly practical significance. In a word, our interest and motivation now became more and more closely aligned with the organism's total cotentive processes in contrast to its habitually divisive, ditentive reactions. It became aligned with organismic man rather than with interpersonal me or the partitive 'I'-persona.

Because of man's subjective bias in favor of his habitually conditioned affects, the discrimination of this line of differentiation is far easier in theory than in practice. The long-continued subordination of the investigator himself to the personal bias of the 'I'-persona or to his own systematization of affects makes it extremely difficult for him to keep consistently in mind the internal and, at the same time, objective nature of his problem. For, though the problem is internal to himself, it is no less physiological and objective than problems presented in other medical fields. The fact is, the student is faced with an immediate and exacting problem in internal orthopaedics. There is, however, a further difficulty. This difficulty consists in the extreme delicacy of the line of demarcation between the two tensional patterns—a line that entails a functional distinction which may be compared with the fine histological discrimination the early students of bacteriology were required to make in attempting to "recognize" a microörganism they had never before seen and of which, therefore, they had no preëxistent image or model.

The reader will, of course, realize that this broader premise of behavior was not achieved overnight. As a matter of fact our research group worked steadily over many years before attaining a consistent sense of this more basic behavioral pattern. While, in looking back, one may relate this experience in a few lines, the research itself covered many years of experimentation and was fraught with many errors in procedure and with many impediments and delays. For, simple and natural as is the primary cotentive pattern, the long-established habit of adhering reflexly to the secondary pattern of ditention makes difficult the recapture of this primary adaptational mode. No matter how simple and natural a pattern of tension, a falsely established contrary pattern makes its recovery all but insuperably difficult by comparison.

But let us turn to a lower level of the organism's homeostatic balance and observe this balance within the restricted somatic reactions of the individual organism. If we will observe the operation of homeostasis in its quite simple ontosomatic expression we shall find comparable instances of cotention and ditention in the most commonplace of our daily activities.[14] I need hardly caution the reader, however, that such instances are definitely not to be confused with the two major phylobiological patterns of behavior; they are by no means commensurate with these patterns but afford only an analogy, on the one hand, to the present interrelational, autopathic or ditentive pattern of behavior and, on the other, to the primary *intra*relational principle of cotention as it operates organismically, phylosomatically, within the species man.

Among our daily ontosomatic expressions it is the analogies to cotention that are the easier to recognize. For wherever worker or player, student or sportsman, child or adult gives whole attention to a particular object or objective; wherever there is coördination and correlation between the senses and the body-musculature, be it in the pursuit of pleasure or of one's daily living, one will find that a quite simple phase of cotention (co-tension)[15] pervades the life of man throughout the species. We see it readily demonstrated among skilled workers of all kinds. We see it in the home, the factory and the workshop. We see it in the artist, the craftsman, the acrobat, and, as mentioned earlier, in the expert swimmer, the skater, the bicycle-rider and the horseman. There is, in fact, no end to these instances. For primarily the single organism is so consistently motivated cotentively in its direct somatic adaptations to the environment that it would be difficult to escape recognizing in all man's simpler physiological activities the immediate influence of this basic principle.

Consider walking, for instance. Of all the obvious movements of the single human organism none is more commonplace than walking. Yet, anatomically speaking, walking is an outstanding achievement in balance and coördination between the senses and the general body-musculature. By merely standing upright and closing the eyes one can readily get a partial feeling-sense of the intricate, coördinated interplay between the many muscles of the body required to sustain this balanced, upright posture. So dependent upon this delicate yet powerful muscular balance is the simple act of standing upright that, if one were to faint and lose this balance for only a second, the body would immediately slump to the ground. Furthermore, once this balance has been achieved in early childhood, one can go through an entire lifetime without feeling any need to give thought to it—not any more than an unmolested, graceful deer gives thought to its ecosomatic processes of adaptation. And, all things being equal, no one ever forgets how to stand upright and walk. Here in the mere act of standing erect and walking, as it is performed by an organism composed of many parts wherein each part has its own particular place and assignment, we have a simple demonstration, equally pragmatic and beautiful, of these many parts functioning together with the sole objective of sustaining a balanced whole. Given the opportunity for expression, the evolution of this coördination and balance never fails. For this is the natural outgrowth of the organism's original protogenic pattern. This is cotention within the restricted somatic activities of the single organism.

But this ultimate achievement of balanced function is by no means the whole picture. There is also the slow, awkward, stumbling stage, the stage of learning that must be laboriously repeated over and over again. This is the trial-and-error period that leads only gradually to the perfect cotentive adaptation—cotentive, that is, in the analogous ontosomatic sense. It requires no feat of intellect or imagination to recognize that in the child's awkward early stages of learning to walk there are the rudiments of all learning processes. What is fundamentally required is timelessness, repeated effort and repeated rest on the part of the child himself; and, in addition, an unobtruding, sympathetic environment of "expert" walkers—not talkers, not people who are forever telling the child how to walk.

Similarly, in learning to talk there are the identical fundamentals. This may seem strange. For all talking, being now affective, is artificially, affectively imparted to the child. As things stand today we may not for a moment forget that, since talking is essentially an interrelational function governed throughout by ditention, the process of talking is necessarily shot through with awkward affecto-symbolic components. Ditentive man talks far too much to the child, and at him. But here too there is required only the sympathetic, unobtrusive environment. There is required only an organismic environment of "expert" talkers, and the child's organism will do the rest in accordance with its needs. Having learned to talk expertly, that is, cotentively, the child will naturally learn to communicate, by means of language, with its cotentive environment. He will use his facility of communication in learning how to do many other things, and do them happily and expertly and with the same interest and confidence with which he learned to walk. With the years there will come the progressive acceleration of healthy reflexes to attest the organism's native strength, capacity, grace and beauty.

So too in learning to run and jump, to play ball, dance, skate and swim; in learning to use a typewriter or to speak fluently in more than one language, there is always more or less—and, as the child's facility develops, less and less—of the awkward, stumbling, learning stage. Similarly with the highly trained mason or cabinet worker, with the surgeon or musician, and in the many skills that present opportunity for interest and expression, expert performance always presupposes this awkward, stumbling period of development—this learning period during which the untrained muscles and senses, at first incoherent and even recalcitrant at times, are slowly but surely brought under the unifying control of the total adaptive tensional pattern and by degrees incorporated into the smoothly functioning cotentive processes of the organism as a coördinated whole.

By way of analogy, but only analogy, this stumbling recalcitrance on the part of an untrained muscle may be likened to autopathic thinking or to the ditentive phase of adaptation that phylic man is now passing through in his socio-neurotic behavior. Incidentally, the single organism that learns to walk expertly in spite of a ditentive environment is the same organism that a little later on completely succumbs to this ditentive environment in everything that has to do with its interrelational behavior. Here, the commentary is not upon the child or upon the adult, not upon man's primary capacity for healthy, integrated, cotentive living, but upon the present reflex blindness of ditentive man to the basic implications of everything cotentive, whether in a single muscle, a single organism or in the phylum man as an organismic whole. This commentary is particularly poignant in the present moment when, following two devastating wars, man is still stumbling—as a child learning to walk never stumbled—over deadly superstitions of his own making that are even more devastating and more horrifying than his endless wars. As a matter of fact, his numinal outlook and his wars stem from the same underlying ditentive pattern of tension.

But in the organism of a child who is learning to walk (we are still keeping to the ontosomatic level), there is demonstrated the healthy process of integrating untrained muscles or parts of the organism into the latently balanced cotentive muscular system of the organism as a whole. If, however, through an unwitting interference of whatever kind, one muscle or set of muscles is favored more than the others; if, for whatever reason, one shoulder is held higher than the other, the organism as a whole is thrown out of balance. While the child would still learn to walk, this shift of interest to one part, with a resulting imbalance of the whole organism, might easily entail a compensatory adjustment that would result in an unnatural curvature of the spine and possibly an eventual undermining of the healthy functioning of the organism. It is in this preponderant shift of interest to one particular part or set of parts, with resulting unnatural strain to a segment of the total organism, that we have within the single organism a relatively simple instance of deviate function that is comparable or analogous to the interrelational dissociation in the behavior of man we have called ditention.

Before going further we may well consider certain broad generalizations. The reader will already have seen that cotention means integration, coördination or health; and that ditention means disintegration, disorder or disease. Cotention is basic or primary. Just as the bony skeleton is the organism's structural framework, so cotention is the organism's functional support. It is the individual's balance wheel; it is the homeostat of organismic man. Through cotention one implements the vast resources of the organism—the organism of man. Ditention, on the other hand, is always secondary and always indicates a shift from the organism's primary matrix of cotention to an over-emphasis upon some special part or part-function of the individual, with resulting tensional imbalance calling for special adaptive treatment.[16] In all stages of learning or of adaptation to one's environment from childhood on, the functional behavior of the single organism is invariably cotentive, unless ditention has intervened. Each new adaptation of whatever sort begins with a relatively difficult, awkward stage during which there is always the latent possibility of ditentive intervention, and ends with the functionally satisfying and pleasurable achievement of cotentive balance. Once the cotentive adaptation has been completed, it sticks; it has become an inseparable part of the organism's balanced, healthy equipment. It has become an integral part of the total functioning organism in much the same sense that the eye or the heart is an integral part of the organism as a whole; and, accordingly, one is no longer aware of it. For instance, the expert surgeon is completely oblivious of the intricate, delicate, yet ever assured and balanced performance of his senses and his body-musculature the while he is performing an operation. This is as it should be. This is healthy, balanced, cotentive function.

There is, however, the circumstance that where there is present a curvature of the spine, here too, nowithstanding that the curvature represents a definite maladaptation, one may be quite uaware of it. But we must bear in mind that in such a maladaptation there is, in general, a trend that directly or indirectly predisposes the organism to disease. In the ontoörganism's cotentive adaptation, on the other hand, there is the unfailing assurance of health. In instances of this kind in which one tends to forget the maladaptation, we need also bear in mind that the powerful, primary, adaptable cotentive pattern of function of the organism as a whole is ever at work in furthering the most favorable adjustment in spite of ditentive handicaps.

These general observations in respect to cotention and ditention apply throughout the life of man in both the ontosoma and the phylosoma. Just as there are functional disorders in the individual organism of which the individual may be unaware, so throughout the phylum man we may become so accustomed to disordered or diseased behavioral ways of living that we take them for granted; and, as I have repeatedly pointed out, we even regard these disorders as normal. I am now referring, of course, to man's inadvertent involvement in retropathic feelings, or affects that are coincident with his use of the symbolic part-brain, and to the consequent confused relation between this part or segment and the basic whole brain. I am referring to man's broad, socially systematized field of disbehavior generally—a disbehavior that starts with the stuttering individual and ends with a stuttering United Nations Organization.

As far as concerns human behavior, man is still in the stumbling stage of his development. Eventually man will come to realize this, but until he does he must continue trying desperately to persuade himself that he has already learned to walk. In the meanwhile, painfully beset as he is with unreal and undependable numinal images, man is naïvely whistling in the dark; he is feverishly rushing about, trying to cure this symptom or that with one palliative after another, when all that is required is the incorporation of the part-brain into the whole brain of man—the integration of the symbolic segment into the whole, healthy functioning of man's organism as a phylum.

There is no doubt that in time man will bring his scatterbrained behavior under the sovereignty of his total phylic organism. He will do this definitely, assuredly, simply, just as every child everywhere always learns to walk. Until this has happened, we can expect only confusion and conflict throughout the world. But sooner or later man will recognize the physiologically common tensional disorder from which his present interrelational confusion—his crime, neurosis and war—arises; and he will then begin to walk and talk phylically, cotentively. For the organism of man, like the individual organism, was originally and primarily patterned not for disease, neurosis and war, but for health, for whole organismic functioning throughout the species.

From this general background of orientation we may consider in more detail the analogy between expert muscular coördination and balance as exemplified in the skilful playing of a game, and the cotentive balance of adaptation that integrates the function of individuals into the larger phylic whole. In both instances, expertness depends primarily upon the kinesthetic awareness of the physiological pattern of tensions that characterize the cotentive or integrated response as contrasted with the ditentive or awkward reaction. In neither case does the symbolic function play an important rôle.

If, for example, I am told to hold up my shoulders or to raise my chin or extend an arm or a leg horizontally before me, I may perform these movements quite accurately from the background of my accustomed proprioceptive or kinesthetic sensations. I need have no intellectual or symbolic education in order to perform these movements with entire accuracy. I need have no systematic knowledge of the anatomy or physiology of arm or leg. So too with the more involved movements entailed in the acquisition of a technique of body-adaptation such as we see in the correct performance of the strokes in a game of tennis. If the technique of my tennis stroke is faulty, I do not "know" it in any sense of behavioral physiology until I have achieved a proprioceptive sense of its inadequacy through the direct experience physiologically of a *correct* stroke. No amount of symbolic knowledge will avail me.

This is where the value of the expert tennis instructor comes in. The instructor analyzes a player's stroke. Having studied the elements that make up a correct stroke he can readily do this. He can dissect out, as it were, and expose the faulty components, one by one, and demonstrate their relation to the elements that enter into a correct stroke. The instructor has not only an internal experience of the appropriate stroke, but he has also a symbolic or mental acquaintance with the separate details of which it is composed.

But what is important is that a tennis stroke is incorrect or faulty because it is not in line with the physiological economy of the organism as a whole. It is not physiologically integrated within the soma to the end of securing the most effective function or performance on the part of the player. Similarly with man and his interrelational behavior. Where in man's interrelational behavior the affect attaches itself to the symbol, his reaction to the environment is awkward and inept; and this awkwardness and ineptness is due to the circumstance that man has failed to integrate the phylosomatic asset of the organism's symbolic function into the function of the phyloörganism as a whole. Instead, affective elements have dissipated the organism's primarily total, coordinated relation to the environment and rendered man's behavior inadequate throughout.

Again, as in the case of the inept tennis player, an habitually partitive interest or ditention rather than direct attention or cotention may characterize my relation to the environment; and, owing to my loss of touch with man's basic cotentive motivation, I shall not "know" this inadequacy in my interrelational behavior except as I experience it from the background of a cotentive or physiologically correct sense of the organism's balanced performance as a whole. Once more my symbolic knowledge will not avail me.

Where there is the possibility of analyzing the elements that enter respectively into cotention and ditention—where we may analyze the elements entering into the neurodynamic function of cotention as compared with the elements that form the partitive function of ditention—we may discriminate the two functions from one another in much the same way that the tennis-player may learn to discriminate an inept stroke from a coördinated one. Like the tennis expert, we will acquire an internal experience of the correct behavior-reaction because we shall have acquired an acquaintance with the separate details of which it is composed. In short, through an analysis of the elements we shall attain an organic synthesis of them and hence a balanced organism-environment relationship. And so, through the technique of phyloanalysis there is the possibility of a student's acquiring a physiological experience of the organism's cotentive, as well as of its ditentive pattern of behavior, and thus of recognizing physiologically and distinguishing proprioceptively the difference between a faulty technique and a correct technique of adaptation to the environment and to other individuals.

As one may reintegrate deviations occurring within the organism of the individual as a whole through a process of practice or physiological training, so through cotention we may reintegrate the social deviations in function that have become artificially dissociated from the function of the phylum as an organismic whole. We may then see disorder and violence, conflict and antagonism, political diplomacies, personal animosities and international intrigues, political, religious and social dissensions—all these we may see as expressions of a part-pattern of reaction that has become detached from the primacy of the organism's total pattern of function. With the tennis-player, we saw that the fault in his stroke is due to the lack of its coördination or integration within the total pattern of the organism as a whole. In this partitive factor in the tennis stroke lies the analogy between the localized "fault" in the individual function of the player and the organismic defect of function brought about through the social systematization of affects embodied in "normality" or in the deviate 'I'-persona of man.

What is true of the tennis-player is also true of the horseman, the swimmer, the skater, the dancer or the trapeze performer. It is true of the mechanic or the artist, the weaver or the singer, the architect or the carpenter in relating him to his environmental occupation. But it is equally true with respect to the technique of behavior that primarily relates the individual and the species to the surrounding environment. In his symbolic capacity man, unlike other animals, possesses a special faculty for relating the organism to the environment. He possesses this faculty in addition to his primary facility for making contact with the external object or situation. The former, as we know, represents man's mental or attentive adaptation; the latter, his cotentive adaptation. But in the individual, as in the species, the two modes of adaptation have become confused. Instead of action and reaction taking place in natural accord with one another, this bionomic function of man is marked throughout by interference and conflict. As in the case of the tennis-player and his faulty stroke, it is necessary now to analyze whatever faults characterize man's effort to produce the correct interrelational reaction of organism to environment. It is necessary to determine precisely the location and nature of the interference or conflict between the neurodynamic pattern that is in keeping with the organism's correct behavior or environmental reaction on the one hand and the pattern responsible for the faulty or incorrect mode of reaction or adaptation on the other. To this end it is necessary first of all to approach this conflict phyloörganismically.

Our interest, after all, is in man's behavior, in man's neurosis and in the physiological basis underlying the external manifestations of his autopathic and abnormal mode of adaptation. Our concern, as is always the concern of medicine, is with the structures and functions to which we must invariably trace the ultimate causation of man's disturbed processes, whether as an individual or as a species.

In man's bionomic awkwardness and neurosis, as in the faulty stroke of the tennis-player, the difficulty consists in the independent withdrawal of a part-function from the primarily integrated function of the organism in its sovereignty as a whole. Whether it is the part-function represented in an hysterical or a depressive reaction, in a local tic or phobia, in the differential confusion of an experimental animal or in the faulty stroke of a tennis-player, the elementary process is essentially an expression of this detachment of a part-function from its biologically normal integration within the functional pattern of the organism as a whole.

But, to reformulate the technique specific to our procedure from the enlarged background of the soma's cotentive function, this technique requires, as far as my own subjective experience discloses, that one recognize his incessant preoccupation with mental images possessing an affect-coloring of greater or less intensity. This is the affect-element which, in attaching itself to the image or symbol, constitutes partitive attention or ditention. So that one's first recourse is to arrest such affect-images because of their functional disparity in relation to the organism as a whole. Through repeated experimentation my associates and I were at pains to verify that the tension about the eyes, while not the primary factor in ditention, constitutes an intrinsic part of the neuromuscular pattern involved in this affecto-symbolic function.

Through daily experiment we found that these autopathic preoccupations invariably consist of obsessive fantasies having to do with one's "normal" satisfactions or denials—with one's liking or disliking, with his claims and frustrations, his rights and their infringement, his happiness or disappointment, and so on *ad infinitum*. These ruminations were seen to form the warp and woof of the loves and lusts of the "normal" as well as of the neurotic, of his greeds and his grouches, his fears, his suspicions, his self-pity, pride, guilt, shame; his righteousness, his hardness and intolerance, his feeble dependence and his wayward sentimentalities. But again and again it was shown that, however unsuspected by the so-called normal wayfarer, such dichotomous preoccupations are in one form or another the confirmed habit of us all. They are the substance of ditention. They are the structure of the social neurosis. Whether waking or sleeping, we are granted no respite from these automatic preoccupations. Indeed, just as one is taken quite out of himself in his pursuit of the flight of a bird or hunted animal, so is one taken out of himself in his pursuit of these idle affects and fantasies.

So that we found ourselves trying to sense and adjust the imbalance of the eyes. As is one's recourse with any other group of muscles, the effort was to place attention upon the eyes and through the internal awareness or observation of them to relax and rest them. But unlike the situation with other local areas of the body-musculature, observation of the functional area localized within the symbolic segment did not readily lead to permanent rest and reintegration of the muscle-contractions involved. So accustomed is this area to discrepant or disparate oculomotor tensions due to man's habitual interrelational affects, that an attempt to bring about a balance of these tensions was unwelcome and caused resistance or stress. It caused resistance or stress from which we tended automatically to seek comfort again in affect-projection or ditention, in turning aside from this imaginal central point of fixation, and automatically darting back to our accustomed images and their precious affect-attachments—to the various interrelational stimuli associated with the preservation of the social self-image or the 'I'-persona.

But as more and more one recalls himself to himself, he is reminded that he is a student and that his field of research is the interrelational activation of man himself. Once more he sets to work. Again the eyes are closed. Again there is the darkness in front of him. Once more there is the central point and the black curtain before his brain. Again its fixated images and their affects are excluded. Again they are replaced by a sense of stress—of stress in the eyes and forehead. But, mind you, one is not *thinking*. One does not reach the phylobiological goal through mental information or knowledge. Not any more than one learns to dance through information or *knowing* about dancing. You dance or you don't dance according to your kinesthetic drill in the proper sequence of the dance steps. Similarly, one does not gain touch with the organism's neurosis through a mental acquaintance with it. One acquires an internal appreciation of tensions internal to his organism, and his observations are based solely upon his internal sense or sensation of these tensions. And so, one's research is now not in the field of thought where all that he has known as research has hitherto lain. The research of the student of phylobiology is within the naked sensation of his own organism—the organism of man. Once more, then, the sense of stress is resumed, and despite the constantly recurring tendency to distraction and to the abandonment of experimentation in favor of tradition and habituation—of affect and the self-image—the student holds on. He devotes himself disinterestedly to his material—to the objective material he senses within a segment of his own organism.

The task is unwelcome, and until this deeper phase of man's consciousness has become familiar, accustomed, he feels himself to be alone in it. Momentarily he *is* alone—alone in his feeling. Man does not like to feel that he is alone. It is not natural, not biological, for man to be alone—not as an individual or as a community cut off from other individuals or communities of his kind. But conscious of himself as a student of research in the field of his own—of man's—internally deviate tensions, the substance of the student's effort is precisely to recover contact with his kind, to recover the function of his organism in its total phylic feeling and integrity, and to renew continuity with other individuals, with all individuals, upon this common organismic basis. And so he works on.

With his increasing observation of the sensation caused by the partitive stress of the affecto-symbolic segment or of the separate 'I'-persona, there develops concurrently the sense of a larger background, of a background that is *not* affective, partitive, ditentive, that is *not* the 'I'-persona, but that is the primary organism of man in its native spontaneous continuity and solidarity. With this phase of his experiment the student begins to sense the positive aspect of his inquiry. He begins to sense his own native organism with its uninhibited, non-affective interests. And thus is born the sensation of syntonicity—of *co*-tention or common tension.

With the sensing of this total organismic tone or balance of tensions and the corresponding absence of partitive images, one's preoccupations with idle fantasies based upon his acquisitive security correspondingly fall away. Instead, the organism senses its relation to the environment and to others as an integral element within an integral organismic unit. Through this procedure the vast material of the organism's personal and social affects becomes increasingly set off from and contrasted with the more permanent matrix of the organism's motivation as a phylum. Where this technique has been persisted in by a group of people over a sufficient period of time, the barriers to common interests and activities artificially set up by the socially prevalent 'I'-persona are let down in behalf of the common interests and activities that make for the survival of the individual and the group as a phylic whole.

The "I" is a dichotomous thing. In its unilateralism and self-interest, it is ever antagonistic to something—something it obsessively believes is opposite and against it. But what in reality is this something? It is the organism. Yet the organism puts up no fight. It remains within its own homeostatic principle. And the "I" just keeps fighting anything and everything, or conniving with anything and everything according as it is against or with the "I". In reality, the "I" is impotent to fight its own organism. Never does it truly envisage the organism. The principle of the organism is never touched by it. The organism never relinquishes its own principle, yet it never gets into the fight. The organism has its duality, but it is a duality of balance, a duality of action and reaction, of quest and quiescence. With the organism of man there is always reciprocity, polarity, bionomic poise. Cotentive man is never perturbed by what ditentive men may do.

The results of our experiments were twofold. First, with repeated observation it was possible to discriminate between the organism's reflexly conditioned behavior-reactions and its centrally motivated pattern of reaction as a whole. Second, as we shall see in Chapter XI, we were able to substantiate this discrimination by means of instrumental measures. Through kymographic recordings of changes in respiration, through measuring alterations of eye-movements by means of photographic and electrical methods of recording, and through electroencephalographic recordings of differences in brain-wave activity, it was possible to discriminate objectively on the one hand the physiological reactions concomitant to the organism's reflexly conditioned or partitive pattern of adaptation and, on the other, the reactions concomitant to the cotentive pattern of behavior or to the organism's primary pattern of adaptation as a whole.[17]

It is because of the partition in the organism's total function responsible for the neurosis of man that phyloanalysis has attempted to assemble all the available physiological elements and, as far as possible, to "dissect out" these elements in the mechanism of part-attention or ditention on the one hand and of whole attention or cotention on the other. If the organism may be shown to react differently in its various mechanisms according as its response is ditentive or cotentive, and if this difference may be shown to be consistent throughout various physiological spheres of the organism's behavior, there is established, through an analysis of the elements of each, the nature of cotention and the nature of ditention, in clear objective terms. If this difference is presented concisely to the student, he may now learn to discriminate, as in the case of the tennis-player, between a correct and a faulty technique of adaptation to the environment through his own internal or physiological experience of the two contrasting modes of adaptation. In any other course our efforts—the efforts of man—toward correcting faulty behavior are purely projective, symbolic, sociocortical; they are merely mental or interpersonal, as contrasted with an appreciation that is physiological and intraorganismic.

From its description, the technique of cotention may appear quite easy, and in a sense it is. That is, when once mastered it is easy. It is the mastery that is the rub. Like swimming, dancing, riding or skating, the cotentive adaptation is very simple once we have learned how, once the new coördination of tensional adjustments has been brought under the sovereignty of the organism's pattern of function as a whole. But with man's various cotensive accomplishments, many are the awkward steps, the inept movements, before the complete organization of the newly acquired skill has been achieved. So with cotention. Here, too, the ups and downs were many, and many our inept attacks upon it. The effort toward its attainment has been a long and hard pull.

This discussion of our phylophysiological technique set out with the description of the muscular tone or tension perceptible about the eyes. But we soon saw that these ocular tensions afforded but a clue—that they were only a fragment of the disordered pattern responsible for man's difficulty of adaptation or for his disbehavior. From this fragmentary beginning, however, a larger area of neurodynamic tension became increasingly susceptible of observation. We now became sensible of an entire brain pattern that more and more lent itself to demarcation and control. Abrogating customary "thinking" with its adherent affects, we intercepted the mechanism of projection and, instead, observed the mechanism that projects. In short, we sensed the stress coincident to the function of the entire affecto-symbolic segment. With this more encompassing sensation of stress or tension there was disclosed the phenomenon of ditention and the numen. But ditention is not the problem of any individual or of any group of individuals. It is the problem of man. The Lifwynn Laboratory is but the nucleus of this larger program of social readjustment. There can be no true laboratory of behavior until there is the laboratory of man. Where it is a question of human conflict, it is the common tension of common men the world over to which we must look for the right answer.

In the preceding pages we have submitted evidence of conflicting patterns of tension within man's organism and have demarcated the tonicity or tension discernible as cotention from the tonicity or tension perceptible as partitive or conditioned attention (ditention). It now remains for us to present instrumental verification of this discrimination between the organism's cotentive or orthotonic behavior-pattern and its ditentive or paratonic pattern of behavior.

NOTES

[1] This area has been designated by Freeman and Watts as the seat of the "consciousness of the self." (Freeman, Walter, and Watts, J. W., "The Frontal Lobes and Consciousness of the Self," *Psychosomatic Medicine,* 1941, Vol.3, pp. 111-19.)

[2] See pages 274-75.

[3] In substantiation of the structural damage done to the brain as a result of the various forms of shock-therapy, Pauline Davis reported functional modifications in these areas. This investigator found that the brain-wave patterns became more

abnormal in schizophrenic patients following insulin and metrazol shock-treatment. (Davis, Pauline A., "Evaluation of the Electroencephalograms of Schizophrenic Patients," *The American Journal of Psychiatry,* 1940, Vol. 96, pp. 851-60.

[4] Burrow, Trigant, *The Structure of Insanity.*

Syz, Hans, "Burrow's Differentiation of Tensional Patterns in Relation to Behavior Disorders," *The Journal of Psychology,* 1940, Vol. 9, pp. 153-63.

[5] Burrow, Trigant, *The Biology of Human Conflict,* Chapter VI.

[6] See Chapter V.

[7] It may be mentioned that while the oculomotor tensions occupied a key position in our initial observations of internal tension and stress, they were of assistance chiefly in the early stages of our experiments. With the progress of our experiment the rôle played by the eyes in relation to perceptible tensions grew steadily less, and correspondingly the deeper cerebral levels of tension came more and more into prominence.

[8] See pages 246-47. See also *The Biology of Human Conflict,* pp. 267, 285-8.

[9] Burrow, Trigant, "Neurosis and War—A Problem in Human Behavior," *The Journal of Psychology,* 1941, Vol. 12, pp. 244-5.

[10] See pages 244-47.

[11] See note 7, page 155.

[12] Burrow, Trigant, *The Biology of Human Conflict,* pp. 158-59, 267-9, 285-8, 329-30.

[13] See note 4, page 338.

[14] See pages 347-48.

[15] See note 11, page 363.

[16] I recall as though it were yesterday a profound interrelational trauma that I experienced many years ago. At the time it represented for me the acme of emotional pain. Under the impact of it the very bottom of things seemed to have dropped out. I was utterly stunned, my feeling and thinking left completely at sea. Needless to say, my "feelings" had got "hurt," and I was reacting to the mauling. But it was my accustomed autopathic feeling, my habitual retroceptive thinking; it was the 'I'-persona that was reeling under the blow of personal frustration and denial. I remember that in my distress my one thought was to find seclusion, to get away from everyone, away from the entire associational medium of wonted relationships. When I had done so—when I had reached my home and the quiet of my study with its outlook upon a wide stretch of lake and fields, a strange thing happened, strange at least in my experience.

The preëminent reaction was a sensation in the chest and abdomen, accompanied by a very slow rate of breathing along with the tendency to marked extension of the period of expiration. The reaction was neither pleasurable nor painful, but was a welcome one. For I seemed to sense in it an instinctive effort of the organism to recover its poise, to regain its equilibrium. The process was wholly automatic, wholly involuntary but, in mitigating the mental stress, it afforded no little relief from the emotional pain. There was no means by which I could later revert to this reaction. There was no palpable avenue to it. While it appeared to serve a purpose in a critical moment, it was wholly beyond my conscious recall.

As I have in later years thought back upon this incident, it has seemed to me unquestionably an expression of the organism's instinctive recourse or effort to abrogate the supremacy of the part-brain and recover its total cotentive pattern of behavior. I had, of course, at the time no inkling of this steadfast orthotonic pattern in man. The phenomenon was completely inexplicable and would have remained so but for my subsequent investigations into the organism's defection from its primary pattern of behavior.

[17] See note 8, page 283.

CHAPTER XI

INSTRUMENTAL EVIDENCE OF MAN'S PRIMARY BIOLOGICAL NORM AND OF DEVIATIONS FROM IT

From what has been said, it must be evident that the solution of man's widespread social neurosis calls for a fundamentally altered orientation. It calls for a sweeping relinquishment of customary ways and means and the acceptance of wholly new and untried principles in the sphere of human behavior. We therefore lost no time in applying ourselves to a radical house-cleaning in the sphere of human relations. We recognized that altered conceptions in the sphere of human behavior demanded a correspondingly altered technique of approach. It was clear that old ways must here give way to new.

Accordingly, in the prevalent speeding up of man's activities throughout the world today, The Lifwynn Laboratory has kept abreast of the accelerated pace. In the widespread development of technical measures of precision our laboratory has not lagged behind. Indeed it may be said that the past few years have marked for us the launching of an era of progressive laboratory instrumentation. The interest of our organization has been the moulding of such tools as would contribute to a closer contact with and understanding of man's behavior. More and more we have attempted to apply units of precise observation and appraisement to the functioning of man's organism. More and more it has been our effort to translate motivation into accurate units of measure. We have employed objective implements with a view primarily to establishing the pattern of behavior that belongs to the unified functioning of man's organism, and to differentiating those partial reaction-patterns that have been artificially diverted into paths of purely personal, partitive enterprise.

Setting aside psychiatric as well as recently adopted surgical measures for the relief of the individual psychoneurosis, we reverted to measures that might answer the need of the wider community—measures that would satisfy man's need as a species. Basing our procedure upon our early experiments with the problems of so-called normal adaptation and upon the physiological conflict evidenced by the presence of tensional stress within the organism, it was to this wider community condition and the physiological phenomena concomitant to it that our interest was henceforth directed.

The story of the instrumental phase of our laboratory work cannot be told without some allusion to the very human story of our early gropings amid internal intimations of behavior-phenomena not hitherto recognized by students of behavior. For some time there had been definite indication of tensions, but as yet there had been no instrumental record of them. So that the physiological account of cotention reported in the preceding chapter hardly gives an adequate picture of the preliminary steps which in all researches are too easily effaced by the more concrete evidences of later experimentation. These initial stages are too indeterminate, too casual a part of one's everyday living readily to achieve the sharp outline of objective data. This circumstance applies very specially to researches in the field of man's own behavior.

There was very early with me the observation of alterations in the respiratory rhythm during attempts at cotention. This, though, was at first but a subjective and quite vague impression. My interest, after all, was not in respiration but in the phenomenon of cotention. After many months it became evident that the rate of my respiration was markedly slowed in the cotentive pattern of reaction. But it was impossible for me to be wholly absorbed in the subjective awareness of tensions of which I was conscious only in cotention, and at the same time occupy myself with the objective observation of my own respirations. So that it was necessary that my colleagues make observations upon me in order to study whatever respiratory modifications were taking place within the organism during the process of cotention.

The situation was similar with regard to changes occurring in the eyes. With the sense of tension in the region of the eyes coincident with the induction of cotention, I experienced a distinct sensation of ocular convergence, along with marked diminution in the number of blink reflexes. Naturally, it was more difficult to observe these ocular changes than to observe changes occurring in respiration. The alterations were slight and therefore not readily observable. Nevertheless it was possible to obtain substantial indication of modifications in the eyes coincident with cotention.

All this, of course, belonged to what I have called the early groping stages of my experiments. As the phylobiologist can take no stock in "internal observations" of total behavior that are unsupported by objective data, the reader will understand my insistent interest in securing measurements of the organism's whole behavior instead of relying on psychiatric "data" derived from a patient's purely "mental reactions." Following these early tentative observations, our course became a decisive one. It became the definite experimental interest of my associates and myself to measure the physiological concomitants of the ditentive and cotentive behavior-patterns, and record any changes in the organism's physiology resulting from a shift from one to the other of these contrasting behavior-modes. Since the cotentive response is not mental, verbal or symbolic, but is predominantly an adjustment affecting the entire physiology of the organism, it seemed natural that interest should be directed toward determining experimentally the physiological changes occurring in this pattern.

We have therefore devoted much experimental work in recent years to the systematic recording of these changes. I should emphasize, however, that this instrumental aspect of our studies is closely correlated with our earlier investigations in phyloanalysis. For it was only the many years spent in the frustration of social affects that ultimately led to our internal discrimination between the cotentive and the ditentive pattern of behavior. It was these years devoted to the analysis of the group as an integral biological unit that afforded us an indispensable background of experience and furnished the conditions that made possible the instrumental experiments which, in recent years, have played so important a rôle in the work of The Lifwynn Laboratory.

Our instrumental studies have centered chiefly on oculomotor behavior, respiratory reactions, and brain-wave patterning in the ditentive and in the cotentive mode of the organism's adaptation. We investigated ocular behavior by both electrical and photographic recording of eye-movements, respiration by the continuous kymograph recording of abdominal and thoracic respiratory patterns, and brain-wave activity by recording the electrical impulses drawn off from the scalp through the employment of a three- and five-channel Grass electroencephalograph. A series of electroencephalographic records were also analyzed by the Grass method of frequency analysis. Some investigations were made of metabolism, and of oxygen absorption and utilization in the two attentional patterns by means of the Jones basal metabolism apparatus, and we conducted exploratory experiments on electrocardiographic responses.

A description of the detailed procedures that were followed in the various experiments, together with graphs and tables presenting the results obtained, is included in the present volume as an appendix (see page 486) and I shall here make brief mention of only the chief findings. These were: (1) A marked and consistent slowing of the respiratory rate in cotention as compared with ditention, the decrease in rate in cotention being accompanied by an increase in the thoracic and abdominal amplitude of the respiratory movements. (2) A reduction in number of eye-movements in cotention. This reduction during cotention occurs not only when the eyes are closed, or when they are directed straight ahead and no specific task or stimulation is imposed, but also under a wide variety of stimulus conditions. (3) A characteristic and consistent alteration in the brain-wave pattern during cotention. This alteration consists of a reduction in alpha-time and a general diminution in cortical potential, which is most pronounced in the motor regions.

As has been repeatedly emphasized, the process of cotention involves a reconstellation of those physiological reaction-patterns that relate the individual to the environment. These internal patterns may be appreciated in greater or less degree as sensations of neuromuscular tension within the organism. These tensional constellations relate, on the one hand, to the organism's affecto-symbolic behavior—man's ditentive (autopathic) feeling and thinking—and, on the other, to the organism's behavior as a whole. The differential activation, and the ability to discriminate these internal adaptive patterns, goes hand in hand with a difference in motivation and in behavioral orientation. It is not surprising that these contrasting tensional constellations, resulting as they do in such differing adaptive modes, should be accompanied by measurable changes in physiological function.

Respiration is, of course, a function of central importance in the maintenance of life. The part it plays in our everyday experience has long been familiar to us in such expressions as "the breath of life," "a sigh of relief," and in the converse implication of the phrase "choked with rage." A great deal of experimentation has been done on the physiological processes and the nervous mechanisms involved in breathing,[1] and on the relation of respiration to behavior and its disorders.[2] Respiratory irregularities and difficulties have been found to have a close association with emotional disturbances and with nervous and mental disorders.[3] We are all familiar with the breathing irregularities produced by an intense emotional response. But a review of the experimental data assembled by various investigators regarding modifications of breathing in attention, in mental effort, in emotional situations and in other psychological or behavioristic action-patterns does not reveal respiratory changes of the type we have found to be consistently present in cotention.

As regards eye-movements, we know that they are intimately connected with the employment of the symbolic mechanism as well as with the organism's total adaptation to the environment. They play an important rôle in thinking and imagination.[4] The eyes are constantly in motion when one is engaged in projective or perceptual processes. So that one might well expect a difference in the motor behavior of the eyes during ditention as compared with cotention, that is, in the restless, competitive mood of "normal" autopathic thinking and feeling as compared with the more collected, integrated mood of the organism's total bionomic orientation. Furthermore, the eye offers special opportunity for study as an element in the organism's behavior because the retina, which forms the base or fundus of this spherical organ, is the direct outgrowth of the brain and hence is a part of the actual brain structure. Indeed the eye appears to be unique in that it is the only part of the brain that comparative anatomy shows to possess an observable motile function.

The innervation of the respiratory system, like that of the visual apparatus, involves two distinct levels of nervous activity. In the functions of both respiration and vision there is an integration of autonomic and cerebrospinal impulses or of involuntary and voluntary nervous mechanisms. In the behavior of man—in his feeling, thinking and doing—there is also an integration of the central, basal areas of the brain and its peripheral, cortical zones. On neuroanatomic grounds, therefore, it is quite understandable that both respiration and eye-movements should constitute indicators of differing behavior-constellations and that the tensional pattern of ditention as of cotention should be reflected in modifications in these physiological systems.

From previous investigations of brain-wave patterns we know

that modifications in the physiological function of the brain are reflected in changes in cortical potential. These changes are most marked in brain lesions and in convulsive disorders.[5] But behavior-disorders of a functional type also show a large percentage of altered electrical pictures.[6] And even such temporary functional states as sleep and sleepiness cause variations in brain-wave patterns.[7] It is therefore not surprising that we should find measurable differences in the electrical activity of the brain in the contrasting types of adaptation represented by cotention and ditention, or that these differences should be reflected in characteristic patterns of cerebral potential. Undoubtedly Berger's prediction of the wide applicability of electroencephalography to social as well as to clinical behavior-disorders will be more and more verified as further studies serve to establish the place of this significant tool in the understanding and betterment of human relations.[8]

Needless to say, increased experience in cotention may add further indication of physiological changes, or may materially modify the indications already obtained. There are other physiological areas of response that could be studied, and it is obvious that the present findings should be checked on a larger series of subjects. It should be remembered, however, that a prerequisite for the subject in such experiments is his acquirement of the consistent ability to abrogate affective projections and regain the organism's central, cotentive pattern. As already noted, this has not proved an easy task—at least for the pioneer students in this field—so that at first only a small number of subjects were available for instrumental experimentation. Keeping these restrictions in mind, we may say that the instrumental studies of The Lifwynn Laboratory have demonstrated the concomitance of marked and consistent physiological alterations with the induction of the pattern of cotention. These physiological alterations provide substantial background for the profound modifications in interrelational motivation and behavior that characterize the cotentive response.

As we have said, the brain mediates two major functions in the adaptation of man to his environment. The first function involves those basal portions of the brain that govern the autonomic or involuntary nervous system, and that relate the organism as a whole to the whole environment. The second function involves the phylogenetically more recently developed brain-cortex that controls the voluntary nervous system, and that relates man to the environment projectively rather than organismically. This second function is largely mediated through the use of commonly agreed tokens or symbols of objects in place of the objects themselves; it relates individuals to one another through the use of symbols or language. When involved in affect, it is identified with the false, partitive basis of motivation inhering in the socially constellated 'I'-persona rather than with the organism's behavioral orientation as a whole.

I have spoken of the differentiation perceptible between neuromuscular tensions concomitant to the process of dition on the one hand, and neuromuscular processes concomitant to cotention on the other. One cannot know, of course, the precise nature or localization of these neural and muscular reactions. From what we know, however, of the broader differentiations of function recognized by the neuroanatomists, and from the internal modifications of function that can be induced experimentally, it may be suggested that cotention accompanies those primary autonomic reactions of the organism which are under the control of the thalamic and infra-thalamic nuclei and which, in mediating the primary organism-environment relationship, are more directly related to man's basic ecology. For this reason I would suggest that the neural substrate of cotention be known as the *ecothalamic system*. The mental or partitive system, on the other hand, as it operates in dition is far more generally controlled through the symbolic function of the cerebral cortex of man, and for this reason I suggest that this constellation be known as the *semio-* or *socio-cortical system*.[9]

It may be that some day we shall discover certain drugs or some combination of drugs which, in influencing special brain-areas, will facilitate the induction and maintenance of the pattern of cotention. We ourselves have as yet made only a few preliminary experiments in this direction, but from these tentative experiments it has seemed to us that the use of very small doses of certain of the barbiturates may, at the outset, aid the investigator's effort to cotend. One difficulty is that, although the pattern of cotention is definitely distinct from that of sleep, the initial state of quiescence so favorable to the induction of cotention may readily induce sleep if it happens that the subject is unduly fatigued. It is a frequent experience of students attempting to induce cotention after retiring that it tends to hasten sleep. So that drugs possessing a narcotic effect may be used only in extremely small doses. The physiological effects of curare upon muscle tonus suggest the possibility of its use in our experiments, but the difficulties of its administration have thus far precluded any attempts by us to employ this drug. When the physiologist, the pharmacologist and the neurologist, working in collaboration with the phylobiologist, can undertake experiments with this and other drugs, perhaps we shall come upon a substance that will materially assist the restoration of cotention.

Certainly there is ground for the expectation that with improved instrumental methods it will be possible to discover technical facilities that will assist students to discriminate between the partitive and the total pattern of reaction. The student will thus be enabled to check objectively his subjective indications of the cotentive pattern as over against the ditentive. In this way he should be materially assisted in freeing himself from the domination of dichotomous images (autopathic or right-wrong response), and in restoring the jurisdiction of the organism's central pattern of motivation, or its primary homeostasis in relation to the environment. As I have repeatedly emphasized, though, this needed behavioral adjustment—an adjustment that liberates man's basic feeling from affective, autopathic entanglements—involves a behavior-pattern that belongs to man as a race or species. Such a behavior-pattern, therefore, can only be reinstated by man as an integral group or community. In the meantime there is here at least the beginning of an attempt to meet a functional anomaly in man's development with a functional technique of adaptation such as should reëstablish man's organismic balance in the field of his socio-biological interrelations.

It should be clearly understood that, valuable and significant as our instrumental recordings may be, they are in a sense quite incidental to our major thesis. No student, of course, should expect to find the millennium in instrumental records, but he must be especially warned against the seductive blandishments of graphs that undertake to chart human behavior. Although these tracings show a difference in the organism's internal reaction according as the organism responds directly or indirectly to its environment, they offer only an external indication of this difference. Undoubtedly, individuals and social communities are in need of a basic alteration in behavior-adaptation, but they will find this needed alteration only through specific physiological adjustments internal to themselves.

And so, while giving full due to instrumental recordings of

alterations in this or that physiological system, I feel it important to emphasize once more that our starting-point and our ending-point is the internal perception of the organism's pattern of behavior as a whole. And by organism as a whole I mean the phylobiological organism of man. Graphs of physiological changes may possess value for us only as they offer corroboration of internal phylic modifications registered by us through the internally controlled technique of phyloanalysis. Through this investigation, may I repeat, we have found evidence in our own sensations and reactions that men, as organismic groups, communities or nations, have become interindividually separated through the replacement of the phyloörganism's total pattern of behavior by a socially partitive pattern. Once more we are brought back to the origin of the social neurosis—to the partitive segmentation within the phylum represented in the socio-symbolic 'I'-persona of each individual as of each group of individuals.

NOTES

[1] Gesell, Robert, "Respiration and its Adjustments," *Annual Review of Physiology*, 1939, Vol. I, pp. 185-216.

Hess, W. R., *Die Regulierungen des Blutkreislaufes und der Atmung*, Leipzig, Georg Thieme, 1931, pp. 137.

——,*Das Zwischenhirn und die Regulation von Kreislauf and Atmung*, Leipzig, Georg Thieme, 1938, pp. 137

Schmidt, Carl F., "The Respiration," in Macleod's *Physiology in Modern Medicine*, St. Louis, The Mosby Co., 1941, pp. 534-710.

Schmidt, Carl F., and Comroe, J. H., "Respiration," *Annual Review of Physiology*, 1941, Vol 3, pp. 151-84.

[2] Finesinger, Jacob E., "Effect of Pleasant and Unpleasant Ideas on Respiration in Psychoneurotic Patients," *Archives of Neurology and Psychiatry*, 1939, Vol. 42, pp. 425--90.

Lehmann, Alfr., *Grundzüge der Psychophysiologie*, Leipzig, O. R. Reisland, 1912, pp. x + 742.

Winkler, C., "Attention and Respiration," *Proceedings of the Royal Academy of Sciences*, Amsterdam, 1899, Vol. 1, pp. 121-38.

Wyss, W. H. von, "Einfluss psychischer Vorgänge auf Atmung, Pulsfrequenz, Blutdruck und Blutverteilung," *Handbuch der normalen und pathologischen Physiologie*, Berlin, Springer, 1931, Vol. 16, pp. 1261-88.

Zoneff, P., and Meumann, E., "Ueber Begleiterscheinungen psychischer Vorgänge in Athem und Puls," *Philosophische Studien*, 1903, Vol. 18, pp. 1-113.

[3] It is noteworthy in this connection that somatic conditions such as pulmonary tuberculosis and asthma have not infrequently been found to be associated with personality conflicts and that these conflicts may be important factors in the onset and course of these diseases.

Brown, Lawrason, "The Mental Aspect in the Etiology and Treatment of Pulmonary Tuberculosis," *International Clinics*, 1933, Vol. III, 43rd Series, pp. 149-74.

French, Thomas N., and Alexander, Franz, "Psychogenic Factors in Bronchial Asthma, Part I," *Psychosomatic Medicine Monograph IV*, 1941, pp. 236.

Hartz, Jerome, "Tuberculosis and Personality Conflicts," *Psychosomatic Medicine*,

1944, Vol. VI, pp. 17-22.

Leavitt, Harry C., "Bronchial Asthma in Functional Psychoses," *Psychosomatic Medicine*, 1943, Vol. V, pp. 39-41.

Rubin, Sidney, and Moses, Leon, "Electoencephalographic Studies in Asthma with some Personality Correlates," *Psychosomatic Medicine*, 1944, Vol. VI, pp. 31-9.

Shultz, Irvin T., "The Emotions of the Tubercular": A Review and an Analysis, *The Journal of Abnormal and Social Psychology*, 1942, Vol. 37, pp. 260-3.

[4] Jacobson, Edmund, "Electrophysiology of Mental Activities," *American Journal of Psychology*, 1932, Vol. XLIV, pp. 677-94.

[5] Case, Theodore J., and Bucy, Paul C., "Localization of Cerebral Lesions by Electroencephalography," *Journal of Neurophysiology*, 1938, Vol. 1, pp. 245-61.

Gibbs, Frederic A., Davis, Hallowell, and Lennox, William G., "The Electroencephalogram in Epilepsy and in Conditions of Impaired Consciousness," *Archives of Neurology and Psychiatry*, 1935, Vol. 34, pp. 1133-48.

Gibbs, Frederic A., Lennox, William G., and Gibbs, Erna L., "The Electroencephalogram in Diagnosis and in Localization of Epileptic Seizures," *Archives of Neurology and Psychiatry*, 1936, Vol. 36, pp. 1225-35.

Walter, W. Grey, "The Electroencephalogram in Cases of Cerebral Tumour," *Proceedings of the Royal Society of Medicine*, 1937, Vol. 30, pp. 579-98.

Gibbs, Frederic A., and Gibbs, Erna L., *Atlas of Electroencephalography*, 1941, Cambridge, Massachusetts, pp. 221.

[6] Davis, Pauline A., and Davis, Hallowell, "The Electroencephalograms of Psychotic Patients," *The American Journal of Psychiatry*, 1939, Vol. 95, pp. 1007-25.

Jasper, Herbert H., Solomon, Philip, and Bradley, Charles, "Electroencephalographic Analyses of Behavior Problem Children," *The American Journal of Psychiatry*, 1938, Vol. 95, pp. 641-58.

Travis, Lee Edward, and Malamud, William, "Brain Potentials from Normal Subjects, Stutterers and Schizophrenic Patients," *The American Journal of Psychiatry*, 1937, Vol. 93, pp. 929-36.

[7] Loomis, Alfred L., Harvey, E. Newton, and Hobart, Garret A., III, "Potential Rhythms of the Cerebral Cortex during Sleep," *Science*, 1935, Vol. 81, pp. 597-98; "Distribution of Disturbance-Patterns in the Human Electroencephalogram, with Special Reference to Sleep," *Journal of Neurophysiology*, 1938, Vol. I, pp. 413-30.

[8] Gibbs, Frederic A., and Gibbs, Erna L., Dedication in *Atlas of Electroencephalography*, 1941, Cambridge, Massachusetts, pp. 221.

[9] See page 367.

CHAPTER XII

THE ORGANISM OF MAN

Many times throughout this book I have spoken of the need for man to expand the function of his brain and senses in respect to the field of his behavior—in respect to those processes that are subjective and internal to man as a species. In one connection or another I have said that there is required a widening of the function of man's perception in regard to himself and his own motivation that would be comparable to the enlargement that has taken place in the function of man's brain with respect to the objective processes to be observed in other fields of science.

From the background of the preceding chapters we are now in a position to consider man, the organism, in a new and greatly expanded concept. We are prepared to consider in a far broader dynamic purview the anatomy and physiology as well as the basic interrelational mechanisms activating this boundless phylic organism. In this purview we shall be in a position to keep dynamically alive the biological identity of individual and phylum, the inseparable continuity between the organism of man as ontosoma or individual and as phylosoma or species. In his autogenous conditioning man has falsely separated ontosoma from phylosoma. This artificial separation has taken place *within man's organism*. It has caused modification in a pattern of tension that is internal to the organism. If the vast millions of individuals or ontosomata that constitute the race or phylosoma of man are to be restored to their intrinsic organismic matrix, it is necessary that man take conscious hold of this abnormal distortion of tension within his own organism; that he recognize within himself the morbid process this artificial dialysis entails. Contrary to popular assumption, man is not a symbolic abstraction; man—man, the phylum—is one's own ontosomatic self.

The biologists have long asserted the principle that regards the development of the individual as a recapitulation of the development of the phylum, the two developmental phases representing but different aspects of the same organism. But when it comes to his own behavior as a species, man has universally abrogated his sense of this biologically indivisible identity. He has unwittingly abrogated it in favor of the partitive bias of the 'I'-persona which posits an artificially separate prerogative of behavior for each individual. If we are to return to the biological rudiments of the human organism and consider behavior from the background of its species solidarity; if we are effectively to challenge the inroads upon man of the false premise of this socially prevalent 'I'-complex, it is necessary that we review the basic structure and function of man's organism in both its phylosomatic and ontosomatic modes.

It is because this factor of species solidarity and its influence upon the underlying processes of human behavior has not received the scientific recognition its importance merits, that I should like to review the anatomical and physiological implications of man's organism-environment relationship in a different and more inclusive envisagement. Regarding the species man or the phylosoma as a vast unitary organism, we shall gain much ground if, in trying to understand its behavior, we consider the various systems composing this organism in their broad generic functions. In this view we shall recognize the structures that serve to relate man, the organism, directly to the environment.

There are of course in man, as in kindred organisms, those feelings, those impulses, those drives or motivations that incite the phyloörganism to secure its primary needs—the impetus to hunger and thirst, the impulse to bodily activity and repose, the drives of sex, of play, and of such self-protective measures as insure shelter, rest and warmth. These functions that maintain the phylosoma's basic internal processes are under the control of the autonomic or involuntary nervous system which through the function of its complementary divisions—the sympathetic and parasympathetic—maintains the organism's internal balance or tonicity. This ramification of nerves, sometimes known as the vegetative system, is distributed for the most part to the internal organs—the alimentary tract, the respiratory, genito-urinary, the vascular and lymphatic systems—and in general controls the innervation of the instinctive or involuntary processes. This system regulates the temperature of the body, its chemical composition, its metabolism, elimination and kindred processes. The maintenance of the balance of function of the internal organs by means of the autonomic system is the process referred to by Cannon as homeostasis.[1]

Corresponding to the autonomic system which regulates the organism's internal drives in relation to the environment, there is, of course, the system of nerves known as the cerebrospinal or voluntary nervous system. Like the autonomic, this system is the carrier of both afferent (incoming) and efferent (outgoing) impulses. The cerebrospinal system innervates the general periphery and sends branches to the visual, tactile, olfactory, auditory and gustatory sense organs. It contributes to the phylosoma's balanced function or homeostasis by determining those properties of the objects or elements in the surrounding environment that are adapted to the organism's internal needs. For example, through the incoming sensory impressions mediated by this system of nerves the phyloörganism becomes acquainted by means of the olfactory and gustatory nerve terminals with the nutritive properties of the elements within its environment. So with other sense modalities. The nerve endings in the skin contribute an appreciation of differences of temperature, while the phyloörganism's sense of the solidarity and security of its surrounding terrain is made possible through its stereognostic and kinesthetic functions. It is by virtue of these sensory provisions afforded by the cerebrospinal system that the phylosoma fulfills its primary needs—needs determined, as we have said, through the activity of the autonomic or involuntary system. The two nervous systems must at all times function in coördination if the organism is to forage successfully for its food, find shelter, shift from conditions of heat and cold, and in general adapt itself to its outer surroundings. In short, it is the function of the autonomic system to give notice of the organism's internal needs, while the voluntary system responds with the suitable choice from among the environmental possibilities.

As we know, the organism's sense of balance in relation to the outer world is maintained through its general kinesthetic and equilibratory sense, and through the organs of vision. The special senses of smell and taste mediate the organism's protective and nutritional needs by relating the body's autonomic system to the products of the soil or vegetation. Through the generative organs and their connection with the deeper autonomic centers of motivation, individuals of the species become related to one another in the process of mating and reproduction. For the phylobiologist, the importance of the autonomic or involuntary system lies in its comprehensive function as the substrate of the phyloörganism's general behavioral feeling or motivation in relating it to the environment. The autonomic nervous system, with its cerebral ganglia and its ramifications of nerves, is genetically the earlier neural structure. Hence we may call this system the first nervous system, and the autonomic centers or midbrain the first brain. The cerebrospinal system, being the more recent development in man's evolution, may be called the second nervous system, and correspondingly its cerebral component or forebrain may be known as the second brain.

In addition to the sensory system of responses that relates the phyloörganism to the external world, there is also, of course, the specific motor function of the cerebrospinal system that mediates the organism's relation to the environment through the external muscular structures. For, lying intermediate in position, roughly speaking, between the periphery and the internal organs of nutrition and elimination, there is the system of skeletal muscles through which the organism operates those major levers of the body constituted of the fore-limbs and the hind-limbs—in man, the arms and legs. Through this intermediate muscular system and through the levers or extremities upon which this system of muscles plays, the organisms composing the species or phylosoma are capable of shifting their position from place to place. In this way the skeletal muscles not only stimulate the function of the general circulatory system but, through effecting changes of location in relation to changing environmental conditions, these muscles greatly aid in promoting the phyloörganism's bionomic well-being and security. In man, these migratory shifts are accomplished chiefly by means of the legs. By means of the anterior extremities, or the arms and hands, aided by the prehensile function of the jaws and mouth, the objects of the phyloörganism's hunt—its food and drink—may be brought within immediate reach and ingested by it.

It will be understood, then, that our interest lies in the various bodily mechanisms that mediate between the phyloörganism's total motivation and its environment. That is, our interest lies in the behavioral function of the phyloörganism as a whole. The processes that relate the internal autonomic system to the objects and conditions of the environment do so in two ways. First, there are the incoming stimuli arising in the environment and reaching the nerve terminals of the periphery—the organism's sensory impressions; and second, there are the outgoing impulses arising in the central nervous system and passing to the external skeletal muscles. Through the system of levers to which they are attached, these muscles, as we have seen, bring the organism into mechanical relation with the objects of the external world. The two nervous functions—afferent and efferent—comprise the two major and primary mechanisms of behavior throughout higher animal forms, from the lowest of the vertebrates, the amphioxus, to the highest of the primates, man.

But we must take account also of the special system of cranial nerves composed, as they are, of elements characteristic of both these major systems. Arising within the cranial cavity, these nerves unite in their conjoined fibres the function of both the autonomic and the cerebrospinal systems. This system of nerves is in large part distributed to the special senses of the head, certain of them sending motor fibres to the face—the ears, eyes and mouth—as also to the tongue and larynx. These latter are the nerves specifically involved in the production of speech.

While the discrimination between the cerebrospinal and the autonomic nervous systems is based partly upon a general difference in topography, the discrimination between these two systems rests also upon a specific difference in function. The differentiation of the cranial nerves though, as their name implies, is mainly topographical, being based on the fact that these nerves originate within and pass out of the cranial cavity to their various points of distribution.

In the foregoing paragraphs I have described briefly the two neural systems which in general mediate man's organism-environment relationship, and I have distinguished them genetically as the "first" and the "second" nervous system or brain. But there is needed the recognition of a further neural agent in relating the organism to its environment. In the course of my phylobiological researches it became evident that this agent possesses so unique a function as to warrant the discrimination in man of a *third nervous system* or *third brain*. I refer to the nervous elements that govern the symbolic mechanism or the function of speech. Basing this discrimination upon its topographical distribution to the special senses of vision and audition as well as to the muscles of the tongue and larynx, I demarcate a specially circumscribed area of neural function within the cranial segment. The pattern of neural function thus discriminated from the organism's general physiology is the pattern embodied in the semiotic or symbolic area of motivation. It is this symbolic nervous system or third brain that is genetically most important to man. The symbolic or third brain is most important to man because this is the brain that has made man—that has afforded him thought and speech—as it is the brain that has unmade him. For it is in the interrelational function of the third nervous system that there has occurred the distortion of function we have recognized as the social neurosis—man's dislocation in attention, interest and motivation.

The discrimination, then, of the neural function of symbol-formation or speech is not proposed on the basis of any rigid anatomical demarcation between it and the other two neural systems already described. This "third nervous system" is discriminated solely on the basis of its *specialization of function* within the organism's motivation as a whole. As with the two main divisions of the nervous anatomy—the cerebrospinal and the autonomic systems—so the system of nervous activation and response I have called the semiotic or symbolic system is delimited into a separate unit on grounds of its special physiological behavior.[2] While there is no rigid anatomical basis for this distinction, yet in consistency with a science of human behavior it is definitely demanded that this third neural system be clearly demarcated from the other two on the strength of its very special socio-biological function.

Our demarcation, then, of a third nervous system or "third brain" permits us to deal in more exact terms with the area of neural function we referred to earlier as the part-brain. In isolating this semiotic or symbolic system of neural activation and response as a distinct reaction entity, we are differentiating a system of neural functions within the organism of man that is quite unlike the functional and topographical systems already described. With our attempt to describe a system of behavior based upon a differentiation in the function of man as a phylum, we are introducing a concept of *behavioral anatomy* that involves a new, phylophysiological sphere of motivation and hence a new, phylophysiological sphere of investigation. Such a behavioral anatomy should be sharply distinguished from the objective descriptions appropriate to systemic or regional anatomy. A brief consideration, therefore, of the implications of such a behavioral anatomy and its contrast with established medical and social concepts of somatic behavior will assist the exposition of the present chapter.

We have seen that a developmental innovation in man's "behavioral anatomy" markedly influenced the function of certain of the cranial nerves and brought about in man a specialization of function that modified the relation of the species to its environment. Through this specialization of function, or through the introduction of speech, the relation of man's organism to the environment underwent a profound alteration. While the behavior of the organism of man is primarily related to its environment as a common and unitary phylum, the gradual development of the function of the third or semiotic nervous system imposed upon the phyloörganism a quite secondary and indirect mode of behavior, both interrelationally and in respect to the environment.

And so the system whereby men now relate themselves to their environment and to one another constitutes a social process that is peculiar to man. It constitutes a process of communication that depends exclusively upon the interindividual code or mark of mutual understanding expressed by the word or symbol. In so far as this process mediates the organism's contact with the environment by means of a restricted, peripheral response—a response occurring largely within the external senses—it was a most propitious one. For this social innovation established within the individuals of the species the recognition of the common nature among them of their external, specialized sense-impressions. In so doing, it established the third or symbolic nervous system as the sponsor of the scientific principle we have called the nomen—the principle that determines the conscious correlation of the organism's behavior in respect to the environment.

If in the course of man's evolution there had been a question merely of man's correlation with the *external environment* by means of the symbolic nervous system, the story of man would have been very different. Man's adaptation would have been consistent, organismic, peaceful. But in mediating man's interindividual relations the behavior of this segment presents a markedly altered picture. Indeed, when this miniature symbolic system undertook to mediate interrelational behavior—man's relation to man—serious trouble arose. It arose within the very system or segment that is responsible for the conscious consistency of man's relation to the outer world. For the fact is that the third nervous system is also responsible for the numen or for the dislocations that have occurred in the sphere of man's feeling and thinking and doing. In its interrelational function this secondary system rudely intercepted and diverted the primary paths of the organism's interest and motivation as a whole—the integrative function of the nomen—causing conflict and impaction within the now overcrowded part-function of the organism. A system negotiable only through outer signs and symbols, or through man's partitive medium of behavior, artificially transformed the organism's total feeling into part-feeling or affect. Here was begotten ditentive, affective, autopathic thinking and feeling, or man's retrofective motivation. It is, therefore, not primarily man's moralistic alternatives of right and wrong, but a bionomic disfunction occcurring within the third or symbolic nervous system that is responsible for disorders in human behavior and for man's inhumanity to man.

We who as individuals of the species man are today affectively involved in the preponderant employment of a symbolic system of neural reactions; we whose very identity has come to be wholly vested in an interrelational code beset with the subjective affects and prejudices that now make up our specially differentiated mode of adaptation both interindividually and in respect to the environment, find it difficult to return to a sense of man's primary neural adaptation either as ontosoma or phylosoma. Having repudiated our original adaptation as a common phylum, we find it difficult to attain an objective sense of the quite radical invasion of the organism's bionomic economy that has come about with this differentiation in man's symbolic mode of adjustment. So overwhelming today is the use of the symbolic system of man interrelationally that we have difficulty in recognizing this mental and social system as a definite neurodynamic impediment to the adaptation of the phyloörganism in respect to the world of external objects and events, as also of individuals, of groups and of nations to one another.

In the absence of a clear scientific recognition of the twofold avenue of approach of phylic man to the environment and of the twofold type of motivation involved, the attempt to understand man's basic adaptation (his behavioral physiology) and reach an intelligent comprehension of its manifold disorders, personal and social, is quite excluded. Versed, as we now are, in a semiotic or ideological mode of adaptation that is activated by an affective or partitive type of attention or interest, all behavioral orientations, all mental evaluations, must of necessity be traced to the zone of man's affecto-symbolic differentiations.

As the third nervous system marks the zone of reactions that constitute "normality" with its inevitable entail of unilateralism and conflict, and as this system is the functional area involved in the vast category of mental and nervous disorders known as the psychoneuroses, it is to this partitive system of neural reactions that man must turn for an understanding of the universal presence of disorders of behavior in both "normal" and "neurotic" individuals. In its behavioral distortion this system of interrelational affects is as alien to the primary bionomic function of man's organism as is a malignant neoplasm to its structure; and in the extent of its social proliferation this partitive system is not less pathological functionally than the most pernicious of structural growths.[3]

Consistent with the trend of the preceding pages we shall consider the structure and mechanism of human behavior from the background of man's species solidarity and not from the point of view of communication as it is now employed by us as socially or symbolically interrelated individuals. We shall regard behavior as the reaction of man to the environment both as a phylosoma and as ontosomata. Consistent with the procedure of biology elsewhere, we shall treat the ontosoma as the individual paradigm, so to speak, of the phylosoma or of the phylum as a whole.

But the adoption of a principle that recognizes the phylosoma as a definite physiological reaction-entity demands a totally altered frame of reference in approaching the study of man and the problem of his behavior-disorders. Replacing the usual concept of the "individual," as represented in his personal and social relations, with that of the ontosma as the interfunctioning element in a common species or phylosoma, involves a fundamental readjustment in human and behavioral values. Adhering to this altered frame of reference, we must keep constantly in mind that our thesis recognizes a primarily integrated phyloörganism comprised of individual components or elements (ontosomata) which interact toward the environment and toward one another under the centrally coördinating sovereignty of this primary phyloörganism or phylosoma.

We must recognize at the outset two major constituents or strata of the phyloörganism—the adult and the infant generations, Barring the functions of respiration and elimination, the relationship of the phyloörganism's infant generation to its environment is largely achieved through the mediation of the adult generation.[4] In the bionomic relationship between the mature component and the immature component of the species, the former provides the latter with nutrition, shelter, body-warmth; insures change of location, shift of posture, etc. That is, the young of the species or phylosoma learns from and is, at first, assisted by the older and more inured contingent. When we speak of man's infancy, therefore, we must keep in mind man's infancy phyloorganismically—not the infancy of this or that individual, not the infancy of the species from an evolutionary viewpoint, but the organismic state of infancy as it exists at any time in human society in contrast to the adult population at that same period.

Because the individuals of the species possess common sense organs, common nervous, vascular and muscular systems, together with identical organs and tissues; because they possess common needs and are activated by common instinctual drives, we can understand how readily habits acquired by the societally maturer generation are absorbed by the younger generation through a process of species assimilation. In this stage of the community's life the needs of the immature contingent are assured by the mature contingent. In mammals, the immature component of the phyloorganism is at first completely dependent for its viability upon the adult component. In the human species it is only after the first year or two that the immature phylosoma begins to fend for itself. But in so fending, it is still materially assisted in its bionomic adaptation or in its intrarelational physiology by the behavior of the more mature generation.

Regarding man as a phyloörganismic unit and the environment as its bionomic source of supply, we find in the phyloorganism's first reaction to the environment as it occurs in respiration the beginning of an environmental correlation in physiological function that is essential to the survival of individual and species. I refer to the balance in functional activity or to the homeostatic rhythm represented in the phyloörganism's alternate inspiration and expiration—an alternating process in the correlation of organism and environment that marks the primary adjustment of man in the interest of his survival. This adjustment consists in the rhythmic balance of functions or in the physiological homeostasis that directly relates the organism as a whole—both as an individual and as a phylum—to the environmental situation.

In this rhythmic alternation between the organism's need and its satiety, between activity and rest, between quest and quiescence as it occurs in the function of respiration, there is typified the balance of function which throughout the biological correlation between phylum and environment maintains the constant equilibrium of the *phyloörganism as a whole* in relation to the whole environment. Throughout the organism's various systems of reaction in respect to the environment there is maintained this same unfailing rhythm between the alternations of quest and quiescence in the organism's effort of survival.

The earliest instance of this bionomic correlation occurs with the infant's first intake of breath at the moment of birth. Up to this moment, of course, the prenascent organism's needed supply of oxygen has been vicariously provided by the maternal organism. But with the infant's direct contact with the outer world, its first physiological reaction is to draw upon the environment for its "breath of life"—for the primary source of subsistence essential to the maintenance of its life and growth.

Next to obtaining oxygen by means of respiration, the chief need of the infant phylosoma is food. Provision for this environmental necessity is the only one in which from the beginning the infant component takes an active part. In response to hunger, the immature contingent communicates its need for food through the physiological signs of discomfort it expresses in the reflex of crying, in its vasomotor modifications, and in the expression of its body-tensions through movements of the arms and legs—tensions later to be integrated with seizing, grasping or with the phyloorganism's independent self-provision. These are the basic and common tensions operating throughout the organismic unit embodied in the species as a whole. Throughout the species man as an organismic unit we see this common internal condition of tension inciting to common external action and leading to the seizure or securing of the required object or condition. With the satisfaction incident to the attainment of the required object there follows a relax of tension commensurate with the organism's fulfillment or with its return from quest to quiescence.

While this general bionomic or ecological interaction exists throughout all forms of life, it is of course far more complex and is woven of far more elaborate integrations the higher we ascend in the animal series. Naturally, the climax of this process in bionomic integration is attained in the more highly developed primates, notably in man and his immediate precursors. It should be recalled, however, that in many of the higher animal forms, including man, the internal tensions of the infant component of the phylosoma are not at first directly related to the environment. The physiological coördination that relates organism and environment is effectively performed only by the adult contingent, and the results of this bionomic coördination are then secondarily conveyed by the adult contingent to the bionomically dependent contingent of the species. This relationship holds until the immature organism develops the necessary physiological patterns of tension and coördination through the processes of maturation, imitation and tuition, and is thus enabled to adapt itself directly to the forces of the environment.

But, unlike other animals, the maturer organism of the human species assists the immature organism through a quite special mode of instruction and communication. In the human organism the parent (again I am speaking, of course, of the phylic parent) trains the young to react to a very specific, localized type of tensions. The infant constituent is trained to a pattern of tensions that is interrelated with certain sounds produced vocally by the parental constituent—sounds functioning as symbols or signs of the objects and conditions about them. For instance, the parental word of warning brings up the image of danger and incites the infant organism to seek protection. Thus, in addition to the larger kinesthetic reactions that maintain phylic communication between parent and infant in their relation commonly to the environment, there exists in the human species the capacity of relating the offspring to the environment quite secondarily or indirectly through the production of certain acquired sounds, signs or gestures.[5]

These sounds or gestures that now relate the child vicariously to the environment through the mediation of the maternal contingent constitute the rudiments of the system of communication we know today as language. This is the interindividual system that tends from the outset to relate the child more to the mental meaning or image of the parent, and to his or her mental images, than to the actual organism of the parent and to the actual objects of their common environment[6] This medium of language operating interindividually is the neuro-social response that removes the organism of man from its direct impact with the environment and with others, and introduces the system of interrelational behavior that is sponsored by the third or symbolic nervous system.

This mode of environmental communication that has arisen in man with his acquisition of language or with his capacity of interaction through the vicarious employment of the symbol, represents a unique bionomic asset. In this phylic innovation man has attained an instrument of adaptation that sharply demarcates him from all other animal forms both in his environmental reactions and in his interrelational behavior. This distinction possesses marked biological advantages by offering an added means of intercommunication among the elements of the species. The function of speech provides man with an especially valuable asset by affording the maturer generation an additional instrument of communication with the less mature. The older stratum or contingent of the species may not only convey instinctively to the younger the processes of behavior it should assimilate in order to maintain itself in a state of homeostatic balance and health in relation to the environment, but the adult generation may also accomplish this end vicariously through the "conscious" employment of the symbol. In this way the adult component augments its instinctual assistance to the growing organism through the instrument of the symbol or spoken word. This short-cut method of interchange characteristic of the human phylosoma constitutes, of course, an enormous economic gain in regulating and expediting communication among the elements of the species. Indeed, it is because the capacity of speech is so powerful an asset to the human phyloörganism that its acquisition has led to its constant and universal use in the hominid.

In this attainment of the symbolic capacity, or of language, through the specialization of function we have described as the third nervous system, the phyloörganism became equipped, as we have said, with a biological advantage that is of inestimable social value. As an adjunct to man's primary relationship to the environment, this secondary mode of interindividual communication and contact is of far-reaching significance to man. It represents for the phylosoma the very matrix of its culture and the rise of civilization. For with the acquisition of the symbolic or projective code the phyloörganism's communication with the outer world was enormously enhanced and elaborated by means of the infinitely varied shades of meaning or mental nuances derived from this mental bond or social covenant. Indeed, so greatly enhanced and specialized was this medium of communication that it may be said that with the development of the symbolic capacity the function of the cortex was automatically relegated to a place among the special peripheral sense organs.

Before the accidental invention of speech, the individuals or elements of the species interacted commonly, with uniformity, in relation to the objects of the environment. This ecosomatic uniformity constituted their common phyloörganismic bond. But, as was most natural, with the attainment of man's handy system of signs and signals, this symbolic or projective code and its marked economic reduction in space-time expenditure came to replace more and more the larger, primary mechanism of man's environmental and social interaction as a phylosoma. Guidance or instruction could now pass from the mature to the immature generation not only through the total behavior of the older component as it is assimilated through imitation by the younger, but instruction now proceeded also by means of a restricted mechanism which demanded no greater physiological activity than the miniature movements required in the production of speech. Communication was shifted from the plane of total physiological demonstration to a plane of mere symbolic intimation or reference.

With this shift we are again brought to the threshold of the principles of cotention and ditention, of total and partitive behavior-responses, of the nomen and the numen. But in this shift we now need to view expressions of the organism's action and reaction—its basic homeostasis—as a function of the phyloörganism. We need to incorporate these principles into the concept of the phylosoma as a biologically functioning whole. For it is here in the phylosoma that we begin to recognize the phyloörganismic origin of the two patterns of tension spoken of in previous chapters: the one primary, total, organismic, and relating organisms commonly to the environment through their direct interaction with it; the other secondary, symbolic, vicarious, and relating organisms to the environment not by means of common organismic interactions, but by means of agreed mental indices or symbols that stand for and replace the organism's direct environmental interrelationship.

Holding firmly to the concept of the organism of man as a unitary and indivisible entity, we shall now consider the influence of the symbolic function upon the phylum's primary integration and continuity in relation to the external world. It is essential that man's facility of communication be regarded in its broad, phylobiological scope. It may not be confined merely to considerations of the interrelations between the single parent and child. It must be regarded in its societal or phyloörganismic aspect. Keeping always in mind the species man as a unitary whole, we must consider the relation of the societal element or continuum comprising the older generation, to the societal element or continuum that constitutes the younger.

The interaction between the two developmental strata or contingents of the species—the parental and the infantile—is an interaction that is social. But, biologically, communication by means of language is at the same time a phylic function. Accordingly, the *faux pas* that occurred in relating these two phases or levels of the phylosoma's growth through the medium of the symbol was also a phylic *faux pas*—a *faux pas* involving the dissociation of man as a species. The point is that, owing to the interpolation in the human species of the symbol or language, a very special, a very unique set or constellation of tensions came into operation between parental and infantile constituents, affording them a specific and unique relation both to the environment and to each other. For the socio-parental contingent not only teaches the child the correct words or symbols with which the child builds its habitual system of thinking and feeling and doing, thereby imbuing it with a purely affecto-symbolic identity or persona, but at the same time the adult contingent inevitably inculcates in the child the "right" attitude or *mood* in relation to the "right" attitude or *mood* of the parent. This is the 'I'-persona—*the social or phylic 'I'-persona* whose sire is the third brain. For such a "right" attitude has now become the mentally or symbolically "right" attitude of every parental *me* or persona with its particular systematization of affects.

Thus where there should have been a marked social asset in assisting the infantile phylosoma to adapt itself to the environment, a heavy liability crept in. There was insinuated an artificial and anomalous division within an organismically indivisible phylum. There was inculcated the sense of "me" as a particular persona when, in reality, this sense of me or of the 'I'-persona represents a phylic phenomenon. It represents a *phylically continuous dissociation from the organism's primary biology*. This contradictory phenomenon is synonymous with *the social neurosis*. For, instead of the immature phylosoma becoming related to the environment more readily through the introduction of speech or through the function of the third nervous system, an element of proprietary affect or personal mood entered in, which had precisely the effect of turning the natural, organismic attention and interest of the immature phylosoma away from its environment as well as *from its physiological continuity with the parent-organism*.

This social affect compelled the immature element to think and feel in accordance with the personally imposed wish or will of the mature element. With this autopathic ultimatum the two contingents became biologically disarticulated. In this affect-innovation consists the phylic fallacy of man's interrelational self-consciousness, of his "right" or "good" behavior. The mature contingent is "right" in its affect and imposes its prerogatory or "right" affect upon the immature. Says the older faction: "I am your guide. I am supreme authority. I am God. It is not the nomen that is your criterion, not the correspondence of your whole (healthy) brain and senses with the objective data surrounding them; it is the numen and the blind conformity of your part or unwhole (unhealthy) brain and senses that must be your criterion. It is not the relation of our organisms to one another, it is your relation to *me* and to what *I* say, that counts. This alone is dependable in the regulating of human behavior." Thus the social 'I'-persona comprised of the older ancestral constituent is law; it is the sum and substance of "truth," of the "good" and the "right." And the answer of the immature faction is a subservient "Amen."

Here is the phylobiological origin of dictatorship, of imperialism, of selfish monarchical and capitalistic forms of government as of the equally unilateral expressions to be seen in a political *party* or in such partitive affiliations as socialism, communism, democracy and the rest. There can be no true communism, no true democracy, no true socialism in this or that community or nation *as a part*. True socialism would be phylobiological and, in abrogating the sovereignty of the part or segment, it would necessarily embrace the one world of man as a race or species.

And so, throughout the species man, an interpersonal, an affecto-symbolic interest came more and more to replace the phylosoma's direct relation to the environment. With the inculcation of the "right" (partitive) mood, or the sense of "right" behavior as it is affectively insinuated by the "right" (partitive) mood of the parental contingent, the youthful contingent learns to feel and think and do in the way it is taught to feel and think and do rather than as the hard-and-fast actuality of the environment demands. We have become a race of marionettes. So much, if not all, of our social interchange consists in saying the "right" thing to the "right" person at the "right" time.

In the child's learning to feel and think affecto-symbolically, as it is affecto-symbolically taught by the adult generation to feel and think, we are confronted with a phylic dislocation in behavior that has its seat in the disturbed function of the third nervous system. In the shifting of the child's *feeling* or *motivation* to the third nervous system at the instigation of the parent, there is enacted a dissociation in the function of the phylum that is as deviate, as pathological as the structural deviations to be seen in cancer or tuberculosis.

Throughout the evolution of living forms there exists no instance of a frank functional disturbance in a species or phylum comparable to this phylic disturbance in man's interrelational behavior. The function or motivation of the child is transmuted into partitive feeling or into affects because, in becoming attached to the word or symbol, the organism's motivation is shunted into a miniature behavior-segment where it becomes automatically blocked and impacted. The organism's total feeling is intercepted in its natural egress to others and to the environment. In such a disturbance of function we are witnessing not an episodic development of imbalance here and there, but a world-wide aberration of function that extends unbroken throughout the phylum. This phylic disturbance in function is biologically unique. In this deviation the function of man's brain is not true to its structure, for the part-brain has now set out upon an independent course of function that is tangential to and subversive of the function of man's brain as a whole.

The element of interference, of conflict, of intercepted motivation in man's relation to the surrounding world is the element which in ontosoma and phylosoma requires to be analyzed. It requires to be dissected out and objectively appreciated by man if this faulty reaction is to be corrected and the appropriate reaction for which it has been substituted is to be restored to its rightful place in the phyloörganism's behavior. It is, then, the major task of phyloanalysis to release the organism's feeling from attachment to the part, sign or symbol of person or object, and to reëstablish the function of individual and community in its total behavior. But how may this be accomplished? How may man extricate himself from this subjectively enveloping glia of personal affects and prejudices? We may dispel our subjective illusions only through recourse to a clear objective definition of them. We may disentangle ourselves from habitual fallacies of inference only as we force them into the perspective of objective diagnosis and control—only as we contrast the ditentive pattern of behavior against the physiological behavior-pattern of man's organism as a whole.

Basically, there need be no discrepancy between man's primary motivation and its symbolic expression through the medium of language. Under biologically normal conditions, total motivation and speech should merge and flow along uniformly and unobstructed. In their complemental accord lies clear thinking and feeling. This is the phyloörganism's homeostasis. It is cotention and the nomen. Thanks to the socio-symbolic inventory embodied in the function of the third or semiotic nervous system and handed down from generation to generation by the older constituent to the younger, man has come to relate himself with streamlined efficiency to the external environment. But it is important to keep in mind that in achieving this unique facility the immature component of the phylum is at the same time the victim of a restrictive, retrofective feeling-tone that has induced in it a false interrelational orientation. For this system of behavior does not now articulate the immature component primarily to the parental organism but to a purely fictitious, affecto-symbolic image of this maturer component. Fortuitously acquired by the older generation and ingeniously transmitted to the younger, this image-relationship begotten of the part-brain has been substituted for the primary interdependence between mature and immature phyloorganisms. Thus the coördination primarily uniting the two contingents has been replaced by a mode of image-dependence or transference on the part of the younger toward the older phyloorganism. "What have I been taught to feel and think and do by my parental seniors?" is the habitual mental attitude of the junior generation in accordance with its vicariously inculcated "right-wrong" dichotomy. "For it is not my organism's coördination, but the ingenuity of my affecto-symbolic part-brain, whether expressed affirmatively ('right') or negatively ('wrong'), that must henceforth determine my relationship to other people and to my objective surroundings." And so we must come to see that while the third brain or the symbolic nervous system was potentially a subsidiary function integrated within and subordinate to the function of the brain as a whole, this subsidiary function gradually came to be the core of man's affecto-symbolic interchange and the dominant factor in his interrelational life.

It is apparent, then, that the relationship of dependence mediated by the third brain is of one cloth with the social conditioning experienced by man as his sense of "right" and its equally conditioned antithesis, his sense of "wrong." For this semiotic part-brain has established not only a social system of symbolic interchange but also a social system of moral alternatives—the compulsive dichotomy of "good" and "bad." The reflexly imbued sense of right regulating the relationship between the socio-parental and the socio-infantile contingents has now established an interchange between them that rests solely upon the social affectivity of one contingent of the phylosomatic unit in relation to the other. This intersocietal standard of conduct in man marks a socio-symbolic basis of adaptation that has artificially replaced the phylosoma's primary kinesthetic balance of tensions whereby the phylic soma as a whole maintains its internal balance of tensions in respect to the environment. Such a phylic mechanism entails for man only conflict and disparity. It represents disorder and pathology. In the phylobiological outlook this disorder is the meaning of *the neurosis of man*.[7]

In the early chapters of Part II we considered the neural aspect of conflict within the organism as this conflict is reflected in man's socially conditioned or partitive processes. These partitive processes we are now in a position to assign to the symbolic or third nervous system. They are related to the socio-cortical or inter-individual system of interchange that operates constantly among us all as elements within a common community or phylum. So that through this relationship the organism's motivation has become inadvertently linked up with the third nervous system, and this linkage has now become systematized into a specific pattern of behavior. In the amalgamation of man's motivation with the symbolic nervous system, there has resulted the distinct type of interrelational behavior whose elements we recognized earlier as consisting of interpersonal affects. The personal and social systematization of these affects constitutes the pseudo-identity we called the 'I'-persona. It is here, then, in the third nervous system or third brain that we may locate the neural substrate of the spurious system of interactions that commonly pass for "normality." This symbolic or semiotic system of neural reactions which now governs the phylosoma and which, from the point of view of its altered behavior-adaptation, we have demarcated from the two major nervous systems as the third or semiotic neural system, is of central importance in phylopathology. For it is here that there resides the very delicate mechanism that determines man's whole or his divisive relationship to the external world—his phylic health or his social neurosis.

With the predominance of normality's artificially differentiated 'I'-persona and the general adoption of this unilateral basis of identity and motivation by the elements or individuals of the species, there inevitably occurred a universal condition of conflict and incompatibility among the individuals composing the phylum man. Being now identified with the partitive pattern or with the affect, the resultant drive or motivation varies according to the personal gain of this or that arbitrary individual, family or community. In this situation the phyloörganism's motivation is not related to a biological norm. On the contrary, its motivation, and hence its action and reaction, its quest and quiescence, is dependent upon the fanciful instigation of each passing affect. In sharp contrast with the trend of Freud's quandary,[8] the fact is that such partitive ("wishful") behavior may readily be the expression of an entire nation or of a whole group of nations. Instead, therefore, of a situation in which the affectively errant individual is singled out, isolated and dubbed neurotic, we have in reality an interindividual situation that is retrofective and in which the adult phylosoma, itself already misguided, intercepts the infant phylosoma's direct interest in its environment by inculcating affective social images or universal neurosis.

In response to the organism's biological norm, the body's various functions, together with its neuromuscular and general tensional systems, would of course react in unison or in conformity with the phylosoma's function as a whole. As within the integrated phylosoma, so within the ontosoma as an integrated unit there would normally be whole tension or cotention. But the 'I'-persona with its unilateral basis of motivation segments and misappropriates to its partitive aim or advantage whatever function of the organism may be brought under the behavioral jurisdiction of the divisive part-brain. Expressed in phylosomatic terms, the partitive function of the semiotic or third nervous system has intervened to split the organism's total motivation into part or divisive functions or into man's socially conditioned system of reactions—his beliefs, wishes and prejudices, in short, his private and ulterior system of affects.

Quite aside from the unwholesomeness of the neurosis in its immediate interrelational pathology, nothing could be more unhygienic from the strictly medical viewpoint than the constant interception of spontaneous function existing throughout the world today. Except as scientists free themselves from the deadening authority of a retrofective 'I'-persona, they cannot possibly conceive of the deleterious effect upon the organism of this bionomically oppressive incubus. People nowadays refer to the vicissitudes of life as a "headache." In truth, it may be said that man actually has a headache throughout his lifetime. It may not reach sufficient severity to be recognized as such, but there it is. Wherever there is the 'I'-persona there is headache, and the major part of the energies of men is spent in ingenious devices designed to suppress the conscious recording of this cerebral stress. Of course, the people who suffer from definitely appreciable headache are legion. Then, too, there are those who all their lives are victims of "eyestrain." Yet many of these visual symptoms are again the result of partitive tensions of which man is as yet unaware. In denying the individual the sense of his organism as a whole—the sense of the organism of man—these partitive tensions and their will-to-self inevitably entail stress or conflict. Under the persistent restraint of conflict one's feelings are not free; they are subordinated to the autopathic dictatorship of the partitive "head" or the affecto-symbolic segment. "What will 'I' get out of property? What will 'I' get out of food? What will 'I' get out of sex?" it asks. With the interposition of the 'I'-persona, all interest, all incitement becomes retroactive interest and incitement.

Medicine cannot properly appraise disease-processes until it has recognized the predisposing influence which this functional maladaptation imposes upon the human organism. It cannot, for example, take thoughtful account of the possible influence of this neurodynamic impediment in furthering such disease-processes in man as tuberculosis, cancer, cardiac and arthritic conditions, not to mention the many disturbances of function occasioned by his various and sundry allergies. I think in particular of cancer because of the maladaptation in structure and function characteristic of this disease. I cannot but think of the aid it might be to the student of cancer-research were he able to reckon with the phylo-organism's distorted tensions in connection with a process whose pathology is characterized by the uncontrollable proliferation of random cells and tissues throughout the body. But as long as students continue to cling to an obfuscating 'I'-persona, they cannot possibly ask themselves to what extent may not this tendency to vicarious growth be influenced by an artificial obstruction to the functional integration and health of the organism as a whole. As we know, carcinoma is largely a miscarriage of growth, of productiveness, but, unlike other pathological invasions of the organism, cancer does not stimulate the body to physiological measures of defense.

As phylobiologists we are faced with a neurodynamic disorder, with a functional dislocation that affects the behavior of man throughout. As phylobiologists, our problem has to do with a disturbance of function that has become systematized within the species man and that can be remedied only by man as a species. Of course we *see* this systematization readily enough in the pseudo-personality of "normality," or in the social plexus of affects that constitutes man's universally prevailing 'I'-persona; but it is possible to *get* this systematization only *in ourselves*—only in the organism that harbors this dissociated 'I'-complex. Again it cannot be too strongly emphasized that the principle of phylobiology is an internal, physiological principle which no amount of theory or symbolic intellectualization can remotely approach.

Earlier in this Report I indicated that fundamentally all disorders of behavior are disorders of communication. In saying this, I attempted to forecast the phyloörganismic basis upon which this statement rests. I said that secondarily a failure of communication through speech, as indicated in such disorders as stammering, is undoubtedly a symptomatic expression of this breach in social or in interindividual contact and communication. But I emphasized the fact that in the present thesis our inquiry relates to a deeper, a more far-reaching impediment to communication; that it relates to a discrepancy that now determines the internal motivation of the phyloörganism of man as a whole.[9]

I think I may say that through our recourse to the scientific investigation of behavior embodied in phyloanalysis, there has come to be the increasing tendency among us to sense the underlying cause of our (of man's) disorder of behavior as a *segmentation*, as a reflex division in the function of our group organism—of the organism of man as a whole. Setting aside the petty claims and pretensions of the agitated Lilliputian whose chief incentive is the ulterior itch to get ahead of other little fellows like himself, the mind of man, as represented in our phyloanalytic group, has begun to crystallize into the unitary conception of man himself, of man the species, as a confluent and unitary organism whose elements are informed and articulated throughout by a principle of behavior that is primary and total. It becomes increasingly apparent that the segmentation of total man into partitive men is a misadaptation in biological unity and continuity that calls for examination within the broad, organismic frame of phyloanalytic inquiry. Experiments with the individual and with groups plainly indicate the presence of this segmentation, as well as its significance in impairing the functional integrity of man's organism as a whole.

The impediments to communication requiring analysis and adjustment, then, are not at all the affective, interpersonal barriers to social and mental well-being commonly envisaged by psychiatry. Although mentation and speech play their undoubted rôle in the dislocations of function evidenced in disorders of behavior, the communication requiring adjustment lies at a deeper level than the customary affect-reactions involved in mental and verbal forms of interchange. It lies deeper than the mere exchange of ideas and affects through the symbol or language. It is this deeper level of communication and contact that phylobiology specifically envisages. For this level embodies the articulation and continuity basically uniting the organisms of the species as these organisms are merged in their common interaction with the environment.[10] In relating the organism to its environmental habitat, this phase of man's interaction or communication is bionomic or ecological.

In order to regard this primary function of the organism's communication as basic or bionomic, we must of necessity view the species man as a phyloörganismic whole or unit. Our insistence upon the necessity of keeping within us, as well as before us, the broad biological concept of man as a unitary, organismic phylum is by no means arbitrary. It is essential to the meaning of the present thesis that this inclusive definition of man as a unitary organism be sustained throughout the field of phylobiology and that we preserve in our own subjective outlook the altered frame of reference coincident with this more encompassing conception of the species man as an organismic whole. Where one's position rests upon the internal, phyloörthopedic process of cotention, nothing could more effectually promote an enlargement of the function of the brain and senses of man in respect to the field of human behavior than a thesis which posits the primacy of man's behavior as a unitary and integrated organism.

Unless we recognize that *cotention* or common tension is basic in man's neurodynamic relation to his environment, we cannot cope with *the neurosis of man*. Ditention or the 'I'-persona is *man's* dissociation. The phenomenon embodied in the 'I'-persona or in ditention marks a phylic dissociation that is internal to the phyloörganism. It is useless, therefore, to look for interpersonal aid. Man's dissociation is itself interpersonal. Neither Gods, parents, teachers, physicians nor psychiatrists can help him. These personæ are but images of man's neurotic projection. In their own autogenous conditioning, physician and psychiatrist, parent and teacher are equal participants in a common neurosis. The condition is internal to man. It is autogenic. Man, therefore, must look within himself. Through the recovery of cotention man must learn to demarcate *within himself* the involuntarily conditioned mode or pattern that is fanciful, specious and unreal, in contrast to a mode or pattern that gives assurance to man of his consistent and dependable relationship to a consistent, objective environment.

It is important, therefore, to realize—to make real within one's own processes—that with the miscarriage of the function of the third brain and the concomitant intrusion of affect, a neurodynamic segmentation has taken place within the organism of man as a species. Man's segmentation has caused a functional division not only among individuals and partitively coalescent groups, but it has caused division also within each individual or organism composing the group. Coincidently, man's part-brain has brought about a generic division in the feeling and motivation of man's organism in relation to the environment. But this bionomic division or segmentation has penetrated far deeper. It has invaded the most vital functions of the phyloörganism. The far-reaching effect of this functional segmentation on the behavior of man will be discussed at greater length in the next chapter.

Undoubtedly the major task ahead of man lies within the field of his own behavior. It is the task of man to see that the acquisition of speech or the symbolic function—falsely linked, as it is, with deflected motivation or affect—has led to inadvertences in his interrelational behavior that have seriously undermined the integrity of his organism in relation to the environment. This division in man's integrity is man's job. After all, a problem of the phylum is the responsibility of the phylum. It is man's task to recover his organism's central principle of motivation. This task is simple; in itself it is simple. But all man's interests, the impetus of all his accustomed traditions and habituations lie in a totally different direction. Man is wholly caught up in these interests. He is immersed in them and completely overwhelmed by them. Yet the task is clear and its accomplishment is, of itself, neither complicated nor difficult. It consists in the reinstatement of man's basic pattern of motivation through its reintegration within the organism's function as a whole, and the coincident alignment of his symbolic capacity with this central motivating principle.

This phylosomatic readjustment is coterminous with the abrogation of ditention. It is coterminous with the abrogation of the purely fanciful images that have replaced the reality of man's organismic security and have led to his bionomic undoing. The realignment of the function of the third or semiotic nervous system with the function of the cerebrospinal and autonomic systems will mean for man the restoration of his organism's uniformity of motivation as a whole. Furthermore, with his concomitantly greater bionomic facility in communication through the spoken word or symbol, this functional realignment will contribute immeasurably to the adjustment of human relations throughout social groups.

NOTES

1 See note 12, page 232.

2 Burrow, Trigant, *The Structure of Insanity*, pp. 15-18, 46-59.

————, *The Biology of Human Conflict*, pp. 386-7.

3 The phylic ramifications of man's partitive behavior explain the limitation of the lobectomists in their attempts to remedy the psychoses through severing the associational paths in this or that particular mental patient. (See pages 366-68.)

4 In the individual or ontosoma, this reciprocity is expressed, of course, in the single mother-infant relationship.

5 Of course there occur such signs or gestures also on a much lower developmental level; for example, the cluck of the hen to its young or the stamping of the doe to warn the fawn of approaching danger.

6 See note 7, page 155.

7 "Neurosis" is really a euphemism. From the point of view of symptomatology man's condition might be better described as a psychosis. But, because of the diplaced neural function of the part-brain or third nervous system and its underlying physiology, as demonstrated through researches in phylobiology, man's dissociation may perhaps, after all, be more fittingly designated as neurosis.

8 See page 180.

9 See pages 253-54, 294-95.

10 This primary mode of communication with the environment has been referred to by Haeckel as man's "relational physiology." (See *The Biology of Human Conflict*, note 3, page 273.)

CHAPTER XIII

OUR COMMON CONSCIOUSNESS IN A COMMON ENVIRONMENT
A SUMMARY

There are in this world two major factors that make for constructive behavior; one is the troubled spirit, the other the inquiring mind. In any moment of crisis in an organism's behavior it is the troubled spirit that gives notice of an underlying state of disturbance, while the inquiring mind seeks to discover what that disturbance is. In the language of human biology with its rapidly broadening frontiers, the troubled spirit becomes transmuted into disorders of the cerebro-sympathetic and parasympathetic nervous systems, while the inquiring mind may be defined as the capacity to correlate consciously such intimations of disturbance with a misadaptation of the organism to the outer environment. Our failure to coördinate these internal maladjustments with the external processes of an increasingly complex environment goes far toward explaining the catastrophic incident in man's evolution we have lately experienced in the uncontrollable convulsions of an all-out world-war.

Throughout history man's perturbations of soul, religious and secular, have sought environmental accommodation under many forms of social and political adaptation. Indeed, the varying adaptations of man are coeval with the processes of history.[1] War itself —notably the recent war in which we have seen one half the world desperately struggling to destroy the life and property of the other half—represents a misguided effort toward the settlement of differences and toward the articulation of man's internal organism with the external environment. Socialism, communism, Marxianism, the ideology of the Soviets, Fascism, labor unions, capitalism, democracy, the Axis Powers, the United Nations—all these political and economic reactions are expressions of man's internal perturbation of spirit.

Born of a world-wide social revolution, these gigantic systems and the mounting billions of dollars with which we are subsidizing their operation betoken a correspondingly vast revolution in the processes of the human organism. In their relation to the human organism, these social and political programs bode the coming of a new science of man—a science which demands that we deal with the organism of man not as a divisible phenomenon, but as a dynamic whole or phylum. In its wide biological perspectives this new science requires that we bring wholly fresh processes of thought to bear upon the problem of man. It requires that we learn to envisage the processes of human behavior in terms of a vast and unitary phyloörganism.

As every organ, so every organism is a center of equilibrium in a delicate balance between the forces of the internal and external environments. The relation of the phyloörganism to the environment, like the relation of the ontoörganism to the environment, entails an equilibrium between internal and external forces. This equilibrium maintains the phyloörganism's balance between action and inaction, and thus preserves man's biologically fitting, as over against his biologically unfitting behavior. No artificial alternatives between choices symbolized socially as "good" and "bad" can with biological impunity be substituted for this basic equilibrium that secures the healthy functioning of the species as a phylic unit. No socio-moral precepts as they affect interindividual conduct can replace this biological solidarity in man's organism-environment relationship. This organism-environment relationship promotes the viability and survival of the species by reason of its balanced function as a whole— its metabolic activity and quiescence, its rhythmic inspiration and expiration, its physiological consumption and elimination, its bionomic activation and subsidence. In short, the security or the health of man is maintained by virtue of a principle of homeostasis that regulates the function of the phyloörganism in relation to the total environment.

Once we have clearly conceived of human behavior in terms of the phyloörganism, we shall be led to study this vast entity as we now study the ontoörganism or the organism of the single individual. Regarding this great phylic unit from the point of view of its basic structure and function, we shall approach our material with the equipment and techniques of medicine and biology. We shall see the behavior of this biological unit in terms of its basic pattern of reaction—its primary cotentive principle of homeostasis

—and we shall study any pathogenic deviations from this pattern as they are made perceptible through measurable physiological modifications.

Misadaptation in the ontoörganism is seen in the obstructions to behavior that characterize neurotic processes in the individual. It is seen in the impactions of motivation that result in purposeless, unproductive behavior. Applying the method of the experimental laboratory to the study of these conditions, my associates and I found that such impactions of function represent a conflict between the ontoörganism's part-reactions and the reactions of the ontoörganism as a whole—between socially conditioned motivations and motivations that are primary and organismic. But as we were led to look deeper beneath the mental perturbations and conflict of social man, we found that behavior-conflict occurs equally in the phyloörganism as a whole, and that this conflict in the phyloörganism is likewise due to a displacement of total behavior-patterns by partial patterns of behavior. Our experimental observations of behavior-conflict, as it occurs both in the neurotic personality and in communities of so-called normal individuals, give indication that these disturbances are traceable to a discrepancy in the phylum's internal patterns of tension, and that the essential conflict is due to the intrusion of partitive patterns of reaction (ditention) upon the supremacy of the phyloörganism's primary reaction as a whole (cotention).[2]

Viewing the status of man's organism with the dispassionate precision of objective analysis, we found that the part-function that is in conflict with the phyloörganism's total reaction consists of the affect-element involved in man's capacity of symbolic behavior or in his use of speech. As a group, we found that in intercepting the organism's total behavior the dominance of this affecto-symbolic part-function has seriously impaired the primary function of man's organism as a phylum. As a group, therefore, it was our express aim to block personalistic affect in mid-career. This procedure was implicit in our early phyloanalytic technique. For it became evident that in supplanting the brain's total function with the partitive activation of the symbolic segment, man, as an individual and as a community, has arbitrarily substituted an artifact of behavior for the primacy of the organism's behavior as a phylic and unitary whole.

These findings have introduced wholly unfamiliar factors into the observation of human behavior, as well as a wholly unfamiliar basis for observing them. But we should recall once more what is meant specifically by the affecto-symbolic segment in its bearing upon impacted motivation and upon the function of the phyloörganism as a whole. The activity of the affecto-symbolic segment is due to a unique specialization in the function of the forebrain. This specialization of function represents the dynamics of the third nervous system or the part-reaction that is outstanding in the behavior of social man. By virtue of this cerebral modification the sensory organs of vision and hearing have combined with the motor function of the tongue and larynx in the production of verbal images or man's symbolic activity. Through the gradual interpolation of this progressively developing social function and through the daily instruction of the infant organism in the use of speech, there has resulted the symbolic conditioning of each individual as an isolated part-entity. There was thus fashioned the separate identity or persona covertly cherished by each of us as "I," or "I myself."

In consequence of this behavioral inadvertence, human conduct has come to be regulated on the basis of the individual's capacity to promote his own partitive gain and enthrone his private interest or advantage above that of others. With this division of the phyloörganism into separate part-reactions, man no longer adjusts his behavior in accordance with the phyloörganism's balanced function—its homeostasis as a whole. His behavior is now regulated in accordance with the reaction-average arbitrarily established by these social part-entities. This behavior-average is determined in respect to the artificial dichotomy of motivation to which man has become socially conditioned and which he now posits symbolically as "right" and "wrong." In this misadaptive process lies the dilemma of the now affectively segregated individual, community, nation or half-world. This vicarious dichotomy of conduct—with its artifacts of social approval or disapproval—has rudely intercepted the phyloörganism's primary balance of function in relation to the environment. As a result, the partitive gain of the individual and his clique, community or country now takes precedence over the behavioral adaptation of the phyloörganism as a unitary whole.

This is the partitive or segmentive mechanism that has begotten man's prerogatory attitude toward possessions (his property-complex); toward social interrelations (his obsessive competitiveness and intrigue); toward the function of sex (man's autoerotic and narcissistic inversions, his homosexuality, that is, his *like*ness- or *image*-sexuality, whether expressed between persons of the same or the opposite sex); toward the function of alimentation (his insatiate greed for an excess of elaborate and often inappropriate food); toward moralistic motives entailing secret guilt and reflected in certain cardiac and circulatory reactions (palpitation, vertigo, fainting), and in the vasomotor reflexes of the skin with their ready response to disturbances in the interrelational sphere (blushing, blanching, sweating, not to mention the elaborate symptomatology we know as "skin-diseases"); toward the function of mating or homing (the superficial marital or non-marital liaisons man substitutes for organismic union); and finally toward the sphere of industry or work, where in his zeal for economic prestige and "face," or in his distorted quest for "life," he not uncommonly works himself to death!

In these various spheres of the organism's activity, the 'I'-persona sets a personal price upon, lays private claim, as it were, to what is called "success," or the achievement that is seen and approved by other people. Because of their overweening desire to think, feel and do as they have been taught to think, feel and do, everyone is actuated by the compulsive drive to aggrandizement; everyone labors under the obsessive urge to do "right" or to do "wrong" in these different domains of the organism's function.[3] At the behest of the "third brain" and its affect-product, the 'I'-persona, each of us madly strives to attain preëminence. We must exceed others. We must lay in ever greater and greater stores. We must have all things for ourselves, for the spectral, metanomic self—the self that is built of the affective image of identity with which man has replaced his organism's unity and identity as a phylically functioning whole.

In saying that the segmenting of the phylosoma into artificial, partitive reaction-units or 'I'-personæ imbues in the individuals thus separated a partitive or segmentive basis of identity, we need again to remind ourselves that we are speaking of a subjective process, of a process internal to ourselves and hence appreciable only within ourselves, within the domain of our own internally perceptible feeling and motivation. In recognizing that all processes coming under the jurisdiction of the 'I'-persona are necessarily partitive or segmented, it is essential that each of us bring this observation home to himself, that he recognize that this spurious persona is his *own* persona, his own affective basis of motivation. Only in this internally subjective awareness of our own spurious identity may each of us, whether individual, community or country, recognize that he has become a discrete part—an artificially divisive and separate entity.

Under the miguided jurisdiction of the 'I'-persona, hunger instead of being the hunger of the ontosoma—of the individual as organism—has become arbitrarily decentered or personalized. It has become "my" hunger. It has become contracted into the subjectively privileged 'I'-persona of each "me," with its enormously exaggerated and distorted image-evaluations. This subjective distortion represents the obsessive intensification of the affect in artificially replacing the organism's behavior or motivation as a confluent and balanced whole. It explains why all the functions within the individual—within the subjective 'I'-persona prevailing upon every hand—take on a false, special, divisive prerogative in contrast to the primary and inclusive behavior sponsored by the organism as a whole.

So that "my" hunger takes on an incalculably inflated and privileged quality, and "I" will eat too much, and though the body grows inordinately fat from this excessive intake, yet "I" still continue to overeat. "I" *like* it. It is *mine*. "I," the segment, will get more than other competing segments. So with "my" sex life. There is no satisfying it. I may only appease it temporarily. It, too, is mine. And the woman I take is mine. And the one woman is not enough. My eyes eagerly, involuntarily seek out others. A world of women would not suffice the partitive 'I'-persona. And what is true of the nutritive and reproductive spheres is equally true of the intellectual and the social—of the now partitive or affective spheres generally. In the *amour propre* of the 'I'-persona I cannot know enough; I cannot be distinguished enough; I cannot be acclaimed enough or in a sufficient number of directions. Economically, too, I am insatiate. The more money "I" make, the more "I" must make, and correspondingly the less may my organism earn, along with other organisms, in our common interest as a phyloörganismic group, community or nation. Under the tyrannical domination of this spurious persona the very organs of one's body become sick. Throughout the world, the body of man becomes a prey to an endless variety of diseases.

Whether it be "God," "love," "property," "success" or "reputation," it is the same; it is "face." All expressions of "face," of the 'I'-persona, may be subsumed under the one head: "What is obtainable *by* me *for* me?" This is the unremitting quest of partitive, autopathic man. This is the thing called "right." The deeds we perpetrate under the ægis of our "rightness" would entitle us all to a place of distinction in an exclusive rogues' gallery. If we took more account of these daily enacted cruelties—of the slow murders that normality commits in the name of what is "right"— we would find less need to high-light the more spectacular brutalities perpetrated in German and Japanese concentration camps. The unbelievable horrors committed in these detention camps will never be understood by looking at this or that individual, group or nation. Such incredibly cruel demonstrations of the depravity of human behavior are but a phase of "man's inhumanity to man" that is consistently demonstrated in endless variations of degree and form in all individuals throughout the species. What is sorely needed is a science of human behavior that envisages the third brain and its 'I'-persona as the seat of man's disordered behavior.

Our rightness, whether represented in individual or community, is segmented and false. It is the conduct we automatically pursue in obedience to the automatic dictates of a "right" or segmented social system. It is feeling and thinking as other people have bid us feel and think. Yet in the manifold combinations and permutations of the sick elements within the 'I'-persona there is to be seen merely the wrong twist to a basic principle of organismic fitness, a principle upon which rests the primary wholeness and health of man as a unitary phyloörganism.

Man's healing, man's being made whole or healthy, awaits man's awareness of his phyloörganism's artificial dispartment or segmentation. It awaits the development of his sense of discrimination between the organism's total pattern of tension and the part-pattern concomitant to the 'I'-persona. Man's subjectively insatiate 'I'-persona—the partitive, affecto-symbolic disbehavior of man—is unrecognized by him because he does not recognize the basis of his divisive, segmented behavior in his own internally appreciable dislocation of function, in his own internal, partitive pattern of reaction. This brings us back to the symbolic or third nervous system; to the miniature behavior-system or the part-brain; to ditention and the numen and the dissociation of the personality of man as a species.

It is here in the function of the part-brain that there is to be found the impaction of feeling and the consequent distortion of the function of the total brain. It is here in the function of this semiotic nervous system, with its ingenious instrument for reproducing in symbolic miniature all the things man sees, hears, smells, tastes and grasps in his hands, that there is to be traced also the inadvertent short-circuiting of man's relation to man and the origin of his partitive, divisive formula of good-bad behavior. It is here in the physiological function of an unrecognized third brain that one must look for the cause of stammering, of manic-depressive states, paranoia, dementia præcox, of crime and war, in short, of man's universal social neurosis, including the impacted feeling to be witnessed in any United Nations Organization that neurotic man may try to build.

Man is sick; not in a few spots here and there, but throughout his whole organism. For the function of the third or symbolic nervous system has got completely out of hand. This function, this affecto-symbolic function, being itself segmented and dissociated, inevitably segments and dissociates the function of the total brain to which it stands opposed. Standing opposed to the total brain, the function of the third nervous system or part-brain segments and dissociates the function of the systems and organs of ontosoma and phylosoma, as it segments and dissociates the behavior of both, interrelationally and in respect to the external world. It is this process of segmentation throughout the world which is the seat of the discord we see in religion, politics, commerce, industry and education; in the individual, in the family, in the State and in the nation—in everything that the adult generation teaches the younger generation to think and feel and do.

The segmented phyloörganism, like the house that is divided against itself, must fall. This is the catastrophe we are witnessing, though with unseeing eyes, in the world today. This is the real fall of man. It is no longer a matter of its mere dramatic portrayal in myth and legend, of its artistic projection in the fanciful dream of the novelist. It is a matter now of the actual fall of man, of the internal disarticulation of bio-social man as a global entity, to which we ourselves are the unconscious witness, as we are the unconscious contributors to it. This real, this bio-social fall of man is evidenced in the growing disintegration of man's institutions, social, political and economic—institutions that are the sick product of our division in feeling and motivation, of man's segmentation as a phyloörganism, as of the individuals spawned of this generically divisive matrix. In view of this pernicious segmentation within the phyloörganism through the interpolation of the functionally deviate third brain or of the 'I'-persona, it is not to be wondered at that man is ever seeking to atone for the division within his organism with mental images of unity that are purely metaphoric and that lie wholly outside the province of the total phylosoma of man. It is no wonder that men are for ever setting up gods supposedly embodying unity, but whose behavior is obviously as divisive and as segmented as the affecto-symbolic part-brain that has projected them.[4]

Throughout the range of evolutionary processes that mark the emergence of man as a species, no step of course is comparable in importance to his acquisition of the capacity of symbol-formation or the production of speech. Only our subjective involvement, as individuals and communities, in this far-reaching modification in the phyloörganism's behavior has permitted us to remain so long insensitive to the magnitude of this modification. But if it is true that speech is the greatest asset in man's development, it is also true that, owing to its partitive misuse, no other factor has so largely contributed to distort the primary behavior of man's organism. Man rightly plumes himself upon being the only rational animal, but he quite overlooks the fact that he is also the only irrational animal. The organismic implications of this partitive innovation in behavior extending throughout the phylum make it imperative that we examine this behavioral inadvertence very carefully. There is need that as an integral species compounded of common and unitary biological antecedents we seriously investigate these affecto-symbolic part-reactions that have so radically impaired the conscious correlation of man's organism with the forces of the external environment.

Speech is thought. With the first word, with the first symbolic gesture of man, there was light—the light of thought through communication. Communication and thought, therefore, are one. But the motivation to communication is the interest of the matter to be communicated. Where interest or attention is undivided, communication is undivided also. The flow of interest is not intercepted by hesitation, deflection or obliquity. It is not obstructed by ditention. The relationship between individual and individual is bona fide, cotentive, assured. But such a condition of complete confluence and contact between organisms is everywhere precluded in human communities because of the interpolation of the partitive, ulterior, politico-social persona with its eye to secret self-advantage. The mentally inculcated ultimatum of "right" is at odds with the complemental impulse to "wrong." Manifest conformity and manifest defection are at loggerheads. In all our interpersonal relationships this dichotomous preoccupation is ever uppermost. Where there is ditention, the light fails. Continuity is broken. There is only *me* versus *you*. The function of the third nervous system is isolated, segmented. The lines of communication are cut and contact ceases throughout the phylosoma.

To take one of the foremost instances of ineptness in communication, we may select an impediment in speech; and of this commonest barrier to communication we may select the most specific instance of it, namely, stammering. In a sense everybody stammers. Even a gathering of professional behavior-students offers no exception. One often witnesses in such a student the utmost difficulty and self-consciousness in presenting a quite simple paper even to familiar colleagues. One sees, for example, marked arhythmic breathing, unclear diction, nervous tension and excitement, awkwardness in delivery and often the fear to lift the eyes from the written page. In casual conversation, too, there is the talk that is interlarded with frequent laughter or giggling, too rapid speech or too slow, speech interspersed with affectations or unconscious imitation, speech that is impaired with affect-mannerisms, in which self-importance or an air of superiority obstructs the speaker's natural delivery. Then, last but not least, there is the prevalent disposition to excessive talk in which an autopathic 'I'-persona attempts obsessively to make good its lack of continuity with the organism's deeper orthopathic processes. And, in envisaging man's interpersonal disorders of speech, we may not overlook the compulsive tendency among people to interrupt one another. Like stammering, all these behavioral oddities are symptoms of social hesitation in communication.

Not everyone stammers, then, according to Hoyle, or clinically; but upon careful analysis everyone's speech shows a trace of this barrier to communication due to the ulterior aim or to the autopathic obliquity inherent in the 'I'-persona. For stammering, as other impediments of speech, is a species of lying—a socially enforced concealment that causes a powerful impaction of tensions concomitant to an artificially enlarged personality-prerogative. It betokens a camouflage in adaptation whose expressions are phyloörganismically false and unwarranted and must, therefore, be concealed. The concealment and impaction constitutes a defect in communication and explains the lying of the stammerer—the prototype of all disorders of speech as they exist in our so-called "normal" communities.

As stammering and lying are social hesitations of speech, we need not be surprised to find such speech-hesitations in parents and relatives, as well as in the wider community in which the overtly clinical stammerer is but an element. The philosophical proposition of ecclesiastical tradition—*homo est mendax*—is very much to the point. We are all tainted with inefficiency in communication. We are all cringing sons of Adam where it is question of our naked integrity! Man's misadaptation in communication is exemplified with such dramatic vividness in the laryngeal spasms of the stammerer because his organism's motivation as a whole surcharges the restricted part-function of speech and becomes impacted there. But if the stammerer is choked with fear and conflict because of his recourse to surreptitious part-reactions—his inveterate habits of evasion—other behavior-types, "normal" as well as "neurotic," are no less choked with conflict and misrepresentation because of these same behavior subterfuges. It merely happens that the choking and impaction are less spectacular where the obstruction takes place along channels that are not so obvious as those of social communication or speech. We shall find, though, that the restricted part-function of the third nervous system is equally responsible wherever there is neurosis, wherever impacted affect has been substituted for confluent, organismic feeling or motivation.

It is really time for man to recognize at last that prayer, repentance and psychotherapy will not save him from either his folly or his sin, and accordingly that he gird himself to grapple with his neuro-social impairments in communication on objective, scientific ground. After all, stammering is only one of many phases of the social neurosis of man. It is the outer interrelational betrayal of a deeper-seated defect in man that is phylophysiological. Briefly, stammering or speech-impediment is a phylosomatic phenomenon. This condition is but part of a disorder in man's ecosomatic relationship that is universal in its pathology.

It is imperative that man recognize the inescapable connection between ineptness of communication among individuals and among peoples, and the presence within him of universal neurosis. For in this hour man's accustomed "normal" environment is crashing about him. It is crashing about him because its structure is insecure. But man has not yet reckoned with his own part in the making of this insecure environment. He has not seen that disordered processes internal to himself are responsible for the flimsy social structure he has built about himself, and as yet he is only concerned with setting it up again. Man must recognize the extent to which his behavior is motivated by affect-pictures of actuality rather than by actuality itself. He must see the direct continuity between the affecto-symbolic part-reactions now governing his behavior, and the artificial social environment his behavior has erected. He must consider the vast difference there is between conduct motivated by a social reaction-average that rests upon purely external standards of "right" and "wrong," and behavior that expresses the organism's reaction as a whole to the whole environment. He must recognize the irreconcilable difference between behavior that is motivated by the segmented function of the third brain, and behavior that is motivated by the whole brain of phyloörganismic man.

Recalling the elementary reactions of the senses of man and of other organisms in respect to the environment, we may acquire a better insight into the psychosocial evolution of the sense impressions of man as a species. Man and other animals obtain a visual impression of objects which, as regards size, markedly contradicts the impression received through the organism's general stereognostic perception. Visually, the impression received may be measured in units of millimetres, while the object itself may be recorded in units of many metres. Similarly with the sense of touch. The tactile impression of an object of considerable size is, of course, compounded of innumerable tiny tactile stimuli. So, too, with the auditory, olfactory and gustatory senses. These sensations are reducible to an almost infinitesimally small element or unit.

The first symbolic stimulus (vocal or gestural) produced by an individual of the species and received by the auditory or visual sense of another individual constituted the interrelational action and reaction (the symbolic impression-response arc) that was elemental in the evolution of man's socio-symbolic synergy or language. The symbolic motor reaction (vocal or gestural) with which the second individual responded to the symbolic impression thus created, completed the psychosocial chain in man's symbolic or associational behavior. These miniature sense impressions with their motor responses marked the beginning of man's mental cognition or his associational communication. For language is the articulate expression of man's mental associations. That is, human congeners (now become mental "associates") attained a level of communication that was symbolic, because this communication was gradually built up of very small signs or substitutive sense impressions plus a relatively small motor response as contrasted with the response of the organism as a total reaction to the total object confronted by it.

In recording his mental associations then, man, unlike other animals, causes a minutely restricted sense impression to discharge into a minutely restricted behavior-response. He "converts" this miniature sense impression into a miniature reaction-process. This reaction-process, as it functions socially among us, constitutes a very special phase of man's behavior—a special phase of his relation to the environment. This is the symbolic, associational or conditioned phase of man's behavior.

It would seem important for us to realize that this symbolic activity of man's phylic organism represents throughout society a very circumscribed, a very miniature type of behavior as contrasted with the whole response of the phyloörganism to its environment. It is important to realize that this restricted, this exceedingly reduced behavior-configuration now mediating man's behavior entails a correspondingly restricted feeling-reaction. One can readily understand, therefore, the unsuitability of this reaction-pattern in negotiating processes belonging to the organism's behavior in its total expression. In prevailing social communities, the senses that function predominantly in symbolic mentation, or in associational communication, are the visual and auditory senses, and the normal motor accompaniment is the vocal gesture produced by the larynx. So that what happens in symbolic behavior is very different, very markedly reduced in scope, from what happens when the organism reacts as a neurodynamic whole to the whole object that engages its interest or incites its activation.

We would do well to realize, if only theoretically at first, how very different must be the behavior of an organism that is activated by its miniature symbolic impressions and their concomitant miniature response, from the behavior that represents the total impression and the concomitant total response of the organism. As we know, of course, the physiological equipment of animals provides them with no less tiny or miniature sense impressions (the elemental visual, auditory and tactile impressions) than is the case with man. For us, however, the important point is the circumstance that in other animals these very small individual impressions are invariably integrated within the organism's cerebrospinal and autonomic systems as a whole; while in man, contrariwise, this peripheral report of the external environmental situation is to a very large extent relayed toward and shunted into a correspondingly small motor pattern of reaction. While in animals there invariably occurs the larger phylosomatic interaction of organism and environment—an interaction that maintains the phyloörganism's ecosomatic coördination and balance—the response in man is largely mediated by the third nervous system and hence is restricted to a purely associational, to a merely graphic or symbolic reaction-process that now relates him to his associates only through a mechanism of mental communication. That is, men are now preponderantly related to one another symbolically, metanomically. Naturally, this associational or miniature type of behavior fails to afford the phylosoma the balanced sense of coördination and security in respect to the environment that man's larger organismic response afforded him.

In man, then, the neurodynamic relation of the phylosoma to the environment may be mediated through the secondary part-function of the symbolic segment or it may take place through the primary function of the brain acting as a whole. In either case this correlation between man and his medium involves the process of attention. Where the act of attention is performed through the phyloörganism's symbolic part-function or through the third nervous system, the element apprehended consists of a part, sign or symbol of the object in question. In this transfiguration of the outer environment into mental parts or symbols, man entered an entirely new universe of experience. For, in the special function achieved through symbolic attention, parts of the environment became mentally separated from other parts in such a way that the composition of the environment was rendered discrete and analyzable.[5]

In its capacity of separating one item from another, therefore, the phyloörganism's attention or adaptation functions differently from the manner in which it functions where the whole brain apprehends the whole object within the setting of the environment as a whole. But whether the pattern of behavior is that of the whole brain acting in relation to the whole environment, or the part-brain acting in relation to parts or symbols of the environment, it was our finding that the organ of vision and its neuromuscular innervation occupies a central position in both patterns.[6]

Because of the importance of the visual organ in the process of attention, its rôle in this vital function should be recalled.[7] In man, as in other animals, the retina of the eye primarily mediates between the outer environment and the whole brain. Consisting of a cup-shaped structure, the retina lies immediately at the back of the dark chamber of the eye. It forms the distal end of the optic nerve and is lined with the visual nerve terminals whose external stimulation is coincident with vision. It is this intermediary function between brain and outer environment that gives to the retina a key position in the process of attention.

As we know, the visual sense organ, like the other special senses, is largely a development of the skin and, like the skin, the function of these special senses was originally a response not of perception but of sensation. It should also be recalled that, in its function as a total, undifferentiated entity, the phyloörganism's visual contact with the environment was one of total, undifferentiated sensation. This matrix of total sensation underlies no less today, of course, man's visual function of partitive discrimination or symbolic perception. But through the dominance of the symbolic segment this primarily sensate function of the organ of vision was gradually submerged. The consequence is that in the course of man's social or symbolic evolution we have come to experience the process of vision almost exclusively in its more recently acquired function of symbolic perception.

When as infants, therefore, we first looked out upon the environment, what we saw was wholly different from what we see now. The retina then functioned as an organ of total sensation. Our impressions were not mentally segregated through the partitive demarcations of the symbol. Objects enlisted only the organism's total process of attention. In other words, it was originally as a whole that the organism back of this visually receptive function reacted to the whole environment before it.[8] And today the retinal hemispheres, when functioning as organs that are an extension of the undifferentiated brain of man, still reflect an external environment that has not been differentiated through the function of the symbolic segment or the third nervous system.

In the maturer organism, however, the retina mediates also between the part-brain and the symbolically segregated objects into which the part-brain separates or "analyzes out" the surrounding environment. When we consider that the retina is an immediate extension of the brain itself and that, as part of the eye, it is an area of the brain that is directly subject to external motor control, we can understand the importance of the eye in its function of total as well as symbolic attention.

Our experiments with eye-movements, as recorded by various cameras and corroborated by The Lifwynn Eye-Movement Camera,[9] show that where the brain ceases to function as a whole—where it assumes a part-function in relation to the environment—the eye too takes on a pattern of movements that corresponds to this cerebral part-function. It, too, adopts a specialized, partitive behavior-reaction. As a constituent in this altered pattern, the eye focuses upon its various objects of interest or attention only in its capacity of symbolic dissection and analysis. In the constellation of functions, therefore, wherein the symbolic segment or part-brain picks out its numberless items by means of verbal signs or indices, the visual function of the eye constitutes an integral and vital component in this altered pattern.

In man, as in other organisms, attention or interest is coterminous with the organism's motivation or behavior. The expression of motivation or behavior that releases itself through the medium of attention possesses special significance in the present thesis. It possesses special significance for us because this type of motivation mediates the conscious correlation of the organism with the environment. Where attention is the function of the whole brain in respect to the environment as a whole, the motivation of the phylosoma is whole, indivisible, organismic. Where attention is derouted into a restricted part-function, the phyloörganism's motivation is correspondingly shifted to a restricted part-reaction. It is this part-reaction, achieved through the legerdemain of the symbol, that has so dramatically transformed the total environment into the hieroglyph of mentally separate elements that it now is.

Owing, then, to the divisive part-reactions into which the brain of man has been artificially segmented, man's interest and incentive has been segmented too. Man's interest and incentive, individually and as a phylum, is no longer a whole reaction. In reacting to the environment partitively or disintegratively, man has reacted partitively or disintegratively toward himself and others. Man's relation to man is now universally separative, interpersonal, discrete. With each individual, the perceptual (symbolic) or partitive interest of the separate persona—of that which I call "me" and "mine"—supersedes the primary interest of man's organism as a total process. Instead of the phyloörganism's incitement to behavior arising from its total motivation, man's behavior has been shunted into the restricted bypaths of mere interpersonal affectivity. For since the interest or motivation of the phyloörganism is now regulated by the part-brain, or by the specialized symbolic segment, the brain of man looks out only from a partitive basis of motivation, and inevitably the objects as well as the fellow beings it looks upon possess only a partitive, retrofective interest for him. As man's attention is now partitive, the motivation to his attention is partitive also. What was primarily the whole and inclusive motivation of the phyloörganism has become the partitive and restricted self-interest of each individual, each community and each nation. So that whatever the individual may identify *himself* with, whether a woman, a whole nation or half the globe, becomes for him a *personal* cause as contrasted with the primary interest of motivation of the ontosoma or of his organism as a whole.

The special function of the part-brain that discriminates it from the brain as a whole involves the area I have already described as the third nervous system or the affecto-symbolic segment of man. Because of the dominance over man's behavior of this affecto-symbolic segment, man's attention and motivation in respect to the external environment is no longer the attention and motivation of his organism as a total phylum. This misadaptation is the basis of the mood-reaction characteristic of the schizophrenic —the mood-reaction that finds its solace in the antisocial regression of behavioral isolationism. But it is also the basis of the mood-reaction that the partitive community of man calls "normal"—a mood or reaction which in its vast numerical preponderance still awaits the scientific challenge of a consensual observation that is world-wide. Because of this split in motivation, man is like the house divided against itself, and his spirit is grievously afflicted. If we are to reëstablish the organism's primary unity of function in relation to the environment, it is necessary that the inquiring mind of man bring experimental observation to bear upon the cerebral processes responsible for his deviate mood-reactions. Only thus may the neurodynamic implications of man's disturbances in behavior be brought to scientific investigation.

The psychiatrists have not tackled the mood of man. They have not tackled this pathological mood in themselves where alone it is observable. They have not recognized within themselves, or phyloanalytically, that man's disordered mood is the product of the symbolic nervous system or "third brain," that it is concomitant with a functional dislocation within this affecto-symbolic segment of the brain of man. They have not seen that man's feeling, his mood or motivation is throughout retropathic, that his thinking is retroceptive, his doing retrofective, that owing to the interpolation of affect or the 'I'-persona the attention or interest of man has recoiled upon itself and that man's thinking, feeling and doing is now everywhere repercussive.

In his repercussive habits of thought and feeling, man has set in motion an environmental system of economic and industrial processes that have turned upon man himself and, in so doing, have now completely escaped his control. Though originally of his own harnessing, these social forces have slipped their bridle and are now plunging headlong in every direction without the guiding restraints of man's conscious mastery. The origin and meaning of these vast social energies have become strange to him. Man has forfeited his one and only source of balanced action and reaction. He has forfeited the principle of cotention. Cotention is the phylo-organism's total sensate pattern of tension in contrast to the affecto-symbolic part-pattern of ditention. Man must return to this primary basis of thought and action. He must recapture the original pattern of cotention if he is to restore his organism's primary sovereignty over these dynamic world processes.

The method which my associates and I adopted in re-inducing cotention within the sphere of man's interrelational function, I have described in Chapter X. As we saw, the procedure consists in bringing about a kinesthetic awareness of the eyes through the consistent maintenance of a steadfast balance in oculomotor tensions. As the result of long-continued practice in this procedure, it was possible to reëstablish the cotentive pattern and, correspondingly, to eliminate the affect-images that prevail in customary attention or ditention. We have seen that in restoring this cotentive pattern one may not do so by fixating the eyes upon a point in the environment but only through an internal equilibration of the physiological tensions in the muscles of the eyes. This sensation of cotention and the sense of the kinesthetic balance of the eyes concomitant to it gradually differentiates itself from the sensation of the affecto-symbolic pattern and gives notice of the partitive stress or tension that ordinarily prevails unrecognized in ditention. That is, the reassertion of the total pattern of behavior gives palpable, objective notice of a stress due to one's habitual ditentive pattern. Thus the symbolic segment is subject at one and the same time to two contrary and opposed patterns of reaction—ditention and cotention.

Cotention or the *intra*relational function of the organism's adaptation is analogous to the neuromuscular tone or balance prevailing throughout the body generally (coten*sion*). The function of ditention or the cerebrum's *inter*relational behavior is analogous, on the other hand, to the partitive stress or tension in the body wherever the body's neuromuscular tone or balance has been disturbed (diten*sion*). Ditention or distortion of the function of the symbolic segment corresponds, for example, to the kinesthetic sense of the outstretched arm as it becomes overfatigued through the interruption of its neuromuscular balance and integration within the total organism. Similarly, ditention or disturbance in this cerebro-ocular area is analogous to the sense of awkwardness and apprehension in the child as it learns to walk, or to the sense of somatic imbalance and uncertainty in the adult when first attempting such unaccustomed adaptations as skating, swimming, bicycling, tennis and the like.[10]

Restoring cotention to the symbolic segment of social man is vitally important for man, because the healthy functioning of his social processes is dependent upon the healthy functioning of the symbolic segment as an integrated element within the total organism. Its importance lies in the fact that the suspension of cotention in man's use of this segment entails an interruption to the organism's conscious correlation with the environment. For the abeyance of cotention permits the artificial dominance of the symbolic part-function over the behavior of man as a species and the consequent induction of impacted motivation or conflict throughout the phyloörganism as a whole. In this mechanism there is seen the neurodynamics of what we have called the social neurosis.

As has been said, our major group experiment consisted in the effort to demarcate man's total motivation as a phyloörganism from the partitive motivation expressed in the reaction-average of communities of individuals now partitively segregated from one another. As a natural adjunct to this group experiment we were interested in establishing whatever objective criteria might serve to differentiate the organism's primary function of cotention from its secondary, affecto-symbolic function of ditention. We were interested in establishing criteria of adaptation that would differentiate man's affecto-symbolic premise of behavior—the social reaction-average symbolized in the autopathic dichotomy of "right" and "wrong"—from the biological norm of behavior governing the organism's reaction as a whole in relation to the environment. These criteria of differentiation were found to consist in physiological alterations that are concomitant to these two discriminable types of attention or adaptation.

To those who are comfortably adapted to and wholly satisfied with the conventional behavior reflexly induced in them and now actuating them at all times—in short, so-called normal or partitively conditioned individuals—it may seem strange that a group of students should find profitable pastime in examining man's social and political behavior in relation to recordable physiological modifications in brain waves, respiration or eye-movements. But as a phylobiologist it would indeed seem strange to me not to do so. Surely if one is to devote serious study to the structure and function of the social institutions which the phyloörganism of man has created, what is more consistent with scientific procedure than to examine the structure and function of the phyloorganismic brain that has created them? After all, when I speak of man's affecto-symbolic reactions and of communities composed of artificially separated individuals, I am not speaking of a phenomenon that has taken place on some remote planet. I am speaking of a reaction that is constantly occurring in those about us—in the man on the street, in our next-door neighbor, in members of our families and, what is still more to the point, in our own naïvely inflated selves.

The daily papers bring us gossipy columns in plenty concerning these artificially segregated behavior-expressions. As an example of such commonplace part-reactions we have read of certain brokers who amassed untold millions by profiteering on war contracts. This is not surprising. Their reaction is an inevitable social response to an affecto-symbolic stimulus. It is the reaction of ditention. Such a socially conditioned part-reaction is now paramount with man. The response of these hungry gentlemen is precisely identical with that of the reflexly conditioned animal that instantly leaps toward his dinner-plate on recognizing the symbol or stimulus that is his dinner-bell. But the point is, we are all reflexly conditioned animals. We are all defense brokers when the bell rings. The behavior of these wily brokers is entirely true to type. It represents in social form the somatic discrepancy between man's total and his partial patterns of behavior. It is idle, therefore, to point to a deviation in this or that individual, group or nation. The experimental animal calling for study is the phylo-organism of man; and since such an experiment has to do with tensions and reactions internal to ourselves, our study can only begin at home or with our own internal tensions.

Or if the conditioning is such that the bell is inhibitory, that inhibition is now the dominant stimulus sounding a note of social alarm that strikes fear into the organism, then people will not take the risk of social trespass and accumulate millions at the expense of others. On the contrary, they will play safe by standing aloof and criticizing the "bad" broker who seeks his personal gain at the expense of others. Yet the response of our "normal" wayfarers to the inhibitory bell is no less the response of the partitive 'I'-persona with its ever keen eye to the main advantage. They are still acquisitive, still brokers—still partitive brokers craftily cashing in. Their "good" reaction is as much a partitive response as their "bad." It is the dichotomous basis of motivation—not one or the other alternative of it—that differentiates the partitive from the total behavior-reaction.

On the artificial basis of man's present social adaptation, dichotomy or political manoeuver now everywhere replaces the homeostasis of function that primarily relates man's organism as a whole to the whole environment. Personal and national intrigues, obsessive aggrandizement, secret dependencies, the competitive deal, covert diplomacies, ulterior pacts, the sharp bargain, in short, a socially refined species of mental cannibalism has now made such ruthless inroads upon man's unity of behavior as a phylum that today this substitutive behavior holds complete sway over man's basic processes. In the formidable array of partitive behavior-discrepancies exemplified in the community's social reaction-average, none of these somatic ironies stands out so conspicuously as the contrast between the behavior prescribed and the behavior practiced by students of behavior themselves.

This organic disharmony between prescription and practice evidences a common pathology in human behavior which as scientists we might profitably take to heart. If there are those who fondly suppose that students of behavior—psychiatrists, neurologists, the clinical psychologists—are themselves exempt from the disorders they attempt to treat in their patients, then they are not familiar with the record. Disorders of feeling are not less frequent among these presumably "normal" representatives of the community than among the laity. Schizophrenia, hysteria, manic-depressive reactions, homosexuality, drug addiction, alcoholism, phobias, obsessions and anxiety states are by no means unusual among the élite of the psychotherapists. The periodic depressions of outstanding students of behavior are well known; and if one views the profession of psychiatry at large, he can hardly fail to detect among its members all the affect-indicators of man's strongly entrenched 'I'-persona. After all, how could it be otherwise? If "normality" is the real disorder, then of course the "normal" psychiatrist, like the rest of "normals," is also a victim of this condition. Certainly nowhere does Bernard Shaw's apt quip, "The professions are a conspiracy against the laity," apply more poignantly than to the profession of psychiatry.[11]

But let it not be thought that such instances of autopathic dichotomy and inconsistency are for a moment an indictment alone of psychiatry or psychiatrists. These manifestations of an imbalance in motivation are in no sense peculiar to our psychiatric groups. The condition exists in individuals and in communities of men throughout. When it comes to the extravagant vagaries and contradictions of the 'I'-persona, we can only point the accusing finger at man—that is, at oneself. Nor should the finger be accusing, even then. For the condition is not moral but neural. The way of all flesh is physiological and it cannot be reached by the symbol. Our dissociation as a species marks a malfunction of the third nervous system and it can be met only with a neurodynamic technique applicable to this disordered behavior-system.

Students of behavior, however, will not take seriously this common pathology of man as long as they continue to posit a behavior-norm that consists of the shifting and uncertain measures represented by the social reaction-average—an average based upon the part-reactions of mere personal bias and clique opinionation. In the conscious correlation of the organism's internal stress with its external surroundings, the arbitrary bent of personal or parochial opinion can play no part. There is the need to approach the behavior of man in the inclusive spirit of an objectively controlled science. Thus far, prior judgment based upon subjective opinion has colored and distorted the clear observation of man's behavior-processes. There can be no stable basis *in regard to* behavior until there is in man himself a stable behavior-basis. We cannot employ criteria to which we are subjectively, affectively, agreed in advance, but, adhering to the method which science applies to the observation of other biological species or phyla, we must base our observations of man upon criteria that have been objectively tested and measured in relation to this established biological norm.[12]

If we are looking for outstanding instances of the deterrent effect of the social mode of ditention upon individual thought and feeling, we cannot cite more patent examples than are on occasion afforded by the behavior of men even of the broadest and most distinguished achievements in public life. Whatever our personal views regarding the policies of the late Franklin Delano Roosevelt, I think that most of us will concede that his outlook upon the problem of human welfare was wide and far-reaching in its scope. That we should see inconsistencies in behavior illustrated in so outstanding a leader and social idealist as President Roosevelt in no way reflects upon the individual leader and idealist but upon the twisted economic and political thinking of the social community—of you and me and the rest of mankind.

It was just before his death in a speech he had planned to deliver on April 13, 1945, that Mr. Roosevelt wrote the unforgettable words that form the legend to this book: "Today we are faced with the preëminent fact that if civilization is to survive we must cultivate the science of human relationships—the ability of peoples of all kinds to live together and work together in the same world, at peace." That was the intentional, the aspirational, the self-dedicated expression of a very earnest, a very great man. Yet it was also Mr. Roosevelt who, in speaking of his political opponents, frequently referred to them with marked hositility as "economic royalist"; who declared that in his first Administration the forces represented by them had met their match and intimated that in his second Administration they would meet their master. In alluding to their opposition to his re-election, Mr. Roosevelt said: "Never before in our history have these forces (he was speaking of business and financial monopoly, speculation, reckless banking, war profiteering, etc.) been so united against one candidate as they stand today. They are united in their hate for me—and I welcome their hatred."[13]

This was not a plea for peace, this was not aspiration, this was not the great vision of a great statesman. It was division, competitiveness. It was the ulterior motive of the 'I'-persona. But this, I repeat, was not Mr. Roosevelt. However much we might like to do so, we cannot single him out; we cannot point at the other fellow. These words of high disdain were the reflex expression by Mr. Roosevelt of a divisive mood, of an unrecognized quirk within the third brain of man—a quirk that causes man to think and feel only divisively, partitively, breeding opposition and resentment against his every aspiration toward human unity and accord. This again is the contradiction between the mood and the mind of man. This again is not clear, whole feeling and thinking. So that we may not unite with those who hate Mr. Roosevelt and his memory. This would not be balanced, intelligent behavior; it would not be the brain of man functioning as a whole. It would be our partitive, divisive, reflexly conditioned 'I'-persona; and we would not be dealing with the internal, neural disturbance responsible for man's disorders of behavior. We would not be employing the basis of feeling and thinking that is alone consistent with man's dispassionate and objective physiological pattern of tension as a whole. We would not be employing man's basic biological norm.

Man has been led far from this basic norm and from an understanding of the wholeness and commonness of human motivation as contrasted with man's partitive behavior ineptitudes.[14] In place of this whole view of whole processes the human organism and its methods of dealing with human behavior are now everywhere divided and at odds. But it is useless to deal with division as it occurs in this faction or that, with the ideology of one nation as opposed to another, with the political systems that motivate the western hemisphere as contrasted with the eastern. It is as useless as the present approach to the part-reactions embodied in mental disturbances. If we are seriously to approach the problem of mental disorder, if we are really to understand, for example, the nature of the divisive, schizoid part-reaction represented in dementia præcox—the disease of which we hear so much and for which we have done so little—we shall have to begin with an understanding of the nature of man's total, undifferentiated behavior as a phyloörganism. Whether it is a question of mollusc or man, science cannot understand the part until it has understood the whole.[15] Sooner or later it must be realized that the partitive deviation expressed in the introversion of dementia præcox is the inevitable complement of the deviation expressed in the partitive extroversion of our prevailing social reaction-average. It is fantastic to attempt to study such a social part-reaction as dementia præcox without having stopped to ask ourselves what is the nature of the whole social reaction of which this pathological manifestation is a part-expression.

In view of the rapidly spreading mental conflict and confusion in the world today as evidenced in our social and economic dislocations, one would think that man's pressing need for a biologically established norm of behavior would give us pause. In view of a social revolution of such ferocity and such world-wide proportions as mark the behavior of man in the present hour, is it possible for us as students of behavior any longer to view dementia præcox from the partitive bias of man's prevalent social reaction-average? Is it possible any longer to advance the view that dementia præcox or any other behavior-deviation embodies a more serious departure from the phyloörganism's total pattern of reaction than the behavior-deviation expressed in the partitive reaction-pattern of our so-called normal community behavior? Considering how recently we were drawn up in a battle line that divided the entire earth; considering that men the world over were but yesterday at the throats of one another in a savage death struggle, surely it is time for us to lay aside our mental projection-lenses and recognize our own affecto-symbolic participation in this world-wide part-reaction. By no process of logic is the student of human behavior warranted in concluding that communities of extroverts who call themselves normal and who place a premium upon motives of cut-throat competition are healthy communities; that they are healthier than the introvert-minority whose schizoid type of secret self-interest prompts them to seek security in images of recessive self-enclosure and withdrawal. Is it not possible for man to enlarge the function of his brain and senses, and recognize that the behavior of the extrovert-majority and the behavior of the introvert-minority are equally part-reactions, and that these part-reactions represent equally a deviation from the phyloörganism's pattern of behavior as a whole? Such are the questions which the student of human behavior must ultimately bring himself to face. For in reckoning with human behavior and its conflicts, we must reckon equally with the 'I'-persona of the adapted and of the non-adapted, of predator and prey.

Where man is embroiled as now in universal revolution and

conflict, the inquiring mind may not envisage this total problem from the habitual part-basis of the social reaction-average. From the background of mere partitive motivation the inquiring mind is necessarily partitive also. Man cannot cope with the enormous disorganization of the social forces lying outside him except as he rediscovers and adopts the primary principle of organization lying within him. The situation in the world today sufficiently attests the extent to which man has permitted these forces to get out of hand. It is only as we view the turmoil of man's world from the phyloörganism's whole and undivided pattern of motivation that the undivided mind of man may correlate consciously his organism's internal disturbances of behavior with his needed adaptation to an external world of complex and changing values.

In this achievement man will have divested the symbol of the false interests and incitements of the 'I'-persona incurred through the adhesion of private affects or through ulterior, dispartive trends. Correspondingly, these adherent affects will have been reconverted into the total feeling requisite to the organism's concinnity and uniformity of motivation as a whole. Man's organism will function without impediment individually and socially, and the "unity" which is now the product of sheer sentimentality, of false beliefs and idle wishes, will have been once more restored to its physiological balance and integrity. Through a biological approach to man's behavior as a phylum, the allegorically conceived notion of the Fall of Man as a descent from virtue into sin and his filial recourses to repentance and amendment will be replaced by his application of a mature scientific principle to his phyloörganismic rehabilitation. The ignorance and superstition of metanomic thinking, or of the numen, will become clearly manifest; and orthonomic thought, or the nomen, will assume supremacy over man's processes as a species or phylum. Not through abject repentance, but through his upstanding recourse to the organism's basic intelligence will man attain his needed reintegration. Man will not leave to the whim of mythical Gods the problem of his salvation, but he will himself assume responsibility for the restoration of his own clear feeling and thinking and doing.

Phyloanalysis has made evident a condition of organization and unity that extends throughout the species or phylosoma as a whole, while parallel with this unitary principle of behavior there was likewise traceable throughout the species a system of reactions that is definitely deviate and disorganized.[16] Our investigations have made out the existence of a biological norm of adaptation that is coincident with the healthy phase of man's behavior and, correspondingly, we have made evident that man's pseudo-normal criterion of adaptation is the product of his deviate plane of behavior. We have emphasized that, contrary to popular supposition, it is not the "mental" faculty or the "mind" of man that is the seat of his disordered behavior, but that a deeper-lying mood or mode of motivation is the pathological factor. Our experiments have aligned this mood or mode with an *internal pattern of behavior* that is definitely physiological in its deviation.[17] Recognizing that the substrate of man's disorder of behavior is physiological and that it may become internally appreciable by him, our researches have centered upon this physiological deviation in the organism's internal patterns of tension. Our researches have brought us to a realization of the primary solidarity of man as a species. They have forced us to recognize the basic unification and coördination of man as a phyloörganism.

This primary coördination and solidarity of man serves to confirm earlier studies in which I attempted to show the importance biologically of the infant organism's primary identification with the mother organism.[18] I have since tried to show how this identification with the mother organism sets a pattern that remains dominant throughout the development of both the individual and the species. For our later researches have shown that it is not alone the individual or ontosoma that carries through life the biological impress of its intraorganismic identity with the mother, but that as a race, species or phylosoma, man's organism bears no less this impress of continuity and solidarity with its maternal source. This genetic pattern inherent in the principle of primary identification is not to be gainsaid. This organismic principle of continuity and solidarity is basic and decisive for the growth and development of man's organism, as of the organisms of other species. And the subsequent cultural, intellectual and symbolic development of man must ever conform to this underlying biological principle. It is only the ditentive dispartment within the function of the third nervous system or within the part-brain of man that has seemingly severed the organismic bonds of which man's continuity and solidarity as a species are wrought.

It is therefore the nature of the organism of man that it is one, not many; and it is likewise the nature of the world surrounding man's organism that it is one, and not many. In the complemental homeostasis between the world within and the world without, between man's internal and external environments, lies the biological health and security of man. Man's health lies not in the many false images, not in the many Gods which in his artificial division as a species he has set up for his purely vicarious comfort and happiness. His health and security lies in the indivisible, organismic interaction between the unitary principle of solidarity within the organism of man and the harmoniously ordered universe outside him.

The identification of infant ontosoma with maternal ontosoma is, then, but the special instance of the identification between infant phylosoma and maternal phylosoma. In this phylic extension of the principle of primary identification we see a principle of continuity and solidarity that is coterminous among all individuals of the species. Here again we return to the basic pattern of tension in ontosoma and phylosoma. We return to the principle of common unity and identity underlying our manifold symbolic interrelations. We return to cotention.

The organism of man is ever in its infancy and ever achieving new maturity; but it is ever one organism, one organismic infant, one organismic adult, one organismic species in relation to its environment. Interrelationship is always, and first of all, between organismic man and his organismic environment. This is primary; all else is secondary. If this primary balance is disturbed, all else is correspondingly disturbed. This organismic frame of reference is the requisite basis from which man can observe and study his own behavior, whether of infant or adult. From this basis man will cultivate and develop his capacity to feel and think organismically; he will observe and handle his own behavior as disaffectively as he observes and handles an object in front of him.[19] This is the manifest destiny of biological man. The concept "man" will become one with the species man as a whole, just as the concept "hammer and nail" is one with the actual hammer and nail in the hands of the carpenter using them. Infancy will come to be the organismic infancy of the species man. So with adult man, with motherhood and with its function within the community. Adaptation will be first and primarily the adaptation of the species as a whole, and individual men will begin to feel and think anew. They will become original, internally creative. Sensing immediately that any disorder in behavior signals a disorder in communication, they will hasten to the task of repair with united effort and intelligence and with unfailing restorative measures.

NOTES

[1] See note 4, page 199.
[2] Burrow, Trigant, *The Biology of Human Conflict*, pp. 175, 266-8, 343.
Syz, Hans, "Burrow's Differentiation of Tensional Patterns in Relation to Behavior Disorders," *The Journal of Psychology*, 1940, Vol. 9, pp. 153-63.
[3] Burrow, Trigant, *The Biology of Human Conflict*, Chapter III.
[4] See pages 165-67, 197-98, 237, 296-99.
[5] Burrow, Trigant, "The Human Equation," *Mental Hygiene*, 1941, Vol. 25, pp. 210-20.
[6] Burrow, Trigant, "Behavior Mechanisms and their Phylopathology," *The Psychonalytic Review*, 1935, Vol. 2, pp. 169-81.
[7] Dodge, Raymond, "Fundamental Steps in the Development of Adaptive Behavior of the Eyes," *Journal of General Psychology*, 1930, Vol. 4, pp. 3-14.
Jacobson, Edmund, "Electrical Measurements of Neuro-muscular States During Mental Activities. III Visual Imagination and Recollection," *American Journal of Physiology*, 1930, Vol. 95, pp. 694-702.
[8] See note 9, page 199.
[9] Syz, Hans, "The Lifwynn Eye-Movement Camera," *Science*, 1946, Vol. 103, pp. 628-9.
[10] See Chapter IX.
[11] An instance of many years ago that is typical of our pseudo-normality is still vivid with me. During the year of my presidency of the American Psychoanalytic Association it was voted that only those holding a medical degree would be eligible to the status of a psychoanalyst; no one having only a Ph.D. degree could qualify for membership in the society. Yet, in that same year, no less than seventeen prominent New York practitioners of this specialty were being "analyzed" by a well-known European analyst then in this country, who himself held only a Ph.D. and, what is more, had been commonly diagnosed by these same colleagues as a hypomanic neurotic! If this does not illustrate the twisted thinking of the ditentive part-brain, I do not know what does.
[12] Studies of animal communities by W. C. Allee, Alfred E. Emerson and others have emphasized the organic solidarity extending throughout these biological units.
Allee, W. C., *Animal Aggregations: A Study in General Sociology*, Chicago, University of Chicago Press, 1931, pp. 431.
——, *Animal Life and Social Growth*, Baltimore, Williams & Wilkins, 1932, pp. 159.
Emerson, Alfred E., "Social Co-ordination and the Superorganism," *American Midland Naturalist*, 1939, Vol. 21, pp. 182-209.
——, "Biological Sociology," *Denison University Bulletin, Journal of Scientific Laboratories*, 1941, Vol. 36, pp. 146-55.
[13] *The Public Papers and Addresses of Franklin D. Roosevelt*, New York, Random House, 1938, p. 569.
[14] See note 12, page 199.
[15] "If the part is conceived without any reference to the whole, it becomes itself a whole—an independent entity; and its relations to existence in general are misapprehended." Spencer, Herbert, *The Principles of Ethics*, New York, D. Appleton & Co., 1898, Vol. I, p. 3.
[16] See page 149.
[17] See note 2, page 199.
[18] See note 13, page 363.
[19] The extent to which moral tradition and superstition may be encouraged to give way to more objective attitudes in respect to the sphere of man's sexual life has been ably and courageously shown through the statistical researches of Alfred C. Kinsey and his associates in this hitherto neglected field of scientific inquiry. (*Sexual*

Behavior in the Human Male, Philadelphia, W. B. Saunders Co., 1948.) To the phylobiologist, Dr. Kinsey's findings are, of course, no revelation. But for the community generally—for the community whose manifest sexual behavior is regarded as "normal"—Dr. Kinsey's incontrovertible studies should be of inestimable value. For myself, as for my associates, man's sexual secrecy and pretense is but symptomatic. It is but an aspect of a secrecy and pretense that is now characteristic of man throughout the various spheres of his behavior. Our sexual misadaptation is but a phase of a larger constellation of reactions that characterize our disbehavior as a species. It reflects an arbitrary "right-wrong" standard of conduct as contrasted with the homeostatic principle of behavior resident within the phyloörganism.

I do not think we shall reconcile the inconsistency and discrepancy between the outer and inner story of human sexuality until we have reconciled the inconsistency and discrepancy in man's behavior generally. I do not think we shall find an avenue for the adjustment of this condition except as we recognize that our excesses and our repressions in the sexual field are traceable to the dissociation and inconsistency inhering in the social 'I'-persona, or to a segmentation in the neurodynamic motivation of man throughout. After all, man's hypocrisy in regard to his sexual life is but a part of normality's open secret of dualism and conflict—an open secret that is by common consent now everywhere kept closed!

CHAPTER XIV

PHYLOBIOLOGICAL REFLECTIONS

The arduous work on which I found myself launched thirty years ago, with its radical alterations in feeling and thinking, was not, as might be supposed, the outcome of some personal disappointment or deep-seated regret. The story of my personal life is, of course, of no general interest and I should not wish to be deliberately tedious. But in a subjective study of interrelational man such as our laboratory represents, with its challenge of prevailing institutions, of man's accustomed motives and feelings, of the entire range of his subjective interests and activities, the reader would hardly sense the essentially human auspices under which our task set out, without at least some pertinent allusion to the background of the particular "subject" who initiated it.

I have never been especially interested in measures of uplift, and would under no circumstances assay to preserve anyone from his chosen path to perdition. It has been my experience that people with ideas about other people's betterment are usually a sorry lot. Neither, as it happens, have I been the forlorn sort who finds himself compelled to search for "a way out" or seek compensation for conditions with which he is beset. The fact is, life has dealt most kindly with me. Having always enjoyed exceptional health, steadfast friends and gracious surroundings, I have in the main had rather a good time of it. I have never known tragedy or loss as have so many people. My only serious loss was a quite voluntary one, but one for which I was amply recompensed in the interest that led me to incur it. I refer to my enforced recognition of the existence of a social neurosis and of my personal share in it. This, I cannot deny, was a serious wrench for me. For having now to adopt an altered basis of inquiry, it was necessary that I forswear completely my psychoanalytic practice and set out anew. Not only this. But, as will be readily understood, the necessity of reckoning with man's ineptitudes in feeling and thinking and doing, as these ineptitudes were daily registered within myself, entailed an acutely painful process.

Then, too, there was the pain of the unavoidable break with my professional colleagues. Certainly no one can lightly wave aside adverse criticism and the loss of the friendly coöperation one has known among his fellow workers. The situation was the more difficult, as in the work I had entered upon it was essential that I forego old outlooks before attaining the new. Not knowing toward what specific objective I was bound, I had perforce to embark for unknown shores. It was this factor of lottery inseparable from the early stages of my scientific adventure that entailed the greatest hardship. But this uncertainty was in time completely dispelled as our consistent investigations gradually brought our laboratory unit to a realization of the solid and dependable course on which we were launched. Barring these untoward, if self-imposed conditions, the circumstances of my life, as I say, have been most fortunate. Indeed, as it turned out, nothing could have been more fortunate than these distressing conditions themselves.

Whatever the incentives, in setting out upon my new field of scientific interest the usual self-comforting compensations played no part. None of the usual noble and self-flattering motives stood sponsor to my endeavors. As the reader will by this time have guessed, I was not for a moment inspired by ideas of doing good in the world, nor had I any thought of helping my fellow man in the ordinary sense of the word. My researches arose quite spontaneously from the recognition that neurosis is pandemic to man and that not only my patients, but also I myself, my family and my friends were necessarily part of this phylic disorder. The motive, therefore, to my phyloanalytic undertaking was no other than to escape this discomfort common to me, to those about me and to the world at large, realizing that my personal discomfort, as that of every other individual, was but the subjective index of this larger constellation.

Here was an interrelational disorder which by its nature involved my very own identity—the complex of reactions embodying my very self. In this situation it was inevitable that, like everyone else, I should be completely caught up in this spurious identity—that everything that was "I" should be obdurately opposed to the relinquishment of this pseudo-personality. It was inevitable that "I" *could not even want* to part with it. Nevertheless, in pursuance of a science of behavior, I was interested in securing a basis of clear *feeling* as a necessary condition of clear *thinking* in the field of man's interrelational reactions, just as scientific observers occupied with phenomena external to them have in the past been interested to put aside a muddled premise of thinking, and substitute for it a scientifically consistent and inclusive process of thought. Since to think clearly or without bias is merely to function without impairment, there is certainly no particular virtue in wishing to think clearly, however painfully one's doing so may offend the prepossessions of the 'I'-persona with its ingrained affects and prejudices. Fundamentally, the urge to clarity of thought and feeling should no more offend one than the urge to preserve unimpaired the facility of any other function. Correspondingly, one can claim no special merit in wishing to escape the discomforts of unclear thinking and motivation, once he has become aware of them. The only reason we are offended by the proposal to seek a clear basis of feeling and of thought is that our own identity, or the 'I'-persona, is now coequal with our partitive (autopathic) habits of unclear thinking and feeling. Yet I have no doubt that once he has recognized it, man the world over, be he statesman or stevedore, will be no less interested in finding relief for his affective imbalance and discomfort than were my associates and myself upon recognizing ours. Such a course is alone consistent with the inescapable processes of the phyloörganism's evolution.

But how will this wider recognition be brought about? Perhaps I can best discuss this question in the light of our own group experience. It early became clear to me that if the neurosis were social, it was only in a social situation that one could seek a remedy for it. This view was responsible for the inception of our group-analytic studies. It was imperative that the student of behavior secure conditions that would afford him social coöperation in his effort to make objective his habitually subjective trends. I felt that he should have conditions that would not only leave him free to voice whatever evidence of affect in himself or others the laboratory setting offered him, but that by the very terms of the laboratory technique he should feel himself under scientific obligation to do so.

It is inconsequential that in our experimental groups the student at first consistently made a fiasco of this opportunity to break through the social covenants commonly posited by accepted social custom. It is inconsequential that at times he was driven to affront egregiously the amenities of orderly social interchange.

For it was inevitable that at the outset he should fail to present his criticisms objectively, that he should invariably have been prompted by motives other than those of calm, objective observation. Often enough, as a matter of fact, he was "mad enough to bite," and in his extremity would, time and again, vent his wrath in tones characteristic of irritation and self-righteous resentment. It could not have been otherwise. The student was not seeing—he was not feeling things clearly. Being himself embroiled in ditentive conflict, he was as yet unfitted to deal circumspectly with conflict and ditention in others. But it was only through such social awkwardness that the student was ultimately led to his phylobiological quarry, to his cultivation of an objective attitude toward habitually subjective reactions—reactions which in every instance we found to be based upon the absolute authority of an autocratic and imperialistic 'I'-persona resident within oneself.

I might say that in the beginning it did not occur to me that the zone of man's internal tensions might prove a profitable field in our investigation of the problem of human behavior. The field of internal tensions was brought to my consideration only as an accidental by-product of my investigations of the motivations of human behavior in their social or interindividual expression. It was brought about only through the consistent obstruction of the customary interests and incitements of "normality." [1]

Our experimental groups, then, came together for the sole purpose of observing our division, our internal lack of social balance and accord. Each of us was automatically thrown back upon himself to find his way through the maze of his own unwarranted affect-projections, of his own spurious thinking and feeling. Certainly, such a process did not make for the "unity," for the "love and confidence" within our groups that one ordinarily understands by these terms. On the contrary, our procedure was a direct challenge to all that we knew as unity, to all that we knew as trust or human affection. There was no leaning upon others, or rather the habit of leaning upon others as commonly expressed throughout normality was at all times material for observation in a social system shot through with pathological moods of transference and dependence. Each of us had to make his own research in his own way at his own desk—his desk being his own organism.

Throughout these pages I have made frequent reference to my associates. But I must emphasize again that my co-workers and I have been associated not through the customary bonds of mutual approval or "liking." Our association has been cemented only through our common adherence to a common principle of human behavior. In phylobiology, no one is his brother's keeper. As laboratory students each of us was compelled to stand on his own feet. No one could act as sponsor for anyone else. None of us could look for any support other than the integrity of his own phylobiological investigations—his own intrarelational principle of behavior. Any other sponsorship could only rest upon the autopathic fallacy of the transference or the parent-child relationship. If, as a result of my own phyloanalysis, I have achieved a degree of synthesis in my own processes as a phylic organism, this and this alone constitutes my credentials as a phylobiologist. And so it is with my associates. While the group set-up was a condition indispensable to our bio-social experiment, the needed *intra*relational adjustment was possible of attainment only as each student maintained the cotentive principle of behavior against the *inter*relational background of ditention prevailing throughout the group and the wider community. In calling attention to this uncompromising premise in our approach to the study of human behavior I am reminded of Huxley's dictum in respect to other domains of science:

All that I have ever proposed to myself is to say, this and this have I learned; thus and thus have I learned it; go thou and learn better; but do not thrust on my shoulders the responsibility for your own laziness if you elect to take, on my authority, conclusions, the value of which you ought to have tested for yourself.[2]

It was this uncompromising phyloanalytic premise to which we adhered in our laboratory approach to human behavior and which brought its own reward in the form of unsuspected observations in the field of our commonplace everyday living. For instance it was apparent that while the outer deportment of the participants in group or phylic analysis became more moderate, yet beneath the outer surface they still remained mad; in their underlying mood they still remained mad enough to bite. They were irritable, resentful and bitterly self-defensive. They no longer showed their teeth, but the habitual mood of the separative 'I'-persona as sponsored by the partitive or third nervous system remained intact.

Time passed. Many and varied were the mental and emotional

reactions. But there was no real progress in dealing with the spurious mood of the 'I'-persona. And there will be no real progress until there is the permanent sense of cotention *as a phylic pattern of behavior*—until there is the student's rigid adherence to this internal, physiological mode. So that it must not be thought that the members of our experimental group were as yet in any sense "cured" of the social neurosis—not any more than a community of tubercular patients who have recovered from their infection is cured of the tendency in man to incur tuberculosis. It is no more possible in the field of behavior than in any other sphere of medicine to bring a satisfactory remedy to a restricted area of an organism while a wider systemic process of infection is raging unabated within that organism. The real problem for man is *man's neurosis*. So let no one imagine that the personnel of The Lifwynn Laboratory presents a shining example of the cotentive life! All that my associates and I have succeeded in doing has been to discover and define the dislocation in neural function responsible for man's disordered behavior, and point the way to the adjustment of this phylic disturbance. If insanity, crime, conflict, neurosis and war are to be remedied it is man's insanity, man's crime, man's conflict, neurosis and war that must be remedied. Ditention and the spurious mood of the 'I'-persona must be made to give way to cotention or to the organism's balanced motivation as a phylic whole.

In the days of early man, if people had trouble with their eyes—if objects became blurred, or appeared double, or looked otherwise unnatural to them—they did not think of an internal difficulty of vision. On the contrary, they thought that they were "conjured," that the objects thus altered in appearance had been distorted by evil spirits. They thought that the evil spirits were responsible for their false visual images and they sought to appease these malign powers with fitting oblations. It was centuries before the oculists came along and, recognizing that the condition was not an external but an internal, physiological one, prescribed glasses. Such an internal, physiological approach ran counter to popular religious tradition and was considered blasphemous. It was regarded as an interference with God's handiwork. Today one does not any longer talk to oculists about evil spirits and what they have done to distort the objects about him.

Owing to the intrusion of the 'I'-persona and its ambivalent affect-images, man dwells today in a world of universal syncretism

—in a world that constantly posits a causal relation between two unrelated phenomena. One reasons: "You are good, so I like you." Or, "You are bad, so I do not like you." But in our study of behavior it has been our effort to dispel these projective affects and prejudices with which we commonly account for reactions occurring in the interrelational world. I may not say that I like one person and do not like another. I may not say, as I am accustomed to say from the background of my habitual prejudice, that such and such a person is "good" and another "bad." On the contrary, I may only say that I have a chronic brain-twist and that because of the distortion in my feeling concomitant to it, I am given to the habit of projecting arbitrary affects. In honesty, I can only say that I am in serious need of an internal, physiological corrective for my mental errors of refraction. And so, consistent with our phylobiological investigations, I have come to see that man's position today in respect to his affect-projections is of one cloth with his invocation of evil spirits yesterday. In short, it is incumbent upon my co-workers and myself to look as definitely for an internal basis of our affects and prejudices as did the oculists of old when, eschewing exorcism, they directed their attention to the eyes in adjusting disturbances in the visual field.

It used sometimes to seem to me that a remedy for the affect-projections of neurotic, war-mongering man would come to pass only when there should occur some vast social convulsion, some basic crisis in the affairs of men and their interrelations—a crisis of such world-enveloping magnitude that there would at last appear nothing outside man to which he could turn for support; that then and only then might man be willing to recognize as one world that his disorder is internal to himself and that the one remedy requisite to this disorder within himself is the balance and integration of his own organism. It seemed to me that in some such all-embracing catastrophe man would be brought to abandon the allurement of his projected affects and look at last to the integrity of his own organism for his own security. One might think that the widespread war we have just experienced would have proved a sufficiently arresting and a sufficiently widespread disaster. One might think that now at last a sufficiently compelling argument had been advanced. Or, if not yet, that perhaps there may intervene the vaster catastrophe of the war between East and West for which the nations are now feverishly, though secretly, preparing and that then man will be finally brought to his needed self-rally. Such are the reflections one might well entertain on the basis of his accustomed habits of "thinking." But, as was the case with the "mental" recognition achieved in our own groups, it is only too apparent that man's "mental" recognition that something is amiss with him is of no avail. Notwithstanding all the mental evidence, certainly no such mental view of the affect-situation existing in the "normal" groups with which I have been associated afforded the slightest instigation to the adoption among us of a more basic, a more internal, physiological principle of inquiry. "Mentally," it is true, people do begin to recognize rather generally that man's disorder—his periodic drives to war—is a mass condition, that man everywhere is in a confused state and that there is no one who has anything to offer to anyone else in the midst of this social maelstrom of neurosis and antagonism. But what does this mental awareness avail us?

In the speech delivered so recently as October 3, 1946, by Secretary Byrnes while at the Paris Peace Conference, he said:

> I do not believe that any responsible official of any Government wants war. The world has had enough of war. The difficulty is that, while no nation wants war, nations may pursue policies or courses of action which lead to war. Nations may seek political and economic advantages which they cannot obtain without war.[3]

This is all very well as far as it goes, *mentally*. But as far as concerns a remedy for a physiological disorder endogenous to man as a species, it leaves us exactly where we started out. From Mr. Byrnes's statement it is plain that a mood in the interest of unilateral advantage, economic and political, dominates the processes of man in spite of all his mental adroitness and agility. But naturally, Mr. Byrnes does not recognize this mood and hence can offer us no remedy for it and its underlying neuropathology. He would therefore have us go on talking, only more gently, more adroitly, more understandingly—as if gentle, adroit, understanding talk had ever yet reached the seat of a disturbance that is internal and physiological. But of this somatic aspect of man's social conditioning the delegates to our peace conferences can, of course, take no account. And so they cannot reckon with the underside of their enticing mood of diplomatic placation, compromise and conciliation. They cannot reckon with the lurking, the ulterior, the sinister self-advantage that ever incites the 'I'-persona within us all. They cannot take account of the secret alternatives of "good" and "bad," of my gain versus your gain, or the ambivalent rightness inherent in the numen—a numen that the dichotomous Gods of Shinto and Christian, of Jew and gentile can so readily reconcile but that is utterly inconsistent with the organismic principle of balanced function inherent in the nomen, in intrarelational integrity, or in cotention. And so they talk. Man is fiddling while the world burns.

Under the autopathic dictates of our present social system, we *should* be suspicious of Russia, and Russia *should* be suspicious of us. We should resent her crude effronteries and she should resent no less our obsequious appeasements. We should be offended by Russia's very bad manners, but she should be offended by our very good manners. For the mood that underlies our enticing amenities is quite as much a threat to Russia as her crude tactics are to us. No matter what the surface manner or appearance may be, we must all be mutually wary of one another. Parents should be suspicious of their children, children of their parents; husband and wife, sister and brother, close friends, and devoted lovers should be mutually suspicious of one another, because there is in man, there is in all people, the dominance of the 'I'-persona or the secret and ulterior purpose to use everything and everybody to one's own secret advantage. Russia and America could keep hammering at each other's *symptoms* of suspicion and antagonism until doomsday. It would avail them nothing. The suspicion and the antagonism of Russia, as of this country and of all countries and individuals, has to do with a mood, mode or pattern that is internal to nation and individual.

This mood or pattern that is internal can be reached and appreciated only internally. Russia and America will attain a basis of peaceful understanding only when each has reached an understanding of its own mood, its own subversive internal pattern of behavior. The Iron Curtain is not Russia's; it is the 'I'-persona's. Where there is a science of human behavior there can be no longer the concern of one nation with the ideology of another. There will be only the concern of each with their common enemy, with an autopathology that is resident within them both. There will be concern with the internal mood or with the dislocation in physiological pattern that is the actual seat of their mutual conflict. In their common recognition of this impediment to their mutual understanding, there will automatically come about a generic sense of the unity and solidarity of man as a total organism.

In their "separate" autopathologies, the two halves into which our world is now divided can only adhere with reflex obduracy to their "separate" premises. Russia and her kinsfolk see things one way; we and our "good neighbors," another. With one world-faction there is honor without principle; with the other, principle without honor. One has its tongue in its cheek when signing a diplomatic pact; the other, when the time comes to make good on it. In the meantime the two signatories continue to wrangle obsessively over their "ideologies." But despite the distinction, I cannot for the life of me see the difference. For the phylobiologist, it's the same tongue and the same cheek, because it's the same retrofective 'I'-persona. Neither the policy of Russia nor that of America is the expression of an immutable biological norm or nomen.

Today man is threatened with extermination through the instrument of the atomic bomb. One would think that surely this devastating weapon would give us pause. But still man goes on with his mental discussions, his obsessive ratiocinations, with his vain search for causes in the external signs and symptoms of disbehavior presented by the other fellow or nation. Yet who is it that threatens man with this heinous instrument of vengeance? None other than man himself. It is no one but man himself with his dichotomous moods of oppositeness and antagonism who is threatening man with extinction. It is the very individuals who represent at this moment man's mental, man's interrelational reactions and their erratic and irreconcilable ideologies. And what is the remedy man fain would provide? It is the organization of a United Nations, of a World Court composed of these same secretly antagonistic elements. It is the establishment of an international "unit" comprising these same autopathic elements with their same inveterate premise of mutually secret suspicions and distrust. Of such is the structure of the organization that is to fashion a basis for mutual world trust, coöperation and order among us! In the blindness of man's own subjective bias he does not see that he is overwhelmingly in favor of mutual suspicion and antagonism rather than of common understanding and accord. Man does not see that in his own mood of disaffection and oppositeness he *prefers* discord to unity; that, owing to the tyranny of the 'I'-persona, he prefers recourse to the secret construction and ownership of atomic bombs to the open disownership and forthright destruction of his own covertly inimical premise of behavior.

And so, not even so great a crisis as is heralded by the loosing upon man of the atomic bomb has proved sufficient to cause him to relinquish his divisive mental habits of feeling, thinking and doing. He continues to talk and "think" in his idle quest for a way out. But man's talking, his thinking and his doing are expressions of sheer dissociation, and his atomic bomb but a reckless bauble in the hands of a heedless and intemperate youth. It really looks as though it were time for little man to put aside his toys, quit his nursery and call it a day. Undoubtedly, in doing so, he will soon learn that the satisfactions of grown-up folk are quite as pleasurable, quite as entertaining as those of childhood and, incidentally, that his present-day equipment and surroundings are far better fitted to his adult stature.

Disavowing a mental premise based upon secret affect and prejudice, is it not possible for man to realize that the weapon of offense we call the atomic bomb has really arisen within his own organism? Is it not possible for him to realize that the correction of this destructive agent can also arise only within his own organism? But if we are to attain a realizing sense that the cause of man's hostility to man lies within ourselves, it is necessary that we somehow recast completely our subjective habits of feeling and thinking—that we recoil with cold, objective analysis upon our own cherished prepossessions.

Viewed in full perspective, how ridiculous is all our concern over the uranium atom. As a matter of fact, the energy that inheres in this chemical atom possesses enormous constructive value for man. We might as well become excited over man's discovery of fire. Surely the use of this phenomenon for constructive ends has through the ages vastly exceeded its destructive uses. So with the physio-chemical process whereby it became possible to split the atom. What should alone excite us is the circumstance that the mind of man today is the product of a divisive mood—of an antagonistic, destructive mood—and that, in its self-interest and unilateralism, this mood has employed an atomic process to create the widest havoc ever recorded in the history of the world. But the harmful agent is not uranium and the splitting of its atom. It is the mind of man and its split mood; it is man's schizophrenic bent toward world inequality and dissension.

There is very urgent need that man employ all his resources to correct this modal split, this misapplication of the organism's energy due to a rift within its own motivation. The split mind, the divided, segmented mind, can only express itself in division and segmentation. It can only express itself in a mood that reverts with hostility upon itself. It is this mood, this internally twisted mode or pattern of motivation that is man's greatest menace. Yet the energy lying back of this distorted mood may become man's greatest resource when harnessed for constructive ends. Like fire or uranium, it can be turned to benign and efficient uses. This twisted mood, however, can be eradicated only when the internal distortion answerable for it has been internally appreciated as a pathological interpolation, and the primary pattern of man's organism as a whole is permitted to resume its biological sovereignty over the larger brain and senses of man. We may eradicate this mood or pattern only when we have relinquished our habitual efforts to explain it away mentally and, instead, apply ourselves directly to the physiological seat of the lesion.

Through the work of our experimental groups we have long been only too aware that the purely "mental" recognition of our behavior-ineptitudes is unavailing, that the lure of social suggestion, of the organism's partitive conditioning, is untouched by any mental or theoretical "recognition" of it. We have seen that our need will be furthered only through a rigid and persistent technique of experimentation whereby the organism of the individual and the community subjects itself to a stark program of self-examination and adjustment. The conditions that prevailed in our group were exactly the conditions with which people are faced throughout the world today. Our groups and the wider community, being of one biological tissue, are of course at all times socially interconnected and continuous. While our phyloanalytic work consisted in the examination of a relatively limited number of individuals, the individuals studied constituted a cross-section of human society. In the experimental specimen that we were able to examine in our social test tube of human reactions, there was embodied the same behavior that exists in the world at large. After all, the groups that assembled came together from the ranks of the wider community.

In these units of "normality" we found that no amount of partitive thinking and feeling provided a remedy for disorders in human behavior. On the basis of their purely partitive conditioning, of their habitually partitive basis of feeling and thinking, it was apparent that no adequate remedy was to be found. So, too, with our families, our friends and the larger community about us. Like ourselves, the larger world-community must somehow make the transition from such habitual thinking to a definite program or technique of internal investigation. The world of man must wrest itself from a condition of unclear thinking and feeling *in regard to* behavior and adopt a definite orthopedic technique that will automatically reëstablish the organism's direction and control of its behavior-processes, personal and social, national and international.

As the condition of conflict existing in the mind and mood of the participants in the experimental groups was identical with the conflict within the mind and mood of man the world over, our analysis of "normal" and "neurotic" groups has been truly a *phylo*analysis—an analysis of the social mind of man. As with ourselves, so throughout the processes of man, the larger brain and senses of the organism as a whole have been denied their whole, their orthonomic interest and motivation. And so, like ourselves, the community, too, whether it shows its teeth or not, is everywhere mad enough to bite. Like ourselves, the community is under the thrall of the 'I'-persona and thus is everywhere addicted to unwarranted, self-reverting images, to affective compensation in sentimental propitiations and in corresponding irritation and resentment. Like ourselves, it is everywhere oppressed with ditentive, unilateral self-seeking. Everywhere—whether in England, Russia, Argentina, China or the United States—*mental* man is feverishly preoccupied in advancing his sick, obsessive, autopathic "rights."

One may perhaps ask, "Does phylobiology advocate depriving man of his rights?" If we are speaking of basic rights, the answer to this question is an emphatic "No." But one must add that the prerogatives that partitive individuals and communities call their "rights" are not their rights. They are presumptive claims that seriously interfere with the basic, prior rights of man's organism as a whole. Biologically, these lesser, these fugitive rights are not assets; they are liabilities. Through these partitive "rights" man as a species has been deprived of his primary unity—a unity that supersedes in importance all the transient claims, all the assumed prerogatives of every individual and of every group. Where the so-called rights of man entail a breach in the organism's primary function, these rights rest upon division and separation. The integrity of the organism of man, like the organism of other animals, rests on the primary solidarity and coördination of the species. The true rights of man are resident within his own tissues. Through invoking the process of cotention we shall the more surely promote man's basic rights, man's inherent organismic rights, and we shall do so without violence or bloodshed. So gently, so naturally will the inalienable privileges inherent in man's organismic rights be restored to him that they will no longer bear the note of defiance implicit in the term "rights" as now employed by partitive men. Such basic rights will be experienced within man as life and happiness, and there will be no need, no wish for the possessive claims that now represent our unilateral retropathic prerogatives. It has been the attempt of phylobiology to rally man to a recognition, to a deep *internal sense* or *feeling* of the priority of this basic principle or right underlying the unity of his organism, a unity that preserves the function of the brain as a whole above the partitively usurped self-discriminations or mental "rights" of the individual, the clique or other socially supported part-expression of man as advocated by the 'I'-persona. There is no common sense in the absence of common sensation.

This whole business of one's "right," as of one's "rights," cries out for careful investigation. People talk of "equal rights" and claim that in them lies the salvation of mankind. But, as things stand, there is no such thing as "equal rights." The constitution of human society, made up as it is of separate and unilateral 'I'-personæ, precludes all equality of rights. In the sight of the 'I'-persona, the very meaning of "right" is *my* right. It is like *my* God, *my* property. It is a God, a right, a property, which of its nature is *mine,* and hence is better than, greater than, enjoys a special priority over, the alleged rights and Gods and property of others. Again, this fallacious "right" is the emanation of a physiological brain-twist, of the distorted brain-function of the third nervous system underlying man's autopathic 'I'-persona. The words that are expended upon every hand *about* this disorder in man's behavior only aggravate this same disorder. Man's talk, his thinking about himself and about his disorder, is futile. It is the brain and its twist, the distorted affecto-symbolic segment with its ditentive feeling and thinking throughout the phylum man, that calls for an adjustment that is physiological and phylic.

We may recall that the devastating plagues which not so long ago used periodically to sweep the countries of Europe and Asia, taking their toll in millions of lives, did not at any time incite man to adopt scientific measures for coping with these widespread afflictions. Fear does not breed science. On the contrary, the more frequent and widespread these human pestilences, the more loudly man prayed to his fanciful "Gods" for deliverance from them. And neither will the pestilences of war or other mass disturbances in behavior induce the scientific spirit necessary to cope with them. In face of these disorders, man's reaction is identical with his reaction to the plague of wide-sweeping infections. He only talks and prays the louder. On every side he only talks and prays with redoubled fervor. The remedy, the answer to the problem of infectious diseases came only when Pasteur, a physiological chemist laboriously studying the processes of bacterial fermentation, extended the domain of his investigations to the human organism and to the production of disease-processes through bacterial agents. In this recourse the medical investigator for the first time turned from futile appeals to superstition and the numen, and applied himself directly to the principle that governs the process of action and reaction observable in the phenomenal world. Science thus established a biological norm or nomen and hence was able to discriminate structures and functions which showed deviation from this biological norm extending throughout the organs and tissues of the phylum.

So it is with human behavior. The horrors of war, the fears that war incites will never bring about a scientific reckoning with the underlying causes of this behavioral disorder. There is required the slow and painstaking investigation of the elements composing the interrelational structure of the material involved, namely, human society. It will be necessary for the scientists in the field of human behavior first to establish the phyloörganism's biological norm. The student of behavior must apply to the interrelational function of the human brain the same consistent observations he has brought to the function of all other organs and tissues. Having established the physiological nature of cotention or the organism's phylobiological norm of behavior in relation to the environment, he will recognize and bring systematic diagnosis and control to whatever ditentive deviations give indication of an interference with the operation of man's primary, cotentive behavior-pattern. In a word, just as the physiological chemist has employed his symbolic capacity in the process of relating his internal perception to the consistent order of functions and relations existing in the external world, so the phylobiologist will employ the function of his total brain and senses in the perception of the phyloörganism's homeostasis or of man's *intra*relational function, and in the perception of whatever *inter*relational processes deviate from it. With the phylobiologist as with the physiological chemist, dintention and the numen must give way to the phyloörganismic principle inherent in cotention and the nomen.

Instead of yielding to the private prejudice of the part-brain with its abject subordination to false numina through supplication and prayer, the physiological chemist set his whole brain the task of fighting to the finish man's real war, the war between health and disease. To do this he employed the controlled methods of the laboratory of chemistry and physiology. Our recourse cannot be other in the effort to resolve the issue between the health and disease of man's own behavior. Here, too, the battle between the forces of clear unbiased feeling and the blind superstitions of sheer personalism and affect must be fought out in the laboratory of behavior. It is only the laboratory of behavior that may seek without bias to evaluate reactions that are unhealthy as contrasted with those that are healthy, that may recognize processes that are consistent with the organism's phylobiological norm, and processes that deviate from this scientifically established criterion of integration and health. It is a battle between the restricted physiological pattern of dintention and the total physiological pattern of cotention; between the divisive function of the part-brain and the function of the brain and senses of man reacting as a whole; between ecosomatic reactions that are governed by tradition or the numen, and the reaction of the organism as a whole to its central constant or nomen.

Nothing, therefore, is so important to man as the welding of his central and peripheral patterns of motivation, as the union between the organism's internal and its external nomen. Nothing is so important as the correlation between man's internal world of reactions and the consistent reactions that form the world of man's external environment—between man's intra-relational behavior and the extra-relational phenomena existing in the world about him. In the absence of this balance between internal and external environments, there is a behavioral hiatus in the processes of man that cannot be bridged. Even the powerful and sustaining instinct uniting man and woman in the relationship of sex is not possible of adequate fulfilment in the absence of the consistent union between man and his environment. If the individual is not basically one with the cotentive organism of mankind, he cannot be conjugally one with the cotentive organism of woman. There can be only the system of partitive mutualities I have called *the conjugal neurosis*.

We are brought back to the thesis with which this report set out. There is urgently demanded in the sphere of man's *feeling* the same scientific spirit that exists in the sphere of man's *thought*. Man is in no less need of a consistent internal constant than of a consistent external constant. Just as in the sphere of thought science demands faithful adherence to the consistent law or nomen operating within the surrounding environment, so in the sphere of feeling there is equally demanded man's faithful adherence to the law or nomen internal to the organism. In the sphere of scientific thought man has recognized that to think clearly it is necessary that the function of the brain and senses conform to a universal and consistent norm. This consistency of function in relation to the outer world is the foundation of science. The science of biology demands the operation of this principle in the study of the tissues and organs objectively observable both in plants and in animals, including man, and reckons as pathological any deviation from this biological norm. But man has yet to apply the law of consistent action and reaction to the behavior of his own brain as it functions in relation to other brains. Man has yet to recognize an internal constant in respect to his own behavior that is comparable to the external constant he posits in respect to the behavior of phenomena existing outside him. The recognition of subjective disorders occurring in man's relation to man yet awaits the adoption of scientific criteria that are as rigid and dependable as the criteria governing other observable processes.

From what has been said it will be evident that the frustration and impasse—economic, religious, social—that exists among peoples today is not basically political, nor is it due to the manipulations of the few political leaders who, in their lack of acquaintance with the basic causations of behavior, are attempting to adjust the lives of the abject millions who constitute their followers. These superficial manifestations are again mental. They are but epiphenomena. Beneath them all there are indications that man will awaken to a deeper self-awareness phylobiologically and that in coming to himself he will experience the throes of new adjustments that will necessarily entail the defeat of the old. The problem of man's behavior, let it be repeated, is neither political, religious nor psychiatric. It is a problem in the internal physiology of man's organism as a phylum as this internal physiology relates man organismically to the reciprocal processes of his environment.

Prompted by their mental interpretations, certain sociologists are for ever shouting for the common man. And by the common man they mean a special class of people who go about in overalls. This sort of thinking is misleading. It tends to incite dissension rather than alleviate it. The phylobiologist does not admit any such allocation as a special common man or group of common men. We are all common men—as common as sky or soil or sea—the sociologists, myself, John Smith and George VI. To take any other view is to create an issue, not remove it. The advocates of a special class or any other form of separatism, would do well to ponder the thesis of an essentially one world composed of men who are essentially one and common. But we shall not achieve one world until *as one world,* as one intrarelational unit phylically continuous and indivisible, we have faced in ourselves the partitive disorder that everywhere thwarts the attainment of it. We shall not attain one world until we have recognized the impediments to unity which as separate 'I'-personæ each of us embodies within the illusory world of his separate self.

Under the jurisdiction, then, of the 'I'-persona, there exists among the interrelated units composing the phyloörganism of man only partition and division of function. Union is never union of the whole but always of some part-function or party—political, religious, national, industrial or what not. Where there is unionization within such part-functioning units or parties—a coalition of nations, the unionization of labor organizations—it is a part-union, the union of a class or party which, far from promoting the solidarity of the species as a whole, only further contributes to distinctions of class, place or opportunity. What is required within the processes of man as a species is a union based upon clear thought and feeling, a union based upon agreements that are determined by the nomen rather than by the numen, by the organism's consistent conformity to the orderly processes existing within and about it. A union based upon consistently clear thought and feeling will necessarily be organized in the interest of mankind at large.

Were it not for socialism, communism, Fascism, democracy as mere part-expressions; were it not for such part-expressions as Catholicism, Protestantism, as democrat and republican; were it not for the partitive manisfestation represented in labor and industry, Jew and gentile, aristocrat and proletarian, negro and white, and a thousand other mass dichotomies based upon man's autopathic ideologies, it would be seen—*it would be felt* that this is a very delightful world, that man's capacity for health and joy, for science and art, for creativeness and play are natural endowments of man that are limitless in scope and in their opportunities for fulfilment. In a world thus divested of the 'I'-persona, there would be no need to set up autocratic Gods especially outfitted to take care of the special interests of *me*! There would be the reality of organismic man and his intrarelational sovereignty as an integrated phylum. One's interrelational health and happiness would consist in functioning freely over the widest possible range and in the completest coöperation with one's kind.

Instead, we have today a moral or ditentive proscription against every conceivable human or interrelational situation. In the clinical reckoning of phylopathology the law represents a frank compulsion neurosis. Similar evidence of man's social pathology is to be found among our religious archives. "Forgive us our trespasses as we forgive those who trespass against us" is a typical plea of normality, as is the remorseful lamentation of the satiated penitent: "We have left undone those things which we ought to have done; and we have done those things which we ought not to have done; and there is no health in us." Here again we are witness to the autopathic plague of man's "good-bad" dichotomy. And we may not overlook the interrelational dichotomy *par excellence* expressed in the familiar motto: "Do unto others as ye would have them do unto you." Of course, in its cynical, autopathic mood the 'I'-persona makes ready quarry of the mutually retropathic covenant latent in the "golden rule." This is the antithesis that forms the impasse to our international peace parleys, to the deliberations of the United Nations Organization. England wants *her* "rights," America *hers*, Russia *hers*, Bulgaria *hers*. So with Italy, Yugoslavia, Greece. Under this dichotomous compulsion, the deliberations of these nations constitute a mere verbal challenge of verbal ideologies. Says England: "Russia is seeking to dominate the world through communist propaganda"; says Russia: "The United States is trying to enslave us and our border nations with capitalistic dollars"; says the United States: "We shall henceforth refrain from conceding loans to people who feel that our loans enslave them"; says Yugoslavia: "Trieste belongs to *me*"; says Italy: "Trieste belongs to *me*." Such goings on!

If in the midst of these behavior-inconsistencies, if in the midst of such "normal" vagaries of mood, there were here and there in the world the individual who realized what a dolt he is in subscribing to such a system of interrelations, there would be the beginning of a better world. Instead of accepting human conflict and pain with our usual futile complaints or noble "long-suffering," and howling for more, we would take heart in the forthright recognition of our pain and observe in it the implications of a world-wide disturbance in our interrelational values. We would recognize a physiological conflict in internal patterns of tension and, consistent with methods of systematic diagnosis and control elsewhere employed in medicine, we would apply the suitable remedy for this disorder. We would see that our mental imprecations upon our behavioral pains are but a plea for the alleviation of mere outer symptoms, and that if our symptoms were once clearly apprehended through the technique of phyloanalysis, these very pains would provide the cue to the physiological disturbance underlying them.

The psychiatrist is ever clamoring for examples, for case histories from the records of phylopathology. Examples? Case histories? Do we really need examples? In this day—after a first world-war and now after a second world-war that was unquestionably global—do we really need the close-to-home example? Are we not ourselves a sufficient example, a sufficiently clear-cut case history? Surely it is evident by now that owing to the interpolation of the 'I'-persona all men are opposed to one another; that as things now stand in this partitive world, every individual is a devout and conscientious hindrance to every other individual; that, after thousands of years of philosophical and religious teachings, man is, as a species, still a prey to differential reflexes that inevitably provoke conflict and war. To posit a psychopathology of the individual apart from the community or phylum is analogous to positing a pathology of individual tissues and organs that denies their phylogenetic import. Psychiatry will not have become a science until we have attained a phylopsychiatry—a phylopathology.

What we call civilization, with its dichotomous basis of good and bad, right and wrong, peace and war, begins with the 'I'-persona and ends with 'I'-persona. The 'I'-persona is the origin and end of civilization's logic, philosophy, religion and similar products of its mental gymnastics. Because as a race or people we are shot through with distorted affects and prejudices there is indeed no health in us. Yet there is no need to be despondent about the world of man's making; we cannot be. All despondency, all depression is again concern for oneself, for one's own partitive interest. Where there is intrarelational solidarity or cotention there can be no depression, no obsessive self-interest, no concern about *me*. There will be only a wholehearted interest in reaching the internal world of man's distorted feeling, and sensing the causal relation of this internal cosmogony to the external world of man's distorted behavior.

No; fear, threat, noble aspiration, the contrite heart—none of these things can aid us. In man's world-wide plight there is only one recourse. That recourse is the scientific curiosity to *know*, to *understand*. It is the scientist's relentless urge to understand phenomena with his whole brain. In the strength of this urge as it relates to the field of man's own behavior we will ask the right question and we will stick to it. We won't bother with the answer. Everybody has the answers. The world is full of them. As research students we'll ask ourselves and we'll keep asking ourselves, what is this pattern of cotention that automatically arrests affect-images and sets at naught the acquisitive claims of an autopathic 'I'-persona? And we'll hold to this question so consistently, so persistently, that the answer will come quite simply in the realization of a healthier motivation in human life. For the answer, as is the case with all research, will be inherent in the question—in the search itself. We might as well face it: The individual neurosis—yours, Reader, and mine—is incurable. Nothing can reach the cause of the individual's disordered adaptation. The cause is phylic. Only this phylic neurosis, only the neurosis of man can be cured, and it can be cured only through scientific research. In that research and in the discovery of the physiological cause of man's phyloneurosis, the individual neurosis will be reached and remedied.

To this end there is required throughout the world the establishment of groups of behavior-students bent upon a strictly physiological technique of behavior-adjustment. Out of the work of such groups will grow a science, a recognized world authority in human behavior. Like the cancer experts, such groups will be interested in healing disorders throughout the organism of man. They will not be interested in modifying the behavior of a particular person, clique, political party or country. They will know that the healing of the phylosoma will alone bring healing to the ontosoma. In applying the function of their whole brain and senses to the larger problem of human behavior, they will embody a world confederacy of cotention or of common feeling and thinking. From this common organismic background they will welcome in common the recognition of whatever ditentive or deviate reactions, whether occurring in themselves or others, tend to obstruct the unified function of the whole—of man as a total phylic organism. Those whose interest lies in phylobiology will represent an altered state of mind among all nations—not a geographical state, not a political state but a fundamentally altered state of mind, because this altered state of mind will be based upon an altered mood, mode or internal pattern of feeling and motivation. It will be the fearless thesis of these students that a democracy which is not physiological is a spurious democracy; that a program of socialism or communism that is not biological is but an empty *symbo*l of a common will in a common world; and they will see that this symbol can only defeat the larger process it would promote. From this cotentive premise they will make clear to the world that their feeling and motivation rests upon full scientific authority, upon a principle of organismic balance and solidarity. They will not truckle to the partitive machinations of political demagogues. The position of these investigators will be: "We are one people, one world, one organism. We will not fight your wars, we will not go to your election polls, we will not take part in political and social conflicts. We will have no patriotism in the narrow, partitive sense of the word. But in all that pertains to man, you can count on us. And you can count on us not to violate any of your laws except as your laws violate the principle of man's biological solidarity as a species."

Granting the possibility that the bionomic thesis which has emerged from our researches becomes accepted by a few people here and there throughout the world, one can readily predict an increased social eagerness to recognize and set aside diseased behavioral processes that are now responsible for the universal phenomenon of human conflict. In this eventuality there would automatically come to pass the universal acceptance of the internal principle of species solidarity as the one basic law governing the behavior of organismic man. While in the small group comprising The Lifwynn Laboratory there are today only the first stirrings of an awareness of this internal constant—of this central principle of behavior and its conscious correlation with the processes inherent in the world of external phenomena—even these first faint inklings give evidence of its overmastering power, its irresistible sovereignty over man's motivation and behavior as an organism. Indeed, as I have earlier indicated, the mere concept of this force resident within man carries with it an unprecedented weight of authority in respect to man's relation to man and to the surrounding world of actuality. How much more significant the day when mankind sets aside mere dreams of unification and accepts the actuality of its native and basic principle of species solidarity.

Under the clarifying influence of a general recognition that the problems of man's behavior are basically physiological and phylic problems, there will be quite spontaneously a world-wide resurgence of those basic cotentive values and capacities that make for organismic communication and production. In the field of education as an intrarelational activity, there will not be between nations the interrelational overtures now expressed in the mere mincing exchange of a handful of university professors. There will be the hearty exchange of youthful scholars—liberal thousands of them—from every country to every other country, and not merely advanced college students but also teen-age boys and girls. This cotentive contact of young minds with other minds the world over would be the beginning of a new world Government—of the only true governing unit that could possibly represent the clear organismic thinking and feeling of all the people for all the people of the world as a phylic whole. Only then will we recognize that it is governments that are the chief obstacle to government; that it is the artificial supremacy we now give to the part-function of man's brain that precludes the operation of man's orderly brain-function as a whole. Today governments are going to pieces on every hand. Governments will continue to go to pieces until they have recognized that they are subjugated to the 'I'-persona or the third brain, that their policies are subjective, not objective, that they are animated solely by self-interest and prejudice, that they lack an inclusive or total basis of motivation and aim.

True government embodies a total autonomic process. In the absence of total, autonomic government, there is no government. There is only tyranny—tyranny over oneself as well as over others due to the domination of man by the third brain. Partitive governments must at last give way to total government. Only then will we have begun to banish from the face of the earth the discriminations and prejudices that rest upon mere superficial differences—differences of color, creed and of merely conditioned habits of adaptation. Then only will the real likenesses, the truly common or organismic identities among human beings begin to be felt—identities of structure and function based upon common neural and muscular systems, common biological needs, organismically common and indivisible reactions to a common and indivisible environment. In some such world-wide confederacy, our cruel barriers—ethnological, political and religious—will be wiped away. The life of man will be motivated and governed by a broad organismic economy,[4] and the narrow incitements of political self-interest and unilateralism will no longer have a place in the sun.

In its phylic reorientation the mind of man will be capable of compassing a far broader outlook, of bringing a wholly altered frame of reference to bear upon the many problems of his behavior—personal, civic and international. In accordance with phylobiological principles we will not shrink from seeing that the social behavior that is called "normal" is measured by purely ditentive standards and that this social norm bears no relation to the biological norm of behavior embodied in the organism's cotentive standards of conduct.[5] We shall not hesitate to concede the biological alignment between the ditentive plane of man's reactions and man's neurosis, between habits of affective thinking and crime.[6] We shall not fear to recognize that the disordered behavior expressed by either the criminal or the neurotic represents a type of reaction that is autopathic and that issues unavoidably out of the interrelational standards of so-called "normal" communities. We shall not fear to see that the recurrent incidence of war is the inevitable complement of the purely numinal charades we know as peace. We shall see without flinching that the type of religion or devotion that is descended from early anthropomorphic traditions is from the outset numinally bonded, that in its ditentive origin this type of thinking and feeling and doing is necessarily irreconcilable with a science of human behavior.[7] Correspondingly, we shall see that science is man's impartial fidelity to organismic law or to the nomen, and that in its rejection of autopathic, self-interested habits of thinking, science embodies man's highest expression of organismic balance or devotion.[8]

While medical and other objective investigations have gone forward by leaps and bounds, the objective observation by man of his own subjective pathology—the scientific study of a radical deviation in the organismic behavior of man himself—still awaits the recognition and participation of the larger community of scientists involved in it. In the work of our small group of investigators, the attempt has been made to bring to controlled laboratory inquiry this all-too-neglected problem of man's unwitting interference with the function of his own organism in its community or species solidarity. We have attempted to bring to objective inquiry the unconscious mechanism of the numen as this social mechanism is observable in the phyloanalysis of social groups.

This investigation requires man's recognition within himself that he has substituted a purely affecto-symbolic nexus of interrelations for his intrarelational integrity of function as a species. It requires our recognition that the insubstantial stuff of human relations is but this cherished numen of man, and that this dislocation in man's mental adaptation imposes a relentless servitude upon the free processes of us all. Only the dominance of this autopathic numen can account for the phylically bizarre and inconsistent situation in which conflict and destructiveness have superseded the integrative forces of unity and coöperation throughout the race of man.[9]

We cannot blink the fact that with the threat that some nation may without warning loose upon other nations the most violent instrument of destruction yet invented or conceived by man, the world still is virtually in a state of war today. There are still the reverberations of man's so-called second World War in the political disagreements existing among the great powers and among the small, in the widespread civil war in China, in the bitter conflict in Palestine, not to mention the internal dissension that divides practically every nation and that may be witnessed in our own country in the ceaseless conflicts between management and labor, and momentarily in our recurrent industrial strikes.

In Chapter VII, I cited many instances of man's projective ingenuity as he applies his symbolic faculty to the external object or situation before him. But none of these extraordinary applications of the brain of man to fields of inquiry outside of himself has in any way promoted man's clearer knowledge of his own behavior. None of these scientific procedures has contributed in the least toward creating a laboratory of inquiry into processes that activate man's own organism. Not only have these inquiries failed to contribute anything to man's basic acquaintance with himself and with the laws of his own organism, but their effect has been precisely to lead his mind away from the study of his own processes.

It is not so much, then, the atomic bomb we need fear as the absence of organismic articulation among us as a species. In view of the indications of a lack of understanding and articulation throughout men's interrelational processes, we need far more to fear man's complete mental breakdown as a species than the many external symptoms of conflict and disharmony of which we make so much ado. Man needs to fear the increasingly lawless assertion of his own distorted mood and the danger it presages of just such a condition of social disarticulation and anarchy as is prefigured in the dream of Dostoevsky's hero. We need to fear the indications throughout the world that man, as a species, is losing his grip and that as a result he is headed toward a condition of social bedlam that is world-wide. The adjustment of this autopathic mood with its interception of man's conscious coördination as a species is the job and the only job of behavioral medicine.

When we consider the widespread presence in man of the troubled spirit, we may gather some idea of the task that confronts the inquiring mind of man. For it is truly extraordinary what affliction of body and mind man will undergo—what contradiction in motive and action, what untiring yet fruitless labor in the interest of personal appearance or distinction; what poverty, what burdensome riches, what meanness, ignorance, false pride and equally false humility; what pain and turmoil, what emotional conflicts of every kind man will undergo rather than yield himself to the internal inquiry necessary to the restoration of his balanced motivation. From generation to generation we endure disease, oppression, insanity and crime. We suffer the agonizing tortures of unbridled warfare with its destruction of human life and property, the permanent crippling of our youth and the ruthless arrest of our cultural processes; and in the interest of these disordered achievements man is ever at meticulous pains to invent and construct the most acutely violent and fabulous of death-dealing instruments.

But where it is a question of recognizing the stupidity and the prodigality of his own affects—where it is a question of looking into those internal reactions that have caused disturbance in his behavior as it interrelates him to his fellows and to their common environment, man is obdurate. Fearing to lose the supremacy of our precious 'I'-persona, we flatly reject whatever ministrations might further the needed objective approach. We do not see that the view which recognizes the organismic basis of man's behavior in no way belittles the power and authority of human individuality. We do not see that in this organismic outlook individuality is greatly strengthened and ennobled. Nor do we see that notwithstanding the precedent of established normal traditions, the momentary importance of this or that discrete little man as he partitively disports himself under the custody of a socially self-concious 'I'-persona is in no way comparable in significance to the total unity and indivisibility of the individual as a phylically conscious organism.

Today there is inescapable evidence that all is not well with man. There is inescapable evidence of a disturbed adaptation in man that is as deep-seated as it is widespread. As yet, though, man has not begun to suspect the presence within him of neurodynamic modifications of which the social manifestations daily enacted by him are but the external index. In a sense we all know the symptoms. In a sense we know that in our social deviations we *are* the symptoms. We know that we ourselves embody them in the phylopathology of the 'I'-persona with its social imbalances of mood, its disordered sex-interests, its autocracy and arrogance, its commercial graft, economic rackets, secret diplomacies, political intrigues; its inequalities of opportunity, its extremes of poverty as of wealth; its moralities and immoralities, its futile recourse to the palliatives of drugs and alcoholism, its neuroses and psychoses, its crimes and its wars. All this we know, and we know that because of these phrenetic behavior-extravagances there are no bounds to man's expendability in human life and property. In a sense we know too that our many remedies are of no avail, that we have tried them for thousands of years, and all to no purpose. We even know that a global war is pathognomonic of a global neurosis. At heart we know that as things stand, there will be no cessation of war, that only the outer form of it will change; that basically, this vast dichotomy in human behavior will not alter so long as man adheres to his present level of adaptation. Deep within us we know that despite all our ideological pretexts, political and economic, man has not yet dimly suspected the essential cause of this conflict and carnage. In our hearts we know that in the present trend of man's thinking and feeling, in the obsessive extravagance of his sick social mood, man must continue to employ the old decoys from generation to generation without the least abatement of his disordered motivation. In reality, we know that man is today no nearer a sane, scientific solution of his insane dichotomies and contradictions than at any time in human history.

All this in a way we know. We know it; but fearing to know, we have not yet put our knowledge to the test of systematic diagnosis and control. For, all that we know of human behavior we know only with the part-brain—with the half-knowing of the symbolic segment that forever leaves intact and unchallenged the artifactual affects and prejudices of the 'I'-persona.[10] We have yet to see that the hoped-for realization of a global condominium of nations and of peoples is but the symbolic projection of the partitive brain of man. We have yet to see that such a guild of commonwealths must await the restoration of man's neural integrity of motivation, that it must await the basic integration of feeling and interest that is internal to man's own organism. For, notwithstanding all that we know, we do not yet know that our global wars, like our global neuroses, are of our own autopathic making. We do not know that the interrelational life of man is completely unstabilized, that it is without biological foundation because of the root of division that underlies the system of motivations now governing the behavior of social man.

We will attain a pattern of social coöperation and harmony among individuals and nations only when we have recognized the functional disturbance within the third nervous system, and have accepted the cotentive pattern of internal balance and coördination within the organism of man as a species. As matters stand today in this world of dichotomy and conflict, the war we have just fought will have been fought in vain. It will have been no less vain than the many political, economic and religious wars that have preceded it. Vain, too, will be the unilateral program of peace that must necessarily issue out of it. Vain all our international covenants, all our diplomatic treaties. For all the peace programs yet to be devised must remain for ever unavailing if our behavior-dichotomies and antagonisms are ultimately traceable to a functional brain-twist resident within the organism of man himself.

The problem of man's behavior is not a problem of politics, of economics or of morals based upon personal "rightness" with its mutable and arbitrary evaluations. It is a problem internal to man. The neurosis of man is a problem of man's self that man must take upon himself. It is the problem of man's organism as a species. The time has come for man to face the unilateral system of behavior that is of his own unilateral making—the system that man alone embodies among all animal species. The moment is at hand for us to take conscious hold of our own unconscious processes by recognizing the false cerebral plane upon which they rest. Only in this way may we accept the fundamental issues at stake and apply ourselves to the study of our own reactions, or to the science of human behavior. Only on this scientific basis will man envisage the intrinsic factors that underlie his interrelational disorganization.

NOTES

[1] See pages 245-47.

[2] *Life and Letters of Thomas Henry Huxley,* New York, D. Appleton & Co., 1902, Vol. II, p. 319.

[3] *The New York Times,* October 4, 1946.

[4] οἶκος = environment, νόμος = law.

[5] Burrow, Trigant, "Preliminary Report of Electroencephalographic Recordings in Relation to Behavior Modifications," *The Journal of Psychology,* 1943, Vol. 15, pp. 109-14.

Burrow, Trigant, and Galt, William E., "Electroencephalographic Recordings of Varying Aspects of Attention in Relation to Behavior Disorders," *The Journal of General Psychology,* 1945, Vol. 32, pp. 269-88.

[6] Crime is derived from Latin, *cernere,* to think, Gr. κρίνειν. Cf. canny, *can,* n., Scot. knowledge, and also cunning, keen and ken, from the Anglo-Saxon *cunnan,* to know (German, *kennen*).

[7] Religion = Latin, *religare,* to bind or hold back.

[8] Devotion = Latin *de,* away from, and *votum,* the wish.

[9] See note 12, page 199.

[10] See note 5, page 455.

APPENDIX*

The following pages dealing with instrumental measures under conditions of ditention and cotention give in detail the experimental procedures followed, and the results obtained in respect to three major physiological systems of the organism—the respiratory, oculomotor and cerebral spheres of reaction.

Respiratory Changes[1]

I shall first describe the modifications in the respiratory function that accompanied the shift from the ditentive to the cotentive pattern of behavior. This reaction is first in order of description because it was first in order of experimentation. We selected this system for study for several reasons: (1) It is the organic reaction-system that is most plainly observable; (2) this system readily permits of instrumental recording; (3) the respiratory function plays an important rôle in mediating man's interchange through speech, or through his socio-symbolic system; (4) respiratory changes are an unfailing accompaniment of affecto-symbolic disorders, both "normal" and neurotic (consider the respiratory disturbances displayed in the psychoneuroses); and (5) the respiratory system is innervated by fibres from both the cerebro-spinal and the sympathetic or autonomic centers, and hence serves a dual function in mediating between the organism and the environment.

The slowed respiratory rhythm that I observed in myself in periods of cotention was amply corroborated by my assistants who, in addition to making observations upon themselves, made careful note of the respiratory alterations observable in each other during cotention. Naturally the observation of this unexpected phenomenon led to our interest in undertaking the more precise study of this reaction as well as to the hope of discovering in ourselves other physiological modifications that might lend themselves to instrumental recording.

Several series of experiments were conducted on the relationship of the respiratory function to the two attentional modes.[2] The first

* I wish to express to Dr. Hans Syz and to Dr. William E. Galt my grateful appreciation for their invaluable aid in the many technical problems connected with our instrumental experimentation, as well as for their assistance in assembling and organizing the material of the present chapter. Acknowledgment is also due to Dr. Charles B. Thompson for his helpful part in working up the data on eye-movements obtained with the "Scanacord," and for assisting in securing certain of the respiratory records.

series of respiratory records was taken in 1937 at the summer research station of The Lifwynn Foundation. In this series and in a later extension of it, the instrument used for recording the respiratory curves was the wax-paper kymograph constructed by Volkmann and Gerbrands at the Harvard Psychological Laboratory, the apparatus having been specially adapted to our purposes. This instrument is electrically driven and permits the taking of continuous records over a period of several hours. Tracings were obtained of the thoracic and of the abdominal respiration by means of rubber-tube pneumographs, and of the carotid pulse by means of a Lombard tambour. The time was registered on the record in intervals of five seconds and there were two signal-markers, one for the subject and one for the experimenter.

Sixteen individuals, eight males and eight females, ranging in age from 17 to 63 years, served as subjects in the first group of experiments. The experimental periods varied from thirty minutes to two hours. With a few individuals the experiments were repeated many times and with several experimental variations, whereas the records of other subjects served chiefly for determining the average conformation of the respiratory curves.

In seven subjects the reaction I have described as cotention was specially investigated. The data are presented for those three subjects on whom most numerous records were obtained. The combined data for the three subjects include respiratory curves for 103 minutes of cotention (56 periods varying from one to ten minutes), and these were compared with 106 one-minute samples of the subjects' respiration during ditention.[3] The most consistent and marked alteration was a decrease in the average respiratory rate of the three subjects which dropped from an average of 13.2 movements per minute in ditention to an average of 4.6 movements per minute for these same three subjects in the cotentive periods. With none of the three subjects was there an overlapping of the respiratory rate in ditention and cotention. The averages and ranges for the three subjects are presented in Table I. An increase in the thoracic and abdominal amplitude of the respiratory movements accompanied the decrease of rate in cotention, but this increase in amplitude was not proportionate in degree or quite so consistent as the decrease in frequency. A graph of respiratory and pulse curves in ditention and in cotention is presented in Fig. 1. In one subject the inspiration-expiration ratio was markedly decreased, that is, the expiration was disproportionately prolonged; but this marked change did not appear so definitely in other subjects. Incidentally, the pulse rate did not show any changes that were statistically reliable.

It should be noted that these respiratory alterations set in immediately with the alteration of the attentional pattern. They occurred automatically and were not brought about by voluntary control or conscious effort. Control experiments showed that the respiratory changes, as they occur in cotention, do not show any similarity to the slight modifications in respiration observed in sleep and sleepiness, in mental effort, emotional excitement, or under conditions in which the subject focuses upon external objects or upon bodily tensions in regions other than those of the symbolic segment. It was interesting that in control periods immediately following cotention there was

TABLE I

AVERAGE FREQUENCY AND RANGE OF RESPIRATORY RATE IN DITENTION AND IN COTENTION

Subject	Ditention.			Cotention.		
	N.	Average Frequency.	Range.	N.	Average Frequency.	Range.
A	33	14·61	11–24	51	3·73	2·5–5·7
B	40	11·26	8·1–14	30	4·22	2·7–6·7
C	33	13·80	12–16·6	22	5·95	4·8–7·0
Average (3 subjects)	106	13·22		103	4·63	

FIG. 1**.—Typical Respiratory and Pulse Curves during Successive Periods of Ditention and Cotention.

Th: thoracic respiration
P: carotid pulse
A: abdominal respiration

Inspiration is recorded on the down-stroke, expiration on the up-stroke.

** Certain of the graphs included here have appeared in articles previously published in the following journals: *Psychosomatic Medicine*, *The Journal of Psychology* and *The Journal of General Psychology*.

no compensatory acceleration in the breathing rate above the normal level. On the other hand, when subjects were instructed to retard consciously the frequency of respiration, there was invariably a compensatory acceleration in respiratory rate in subsequent control periods.

In a second series of experiments on the same three subjects, respiratory measurements were taken with the Jones basal metabolism apparatus. These observations were made under the direction of Dr. Henry B. Turner in the medical laboratory of the Guardian Life Insurance Company, New York. The procedure adopted was that ordinarily employed in basal metabolism tests. With this method dependable spirometric curves were obtained. All tests were made in the early morning before the subjects had had any food. The subjects rested in a supine position for one half hour, before each test. We shall first present only those results which may serve as a control and amplification of the experimental series on respiration just reported. The findings on basal metabolism will be reported in subsequent pages.

A glance at Table II will show that in these experiments the trend is similar to that shown in the earlier series.[4] For all three subjects the frequency of respiration was markedly lower in cotention than in ditention. By combining the data for the three subjects, we compared 239 minutes of cotention in 56 periods, ranging from two to five minutes each, with 249 minutes of ditention comprising 64 periods of three and four minutes each. The respiratory rate dropped from an average of 9.7 movements per minute for the three subjects in ditention to an average of 2.6 in the cotentive periods. Again there was no overlapping for any one of the three subjects in the distribution of the respiratory rates in ditention and cotention. There can be no question, therefore, as to the validity of the difference in rate under the two conditions.

The records obtained from the basal metabolism apparatus made it possible to secure additional respiratory data, namely, the *minute-volume* of air inspired, the *tidal air,* and the *oxygen-utilization* of the subjects. The *minute-volume* was calculated by measuring the individual inspiratory strokes through a specified portion of the experimental periods and adding the figures obtained. As it is known what amount of air-volume a specified length of amplitude represents, the minute-volume may be directly calculated from the basal metabolism charts. This procedure is laborious but it is more exact than merely determining the mean respiratory amplitude and multiplying it by the respiratory rate. It will be seen from Table II that in all three subjects the minute-volume in cotention was markedly less than in ditention. If we pool the results we find that the average minute-volume of air inspired by the three subjects dropped from 6.95 litres in ditention to 4.08 litres in cotention. As there was no overlapping in the distribution of minute-volumes during cotention and ditention for any of the three subjects, again there can be no question as to the validity of the difference in minute-volumes under the two experimental conditions.

TABLE II

AVERAGE FREQUENCY OF RESPIRATORY RATE, MINUTE-VOLUME OF INSPIRED AIR, AND TIDAL AIR IN DITENTION AND IN COTENTION

Subject.	Ditention.			Cotention.		
	N.	Average Frequency.	Range.	N.	Average Frequency.	Range.
A	61	9·42	7·7–11	48	1·72	1·3–2·3
B	97	10·76	9·3–13·1	98	3·00	2·1–4·4
C	91	9·03	6·8–11	93	3·20	2·8–3·9
Average (3 subjects)	249	9·74		239	2·64	

Subject.	N.	Average Minute-Vol.	Range.	N.	Average Minute-Vol.	Range.
A	61	5·08 litres	4·3–6·4	48	3·27 litres	2·5–3·9
B	97	8·64 ,,	6·2–12·1	98	4·44 ,,	3·2–5·4
C	91	7·15 ,,	5·8–8·3	93	4·53 ,,	3·9–5·6
Average (3 subjects)	249	6·95 ,,		239	4·08 ,,	

Subject.	N.	Average Tidal Air.	N.	Average Tidal Air.
A	61	0·53 litre	48	1·90 litres
B	97	0·80 ,,	98	1·48 ,,
C	91	0·79 ,,	93	1·41 ,,
Average (3 subjects)	249	0·71 ,,	239	1·60 ,,

These values may also be expressed in terms of *tidal air*. Although the drop in minute-volume is definite and consistent in each of the three subjects, it is not so great as is the case in regard to frequency of respiration. In other words, the amount of air-intake per inspiration was greater in cotention than in ditention. This measure of the tidal air is calculated by dividing the minute-volume by the respiratory rate. The average tidal air for the three subjects was 0.71 litre in ditention and 1.59 litres in cotention. This corroborates the finding, made by direct observation as well as by the kymograph and by the metabolism apparatus, that the respiratory movements are deeper in cotention than in ditention. On the other hand, as just mentioned, the total air inspired per minute in cotention does not equal the total amount of air inspired per minute in ditention.

The oxygen absorbed per minute, when averaged for the three subjects (Table III), was the same in ditention and in cotention, namely, 0.22 litre. From these data we can calculate the *oxygen-utilization*, that is, the relation of the oxygen absorbed to the total volume of air respired per minute. We realize, of course, that it was not pure oxygen but an air-mixture of high oxygen content which the subjects breathed and which is to be compared with the oxygen actually absorbed. The percentage is obtained by dividing the oxygen absorbed per minute by the minute-volume of air. As would be expected on the basis of the values already given, the results show that the average percentage of oxygen utilized by the three subjects was markedly higher in cotention than in ditention, namely, 5.4 per cent. as compared with 3.3 per cent. This means that although a smaller volume of air is breathed per minute in cotention, a larger part of the available oxygen is utilized than in ditention. The average amount of oxygen actually absorbed during the ditentive and cotentive reactions is, however, about the same.

TABLE III

AVERAGE OXYGEN ABSORBED PER MINUTE AND PERCENTAGE OF OXYGEN-UTILIZATION IN DITENTION AND IN COTENTION

Subject.	Ditention.			Cotention.		
	N.	Average Oxygen Absorption.	Oxygen-Utilization.	N.	Average Oxygen Absorption.	Oxygen-Utilization.
A	61	0.19 litre	3.7%	48	0.21 litre	6.4%
B	97	0.24 ,,	2.8%	98	0.22 ,,	5.0%
C	91	0.24 ,,	3.3%	93	0.22 ,,	4.9%
Average (3 subjects)	249	0.22 ,,	3.3%	239	0.22 ,,	5.4%

Regarding *basal metabolism*, the following number of readings during ditention and cotention were secured on the same three subjects: Subject A—ditention 16, cotention 12; subject B—ditention 26, cotention 21; subject C—ditention 24, cotention 20. The periods for both ditention and cotention averaged four minutes. A comparison of the records of each subject during ditention and cotention indicated a consistent trend of the metabolic rate for each of the subjects, but the trend was not the same for all subjects. In subject A, the basal metabolic rate in cotention was reliably higher than the rate in ditention. In shifting from a period of ditention to a period of cotention the basal metabolic rate always increased, while in shifting from cotention to ditention the basal metabolism always decreased. This fact shows clearly that the changes could not have been caused by the sequence of the experimental periods. The average change in metabolic rate in passing from ditention to cotention was+12; the average change in shifting from cotention to ditention was—13.

In subjects B and C, on the other hand, the basal metabolic rate tended to be consistently lower in cotention than in ditention. In shifting from a period of ditention to a period of cotention the basal metabolism of these two subjects decreased in almost every instance (29 out of 31), and in shifting from a period of cotention to one of ditention, the basal metabolic rate increased in 15 out of 23 shifts. The average change in metabolic rate in shifting from ditention to cotention was—8.6 for subject B and—15.5 for subject C; the average change in shifting from cotention to ditention was + 3.6 for subject B and+8.3 for subject C. The averages and ranges of the metabolic rates for the three subjects in ditention and in cotention are presented in Table IV. It is evident, then, that the change in physiological orien-

TABLE IV

AVERAGE AND RANGE OF METABOLIC RATES
IN DITENTION AND IN COTENTION

Subject.	Ditention.			Cotention.		
	N.	Average.	Range.	N.	Average.	Range.
A . . .	16	95	84–105	12	107	100–114
B . . .	26	104	89–113	21	97	87–109
C . . .	24	109	91–126	20	97	86–114

tation involved in the shift from ditention to cotention modifies the individual's metabolic rate and that the resultant change is fairly consistent during a series of tests on that individual. Results from different individuals, however, have so far given conflicting evidence in regard to the direction of the difference in rate in the contrasting attentional modes. Additional investigations are required in this respect.

Cardiovascular Functions

As already mentioned, in connection with the kymograph recordings of respiration numerous tracings of the carotid pulse were obtained. However, no characteristic or consistent differences in *pulse rate* were found in the two attentional patterns.

In order to secure more exact information regarding possible differences in the pulse curves, sphygmographic recordings were taken by Dr. Dayton J. Edwards at the Cornell University Medical School. In the technique employed by Dr. Edwards, the fluctuations of pressure from the carotid artery are transmitted to a membrane to which a small mirror is attached. The reflections from this mirror are recorded on a rolling photographic film that permits a very exact registration of the pressure changes. The *sphygmograms* thus obtained did not show any specific differences between ditention and cotention; the systole-diastole relation was not changed, nor was there any consistent difference in the pulse rate.

As to *blood pressure*, recordings taken in ditention and in cotention gave no consistent differences. In order to detect the possibility of finer fluctuations, the continuous recording of blood pressure would have been necessary. But a survey of the literature, and information from authorities in this field indicated that the methods thus far developed for the continuous registering of blood pressure are not satisfactory, except for the intra-arterial method which, however, necessitates surgical intervention and is practically restricted to animal experimentation.

In a series of *electrocardiograms* taken by Dr. Turner, different leads were employed in order to obtain as complete a picture as possible. The electrocardiographic curves were of the normal type, showing no specific difference in form between ditention and cotention. One finding that was somewhat unusual was the presence of fine somatic oscillations during the cotentive phase. These oscillations were different in consistency on different days; but on the whole they were preponderant in cotention. Apparently this phenomenon has nothing to do with the cardiac function but is probably caused by the increased muscular tonus of the respiratory musculature during the deeper respiratory movements in cotention.

Oculomotor Changes[5]

In the course of our experimentation on the contrasting respiratory patterns exhibited in ditention and cotention, incidental observations had also been made on eye-movements. Through direct inspection, and through the use of an interpupillary distance gauge, it was found that the frequency of both eye-movements and lid-movements was markedly reduced during periods of cotention. The movements that occurred during cotention also appeared to be of lesser amplitude. Other oculomotor changes noted in cotention were diminution in the size of the pupil and an increase of convergence.

These incidental observations were followed by several studies in which the eye-movements were recorded photographically and electrically. In a preliminary series of observations the eye-movements were recorded by a motion-picture camera (Eastman Kodak K). While the projection of the films showed roughly the difference of eye-movements in ditention and cotention, there was required a procedure that would lend itself to more specific and detailed analysis. With this in view, pictures were taken of the eye-movements of two subjects with the two-film camera of Dr. G. T. Buswell of The University of Chicago. Tracings obtained from these records showed a marked diminution in the number of eye-movements and a decided decrease in their complexity in cotention as compared with ordinary (affecto-symbolic) attention or ditention.[6] There were correspondingly longer periods of fixation in cotention than in ditention, and the number of eye-blinks was reduced in cotention. Certain experiments also confirmed the observation made earlier by means of the interpupillary distance gauge, that in some cases cotention is accompanied by ocular convergence. The data given in Table V are a summary of the results secured on two subjects during these preliminary experiments in Dr. Buswell's laboratory. For subject A, they represent averages for 18 ten-second periods of ditention compared with 10 ten-second periods of cotention; for subject B, 8 ten-second periods of ditention are compared with 4 ten-second periods of cotention. Fig. 2 presents a graphic reproduction of the eye-movements of subject A during a twenty-second period of ditention and during a twenty-second period of cotention immediately succeeding it.

In connection with a series of electroencephalographic studies reported later in this chapter, eye-movements of two subjects were electrically recorded during extended periods of cotention and ditention. Electrodes were placed directly above and below the right orbit of these subjects in order to register the changes in corneo-retinal potential accompanying the eye-movements. A graphic record of the changes was obtained on the moving tape by means of an ink-writer oscillograph. It has been established that changes thus recorded are comparable to the results obtained by the photographic corneal reflection technique.[7] Our experimental series consisted of 54 periods of ditention and 44 periods of cotention for subject A, and 35 periods of ditention and 34 periods of cotention for subject B. Each experimental period was of two minutes' duration. The results obtained in this series of electrically recorded eye-movements are presented in Table VI. It will be seen that for both subjects the average number of eye-movements occurring in ditention greatly exceeds the average number occurring in cotention. Furthermore, the differences are of such magnitude as to possess complete statistical reliability.

Further series of experiments on differences in ocular responses during ditention and cotention were made by means of a motion-picture type of ophthalmograph, a modification of the "Scanacord," developed by Herbert A. Thompson and Leonard E. Luce of Arthur Kudner, Inc., of New York. This camera is operated according to the motion-picture technique, five frames being exposed per second. On each frame

TABLE V

AVERAGE NUMBER OF BLINKS AND EYE-MOVEMENTS IN TEN-SECOND PERIODS OF DITENTION AND COTENTION

Subject.	Ditention.			Cotention.		
	N.	Av. No. of Blinks.	Av. No. of Eye-Movements.	N.	Av. No. of Blinks.	Av. No. of Eye-Movements.
A	18	4·3	13·0	10	0·30	5·4
B	8	5·8	23·1	4	0·00	7·7

FIG. 2.—Graphic Reproduction of Eye-Movements during Twenty-Second Periods of Ditention and Cotention.

DITENTION   COTENTION

Subject A.

a dot of light is recorded, showing the corneal reflection at a fixation point. From these dots on successive frames one may trace by projection and superposition the actual location, duration and sequence of the ocular fixations. The tracings thus obtained may be superimposed upon the pictures looked at, thus giving a workable record of the fixation points in relation to the visual material used in the experiments.

Four subjects were used in this series of experiments. It was our objective to determine whether the difference in number of eye-move-

TABLE VI

NUMBER OF EYE-MOVEMENTS IN TWO-MINUTE PERIODS
OF DITENTION AND COTENTION

Subject.	Ditention.			Cotention.				
	N.	Mean.	S.D.	N.	Mean.	S.D.	C.R.	Level of Significance.
A . . .	54	59·4	30·44	44	19·0	9·85	9·20	0·1%*
B . . .	35	103·5	18·41	34	22·6	19·34	17·78	0·1%

* A level of significance of 0·1% means that there is only one chance in 1,000 that the obtained decrease in average number of eye-movements during cotention could be attributable to chance, or to fluctuations of sampling.

ments recorded in cotention and in ditention persisted under varying conditions, for example, when the subject was actually looking at pictures, or calling up mental images of pictures, or listening to affectively toned stimulus words. In the first experiment, thirty pictures in two series of ten and two series of five each were presented to the subjects, each picture being exposed for a period of ten seconds. Half of the pictures were looked at first in ditention and then in cotention, while the other half were looked at first in cotention and then in ditention. The pictures were selected for the affective response they were likely to elicit. Four types of measurements were secured: (1) Number of eye-movements, (2) extent of eye-movements (distance between successive fixations), (3) extreme vertical extent of eye-movement pattern, and (4) extreme horizontal extent of eye-movement pattern.

The results of this experiment are summarized in Table VII. It will be seen that the average number of eye-movements was consistently reduced in cotention. Conversely, single fixations were of longer duration in cotention than in ditention. There was no consistent difference in the extent of individual eye-movements in ditention and cotention, but the extreme horizontal distance in the eye-movement pattern was consistently reduced in cotention for all four subjects. The extreme vertical distance in the eye-movement pattern was also reduced in cotention for three of the four subjects. Projection of the pattern of eye-movements on the pictures that were looked at showed that in cotention, in contrast to ditention, the eyes tended to fixate more often on neutral points or on points less likely to provoke affect.

In another experiment on three of the same four subjects, pictures were first looked at and then recalled in ditention and in cotention. The procedure was as follows: first, the subject looked at the picture for five seconds; then he closed his eyes for five seconds, and finally opened and directed them toward a neutral grey background for another five seconds, during which time he recalled the picture. The eye-

TABLE VII

AVERAGE NUMBER, EXTENT, AND EXTREME VERTICAL AND HORIZONTAL MOVEMENTS OF EYES PER PICTURE IN DITENTION AND COTENTION

Subject.	N.	Av. Number of Eye-Movements.		Av. Extent of Eye-Movements (cms.).		Av. of Extreme Vertical Distance in Eye-Movement Pattern (cms.).		Av. of Extreme Horizontal Distance in Eye-Movement Pattern (cms.).	
		Diten.	Coten.	Diten.	Coten.	Diten.	Coten.	Diten.	Coten.
A	30	9.4	5.9	7.9	7.7	16.9	13.3	17.4	14.9
B	10	9.3	5.6	8.4	7.6	16.4	13.7	19.8	14.1
C	30	11.1	6.5	8.2	8.4	18.0	14.1	19.0	15.7
D	20	8.1	6.4	8.3	8.3	14.5	14.5	16.1	14.8

movements were photographed during this five-second recall period. Ten pictures were used in the experiment. The subjects recalled five of the pictures first in ditention and then in cotention. For the other five pictures, the sequence of attentional patterns during recall was reversed.

The results of this experiment are presented in Table VIII. It will be seen that in general they are in agreement with those obtained when the subject was looking directly at the pictures (Table VII). The eye-movement patterns accompanying the recall of pictures showed the same general alterations when the subject shifts from ditention to cotention. There was a reduction in the number of eye-movements in cotention, and the vertical and horizontal diameters of the eye-movement pattern were shorter in cotention.

In a further series of experiments, words were employed as stimuli, and records were made of the eye-movements of four subjects in the two attentional modes. Two series of ten words each and one series of five words were used. Some of the words were presented orally and others graphically. In the oral presentation, the word was read to the subject while he looked at a neutral grey background, and pictures were made of the eye-movements during the succeeding five-second period. In the graphic presentation, the subject read the word and then looked immediately at a neutral grey background for five seconds during which time the eye-movements were photographed. The words were chosen, some for their neutral and some for their affect-provoking quality. The sequence of presentation was arranged in such a way that one-half the words were initially presented while the subject maintained the cotentive pattern, the other half being initially presented while the subject's pattern of response was ditentive. The results are given in Table IX. They are similar to those already reported for pictures. The average number of eye-movements per word was reduced in all subjects during cotention and the extreme vertical and horizontal movements of the eyes tended to be less in cotention than in ditention.

TABLE VIII

AVERAGE NUMBER, EXTENT, AND EXTREME VERTICAL AND HORIZONTAL MOVEMENTS OF EYES WHILE RECALLING PICTURES IN DITENTION AND COTENTION

Subject.	N.	Av. Number of Eye-Movements.		Av. Extent of Eye-Movements (cms.).		Av. of Extreme Vertical Distance in Eye-Movement Pattern (cms.).		Av. of Extreme Horizontal Distance in Eye-Movement Pattern (cms.).	
		Diten.	Coten.	Diten.	Coten.	Diten.	Coten.	Diten.	Coten.
A	10	8·6	4·4	7·7	8·7	16·4	11·6	16·5	13·0
C	10	6·0	4·0	8·9	8·4	14·6	11·1	18·0	13·9
D	10	5·1	4·2	9·9	8·2	15·3	11·6	15·3	12·7

The results on the series of experiments measuring eye-movements by means of the "Scanacord" thus confirmed our finding that there is a reduction in number of eye-movements during cotention—a result that had been obtained in the earlier observations by means of the interpupillary distance gauge, the experiments with the Buswell camera, and the electrical recording of eye-movements. They also showed that this characteristic reduction takes place during cotention not only when the eyes are closed, or when they are directed straight ahead and no specific task or stimulation is imposed, but that it also occurs when the subject is presented with pictures or words, or when he recalls pictures or words, many of which contain affect-associations. The experiments thus indicate that cotention is accompanied by a decrease in number of eye-movements under a wide variety of stimulus conditions, and that the subject who is practiced in cotention can maintain the cotentive pattern and set aside his accustomed affective response even when presented with affect-inducing stimuli.

The results obtained in these experiments on oculomotor changes led to a prolonged search for an eye-movement camera that would give us a more direct and immediate record of the eye-movements and fixations in ditention and cotention and that would also permit us to study certain aspects such as the course and velocity of the movements on single frames of the recording film without calculations or other complicated procedures. A careful survey of available cameras showed that none of them was adequate to meet our requirements. We were fortunate, however, in securing the assistance of Dr. Henry Roger of the Rolab Laboratories at Sandy Hook, Connecticut, who developed and constructed a camera in accordance with our specifications.[8] This ap-

TABLE IX

AVERAGE NUMBER, EXTENT, AND EXTREME VERTICAL AND HORIZONTAL MOVEMENTS OF EYES IN RESPONSE TO STIMULUS WORDS IN DITENTION AND COTENTION

Subject.	N.	Av. Number of Eye-Movements.		Av. Extent of Eye-Movements (cms.).		Av. of Extreme Vertical Distance in Eye-Movement Pattern (cms.).		Av. of Extreme Horizontal Distance in Eye-Movement Pattern (cms.).	
		Diten.	Coten.	Diten.	Coten.	Diten.	Coten.	Diten.	Coten.
A . .	25	7.5	5.3	5.2	5.5	9.2	8.2	11.2	10.2
B . .	15	5.6	3.9	5.1	4.8	6.5	6.0	11.1	8.3
C . .	25	5.1	4.1	4.7	5.4	8.3	7.1	9.0	8.1
D . .	10	5.3	4.1	7.6	7.2	10.0	7.9	11.0	11.3

paratus combines the principles of a still camera with certain features of the motion-picture technique, using a 35-mm. film. All parts of the apparatus are interconnected by electrical cables and operated from a central electrical control-panel. The frame change is timed to take effect automatically once every second, but by manual control any number of seconds may be allowed to elapse between frame changes. The exposures are of very short duration and are controlled by a stroboscopic mechanism. The frequency of exposures can be varied from 5 to 30 per second, and higher frequencies can be added should this prove necessary. In order to register the sequence of the eye-movements and the duration of the fixations, a rotating dial is employed through which the flashes of the light-source are projected on the cornea and from there reflected into the camera. The dial performs one revolution per second, so that one revolution is automatically recorded on each frame. In these experiments the apparatus is adjusted so that the dial

FIG. 3. Photograms Showing Eye-Movements and Fixation with Five Exposures per Second.

A. EYE-MOVEMENTS

B. FIXATION

The dial moves clockwise in these illustrations as in all subsequent illustrations dealing with eye-movements. The course of the eye-movements can be determined by following the successive positions of the dial.

Fig. 4. Photograms Showing Eye-Movements and Fixation with Ten Exposures per Second.

A. EYE-MOVEMENTS

B. FIXATION

FIG. 5. Photograms of Eye-Movements for Periods of Two and Three Seconds.

A. TWO SECONDS

B. THREE SECONDS

Exposure frequency ten per second.

Fig. 6. Photograms of Eye-Movements when Subject was looking at Black Background without Focusing on any special Point.

A. DITENTION

B. COTENTION

Exposure frequency ten per second.

moves clockwise on the cornea and the changing positions of its bar can be analyzed readily on the projected photogram. A projection device permits one not only to analyze individual frames but also to trace a composite record by superimposing a series of frames. The track of the eye-movements may also be superimposed upon the pictures or other visual material that the subject may be asked to observe during the experiment.

The subject is comfortably seated in front of the camera, his head being supported and held in position by a chin and head rest. A blackened board is placed at a convenient distance in front of the subject's eyes and may be used as a rack to support pictures or other material to be looked at in the experiments. This board is provided with point-like sources of light placed at the four corners and at the center of a ten-inch square. These light bulbs can be individually controlled from the main panel. By having the subject focus on the lights it is possible to correlate the course of the corneal reflection, as recorded photographically, with the visual axis when the eyes follow an arbitrarily chosen and accurately known course.

The reproduction of typical films obtained by this method shows the varying positions of the reflected dial. Fig. 3 gives frames with five exposures per second, Fig. 4 with ten exposures. In general, it may be said that of the different frequencies employed in a preliminary series of experiments, ten per second was found most satisfactory. The positions of the dial bar when read in clockwise sequence indicate the direction of the eye-movements. Fixations occur wherever two or more dial impressions are superimposed, the number of the progressive positions of the dial bar showing the duration of the fixations. Figs. 3b and 4b show fixations lasting throughout the entire presentation of the frame (1 second). For determining the actual duration of these fixations, however, it would be necessary to examine also the dial impressions on preceding and succeeding frames. Fig. 5 gives photograms of frames presented for several seconds each, with an exposure frequency of 10 per second. It may be seen that the subject performed a rotating movement that was interrupted by many fixations.

One of the advantages of this camera is the possibility of obtaining on single frames of the film relatively large sections of the eye-movements. One may not only follow the location and duration of the successive fixations but, because of the short duration of the individual exposures, impressions of the corneal reflection obtained while the eye is moving are recorded at regular time intervals between the fixation points. The moving bar of the dial impressions makes it easy to follow the sequence and course of the eye-movements. This is of importance especially where the movement of the eye does not follow a course prearranged by the experimental routine but where the subject, in a state of relaxation, is allowed to move his eyes about freely and at random, or when he is asked to look at pictures or other material. Figs. 6 to 9 give samples of such experiments. While the room was kept in semi-darkness the subject was asked to look ahead in a normal way without attempting to focus on any special point. He was asked to do this in the two attentional modes under investigation, namely, in ditention and cotention. Figs. 6a and 6b show characteristic photographic recordings in these two modalities of attention. The decreased number and extent of the eye-movements in cotention is evident. Fig. 7 gives drawings of five successive one-second periods in each mode of attention, indicating the consistency of these differences.

FIG. 7.—Drawings of Photograms of Five Successive One-Second Periods in Ditention and in Cotention.

DITENTION

COTENTION

The same experimental conditions prevailed as for Fig. 6.

Another series of photographic records was obtained while the subject was looking at pictures. Figs. 8a and 8b give typical frames of these experiments, indicating again the lessened frequency and excursion of the eye-movements in cotention. Fig. 9 represents drawings of several successive frames obtained in ditention and in cotention while the subject was looking at pictures presented to him. Here again the difference is quite marked and consistent throughout these longer periods of the experiment.

The novel features included in our apparatus necessitated a great deal of exploratory experimentation which resulted in many technical adjustments and minor modifications of the instrument, thus delaying its full use. So that we are giving here only certain preliminary findings, without attempting to treat the results in a more comprehensive and statistical manner. A fuller report including additional experimental settings as well as a consideration of other qualitative aspects of the eye-movements will be presented later. However, we may say that, besides affording a short-cut method, these experiments add confirmation to our findings arrived at by means of other eye-movement cameras.

FIG. 8. Photograms of Eye-Movements When Subject was Looking at a Picture.

A. DITENTION

B. COTENTION

Exposure frequency ten per second.

APPENDIX

Electroencephalographic Changes[9]

The study of the neural function of the brain by recording electrical potentials, led off from the scalp, has been given much attention in recent investigations of behavioral disfunctions. Naturally, we were interested in determining whether there were any differences in the

FIG. 9.—Drawings of Photograms of Successive One-Second Periods in Ditention and in Cotention.

DITENTION

COTENTION

The same experimental conditions prevailed as for Fig. 8.

pattern of electrical activity of the brain in ditention and in cotention. With the assitance of Dr. Margaret Rheinberger, and of Dr. Marcel Goldenberg, we studied the brain-wave patterns led off from the frontal, motor, temporal and occipital areas in these two attentional modes.[10] Our records were secured in part with a three-channel and in part with a five-channel Grass electroencephalograph.

A total of fifty EEG records on four subjects was included in the experimental series. Each record contained four sequences, a sample of which is presented below:

Half of the records for each subject began with a series with open eyes and half with a series with closed eyes. In half of the records for each subject the record began and ended with a period of cotention; in the other half, the record began and ended with a period of ditention. Each experimental period of ditention and cotention was of two minutes' duration. The series with eyes open was always preceded by an adaptation period of at least ten minutes in which the eyes were kept open.

An inspection of the records of three of the four subjects used showed that there was an obvious difference in brain-wave patterns during ditention and cotention. (The frequent occurrence of sleepiness

FIG. 10.—Typical Tracings of Brain Waves from Right Motor and Left Motor Areas during Successive Periods of Ditention and Cotention.

DITENTION
R.M.
L.M.
R.M.-L.M.

COTENTION
R.M.
L.M.
R.M.-L.M.

Subject B.   Eyes Closed.

so vitiated the records of the fourth subject that the results could not be considered valid.) This difference seemed to consist chiefly in a reduction in the percentage of alpha-time and a decrease in the amplitude of the alpha waves during cotention. These two changes are shown in Fig. 10 which consists of two sections. The upper line in each section is a tracing from bipolar leads in the right motor area, the middle line from bipolar leads in the left motor area, and the lower line from leads in the right motor and left motor areas. The upper section is a record taken from a typical period of ditention, and the lower section is taken from the immediately succeeding period of cotention, with all other conditions held constant.

Inspection of the records also showed that the changes typical of cotention—the drop in alpha-percentage and amplitude—was most pronounced in the motor regions, considerably less in the temporal, frontal and occipital regions M > T > F > O. The differential effect of cotention on brain-wave activity from the motor and occipital regions is shown graphically in Fig. 11.

FIG. 11.—Typical Tracings of Brain Waves from Right and Left Motor, and Right and Left Occipital Areas during Successive Periods of Ditention and Cotention.

Subject B. Eyes closed. The figure is in two sections. The upper line in each section is a tracing of the electrocardiograph; the second, third and fourth lines are tracings of electrical activity in the right motor, left motor and right occipital areas of the brain respectively; and the bottom line records electrical activity in the left occipital area. The upper section is a record taken from a typical period of ditention, and the lower section is taken from the immediately succeeding period of cotention with all other conditions held constant.

In a detailed statistical analysis, representative records of three subjects were counted to determine the percentage of time during which alpha waves were present. In this analysis, alpha waves were interpreted as those waves having a frequency of 8.5 to 12.5 per second. Two thirty-second samples from the middle of each period of ditention and cotention were chosen as most reliable for purposes of counting. Since the inducing of the cotentive pattern brought about comparable changes in the brain-wave pattern irrespective of whether the eyes were open or closed, the data for the two conditions of the eyes were grouped and treated together. In addition, some of the records were counted with a view to establishing the average amplitude and frequency of the alpha waves in ditention and in cotention. The records submitted to this more detailed analysis were secured with a three-channel Grass electroencephalograph. We made use of bipolar leads, placing the electrodes at a distance of 4-5cms. in transverse or in sagittal rows. In the right motor area, 170 thirty-second periods of cotention were counted and compared with 134 thirty-second periods of ditention; in the left motor area, 148 thirty-second periods of cotention were counted and compared with 119 thirty-second periods of ditention. The average percentages of alpha waves present in the right and left motor areas of each of the three subjects during ditention and cotention, together with standard deviations, critical ratios and level of significance of the obtained differences, are presented in Table X. The number of periods of ditention and cotention which were counted for the right and left motor areas of each subject is given in the column under N.

TABLE X

Percentage of Alpha-Wave Activity recorded from Right Motor and Left Motor Brain-Areas in Thirty-Second Periods of Ditention and Cotention

Subject.	Brain Area.	Ditention. N.	Mean.	S.D.	Cotention. N.	Mean.	S.D.	C.R.	Level of Significance.
A	R.M.	47	67·64	13·02	41	56·44	20·03	3·03	1%*
A	L.M.	47	60·61	15·32	41	47·49	22·37	3·12	1%
B	R.M.	89	75·30	11·88	67	54·92	16·98	8·35	0·1%
B	L.M.	69	73·66	13·58	54	61·94	14·22	4·58	0·1%
C	R.M.	34	52·33	8·49	26	46·61	10·61	2·22	3%
C	L.M.	32	48·58	7·81	24	41·45	13·58	2·26	2%

* A level of significance of 1% can be interpreted to mean that there is only one chance in 100 that the obtained decrease in average alpha-percentage during cotention is attributable to chance, or to fluctuations of sampling.

It will be seen that all three subjects showed an average decrease in alpha-percentage in both the right and left motor areas during cotention, and that this decrease was of sufficient magnitude and consistency in both right and left motor areas to be statistically significant for all three subjects. The amount of decrease in alpha-percentage during cotention varied among the three subjects, but it was relatively constant for a given subject, as was indicated by a comparison of the various ditentive and cotentive periods for the same subject.

Figs. 12 and 13 present graphically the distribution of alpha-percentages for subject B during 44 matched periods of ditention and of cotention. The number of periods during which a given alpha-percentage occurred is represented on the vertical axis, and the alpha-percentage is given on the horizontal axis. Fig. 12 gives results from the right motor, and Fig. 13 from the left motor area. It will be seen that in cotention (marked by interrupted hatching) the periods with low alpha-percentage (50-65) occur most frequently, whereas in ditention the mode in both the right and left motor areas falls on a considerably higher percentage (80-85). Fig. 14 gives data from an individual record in which the alpha-percentages from the right and left motor areas in consecutive periods of ditention and cotention are represented in graphic form. It will be noted that in every transition from ditention to cotention there is a decrease in the alpha-percentage in both right and left motor areas, and that in each transition from cotention to ditention there is an increase in the alpha-percentage in each of the motor areas.

FIG. 12.—Distribution of Alpha-Percentages in the EEG during Ditention and Cotention.

Figs. 15 and 16 present the distribution of amplitudes from an individual record of subject A in which the amplitudes from the right and left motor areas in consecutive periods of ditention and cotention

FIG. 13.—Distribution of Alpha-Percentages in the EEG during Ditention and Cotention.

Subject B.

FIG. 14.—Alpha-Percentages in Successive Periods of Ditention and Cotention.

Subject A. Right and Left Motor Areas.

APPENDIX

are represented in graphic form. The amplitudes are expressed in microvolt units (5-25) along the horizontal axis, and the number of alpha waves in each amplitude group is indicated on the vertical axis.

FIG. 15.—Distribution of Alpha Amplitudes in the EEG during Successive Periods of Ditention and Cotention.

Subject A.   Right Motor Area.

FIG. 16.—Distribution of Alpha Amplitudes in the EEG during Successive Periods of Ditention and Cotention.

Subject A.   Left Motor Area.

It will be readily seen that in cotention we have a larger number of waves in the low amplitude group, whereas in ditention there are fewer waves of low and relatively more of higher amplitude. The consistency of this difference is indicated in the Figures. Amplitudes of 15-20, and higher, practically disappear in cotention.

Control experiments were run on the same subjects to determine whether the decrease in alpha-percentage and amplitude found to occur in cotention could be attributed to an increase in muscular tension in this attentional pattern. This likelihood seemed doubtful, since cotention does not appear subjectively to be characterized by an increase

FIG. 17.—Typical Tracings of Brain Waves from Right and Left Motor Areas and of Eye-Movements during Periods of Ditention, Muscle-Tension, and Cotention.

DITENTION

R.M. $A_3 F_3$

L.M. $A_3 F_3$

EYE-MOVEMENTS $A_7 F_3$

MUSCLE TENSION—JAW

R.M. $A_3 F_3$

L.M. $A_3 F_3$

EYE-MOVEMENTS $A_7 F_3$

COTENTION

R.M. $A_3 F_3$

L.M. $A_3 F_3$

EYE-MOVEMENTS $A_7 F_3$

in tension. In the control experiments, tensions were set up by clenching the fist or holding the jaw rigid, and periods of such muscular tension were interspersed with periods of ditention and cotention. While there was some decrease in alpha-percentage and amplitude during the periods of muscle-tension, the decrease was markedly less than in cotention. In passing from periods of muscle-tension to cotention there was invariably a further decrease in the amplitude and percentage of the alpha waves. Fig. 17, which is in three sections, shows representative strips from an EEG record in which there were periods of ditention, muscle-tension and cotention, other conditions being held constant. The upper line in each section is a tracing from the right motor area, the middle line from the left motor area, and the lower line is an electrical record of eye-movements. It will be noted that cotention has a much greater effect on the alpha-percentage and amplitude than does muscular tension.

Check of Ink-Writer Records by Grass Method of Frequency Analysis

In order to check the ordinary ink-writer records against the Grass method of frequency analysis,[11] certain of the electroencephalographic series were repeated in the laboratory of Dr. Frederic A. Gibbs of the Neurological Unit of the Boston City Hospital.[12] The cortical activity of the right and left motor, and of the right and left occipital areas was studied, and simultaneous spectra were recorded from two regions and, on occasion, from three. Series were made with the eyes open and with the eyes closed. Records were taken under conditions of cotention, of ditention, and of reading in cotention and in ditention. Control records were also obtained during periods of intense attention (mental work).[13] Two subjects were used in the experiments and for the most part both showed similar changes. Over 200 spectra were secured for the two subjects. The spectra were carefully compared with the simultaneously obtained ink-writer records, and those spectra were discarded in which there was evidence of artifacts, sleepiness or other extraneous factors. The present discussion is based upon an analysis of the 125 spectra which met our criteria for inclusion. A planimeter was used in analyzing the spectra in order to determine for each graph the areas lying in the different frequency-bands. In these experiments bipolar leads were used in the motor areas, and the distance between the two electrodes was 5.0 cms. Monopolar leads were used in the occipital areas.

Comparison of Ditention with Cotention

As already reported, analysis of the ink-writer records showed that the shift from ditention to cotention is accompanied by a decrease in alpha-percentage and amplitude which is most pronounced in the motor regions, and much less in the temporal, frontal and occipital regions. An analysis of the frequency-spectra showed that in cotention there was a drop in the total energy-output in the 2-40 frequency-range when thirty-second samples of cotention were compared with

FIG. 18.—Spectra of Brain-Wave Activity from Motor Area during Successive Periods of Ditention and Cotention.

A. Ditention.

B. Cotention

Subject A.   Eyes Closed.   Left Motor Area.

thirty-second samples of ditention, and that this drop was considerably more marked in the motor than in the occipital regions. In all cases the samples were taken from the middle of the experimental periods. In half the series, the sequence was from ditention to cotention; in the other half, the sequence was reversed. The most marked drop in

APPENDIX 513

FIG. 19.—Spectra of Brain-Wave Activity from Occipital Area during Successive Periods of Ditention and Cotention.

A. Ditention.

B. Cotention.

Subject A. Eyes closed. Left Occipital Area.

energy-output occurred in the 8-12 frequency-range (alpha component). Basing our results on the planimetric analysis of 31 spectra secured during 31 periods of cotention, and an equal number obtained during ditention, the average area of the spectra (indicating the energy-output) included in the 2-40 frequency-range was 17.3 per cent. less in cotention than in ditention for the motor areas; in the 8-12 range, it averaged 35.4 per cent. less in cotention for the motor areas. The data on which these averages are based show practically no overlapping. In the occipital regions the average decrease of energy-output in cotention was 7.4 per cent. for the 2-40 frequency-range and 12 per cent. for the 8-12 range. Figs. 18 and 19 reproduce spectra of typical brain-wave activity in the motor and occipital areas during successive periods of ditention and cotention. The differential effect of cotention on the two brain-areas is clearly shown.

In cotention as compared with ditention, very few experiments show an increase in the energy-output in the slow-wave range (below 6 per second) in the motor regions. In the fast-wave range (above 30 per second) there is a tendency to an increase of energy-output in cotention. But these minor increases are not sufficient to counteract the marked decrease of energy-output in the 8-12 range during cotention. A careful inspection of the series of spectra showed that there was no tendency for the alpha peak to shift to a slower frequency in cotention. In 58 per cent. of the observations in the motor regions there occurred a shift of alpha peak to a slightly faster frequency in cotention; the average shift being from a frequency of 9.7 per second in ditention to 10.3 per second in cotention. This fact may be used as an added criterion to differentiate cotention from sleepiness in the EEG, since sleepiness results in a shift of the alpha peak to a slower frequency. There was no appreciable shift of alpha peak in the occipital region during cotention, and the changes in the slow- and fast-wave ranges were too small to be of significance.

Comparison of Reading in Ditention with Reading in Cotention

The reading material consisted of a technical article of a psychological nature, and the subject read continuously throughout the series. In all instances the reading was silent. The eyes were open for at least ten minutes prior to these experiments in order to allow for adaptation. The ceiling light in the room was kept on. In half of the series the subject read first in ditention and then in cotention; in the other half, the sequence was reversed. Two subjects were used.

When the spectra for *reading in ditention* were compared with the spectra for *reading in cotention* taken in the same experimental period, a planimetric analysis of eight spectra showed that in cotentive reading there was in the motor region an average decrease of 17 per cent. in energy-output in the 2-40 frequency-range and of 24 per cent.

APPENDIX 515

in the 8-12 range. The alpha peak shifts to a slightly faster frequency in cotentive reading (see Fig. 20). In cotentive reading, as compared with ditentive reading, there was in the occipital region an average

FIG. 20.—Spectra of Brain-Wave Activity from Motor Area during Successive Periods of Reading in Ditention and Reading in Cotention.

A. Reading in Ditention.

B. Reading in Cotention.

Subject B. Right Motor Area.

decrease in energy-output of 21 per cent. in the 2-40 frequency-range and a decrease of 24 per cent. in the 8-12 range. There was again a tendency for the alpha peak to shift to the right (or toward a faster frequency) in cotentive reading. In both the motor and occipital regions the energy-output in cotentive reading was consistently lower throughout the entire range of frequencies. The results from this

FIG. 21.—Spectra of Brain-Wave Activity from Occipital Area during Successive Periods of Reading in Ditention and Reading in Cotention.

A. Reading in Ditention.

B. Reading in Cotention.

Subject A. Left Occipital Area.

series are thus consonant with those obtained in the earlier ditentive and cotentive series (without reading), and substantiate the evidence that cotention causes specific modifications in the pattern of the electrical activity of the brain.

APPENDIX

The graphs in Fig. 20 show spectra of brain-wave activity in the motor area under conditions of reading in ditention and reading in cotention in successive experimental periods. Fig. 21 presents spectra

FIG. 22.—Differential Effect of Reading in Ditention and Reading in Cotention on Brain-Wave Activity from Occipital Area.

SOLID LINE = READING IN DITENTION
BROKEN LINE = READING IN COTENTION

Subject A. Left Occipital Area.

from the occipital area under the same two conditions. Fig. 22 is a composite graph showing the differential effect of reading in cotention and reading in ditention on brain-wave activity in the occipital area.

COMPARISON OF INTENSE ATTENTION WITH DITENTION AND WITH COTENTION

In order to check the possibility that the changes in the spectra of brain-wave activity noted in cotention might be due to an intensification of the attentive process, control experiments were run in which the subjects were required to perform an exercise in complex mental arithmetic. In this series, 16 spectra secured under conditions of *intense attention* or mental work were compared with 32 spectra of *ditention* obtained during the same experimental periods. The series included sixteen shifts from ditention to intense attention and sixteen shifts from intense attention to ditention. The results from the planimetric analyses of these spectra showed that there was a small average decrease in energy-output in intense attention but that this decrease was not consistent. Intense attention shows in the motor region an average energy-output that is 6 per cent. smaller than the energy-output in ditention both for the 2-40 and for the 8-12 frequency-range. In the occipital regions the decreases were 3.6 per cent. in the 2-40 range and

FIG. 23.—Spectra of Brain-Wave Activity from Motor Area during Successive Periods of Ditention and Intense Attention.

A. Ditention.

B. Intense Attention.

Subject B. Eyes Closed. Right Motor Area.

8.8 per cent. in the 8-12 range. The range of the changes in energy output from ditention to intense attention varied in the motor region between $+$ 8 per cent. and $-$ 17 per cent. for the 2-40 frequencies, and between + 18 per cent. and — 27 per cent. for the 8-12 frequencies. The corresponding values for the occipital region were + 10 per cent. and — 17 per cent., and + 3 per cent. and — 21 per cent.

FIG. 24.—Spectra of Brain-Wave Activity from Occipital Area during Successive Periods of Ditention and Intense Attention.

A. Ditention.

B. Intense Attention.

Subject A. Eyes Closed. Left Occipital Area.

Although there is an average decrease in energy-output in intense attention, the decrease is so small and the ranges so wide that at least for these experiments any consistent link between intense attention and changes of energy-output must be denied. There was no indication of increase in fast-wave activity in intense attention for either the motor or occipital regions. In the motor regions there was a shift in the alpha peak in intense attention to a faster frequency, namely, from an average of 9.4 to an average of 10.2. In the occipital region there was no shift in the alpha peak. Fig. 23 reproduces spectra of electrical activity in the motor area during ditention and intense attention, while Fig. 24 presents spectra for the occipital area under the same experimental conditions.

The differential findings in regard to the spectra recorded under conditions of *cotention* and *intense attention* are of interest since they serve to indicate that cotention may not be regarded as a heightened form of attention, just as earlier control experiments with ink-writer of increased muscular tension. In cotention, as we have seen, the diminution in energy-output is marked and consistent, while this is not true in intense attention.

We have seen that in *intense attention* as compared with *ditention* the average drop in energy-output in the alpha range tended to be slightly greater in the occipital (8.8 per cent.) than in the motor regions (6 per cent.). It will be recalled that precisely the opposite situation prevailed in a comparison of the spectra of *cotention* and *ditention* where the drop in energy-output in the alpha range in cotention was markedly and consistently more pronounced in the motor (35.4 per cent.) than in the occipital regions (12 per cent.). Compare Figs. 18 and 19.

FIG. 25.—Differential Effect of Intense Attention and Cotention on Brain-Wave Activity from Motor Area.

SOLID LINE = INTENSE ATTENTION
BROKEN LINE = COTENTION

Subject B. Eyes Closed. Right Motor Area.

APPENDIX 521

On the basis of previous EEG investigations it was surprising to find that the drop in energy-output in the alpha range was not more marked in intense attention.[14] Whether the difference is due to the quite different electrode-placement (closely spaced bipolar leads instead of monopolar leads as mostly used in psychological EEG studies), or whether there was any special conditioning with our subjects which may have influenced the results, will have to be determined by further experimentation. No previous studies of spectra in various phases of attention are available for comparison.[15]

Further data in regard to the differentiation of cotention from intense attention were secured by running a number of series in which there were immediate shifts from intense attention to cotention, and vice versa. Planimetric analyses of the 14 spectra from these series showed that in cotention, as compared with intense attention, there was a consistent reduction of energy-output. In the motor regions

Fig. 26.—Summary Graph showing Three Types of Physiological Changes occurring most consistently in Cotention.

DITENTION
R.M. $A_3 F_3$
EYE-MOVEMENTS $A_7 F_3$
RESPIRATION

COTENTION
R.M. $A_3 F_3$
EYE-MOVEMENTS $A_7 F_3$
RESPIRATION

Subject B.   Eyes Closed.

this decrease averaged 11 per cent. in the 2-40 frequency-range and 9.2 per cent. in the 8-12 frequency-range; in the occipital regions the decrease averaged 7.6 per cent. in the 2-40 range and 14.4 per cent. in the 8-12 range. Fig. 25 is a composite graph showing the differential effect of intense attention and cotention on spectra of brain-wave activity in the right motor region.

In summarizing the physiological alterations that we have thus far been able to record instrumentally and that we have found to occur concomitantly with the adoption of the cotentive pattern of response,

I should like to invite attention to Fig. 26 in which the three types of changes most characteristic of cotention were simultaneously recorded. The simultaneous recording of changes in these three physiological systems was made possible by a hookup of elements of the pneumograph with the electroencephalograph. The upper line is a record of the brain-wave pattern from the right motor area, the middle line represents an electrical recording of eye-movements by registering changes in the corneo-retinal potential, while the bottom line records respiratory movements. A comparison of the sections of the graph recorded in ditention and in cotention shows the marked diminution in the frequency of eye-movements and respiration in cotention, and the alteration in brain-wave pattern involving a reduction in alpha-time and a general diminution in cortical potential.

NOTES

[1] For their valuable advice, suggestions and coöperation in our observations on respiratory and cardiovascular phenomena I should like to express my appreciation to: Professors Eugene F. Du Bois, Dayton J. Edwards and Joseph C. Hinsey of Cornell Medical College; Dr. Carney Landis of New York State Psychiatric Institute; Dr. Horatio B. Williams, College of Physicians and Surgeons, Columbia University; and to Professor W. R. Hess, University of Zurich. I am deeply indebted to Dr. Grace Whitford and the Morton F. Plant Hospital for graciously providing us with laboratory accommodations in Clearwater, Florida. Special appreciation is due to Dr. Henry B. Turner of the Medical Department of the Guardian Life Insurance Company, New York, for taking a series of electrocardiograms, and for making, with the assistance of Miss Mary Gaillard, the observations on basal metabolism. The wax-paper kymograph used for recording respiration and pulse was constructed by Mr. Ralph Gerbrands under the supervision of Dr. John Volkmann, through the courtesy of the Department of Psychology, Harvard University.

[2] Burrow, Trigant, "The Economic Factor in Disorders of Behavior," *The American Journal of Orthopsychiatry,* 1939, Vol. IX, pp. 102-8.

———, "Kymograph Studies of Physiological (Respiratory) Concomitants in Two Types of Attentional Adaptation," *Nature* (London), 1938, Vol. 142, p. 156.

———, "Kymograph Records of Neuromuscular (Respiratory) Patterns in Relation to Behavior Disorders," *Psychosomatic Medicine,* 1941, Vol. III, pp. 174-86.

[3] In my first published reports of instrumental results, partitive or deflected attention was referred to as "attention" in contrast to total attention or cotention. Later, in describing the type of attention I discriminate as partitive or deflected attention, I adopted the term "ditention."

[4] The fact that the respiratory rates in both ditention and cotention were generally slower in the recordings with the metabolism apparatus as compared with the earlier recordings with the kymograph is perhaps accounted for by the circumstance that in the metabolism series a mixture was inspired which was richer in oxygen than is ordinary air.

[5] I want to express my appreciation to the many colleagues and technical experts who gave so generously of their advice regarding the various aspects of the behavior of the eyes studied by us, and who coöperated in devising adequate means for the recording of these phenomena: Dr. Conrad Berens, Dr. Daniel B. Kirby, Dr. Le Grand H. Hardy, New York; Dr. Norman Cameron, New York Hospital; Dr. R. Lorente de Nó, Rockefeller Institute; Dr. Otto Lowenstein, New York University College of Medicine; Dr. H. F. Pierce, New York Hospital; Professor Robert T.

Rock, Department of Educational Psychology, Fordham University; Dr. Stella Center, Reading Clinic, New York University; Professors C. E. Benson, E. R. Wood and B. E. Tomlinson, Department of Educational Psychology, New York University; Professors Walter R. Miles and Donald G. Marquis, Yale University; Dr. H. E. Edgerton, Massachusetts Institute of Technology; Dr. Herman F. Brandt, Visual Research Laboratories, Drake University.

To Professor G. T. Buswell, Department of Education, The University of Chicago, we are indebted for a number of exploratory observations with his two-film camera as well as with his modified ophthalmograph; to Mr. Herbert A. Thompson of Arthur Kudner, Inc., who kindly loaned us his camera for an extended series of experiments, as reported here. Further technical advice and coöperation was received from Dr. Turner Veith and Dr. J. F. Morrow, Jr., of the American Optical Company, New York; from Dr. Julius Neumueller, Director, Bureau of Visual Science, American Optical Company, Southbridge, Massachusetts; Mr. Kern Larkin, technician, and Mr. Adolfo Marfaing, photographer, Institute of Ophthalmology, Presbyterian Hospital, New York; Mr. Fred Kerwer, Douglas Leigh, Inc., New York; Mr. Dagobert Horn, Mr. Gjon Mili, Mr. Carl Oswald, Mr. Albert Paganelli and Mr. Carl Schleicher, all of New York. A tentative plan for the development of a new camera was suggested by Dr. F. M. Bishop, Mr. R. E. McAdam and associates of the Development Department, Eastman Kodak Company, Rochester, New York. Owing to restrictions incident to the war, this plan could not be followed through. The camera now used by us was developed and constructed by Dr. Henry Roger and Mr. Charles Robinson at the former's laboratory at Sandy Hook, Connecticut. Dr. Herbert E. Grier, Massachusetts Institute of Technology, gave valuable advice regarding certain electro-technical features of the apparatus.

[6] Burrow, Trigant, "Neurosis and War: A Problem in Human Behavior," *The Journal of Psychology*, 1941, Vol. 12, pp. 235-49.

[7] Carmichael, Leonard, Hoffman, Arthur C., and Wellman, Bertram, "A Qualitative Comparison of the Electrical and Photographic Techniques of Eye-Movement Recording," *Journal of Experimental Psychology*, 1939, Vol. 24, pp. 40-53.

[8] Syz, Hans, "The Lifwynn Eye-Movement Camera," *Science*, 1946, Vol. 103, pp. 628-29.

[9] For advice and coöperation in taking the electroencephalograms I should like to express my appreciation to Dr. Margaret Rheinberger, The Jewish Hospital of Brooklyn; to Dr. Marcel Goldenberg, New York; to Dr. Frederic A. Gibbs, Boston City Hospital; and to Mr. Albert M. Grass, Quincy, Massachusetts.

[10] Burrow, Trigant, "Preliminary Report of Electroencephalographic Recordings in Relation to Behavior Modifications," *The Journal of Psychology*, 1943, Vol. 5, pp. 109-14.

[11] This method offers an objective analysis based on a Fourier transformation of the EEG or, in other words, an automatic record of the energy-distribution over different frequencies. (Grass, A. M., and Gibbs, Frederic A., "A Fourier Transform of the Electroencephalogram," *Journal of Neurophysiology*, 1938, Vol. 1, pp. 521-26.)

[12] It should be stated that Dr. Gibbs had, of course, no part in our formulations regarding cotention—formulations which constitute the major premise of our phylobiological thesis and are derived solely from group experimentation.

[13] Burrow, Trigant, and Galt, William E., "Electroencephalographic Recordings of Varying Aspects of Attention in Relation to Behavior," *The Journal of General Psychology*, 1945, Vol. 32, pp. 269-88.

[14] Berger, H., "Ueber das Elektrenkephalogramm des Menschen," *Journal für Psychologie und Neurologie*, 1930, Vol. 40, p. 160.

Knott, John R., "Brain Potentials during Silent and Oral Reading," *The Journal of General Psychology*, 1938, Vol. 18, pp. 57-62.

[15] Gibbs *et al* have reported on further aspects of cortical frequency, using the spectral method of analysis. Further information as to the way in which the analyzer functions may be found in the following papers:

Gibbs, Frederic A., "Cortical Frequency Spectra of Healthy Adults," *The Journal of Nervous and Mental Disease*, 1942, Vol. 95, pp. 417-26.

Gibbs, Frederic A., Lennox, William G., and Gibbs, Erna L., "The Cortical Frequency Spectrum in Epilepsy," *Archives of Neurology and Psychiatry*, 1941, Vol. 46, pp. 613-20.

GLOSSARY[1]

(Terms originated by the author are indicated by an asterisk.)

Affect: As used in phylobiology, affect is a reaction that is subjectively biased through the artificial linkage of feeling and symbol, leading to imbalance and distortion of interrelational behavior. (Synonyms: autopathic feeling, partitive feeling. Contrasted with primary, total feeling.)

*Affecto-symbolic: Author's term to describe type of behavior characterized by mental bias. (See *Ditentive.* Contrasted with cotentive.)

Allergy: As used in phylobiology, this term indicates disturbances in man's interrelational function. (Synonym: allogenic function. Contrasted with protergy, protogenic function.)

Allogenic function: See *Allergy.*

Alloplasm: In phylobiology this term is applied to disordered protoplasm.

Anthroponomic: Referring to the laws that regulate the development of man in relation to the environment and to other organisms.

*Auto-empathic: Term used to describe a reaction that is ulterior, ditentive or self-reversive. In his feeling-illusion the subject seeks constantly to identify others with himself rather than himself with them. (See also *Empathy.*)

*Automorphic: Term indicating reaction patterned after one's self-image. (From αὐτός, self, and μορφή, form.)

Autonomic Nervous System: The unit of the nervous system that is largely independent of the cerebrospinal or central nervous system, and that regulates the action of the ductless glands, the viscera, blood vessels, and other organs possessing involuntary muscles. It consists of sympathetic and parasympathetic divisions.

*Autopathic: Term signifying feeling that has been distorted by self-consciousness and bias. (See *Ditentive.* Contrasted with orthopathic. From αὐτός, self, and πάθος, feeling.)

---

[1] Fuller definitions of many of the phylobiological terms listed here may be found in the glossary of *The Biology of Human Conflict* and in the *Psychiatric Dictionary* compiled by Leland E. Hinsie and Jacob Shatzky (New York, Oxford University Press, 1940, pp. vi + 559.)

The glossary has been compiled for the benefit of lay readers as well as professional, so that terms are included besides those having special phylobiological significance.

Behavioral anatomy: Term used by the author in connection with morphological change involved in the phyloörganism's shift of behavior from its primary, total reaction to its secondary symbolic function. This concept should be distinguished from the objective descriptions of regional anatomy.

Biological norm: As used in phylobiology, this term refers to the organism's primary bionomic balance, or cotention. (Contrasted with numen, social reaction-average, or "normality." See also *Cotention, Homeostasis, Nomen.*)

Bionomics: The branch of biology that deals with the relation between organism and environment. (Synonym: ecology. See also *Anthroponomic, Ecosomatic.*)

Bio-social: In phylobiology this term refers to the primary biological principle of species solidarity. (Synonyms: organismic, total. Contrasted with numen, politico-social, psychosocial.)

*Central constant: The primary principle governing the organism's total action-pattern, and relating man as a species to his environment. (Synonyms: common constant, internal constant. Compare external constant.)

Cephalic: Pertaining to the head.

Cerebro-ocular: Term used to describe behavior-reactions involving combined function of brain and organ of vision.

Cerebrospinal nervous system: The brain, spinal cord and their branches. This system regulates the organism's voluntary musculature.

Coenesthetic: Having to do with the body's general internal sensibility. (See also *Kinesthetic.*)

Collective whole: Sum of the parts composing a unit or substance. In phylobiology, "normality" or the social reaction-average represents a collective whole in contrast to the primary organismic unit represented by the phylum man. (Contrasted with organic whole.)

*Common constant: See *Central constant.*

*Cotension: Term descriptive of the tensional norm of the body that controls its coördinated neuromuscular function. (Contrasted with ditension. See also *Cotention.*)

*Cotention: The type of attention that marks the organism's total tensional reaction in relation to the environment, and that precludes the usual play of wishful fantasies with their interrelational affects and strivings. (Contrasted with ditention. See also *Biological norm, Homeostasis, Nomen.*)

*Cotentive: See *Cotention.* (Contrasted with ditentive. See also *Homeostatic, Orthonomic, Orthopathic, Orthotonic, Protogenic, Syntonic, Total.*)

Dialysis: Separation of elements normally united; discontinuity. (See also *Dichotomy.*)

Dichotomy: As used in phylobiology, this term expresses the two-way policy of feeling and thinking coincident with man's ditentive pattern of reaction.

*Ditension: Disturbance in the body's tensional norm, resulting in faulty neuromuscular adaptation to the environment. (Contrasted with cotension. See also *Ditention*.)

*Ditention: Term used to indicate the intrusion of affect-elements or bias into ordinary attention. Ditention is a reaction that characterizes man's interrelational behavior throughout. (Contrasted with cotention.)

*Ditentive: See *Ditention*. (Contrasted with cotentive. See also *Affectosymbolic, Autopathic, Ditonic, Metanomic, Numinal, Paratonic, Partitive*.)

*Ditonic: See *Ditentive*. (Contrasted with syntonic.)

Ecology: See *Bionomics*.

*Ecosomatic: Word used as variant of term "organism-environment." (From οἶχος, environment, and σῶμα, organism.)

Electroencephalograph: An instrument for measuring and recording the electrical activity of the brain. Abbreviation: EEG.

Empathy: The feeling-identification of oneself with another. (See also *Autoempathic*.)

Endogenous: Originating from or due to internal causes.

*Endophatic: Term used to indicate primary feeling. (From ἔνδον, within, and πάθος, feeling.)

*External constant: The principle governing the consistency of the organism's symbolic behavior in relation to the environment. (Compare internal or central constant. See also *Nomen*.)

Feeling: As used in phylobiology, the total response of the organism to stimuli naturally affecting its primary motivation. Feeling arises as a spontaneous reaction within the organism as a whole. (Synonym: orthopathic reaction. Contrasted with affect or autopathic reaction.)

Generic: See *Phylic*.

Glia: The connective tissue supporting cells of brain and spinal cord. Used by the author in a figurative sense.

*Group-analysis: Term originally applied by the author to his investigation of the impediment to coördinated group function. As used by him, the term "group" signifies an organic unit, not a collection of individuals. The studies in group or community pathology were begun in 1918. This method involves the subjective participation of all the elements comprising a social group, wherein each investigator is not only an observer but is also himself material to be observed. In its later development this method was called phyloanalysis. (Synonym: phyloanalysis. Not to be confused with group-therapy.)

Group-therapy: A psychiatric method of recent development in which patients are treated collectively. They discuss their problems, reactions and ideologies under the guidance of a psychiatrist, and receive advice or assistance from him with a view to reinterpreting and readjusting their feelings and behavior in a "more normal manner." (To be distinguished from group-analysis, phyloanalysis.)

Homeostasis: Term originated by W. B. Cannon to designate "the coördinated physiological processes which maintain most of the steady states in the organism." In its phylobiological application the scope of this term is widened to include the internal balance of function maintained by every organism as a whole, and by every species as a whole, in relation to the environment. (See also *Biological norm, Cotention, Nomen.*)

Hominid: Human being.

Hypothalamic: Pertaining to the ventral or lower portion of the interbrain or diencephalon. (See also *Thalamic, Phylothalamic.*)

*'I'-complex: See *'I'-persona.*

*'I'-persona: The restricted part-expression of the personality, or the affective identity through which man, individual and social, achieves his symbolic interchange. The 'I'-persona represents the systematized sum of the individual's projective, symbolic processes with their divisive "feelings" or affects, in contrast to the primary coördination of function motivating the behavior of the organism as a whole. (Synonyms: 'I'-complex, social substantive 'I'. Contrasted with total organism. See also *Affect, Part-brain, Social image, Social neurosis.*)

*Internal constant: See *Central constant.*

Interrelational: Term used by the author to describe the disfunction in the phylum expressed in social interactions resultant from man's neurosis. (Contrasted with intrarelational.)

*Intraorganismic: Term describing reactions internal to the organism of man as a phylum. (See also *Intrarelational.*)

*Intrarelational: Term used to describe total coördinated function in man as a phylum. (Contrasted with interrelational. See also *Intraorganismic.*)

Involuntary nervous system: See *Autonomic nervous system.*

Kinesthetic: Pertaining to muscle sense. (See also *Coenesthetic.*)

Kymograph: An instrument for recording variations in physiological processes, for instance, those of respiration and pulse.

*Metanomic: This term refers to the organism's part-reactions to the environment, that is, to its secondary, affectively conditioned system of reactions. (Contrasted with orthonomic. See also *Ditentive.* From μετά, beyond, and νόμος, law.)

GLOSSARY

Miniature behavior-segment: The symbolic part-system mediated chiefly by the cortex. (Contrasted with the organism as a whole. See also *Parencephalon, Part-brain, Third nervous system, "Third brain."*)

Modal: In phylobiology this term has to do with the mood or mode of man.

Morphology: In phylobiological usage this term relates specifically to those functional innovations in man that have induced structural modifications in the process of his evolution as a species.

Neurodynamics: Term used by the author in connection with investigations which posit the thesis that the interrelational disorders of man are due to disturbance in the organism's internal tensional patterns.

Neurosis: See *Social neurosis*.

**Neuro-social:* Term describing the deflection or interruption in the direct relation of the organism of man to the environment that was coincident with the development of the symbolic system or the function of speech. (See also *Socio-cortical*.)

Neurotic: This term is applied in phylopathology not only to the psychoneurotic patient but also to the autopathic behavior of the so-called "normal" individual. (Contrasted with phyloörganismic. See also *Social neurosis*.)

**Nomen:* Term employed to indicate the consistency of man's organismic response to environmental phenomena. (Contrasted with numen. See also *Biological norm, Cotention, Homeostasis*. From νόμος, law.)

Normality: From the viewpoint of phylobiology normality represents a social reaction-average that is characterized by affecto-symbolic or ditentive behavior and hence lacks the validity of a biological norm. This deviate mode of adaptation is now common to individuals throughout the race of man, activating the behavior of the socially adjusted individual no less than that of the so-called psychoneurotic patient. (Synonym: social reaction-average. Contrasted with biological norm.)

**Numen:* Indicates the affecto-symbolic deflection superimposed upon man's primary feeling-reactions through the process of social conditioning. The consequent distortion of man's senses disrupts his relation to the environment, especially to other members of the species or to the community generally. (Contrasted with nomen. See also *Social image*. L. *numen* = nod, acquiescence.)

**Ontoörganism:* The single individual or element of a species. From the background of phylobiology the individual is viewed as an integrated unit within the phylic whole. (Synonym: ontosoma. See also *Phyloörganism*.)

Ontosoma: See Ontoörganism.

Organic whole: See *Organism as a whole.*

Organism as a whole: This term refers to a principle of integration that unites and correlates the functions of the elements composing a living organism. In phylobiology this term is applied to the species as well as to the individual. (Contrasted with collective whole.)

Organismic: See *Organism as a whole.*

**Orthencephalon:* The cerebral system that regulates the organism's primary or total pattern of reaction. (Contrasted with parencephalon, part-brain, third nervous system, "third brain." From ὀρθός, straight, and ἐγκέφαλος, brain.)

**Orthonomic:* In phylobiology this term refers to the organism's total coördinative function. The orthonomic mechanism preserves the balance of the organism as a whole in its relation to the environment. (Contrasted with metanomic. See also *Cotentive.* From ὀρθός, straight, and νόμος, law.)

**Orthopathic:* Term describing feeling that is primary, direct, whole. (Contrasted with authpathic. See also *Cotentive.* From ὀρθός, straight, and πάθος, feeling.)

**Orthotonic:* This term describes the internal tone or tension characterizing the organism's total pattern of reaction. (Contrasted with paratonic. See also *Cotentive.* From ὀρθός, straight, and τόνος, tension.)

Parasympathetic nervous system: A division of the autonomic system which, along with the sympathetic system, contributes to the maintenance of the organism's internal balance of function.

**Paratonic:* Term describing the internal tone or tension that characterizes the secondary, affectively conditioned system of response. (Contrasted with orthotonic. See also *Ditentive.* From παρά, beside, and τόνος, tension.)

**Parencephalon:* See part-brain. (Contrasted with orthencephalon. From παρά, beside, and ἐγκέφαλος, brain.)

**Part-brain:* The restricted cerebral system that controls the secondary or partitive pattern of tensions and relates individuals only symbolically, vicariously to one another. The part-brain has brought about a generic division in man's feeling and motivation and has distorted the most vital functions of his organism. (Synonyms: parencephalon, third nervous system, "third brain." Contrasted with orthencephalon.)

**Partitive:* Phylobiology employs this term in signifying processes that are mediated by the organism's part-functions restricted to the cephalic segment, and that make contact only with the part-features (symbols) of outer objects. The artificial supremacy of man's partitive or affecto-symbolic mode of behavior over the primary motivation of the organism as a whole constitutes the physiological basis of both individual and social neurosis. (Contrasted with total. See also *Ditentive*.)

Pathognomonic: Referring to signs and symptoms indicative of a specific disease.

Periphery: This term refers to those external body-structures through which the organism reacts to the surrounding environment.

Phylic: Refers to man as a species. (Synonyms: generic, racial, phyloorganismic, phylosomatic. Contrasted with individual, ontoörganismic, ontosomatic, social.)

**Phyloanalysis:* A method developed by the author for investigating disorders in human behavior. Originally called group-analysis. Phyloanalysis regards the symptoms of individual and society as but the outer aspect of impaired tensional processes that affect the balance of the organism's internal reaction as a whole. Through the technique of phyloanalysis there is induced in individual and group an awareness of partitive or deviate behavior. This discrimination is made possible by contrasting the internal tensions concomitant to this type of behavior-reaction with the internal pattern of tension concomitant to the organism's motivation as a whole. (Synonym: group-analysis. Not to be confused with group-therapy. From φῦλον, phylum, race.)

**Phylobiology:* The science of behavior that studies the relation of the organism as a whole in its adaptation to the environment and to other organisms. Phylobiology posits a principle of functional unity and solidarity activating the behavior of individual and species.

**Phyloneurology:* Term applied to neural modifications that affect the behavior of man as a phylum.

**Phyloneurosis:* See *Social neurosis*.

*Phyloörganism: The species man regarded as an organismic whole in which the element or individual is a phylically integrated unit. (Synonym: phylosoma. See also *Ontoörganism, Ontosoma*.)

**Phyloörthopedic:* Term used to describe the internal technique for reactivating the organism's tensional coördination as a whole. (See also *Cotention*.)

**Phylopathology:* Term denoting the scientific investigation of the underlying factors in behavior-disorders envisaged from the background of phylobiology. It represents a broad organismic approach to deviations in behavior, and includes oneself and the so-called normal community along with the neurotic patient.

**Phylophysiology:* This term refers to the physiological tensions that underlie the manifest expressions of individual and social behavior.

Phylosoma: The species man as a unitary organism. (Synonyms: phyloörganism, phylum. See also *Ontosoma.*)

Phylosynthesis: This term refers to the adjustment of man's conflict upon a basis that is both physiological and phylic.

Phylothalamic: Refers to the structures and functions that regulate the behavior of man as an organismic whole. (See also *Hypothalamic, Thalamic.*)

Phylum: In phylobiology this word is used to include the human race irrespective of ethnological or geographical differentiations. (Synonyms: race, species.)

Physiological: In phylobiology the term refers to perceptible processes internal to the organism. Nervous or behavior disorders are regarded as due to definite physiological conflict within man's organism as individual and species. (Contrasted with mental, psychic. See also *Phylophysiology.*)

Politico-social: Term referring to the secondary, affecto-symbolic processes characterizing man's interrelational adaptation. (Contrasted with bio-social, organismic, total. See also *Numen, Psychosocial.*)

Preconscious, The: See *Primary Identification.*

Primary Identification: The primary phase or mode of consciousness of the infant in which there is complete identification with the mother organism. This preconscious mode represents the non-libidinal, pre-objective phase of the organism's development. In later life it finds symbolic expression in art, poetry, folklore, religion, in the dreams and fantasies of the "normal" individual as well as of the psychoneurotic. (Synonym: The Preconscious.)

Projection: In phylobiology emphasis is placed upon the phylic aspect of this mechanism whereby one holds others responsible for ideas or impulses arising within oneself. This reaction developed coincidently with the symbolic segment or with man's acquisition of the language-forming function.

Protergy: The principle of the organism's primary motivation or function (Synonym: protogenic function. Contrasted with allergy, allogenic function. From πρῶτος, primary, and ἔργον, force.)

Protogenic function: See *Protergy.*

Psychic: As used in phylobiology, this term refers to the domain of man's mental or symbolic activities. Unlike psychiatry and psychoanalysis, phylobiology does not regard the cause of man's behavior-disturbances as residing in the psychic sphere. The cause resides rather in certain inappropriate tensional constellations affecting man as individual and species. The approach to these conditions should therefore be an internal, organismic or physiological approach. (Synonyms: mental, symbolic. Contrasted with physiological, organismic.)

Psychosocial: Term applied to man's affecto-symbolic behavior in its social expressions. (Contrasted with bio-social. See also *Numen, Politico-social, Socio-symbolic*.)

Race: See *Phylum.*

Resistance: As used in phylobiology, this word possesses broad biological significance. It refers to the presence in individuals and groups of a socially constellated defense-reaction which automatically preserves them against a realization of the illusory nature of of their neurotic and "normal" contact and communication.

**Retroceptive thinking:* Self-conscious type of thinking that has been distorted by the bias of affect. (See also retropathic feeling, retrofective action. From L. *retro,* backward, and [*con-*]*cipere,* to conceive, to take in.)

**Retrofective action:* Type of action that has been self-consciously distorted by affect. (From L. *retro,* backward, and *facere,* to do.)

*ature*Retropathic feeling:* Type of feeling that recoils affectively upon the subject. (Contrasted with orthopathic. See also *Autopathic, Autoempathic*. From L. *retro,* backward, and πάθος, feeling.)

Segmentation: Used in phylobiology in referring to the division that has taken place within the unitary organism of man as a species through his misuse of the symbol-forming mechanism. This division or segmentation has occurred within each individual as well as between individuals and among social groups. It has interrupted man's direct relation to the environment and has distorted the most vital functions of his organism. (See also *Affect, Part-brain, Social neurosis, Third nervous system, "Third brain."*)

**Semiosomatic:* Term used to describe the partitive modification that has occurred within the organism as the result of reflex conditioning. (From σημεῖον, sign, and σῶμα, body.)

Semiotic: This term is applied by the author to man's symbol-forming capacity.

**Semiotic nervous system:* See *Third nervous system.*

Social: In phylobiology this word refers to man's word-conditioned interrelations as they are mediated through the affecto-symbolic mechanism. (Contrasted with organismic, phylic, societal.)

**Social image:* An affective impression representing socially crystallized opinions, beliefs and prejudices which are deeply ingrained in the individual and are corroborated by society, but for which there is no objective, demonstrable foundation. These images, or socially sanctioned illusions, are emotionally conditioned and are to be sharply distinguished from the legitimate images one forms of some object or phenomenon as determined by its structure or inherent meaning. Examples of the social image are to be found in the constellations of affective ideas or images that are bound up with one's conception of the Church, the State, the home, marriage, God, one's country, one's neighbor, one's self. (See also *Numen*. Contrasted with nomen.)

Social neurosis: The disorder and conflict existing throughout man's social structure, though universally unrecognized by him. Viewed phylobiologically, the social neurosis is the generic condition of which the individual manifestations of mental and nervous disorders, crime and social conflict are merely symptomatic expressions. (Synonym: phyloneurosis.)

Social reaction-average: See *Normality*.

Social substantive 'I': See *'I'-persona*.

Societal: As used in phylobiology this word is closely related to such terms as organismic, phylic, total. It has a broader significance than that ordinarily attaching to this term. (Contrasted with social.)

Socio-biological: This term is used with a view to reintegrating the two aspects of man's behavior—external social phenomena and the fundamental biology of man—which, according to phylobiology, embody an essential totality. (See also *Socio-cortical, Socio-symbolic*.)

Socio-cortical: This term refers to the organism's social interchange by means of symbol and speech. (Synonym: socio-symbolic. Compare socio-biological. See also *Neuro-social*.)

Socio-neurotic: This term refers to the conditioned, affecto-symbolic behavior of social man today. (See also *Social neurosis*.)

Socio-symbolic: See *Socio-cortical*.

Soma: The body or organism. (See also *Ontosoma, Phylosoma*.)

Species: See *Phylum*.

Species solidarity: The principle that insures the uniform and consistent pattern of structure and function within the individual element and throughout the species as a whole.

Symbolic attention: See *Ditention*.

Sympathetic nervous system: A division of the autonomic system which, along with the parasympathetic system, maintains the organism's internal functional balance.

Syncretism: The fallacious reconcilement of incompatible concepts.

Synergy: Combined action or operation of two or more entities.

Syntonic: In phylobiology this term applies to the primary tensional state of the organism. The syntonic pattern controls the balance of function and behavior in the individual and in the species as a whole. (Synonym: cotentive. Contrasted with ditonic.)

Tension: In phylobiology this term refers to internally appreciable patterns of strain or stress. Distinction is made between two patterns of tension, the one primary, total, organismic, and constituting the organism's biological norm; the other secondary, restricted and underlying the social neurosis in its individual and community expression. (See also *Ditonic, Syntonic, Tonicity*.)

Thalamic: Pertaining to the thalamus, the largest division of the interbrain or diencephalon. (See also *Hypothalamic, Phylothalamic*.)

**Third brain:* See *Third nervous system*.

**Third nervous system:* This system embodies the neural structures that govern man's symbolic interchange or the function of speech. It is differentiated by the author on the basis of its specialization of function, not on the basis of anatomical demarcation. Through its misuse, the third nervous system is responsible for man's ditentive or autopathic behavior. (Synonym: "third brain." See also *Parencephalon, Part-brain*.)

Tonicity: The condition or property of possessing tone or tension. As used in phylobiology, this term is synonymous with internal baance. (See also *Cotention, Syntonic*.)

Total organism: See *Organism as a whole*.

Transference: As used in phylobiology, this term refers to the system of socially conditioned, affecto-symbolic relationships that actuate individuals and communities and that substitute for man's primary organismic interrelations.

Vegetative nervous system: See *Autonomic nervous system*.

Voluntary nervous system: See *Cerebrospinal nervous system*.

NAME INDEX

AEschylus, 334
Albrecht, W. A., 363 note 5
Alexander, F., 400 note 3
Allee, W. C., 73 note 1, 455 note 12
Allport, G. W., 76-7, 81, 86
Anderson, O. D., 283 note 4
Anderson, S., 158, 178 note 4
Aristotle, 225
Arnold, M., 334

Bailey, H. S., 68-9
Baldwin, J. M., 210
Baruch, B., 145-46, 155 note 9
Beaumont, Lady Margaret, 5
Beethoven, L v., 335
Benson, C. E., 523 note 5
Bentley, A. F., 19, 21, 105-07
Berens, C., 523 note 5
Berger, H., 88, 397, 524 note 16
Bernard, C., 213, 232 note 12, 341, 363 note 9
Bishop, F. M., 523 note 5
Bleuler, E., 85, 355, 364 note 14
Boas, G., 23-4, 28
Boring, E. G. 76,
Bradley, C., 401 note 6
Brandt, H. F., 523 note 5
Bridgman, P. W., 72-3
Brooke, R., 251, 258 note 24
Brown, L. 400 note 3
Bucy, P. C., 401 note 5
Burke, E., 178 note 1
Buswell, G. T., 495-96, 499, 523 note 5
Byrnes, J. F., 464

Calvin, J., 225
Cameron, N., 523 note 5
Cannon, W. B., 213, 232 note 12, 341-43, 363 notes 7, 8, 9, 403
Carlson, A. J., 15, 23, 25, 28
Carmichael, L., 523 note 8
Case, T. J., 401 note 5
Castiglioni, A., 311 note 2
Center, S., 523 note 5

Charcot, J. M., 210, 225
Coghill, G. E., 88, 283-84 note 11
Columbus, C., 237
Compton, K. T., 145
Comroe, J. H., 400 note 1
Conant, J. B., 145
Cooley, C. H., 87

Darwin, C., 9, 179 note 20, 288
Davis, H., 401 notes 5, 6
Davis, P. A., 390-91 note 3, 401 note 6
Delgado, H., 56
Dewey, J., 14, 46, 52, 87, 134
Dodge, R., 455 note 7
Dostoevsky, F., 189, 199 note 7, 482
Du Bois, E. F., 522 note 1

Edgerton, H. E., 523 note 5
Edwards, D. J., 493-94, 522 note 1
Einstein, A., 62, 288, 311 note 6
Elsberg, C. A., 338-39 note 9
Emerson, A. E., 20, 455 note 12

Fields, P. E., 283 note 5
Finesinger, J. E., 400 note 2
Forel, A., 210
Freeman, W., 390 note 1
French, T. N., 400 note 3
Freud, S., 76, 88, 120, 189, 199 note 1, 217, 225, 239-41, 250, 252, **261, 313,** 318, 421

Gaillard, M., 522 note 1
Galileo, 9
Galt, W. E., 199 note 12, 232 note 13, 257 note 13, 283 notes 5, 8, 284 note 12, 312 note 19, 485 note 5, 522 note*, 523 note 15
Gantt, W. H., 283 notes 4, 7
Garrison, F. H., 199 notes 10, 11
Gerard, R. W., 43, 66-7
Gerbrands, R., 487, 522 note 1
Gesell, R., 400 note 1
Gibbs, E. L., 401 notes 5, 8, 524 note 17

537

Gibbs, F. A., 401 notes 5, 8, 511, 523 notes 10, 13, 14, 524 note 17
Gibbs, W., 255, 288, 311 note 5
Glaser, N. M., 283 note 4
Goethe, J. W. v., 213
Goldenberg, M., 503, 523 note 10
Goldstein, K., 19
Grass, A. M., 394, 503, 506, 511, 523 notes 10, 13
Gregg, A., 5, 12 note 1, 18, 21, 23, 28, 104-05
Grier, H. E., 523 note 5
Gurevitch, 85

Haeckel, E., 231-32 notes 1, 9, 426 note 10
Haggard, H. W., 311 note 2
Haldane, H. S., 363 note 9
Hardy, L. H., 523 note 5
Hargreaves, R., 24
Hartz, J., 400 note 3
Harvey, E. N., 401 note 7
Hayakawa, S. I., 52
Head, H., 243, 258 note 17
Herrick, C. J., 11, 20-1, 44 note 2, 70-1, 74 notes 3-4, 99-100
Herskovits, M. J., 45, 47
Hess, W. R., 400 note 1, 522 note 1
Hinsey, J. C., 522 note 1
Hinsie, L. E., 17, 21
Hitler, A., 7, 9, 110, 184-86, 188
Hobart, G. A., III, 401 note 7
Hoffman, A. C., 523 note 8
Horn, D., 523 note 5
Huss, J., 7
Huxley, T. H., 145, 155 note 8, 313, 461, 485 note 2

Infeld, L., 311 note 6

Jacobson, E., 401 note 4, 455 note 7
Jaensch, E., 85-6
James, W., 76, 191, 199 note 8
Janet, P., 210
Jasper, H. H., 401 note 6
Jennings, H. S., 56
Jesus, 333
Joan of Arc, 7

Kant, I., 225
Karn, H. W., 283 note 5
Katz, D., 34, 97-8
Kerwer, F., 523 note 5
Kinsey, A. C., 455-56 note 19

Kirby, D. B., 523 note 5
Kluckhohn, Clyde, 102-03
Knott, J. R., 524 note 16
Koch, R., 194, 288
Korzybski, A., 295
Krogman, W. M., 40

Landis, C., 18, 101-02, 522 note 1
Larkin, K., 523 note 5
La Rochefoucauld, F., 178 note 1
Leavitt, H. C., 401 note 3
Lehmann, A., 400 note 2
Lennox, W. G., 401 note 5, 524 note 17
Lewin, K., 77
Liddell, H. S., 283 note 4
Lillie, R. S., 18, 51, 56, 59, 61, 63-4, 66, 257 note 12
Lindeman, E. C., 86, 88
Livingstone, R., 9, 12 note 2
Loomis, A. L., 401 note 7
Lorente de Nó, R., 523 note 5
Lowenstein, O., 523 note 5
Lucas, J. G., 179 note 23
Luce, L. E., 497
Luther, M., 225

McAdam, R. E., 523 note 5
Maier, N. R. F., 283 note 4
Malamud, W., 401 note 6
Marconi, G., 288
Marfaing, A., 523 note 5
Marquis, D. G., 523 note 5
Mather, C., 7
Meumann, E., 400 note 2
Meyer, A., 85, 108, 218
Miles, W. R., 523 note 5
Mili, G., 523 note 5
Montaigne, M. E. de, 198, 199 note 13
Morrow, J. F., Jr., 523 note 5
Moses, L., 401 note 3
Murphy, G., 55, 57

Neumueller, J., 523 note 5
Newton, I., 9

Odegard, O., 56, 84-6
Ogburn, W. F., 84-5
Ogden, C. K., 126
Oswald, C., 523 note 5

Paganelli, A., 523 note 5
Paget, R., 311 note 9
Pasteur, L., 9, 194, 288, 471
Paul, the Apostle, 225

NAME INDEX

Pavlov, I. P., 88, 283 note 4
Pierce, H. F., 523 note 5
Plato, 9, 225
Pope, A., 143

Rashevsky, N., 29, 31, 33 note 2
Razran, G. H. S., 283 note 7
Read, H., 91, 126, 334-35
Reves, E., 178 note 11
Rheinberger, M., 503, 523 note 10
Richter, C. P., 363 note 5
Robinson, C., 523 note 5
Robinson, J. H., 161, 178 note 5
Rock, R. T., 523 note 5
Roger, H., 500, 523 note 5
Roosevelt, F. D., 117, 449-50, 455 note 13
Rubin, S., 401 note 3
Rukeyser, M., 311 note 5

Sanborn, F. B., 179 note 13
Savonarola, G., 225
Schleicher, C., 523 note 5
Schmidt, C. F., 400 note 1
Shakespeare, W., 158, 171, 335
Shaw, B., 57, 448
Shields, C., 49, 119, 122, 124, 180, 335
Shultz, I. T., 401 note 3
Sill, A. P., 33 note 1
Socrates, 225
Solomon, P., 401 note 6
Sorokin, P. A., 82-3
Spencer, H., 205, 231 note 8, 363 note 9, 455 note 15
Spinoza, B., 225
Stein, L., 94
Stockard, C., 104-05
Stratton, G. M., 54-6
Syz, H., 44 note 1, 155 note 1, 232 note 20, 257 note 12, 258 note 27, 284 note 12, 339 note 15, 391 note 4, 455 notes 2, 9, 522 note*, 523 note 9

Thompson, C. B., 33 note 1, 338 note 8, 522 note*
Thompson, F., 334
Thompson, H. A., 497, 523 note 5
Thoreau, H. D., 170, 179 note 13
Thouless, R. H., 24, 82
Tolman, E., 76
Tomlinson, B. E., 523 note 5
Travis, L. E., 401 note 6
Truman, H. S., 355
Turner, H. B., 490, 494, 522 note 1

Veith, T., 523 note 5
Volkmann, J., 487, 522 note 1
von Bertalanffy, L., 63, 74 note 2
von Wyss, W. H., 400 note 2

Wagner, R., 157-58, 178 note 2
Walter, W. G., 401 note 5
Watts, J. W., 390 note 1
Wellman, B., 523 note 8
Wertheimer, M., 231 note 2
Westgate, L. G., 356, 364 note 17
White, Leslie, 71
Whitford, G., 522 note 1
Wilde, O., 136
Williams, H. B., 522 note 1
Winkler, C., 400 note 2
Wood, E. R., 523 note 5
Wordsworth, W., 5
Wunderlich, C. R. A., 199 note 10

Xavier, St. Francis, 225

Yerkes, R. M., 53-4
Young, B., 225

Zoneff, P., 400 note 2

SUBJECT INDEX*

Absolutism, 38-9, 183, 185, 242-43, 274, 316-18
  see also Unilateralism
Ache—
  see Pain
Action and reaction—
  see Law of action and reaction
Adaptation—
  see Attention; Bionomic adaptation; Ontosomatic adaptation
Admire—
  derivation of, 179 note 15
Adult and infant generations, 410-11, *412-20*
  see also Parent-child relationship
Affability, 174, 243
Affect—
  attention and interest deflected by, 29, 169, 174, 204-05, *207-08*, 209-10, 230
  brain-function and, 102-03, 203-04, 248-49, 328, 331-32
  and conditioning, 266, *267*, 270-71, 273-74
  contagion of, 362
  definition of, 160
  encysted feeling, 306
  examples of, 165-169
  and "face", 172-73, 197-98, 352
  frustration of, 95, 247
  and 'I'-persona, 53, 188, 229, 233, 268, 272, 278, 293, 298, 306, 328, 342, 350, 362, 368, 384, 398, 420, 423
  identical with prejudice, 160-61, 168-69
  inception of, 293, 418
  incitement to conflict and war, 57, 168, 351
  in man only, 273
  and man's behavior, 29, 164-65, 248, *272-73*, 293, 328, 421, 432, 483
  and money, 229
  and neuromuscular stress, 68
  and the numen, 255
  and organism-environment relationship, 83, 383, 430
  phylobiological approach to, 11, 29, 160-61, 164, 167-69, 208, **210-11**, *213-15*, 219-21, 223-24, 226, 240-41, 243-44, 246-48, 257, 262, *309-10*, 357, *368-69*, 429, 462-63
  physiological substrate of, 68, 262, 368-69
  possessive quality of, 274
  and primary feeling, 83, 272-74, 295-96, 332, 361, 452
  and psychiatry, 160, *262*
  resurgent feeling, 296
  scientific understanding of, 18
  a social condition, 28, 167-68, *169*
  and symbolic system, 100, 106-07, 235, 264, 277, *293-96*, 409, 429
  systematization of, 64, 66, 83, 105, 233, 267-68, 271-74, 292, 295, 305-06, 316, 329, 342, 376, 384, 416, 420, 423
  and traditional beliefs, 163
  see also *Amour Propre;* Bias; Experimental affect; "Face"; Prejudice
Affect-dichotomy, 185-86, 188, 215, 217
Affect-image, 262
  and dichotomous fantasies, 385-86
  elimination of, 372, 374, 385, 444
  and 'I'-persona, 353
  in parent-child relationship, 215-17
  and physiological tensions, 91, *246-49*, 374
  see also Projection
Affect-linkage—
  phylobiological approach to, *310*, 347, 371
  with symbol, 38, 83, 270, 280
Affect-paranoia, 168
Affect-projection, 79, 249, 460
Affectation, 160

*The more important entries are indicated by italics

Affection, 137, 168, 460
Affectivity, 12, 169, 184, 193, 309, 316-18, 354, 443
Affecto-symbolic behavior, 28
  in child-conditioning, 276, 378
  pain involved in, 243
  phylobiological approach to, 335, 375, 446
  and total pattern, 235, 331-32, 375, 446
Affecto-symbolic segment—
  conditioned reflex localized in, 366
  and man's behavior, 422, 438, 443, 470
  phylobiological approach to, 256, 306, 309, 375, 390, 430, 481
  specialization within forebrain, 430
  see also Miniature symbolic system; Socio-symbolic segment
Afferent impulses
  see Impulses
Agreement, 9-10
Alcohol—
  used as an anodyne, 253-54, 339 note 13
  see also Drugs; Tobacco
Allegorical expression—
  of organic unity, 334
  unconscious symbolism, 297
Allergy, 322, 332
All-might, 64
Allogenic function—
  see Intrarelational function
Alloplasm, 320, 322
  see also Protoplasm
Altered frame of reference—
  and author's personal experience, 457-459
  difficulty of communication, 88
  in man's behavior, 9, 92, *296*
  in phylobiological research, 12, 15, 21-2, 26, 80, 249, 307, 309-10, 410, 478, 480
  in science, 21
Ambivalence, 261-62, 281, 318
  see also Dichotomy
Amour propre—
  attention intercepted by, 209
  and 'I'-persona, 328, 432
  identical with "face", 171, 292, 328, 353, 375
  and interrelational behavior, 170-71, 328
  see also Affect
Animal life—
  biological fitness in, 35
  fighting in, 55-7
  induction of rudimentary affect in, 273-74
  organism-environment relationship in, 202, 233, 263, 341-42
  sense-impressions in, 439-40
  subsistence in, 229
Anodyne—
  see Palliatives
Antagonism—
  in animal life, 56-7
  in human life, 56-7
  see also Competitiveness; Conflict; Dichotomy; Social discord
Anthropology, 47, 85, 152-53, 187
Anthropomorphism, 236-37, 239, 269
Anthroponomic behavior, 210, 212-13, 257, 280, 367
Apparent—
  derivation of, 232 note 15
Art, 151, *334-35*
Associational system—
  involved in man's conditioning, 269-70
  primary composition of, 368
  same in individual and community, 365-66
  symbolic function of, 438-39
Asylums—
  see Institutions
Atheist, 84, 188
Atomic Bomb, 153-54, 156, *466-67*, 481-482
Atomic energy, 153-54, 467
Attention—
  in animal life, 202
  author's early interest in, 210
  and behavior-students, 209
  deflected by affect, 29, 230
  an ecological process, 29, 201, *202*, 203-05, 209-11, 230, 317, 328, 384-85, *442*
  impairment of, 27, 49, 71-2, 169, 174, 204-05, *207*, *209*, 211-13, 315-17, 342, 442-44
  originally a total process, 203, *345*, 441
  phylobiological approach to, 202-05, 209-11, 305, 317, 344-46, 441-43
  physiological aspects of, 29, 209-10
  and symbolic system, 202, 204, 337, 440, 442-43
  two types of, 29, 346-48
  see also Cotention; Ditention; Symbolic attention
Autistic thinking, 85, 355

SUBJECT INDEX

Autogenic conditioning, 273, 402, 425
Automorphism—
  see Anthropomorphism
Autonomic nervous system—
  afferent and efferent impulses carried by, 406
  conditioning and, 280
  designated as first nervous system, 405
  involved in respiration and vision, 396
  motivation of man and animal governed by, 403-05
  and organism-environment relationship, 397, 404, *405-06*
  realignment of third nervous system with, 426
  relation to cerebrospinal nervous system, 396-98, 404-06
  relation to socio-symbolic segment, 341
  see also Cerebrospinal nervous system
Autopathic—
  derivation of, 179 note 19
Autopathic motivation—
  analogy in untrained muscle, 379
  attention and interest deflected by, 174
  in the behavior of man, 173, 188-89, 196, 204, 208, 217, 229, *305*, 329, 342, 362, 375, 433, 480, 482
  and 'I'-persona, 186
  a phylic phenomenon, 190, 295
  phylobiological approach to, 186-87, 277, 340
  tensional substrate of, 360, 362
  and third nervous system, 408
  see also Affect; Orthopathic behavior
Autopathology, 465-66
Autosexuality—
  see Homosexuality
Avidity, 242
  derivation of, 257 note 14

Bacteriology—
  achievements of, 138-39
  analogy between phylobiology and, 26-7, 69, 96-7, 101, 164, *194-95*, 239, 244, 254-55, 361, 376, 471
  and infectious disease, 139, 289, 361-362, *470-71*
Balance—
  see Homeostasis; Muscular balance; Organismic balance; Walking
Basal metabolism—
  see Instrumental experimentation
Basic behavior of man—
  see Primary motivation of man
Behavior—
  altered frame of reference regarding, 5-6, 9, 12, 15, 26, 92, 249, 428
  and culture, 45-7, 52
  a dichotomous expression, 42, 188, 226-227
  everyone an authority, 6-7, 135, 143, 196
  external expressions of, 47
  C. J. Herrick's analysis of, 70
  and 'I'-persona, 289, 306
  lack of scientific approach to, 6-7, 11, *138-47, 152-53,* 190, 192-94, 198-99, 211-12, 288-90, 303, 307-08, 325, 354, 360, 365, 381-82, 403, 448-49, 481
  motivated by affect, 164-65, 168, 236, *272,* 438, 443
  motivated by feeling, 76, 443
  and the nomen, 239, 255, 290-91
  and the numen, 236-39, *255,* 289-91, 315-16
  objective approach required, 9, 21, 448
  phylobiological approach to, 7, 11, 22, 25, 28, 43, *61-2,* 84, *97,* 100, 105, 135-**136,** 141-43, 148-49, 164, 187, 198, 208-09, 219-20, 248-49, *256-57,* 259, *305-10,* 316-17, 320-22, *350-51,* 385, 392, *410, 425-26, 477-79,* 481, 485
  physiological substrate of, 20, 94, 247, 281-82, 318, 345, 396
  and "right," 39-40, 57-8, 292
  study by layman, 19
  subject to change, 43
  see also Anthroponomic behavior; Collective behavior; Disbehavior; Instinctive behavior; Interrelational behavior; Man's relation to man; Neural basis of behavior; Neurodynamics of behavior; Paleontology of behavior; Science of human behavior
Behavior-disorders—
  author's early interest in, 147, 210
  common to man, 146-47, *153,* 195-96, 208, 230, 254, 264, 324, 423, 462
  and communication, 423, 437
  and conditioning, 45
  deviation from functional norm, 321, 325, 329-30
  and "face," 173-74, 235

Behavior-disorders *(contd.)* —
 a functional imbalance, 109
 implicit in unilateralism, 188
 inadequate approach to, 144, 152, 193-196, 255-56, 264, 288-90, *307-08,* 319, 321, 358, 365, 382, 450, *482-84*
 a medical problem, 260, 264, 282
 and the numen, 237-40, *255*
 phylic implications of, 11-12, 69
 phylobiological approach to, 22, 68-9, 84, 101-04, 198, 211, 226-27, *240-43,* 264, *301-03, 317-18,* 323-26, 357, *369,* 450, 462-63, *468*
 physiological substrate of, 103-04, 169-170, 199 note 14, 262, 264, 277, 476
 reflected in literature and newspapers, 157-59, 193
 segmentation cause of, 423
 and the social community, *192-93,* 260-61, 480, *483-84*
 and third nervous system, 409, 418, 448
 See also Affecto-symbolic behavior; Conflict; Neurosis of man; Neurotic individual; Schizophrenia; Social neurosis; Socio-symbolic behavior
Behavior-inconsistency, 164-65, 245, 260
 evidenced in normality, 181, 304
 material of group-analysis, 306
 objective recognition required, 331, 476
 a universal phenomenon, 268, *331,* 448-49
 see also Feeling-inconsistency
Behavior-norm—
 and cotention, 323, 325
 deviations from, 37, 319-20, *329-30,* 331-32, 344, 421, 450
 in interrelational sphere, 30-2
 not yet established, *319,* 321, 323-24
 phylobiological approach to, 15-16, 28, *213,* 320, *322-24,* 344, 446, 471, 480
 restoration of, 273, 341
 and species solidarity, 324
  see also Biological norm; Central constant; Homeostasis
Behavior-patterns—
 altered by development of symbolic system, 295-96
 conflict between primary and total, 373, 384-85, *428-29,* 447
 instrumental differentiation of, 389, 392-93, 399, *487-522*
 reinstatement of total pattern, 108, 399,
 relation of eyes to, *371-73,* 440-41
 thinking determined by, *212-13,* 230
 two types discriminable, 108, 256, 301-02, 306, 344, 346, 369-70, *374-75,* 388-89
 see also Internal pattern; Tensional patterns
Behavior-schools, 276, 367
 see also General Semantics; Group-therapy; Psychiatry; Psychoanalysis
Behavior-students, 310, 338
 and attention, 209
 establishment of groups of, 477-78
 inadequate interpretations by, 11, 147, 213, *219,* 220, 282, 305, 319, 324, 448, 451
 not immune to behavior-disorders, 447-48
 use of alien tongues, 224
 see also Phylobiological students
Behavioral anatomy, 407-08
Belief, 163
 derivation of, 155 note 5
Bias, 160, 164-65, 193-94, 209, 376, 466
 see also Affect; Prejudice
Biological norm, 35, 39, 43, 60-1, 92, 319-20, 324, 421, 471, 473
 see also Behavior-norm
Bionomic adaptation—
 and development of symbolic system, 263, 341, 425
 impediment to, 354, 408-09
 throughout all forms of life, 279
 two modes of, 301-02, 385
 see also Ecology; Ecosomatic relationship; Ontosomatic adaptation; Organism - environment relationship; Primary motivation of man
Biophysiological basis of behavior disturbances, 277
Blink reflexes, 393, 495-96
Blushing, 179 note 20
Body—
 see Soma
Brain—
 affect referred back to, 248-49
 compared with other organs, 103, 326-327, 330
 differentiation of part-brain, 318, 330-332, 336-38, 356, 370-71, 381, 418, 433, 443, 479
 and 'I'-persona, 318
 of man and other animals, 103

SUBJECT INDEX

(contd.) —
means of communication, 103, 327
and organism-environment relationship, 255, 285, 287, 327-29, *370*, 397-398
in relation to man's behavior, *247-48*, 255-56, 291, 315-16, *318*, *330-33*, 340, 390, 396, 469
retina outgrowth of, 396
subjective knowledge of, lacking, 327-328, 330
see also Autonomic nervous system; Cerebrospinal nervous system; Cortex; Forebrain, Orthencephalon; Parencephalon; Part-brain; Thalamus

Brain-function—
and affect, 102-03
and behavior of man, 48, 68, 107, 328-32
deviation of, 71-2, 329-30, 366
enlargement of, 103, 256, 285, 288, 336-337, 341, 370-71, 402, 424, 451
and organism-environment relationship, 290, 327-28, 354, 365
relation of eye-movements to, 442
scientific knowledge of, 101-02, 329
and use of symbols, 103, 336-37

Brain-twist, 102, 463, 470, 485
Brain waves, 95, 394-97
see also Electroencephalography; Instrumental experimentation

Breathing—
see Respiration

Camera—
see Lifwynn Eye-movement Camera
Cancer, 422-23
Cardiovascular function—
see Instrumental experimentation
Central constant—
motivating principle in human behavior, 47, 176, 336, *340-41*, *344*, 473, 479
relation of external constant to, 340-341, 473
see also Behavior-norm; Biological norm; External constant

Cephalic region—
see Physiological tensions
Cerebral cortex—
see Cortex
Cerebral tensions—
see Headache; Physiological tensions

Cerebrospinal nervous system—
afferent and efferent impulses carried by, 404
designated as second nervous system, 405
and homeostasis, 404
involved in respiration and vision, 396
and organism-environment relationship, 404-05
realignment of third nervous system with, 426
relation between autonomic nervous system and, 396-98, 404-06
see also Autonomic nervous system

Challenge inherent in phylobiology, 36, 47, 64, 79-81
Character, 170, 217
Child—
biological health of, 35-7
conditioning of, *188*, *214-17*, 275-76, 320, 430
learning to walk, 378-80
talking in relation to, 378-79
see also Adult and infant generations; Infant; Motherhood; Parent-child relationship

Civilization, 103, 216, 414, *477*
due to symbolic system, 103
Collective whole, 308
see also Organic whole
Color blindness, 36
Columbia-Greystone project, 102
Common consciousness, 43
see also Consciousness
Common constant—
see Central constant
Common man, 14, 390, 474
Common tension—
see Cotention
Communication—
and affect, 294
author's interest in, 111
behavior-disorders related to, 423-24
and "face," 172-74
and group-therapy, 225
impediments to, 254, 424, 436
in parent-child relationship, 379, 413-416
phylobiological approach to, 135, 415-416, 423, *424*, 426, 435, 479
and speech-disorders, 423, 436-37
and thought, 135, 435
through symbolic system, 135, 143,

Communication (Contd.)—
151, 294, 336-37, 408, *413-15*, 435, 438-39
  see also Interrelational behavior; Organism-environment relationship
Communism, 16, 417, 475
Community—
  and behavior-disorders, 261, 365-66, 469
  dichotomous attitude of, 261, 279
  health of, 181, 282-83 note 1
  phylobiology and, 75
  see also Group; Normal community
Community mind—
  see Social mind
Competitiveness—
  and *amour propre*, 353
  and ditention, 353
  and "face," 196-97, 353
  and grab reflex, 353
  and 'I'-persona, 353, 359, *431-32*
  illustration of, 449-50
  inculcated in child, 216
  and segmentation, 430-31
  and self-interest, 196-97
  see also Possessiveness
Conceit—
  meaning of, 258 note 25
Concentration camps, 433
  see also Germany; Japan
Conditioned reflex—
  in animals, 104, *264-66*
  localized in affecto-symbolic segment, 366
  in man, *266-68*, 270
  physiological substrate of, 371
Conditioning—
  analogous in man and animal, 105, 266, 268, *269-73*, *275*, *278-80*, 281-282, 368-69, 446-47
  associational function involved in, 269-70
  of child, 273, 276, 320, 430
  conflict and, 268-69, 368
  dichotomy bred of, 214, 430
  differential, 268
  experimental procedure, 264-66, 269-270
  hypothetical procedure, 105
  and 'I'-persona, 268, 271-72, 274, 291, 430, 447
  illustration of, 446-47
  man's outlook distorted by, 256, *267-269*, 280, 286
  Pavlov's study analogous to phylobiological thesis, 88
  phylobiological approach to, 269-77, 279-82
  physiological reaction to, 267, 269, 276, 280
  in response to symbols of objects, 266-267, *270-71*, 275, 279-80
  throughout the species man, *272-74*, 280-81
  and transference, 268
  see also Autogenic conditioning; Social conditioning
Conflict—
  and conditioning, 268-69, 368
  different in man and other animals, 56-7
  and 'I'-persona, 18, 421, 451, *476-77*
  illustrative material, 157-59, 189-90
  incited by affect, 168, 351
  in interrelational life, 27-8, 42-3, 83, 159, 226, 243, *254*, 277, 340
  and man's symbolic capacity, 52-3, 65, 170, 263-64, *294*, *336-38*, *420*
  national expression of, 190-91, 465
  in neurotic and normal individual, 318, *429*, 437
  and pain, 243, 329-30, 332, 336
  a phylic phenomenon, 15, *156-57*, 240, 282, 318, 335-36, *338*, 362, 429, 451
  phylobiological approach to, 8, 58, 107, 208-09, 318, 340, 390, *429* 451-52, 479
  physiological substrate of, 105, 195, *249*, 281-82, 350
  Raskolnikov's dream, 189-90, 482
  restricted to man, 170
  scientific approach lacking, 193, 195, 240, 262, *288-89*
  social neurosis entailed in, 330
  traceable to ditention, 204, 213
  and war, 193, 195, 330, 332-33
  see also Antagonism; Dichotomy; Industrial conflict; Mental conflict; Social discord; War
Conjugal neurosis, 473
Conscience, 262, 281
Consciousness, 103, 216, 233-34, 296, 304, *337*, 354
  see also Common consciousness; Self-consciousness
"Consciousness of the self," 390 note 1
Constant—
  see Central constant; External constant

Continuity, 87-8, 110
Convergence—
  see Ocular convergence
Coördination—
  see Central constant; Homeostasis; Law of the organism
Cortex, 358, 397, 414
  see also Socio-cortical system
Cotension, 363 note 11, 377, 389, 445
  see also Ditension
Cotention—
  analogy in ontosomatic adaptation, 94, *347-48, 351-52, 377-80,* 382-85, 389, 445
  community need of, 105
  criterion of healthy behavior, 93, 323, 380-82
  definition of, 29, 323, 344, *347*
  drugs in relation to, 398-99
  exclusion of mental images, 93-4
  eye-movements and, 98-9, 393-94, 396, 444
  instrumental experimentation and, 394-95, 397, 399, *487-522*
  not a verbal process, 93
  and organism-environment relationship, 54, 346-48, 353, 395
  and personality types, 86
  phylobiological approach to, 97, 346, *385-88, 424-25,* 462
  physiological substrate of, 91, 93, 105, 397
  and primitive man, 55
  rediscovery of 91, 96, 99
  relation of ditention to, 99, 112 note 4, 323-32, 338, 342, *347-49,* 351, 353, 359-60, 370-71, *376-77,* 380, *383-85, 389,* 394, 418-19, 429, 444-45, 462, 471-72
  relation of sleep to, 398
  relation of thalamus to, 398
  respiration and, 95, 97-8, 393, 395-96
  and the symbolic function, 342, 348, 415, 419, 445
  total pattern of motivation, 105, 317, 345-46, *347,* 348-50, *353-54,* 375-76, 380-81, 384-, 421, 444, 454, 462
  see also Ditention; Homeostasis; Internal orthopedics; Primary motivation of man; Technique of cotention

Cotentive pattern, *92-3*
  physiological substrate of, 348, 369, *372-74,* 375-76, 397

reëstablishment of, *93,* 94, *348-51,* 352, 354, 357, 359, 370-71, 444
Cranial nerves, 406
Crime, 83, 480
  derivation of, 485 note 6
Cross-cultural thinking, 45, 47

Deity—
  see God
Dementia praecox, 450-51
  see also Schizophrenia
Democracy, 16, 417, 475
Dependence, 136-38, 142-43, *144-45,* 216, 419
  see also Transference
Depression, 366, 448, *477*
Devotion, 83, 480-81
  derivation of, 485 note 8
Dichotomy—
  artificially induced in conditioning, 214, 368, 430
  characteristic of normality, *183,* 185
  of community and State, 191, 261, 279
  in economic system, 227-28
  expressed in peace and in war, 156-57, 193, 227-28, 484
  of 'I'-persona, 184, 268, 368, 388, 462-463
  individual expression of, 277-28, *260-262,* 278-79, *304*
  inherent in parent-child relationship, 40, 188, 214-17
  in interrelational behavior, 136-37, *156-57, 217-19,* 243, 251, 386, 436
  phylobiological approach to, *226-27,* 318, 340
  in relation to group-therapy, 220, 223, 225
  of religious belief, *188,* 237, 475
  total motivation interrupted by, 188, 318, 337-38
  see also Affect-dichotomy; Ambivalence; Behavior-inconsistency; Conflict; Divisive mood; Feeling-inconsistency; Nature-nurture dichotomy; Partitiveness; Right and wrong
Dictatorship, 417
  see also Hitlerism; Leader; Ruler
Differentiation, 107-08
Diplomacy—
  derivation of, 179 note 21
Disbehavior, 139, 141-42, 155 note 3, 301, 381, 390, 466
Discord—
  see Dissociation; Social discord

Disease, 263, 289, 360
   see also Somatic disease
Disliking—
   see Liking-disliking
Dissociation, 75, 241, 328, 358, 380, *416*, 425, 433, 448, 467
Ditension, 363 note 11, 445
   see also Cotension
Ditention—
   analogy in faulty ontosomatic adaptation, *379-82*, 383-85, *445*
   attention obstructed by, 209-10, 216-17, 226-27, 231, 268, 315-16, 348
   behavior affected by, 54, 209-10, *225*, 226-27, 235, *305*, *315*, 328-29, 338, 380, *386*, *480*
   and conditioning, 268, 299, 342
   constituted of linkage of affect and symbol, 385
   and cotention, 99, 112 note 4, 323, 331-332, 338, 342, *347-49*, 351, 353, 359-360, 370-71, *376-77*, 380, *383-85*, *389*, 394, 418-19, 429, 444-45, 462, 471-72
   definition of, 29, 86, *204-05*, 344-45, 347, 380
   effect on childhood, 54, 214, 216-17, 378
   embodied in right-wrong dichotomy, *214*, 340
   expressed in peace and war, 356, 379-80, 480
   and group-therapy, *220-21*, 224-25
   and 'I'-persona, 317, 328, 342, 349, 353, 357, 425
   illustrations of, 205-06, 227-29, 446-47, 449
   instrumental experimentation and, 395,, 397, 399, *487-522*
   and normality, 225
   and the numen, 248, 255, 315-17, 328-330, 371
   organism - environment relationship modified by, 210, 231, 315, 328, 342, *379*
   and personality types, 86
   phyloanalytic approach to, 213-14, *219-21*, *225-27*, 231, 243-44, 305-07, 344-45, 347, *375-76*, 380, 389-90, 394, 426, 445-46, 462
   physiological substrate of, 91, 98, 105, 212, 226, 360, 369, 373, 375, 396, 398
   and primitive man, 55
   reflected in literary publications, 229
   relation to brain-function, 50, 330, 370-71, 398
   relation of ocular segment to, 386, *396*
   and respiration, 95, 98
   and sense of right, 51
   a social phenomenon, *205-07*, 224-26, 228-29, 254, 305, 329
   substance of social neurosis, 220, 480
   and symbolic system, 213, 217, 317, 347, 398, *415*
   see also Cotention; Symbolic attention
Ditonic condition, 263-64
   see also Syntonicity
Division—
   see Conflict
Divisive mood—
   illustration of, 449-50
   and religious belief, 333
   a social phenomenon, *292-93*, 296-97, 332-33, 467-68
Divorce, 183, 217
Dreams, 208
   see also Raskolnikov's dream
Drives—
   see Impulses
Drugs, 253, 339 note 13, 398-99
   see also Alcohol; Tobacco
Duality—
   see Dichotomy

Ecology, 209 231-32 note 9, 235-36, 426 note 10
   ..see also Bionomic adaptation; Organism-environment relationship
Economic system, *227-29*, 444
Economy—
   derivation of, 485 note 4
Ecosomatic—
   derivation of, 231 note 1
Ecosomatic relationship, 71-2, 201, 204-205, 322, 342, 344, 415, 437, 440, 472
   see also Organism-environment relationship
Ecothalamic system, 398
Education, 479
Efferent impulses—
   see Impulses
Electro-shock therapy—
   see Shock therapy
Electrocardiography—
   see Instrumental experimentation
Electroencephalography, 88, 397
   see also Brain waves; Instrumental experimentation

SUBJECT INDEX

Emotion—
see Affect
Endopathic lesion, 362
Evolution—
see Social evolution
Experimental affect, 266
Experimental neurosis, 88, 104-05, 265-266, *269*
External constant, 233, 239, 341, 473
see also Central constant; Nomen
Extroversion, 451
Eye-movements—
during cotention in contrast to ditention, 95, 389, 395-96, 442
related to symbolic mechanism and total organism, 396
see also Instrumental experimentation; Lifwynn Eye-movement Camera
Eyes—
and early man, 462
and phylobiological experimentation, 94-5, 98, *371-75*, 386-87, 390, 440-41, 444
related to attention, 441-42
related to behavior-patterns, 371-72, 396, 440-41, 444
see also Blink reflexes; Ocular convergence; Oculomotor tension; Retina

Face, 171-74
"Face"—
and behavior of man, *171-74*, 196-98, 204, 224, 229, 235, 251, 328, 353, 432-33
saving of, 171-72
tensional pattern underlying, 360
see also Affect
Fact, faction—
derivation of, 179 note 14
Fall of man, 238, 297, 299, 434, *452*
Fancy, 179 note 16
Fantasies, 386, 388
Father-image, 186, 239, *241*
see also Mother-image; Parent-child relationship
Favor—
meanings of, 179 note 16
see also Liking-disliking
Fear, 216 note 12, 471, 477
Feeling—
and affect, 66, 83, 173, 272-74, 296, 306, 361, 452

distortion in, 49, 63, 65-6
handed down by arbitrary teaching, *137*, 140-41, 173, 188, 198, 206, 215, 218, 225, 229, 244, 255, 276, 296, *416-19*, 431, 433-34
and human behavior, 76, 197, 204, *211-213*, 255, 292-94, 417-18, 439
and 'I'-persona, 66, 102
need for a science of, 211, 473
phyloanalytic approach to, 66, 97, 103, 219, 222, 244, 323, 362, 418, *458-59*, 467
transformed into symbol, 103, 109
with our mouths, 102
see also Affect; Instinctive behavior
Feeling-inconsistency, *164-67*, 168-69
see also Behavior-inconsistency
Fever, 199 note 10, 250
Fighting, 55-6, 60
see also Antagonism; Conflict; War
First nervous system—
see Autonomic nervous system
Folk mind, 238, 297
Fond—
derivation of, 232 note 14
Forebrain, 63, 104, 106, 332, 336
supremacy of, 102
see also Part-brain
Frame of reference—
see Altered frame of reference
Freudian formulations, 18
Frustration, 144, 473
and conditioned reflex, 265-66, 281
of ditentive behavior, 347, 372
involved in phyloanalytic experimentation, 79, 95, 242, *245-47*, 281, *306*, 372, 394
pain involved in, 243, 372
personal experience of, 391 note 16
Function—
see Allogenic function; Brain-function; Intrarelational function; Kinesthetic function; Motor function; Socio-biological function; Stereognostic function

Gastronomic system, 253
Genealogy of behavior—
see Paleontology of behavior
General Semantics, 53, 276, 278, 294-95
General system theory, 63
Genius, 66
Germany, 186-87, 190, 433
Gestalt psychology, 76, 231 note 2

God—
  and affect, 274
  belief in, 82, 161-62, 165, 188, 227-28, 234-35, *297-98*, 452, 454
  and 'I'-persona, 335, 470, 472, 475
  a social image, 83, 161-63, 188, 198, 228, *237*, *297-99*, 333, 435
  and war, 227-28, 333
  see also Religion
Good and bad—
  see Right and wrong
Gossip, 206, 314
  see also Rumor
Government, 191, 479-80
  see also Dictatorship; Nationalism; Patriotism; State; World government
Grasp reflex perverted to grab reflex, 353
"Great men," 185, 250
  see also Hitlerism; Ruler
Group, *222-23*, 301
  see also Community
Group-analysis—
  challenge inherent in, 36, 47, 64, 79-81, 183, 302, 306
  defense-reactions and, 183
  inception of, 25-6, 28, *180-81*, *198*, 210-11, 222, 242, 302, *306-07*, 458-60
  not a statistical process, 49
  personnel of, 14, 49-50, 78, 302
  and the species man, 68, 76
  term changed to phyloanalysis, 223
  see also Phyloanalysis; Phylobiology
Group-regarding characters—
  see Species-regarding characters
Group-therapy, 25, 81, *220-25*, 303
Guilt—
  see Morality

Harmony—
  mental concept of, 82-3
Headache, 422
Health—
  basic to man as a phylum, 164
  cotention the criterion of, 323
  homeostasis and, 428, *454*
  and somatic disease, 33, 69, 320-21, 323-24
  tensional patterns and, 360
Hearing—
  see Special senses
Heart—
  see Instrumental experimentation
Hitlerism, 184-87

Hoarding of wealth, 49, 305
Homeostasis—
  balanced function of organism, 35, 213, 229-30, 257, *263-64*, 279, 321, 341-42, *428*
  behavior-disorders due to deviations in, 213, 264, 321-23, 447
  cotention a form of, 347, 380, 419
  first described by Claude Bernard, 213, 341
  and health, 428, *454*
  in individual organism, 213, 341-43, 377
  in interrelational behavior, 223, 231, 342, 419
  named by Walter B. Cannon, 213, 341, 403
  and organism-environment relationship, 213, 287, 292, 323, 404, 411, 428, 454
  present social institutions not governed by, 343
  relation of phylobiology to, 287, 472
  replaced by 'I'-persona, 292
  see also Behavior-norm; Law of action and reaction; Law of the organism; Primary motivation of man; Synergy; Syntonicity
Hominid—
  conditioning of, 267-69, 273, 276, 280-282
  in phylobiological research, 260, 273
  use of speech by, 414
  see also Man
Homogenic perversions, 252
Homosexuality, 252-53, 431
Human behavior—
  see Behavior
"Human nature," 26, 43, 45
Human relations—
  see Behavior
Hunger, 432
  see also Nutritional needs
Hypothalamus—
  see Thalamus

'I'-persona—
  and affect, 53, 64, 188, 203, 229, 233, 268, *271-72*, 274, *277-78*, 293, 298, 306, 316, 328-29, 342, 350, 354, 362, 368, 384, 386, 398, 420, 423, 432, 452, 469, 483
  and *amour propre*, 328, 432
  and art, 335

SUBJECT INDEX

'I'-persona *(Contd.)*—
  of author, 78
  and the behavior of man, 26, *48*, 59-61, 63-4, 67, 236, *251*, 289, *299-300*, 305-06, 318, 342, 357, 360, 403, 417, 430, 433, 483
  and conditioning, 271-72, *274*, 291, 368, 430, 447
  and conflict, 18, 421, 451, 476
  definition of, 184, *291*
  dichotomous attitude of, 184, 188, 190, 206, 230, 268, *304*, 388, 425
  and dissociation, 75
  and ditention, 236, 291, 317, 328, 342, 349, 353, 357
  dominant in group-therapy, 222-23
  and feeling, 66, 102, 107
  and God, 299, 475
  governments based on, 417, 479-80
  illustration of, 449-50
  inception of, 48, 274, 430
  none in animal, 271
  not a cultural phenomenon, 48, 51
  obstructive character of, 188, 193, 196-97, 204, 209, *230*, 236, 254, *291*, 292-93, 328, 331, 342, 421-422, 474
  and organism-environment relationship, 59, 259, 291, 298, 329
  in parent-child relationship, 216, *416-417*
  and part-brain, 278, 316, 318, 338, 356, 416, 421
  a phylic phenomenon, 48, 72, 86, 109, 416
  phyloanalytic approach to, 36, 70, 72, 104-05, 108, *184*, 187-88, 190, 224, 233, *242-44*, *250-51*, 277-78, 295-96, *299*, 305-07, *310*, 318, 340, 350, 354, 359, 362, 375-76, 403, 448, 462
  physiological substrate of, 105, 248, 270, 318, 350, 360-61, 369, 375, 470
  and possessiveness, 300, *305*, *432-33*, 470
  reflected in literary publications, 229
  and "right," 53, 292, 353, 470
  and segmentation, 251, 254, 421, 431
  and sex, *250-51*, 432
  and social neurosis, 66-7, 293, 357, *360*, 416
  and speech-disorders, 253, 436
  and symbolic system, 53, 104-05, 292-293, 296, 430
  systematization of, 64, 73
  and war, 57, 355, 466
Identification—
  see Principle of primary identification
Image, 110
  see also Affect-image; Father-image; Mother-image; Parental image; Self-image; Social image
Image of unity, 297, 337, 435, 452
Inconsistency—
  see Behavior-inconsistency; Feeling-inconsistency
Individual—
  constantly reconditioned, 273
  creativeness of, 66
  hampered by social neurosis, 66
  original functioning of, 63
  outgrowth of an organismic pattern, 153, *301*, 402-03, 410
  relation to species, 20, 59, 61, 66-73, 83, 92, 109-10
  see also Neurotic individual; Normal individual; Ontosoma
Individual organisms, 65, *323-24*, 325-26
Individuals, 60
  differences among, 51, 60, 64, 70
  importance of, 51, 61, 68
Individuality, 56-7, 59, 61
Industrial conflict, 11, 259-60, 332-33, 343, 481
Infant, 35-6, 273, 320
  see also Adult and infant generations; Child; Parent-child relationship
Infectious disease—
  see Bacteriology; Malaria; Tuberculosis; Typhoid fever
Infidel, 84
Information, 305
Insanity—
  see Psychosis
Instinctive behavior, 197, 202, 263, 345
  conflict in, 294
  of lower orders of animals, 263, 341-42
  of man as a phylic organism, 175-76
  see also Primary motivation of man
Institutions, 41-2, 181, *192*
  see also Social institutions
Instrumental experimentation—
  basal metabolism tests, 395, *490-93*
  cardiovascular functions, 395, *493-94*
  discrimination of behavior-patterns, 388-89, 394-95
  electroencephalographic changes, 394-395, 397, *503-21*
  oculomotor changes, 395, 442, *494-502*
  in phylobiology, 29, 95, *393-95*, 399-400, 446
  respiratory changes, 395, *487-92*

Interest—
    see Attention
Internal balance—
    see Cotention; Homeostasis; Syntonicity
Internal constant—
    see Central constant
Internal environment, 213, 472
Internal orthopedics, 376, 469
    see also Phyloörthopedic process
Internal pattern of behavior, 453, 465
    see also Behavior-patterns; Tensional patterns
Internal processes—
    material of phylobiological research, 88, 349, *423-24*, 431-32, 447
    regulated by central constant, 65, 340-341, 473
    underlying social disorders, 438, 463
    see also Physiological processes
Internal tensions—
    see Physiological tensions; Tensional patterns
Interrelational behavior—
    and affect, 64, 160, 162, 165, 184, *197*, 231 note 2, 267, 272, 289-90, *293-94*, 328, 383
    and brain-function, 327-28, 370
    characterized by dichotomy, *136-37*, 140, *183*, 217-18, 293, 436
    conflict in, 159, *254*, 277, 340
    cotention and, *323*, 383, 397, 435
    ditention and, 72, 210, 213-14, 235, 328, 342, 380, 383
    ignorance of, 63, 83, 141, 287-88, 321, *484*
    interrupted by the numen, 236, 239, 259, *290-91*
    mediated by face, 171-72, *173-74*
    and the nomen, 341, 370
    obstructed by the 'I'-persona, 48, 236, 254, *291-92*, 331, 342
    organismic consistency in, 235, 341, 345
    phylic impairment of, 27, 211-12, *418*
    phyloanalytic approach to, 8, 19, 47, 62, 65, 88, 100-01, 193, 226, 233, 287, *306*, *322-24*, 340, 360, 386-87, *485*
    and prejudice, 57-8, 64
    and segmentation, 254, 430
    and symbolic system, 55, 172, 235, 287, *293*, 295-96, *300*, 316, 318, 348, 350, 398, *408-09*, 413-15, *419-20*
    see also Anthroponomic behavior; Communication; Man's relation to man; Organism-environment relationship
Intraorganismic research, 317
Intrarelational function—
    disorder in, *322-23*, 332
    see also Cotention; Homeostasis
Introversion, 451
Involuntary nervous system—
    see Autonomic nervous system
Isolationism, 75
    see also Lone wolf criticism

Japan, 168-69, 186, 190, 433

Kinesthetic function, 246, 382, 404
    see also Proprioceptive sensation; Tensional patterns

Laboratory—
    authority of the, 89-90
Language, 107
    and attention, 204, 345
    and behavior-disorder, 48, 52
    and communication, 438-39
    and conditioning, 267, 270, 273
    Paget's theory of, 311 note 9
    in relation to man's primary motivation, 65, 111, 419
    and self-consciousness, 56, 292
    see also Speech; Symbol
Law, 169, 181, 192, 475
Law of action and reaction, 229, 332, 471, 473
    expression in man marked by conflict, 385, 421
    phyloörganismic balance, 151, 161, 341, 388, 415, 444
    and symbolic system, 438
    see also Homeostasis; Species solidarity
Law of the organism, 233, 239, 340
    see also Homeostasis; Nomen
Leader, 61, 186
    see also Dictatorship; Ruler
Lesion—
    see Endophathic lesion
Leucotomy—
    see Surgical therapy
Lifwynn Eye-Movement Camera, 442, *500-02*
Lifwynn Foundation, The, 6, 49, 335, 487
Lifwynn Laboratory, The, 81, 97, 108, 286, 349, 357, 370, 394, 397, 462, 479

SUBJECT INDEX

Liking-disliking, 65, 171, *205*, 218, *293*, 463
Literature—
 behavior-disorder reflected in, *157-59*, 169, *189-90*, 229, *334*
 see also Newspapers; Poetry
Lobectomy—
 see Surgical therapy
Lone wolf criticism, 76-80
Love and hatred—
 see Dichotomy; Liking-disliking
Lying—
 see Stammering

Malaria, 27
Man, 33, 83, *354*, 402, *425-26*, 434-35
 as a species, 46
 see also Common man; Fall of man; "Great men"; Hominid; Individual; Ontosoma; Paleontology of behavior; Phyloörganism; Phylosoma; Phylum; Primary motivation of man; Primitive man
Man's relation to man, 27
 alteration in, 48, 296, 315
 false signals, 104-05
 inhumanity in, 83, 409, *433*, 467
 and language, 48
 phylobiological approach to, *61-2*, 291, 370, 479
 scientific attitude lacking, 83, 139-40, 142, 288, 473
 and symbolic system, 295-96, 408, 434, 442
 see also Interrelational behavior; Organism-environment relationship
Manifest destiny of man, 454
Marriage, 217
 see also Conjugal neurosis
Medicine—
 beginning of, 69, 144
 and behavior-disorders, 19, 144, 152, *193-95*, 259-61, 308, *321*, *324-25*, 358
 establishment of norm, 323-24
 and phylobiology, 99-100, 111-12 note 4
 preceded by mysticism and magic, 287
 and somatic disease, 6, 8, 62, 139, 193-195, *289*, 308, *320-21*, 323-24, 326, 335-36, *422*
 see also Bacteriology; Disease; Psychiatry; Somatic disease
Mental conflict, 261
Mental disorders—
 see Behavior-disorders

Mental hygiene, 282 note 1
Mental image—
 see Affect-image; Father-image; Image of unity; Mother-image; Parental image; Self-image; Social image
Metanomic reaction, 292, 357, 440
 an affective expression, 274-75, 367-69
 in thinking and feeling, 344, 362, 452
 see also Orthonomic response; Paratonic pattern; Part-reaction
Metaphor—
 see Physiological metaphor; Symbol
Mind—
 see Folk mind; Social mind
Miniature symbolic system, 408, 415, *418*, *433-34*, *438-40*
 see also Affecto-symbolic segment; Socio-symbolic behavior
Misbehavior—
 disbehavior distinguished from, 155 note 3
Mode—
 see Mood
Money, 229
Mood, 199 note 2, *355*, 357, 443-44
 see also Divisive mood; Preconscious mode; Social mood
Mood-affectivity—
 see Affectivity
Morality, 172, 188-89, 199-200 note 14
 derivation of, 44 note 3
 inadequate criterion, 41-2, 65-6
 phylobiological approach to, 34-6, 84
 see also Right and wrong
Mother-complex—
 see Mother-image
Mother-image, 207-08, 260-61, 275-76, 278-79
 see also Father-image; Parent-child relationship; Parental image
Mother-love—
 see Mother-image
Motherhood, 159, 236-37
Motivation—
 see Autopathic motivation; Behavior; Feeling; Impulses; Instinctive behavior; Primary motivation of man
Motor function—
 of cerebrospinal system, 405
 of eyes, 396, 442
Muscular balance, 377-78, 380, 382
Musculature, 380-81
 see also Physical exercise
Music, 110

Nationalism, 187, 217
  See also Government; Patriotism; State
Nature-nurture dichotomy, 45
Nazism, 333
  see also Hitlerism
Nerves—
  see Cranial nerves
Nervous disorders—
  see Behavior-disorders
Nervous system—
  see Autonomic nervous system; Cerebrospinal nervous system; Third nervous system
Neural basis of behavior, 358, 484
  see also Phyloneurology
Neuroanatomy—
  see Neurophysiology
Neurodynamics of behavior, 15, 19, 49, 100, 208, 248-49, 285, 317, 340, 371, 423, 443
Neurology of behavior-disorders, 325
Neuromuscular patterns—
  see Tensional patterns
Neuromuscular tensions—
  see Physiological tensions
Neurophysiology, 20, 62, 99-100, 316
Neurosis, 426 note 7
  see also Behavior-disorders; Conjugal neurosis; Experimental neurosis; Neurosis of man; Social neurosis
Neurosis of man, 52, 69, 146, 269, 310, 365, 367, *420*, 425, 462, 477, *485*
  see also Social neurosis
Neurosis of Man, The (book), 13, 21, 68, 88, 95, 105, 111 note 4
Neurotic individual—
  dichotomous attitude of 207-08, *260-262*, 278-79
  and mother-complex, 260, 278-79
  relation between physician and, 195-196, 302-03, 365-66
  same characteristics as those of normal, 26, 28, 89, 144, 195, 207-08, 226-27, *318-20*, 344, 386, 429, 437
  symptom of social neurosis, 196
  see also Normal individual
Newspapers, 17, 42, 157, 206, 229, 446
Nomen—
  consistent response to environment, *233*, 329, *340-41*
  ditention an obstacle to, 342, 371
  in human behavior, 289-90, 317, 472
  and numen, *237-39*, 248-49, 255, 268, 290-91, 315, 329, 360, 370-71, 415, 417, 452, 465, 472, 481

in relation to science, 77, 471, 473
and symbolic system, 408-09, 419
tensional pattern underlying, 360
and third nervous system, 408
see also Law of the organism; Numen
Norm—
  see Behavior-norm; Biological norm; Social norm
Normal—
  identified with average, habitual, 24, 32
  meaning of, 24-5
Normal community, 192, *318-19*, 451
Normal individual—
  conflict in, 437
  dichotomous attitude of, 279
  same characteristics as those of neurotic, 26, 28, 89, 144, 195, 207-08, 226-27, *318-20*, 344, 386, 429, 437
  see also Neurotic individual
Normality—
  and affect, 185, 318, 384, 423
  characteristics of, *182-84*, 443
  ditention and, 225
  false criterion of behavior, 26, 32, 76, *181-84*, 273, 319, 321, 324, 329
  'I'-persona embodied in, 184, 360, 421
  and sex, 251-52
  subject of phylobiological study, 6, 15, 23, 25, 28, 32, 49-50, 73, 76, *180-184*, 198, 242, 316, 318-19, 480
  thesis questioned by G. Boas, 23, 28
  thesis questioned by A. Gregg, 23-4
  thesis questioned by M. Herskovits, 45-6
  thesis questioned by N. Rashevsky, 29-31
  and third nervous system, 409, 420, 443
  see also Social reaction-average
Numen—
  definition of, 236, 257 note 5
  and ditention, 248, 255, 315-17, 362, *371*, 390
  and God, 297-99, 465
  in human behavior, 236, *237-39*, 255-256, 289-90, *291*, 315-16, 329, 357, 360, *481*
  and nomen, *237-39*, 248-49, 255, 268, 290-91, 315, 329, 360, 370-71, 415, 417, 452, 465, 472, 481
  organism-environment relationship interrupted by, 236-39, 259, 315-16, 328-29
  in parent-child relationship, 236, 417

SUBJECT INDEX

Numen *(Contd.)* —
  in psychiatry, 239-40, 256
  in relation to symptoms, 249-50
  and the social neurosis, 239
  and third nervous system, 408
  see also Nomen
Nutritional needs, 404, 412
  see also Hunger

Ocular convergence, 393
Oculomotor tension, 247, 350, *371-75,* 386-87, 390, 393, 444
  see also Eye-movements
One world, 15, 474, 484
Oneness, 176, 299-300, 453-54
  see also Principle of unity
Ontosoma, 381, 402, 410, 421
  see also Individual; Phylosoma
Ontosomatic adaptation, *377-82,* 384-85
  see also Bionomic adaptation; Physical exercise
Opiates—
  see Drugs
Organic unity—
  see Principle of unity
Organic whole, 308
  see also Collective whole
Organism as a whole—
  disorder in, 277, 292-93, 295
  distinguished from collective whole, 308
  encroached upon by symbolic system, 107, 235, 275, *295-96,* 357, 418-19, 445
  material of phylobiological research, 236, *400*
  in medicine, 62
  relation of organs to, 213, 326
  theoretical concept of, 63, 278
  see also Organism of man; Phyloörganism; Phylosoma; Primary motivation of man; Principle of unity; Total organism
Organism-environment relationship—
  analogy in ontosomatic adaptation, 383-85, 389
  in animal life, 202, 233, 263
  and attention, 29, *201-05,* 209-12, 317, 328, 344-45
  and cotention, 54, 344, *346-48,* 353-54, 395
  and homeostasis, 213, 342, *428*
  and image of God, 234-35, 237
  of infant generation, 215, 410, 412-18
  and language, 48

  mediated by brain, 327-29, 341, 370, 405-06
  modified by ditention, 315, 328
  and the nomen, 341, 370, 408, 473
  not consistent in early man, 234-35
  obstruction of, 48, 173-74, 204, 209, 212-13, 235, *238-39,* 259-60, 262, 290-91, 298, 342, 354, 383, 483
  phylobiological approach to, 20, 65, 101, 210-11, 213-14, *255-56, 287-88,* 316-17, 322, 340, 344, 403, 424-25
  physiological processes involved in, 213, 316-18, 322-23, 340, 345-47, 369, 403-04, 415
  respiration and, 411-12
  and sense of right, 57
  and symbolic system, 204, 236, *239,* 263, *296-97,* 316, 341, 370, 383-84, 397-98, 408-09, *413-16,* 439-41
  and third brain, *406-08,* 413, 419
  see also Bionomic adaptation; Ecosomatic relationship
Organism of man, 76, 297-98, 317, 328, 362, *388,* 453
Organismic balance, 347, 381, 388, 404, 428
Organismic principle of motivation—
  see Principle of unity
Organs of body, 51, 65, 213, *326-27,* 329-30
Orthencephalon, 367
  see also Parencephalon
Orthogenic behavior—
  see Primary motivation of man
Orthonomic response, 274, 292, 369, 452, 469
  see also Metanomic reaction; Paratonic pattern
Orthopathic—
  derivation of, 179 note 19, 257 note 4
Orthopathic behavior, 174, 187, 235, 239, 274, 280, 363 note 12
  see also Autopathic motivation; Cotention
Orthopedics—
  see Internal orthopedics; Phyloörthopedic process
Orthotonic pattern, 275, 367, 371, 374-75
  see also Orthonomic response; Paratonic pattern

Pain, 248, 326, 328, 336
  involved in conflict, 83, 243, 329-30, 332, 361
  involved in phylobiological experi-

Pain (*Contd.*)—
 mentation, 243, 372
 and social neurosis, 67, 330, 360-61
Paleontology of behavior, 233, 236, *237-239, 296-98*
 see also Numen
Palliatives, 253-54, 382
 see also Alcohol; Drugs; Tobacco
Paranoia—
 see Affect-paranoia
Parasympathetic nervous system—
 see Autonomic nervous system
Paratonic pattern, 275, 367, 371, 374-75
 see also Metanomic reaction; Orthotonic pattern
Parencephalon, 367-68
 see also Orthencephalon
Parent—
 derivation of, 232 note 15
Parent-child relationship—
 affect-dichotomy in, 188, *214-16*, 417-418
 in animal life, 215-16
 conditioning in, 275-76
 and dition, 54
 image-transference in, 216-17
 importance of face in, 172-73
 sense of right in, *37-40*, 57
 third nervous system involved in, 417-418
 in unhappy marriage, 217
 see also Adult and infant generations; Motherhood; Parental image
Parental image—
 and 'I'-persona, 216, *298*
 imbued in child, 215-17, 413, *419*
 involved in transference, 219, *239-40*
 see also Father-image; Mother-image
Part-attention—
 see Ditention
Part-brain—
 and affect, 203, 278, 316
 and creativeness, 61
 dominant rôle assumed by, 337-38
 and 'I'-persona, 278, 316, 318, 338, 356
 and maladjustment, 61
 in relation to man's behavior, 256, 304, 316, *318*, 356-57, 381, 419-20, 425, 484
 relation to whole brain, 318, *330*, 331-332, *336-37*, 356, 370-71, 381-82, 418, 434, 443, 472, 479
 and segmentation, 425, 434, 442
 and symbolic system, 202, 316, 336-37, 407, 420
 and war, 338, 355-56
 see also Affecto-symbolic segment; Forebrain; Symbolic attention; Third nervous system
Part-reaction—
 behavior-disorders an expression of, 272, 384-85, 429, 451
 total reaction replaced by, 275, 435, *442-43*
 see also Metanomic reaction
Part-whole relationship, 110, 157, 231 note 2, 300-01, 325, 450, 474-75
Partitive motivation—
 see Affect
Partitive reaction—
 see Metanomic reaction; Part-reaction
Partitiveness, 89, 108, 110, 157, 421, 474-475
 see also Dichotomy
Pathology of society, 33
 see also Social neurosis
Patient-physician relationship—
 see Physician-patient relationship
Patriotism, 24
 see also Government; Nationalism; State
Pattern—
 kinship in meaning with mood, 199 note 2
 see also Behavior-patterns; Orthotonic pattern; Paratonic pattern; Tensional patterns
Peace, 107, 140, 156, 191, 193, 333, 338
Peace conferences, 39, 140, 227, 274, 464, 475
Pedagogy—
 see Education
Persona, 179 note 22
 see also 'I'-persona
Persona-regarding characters—
 see Self-regarding characters
Personality, 145, 148, 150-51, 305
Perversions—
 see Homogenic perversions
Philosophy, 54, 83, 87, 107, 169, *197-98*, 225, 238
Phylic neurosis—
 see Neurosis of man; Social neurosis
Phylic organism—
 see Organism as a whole
Phyloanalysis—
 application to mankind, 8, 14-16
 approach to 'I'-persona, 224, *299*, 306-07, 310

Phyloanalysis *(Contd.)* —
experimental material internal to participants, 149, 226, 310, 349, 468
frustration involved in, 79, 242-43, 245-247, 281, 306, 309
not a mental process, 47, *78,* 79, 81, 97, 303, 464
organismic principle of researches, 223, 261-62, 303, 307-09, 418
resistance to, 89, 149-51, 220, 243-44, 307
see also Group-analysis; Phylobiological technique; Phylobiology

Phyloanalytic technique—
see Phylobiological technique

Phylobiological students, 96, 153, 460-61, 468-69

Phylobiological technique, 101, 149, 153, 219, *371-76,* 384

Phylobiology—
and affect, 208, 211, 213-14, *219-20,* 224, 243-44, 276-78, *310*
altered frame of reference, 5, 12, 15, 22, 25-6, 80-1, 249, 307-10, 410, 424, *478*
analogy between bacteriology and, 26-7, 69, 96-7, 101, 164, 194-95, 239, 244, 254-55, 361, 376, 471
approach to man's behavior, 6-7, 13, 51, 78-9, 86, 111, 208, 242, 256, 260, 281, *287-88,* 306, *309, 320-25,* 344, 350, 423, 460-61, 472, *481*
and attention, 204, 209, 211, 345
and conflict, 340, 429
derivation of, 74 note 1
difficulty of communication, 79-80, 88-9
and General Semantics, 53, *276,* 278, 295
group-therapy not related to, 25, 81, 221-25, 303
an internal process, 88, 310, 317, 376, 387, *423*
laboratory of, 90
man's brain-function enlarged by, 285, 424
material of, 12, 14, 25-6, 28, 49, 51, 80, 149, 153, 220, 226, 230, 277, 285-286, 306, 310, 317, 324-25, 344, *358-59,* 361
and mood of man, 78-9
and mother-complex, 275
not concerned with symptoms, 208, 322, *325*
not popular, 90
not the product of one mind, 75-6
and organism-environment relationship, 211, 213, 260, 340-41, *344,* 424
outgrowth of Freud's thesis, 88
parallel with other sciences, 62
and philosophy, 87
and phyloörganism as a whole, 67, 321-22, 346, *405,* 410, 423-25
and psychiatry, 99-100, 111-12 note 4, 219, 276-78, 285, 307
and psychology, 85
research incomplete, 101
results accidental, 81
and rights of man, 469-70
and segmentation, 423
significance of individual, 51, 66
social characteristics not important, 50
study of physiological processes, 220, 226, 244-45, *358-60,* 362, 374-75, 394
see also Instrumental experimentation; Intraorganismic research

Phyloneurology, 316

Phyloneurosis, 330
see also Neurosis of man; Social neurosis

Phyloörganism—
consistent pattern of structure and function in, 323
division within, 28, 430, 434, *474*
internal balance of, 213, 263
motivation of, checked by self-interest, 197
phylobiological interest in, 20, 405, 410, 424, 428, 445-46, 453
physiological function of, 343
see also Organism as a whole; Phylosoma; Phylum; Total organism

Phyloörthopedic process of cotention, 424
see also Internal orthopedics

Phylopathic reactions—
see Orthopathic behavior

Phylopathology, 231, 261, 420, 476

Phylophysiological processes, 53, 249, 277, 295, 367, 407, 437

Phylosoma, 321, 367, 370, 402-03, 410, 415, 421, 431
see also Ontosoma; Phyloörganism; Phylum; Soma

Phylosomatic processes, 403, 426, 437, 440

Phylothalamic processes, 358, 367

Phylum, 300-01, 402-03, 425
  phylobiological use of term, 68, 73-4 note 1
  see also Phyloörganism; Phylosoma
Physical disease—
  see Somatic disease
Physical exercise, 94, *377-79*, 384, 445
  see also Musculature; Ontosomatic adaptation; Swimming; Tennis; Walking
Physician-patient relationship, 33, 147, 240, *302-03*
Physiological metaphor, 280
Physiological processes—
  and conditioning, 267, 269, *270-71*, 276, 280-82, 371
  material of phylobiology, 211, 220, 226, 244-45, 249, 277, 288, *316-18*, 322, 358-59, 369, 385, 392-94, 446, 453
  underlying behavior, 72, 103-04, 106, 211, 226, 247, 262, 281-82, 318, 358, 369, 385, 446
  see also Autonomic nervous system; Internal processes; Phylophysiological processes
Physiological tensions—
  in cephalic region, *254-49*, 350, 369, *372-75*, 422
  and mental images, 246-48, 372
  and man's behavior, 85, 88, 91-2, 94-6, 112 note 4, 247-49, 322, *346*, 350, 360, 390, 395, 447, 460
  and somatic disorder, 92
  see also Oculomotor tension; Tensional patterns
Physiology, 51, 211-12, 294
  see also Biophysiological basis of behavior-disturbances; Phylophysiological processes
Poetry, 143, 334
Political parties, 417, 427-28, 478
  see also Communism; Democracy; Socialism
Politico-social persona, 435
  see also 'I'-persona
Possessiveness, 271-72, 274, 305, 332, *430-34*, 470
  see also Competitiveness
Preconscious mode, 354
  see also Principle of primary identification
Prejudice—
  and affect, 66, 160-61, 168-69, 226
  basis of thinking, 42, 162, 171, 207
  definition of, 155 note 4
  encysted feeling, 306
  expressed in war and crime, 163, 171
  God fashioned of, 161-62
  hindrance to knowledge, 19
  and man's behavior, 26-8, 52, 57-8, 160-164, 171, 174, 183, 234
  phylobiological approach to, 8, 11, 226, 243-44, 281, 310
  a somatic reaction, 281
  systematization of, 105
  see also Affect; Bias
Prestige, 170-72
  derivation of, 179 note 12
  see also Amour propre
Primary motivation of man—
  and affect, 296, 432, 443
  and allergy and protergy, 322
  conflict between part-function and, 429
  and cotention, *354*, 358
  division in, 292-93, 333, 443
  fundamental to behavior, 357, 452
  and the 'I'-persona, 291, 357, 433
  and language, 111
  and the numen, 236, 297
  obstacles to, 109
  phyloanalytic approach to, *149*, 211, 256, *261*, 298, 301, 340, 357, 359, 376, *387-88*, 423-24
  restoration of, 359, 382, 388, 399, *425-426*, 452, 468, *479*, *484*
  symbolic expression of, 334
  symbolic system in relation to, 295-96, 341, 357-58, 418-20, 435, 438, 443
  see also Cotention; Homeostasis; Instinctive behavior; Organism as a whole; Phyloörganism; Phylosoma; Total organism
Primitive man, 55
Principle of primary identification, 454
  See also Preconscious mode
Principle of unity, 107, 162, 228, 454
  See also Image of Unity; Oneness; Organism as a whole; Primary motivation of man; Total organism
Profiteering, 446-47
Projection, 80, 94-5, 104, 107, 291-97, 300, 327-30, 390
  see also Affect-projection
Proprietary (Proper, Property) —
  meaning of, 179 note 18
Proprioceptive Sensation, 382-83
  see also Kinesthetic function

SUBJECT INDEX

Protergy, 322-23, 332
   see also Intrarelational function
Protogenic pattern—
   see Cotention; Cotentive pattern
Protoplasm, 320, 324, 357
   see also Alloplasm
Pseudo-feeling—
   see Affect
Pseudo-identity—
   see 'I'-persona
Pseudo-normality—
   see Normality
Pseudo-science—
   see Sciolism
Pseudo-sexuality—
   see Sex
Psychiatrists—
   approach to "tensions," 346
   behavior of, 240, 286, 443-44, 447-448
   and Freud, 240-41, 261
   of The Lifwynn Laboratory, 286
   and patients, 147, 191-92, 196, 218, 230, 240, 302-03
Psychiatry—
   contrasted with phylobiology, 99-101, 111-12 note 4, 208, 260-61, 276-78, *285-86*, 304, 307, *476-77*
   everyone an authority, 196
   inadequacy of, 147-48, 160, 192, *193-96*, 206, 231, *237*, 240, 256, 262, 278, 325, 365-67, 443-44
   and the neurotic patient, 46-7, 218
   see also Group-therapy; Mental hygiene; Psychoanalysis; Shock Therapy; Surgical therapy
Psychoanalysis, 18, 239-42, 455 note 11
Psychology, 62-3, 76, 85, 101
Psychoneurosis—
   see Neurosis of man; Social neurosis
Psychopathology—
   see Psychiatry
Psychopractice, 144, 194, 198-99
Psychosis, phylic, 83, 234, 296, 426 note 7
   see also Behavior-disorders
Psychosocial process, 171, 369, 438
Psychotherapy—
   see Psychiatry
Public Health Movement, 282 note 1

Race—
   see Phyloörganism; Phylosoma; Phylum
Raskolnikov's dream, 189-90
Reaction-average—
   see Social reaction-average
Reaction-patterns—
   see Behavior-patterns
Reflex—
   see Blink reflexes; Conditioned reflex
Relational physiology—
   see Ecology
Relativity, 31, 62
Religion, 61, 66, 333, 480-81
   author's attitude toward, 82, 84
   and behavior-disorders, 11, 169, 198, 225, 238-39
   contrasted with devotion, 83
   derivation of, 90 note 1, 485 note 7
   and group-therapy, 225
   parental image and, 161-62
   and social neurosis, 54
   sects irreconcilable with one another, 157, 168
   symbolic striving for harmony, 65, 82-3
   see also God
Repression, 144
Respiration, 95, 97-8, 253, 363 note 12, 391 note 16, 393, 395-96, 411-12
   see also Instrumental experimentation
Retina, 396, *441*, 442
Retroceptive thinking, 188, 207, 347, 444
Retrofective doing, 188, 296, 409, 444
Retropathic feeling and thinking, 173, 179 note 19, 188, 444
   see also Autopathic motivation
Right—
   see Sense of right
Right and wrong—
   biological standards of, 35
   bred of conditioning, 214, 419-20, 430
   in community, 42, 184, 214, 217-19, 226-27 229-30, 261, 296, 431, 436, 438
   and education, 34, 42
   and the neurosis, 238, *261-62*, 278-79
   in parent-child relationship, 173, *214-215*, 217, *416-17*, 419-20
   phylobiological approach to, 6, *34-6*, 42, 99, 148, 279, 281-82, *300*
   tensional substrate of, 374
   thesis questioned by D. Katz, 34-5
   an undependable criterion, 143, 148, 151-52, 195, 214, 358
   see also Morality; Sense of right
Ruler, 191
   see also Dictatorship; Leader
Rumor, 135, 143, 206
   see also Gossip

Russia, 42, 186-87, 190, 333, 465-66

Schizophrenia, 355, 443, 450
see also Autistic thinking; Dementia praecox

Schools—
see Behavior-schools; General Semantics; Group-therapy

Science, 6, 111, 298
accomplishment in field of external adaptation, 5, *138-39*, 141, 255, 287, *288*
and animal life, 138
and atomic energy, 154
atomistic purview of, 62-3
Huxley's dicta, 145, 461
limitations of, 60
material of, 225-26
modern trend in, 62
not bred of fear, 471
objective approach of, 10-11, 13-14, 138-39, 142, 145, 226, 233-34, 473, 481
relation of part to whole, 325, 450
and the symbol, 103, 203, 233, *234*, 255
see also Sciolism

Science of human behavior—
author's early approach to, 457-58, 460
broader evaluations of, 14-16, 195, 285-87, *310*, 340, *428-29*, 465, *478*
need for, 5, 11, 13, 15, 17, 43, 71, 143-44, 154, 192-93, *288-89*, 299, 303-304, 325-26, 330-31, 350, 357, 448-49, 473, 477, *481-82*, 485
see also Behavior; Phylobiology

Scientists, 250, 252-53
and human behavior, *8*, *16*, 19-21, 111, 245, 344
letter to, 8-9, 13-17
prejudice among, 19
replies from, 9, *10-11*, 17-21, 23, 45

Sciolism, 287
see also Science

Second brain—
see Cerebrospinal nervous system; Forebrain

Segment—
see Affecto-symbolic segment; Socio-symbolic segment

Segmentation, *251-52*, *254*, 400, 421, *423-425*, 430, 433, *434*, 442, *468*

Self-awareness, 56, 291-92

Self-consciousness, 72, 104, 216, *292-93*, *296-97*, 299, 337

Self-image, 36, 57, 110, 168, 173, 237-38, 251, 268, 337

Self-interest—
attention altered by, 174, 204, 207, 209
human behavior distorted by, 159, 173, *196-97*, 243, 292-93, 430, 467
see also Amour propre; "Face"

Self-regarding characters, 18, 59-60, 63
see also Species-regarding characters

Semio-cortical capacity—
see Socio-cortical system; Symbolic system

Semiotic capacity—
see Socio-cortical system; Symbolic system

Semiotic nervous system—
see Third nervous system

Sensation—
see Kinesthetic function; Proprioceptive sensation

Sense organs—
see Special senses

Sense of right—
ditention and, 51
and human behavior, 7, 39-40, 42-3, 57-8, 64, 72, 197, 214, 217-18, 227, 292, 332, 353, *469-70*
inconsistency in, 41
not present in animal life, 229
in parent-child relationship, *37-40*, 57
at peace conferences, 274
in organism-environment relationship, 57
phylobiological approach to, 7, *36-7*, *41*, 170, 174, *469-70*
and war, 39, 58
see also Right and wrong

Sex, 173, *250-52*, 430-32, 455-56 note 19, 472-73
see also Conjugal neurosis; Homosexuality; Marriage

Shock therapy, 365, 368
see also Surgical therapy

Sign—
see Symbol

Sin, 238, 297
see also Fall of man

Sisyphus complex, 42

Skin, 106, 404, 431, 441

Smell—
see Special senses

Smoking—
see Tobacco

Social conditioning, 40, 184, 316, 342, 419

SUBJECT INDEX

Social conflict—
see Conflict
Social discord—
  discussed by Freud, 180, 184, 189, 318-19
  expressed in man's behavior, 11, 207, 466, 483
  illustrative material, 158-60, 189-90
  physiological tensions underlying, 343, 384
  reflected in literature and newspapers, 157
  see also Conflict; Dissociation; Divisive mood
Social evolution, 43, 144
  faux pas in, 295
Social image—
  and antagonism, 57
  in conditioning, 275
  embodied in liking or disliking, 171
  and God, 163, 198, *237*, 297-98
  in human relationships, 6, 104, 147, 219, 240, 275-76
  and 'I'-persona, 184, 292, 297, 340
  motion pictures an expression of, 252
  in organism-environment relationship, 262, 340
  in parent-child relationship, 217, 421
  and the "personality," 145
  in physician-patient relationship, 302-303
  and psychiatry, 239-40, 262
  reversal of spontaneous motivation, 238, 426
  see also Affect-image; Father-image; Image of unity; Mother-image; Parental image; Self-image
Social institutions—
  homeostasis not traceable in, 343
  product of segmentation, 434
  reflection of internal processes, 280-81, 446
  see also Economic system
Social mind—
  and phylobiology, 469, 480
  relation between social mood and, 355-356, 443, 450, 453, 464, *467-69*
  in relation to war, 355-56, 464
Social mood—
  confusion and division traceable to, 190, *354-55*
  material of phylobiology, 78-9
  in need of scientific observation, 357, 465
  psychiatry in relation to, 443-44

  relation of social mind to, 355-56, 443, 450, 453, 464, *467-69*
  third brain responsible for disordered, 444
  underlying antagonism, 39, *467-68*, 482
  underlying normality, 183-84
  and war, 355-56, 464
  see also Autopathic motivation; 'I'-persona
Social neurosis—
  art and, 335
  cleavage in organism-environment relationship, 212-13, 420-21
  a cultural problem, 46
  ditention substance of, 220, 386, 480
  expressed in morality, 199-200 note 14
  and 'I'-persona, 67, 104-05, 357, *360*, 400, *416*
  illustration of, 228
  inception of, 238-39, 293, 297, 400, *416*, 445
  interception of man's function, 66, 240, 421-22
  and the numen, 238-40, 342
  outgrowth of author's interest in Freud's thesis, 88
  and philosophy, 54
  a phylic phenomenon, 26-7, 33, 40, 43, 47, 67, 76, 254, 282, 416
  phylobiological approach to, 15-16, 23, 25-6, 40, 69, 72, 102-04, 136-37, 250, 276, *322*, 385, 392, 458-59, 462
  and religion, 54
  tensional substrate of, 359, 382
  thesis questioned by H. S. Bailey, 68
  thesis questioned by A. J. Carlson, 23
  thesis questioned by J. Dewey, 46
  thesis questioned by C. J. Herrick, 71
  thesis questioned by R. S. Lillie, 60-1
  thesis questioned by R. H. Thouless, 24
  thesis questioned by R. M. Yerkes, 53
  and third nervous system, 407, 434
  and war, 483-84
  see also Behavior-disorders; Neurosis of man; Neurotic individual
Social norm, 39, 70-1
Social reaction-average, 25, 181, 183, 319, 321, 430, 451
  see also Normality
Social revolution, 17, 427-28, 451
Social substantive 'I', 306
  see also 'I'-persona
Social transference—
see Transference

Social values, 34, 40-1, 57-8
Socialism, 417, 475
Socio-biological function, 399, 407
Socio-cortical system, 398
Socio-neurotic behavior, 379
Socio-symbolic behavior, 331, 337, 359, 439
Socio-symbolic segment, 316, 359
  and affect, 102, 106-07
  and human behavior, 102
  and physiological tensions, 316, 369, *374-75*
  reintegration within total organism, 382, 426, 445
  relation to autonomic nervous system, 341
  relation to man's behavior, 484
  see also Affecto-symbolic segment; Symbolic system
Sociology, 47, 85, 99-100, 111-12 note 4
Soma, 170, 205, 275
  see also Ontosoma; Phylosoma
Somatic disease, 33, 194, 319-21, 323-24, 335-36, 422, 432
  see also Cancer; Malaria; Tuberculosis; Typhoid fever
Somatic processes—
  see Physiological processes
Soviet Union—
  see Russia
Special senses—
  of animals, 439-40
  correlated with body-musculature, 377-381
  media of contact with outer world, 65, 202, *233-34,* 363 note 5, 404, *438-440*
  relation to nervous systems, 404, 406
Species—
  social unit, 74 note 4
  see also Phyloörganism; Phylosoma; Phylum
Species norm, 70-1
Species-regarding characters, 18, 56, 59-60, 63
  see also Self-regarding characters
Species solidarity, 71
  and cotention, 323, 325, 454
  during war, 175-77
  evident in individual organism, 69-70, 323-24, 329
  interruptions to, 27, 47-8, 50, 65, 259, *296-97,* 342
  motivating principle in human behavior, 69-70, 175-78, *403,* 454, 465-466, 470, 478-79
  and the nomen, 341
  phylobiological approach to, 256-57, 325-26, *453*
  premise of medical science, 194-95, *326*
  primitive man and, 55
  relation of individual to, 69-70
  see also Central constant; Cotention; Homeostasis
Speech, 293, 295, 406-08, 414, 429-30, *435*
  see also Language; Symbol; Symbolic system
Speech-disorders, 253, 423, 436-37
Spirit possession, 46, 48-9
Stammering, 436-37
State, 191, 333
  see also Government; Nationalism; Patriotism
Stereognostic function, 404, 438
Students of behavior—
  see Behavior-students
Summum organum, 110
Superstition, 40, 234, 257 note 6, 287, 362
Surgical therapy, 88, 366-68, 426 note 3
  see also Shock therapy
Swimming, 351-52
Symbol—
  and affect, 38, 235, 264, *277,* 293, 295-296, *310,* 357-58, 383
  and civilization, 103
  in conditioning, *266-67, 269-71,* 275, 280
  and feeling, 103
  and General Semantics, 294-95
  an invaluable asset, 143, 280, 295, 335, 357, *413-14,* 435
  means of communication, 103, 135, 143, 204, 294
  misuse of, 147-48, 213, *234-35,* 238, 435
  and neurosis, 104-05
  phylobiological approach to, 52, 104, 147, 277, *357-58*
  and science, 103, 233-34
  and sex, 251-52
  substituted for total reaction, 83, 110, 235, 266, 296
  and total brain-function, 256, *335*
  see also Affect-linkage
Symbol of unity—
  see Image of unity
Symbolic attention, 202-04, 440, 442
  see also Ditention; Part-brain

SUBJECT INDEX

Symbolic nervous system—
see Third nervous system
Symbolic segment—
see Socio-symbolic segment
Symbolic system—
and affect, 100
and conflict, 170, 262-64, 294
cotention and ditention in relation to, 213, 217, 347-48
encroachment of, upon total organism, 203, *295-96*, 357, 369, 418, 429, 445
faux pas associated with, 295, 337, 416
and 'I'-persona, 53, 292-93, 296, 360
and man's interrelational behavior, 52, 55, 172-73, 204, 235, *294-96*, 300, 318, 348, 370, 398, 409, *414-15*, 425, *438-39*
mediated by brain, 256, 358, 398
and organism-environment relationship, 233, 236, *239*, 263, 296, 336-37, 340-42, 370, 384, 397-98, *407-09*, 413-16, 425
origin of, in psychosis, 234, 296
and parent-child relationship, 172-73, *413-14*, 416
peculiar to man, 408, 413-14
and right-wrong dichotomy, 336-37, 416
tensional substrate of, 359-60, 416
see also Affecto-symbolic segment; Language; Miniature symbolic system; Socio-symbolic segment; Speech; Third nervous system
Sympathetic nervous system—
see Autonomic nervous system
Symptoms—
of behavior-disorders, 100-01, 104, 311, 483
numen in relation to, 249-50
phylobiology not concerned with, 208, 322, 325
psychiatric interest in, 194, 285
and psychoanalysts, 241
of somatic disease, 69, 320-21
see also Fever
Syncretism, 462
Synergy, 345, 438
Syntonicity, 263-64, 275, 388, 403

Talking, 378, 436, 465, 467, 470-71
Taste—
see Special senses
Technique of cotention, 94-5, 365, *385-390*, 444-45
see also Cotention; Phylobiological technique
Tennis, 94, 383-85
Tensional patterns—
conflict between, 340, 369, *429*, 476
discrimination of two, 94-5, 97, 105, *317*, 346-47, *359-62*, *369-70*, 372, 375-76, 395, 398, 415
functional shift between, 100
kinesthetic awareness of, 382
in relation to behavior, 62, 105, 359-360, *375-76*
relation of eyes to, 371-74, 390, 440-42, 444
see also Oculomotor tension; Organismic balance; Physiological tensions
Tensions—
see Physiological tensions
Terminology, 74 note 1, 85-6, 224
Thalamus, 341, 358, 398
see also Ecothalamic system; Phylothalamic processes
Therapy—
see Group-therapy; Shock therapy; Surgical therapy
Thinking, 92, 94-6, 109, 212-13, 230, 387, 390, 435, 459, 464, 467, 470
with our mouths, 102
see also Autistic thinking; Cross-cultural thinking
Third brain—
see Third nervous system
Third nervous system—
and behavior-disorders, 100, *406-10*, 418, *419-21*, 433-34, 437-38, 443-444, 448, 484
and behavioral anatomy, 407-08
genetic importance of, 406-07
and 'I'-persona, 416, 431
nomen and numen in relation to, 408
and normality, 409-10, 420
and organism-environment relationship, 406, *408*, 413, *416*, 419, 440
realignment with total system, 426
and segmentation, 425, *433*, 436
specialized function of, *407*, 430
species solidarity severed by, 453
and speech, 406-07, 414
see also Affecto-symbolic segment; Socio-symbolic segment; Symbolic system
Tobacco, a palliative, 254, 339 note 13
see also Alcohol; Drugs
Tonicity—
see Syntonicity

Total motivation, 110
 see also Instinctive behavior; Primary motivation of man
Total organism, 35, 97, *308*, *336-37*, 345-46
 instrument of observation, 290
 see also Organism as a whole
Total response—
 see Orthonomic response
Touch—
 see Special senses
Transference—
 and conditioning, 268
 expressed in normality, 184
 and Freud, 239-40
 in parent-child relationship, 216-19, 419
 phyloanalytic interpretation of, 219, *240*, 268, 322-23
 toward God, 163, 237
 see also Dependence; Social image
Tuberculosis, 164, 319-20
Typhoid fever, 33, 323

Unconscious processes, 485
Unilateralism, 188, 353-54, 388, 467, 480
 see also Absolutism
United Nations Organization, 6-7, 71, 177, 193, 274, 281, 355, 381, 434, 466, 475
United States of America, 42, 187, 333, 465-66
Unity—
 see Image of unity; Oneness; Peace; Principle of unity

Values—
 see Social values
Vegetative nervous system—
 see Autonomic nervous system
Verbal conditioning—
 see Conditioning; Language; Speech; Symbol
Vision—
 see Eyes; Stereognostic function
Voluntary nervous system—
 see Cerebrospinal nervous system
Vote, 241-42

Walking, 377-80
War, 11, 83-4, 217, 330
 and ditention, 379
 an expression of affect and prejudice, 28, 163, 168, 171, 197, 230-31
 global character of, 7, 140, 153, 156, 193, 333, 362, 484
 and God, 227-28, *333*
 inconsistency in, 228, 260
 a medical problem, 15
 mind and mood of man in relation to, 58, *355-56*, 464, 467, 482-84
 and normality, 181, 333
 and part-brain, 338, 355-56
 relation between peace and, 107, *191*, 193, 333, 338, 480
 and sense of right, 39, 58
 species solidarity evidenced during, 175-77
 succeeded by conflict, 259-60, 332
 see also Antagonism; Atomic bomb; Fighting; Peace; World War I; World War II
Wealth—
 see Hoarding of wealth
Whole-part relationship, 110, 157, 301, 325, 450-51, 474
 see also Collective whole; Organic whole
Wisdom of the body, 343
Wish, 26, 208, 234, 241-42, 262, 342
Words—
 see Language; Speech; Symbol
World Court—
 see United Nations Organization
World War I, 355
World War II, 193, 195, 259, 355, 427, 451, 481, 484-85
 see also Germany; Japan; Profiteering
Writing—
 see Communication
Wrong—
 see Right and wrong